Cooperative enterprises, workers' self-management and new forms of industrial democracy – these are the stirring themes animating Marcelo Vieta's original and exciting book. Using a stunning set of interviews, buttressed by historical investigation and deep theoretical inquiry, *Workers' Self-Management in Argentina* illuminates movements of occupation, recuperation and *autogestion* in Argentina in recent years. There is virtually nothing like this book when it comes to the study of lived practices of workers' control today. Everyone searching for alternatives to neoliberalism and the domination of labor will relish this powerful and important work.

–*David McNally, Cullen Distinguished Professor of History and Business, University of Houston. He is the author of* Against the Market: Political Economy, Market Socialism, and the Marxist Critique (*Verso, 1992*) *and* Global Slump: The Economics and Politics of Crisis and Resistance (*PM Press, 2010*).

Marcelo Vieta's *Workers' Self-Management in Argentina* is one of the most important books on contemporary labour and democracy. The volume masterfully revisits and extends theory on *autogestión* (loosely translated as self-management in English) and places it in richly detailed historical, economic, and social contexts. The book employs three in-depth case studies of "worker-recuperated" firms in today's Argentina and at the same time beautifully integrates those with an analysis of work and economy in Argentina especially over the past two decades. The comparisons of lessons from the experiences of workers in those firms for other national contexts gives the analysis an expansiveness seldom found in case-based studies of worklife and labour arrangements. Vieta's longitudinal study and insightful commentary provide must reading for anyone interested in the intricacies of and possibilities for democratic revival from the shop floor and board rooms to communities and the global economy.

–*George Cheney, Professor of Communication, University of Colorado at Colorado Springs. He is the author of* Values at Work: Employee Participation Meets Market Pressure at Mondragon (*Cornell University Press, 2002*) *and co-editor of* The Routledge Companion to Alternative Organization (*Routledge, 2014*).

Marcelo Vieta's book ranges far beyond the bounds of its Argentine analysis. It is thoroughly researched and grounded in "class struggle Marxist" theory and reflects a prolonged and deep understanding of and commitment to global working-class enterprise autonomy struggles. In this Vieta provides a powerful and meaningful critique and alternative to neo-liberal capitalism.

–*Peter Ranis is Professor Emeritus/Political Sci~~~~ ~~~~~~~~ ~~~~~~ ~~~ ~~~~~~~~~~y of New York. He is the author of* Cooperatives ~~~~~~~~~~~~~~~~~~~~~~~~~~~~~~~ he Neo-liberal Economy (*Zed Books, 2016*) *and* ~~~~~~~~~~~~~~~~~~~~~~ n-temporary Class Consciousness (*University ~~*

D1213854

I was consistently impressed by Vieta's impeccable scholarship and deeply-thought argumentation. Theoretically, this work is oriented around the perspective of class-struggle Marxism, but is also informed by a deep knowledge of the history and practices of trades unionism, cooperativism, and social and solidarity economics in Argentina, Latin America and internationally. The work situates *empresas recuperadas* (ERTS) within the history of the Argentine class-composition and workers movements. It shows how the ERT practice of "occupy, resist, produce" generated a series of "radical social innovations" affecting economic activities, political formations and trans-individual subject formation. From this study Vieta draws important conclusions about the circumstances in which the potential for self-directed worker activities is actualized in ways that point beyond the existing system of production relations. I want to reiterate how impressed I am by this work. It is a major contribution to scholarship on the global worker of the twenty first century.

–*Nick Dyer-Witheford is Associate Professor in the Faculty of Information and Media Studies at University of Western Ontario. He is the author of* Cyber-Marx: Cycles and Circuits of Struggle in High Technology Capitalism (*University of Illinois, 1999*) *and* Cyber-Proletariat: Global Labour in the Digital Vortex (*Pluto Press, 2015*).

This book is a tremendous gift. A must read for scholars, activists and all who want to learn how to retake our lives and create something new. Within these pages Vieta has detailed the history of class struggle in Argentina, bringing us to this historical moment, grounded in a new conceptualization of *autogestión*. Workers taking back – recuperating – their sense of worth and dignity though directly democratic workplace recuperations. Distinct from occupations, making demands on bosses and states, in recuperations workers re-claim what is theirs/ours. Vieta's lens offers a unique insider/outsider perspective, as an Argentine scholar based in Canada. His methodological approach, also innovative, combines global ethnography, history, political science, economics and sociology. Most of all, in *Workers' Self-Management in Argentina*, Vieta shows, by way of extended examples, that people can self-organize their work and life, in ways that are horizontal, effective and affective.

–*Marina Sitrin, Assistant Professor of Sociology at the State University of New York at Binghamton. She is the author of* Everyday Revolutions: Horizontalism and Autonomy in Argentina (*Zed Books, 2012*) *and* They Can't Represent Us! Reinventing Democracy from Greece to Occupy, *co-authored with Dario Azzellini* (*Verso Press, 2014*).

Workers' Self-Management in Argentina

Historical Materialism Book Series

The Historical Materialism Book Series is a major publishing initiative of the radical left. The capitalist crisis of the twenty-first century has been met by a resurgence of interest in critical Marxist theory. At the same time, the publishing institutions committed to Marxism have contracted markedly since the high point of the 1970s. The Historical Materialism Book Series is dedicated to addressing this situation by making available important works of Marxist theory. The aim of the series is to publish important theoretical contributions as the basis for vigorous intellectual debate and exchange on the left.

The peer-reviewed series publishes original monographs, translated texts, and reprints of classics across the bounds of academic disciplinary agendas and across the divisions of the left. The series is particularly concerned to encourage the internationalization of Marxist debate and aims to translate significant studies from beyond the English-speaking world.

For a full list of titles in the Historical Materialism Book Series
available in paperback from Haymarket Books, visit:
https://www.haymarketbooks.org/series_collections/1-historical-materialism

Workers' Self-Management in Argentina

Contesting Neo-Liberalism by Occupying Companies, Creating Cooperatives, and Recuperating Autogestión

Marcelo Vieta

Haymarket Books
Chicago, IL

First published in 2019 by Brill Academic Publishers, The Netherlands
© 2019 Koninklijke Brill NV, Leiden, The Netherlands

Published in paperback in 2020 by
Haymarket Books
P.O. Box 180165
Chicago, IL 60618
773-583-7884
www.haymarketbooks.org

ISBN: 978-1-64259-339-6

Distributed to the trade in the US through Consortium Book Sales and
Distribution (www.cbsd.com) and internationally through Ingram
Publisher Services International (www.ingramcontent.com).

This book was published with the generous support of Lannan
Foundation and Wallace Action Fund.

Special discounts are available for bulk purchases by organizations and
institutions. Please call 773-583-7884 or email info@haymarketbooks.org
for more information.

Cover design by Jamie Kerry and Ragina Johnson.

Printed in the United States.

10 9 8 7 6 5 4 3 2 1

Library of Congress Cataloging-in-Publication data is available.

To the workers of the empresas recuperadas,
for prefiguring another world

To my son, Adrián,
for teaching me that another world is already here in so many ways

∴

Contents

Preface

Do class-based differences still exist? Can we 'see' class today? Is there still a working class, or have we in advanced so-called post-Fordist capitalism bid 'farewell' to it, as André Gorz so confidently concluded in the early 1980s?[1] If we haven't yet given the working class its final *adieu*, is class still 'determined by one's position within the labour–capital *social relation of production*'?[2] And, if the notion of class is still relevant, can the waged and the marginalised come to a critical awareness of their class situation and state of subjugation?[3] In short, does class still matter? Ample evidence of persistent inequality today[4] – made visible by the deplorable material conditions of millions around the world while a smaller number of people bask in abundance – suggests it still does. Indeed, the plight and struggles of workers, the marginalised, and the dispossessed the world over are to a large extent still shaped and driven by class-based differences that continue to persist in our existing neo-liberal capitalist world order.

This book brings a contemporary instantiation of working-class struggle to light through the story of one group of workers in Argentina – the protagonists of the *empresas recuperadas por sus trabajadores* (worker-recuperated enterprises).[5] These workers have been engaged for over two decades in their own self-determination as they take over and recuperate the former capitalist workplaces that had employed them and reinvent them as worker cooperatives. We will come to know these workplaces reconstituted along notions of *autogestión* (self-management) more simply by their Spanish acronym: ERT.

The struggle of these workers to stabilise and self-determine their working lives, however, has been anything but simple. Despite continued challenges – especially as the Argentine political economy re-embraced a clear neo-liberal path in late 2015 after 12 years of relative reprieve from austerity and anti-labour, pro-market policies – the story of Argentina's ERTs is, more than ever, full of promise for all workers desiring to control and re-envision their own

---

1 Gorz 1982.

2 Allman 2007, p. 74 (emphasis in original).

3 Paulo Freire termed this critical awareness, or 'critical consciousness', the '*conscientização*' of the 'social, political, and economic contradictions' of one's historical and material situation, which includes 'tak[ing] action against the oppressive elements of reality' (Freire 1970, pp. 35, 109).

4 See, for instance, Cohen 2015; Doob 2013; Glenn 2009; Piketty 2014; Stiglitz 2012; and Wilkinson and Pickett 2010.

5 Unless indicated, all translations in this book are the author's.

socio-economic destinies. This is a book about the attempted unmaking of the
working class by neo-liberal capital in Argentina and the working class's continued struggle for its own remaking. It is a story of workers recomposing their
places of work and, in the process, regaining their livelihoods and dignity in an
Argentina pockmarked by constant macro- and micro-economic crises that in
recent decades unfolded within a waxing and waning neo-liberal backdrop.

In 2005 I began a journey that would see me face-to-face with the working
class in the (re)making. It involves workers in Argentina confronting capitals,
capitalists, and the state in a struggle that begins at the point of production or
service delivery, from within the failing firms where they had been employed.
On several research trips since the mid-2000s, and in more recent follow-up
visits to Argentina, I have witnessed first-hand workers acting collectively in
their shops, in their factories, and in their neighbourhoods in order to save their
jobs, secure their livelihoods, and ultimately reconstitute their socio-economic
circumstances. Most palpably, ERT protagonists transform once-capitalist businesses into worker-run, directly democratic, and horizontally organised productive entities. But they change much more than that, as I have learned over
the years. Since beginning this research, I have not only seen workers creating new worker cooperatives from out of the ashes of failed capitalist firms;[6] I
have also seen them transforming these recuperated workplaces into socially
focused enterprises that become deeply concerned with the wellbeing of surrounding communities and neighbourhoods and that respond directly and locally to social distress and economic depletion. As I came to know better these
workers and the enterprises they revived, I began to also realise that in recuperating their workplaces and engaging actively with their communities they
begin to overturn and take back – again, collectively – that most sacrosanct of
class-based institutions: private property as embodied in the capital-centred
firm and its hierarchically managed labour process. And, most fundamentally
I have learned, ERT workers begin to recuperate for themselves their very productive capacities as creative human beings working cooperatively in associated labour.

Contemporary ERTs in Argentina first emerged from out of the crisis of
the country's neo-liberal model that escalated throughout the late 1990s and

---

6 By *capitalist firms*, *capitalist businesses*, or *capitalist enterprises*, I mean businesses driven
   mainly by the pursuit of profits (rather than social aims), that hire wage-labour, that extract
   surplus-value from the work conducted by employees, and that are organised by exclusionary forms of ownership and administrative control whereby employees have no or little say
   in decision-making, strategic planning, or in constituting the ownership and administration
   of the firm.

early 2000s. Driven in part by the implementation of IMF-sanctioned structural reforms under the reconfigured right-leaning Peronism of President Carlos Menem (1989–99) and the centre-right coalition government led by the
Union Cívica Radical (UCR, Radical Civic Union) party of Fernando de la Rúa
(1999–2001), Argentina's version of the neo-liberal model would eventually – if
temporarily – implode during the years spanning the turn of the millennium.
As local businesses began to fail at record rates, finding it harder and harder to
compete with multinationals and imported goods that had flooded local markets, many Argentine business owners compensated by not paying wages and
engaging in the *vaciamiento* (asset stripping, or literally 'emptying') of their
dying firms. At the same time, and with an overvalued peso pegged to the
US dollar compromising Argentine firms' competitiveness and compounding
their difficulties, workers began to increasingly experience heightened levels
of exploitation on shop floors. With traditional union strategies proving unresponsive to the neo-liberal juggernaut, an Argentine state indifferent to the
plight of the country's workers, and with no alternative jobs available, more
and more workers from a broad cross-section of Argentina's urban-based economy would begin to take matters into their own hands by occupying and
subsequently self-managing their troubled workplaces.

Reviving a form of bottom-up labour action and organising centred explicitly in the notion of *autogestión*, as of mid-2016 there were in Argentina almost
16,000 workers self-managing their workplaces in close to 370 *empresas recuperadas* in sectors as varied as printing and publishing, media, metalwork,
gastronomy, textiles, health care, foodstuffs, shipbuilding, waste management,
construction, education, rubber and plastics, fuel provisioning, and tourism.[7]
Found across the national territory, Argentina's ERTs make up – by far – the
largest movement in the world of worker-led conversions of capitalist businesses into cooperatives.

While still small in numbers when situated within the broader Argentine
economy, ERTs have defied their numerical weight and have stepped up to the
task of saving companies from closure, addressing under- and unemployment,
stabilising local economies, and securing the social wellbeing of surrounding communities. Because of this, ERTs have gained the broad support of the
Argentine people as well as inspiring other workers' struggles and proposals for
social change in Argentina and beyond.[8] Since coming to the world's attention
during the political turmoil, economic collapse, and debt default of December

---

7 See Kennard and Caistor-Arendar 2016; Lewkowicz 2016; Palomino, Bleynat, Garro, and Giacomuzzi 2010; Ranis 2016; Ruggeri 2016; and Ruggeri and Vieta 2015.
8 Fajn 2003; Magnani 2009; Palomino 2003; Ranis 2016; Vieta and Ruggeri 2009.

2001 and the immediate years thereafter – by which time around 200 ERTs had emerged[9] – the *empresas recuperadas* have stimulated new expectations for socio-economic change while actually helping to forge new labour relations in Argentina.[10]

As the country began to recover under more favourable global economic conditions throughout the first decade of the 2000s, aided by the left-populist and nationalist-developmentalist policies of the Peronist governments of Néstor Kirchner (2003–7) and Cristina Fernández de Kirchner (2007–15),[11] workplace takeovers and conversions to worker cooperatives would continue to occur, although at a slower rate per year than in the 2001–4 period of crisis.[12] By the mid-2000s, and in no small part due to the lobbying and organising efforts of the ERT movements' leaders and new self-managed workers' associations, ERTs had become a viable solution to firm failure and unemployment in Argentina. And ERTs have surged again in recent years as the post-2008 global financial crisis touched down in the country and brought with it new economic difficulties and new firm closures.

While new ERTs had continued to emerge during President Mauricio Macri's Cambiemos coalition government (2015–19), *macrismo*'s revival of explicitly neo-liberal policies brought new challenges to ERTs and other social justice and community groups, challenges that had been partly overcome throughout the first decade and a half of the 2000s. Though this neo-liberal redux confronted ERTs and other social and solidarity economy organisations as new reactionary forces,[13] these self-managed firms' broad legitimacy amongst the Argentine public and their proven net-positive effects for Argentina's economic wellbeing did not make it easy for *macrismo*'s brand of neo-liberalism to quell the still-growing movement of recuperated enterprises. As this book will show, ERT worker-protagonists' political savvy; their capacity for self-organising; and

9   Ruggeri 2016; Ruggeri, Antivero, Elena, Polti, et al. 2014. See also Chapter 2.

10   Palomino 2003; Rebón 2007; Vieta 2010a, 2014b.

11   The Kirchner years (2003–15) have been understood as forming part of the broader tendency of the 'pink tide' of left-leaning, neo-developmentalist, and anti-Washington Consensus governments across Latin America that emerged throughout the first decade of the 2000s (see Kozloff 2008; Pozzi and Nigra 2015a, 2015b; Schuster 2008; Spronk and Webber 2014; and Wylde 2011).

12   See Chapter 2. As will be discussed there, the rate of creation of new ERTs would diminish and plateau between 2004 and 2010 due to various factors, including better economic conditions and the return to more traditional forms of union organising and representation as outlets for workers' demands.

13   The 'social and solidarity economy', known in the global North mostly as the 'social economy' or the 'third sector', encompasses economic practices and organisations that are primarily driven by social aims rather than private gain (see, for example, McMurtry 2010;

their demonstrated creativity, innovation, and tenacity over the years provide a solid foundation for the ERT movement to directly contest the new political economic environment and continue to invigorate working-class self-activity in Argentina.

In the midst of persistent socio-economic difficulties, ERT workers have been directly addressing Argentina's chronic under- and unemployment. They have also been reviving (for over two decades now) radical, bottom-up working-class protagonism. Over the first decade and a half of the new century, ERT worker-protagonists and movement leaders have also influenced the reform of national bankruptcy and expropriation laws to favour workplace conversions to cooperatives. Moreover, they have been socialising wealth by transforming capital-centred firms into worker-managed cooperatives, returning productive entities to the communities and neighbourhoods that surround them. They especially do so when ERTs bring the community into a workplace by doubling as cultural centres, free medical clinics, and spaces for alternative educational initiatives. They also do so when they extend out territorially into the community by contributing portions of their surpluses to local community revitalisation and economic and cultural development. Because of this enterprise-community fusion, as this book's case studies will show, ERTs symbolically tear down the walls that segregate a workplace from the community. Most promising for those seeking less exploitative and more humane labour practices and workplaces, ERTs have begun to return control to workers, even though they still struggle with the realities and tensions of having to exist – at least in part – within competitive capitalist markets.

ERTs have also inspired the imaginaries of workers throughout Argentina and outside of its borders by proving – despite the contrary claims of orthodox economists, pro-market politicians, and mainstream business media punditry – that workers *can* effectively run productive enterprises without bosses. In sum, as we will see throughout this book, ERTs place into question capital-labour relations, the commodification of labour-power, the privileging of property rights over the dignity and wellbeing of workers, and the segregation of businesses from surrounding communities. They do so while, at the same time, bringing to light and addressing myriad other dimensions of injustice and inequality related to the capitalist mode of production. ERTs are thus exem-

---

Quarter, Mook, and Armstrong 2009). ERTs can indeed be considered social and solidarity economy organisations, in particular due to their main objectives of securing jobs, their cooperative structures, and the community development projects that many of them take on.

plary of both the possibilities and challenges for workers' self-management in our continuing neo-liberal context, providing rich cases for studying the continued relevance of working-class protagonism, self-organisation, and cooperation.

Why did ERTs emerge in Argentina at this particular historical conjuncture? What are their connections to historical workers' struggles in Argentina and elsewhere? What is at stake for these workers in their strategies and tactics of 'ocupar, resistir, producir' ('occupy, resist, produce'), the slogan borrowed from Brazil's landless peasants' and workers' movement that evocatively captures ERT workers' paths to *autogestión*? What exactly are ERT protagonists 'recuperating' when they take over troubled businesses in order to self-manage them? How do ERT workers learn cooperative values and practices? How are they bringing to light the continued relevance of working-class struggles? How do their lived experiences of crises and their subsequent practices of *autogestión* contribute to our understanding of work beyond capital? What can workers' struggles throughout the world today learn from Argentina's ERTs? These are the guiding questions that drive this book. In addressing these questions, the book takes the position that, as Argentina's ERT protagonists repeatedly show, workers have the capacities to lay claim to their creative abilities, run their own places of work, and collectively manage the production of social wealth.

This book seeks to understand ERTs' promise for worker-led alternative economic realities today in light of and as paths beyond persistent neo-liberal enclosures and crises. It takes seriously workers' continued agency in praxis, their implicit and often explicit desire for autonomy from arbitrary control, and their ongoing ability to self-manage their own productive lives despite the contradictions inherent to the capital–labour relationship. The book particularly recognises the possibilities that open up for workers' control and self-management during moments of crises in the political economy of a country or at the point of production of a firm; such macro- or micro-economic crises can put into sharp relief for workers their situations of exploitation *as well as* the capacities for solidarity and cooperation that they already possess from having been brought together by capital within the labour process.[14] At bottom, the following pages delve into the historical-material conditions from out of which ERTs emerge, their connections to the self-activity of workers within the labour process under capitalism and Argentina's long tradition of working-class militancy, and how ERT protagonists face socio-economic crises head-on by taking

---

14   Antunes 2013; Atzeni 2010; Bell and Cleaver 2002; Burawoy 1985; Lebowitz 2003; Marx 1967; Vieta 2014b.

their productive and creative destinies into their own hands. And in the process of taking control of their workplaces and working lives, these protagonists transform themselves from managed employees to self-managed workers.

Class Matters

Most broadly, this study adheres to a historical-materialist understanding of the concept of *the working class*, or 'the-class-that-lives-from-labour', as Brazilian Marxist sociologist Ricardo Antunes succinctly defines it.[15] A historical-materialist perspective most fundamentally posits that in the capitalist system the working class consists of those who must survive by selling their labour-power to those who own the means of production in order to produce surplus-value. With this perspective, class is thus not a 'thing' but rather a social relation, 'viz. the internal relation between labour and capital'.[16] Through a historical materialist-based critical theoretical and sociological analysis of the emergence and circumstances of Argentina's ERTs, this book ultimately manifests the possibilities that remain available to those that live from labour – the working class – for beginning to free themselves from today's neo-liberal capitalist order.

Specifically, this book's approach adopts a 'class struggle' standpoint. As E.P. Thompson teaches us, class does not consist of neat sociological categories but, rather, 'happens' in everyday experiences, actions, and struggles as people together 'live [out] their own history' immanently, as a class-in-the-making.[17] The experiences of Argentina's ERT protagonists, as I will argue, provide us with sketches of how those that live from their labour can act collectively, for themselves and in their own interest, as they struggle against capitalist contradictions, exploitations, and perpetual crises. In the process, ERT protagonists teach us how workers may come to a critical awareness of their class situation and start to move beyond the tensions inherent in the social relations of capitalist production. ERT workers' resistances and innovations in *autogestión* begin to map out – via the cooperativisation of their work, the socialisation of the products of their labour, and their forms of horizontal organising – how the working class can forge its own path beyond capital-induced crises and enclosures. In short, ERT protagonists' audacious projects to take over and subsequently self-manage once-capitalist businesses, and the continued existence

---

15   Antunes 2013, pp. 80–95.
16   Allman 2007, p. 9. See also Thompson 1963.
17   Thompson 1963, pp. 9, 11. See also Allman 2007, pp. 8–10, 74.

and emergence of the worker cooperatives they create, remind us of the paths still available to the working class for its own (re)making.

This book, then, not only strives to better understand how and why Argentina's ERTs have emerged and evolved, but also seeks, via the ERT phenomenon as case study, to come to grips with how the working class comes to know itself and act for itself in the face of capitalism's exploitative tendencies and recurring bouts of macro- and micro-economic crises. From out of the lived experiences of Argentina's ERT protagonists, the book fundamentally aspires to return to the agentic capacities always already possessed by workers, which is not only about responding to crises and resisting capitals' continued encroachments on their lives, but also about inventing new socio-economic realities beyond them.

As made clear by recent experiences with worker-recuperated firms in Argentina and elsewhere – in such diverse places as Brazil, Uruguay, Greece, Italy, France, Spain, Turkey, South Korea, and in pockets of the United States and Canada – recurrent structural crises of the capitalist system offer moments of rupture[18] that can potentially become openings for new experiments with workers' control and self-management. Moments of systemic crises often raise the level of exploitation on shop floors and bring extra hardship to the daily lives of millions – augmented when orthodox economic gurus and neo-liberal governments try to counter crises with austerity. But moments of crises are also, history has shown, openings for possibilities for that 'other world' that can seize the imaginary of the marginalised and working people, while putting in sharp relief already existing class distinctions and antagonisms.[19]

In the time it took to write this book, we have witnessed not only the continued growth of the ERT phenomenon in Argentina, throughout Latin America, and in other countries, but also the ongoing and broader mobilisations of 'those without' and on 'the margins of society',[20] as working people, the marginalised, and the dispossessed creatively resist and begin to counter neo-liberal ideologies, policies, and practices. Take, for instance, the initial promises of Egypt's Tahrir Square demonstrations and the Arab Spring of 2011; the situation of massive inequality brought to light by the Occupy Movement in 2011 and 2012; the rise of Spain's *Indignados* against austerity in 2011; the Chilean, Brazilian,

---

18   Bell and Cleaver 2002.
19   Vieta 2016a, 2016b, 2017.
20   Zibechi 2012, p. 61. For Zibechi, groups 'on the margins of society' are those that are either excluded or left out of the rights and privileges promised by liberal states. For him, 'those without' are people on the margins 'without homes, without land, without work, without rights' (Ibid).

and Québec student movements against the neo-liberalisation of public education in 2012; Turkey's Taksim Square protests and Gezi Park occupation of 2013; the renewed wave of anti-austerity protests in Greece in 2014 and 2015; Hong Kong's Umbrella Revolution sit-in street protests of 2014 demanding democratic participation and self-governance; and, more recently, France's Nuit Debout movement and related mass protests against reforms to labour legislation that threaten to continue the precarisation of jobs and life; the Idle No More and the Standing Rock organising and resistance against continued imperialist-capitalist encroachments on Indigenous cultures and ways of life; and the growing wave of protests and organising in the US in the wake of President Donald Trump's misogynistic, racist, anti-immigrant, and anti-environmental policies. With all of these and in many other recent movements, protests, and revolts, occupations of public and private spaces have merged with actions of solidarity across social justice and identity groups while workers, students, Indigenous peoples, and the marginalised have taken to the streets *en masse* to demand and fight for better life conditions and an end to exorbitant income inequalities, political and state repression, cultural genocide, and neo-liberal austerity (the latter often most viscerally felt by working people as nothing less than economic repression). Peter Ranis has recently written that these contemporary mass revolts against neo-liberal injustices and recalcitrant state power show how people's resistance from below develop

> islands of political and economic autonomy that [draw] attention to what people can do on their own and for themselves. From many walks of life they [stand] up and [speak] with measured purpose and [are] heard.[21]

Inspired by the popular revolts of another era, Herbert Marcuse in a similar vein reminds us that social changes spawned by political and economic crises *and* the very struggles of the marginalised against power from above show how social transformation can begin through inventive and non-vanguardist forms of political expression 'from below' and 'from the margins'.[22]

In all of these moments of visceral struggles of the marginalised over work, life, and meaning, we again and again witness the working class in a state of unmaking and remaking.[23] For workers, it is often during moments of broader

---

21   Ranis 2016, p. 34.

22   Marcuse 1969, p. 87. See also Vieta, 2016a, 2016b, 2017.

23   My conceptualisation of the unmaking and remaking of the working class draws on the work of E.P. Thompson (1963) and notions of working-class composition, decomposition,

crises of the status quo economic system or micro-economic crises on shop floors when their circumstances of exploitation, emerging from out of the internal contradictions inherent to capitalist society, become obvious.[24] And in the thick of crisis moments, through solidary acts of refusal and reinvention, these circumstances can begin to give way, imaginatively and practically, to new possibilities for working and living. As Michael Lebowitz[25] and Maurizio Atzeni[26] have argued, the exploitative nature of the capitalist labour process can be made excruciatingly visible to workers as egregious violations of the wage-labour contract when work intensifies, salaries fall, and redundancies increase. Workers' initially spontaneous self-defensive responses spawned by need can eventually lead to them consciously organising to overcome their exploitation, generating in the process another reality for themselves, their families, and surrounding communities. At times, as with Argentina's ERTs, collective memories and traditions of past working-class militancy also re-emerge during these moments and combine with new modes of collective action that compel new generations of working people to propose and struggle for different socio-economic circumstances. And this can begin with the seizure of the very sites of continued capitalist exploitation: the workplace.

For many in the movements of the exploited and the marginalised over the past two decades, their struggles for self-determination have extended beyond reactive protests and revolts to include, as with Argentina's ERTs, actual proposals and practices for alternatively organising work and economic activity. As we will see throughout this book, ERTs highlight workers' ongoing capacities to both engage in direct responses to capitalist enclosures and exploitations *and* invent socio-economic alternatives beyond them. Argentina's experiences with ERTs, I argue, bring to light the potential for working people to create another socio-economic reality – a potential, I suggest, that exists at the heart of working-class initiatives. These initiatives are rooted in the working class's creative force that can be unleashed at the right conjunctural moment. For Argentina's ERT workers, that moment arrived with the country's deep crisis of its neo-liberal model at the turn of the millennium. And it is a story that is still unfolding.

---

and recompositon developed by other Marxist thinkers such as Negri 1988, 1991, 2005; Thompson 1963; Tronti 1973; Virno 2004; Wright 2010; and Wright 2002.

24   McNally 1993, p. 153. See also Atzeni 2010; Atzeni and Vieta 2014; and Bell and Cleaver 2002.
25   Lebowitz 2003.
26   Atzeni 2010.

Why I Wrote This Book

Without doubt, this project has been a personal journey for me. Born in Quilmes, Argentina in 1970 to a family of working-class Italian immigrants on both sides, I grew up in Canada, immigrating to Vancouver, BC with my parents when I was five. Growing up in multiple cultures – that of Italo-Argentines at home and as an English-speaking Canadian outside of the home – I have always desired to know better where I come from and who I am in the midst of what has been a polyglot existence.

I was taken by Argentina's *empresas recuperadas* early on in my PhD studies in the Graduate Program in Social and Political Thought at York University in Toronto. In the mid-2000s, when I began to work with and study them, the *empresas recuperadas* made up a radical labour and social movement in bloom in the midst of a still-smouldering post-2001 Argentina. What particularly struck me at the beginning of my engagement with ERTs – besides the audacity of workers taking over their former places of employment – was that a fair number of them emerged from the metallurgic and construction sectors, and that many of them were also located in the southern suburbs of Buenos Aires, the heavily working-class and immigrant-based region where I had spent the first five years of my life. This resonated with me. My grandfather on my fathers' side, who immigrated from the northern Italian town of Forno Canavese in the province of Torino to the industrial city of Avellaneda just to the south of the city of Buenos Aires as a young child in the early 1920s, eventually became a welder and a member of the Argentine steelworkers' union, the Unión Obrera Metalúrgica (UOM, Metalurgical Workers' Union). I soon discovered that this was one of the few unions that actively supported Argentina's ERTs early on – especially in the Avellaneda and Quilmes suburbs of Buenos Aires, exactly where my family had immigrated to from Italy and where I was born. My grandfather on my mother's side was, amongst many other things, a mason and carpenter, occupations also taken up by ERTs. My mother's father had arrived in Argentina from Lanciano, Italy in 1950 when then-president Juán Domingo Perón's administration was promoting a new wave of immigration of skilled workers from Europe to Argentina. Four years later, my grandfather would bring the rest of his family, including my mother, to join him in Quilmes (a typical Italian immigrant story of the early-to-mid twentieth century). And my father has worked in the automotive sector most of his life, starting out as an elevator repair apprentice in Argentina at the age of 12 in order to provide for his family after the early death of his father, and soon learning the craft of auto body repair, which still occupied him in his formal working hours until he retired in early 2017.

This research project has thus offered me an opportunity to return, intellectually and autobiographically, to my origins, a project I had wanted to engage in since my early 20s. The project eventually merged into my own personal journey of radicalisation that began to grow in the late 1990s and early 2000s. As I travelled throughout Latin America on several trips during this period, I began to become deeply disappointed with the inequalities and social divisions that were plainly visible – inequities intrinsic to the neo-liberal capitalist system that has had such a tumultuous passage throughout the region in recent decades. Increasingly in my academic studies, I began to explore why it is that our world is possessed of so much inequality, oppression, and poverty when we have at hand, technologically speaking, the capacity to overcome scarcity and reduce the perpetuation of 'toil, aggressiveness, misery, and injustice' for all, as Marcuse put it in *One Dimensional Man* in 1964.[27] As I embarked on my MA work at Simon Fraser University and immediately thereafter my PhD studies at York University, where I read critical theory, Marxist and anarchist analyses, and Latin American history, I began to understand more deeply how the capitalist reordering of our planet has had much to do with these inequalities and injustices.

This research project has encouraged me to merge these autobiographical dimensions with my desire to understand better why these inequities have taken such deep root in Argentina in recent years. Why had Argentina, at the expense of the wellbeing of so many of its people, embarked on such a sharp turn to neo-liberalism in the 1990s? Why had many of its people – including my extended family in Argentina – suffered so much in the eventual, if temporary, collapse of the model in the late 1990s and early 2000s? And why was it that so many Argentines had not stood by idly but had, instead, gone to great lengths to restart their lives via myriad experiments in solidarity-based socioeconomic arrangements and direct democracy? My turn to historical materialism, critical theory, the sociology of work, the philosophy of technology, political economy, and Argentine and Latin American history during my MA and PhD studies provided me with a critical intellectual foundation from which to begin to answer these questions. And this foundation has helped me better understand the particularity of Argentina's recent history and political economy from macro- and micro-sociological perspectives. The ERT phenomenon was, I began to realise, a rich terrain of study for both satiating my personal interests and responding to my radicalisation while engaging and working with a social movement that seemed to be illustrating vividly how workers them-

---

27   Marcuse 1964, p. 5.

selves, despite continued crises and stubborn hierarchies of power and exploit-ation, were taking their social, economic, and productive lives into their own hands. Here then, with Argentina's ERTs, was a chance to contribute to a project where I could help disseminate the experiences and stories of workers attempt-ing to overcome much hardship in their professional and personal lives, assist in articulating a contemporary instance of working-class recomposition and self-activity, and be passionate enough about the field of study to sustain me throughout the years it took to work on and complete this book.

This text is the outcome of this intellectual, political, and autobiographical journey that continues still for me as faculty in the Program in Adult Education and Community Development at the University of Toronto's Ontario Institute for Studies in Education (OISE/UT). It is my deepest hope that the book has done justice to the stories and experiences of the workers and activists who helped me write it with their stories and their time. The validation of this pro-ject by the ERT workers with whom I have shared parts of this book begins to set me at ease in this regard.

Marcelo Vieta
Buenos Aires and Toronto
November 2016–May 2017

Acknowledgements

A book is rarely written entirely by one person in isolation. This one is no exception. I could not have found the time and space to carry out and complete this research project without the care, kindness, generosity, enthusiasm, patience, frankness, forgiveness, and love of numerous people. In one way or another, they all traverse these pages.

First and foremost, I would like to profoundly thank my partner, Patricia Díaz Barrero, and my son, Adrián Däxa Vieta Díaz: For tolerating my idiosyncrasies, for granting me so much undeserved grace, and for surrounding me with overflowing love. The sweetest moments of this project were always when I would reunite with you both after a long day of reading or writing, or after returning from research or conference trips.

Second, I would like to thank my parents, Clelia and Eduardo Vieta: For your boundless encouragement and unconditional generosity. In so many ways you both prefigure the world many of us would like to see. *¡Están en mis pensamientos siempre!*

The deepest thanks also to the mentors, colleagues, and friends who have influenced and continue to shape my intellectual journey and who have over the years supported this project. To my PhD committee, David McNally (my supervisor) and Viviana Patroni and J.J. McMurtry: Thank you so much for your time, guidance, assistance, and engaged interest in this research over the years! And many thanks also to Nick Dyer-Witheford, Sam Gindin, Mark Thomas, Daniel Schugurensky, Peter Sawchuk, Greig de Peuter, Stephen Dobson, Maurizio Atzeni, Richard J.F. Day, Andrew Feenberg, and Peter Ranis. You too have all been vital in helping me see this project to completion. Collectively, all of you have not only extended your enthusiastic support to me, but have also taken the time to provide me with the sharp feedback, probing questions, and keen observations that have invaluably shaped this book. Moreover, your commitments to creating a better world have been an inspiration to me.

I would also like to remember three intellectual and pedagogical giants who are tragically no longer with us and whom I had the privilege of calling mentors and friends: Jack Quarter, David F. Noble, and Roman Onufrijchuk. Their abounding kindness (especially with time), their deep understanding of the ethics of mentorship, and their inspiring teaching have left indelible marks in this book and in my life. You are all missed!

A special note of deep gratitude must go to my friend and frequent collaborator, Andrés Ruggeri, co-author of a section of Chapter 2 and Chapter 6 of this book. Thank you for helping me understand the intricacies and history of *auto-*

gestión, and for all of your assistance and wisdom during my stays in Argentina. Thank you also for including me in some of the work of the Programa Facultad Abierta of the University of Buenos Aires, the Centro de Documentación de Empresas Recuperadas, and for inviting me early on to be a part of the International Gatherings of the 'Workers' Economy'. *¡Gracias por tu generosidad, amigo!* And to Carlos Martínez, Natalia Polti, Javier Antivero, and Gabriel Clark of the Programa Facultad Abierta: *¡muchas gracias, también!* You have all opened so many doors for me and have been generous with sharing the invaluable data you have collected over the years. Your commitment to university extension and activist scholarship and your *acompañamiento* of the workers of the *empresas recuperadas* is to be emulated. Much gratitude also to Graciela Monteagudo for helping me better understand Argentina's labour and social movement traditions as part of the Argentina Autonomista Project research and study tour, and to the many friends and mentors I met during that study trip in 2005, especially Pablo Pozzi, Rhiannon Edwards, and Michael Gould-Wartofsky.

And again, to Stephan Dobson, this book's astute editor: Many, many thanks for your time, for the engaging conversations that helped me clarify so much, for helping me see from the beginning that it is about the voices of the workers, for your editorial work and advice, for opening up your home to me, and, and, and ... Thanks also to Ashish Pillai for assisting me so adeptly with the in-text references and bibliography, to Dina Theleritis for indexing help, and to the editorial team at the Historical Materialism Book Series for taking an early interest in this project and for their patience and support throughout the editorial process.

To the rest of my Toronto *compañeros*, to my Vancouver friendships that have stayed strong despite the distance, and to the *amistades* that have unfolded in Canada, Argentina, Italy, and beyond since I started this project: Thank you Albert Banerjee, Enda Brophy, Fiona Duguid, Chris Bradd, Sonya Scott, Manuel Larrabure, Adrian Blackwell, Laureano Ralón, Gonzalo Ralón, Sean Smith, Mark Macool, Sean Matvenko, Cedric Johnson, Sonja Novkovic, Darryl Reed, Angie Hsieh, Dan Schick, Michael Felczak, Mike Newson, Christine Shaw, Marnina Norris, Dave Myles, James Wanless, Sheila Grant, Pablo Bose, Ryan Rogerson, Burgundy Code, Camila Piñeiro Harnecker, Wendy Holm, Heather Haynes, Sebastian Touza, Ron Vida, Scott Uzelman, Doug Lionais, Jorge Sousa, George Cheney, Larry Haiven, Giulia Galera, Barbara Franchini, Antonella Carrano, Carlo Borzaga, and Alberto Zevi. Without all of you in my life at key moments I would have been lost at sea in the depths of the details. The *compañerismo* of all of you – however far back or recently it extends, however brief or long lasting it has been – is precious to me.

I would like to also recognise the financial support that I received for parts of this project from the Social Sciences and Humanities Research Council of Canada (SSHRC) through their Doctoral (2006–8) and Post-Doctoral awards (2013–14), from several SSHRC Institutional Grants (2015–17), and from a SSHRC Partnership Development Grant (2018–21). The University of Toronto's Connaught New Researcher Award (2016–19) was also helpful in the final stages of this project. Many thanks also to my colleagues in the Department of Leadership, Higher and Adult Education at the University of Toronto's Ontario Institute for Studies in Education for encouraging and supporting me in countless ways during the final stages of preparing this manuscript.

To my Argentine family: Carina Vieta, Paola Vieta, Gustavo Satriano, Guido Satriano, Delia Steinbauer, Maria Rullo, Adriana Rullo, Sergio Rullo, Florencia Rullo, and Laura Rullo. *Gracias* for taking care of me on my trips to Argentina.

And to my Colombian family: *Gracias* Gloria Barrero, my mother-in-law, in whose home I wrote several sections of this book. Your generosity has been boundless. And *gracias* to my brother-in-law Henry Díaz and sister-in-law Ingrid Pinto, for helping us out in so many untold ways while we lived in Colombia, and now while you live in Toronto.

Above all, I would like to thank the workers of the *empresas recuperadas* and each person that I have interviewed and talked to in Argentina since 2005 about the themes in this book. I have learned so, so much from all of you. You have entrusted me with the stories of your experiences; given freely of your time; and have opened up your workplaces, assemblies, and homes to me. This work would have been impossible without you. I would especially like to thank Plácido Peñarrieta, Cándido González, Ernesto González, Mario Alberto Barrios, Oscar Barrios, Diego Ledezma, Javier De Pascuale, Esteban Torletti, Alejandro Torres, José López, and Eduardo Murúa: For the innumerable ways you have helped me better understand the political economy and history of Argentina's *obreros*, and for helping me see how your struggles to save your jobs and start a new life with your *compañeros* extend far beyond keeping a company afloat. *¡Gracias por enseñarnos nuevos caminos a ese otro mundo que buscamos!*

All of these people, and many others, are the hidden co-authors of this book. Despite this, any missteps and glitches are solely mine.

Figures and Tables

Figures

Tables

Abbreviations and Acronyms

ACTRA	Federación Autogestión, Cooperativismo y Trabajo (Federation of Self-Management, Cooperativism and Work)
ADS/CUT	Agência de Desenvolvimento Solidário (Agency of Solidary Development) (Brazil)
AGOEC	Asociación Gremial Obreros y Empledos de Ceamse (Association of Unionised Workers and Employees of CEAMSE)
ALBA	Alianza Bolivariana para los Pueblos de Nuestra América (Bolivarian Alliance for the Peoples of Our America). Before 2009, the word 'Alternative' was used instead of 'Alliance'.
ANERT	Asociación Nacional de Empresas Recuperadas por sus Trabajadores (National Association of Worker-Recuperated Enterprises) (Uruguay)
ANTA	Asociación Nacional de Trabajadores Autogestionados (National Association of Self-Managed Workers)
ANTEAG	Associação Nacional dos Trabalhadores em Empresas de Autogestão e Participação Acionária (National Association of Workers of Self-Managed and Participatory Share Enterprises) (Brazil)
AOTRA	Asociación Obrera Textil de la República Argentina (Textile Workers' Association of the Republic of Argentina)
CAW	Canadian Auto Workers
CCC	Corriente Clasista y Combativa (Classist and Combative Current)
CEAMSE	Coordinación Ecológica Area Metropolitana Sociedad del Estado (Ecological Coordination Metropolitan Area Society of the State)
CF	Capitalist firm
CFI	Cooperazione Finanza Impresa (Enterprise Finance Cooperation) (Italy)
CGT	Confederación General del Trabajo de la República Argentina (General Confederation of Labour of the Republic of Argentina)
CGTFB	Confederación General de Trabajadores Fabriles de Bolivia (General Confederation of Industrial Workers of Bolivia)
CLAP	Camere del Lavoro Autonomo e Precario (Chamber of Autonomous and Precarious Work) (Italy)
CNCT	Confederación Nacional de Cooperativas de Trabajo (National Confederation of Worker Cooperatives)
Confcooperative	Confederazione Cooperative Italiane (Italian Cooperative Confederation)

CMC	Co-operatives and Mutuals Canada
CPU	Canadian Paperworkers Union
CSN	Confédération des Sindicats Nationaux (National Confederation of Unions) (Québec)
CSR	Corporate social responsibility
CTEP	Confederación de Trabajadores de la Economía Popular (Confederation of Workers of the Popular Economy)
CTA	Central de Trabajadores de la Argentina (Argentine Workers Central)
CUT	Central Única dos Trabalhadores (Unified Workers' Central) (Brazil)
CWCF	Canadian Worker Co-operative Federation
DİH	Devrimci İşçi Hareketi (Revolutionary Workers' Movement) (Turkey)
DyPRA	Diaros y Períodicos Regionales Argentinos (Cooperative of Regional Argentine Newspapers and Periodicals)
ERT	Empresa recuperada por sus trabajadores (worker-recuperated enterprise); also, empresa recuperada por los trabajadores (enterprise recuperated by the workers)
ESOP	Employee share-ownership plan
EURICSE	European Research Institute of Cooperative and Social Enterprises (Italy)
FACTA	Federación Argentina de Cooperativas de Trabajadores Autogestionados (Argentine Federation of Self-Managed Worker Cooperatives)
FADICCRA	Federación Asociativa de Diarios y Comunicadores Cooperativos de la República Argentina (Associational Federation of Cooperative Newspapers and Communicators of the Republic of Argentina)
FCPU	Federación de Cooperativas de Producción del Uruguay (Federation of Producer Cooperatives of Uruguay)
FECOOTRA	Federación de Cooperativas de Trabajo de la República Argentina (Federation of Worker Cooperatives of the Republic of Argentina)
FEDECABA	Federación de Cooperativas Autogestionadas de Buenos Aires (Federation of Self-Managed Cooperatives of Buenos Aires)
FETERA	Federación de Trabajadores de la Energía de la República Argentina (Federation of Energy Workers of the Republic of Argentina)
FGB	Federación Gráfica Bonaerense (Buenos Aires Graphics Federation)

FRETECO	Frente Revoloucionario de Trabajadores de Empresas en Cogestión y Ocupadas (Revolutionary Front of Enterprises Co-managed and Occupied by Workers) (Venezuela)
GESTARA	Grupo de Empresas Sociales y Trabajadores Autogestionados de la República Argentina (Group of Social Enterprises and Self-Managed Workers of the Republic of Argentina)
HRM	Human Resource Management
HRS	Human Relations School
ICOM	Industrial Common Ownership Movement (United Kingdom)
ICA	International Co-operative Alliance
IIFAP	Instituto de Investigación y Formación en Administración Pública (Institute of Research and Education in Public Administration, National University of Córdoba)
INAES	Instituto Nacional de Asociativismo y Economía Social (National Institute for Associationalism and the Social Economy)
INDEC	Instituto Nacional de Estadísticas y Censos (National Institute of Statistics and Census)
INTI	Instituto Nacional de Tecnología Industrial (National Institute of Industrial Technology)
IMPA	Industria Metalúrgica y Plástica Argentina (Metalurgic and Plastics Indusry of Argentina)
ISI	Import substitution industrialisation
IWW	Industrial Workers of the World
KMF	Capital-managed firm
Legacoop	Lega Nazionale delle Cooperative e Mutue (National League of Cooperatives and Mutuals) (Italy)
LMF	Labour-managed firm
MCC	Mondragón Cooperative Corporation
MERPBA	Mesa de Empresas Recuparadas de la Provincia de Buenos Aires (Committee of Recuperated Enterprises of the Province of Buenos Aires)
MNER	Movimiento Nacional de Empresas Recuperadas (National Movement of Recuperated Enterprises)
MNFRT	Movimiento Nacional de Fábricas Recuperadas por los Trabajadores (National Movement of Worker-Recuperated Factories)
MTD	Movimiento de Trabajadores Desocupados (Movement of Unemployed Workers)
MTS	Movimento dos Trabalhadores Rurais Sem Terra (Movement of Landless Rural Workers) (Brazil)
NDP	New Democratic Party (Canada)

NGO	Non-governmental organisation
OEOC	Ohio Employee Ownership Center
OSERA	Observatorio Social sobre Empresas Recupradas y Autogestionadas (Social Observatory on Recuperated and Self-Managed Enterprises)
PIT–CNT	Plenario Intersindical de Trabajadores–Convención Nacional de Trabajadores (Inter-Union Assembly of Workers–National Workers' Central)
PJ	Partido Justicialista (Jusiticialist Party)
PTS	Partido de los Trabajadores Socialistas (Socialist Workers' Party)
PyMES	Pequeñas y medianas empresas (small- and medium-sized enterprises) (English: SMES)
SAL	Sociedades laborales (labour societies) (Spain)
SCOP	Société coopérative ouvrières de production (society of workers' cooperatives of production); also, sociétés coopératives et participatives (cooperative and participative society) (France)
SETIA	Sindicato de Empleados Textiles de la Industria y Afines (Union of Employees of Textile and Related Industries)
SMATA	Sindicato de Mecánicos y Afines del Transporte Automotor de la República Argentina (Union of Mechanics and Allied Automotive Transport Workers of the Republic of Argentina).
SMES	Small- and medium-sized enterprises (Spanish: PyMES)
SOECN	Sindicato de Obreros y Empleados Ceramistas de Neuquén (Union of Ceramics Workers and Employees of Neuquén)
SOIVA	Sindicato Obrero de la Industria del Vestido y Afines (Workers' Union of Clothing and Related Industries)
SOE	State-owned enterprise
SOFICOOP	Società Finanza Cooperazione (Cooperation Finance Society) (Italy)
SUOEM	Sindicato Unión Obreros y Empleados Municipales (Municipal Workers' and Employees Union of Córdoba)
SPE	Unidades/empresas de producción socialista/social (Socialist/social production enterprise) (Venezuela)
SRL	Sociedad de responsabilidad limitada (limited liability company)
SSE	Social and solidarity economy
SYUSA	Saneamiento y Urbanización Sociedad Anónima (Sanitation and Urbanisation Anonymous Society)
UAW	United Automobile, Aerospace and Agricultural Implement Workers of America, also United Automobile Workers (United States)

UCR	Unión Cívica Radical (Radical Civic Union)
UE	United Electrical, Radio and Machine Workers of America
UNISOL Brasil	Central de Cooperativas e Empreendimentos Solidários de Economia Social do Brasil (Central of Cooperatives and Solidarity Enterprises of the Social Economy of Brazil)
UNISOL São Paulo	União e Solidariedade das Cooperativas de São Paulo (Union and Solidarity of Cooperatives of Sao Paulo)
UOGC	Unión Obrera Gráfica Cordobesa (Graphic Workers' Union of Cordoba)
UOCRA	Unón Obrera de la Construcción de la República Argentina (Construction Workers' Union of the Republic of Argentina)
UOM	Unión Obrera Metalúrgica (Metalurgical Workers' Union)
UPEA	Unión Productiva de Empresas Autogestionadas (Productive Union of Self-Managed Enterprises)
USFWC	US Federation of Worker Cooperatives
UST	Cooperativata de Trabajo 'Unión Solidaria de Trabajadores' ('Solidarity Gathering of Workers' Worker Cooperative)
USW	United Steel, Paper and Forestry, Rubber, Manufacturing, Energy, Allied Industrial and Service Workers International Union, also United Steelworkers (United States, Canada, and Caribbean)
UTE	Unión transitoria/temporaria de empresas (transitory/temporary association of firms)
UTHGRA	Unión de Trabajadores del Turismo, Hoteleros y Gastronómicos (Union of Tourism, Hotel, and Gastronomy Workers)
WBO	Worker buyouts
WISE	Work-integration social enterprise
WOF	worker-owned firm

Introduction

> This path that we have begun to travel on together is an historic chal
> lenge. We need to take up this challenge with the best that we have in
> order to strengthen over time the idea that we workers are indeed capable
> of forging a future where a social economy is the considered reality. Yet,
> we need to always keep in mind that we came from a dark night where
> egoism, fear, and ignorance marked [the other] path towards the abyss.
> Since the beginning of time rebels have emerged, rebels ready to search
> out other destinies and change directions so that fraternity and reason
> mould the soul of the new person.
>
> HUGO CABRERA and GABRIEL ROJAS[1]

∴

1   Neo-liberal Crisis, Popular Revolt, and *Autogestión*

On 19 and 20 December 2001 Argentina became the site of a massive popular uprising that brought the economic and political crisis of its neo-liberal
experiment to a breaking point. With a broad cross-section of the population
rising momentarily in unison during these days and the weeks that followed,
banging pots and pans, occupying streets and plazas, and chanting *'¡Qué se
vayan todos, que no quede ni uno sólo!'* ('Everyone [in the political and economic
establishment] must leave now, let not even one stay!'), the collective scream
of popular fury radiating from Argentina resonated throughout the world in a
rejoinder to diminished economic prospects, dwindling political voice, frozen
bank accounts, lost jobs, heightened government corruption, and rapidly rising
poverty. Throughout December 2001 the nation experienced escalating social
turmoil and in the week or so following the 19 and 20 December events went
through five presidents in quick succession.[2] In the subsequent months, with a
devalued peso and in the wake of what was at the time the largest national debt

---

1   Cabrera and Rojas n.d., p. 1 (*Curso básico sobre cooperativas de trabajo*).
2   These five presidents included: the fall of Fernando de la Rúa, three short-lived interim presidencies following the line of succession, and the eventual congressional appointment of
    Eduardo Duhalde as caretaker president.

default in history, Argentina's social and economic crisis worsened to unprecedented levels as unemployment soared and poverty engulfed around half of its population. Between December 2001 and mid-2003, the country meandered from the collapse of Fernando de la Rúa's presidency (1999–2001),[3] to relative political stabilisation (but continued socio-economic instability) by the end of 2002 under the caretaker administration of President Eduardo Duhalde[4] (2002–3), to the restitution of relative social peace and eventual economic steadying with the nationalist-developmentalist policies of President Néstor Kirchner's administration beginning in 2003.

In response to the prolonged crisis and the eventual blighting of the lives of millions of Argentina's working people – instigated in no small part by the government of President Carlos Menem's (1989–99) earlier acquiescence to IMF-sanctioned deregulation, privatisation, and austerity – already by the mid-to-late 1990s myriad spaces for social and economic renewal from below were being created by organised movements of the unemployed, neighbourhood assemblies, housing and human-rights groups, and the *empresas recuperadas por sus trabajadores* (ERTs, worker-recuperated enterprises[5]) – the group at the heart of this book.[6] Through community-based projects centred on values of social justice, a desire for economic self-reliance, and practices of direct democracy and horizontal organising – all of which stood in stark contrast to neo-liberal values and practices of individualism, consumerism, and free market competition that had dominated Argentina throughout the 1990s – these bottom-up movements managed to directly address the inability of the country's traditional institutions to contain record levels of socio-economic exclusion and poverty.[7]

Argentina's *empresas recuperadas* thus predate the social and political upheavals of what became known as *el Argentinazo* of 19 and 20 December 2001. The contemporary phenomenon of workers' recuperations of workplaces began to slowly emerge some years before, during the first signs of the neo-

---

3 De la Rúa was the Unión Cívica Radical (UCR) politician who had led the coalition-based administration that, despite its initial opposition to *menemismo*, had paradoxically continued most of the neo-liberal policies of the preceding regime of President Carlos Menem.

4 Before his brief Senate-appointed caretaker presidency, Peronist politician Eduardo Duhalde had been Menem's first vice-president (1989–91) and then governor of the province of Buenos Aires (1991–9).

5 Also called *empresas recuperadas por los trabajadores* (enterprises recuperated by the workers).

6 Pozzi and Nigra 2015b; Svampa and Pereyra 2004; Zibechi 2012.

7 Castro Soto 2008; Damill 2005; Palomino 2003, 2005; Pozzi and Nigra 2015a, 2015b.

liberal model's unravelling in the early 1990s.[8] The *empresas recuperadas* would thus act as socio-economic canaries in the narrowing mineshaft that was sinking Argentina deeper and deeper into social, political, and economic despair throughout the last decade of the twentieth century.

As Argentina's free-market economy began collapsing by the mid-1990s, small- and medium-sized enterprises (SMEs; in Spanish, *pequeñas y medianas empresas*, or PyMEs), unable to compete against the wave of foreign products saturating local markets and tied down by an artificially inflated peso, began to declare bankruptcy in historically exceptional numbers.[9] On the one hand, and most immediately, this massive failure of firms – together with the growing immiseration of working people – was intimately linked to Argentina's 'financial and economic deregulation, privatisation, the shedding of protective tariffs', deindustrialisation, and a starkly anti-labour political environment.[10] An overvalued peso legally set to a one-to-one exchange rate with the US dollar also compounded business failures. Known as the Plan de Covertibilidad (Convertability Plan), this fixed exchange rate policy was introduced in 1991 by Menem's economics minister Domingo Cavallo to combat the high inflation of the late 1980s. The policy of *convertibilidad* would ultimately prove devastating for the country's SMEs, making the purchasing of business inputs and the regular payment of wages increasingly challenging.[11]

On the other hand, these business failures were also due to desperate moves by business owners who, anxious to stave off permanent closure, increasingly resorted to heightening the rate of exploitation on shop floors and, eventually, to laying off, locking out, or firing employees. At times owners would, in obviously illegal manoeuvres, asset strip their own firms while in the midst of debt refinancing or bankruptcy proceedings. Sometimes they would collude with or pay off bankruptcy court trustees while in the process of closing shops without telling the businesses' employees, who had often already been suffering weeks or months of dwindling job security and pay reductions, had not been receiving the employer's portion of benefits and overtime pay, or, in the worst cases, had not been receiving *any* remuneration. And some of these swindling, incompetent, or overwhelmed business owners would even take their firm's assets and open up shop elsewhere employing cheaper labour.

---

8   Fajn 2003; Rebón 2004; Ruggeri, Polti, Clark, Antivero, Delegdisch, et al. 2010. See Figures 7
     and 12.
9   Magnani 2009.
10   Zibechi 2012, p. 92.
11   Patroni 2002, 2004.

Already by 1995 it was becoming clear that more and more workers were falling into the population of the structurally unemployed at rates that were expanding the ranks of Argentina's reserve army of labour to extraordinary proportions;[12] by late 2001 and early 2002, the rate of structural unemployment had reached well over 20 percent of the adult population willing and able to work.[13] It is no accident, then, that the apex of new ERT growth occurred between 2001–4, the most intense period of socio-economic crisis in Argentina's recent history.[14]

With many in the established labour movement's leadership co-opted into supporting the state's neo-liberal policies by the Menem regime; with traditional union tactics of strikes or strike threats proving incapable of adequately addressing workers' immediate needs in this starkly anti-labour environment; and with an impotent state on the defensive as social, economic, and political crises rendered it incapable of adequately responding to soaring immiseration and business failures, some workers began taking matters into their own hands by occupying and reopening the collapsing or bankrupted firms that had been employing them, converting these occupied workplaces into worker cooperatives in the process. Rather than being impelled (at first) by a desire for broad social change or by traditional union demands, these bottom-up worker

---

12   Neo-classical economists consider 'structural unemployment' as being the gap between the population of workers not working but actively seeking full-time work and those workers still employed, specifically when this gap is a result of labour not being able to 'adjust' to the structural changes in a national or regional economy's work conditions due either to economic growth or contraction or changing demands in skills related to technological change in the extant regime of production (Ragan and Lipsey 2004). As Viviana Patroni points out, for the first time in Argentina's modern history, the initial spurt of economic growth of the early 1990s brought with it structural unemployment rather than more employment (Patroni 2004, p. 104). As the decade wore on, the continued deindustrialisation and multinationalisation of much of Argentina's economy caused the demand for labour to decrease even further, especially related to the widespread business practice of replacing workers with labour-saving machinery from abroad; such machinery became cheaper and more accessible for businesses during these years as a result of the dollarised peso. Additionally, as dismissed former public- and private-sector workers found it harder and harder to find similar work in their sectors, growing structural unemployment was paralleled by the growing rate of underemployment and unregulated part-time work, contract work, and other precarious forms of employment devoid of social security guarantees. Thus, the neo-liberal model in 1990s Argentina was also effectively about the cheapening of labour costs, the flexibilisation of labour, and, ultimately, the fragmentation of organised labour (Patroni 2002, 2004).

13   INDEC 2016; Levy Yeyati, and Valenzuela 2013; Lozano 2005.

14   Palomino, Bleynat, Garro, and Giacomuzzi 2010, p. 256; Ruggeri, Polti, Clark, Antivero, Delegdisch, et al. 2010, p. 12. See Figure 12.

responses would emerge locally on shop floors – and predominantly in SMEs – as mobilising grievances at the point of production.[15] These collective grievances would mobilise workforces that had been experiencing blatant violations of wage contracts, or that were most at risk of lockouts, firings, or the closure of their places of employment. That is, ERT protagonists' *initial* actions of workplace occupations were – and are to this day – mostly *defensive*, arising out of necessity (saving their jobs, securing a livelihood for themselves and their families), out of fear of never finding similar work again or any work at all,[16] or out of indignation at being *estafado* (literally, shafted) by managers and bosses. Moreover, given the age-old threat of institutional violence in Argentina, these direct-action responses can be seen as highly risky localised tactics that emerge on some of the shop floors most impelled by micro-economic difficulties, carried out by desperate workers' collectives willing to face violent repression by the state or returning owners in order to save their jobs and safeguard their self-dignity. During the most acute years of socio-economic crisis spanning the turn of the millennium, workplace occupation actions were further propelled by a morally bankrupt political system that looked the other way while countless business owners engaged in highly questionable schemes to save dying firms or sought to profit from running them into the ground at the expense of the wellbeing of employees. Most ERTs, then, first emerge from their employees' pragmatic and immanent responses to their boss's *blatant contraventions of labour contracts* and from workers' own *deep worries of becoming structurally unemployed*, a life situation that Argentine workers have since termed, for reasons that will become clear as this book unfolds, '*muerte en vida*' ('death in life').[17]

The direct action strategies and tactics of occupation, resistance to repression and eviction, and subsequent self-managed production under the legal

---

15   Within social movement theory, 'mobilising grievances' are 'grievances [or perceived injustices] that are shared among some number of actors, be they individuals or organizations, and that are felt to be sufficiently serious to warrant some kind of corrective, collective action' (Snow and Soule 2010, p. 24; see also Dahrendorf 1959). ERTs are examples of such a collective of actors – made up of protagonists from a subset of Argentina's working class – that held such grievances and that acted collectively by mobilising to fight for their jobs and the recuperation of their firms in order to rectify injustices they felt were committed against them by bosses and the state-capitalist establishment. I specifically discuss the motivations of this subset of Argentina's working class for taking over and self-managing their failing firms in Chapter 6 and as a struggle rooted in a 'moral economy of work' at the end of this book's Introduction.

16   This was a common fear amongst workers during the crisis years spanning the turn of the millennium.

17   Vieta and Ruggeri 2009, p. 202.

framework of a worker cooperative are, then, important *defensive manoeuvres* for its worker protagonists, especially during the first precarious days of an ERT. These are manoeuvres that, at first, directly respond to the dire conjunctural and micro-economic situations that, in innumerable ways, continue to make the lives of Argentina's workers precarious. Eventually, and for reasons I will explore throughout this book, over the course of reopening the firm as a worker cooperative, these defensive manoeuvres born out of necessity transform into workers' pro-active and long-term visions and practices of self-managing their own economic and productive lives, which they call '*autogestión*'.

In Argentina, *autogestión* – this book's key concept – means to self-determine and self-manage productive activity cooperatively and democratically as an alternative to strictly capitalist organisations of work. More profoundly, for many self-managed workers' collectives in Argentina and throughout Latin America, *autogestión* means *to self-constitute and self-direct production and economic life while attempting to minimise the intrusive mediation of free markets, hierarchical organisation, or state and union bureaucracies*. In Argentina and across Latin America, myriad social justice groups and movements, including ERTs, have been using the concept of *autogestión* to articulate for themselves and to others how the (re)invention and (re)construction of their organisations, their labour processes, and the social relations therein, are to take place under more humane values than those offered by the capitalist system of work organisation and its principal interest: the pursuit of profit.[18]

For the protagonists of Argentina's ERTs, their initial tactics of taking over the troubled firms that had been employing them in order to protect jobs and maintain life-security eventually can become, they discover, viable strategies for reorganising workplaces and working life *cooperatively*. As many ERT workers and activists have told me since I began this research in 2005, and as the three recuperation stories in Chapter 1 will show, their initial fear of being without work in dire economic times and their anger towards the empty promises and callousness of former bosses usually foment their workplace occupation direct actions. But gradually, throughout the struggle to save their jobs and, subsequently, after beginning to self-manage their workplaces, these workers, for the first time in their lives, come to discover that it is indeed possible to change and self-control their own social and economic circumstances. And this in spite of – and, indeed, perhaps because of – a political and economic

---

18   On *autogestión*, see also Buendía Garcia 2005; Del Mar Araus 2004; Peixoto de Albuquerque 2004; Ruggeri 2009; Vieta 2010b, 2014a, 2014b, 2016b; and Wyczykier 2009b. I provide a genealogical study of the term in Chapter 5.

system that in many ways has continued to remain unresponsive to their quotidian needs, as we will soon see. Eventually, these multifaceted experiences of heightened exploitation and ERT workers' self-determined and collective responses to them combine to ground and strengthen their commitments to cooperativised labour processes and divisions of labour. And at times in many ERTs, these experiences eventually inspire new and promising solidarity economies with other ERTs and the communities and *barrios* (neighbourhoods) that surround them.

In short, ERT workers *immanently* and, as I will explore later in the book, *informally* learn the practices of *autogestión* and cooperativism '*sobre la marcha*', or 'on the path of doing', as ERT protagonists have told me.[19] That is, they learn in the process of struggle.[20] In the beginning, these practices emerge out of need. Subsequently, as the months and years of *autogestión* unfold, their ideas of a self-directed and collectively controlled work life concretise and expand in these workers' very actions, transforming into viable projects for not only securing jobs, but also providing for their communities' needs and, perhaps, even as foundations for a new, less exploitative and more egalitarian socio-economic reality for Argentina. Thus, additional key themes that drive this study and that will begin to unfold with more clarity as we proceed include: ERT protagonists' immanently emergent 'conscientisation', or a coming to an awareness of their exploitation and how to address and move beyond it;[21] their protagonism as a 'class-in-the-making'; and their 'learning by doing' and 'in struggle', all rooted in their lived experiences of crises and their bottom-up collective actions against and beyond crises.

2 The Approach

The overarching argument that guides this book is that ERTs are exemplars of the potential for alternative socio-economic arrangements still possible in the self-activity and agency of working people – despite the continued preponderance of neo-liberal capitalism, its incessant imposition of market logics, and its waves of macro- and micro-economic crises. To begin to sketch out this potential, Part 1 of the book begins from the standpoint of the lived experiences

---

19   This can be equated to the Zapatistas' notion of 'making the path by walking' (Holloway 2011).

20   See also Vieta 2014b.

21   Here I am drawing on Paulo Freire's notion of *conscientização* (concientisation) (Freire 1970, pp. 35, 109).

and voices of Argentina's ERT worker protagonists and maps out the conjunctural dimensions of the emergence of the ERT phenomenon.[22] Part 2 theorises
and historicises the agentic capacities of the working class and, specifically,
workers' self-managed production encapsulated in the concept of *autogestión*.
It also begins to explore the broader implications of *autogestión* for alternative economic arrangements as suggested by Argentina's ERTs. Part 3, in turn,
returns to ERT protagonists' lived experiences, exploring in detail the radical
social innovations and challenges of their projects and practices of *autogestión*. Finally, Part 4 reviews the book's key findings and seeks to re-theorise
the potential of *autogestión* for the project of reconstituting work and socio-
economic life beyond capitalism.

An important aim of the book is to show that coming to know ERTs and
their protagonists' lived experiences of *autogestión* results in important contributions to a critical sociology of work, to theories of working-class agency,
to the study of alternative work organisations[23] such as worker cooperatives,
and for better understanding the dynamics of conversions of capitalist businesses to labour-managed firms. Overall, an engaged study of Argentina's ERTs,
I contend, can contribute much to broader social justice projects that seek new
socio-economic realities rooted in more solidarity-based and egalitarian relations of working and living. For the study of alternative work organisations,
the book seeks to learn from the experiences of Argentina's ERTs in the hope
of building on theories and practices of workers' self-management. For critical sociologies of work and theories of the labour-managed firm, the evidence
offered in this book shows that a worker collective's *shared experiences of crises
at the point of production* and *having to overcome crises together* (crises that
are in no small part prolonged when having to exist within capitalist markets)
can sustain and radicalise a cooperative project, catalyse the organisational
potential of workers' self-management, and ultimately strengthen the solidarity and commitment of a cooperative's worker-members. For better understanding working-class struggle and the motivations that drive initiatives for

---

22   As I discuss in detail in Chapter 9, and in the spirit of the historical materialist and crit-
      ical theoretical approaches of the book, this study embraces a *conjunctural analysis* of
      the emergence of Argentina's ERTs. For Antonio Gramsci, the conjuncture is 'the set of
      [immanent socio-political and socio-economic] circumstances ... constituting a process
      of ever-changing combinations ... [inherent to] ... the economic cycle' (Gramsci 1971a,
      p. 177). Immanent to a given historical moment, according to Gramsci, *the conjunctural*
      can emerge out of capitalist economic crises and may potentially open up the space for
      oppositional forces to counter the hegemonic socio-economic system (Ibid; see also For-
      gacs 2000).

23   Atzeni 2012; Parker, Cheney, Fournier, and Land 2014.

social justice in the workplace, theorised and historicised in Chapters 4 and 5, the book aspires to learn from ERT protagonists' modes of organising and how they, as we will further explore in Chapter 8, cooperatively 'learn in struggle' and 'by doing' *autogestión*. In short, the book strives to better understand a specific and contemporary example of how workers living within a national conjuncture of neo-liberal capitalism can indeed, as an ERT pamphlet suggests, '*take destiny in [their] own hands*'.[24]

Relying on the experiences of Argentina's ERT protagonists, the book ultimately theorises what it is that workers *recuperate* (or take back) for themselves when they take over and self-manage the capitalist workplaces that formerly employed them. As I will introduce shortly, this includes the recuperation of workers' labour-power, *their* labour processes, *their* surpluses, and, overall, workers' very dignity as creative and socially embedded human beings. ERT protagonists' struggles for recuperating and recomposing their workplaces and working lives, I contend throughout the book, are thus relevant in two major ways: they practically suggest the continued capacities of workers to collectively self-control their own productive destinies *and*, in the very act of taking over and self-managing their former capitalist places of employment, they allude to the fundamental things that are at stake in the capital-labour relationship for working people.

In sum, in the following pages I set out to empirically and theoretically explore, from historical materialist, critical theoretical, and critical sociological perspectives, *the agentic potential* always already present with workers – at times surfacing into struggles to collectively control their own socio-economic destinies – and *the transformative force* that is unleashed when workers involve themselves cooperatively in projects of *autogestión* that seek to overcome micro-economic crises at their places of work and macro-economic crises in the political economy. As the following chapters highlight, workers' agentic potential and transformative force are witnessed in ERT protagonists' very collective responses to crises that, in the recent conjuncture of Argentina, has transformed their subjectivities (from managed employees to self-managed workers), their organisations (from capitalist enterprises to cooperative workplaces), and their communities (from depleted and fragmented localities to places of collective self-provision).

24　Cooperativa 'Unión Solidaria de Trabajadores' 2007 (emphasis in original).

2.1   A Critical Theoretical Research Programme

The book is grounded in two closely related historical materialist traditions: critical theories of capitalist processes of production and working-class political economy, the latter including theories and histories of workers' self-activity and *autogestión*. As I expand on more fully in Chapter 4, these two complementary traditions are appropriate for helping us work through ERTs' practical and theoretical implications because they look critically at two interrelated dimensions intersecting capitalist economics and socio-technical organisation: the constraining of labour-power[25] via the exploitation and alienation of workers *and* the possibilities for opening up the capitalist labour process to workers' control beyond alienation and exploitation when the capitalist technological inheritance merges with workers' innate abilities to cooperate. Despite their challenges and continued situatedness within capitalist markets, ERTs, I argue throughout this book, are one contemporary and powerful manifestation of workers' capacities to move beyond capital-labour relations, embracing the possibilities for another kind of socio-economic present and future.

In this spirit, the book proceeds on a two-pronged methodological trajectory. A macro-level historical and political economic dimension roots Argentina's ERTs in a past of bottom-up working-class militancy that has often seen Argentina's workers act collectively as a counterforce to the episodic authoritarian tendencies of its political economic history. This historical working-class militancy, as I will specifically trace out in Chapter 3, has unfolded both within and, more often than is accounted for in the scholarly literature, outside of the auspices of Argentina's organised labour movement. In order to trace out this history, I rely on Argentine secondary documents gathered from scholarly, government, union, journalistic, and social movement sources.

Concurrently, a micro-sociological dimension takes inspiration from workers' and labour process ethnographies[26] and the semi-structured interview approach of Latin American and Argentine oral labour history.[27] The book's micro-level empirical findings emerge from interviews and ethnographic evidence I gathered on extended research trips to Argentina between 2005 and 2009 and in follow-up trips since. During these research trips, I visited many ERTs and spent extended periods of time conducting formal interviews, enga-

---

25   Explored further in Chapter 4, labour-power is the potential capacity of workers to labour and create value.

26   For instance, Burawoy 1979, 1998; Juravich 1985; and Willis 1977.

27   For instance, Carey 2017; Fals Borda 1971, 2001; James 1988; Pozzi 1988, 2012; Schneider 2005; and Werner and Aguirre 2007.

ging in informal conversations, and carrying out in-situ observations at various *empresas recuperadas* while focusing on three exemplar ERT case studies: the print shop Cooperativa de Trabajo Chilavert Artés Gráficas in the city of Buenos Aires (where I also engaged in non-remunerated work-related activity as a student-intern for a month in July 2005); the waste management, parks maintenance, and construction firm Cooperativa de Trabajo 'Unión Solidaria de Trabajadores' (UST, Solidarity Gathering of Workers) in the province of Buenos Aires; and the health clinic Cooperativa de Trabajo Salud Junín in the city of Córdoba. In selecting these three case studies, I deployed a strategy of 'diversification'.[28] That is, these three ERTs are exemplary for this book because of the distinct economic sectors they operate in; the different labour processes they employ; their diverse workers' struggles, paths to self-management, and histories of conflicts with each firm's previous owners and the legal system; their varied sizes; and the unique political, cultural, and regional contexts in which they find themselves.[29] In total I conducted 65 formal, in-depth, and semi-structured key informant interviews for this study, including ERT workers from the three case studies and from other ERTs; labour leaders; municipal, provincial, and national government officials; social movement activists; and academic researchers.[30]

Since 2006, I have also been working collaboratively with the team of social anthropologists, sociologists, labour historians, social movement researchers, and activists of the Programa Facultad Abierta (Open University Program) at

---

28 Atzeni and Ghigliani 2007, p. 658. See also Atzeni 2010.

29 Not only did I look for diversification in selecting my ERT case studies, I also aimed to do so in securing interviews within each ERT. My sample of key informants for my semi-structured interviews in each case study took on a snowball approach. In all cases I first interviewed a former or current leader or president of the ERT and was eventually introduced to other workers as I conducted my interviews. I was sensitive to interviewing both founders and newer members of each ERT and, where applicable, strove to attain a gender balance and age balance, as well.

30 See Appendix. It is important to note up front that I use the actual names of the people I have interviewed, with their permission, in order to honour and recognise their stories and give voice to the actual protagonists of Argentina's ERTs in the spirit of collaborative co-research. As Salud Junín's Edith Allende emphatically told me, capturing the sentiment of all of the ERT workers I have talked to over the years: 'We have no problems with you naming us. What's more, we carry our name with pride and we have no issues with others using our name when we speak, or with showing [the name of our cooperative] to the entire world' (Allende 2009, personal interview). I have also endeavoured to share copies of the recordings and transcripts of the interviews with key informants, as well as earlier versions of this book's manuscript. In situations where I use testimony material gathered from informal conversations, or in the few cases where particular narratives might compromise key informants, no names are disclosed.

the University of Buenos Aires's Faculty of Philosophy and Letters,[31] a team that has been studying and working in solidarity with Argentina's ERTs since 2002. In a spirit of collaborative research, key sections of Chapter 2 and Chapter 6 are a collective effort with the Programa Facultad Abierta's director, Andrés Ruggeri. Moreover, many of the book's figures and tables rely on the Programa Facultad Abierta's primary quantitative data collected between 2002–16.[32] Consistently cited in most scholarly and journalistic publications on ERTs throughout the world, the team's data on the Argentine ERT phenomenon is undoubtedly the most thorough, reliable, rigorously collected, and up to date.

My research for this book has also drawn particular inspiration from Michael Burawoy's iteration of workplace sociology,[33] most recently articulated in his 'global ethnography' approach.[34] Commensurate with this book's broader research aims, the global ethnography approach aspires to unravel the macro *and* micro forces and tensions at play within an organisation's labour process operating under a particular production regime. Central to this approach is the 'extended case method' of assessing workplace labour processes,[35] wherein the observations of the researcher on the ground *extends* the understanding (and theories) of 'micro processes to macro forces, from the space-time rhythms of the site to the geographical and historical context of the field'.[36] Guided by this

---

31   See, for instance, Ruggeri 2006; Vieta 2009a, 2009b; Vieta and Ruggeri 2009; and Ruggeri and Vieta 2015.

32   As of this writing, the Programa Facultad Abierta team has produced and published five country-wide ERT surveys (Programa Facultad Abierta 2002; Ruggeri, Martínez, and Trinchero 2005; Ruggeri, Polti, Clark, Antivero, Delegdisch, et al. 2010; Ruggeri, Antivero, Elena, Polti, et al. 2014; Ruggeri 2016), fourteen books or reports on Argentina's ERTs and the topic of workers' self-management, and numerous educational booklets and pamphlets directed at Argentina's ERT workers. Many of their books and reports have been translated into English, Portuguese, Italian, Greek, and other languages. The Programa Facultad Abierta also runs the ERT Documentation Centre out of Artes Gráficas Chilavert, which is one of this book's case study ERTs. The team has also been the lead organiser of the international 'Workers' Economy' conferences (see Chapter 7).

33   Burawoy 1979, 1985.

34   Burawoy 2000.

35   Burawoy 1998, p. 4.

36   Burawoy 2000, p. 27. For this book, this necessarily also means the possible 'extension of theory' (Burawoy 2000, p. 28) emerging at times, and in unexpected ways, from ERT protagonists' lived experiences of recuperating firms and then self-managing them. That is, not only is this study's theoretical framework used to understand the specificities of the practices of self-management I encountered in the field in Argentina, but the theoretical framework is pushed or even yields, at times, to the anomalies unearthed, or, as Burawoy articulates it, to the 'discrepancies [that] challenge ... the theory we want to improve'

way of proceeding, this book's case studies and empirical analysis are my effort to put into relief the macro-political and macro-economic forces that meet and entangle the processes of workplace recuperation and the subsequent everyday organisational practices of ERTs at their point of production or point of service delivery.[37]

2.2 The Stream of Self-Determination, Class Struggle, and the Political Economy of the Working Class

Threading throughout the historical materialist traditions that frame the book is what I call 'the stream of self-determination' of modern socialism. The stream of self-determination is a praxical current of critical thought that courses through nineteenth-century utopian socialism and classical social anarchism, fragments of Marx and Engels' works, as well as twentieth- and twenty-first century veins of libertarian socialist and social anarchist theory. The stream of self-determination of modern socialism focuses on the cooperative capacities of working people and their continued agency. It draws inspiration from both the historical struggles of working people before capitalism took root as the world's central economic paradigm and the ongoing struggles of workers as a counterforce to the rise and consolidation of capitalism itself. Rather than remaining fixed on how workers and the marginalised are acted upon by capital and state power, the stream of self-determination homes in on the self-activity of communities, people's 'individual autonomy' and the continued freedom they have to choose 'ethical' ways of reorganising their own and society's economic needs,[38] and the potentiality open to workers to *re-appropriate* the capitalist technological paradigm in order to counteract and find alternatives to exploitation and alienation.[39]

For the task of working out the conjunctural realities and alternative economic possibilities of ERTs' practices of *autogestión*, this book's analysis is spe-

---

(Burawoy 2000, p. 28). It is in these discrepancies that the critical theories of capitalist production, *autogestión*, and working-class struggle we will engage with are 'extended' (Burawoy 2000, p. 27).

37   Burawoy's labour process-based workplace sociology, informed especially by his global ethnography/extended case method approach, is adequate for tackling my research questions because it considers the micro-level dimensions I am after – that is, at the level of *the lived experiences* of ERT workers – while also considering, to appropriate Dorothy Smith's standpoint for studying everyday life, how these 'micro-structures of everyday life' (Smith, in Burawoy 2000, pp. 26, 40) are 'knitted into broader forms of [macro-level] social organization' and institutions (Grahame 1998, p. 347).

38   Bookchin 1990, pp. 99, 119–20.

39   See, for instance, Feenberg 2002; Marcuse 1964; and Marx 1973.

cifically located in a theoretical tributary of the stream of self-determination that some contemporary Marxist socialist theorists have come to call '"class-struggle" Marxism'.[40] This 'class-struggle' tributary, while certainly not shunning the political-economic analysis of capital, specifically sets its sights on the self-activity of the working class. Disdaining the strict 'economism' that, as Michael Lebowitz points out, affects classical 'one-sided [or objectivist] Marxism'[41] (with its traditional focus on the laws of capital), class-struggle Marxism instead draws inspiration from the continuing agency that remains with those exploited by capital. Class-struggle Marxism does indeed consider the dynamics, lived experiences, and effects of exploitation, alienation, and class conflict within capitalism. But it also focuses on: (1) workers' ongoing capacities to do something about their situation of exploitation within the capital-labour relation, and the vitality and varieties of working-class resistances to capitalist logics of domination;[42] (2) the richness of working-class culture and workers' self-activity[43] (such as the 'cultures of solidarity'[44] workers subsequently forge within and beyond the labour process that act as counterweights to capitalism's modes of control and its exploitations and crises); (3) the recognition of workers as active agents of history (rather than passive objects);[45] and (4) how workers, in turn, potentially transform themselves and their circumstances as they 'live [and make] their own history'.[46] In other words, in what has been called a 'heretical strain of Marxism', the class-struggle approach analyses 'not just the dominative power of capital, but [also] people's capacity to contest that power'.[47]

Class-struggle Marxists thus devote a good portion of their critical work to analysing the potential for the working class to transform, move beyond, or generally overcome the technological rationalities and dominative logics of capitalism. Class-struggle Marxism does so by: recognising the cracks and strains inherent to the contradictions of the capitalist system that particularly come to

---

40   Dyer-Witheford 1999, p. 62. See also So 1991; So and Hikam 1989; and Meiksins 1987. Class-struggle Marxism is also widely (but perhaps too broadly) known as 'subjectivist Marxism' (Hudis 2012). This critical theoretical position situated within modern socialism's stream of self-determination has been taken up by numerous mid-to-late twentieth and early twenty-first century writers that I review in Chapter 4.

41   Michael Lebowitz 2003, pp. 9–10.

42   Cleaver 2000; Dyer-Witheford 1999.

43   Ranciere 1989; Thompson 1963.

44   Fantasia 1988.

45   Thompson 1963.

46   Thompson 1963, p. 11. See also Lebowitz 2003; Marx 1976a; and Wood 1982, 1986, 1988, 1995.

47   Dyer-Witheford, 1999, p. 62.

the surface in moments of crises, the force of workers' cooperation unleashed by the capitalist labour process that forge solidarities beyond the controlling reach of capitalist administrators, the potentiality opened up by new technologies for working-class emancipation, and, most broadly, the possibilities that the very capitalist mode of production transmits to the class struggle itself by bringing workers together.

Class-struggle Marxist theorists and historians have taken off from a re-reading of Marx's more explicit analysis of working-class self-activity sketched out throughout his mature writings.[48] In the 'Inaugural Address of the Working Men's International Association', for example, Marx himself termed this approach 'the political economy of the working class'.[49] For Marx, two examples from his own time that vividly illustrated this working-class political economy and the prefigurative nature of workers' self-activity were the struggle for the 10-hour workday and the existence of worker/producer cooperatives. Marx theoretically positioned these two examples as instantiations of 'the political economy of labour over the political economy of property'.[50] Worker cooperatives, of course, are particularly relevant for the study of ERTs; most directly, worker cooperatives showed in practice, for Marx, that owners and managers were superfluous for the organisation of production and for meeting humanity's socio-economic needs.[51] Worker cooperatives also demonstrated for Marx (although not without tensions and contradictions, as we will soon see) how 'the opposition between capital and labour' could be abolished in 'a new mode of production' based on associated labour.[52] Argentina's ERT phenomenon, I contend, adds one more significant moment to the political economy of the working class. In short, taking up a class-struggle Marxist perspective offers historical materialist force and analytical strength for helping us answer the major questions that drive this book[53] – in particular, for more precisely understanding what it is that ERT protagonists recuperate when they take over and self-manage formerly capitalist firms.

Rather than remaining fixed on how the exploitative and dominative logics of capitalism and its neo-liberal variant have restrained Argentina's workers,

---

48   For instance, Marx 1973, pp. 690–712; Marx 1978a, 1978b, 1978c, 1985, 1988. But also in Marx 2007, Marx and Engels 1998. See also Hudis 2012.

49   Marx 1978a, p. 517.

50   Ibid.

51   Marx 1981, p. 511. On the importance of worker cooperatives for Marx's political economy of the working class, see Lebowitz 2003, p. 89; Jossa 2005, 2014, 2017.

52   Marx 1981, p. 571. Se also Marx 1985, 1988.

53   As presented in this book's Preface.

this book's empirical analysis is centred on the point of view of ERT protagonists, jumping off from the standpoint of their lived experiences of exploitation
and their struggles to restart their working lives under the rubric of *autogestión*. The bulk of this book's exposition thus rests on the empirical evidence
offered by the actual words and experiences of ERT protagonists, shaped also,
of course, by my interpretation of these words and experiences and my own
in situ observations of Argentine ERTs. Grounded in the traditions of critical
theories of capitalist processes of production and working-class political economy, this book thus treats the ERT phenomenon as both a continuation of
workers' long history of bottom-up resistance and also as a remarkable contemporary instance of working-class self-activity within the particular conjuncture
of a country caught in the ebbs and flows of a neo-liberal capitalist political-
economic system in continual flux.

3   What We Will Learn

Theoretically, ERTs contribute rich experiences for pushing forward critical
sociologies of work, theories of alternative economic organisations and labour-
managed firms, and especially for our deeper understanding of the dynamics
of conversions of capitalist firms to worker cooperatives. Practically, ERTs suggest paths that still exist for workers beyond neo-liberal crises, exploitation,
and alienation. While caught in a tension between worker-led alternative economies and capitalist-led market realities, ERTs are, I ultimately argue, hopeful beacons for those seeking social change emanating from reconfigured and
democratised workplaces. They demonstrate – prefiguratively – what workers
entrenched in the capital-labour relationship *can still do* to free themselves
from the dominative logics of capital.

3.1   *ERTs' Prefigurative Force*
Taking cues from utopian socialist, classical and contemporary social anarchist,
and autonomist Marxist thought, prefigurative socio-economic practices chart
aspects of another, post-capitalist world 'in the now'.[54] They do so by experi-

---

[54]   As I will discuss further in Chapter 4, the concept of prefiguration is most explicitly present
in utopian socialist, classical anarchist, and autonomist Marxist writings. However, I also
recognise, following Martin Buber (Buber 1996, pp. 13–16) and Norman Geras (Geras 2000,
sec. 1), that the concept is implicitly present in some of Marx and Engels' texts, especially
in the brief but evocative writings where they engaged with the 'political economy of the
working class' (see, for instance Marx 1973, 1978a, 1978b, 1978c, 1981; and Marx and Engels
1998). For a similar reading of Marx, see also Allman 2001; Hudis 2012; and Lebowitz 2003.

menting with and interlacing alternative socio-economic arrangements with the ethics, values, and practices that are being struggled over and desired.[55] In short, prefigurative social and economic arrangements begin to create, to quote the old socialist maxim, 'the new inside of the shell of the old'.[56]

ERTs, as well as worker cooperatives, community collectives, and other people-centred organisations that practice *autogestión*, are some of the articulations of working-class self-activity pregnant with prefigurative realities for socio-economic life. Despite ERTs' many challenges, induced in no small part, as we will see, from having to continue to produce in competitive markets, ERTs not only highlight their workers' innovative capacities for saving jobs and avoiding the fate of precarious welfare plans or structural unemployment, they also underscore – and begin to *recuperate*, as I expand on shortly and more fully in Chapters 4, 8 and 9 – workers' always already innate capacities for adeptly managing their own productive and social lives. Most promising for contemplating alternatives to capital-labour relations, ERTs begin to prefiguratively articulate ways of critically thinking about the very 'right' of employers to determine the working conditions of employees, pointing towards, if incipiently at present, an alternative, non-capitalist model for working life free from the coercions of markets, bosses, managers, wage-labour contracts, and competition. Threading through this book, then, is the contention that ERT workers' resistances to capital and their self-directed activities beyond it – as part of the myriad forms of resistances and self-activity available to working people – have *prefigurative force* for delineating different socio-economic circumstances *for the future in the present.*

3.2   *Our Guiding Concept:* Autogestión

Autogestión – a central term that ERT workers themselves use when describing their cooperative projects – is the guiding concept that will help us unpack the transformative and prefigurative forces that are explicitly and latently present in the ERT phenomenon, and, more broadly, in working-class practices of self-organisation. I will let the words of Javier De Pascuale, editorial director and former president of the worker-recuperated newspaper *Comercio y Justicia Editores Cooperativa de Trabajo* in the city of Córdoba, explain what *autogestión* means, theorised from his own lived experience of it; there is, in my opinion, no better précis of the term. In a long conversation I had with Javier in July 2009, he poignantly told me that *autogestión* is, for him,

---

55   Franks 2006; Gordon 2008; Graeber 2004, 2009.
56   Bakunin 1990; Boggs 1977.

the possibility that we – all people – have to realise ourselves profession-
ally, economically, and in our capacities to labour. It emerges from within
ourselves and together with the people with whom we want to share this
realisation, but without sacrificing personal freedom, without sacrificing
personal dignity, and from our own developmental potential. It is, in other
words, about the possibility of the full development of the person.[57]

Imperfectly translated into English as *self-management*, the present work
spends time working through the concept of *autogestión* and how ERT workers have come to understand and live it. The concept began to take root in
Argentina in the 1960s and 1970s from the merger of its bottom-up workers'
struggles of the period with experiences of workers' control around the world
at the time, such as those expressed by the events, desires, and after-effects
of the worldwide student and worker uprisings of 1968 and in Argentina in
1969.[58] The term became more widely known in Argentina via the translated
works of European radical theory and histories.[59] These experiences and theories of *autogestión* would eventually combine with the long-held Argentine
notion of the 'dignity of work'[60] and the collective memory of the country's
storied history of working-class militancy and self-activity. In the late 1990s
and early 2000s – the apex years for the emergence of ERTs – the concept
of *autogestión* for Argentina's workers would return, merging with the practices and values of other social movements of the period.[61] The theory, practice, and meaning of *autogestión*, then, are further nuanced throughout the
book by the actual stories and experiences of the ERT workers I interviewed
and spent time with. By the end of Chapter 5, we will arrive at the following genealogically and experientially informed working definition of *autogestión*: *the collective and democratic self-constitution, self-organisation, and self-
direction of the productive, social, cultural, or economic spheres of life by the very
people and communities that most directly benefit from or are affected by these*

---

57   De Pascuale 2009, personal interview.
58   Wyczykier 2009b. See my discussion of *el Cordobazo* and other Argentine student and
      workers' revolts of the late 1960s and early 1970s in Chapters 2 and 3.
59   See Chapter 5.
60   Used effectively by Juán Domingo Perón in the 1940s and 1950s to, at first, ingratiate his
      political ambitions with the country's working class, the term 'dignity of work' would even-
      tually be taken up enthusiastically by many in Argentina's working class as a clarion call
      for their struggles for better working and living conditions (Munck, Falcón, and Galitelli
      1987, p. 133). See Chapters 3 and 5.
61   Sitrin and Azzellini 2012, 2014; Svampa and Pereyra 2004; Vieta 2010a, 2013, 2014a;
      Wyczykier 2009b. See Chapter 3.

activities, while attempting to minimise the intrusive mediation of markets, hier-archical organisation, or the state. In short, *autogestión* is the desire and lived experience of striving to self-determine a collective's own socio-economic destiny.

The concept of *autogestión* is, I believe, one of the ERT movement's major contributions for people struggling for more democratic workplaces and lives free from alienation and exploitation. Exploring the concept of *autogestión* from out of the lived experiences of ERT protagonists and helping to introduce it into the English lexicon is, I hope, one of the book's major contributions for thinking through the possibilities for alternative work and economic organisations. In a way, this book serves as a medium for communicating to readers the *praxis* – that is, the theory in practice – of *autogestión* that ERT workers themselves have been living and working through for some years now, via the reorganisation of their workplaces and communities. *Autogestión* is, most crucially for me, ERT workers' and, by association, this book's major contribution for other groups and movements struggling and searching for their own alternative economic realities today. My understanding of the concept is thus heavily indebted to the actual praxis of ERT workers themselves.

3.3   ERTs' 'Radical Social Innovations' and 'Recuperative Moments'

Two additional conceptual dimensions will emerge throughout this book to help articulate ERTs' prefigurative promises of *autogestión* for workers' struggles: their *radical social innovations* and their *recuperative moments*.

3.3.1   Seven Radical Social Innovations

My hope is that in this study we will learn from the actual experiences of ERT worker-protagonists in order to assess the possibilities for a 'new mode of production' developing 'naturally out of the old', as Marx critically concluded concerning the worker cooperatives of his time.[62] This book brings these possibilities into relief by pinpointing what I call ERTs' *radical social innovations* fostered by their worker-protagonists' practices of *autogestión*. As we will learn, these radical social innovations emerge out of the intense levels of solidarity catalysed by ERT workers collectively striving to overcome crises together.[63]

Writing in the *Stanford Social Innovation Review*, James Phills Jr., Kriss Deiglmeier, and Dale Miller define *social innovations* as 'novel solution[s] to ... social

---

62   Marx 1981, p. 571.
63   Ruggeri 2009; Vieta and Ruggeri 2009; Vieta 2009a, 2009b, 2010a.

problem[s] that [are] more effective, efficient, sustainable, or just than existing solutions and for which the value created accrues primarily to society as
a whole rather than private individuals'.[64] Social innovations are, according
to the authors, rooted in innovating *processes* such as 'individual creativity,
organizational structure, ... and social and economic factors' and innovating
outcomes such as 'new products, product features, and production methods'
for social needs.[65]

For the Programa Facultad Abierta at the University of Buenos Aires, which
approaches the concept from the perspectives of critical social anthropology
and Latin American social movement and radical labour history, social innovation takes on a more radical tone, especially with regard to Argentina's ERTs.
For them, the social innovations of ERTs encompass the ways its worker-
protagonists (re)appropriate and transform the businesses they take over, overturning the logic of profit-centred entrepreneurialism that previously determined the firm and replacing it with a new logic of collectively determined social
objectives. As Andrés Ruggeri, lead researcher of this group, writes:

> We can characterise ERTs' social innovations as processes that alter, con-
> dition, replace, or generate alternatives to the management methods
> and rationalised economic logics of the capitalist enterprise, over which
> is mounted the processes of *autogestión*. These *transformations* do not
> necessarily only implicate the labour process or the productive or techno-
> logical model. Rather, they also – and up until now, principally – impact
> upon social questions once unimaginable in the capitalist business con-
> text, such as the rupturing of the entrepreneurial 'secret' [that pervades
> the competitive capitalist model of doing business], or the expansion of
> the social uses of an enterprise in order to include class or community
> solidarity, or the political implications of ERTs and their [new modes] of
> sector-wide organisation ...[66]

Taking off from Phills Jr., Deiglmeier, and Miller's definition of social innovation
and merging it with Ruggeri's more worker-centred definition, what I call ERTs'
radical social innovations include two crucial dimensions: First, ERT protagonists socially innovate via the *processes* of cooperativism they adopt, infused as
they are with directly democratic values and practices that re-appropriate and

---

64   Phills Jr., Deiglmeier, and Miller 2008, p. 34.
65   Phills Jr. et al. 2008, p. 37.
66   Ruggeri 2009, p. 79 (emphasis added).

re-articulate once-capitalist organisational and production structures and re-rationalise business logics along the lines of strong social prerogatives. Second, they socially innovate *outcomes* of socialised production and social wealth generation and redistribution via the links ERTs forge with each other and the neighbourhoods and communities that surround them, extending the workshop into the community and the community into the workshop and, in effect, socialising surpluses. ERTs' radical social innovations, in short, are the modes of restructuring a work organisation's *governance, production processes, culture, goals*, and *outputs* through *social values and practices* of solidarity, cooperation, and mutual aid. ERTs' social innovations are *radical* because they fundamentally critique and contest capitalist ideologies of self-interest and competition and begin to replace them with new socialised values and practices of collective interest and cooperation. Specifically, ERTs' seven radical social innovations, and the chapters where they are presented and where evidence for them is found, include:

– *ERTs' first radical social innovation*: The mobilisation of direct action strategies and the re-forging of workplace solidarity in order for workers to keep their jobs and safeguard their places of work via the occupation of the firms that had been employing them and their subsequent pursuit of self-managed production (Chapter 1).
– *ERTs' second radical social innovation*: The ongoing lobbying of the political and legal establishments, the re-appropriation and reform of extant laws, and the application of cooperative values in order to reconstitute their work and begin to consolidate their projects of *autogestión* (Chapter 6).
– *ERTs' third radical social innovation*: The re-incorporation of working-class organising strategies between ERTs and between ERTs and the community in order to collectively respond to their production, financial, and legal challenges and begin to create a new organised labour environment that extends beyond traditional union strategies and tactics (Chapter 7).
– *ERTs' fourth radical social innovation*: The redefinition of social production as ERT workers democratise the labour process, reclaim their surpluses and, ultimately, contest notions of surplus-value, surplus-labour, and worker alienation, even as they produce in part for capitalist markets (Chapter 8).
– *ERTs' fifth radical social innovation*: The recomposition of working-class subjectivities and multidimensional skills via informal learning processes such as shop floor apprenticing and the sharing of expertise and knowledge (Chapter 8).
– *ERTs' sixth radical social innovation*: The production and redistribution of social wealth that inwardly open up workplaces to the communities and neighbourhoods that surround them and, in the process, strengthen the social value of ERTs (Chapter 8).

– ERTS' *seventh radical social innovation*: The reclamation and redistribution of portions of workers' surpluses for outward community development, and their engagement in economies of solidarity with other cooperatives, ERTS, and community organisations (Chapter 8).

ERTS' seven radical social innovations can be boiled down to four overarching social innovations that unfold when its workers collectively take over and self-manage formerly capitalist firms in Argentina:

(1) *responding collectively and creatively* to socio-economic crises, intensive market competition, and financial and production challenges;

(2) *embracing practices of direct democracy* that, at the level of the firm, re-contour a work organisation's governance and decision-making;

(3) *re-rationalising labour processes and divisions of labour* in such a way that ERTS reconstruct workplaces horizontally, humanise work, and return surpluses to workers and local communities; and

(4) *nurturing tight bonds of solidarity* that open up workplaces to the community, extend them out territorially into the community, and that are co-created between workers, different ERTS, surrounding communities, and other groups struggling for socio-economic justice in Argentina.

Together, ERTS' radical social innovations will help us position the ERT phenomenon as a labour *and* social movement engaged in broader struggles against capital, all the while suggesting more humane and inclusive ways of reorganising socio-economic life.

3.3.2   Six Recuperative Moments

ERTS' seven radical social innovations are further interwoven by what I call ERTS' six fundamental *recuperative moments* unleashed by workers' very actions of taking over and self-managing the capitalist firms that had formerly employed them. These six recuperative moments are, at core, *what ERT workers fundamentally recuperate* – or *recover* and *take back control of* – in their very actions of occupying and subsequently re-purposing once capitalist workplaces into socially focused worker cooperatives.[67] Worked out theoretically in Chapter 4, implicitly throughout the ensuing chapters, and then again in my concluding comments in Chapter 9, ERT protagonists' six recuperative moments are, in brief:

(1)   the recuperation of the creative skills inherent to workers' *labour-power*;

(2)   the recuperation of workers' *surpluses*;

---

67   See Chapter 9 for my concluding definition of 'recuperation' built on the evidence provided by Argentina's ERTS and their contributions to the practices of *autogestión*.

(3) the recuperation of workers' expansive powers of production in *voluntary cooperation* (a cooperation forged by workplace solidarity in the labour process);

(4) the recuperation of *the labour process* in general;

(5) the recuperation of *the division of labour*; and

(6) the recuperation of *social production* for producing *social wealth*.

These six recuperative moments, I theorise in Chapters 4 and 9, emerge out of the praxical actions of ERT workers that are also engrained within the strategies and tactics of 'occupy, resist, produce', whereby ERT workers not only symbolically, but *actually* take back for themselves their inherently human capacities to create and work that they had previously sold off to employers when they signed the wage-labour contract. Together, these six recuperative moments also return dignity to workers who had suffered under the yoke of an exclusionary capitalist system in perpetual crisis. As Marina Sitrin and Dario Azzellini underscore in their analysis of the Occupy movement,

> [t]he term *recuperate*, in an emancipatory context, refers to the re-appropriation of something concrete, conceptual, or historical, by the people. This is anything from a factory to historical memory. The prefix 're' indicates that it is understood as having belonged to the people before.[68]

In a similar vein, ERT protagonists' six recuperative moments delineate the key human capacities, values, and experiences that are common to all working people. These *begin to be fundamentally recuperated* by workers, I argue, when they start to control their own work, co-own the means of production, and co-determine the outcomes of their own productive activities.

Taken together, ERTs' six recuperative moments, as well as their seven radical social innovations, gradually emerge over the years as ERT workers learn how to deal with the manifold crises and challenges involved in reopening and self-managing formerly bankrupt or failing capitalist firms. In other words, they develop praxically, immanently, and intersubjectively from out of ERT protagonists' shared experiences of exploitation and within and beyond moments of micro-economic crises on shop floors that, especially in the ERT phenomenon's first years, were engrained in a conjuncture of macro-economic and macro-political precariousness within a collapsing neo-liberal regime.[69] In the process of recuperating workplaces and saving jobs, as I elaborate on in Chapters 1 and

---

68   Sitrin and Azzellini 2012, p. 12 (emphasis added).

69   See Chapters 2 and 3.

8, ERT protagonists *learn informally from each other* and *in the act of doing and struggling together* as they unfold their projects of *autogestión* over the ensuing months and years. In short, ERTs' recuperative moments underscore how, in taking control of their workplaces and working lives, ERT protagonists transform themselves from managed employees to self-managed workers and, in the process, change their circumstances.

4   ERTs' Symbolic Dimension, Legitimacy, and the 'Moral Economy of Work'

Most poignant for inspiring other workers' struggles is the way in which ERTs show that workers can punch well above their numerical or economic weight and can indeed self-manage their working lives, often in less-than-ideal circumstances. In this regard, labour sociologist Hector Palomino points out that despite their small numbers, ERTs have inspired 'new expectations for social change among the broader [Argentine] population' and, indeed, even beyond Argentina's borders.[70] Thus, as Palomino has further suggested, Argentina's ERTs are more 'related to [their] symbolic dimension' than to the strength of their numbers or economic force,[71] given the multiple social innovations being forged by ERTs, the phenomenon's longevity, and the increasing support for and legitimacy of ERT workers and their self-management projects amongst the general populace throughout the last two decades. Part of the importance of ERTs' 'symbolic dimension' also rests with how they are fundamentally showing 'new institutional relations' for Argentina's working class[72] as they pave the way for new modes of constituting workspaces horizontally and democratically, new forms of labour organising, and new ways of engaging with state power and market regulation while remaining, in other ways that I will also detail throughout the book, autonomous from the state and market dynamics. I thus extend Palomino's analysis of ERTs' symbolic dimension in the following pages by suggesting that it is in their very existence within a sea of capitalist economic arrangements that these self-managed firms both implicitly critique capital-labour relations and the liberal sanctity of private property while beginning to explicitly and prefiguratively move beyond them.

As more and more businesses were going under throughout the mid-to-late 1990s, people from across Argentina were witnessing in televised news

---

70   Palomino 2003, p. 71.
71   Ibid.
72   Ibid.

reports, reading in their daily papers, or experiencing in their own neighbourhoods workers occupying and taking over their places of work. And even
though these workers were violating national property laws, most Argentines
were supportive of such actions because something more serious than the violation of property rights was occurring regularly and touching the everyday lives
of most middle- and working-class people: the loss of national productivity,
the erosion of job security, the rise of precariousness in everyday life, and the
explicit violation of labour contracts. The latter is that ostensibly inviolable
agreement, as Marx has convincingly critiqued, between two 'free' but, in reality, unequal individuals: the 'seller' of the commodity labour-power – inherent
to the worker but put up for sale when workers look for employment in the
labour-market – and the 'owner' of this commodity once it is 'purchased' for
the price of a wage – the capitalist.[73] Argentines from across social sectors were
coming to understand that this 'sacrosanct' contract was clearly being violated by the actions of countless business-owners and managers who were more
interested in saving their own skins than in the wellbeing of workers – workers
who had often given decades of their lives to their jobs and the businesses that
had employed them. And, in the eyes of many Argentines, these workers who
were occupying their places of work and attempting to keep their jobs were not,
after all, 'further burdening' already depleted state coffers by relying on welfare
or work-for-welfare plans. Rather, these recalcitrant workers simply wanted to
keep on working, provide for their families, and ensure that their workplaces
remained open in order to preserve their livelihoods.

These widely held positive perceptions of ERTs during the conjuncture of
turn-of-the-millennium Argentina – perceptions that continue to this day[74] –
have helped *legitimise* workers' actions of taking over companies in trouble,
making it unpopular and infinitely harder for the political and judicial establishment or the police to reprove, repress, or evict these workers.[75] José Luís
Coraggio and Maria Sol Arroyo have framed the legitimacy of Argentine work-

---

73 Marx 1967, p. 168.

74 The overwhelming support of ERTs by the Argentine populace was underscored in a
recent survey that found that 73 percent of Argentines know about the ERT phenomenon,
and that of these, 96.7 percent view them positively and over 80 percent see ERTs as a
way of preserving jobs (Instituto de Investigaciones Gino Germani 2012; see also Ranis
2016, p. 112).

75 Although there is no doubt, as I will discuss in Chapters 3, 6, and 7, that the repressive
actions of the state via the threat of or actual forced evictions was and continues to be an
important challenge faced by ERT workers, especially so today after the return of an explicitly neo-liberal agenda with the national administration of President Mauricio Macri
beginning December 2015.

ers' takeovers of the businesses that had formerly employed them and the cooperative restructuring of these firms as part of a *moral economy* centred on the notion of work.[76] Here, Coraggio and Arroyo borrow from E.P. Thompson's concept of the moral economy to understand the legitimacy enfolding ERT workers' self-directed actions. Recurring throughout this book, I would like to define here these two related terms – *legitimacy* and *moral economy* – in order to be clear about what I mean when I apply them to ERTs' historical emergence, recuperative moments, and continued presence in Argentina.

Borrowing from organisational theory, by *legitimacy* I mean the 'social judgment'[77] or 'generalized perception or assumption that the actions of an entity [or group] are desirable, proper or appropriate within some socially constructed system of norms, values, beliefs and definitions'.[78] By *moral legitimacy*, in turn, I refer to 'the evaluation of outputs and consequences'[79] of an entity or group's activities as judged by and compared to other entities or groups within the greater social and normative milieu within which they are situated. What gets evaluated as 'desirable, proper or appropriate' is whether such entities or groups: (1) possess 'the right procedures and structures'; (2) have leaders and members with acceptable ethical dispositions as held up against social norms, cultural standards, or legal definitions; or (3) embrace interpersonal, social, professional, organisational, or business practices that are perceived to be virtuous and worthy.[80]

Thompson's concept of the *moral economy*[81] includes the moral legitimacy rooted in the self-conscious and consensus-based popular actions of working people or the poor struggling to preserve socio-economic traditions and customs threatened by encroaching government policies, new laws, and deregulated markets.[82] Expanding on Thompson's and Coraggio and Arroyo's con-

---

76   Coraggio and Aroyo 2009, p. 140.

77   Ashforth and Gibbs 1990, p. 177.

78   Suchman 1995, p. 574.

79   Singh and Point 2009, p. 25.

80   Ibid. See also Dart 2004; and McInerney 2012.

81   Thompson 1993.

82   *Moral economy*, which E.P. Thompson (1993) discusses at length in his influential article 'The Moral Economy of the English Crowd in the Eighteenth Century', is suffused in the historical responses by working people and the poor to the enclosures of the commons, rising market encroachments, and the effects of these enclosures and encroachments on traditional ways of life. These responses would often include rioting and various forms of consumer protest and resistance. Thompson's specific example in this article are the riots and protests of the poor that occurred throughout eighteenth-century England when the traditionally regulated price of bread and the means of producing and distributing it were increasingly left to unregulated markets, middlemen, and practices of privatisation within

ceptualisations, throughout this book I frame the moral legitimacy that saturates Argentina's ERTS as *the moral economy of work*. ERT protagonists' moral economy of work draws to our attention: (1) what ERT workers are struggling against (for example, violations of the basic tenets of the wage-labour contract when workers are pushed to work for reduced pay or without remuneration, are locked out, made redundant, and so on); (2) what they eventually struggle for (for example, the return of dignity to and the collective self-determination of their own working lives); and (3) the social transformations for Argentina's working class prefigured by the very existence of ERTS (for example, a non-commodified, non-capitalist mode of provisioning for life's needs within a social and solidarity economy where wealth is distributed and produced much more equitably than what capitalism proposes and practices). ERTS' moral economy of work is the concept I use to signify what motivates workers to take over the firms that had previously employed them, what they are struggling for in the process, how they justify and legitimise their strategies and tactics of taking over private firms to the broader Argentine society, and how the broader Argentine society in general positively views these strategies and tactics as morally legitimate.

A moral economy of work would eventually be articulated by ERT workers as the rising exploitation they experienced on shop floors became increasingly unbearable to them, as labour-contracts were explicitly violated by employers, and as the political economic system which had promised workers so much in the past slowly corroded around them. The moral economy of work that first led some of Argentina's workers to ultimately mobilise via the direct actions of workplace occupations is thus intimately related to the broader erosion of the decades-old class compromise in Argentina which had seen, on the whole, labour give their consent to capital to accumulate in return for job security, relatively high wages, and myriad social benefits that Peronism first consolidated in the early-to-mid 1940s.

Slow-downs and soldiering,[83] or putting down tools or striking, have been useful working-class methods for demanding better work conditions or wage

---

the emergent capitalist system. People rioted often throughout this period when the price of bread rose, recounts Thompson, because the traditions and customs that the poor had been habituated to and that enabled them to plan their daily lives and their alimentary needs around a 'just price' were fundamentally transforming. Moreover, he explains, the rioting and direct actions of the poor were not random or 'spasmodic' responses (p. 185) but, rather, were *self-consciously* carried out and undergirded by a 'legitimising notion' of defending their 'traditional rights and customs' and supported by, as has been the case with Argentina's ERTS, 'the wider consensus of the community' (p. 188).

83   That is, working-to-rule or purposefully slowing down the pace of production.

increases during more stable economic times. These options are less effective during severe economic downturns or crises when firms are closing throughout the economy; micro-economic hardship is rampant; the unemployment rate is high; and employers can, with increased impunity, engage in systematic lock-outs, asset theft, and other blatant infringements to the standard employment contract. In a situation where the class compromise between workers, employers, and the state had ruptured and where struggles for decent wages and shop floor conditions had given way to struggles over the preservation of jobs and the securing of livelihoods, the only solution an increasing number of Argentine workers had in the years spanning the turn of the millennium was to rely on the solidarity that they had already been forging over the years on shop floors and that had solidified further during the increasing periods of acute socio-economic crisis. Eventually, their moral economy of work would clash with experiences of heightened exploitation on shop floors and the broader political economic realities of crisis the country was facing, leading more and more workers throughout Argentina to risk all in occupying their workplaces.

Maurizio Atzeni succinctly articulates the major driving force for workers' bottom-up mobilisations throughout the country during the 1990s, tapping into the possibilities always present for workers toiling within the capitalist labour process: '[W]orkers struggle not just about money but also *their conditions as human beings*'.[84] Struggles in the workplace over working conditions *and* the conditions of life outside of it – articulating a moral economy of work – can especially come to the fore during periods of acute socio-economic crises when the so-called 'class compromise' is broken. In these situations, workers cease to accommodate to capital's prerogatives and employers can no longer hide the exploitative nature of the capitalist labour process. Here, Atzeni embeds the newfound legitimacy of workers' emboldened drive to take on more dramatic and spontaneous acts, such as workplace occupations, to the increasing rate of exploitation during periods of sharp economic downturns.[85] That is, in periods of macro-economic crises coupled with intensifying workloads, falling salaries, and a rise in redundancies, the exploitation always already present within the capitalist labour process is made readily visible to workers as egregious violations of the wage-labour contract. During these moments, as Atzeni further asserts, '[w]hen the impelling need of capitalists for profitability breaks even the illusion of an equal exchange relation' between workers and bosses, the actual 'exploitation [of the capitalist labour process] is

---

84   Atzeni 2010, p. 24 (emphasis added).
85   See also Patroni 2004.

revealed'.[86] As happened in Argentina during the years spanning the implosion of the neo-liberal model, spontaneous and bottom-up mobilisation and direct actions by workers during conjunctures of extreme socio-political and socio-economic rupture can and do arise outside of the purview of traditional union strategies and tactics. Moreover, when Argentina's workers no longer had *el patrón* (the boss) to demand better and more secure working conditions from, their moral economy of work extended to a new *patronal* – the state.[87]

In sum, ERT workers' actions and radical social innovations have been grounded in a moral economy of work stimulated by the following convictions: that all Argentines have a right to work in a 'dignified' job;[88] that, as has long been held in Argentina, emphasis must be placed on the 'dignity of work'; and that the conversions of firms in trouble into worker-controlled entities are a better *salida*[89] to crises than bankruptcy and business closures, given that jobs are saved, that these workers are avoiding unemployment and long-term costs to the state, and that ERTs engage in community revitalisation and economic development as their projects of *autogestión* gradually unfold.

---

86   Atzeni 2010, p. 24. In Chapters 3 and 4 we will look in some detail at how the exploitation inherent to the labour process under capitalism, to paraphrase Michael Burawoy (1985), *obscures and secures the extraction of surplus* under the class compromise. Chapters 1, 3, and 6 will show how the violation of this compromise was revealed to workers in their lived experiences of the crisis of the Argentine neo-liberal system during the years spanning the turn of the millennium. As happened with most capitalist workspaces that transformed into ERTs, '[c]hanges in workers' everyday working conditions ..., despotic managerial control ... [and] reduction of wages and redundancies' (Atzeni 2010, p. 24) were some of the ways that this exploitation was revealed to Argentine workers living through micro-economic crises at the point of production in thousands of firms across the Argentine economy.

87   As I touch on in more depth in Chapters 3, 6, and 7, treating the state as the new *patronal* that ERTs and other self-managed organisations in Argentina must lobby is the specific position adopted by most associations of self-managed workers that have formed since the emergence of ERTs.

88   The right to a dignified job was entrenched in Article 14 of the Argentine constitution of 1994, originally drafted and passed during Perón's first presidency (Rudi 1974). The practice among workers of appealing to extant and long-accepted legislation to defend their rights has also been documented as part of a moral economy by Thompson (1991).

89   Literally meaning 'exit', in Argentina the term *salida* is also used to mean an 'out' or a solution to a problem.

5   Anticipating the 'Dual Reality' of Argentina's ERTs

Before fully launching into the book, I would like to leave the reader with a proviso: While ERTs are indeed, as I argue throughout, prefigurative of another way of organising working life, their prefigurative potential continues to be challenged by the capitalist reality that still surrounds them. This reality might be glossed over when reading some accounts of Argentina's ERTs, including, admittedly, some of my earliest published works on ERTs. For radical commentators hungry for models of social change – a hunger that is especially palpable in the writings of Northern observers perhaps caught up in the excitement of Latin America's 'left-turn' of recent years – ERTs are seen as poignant examples of non-capitalist economic arrangements whereby the means of production are owned in common.[90] For these commentators, ERTs offer concrete proof that bosses are not needed to control and manage employees and that workers can actually self-manage themselves, and even begin to reinvent a more equitable economic system. ERTs are also showing them that, indeed, the capitalist wage-labour contract is deeply flawed and exploitative and that workers *should* control their own labour-power and even possibly move beyond productivist discourses by increasingly 'refusing' to work under compulsion. Most broadly, these commentators generally point to the possibilities foreshadowed by ERTs for non-commodified production, possibilities that could be laying the groundwork for a new, grassroots-driven socialised economy that extricates itself from the control of the capitalist state, free markets, or the whims of global financial institutions.

I am sympathetic to the enthusiasms of these radical views of ERTs. I agree with them that ERTs do indeed suggest a new mode of economic and productive life whereby workers, as the 'free association of the producers',[91] could democratically control the means of production and the greater economy. Their conclusions, however, including, again, some of my earliest writings on ERTs, are often drawn too hastily, and at times do not consider the complexity of the challenges, tensions, and contradictions present within these firms that keep their workers from leaving the market system entirely. Delving into these issues specifically in Chapters 6–8, we must remember that prefiguring new socio-economic realities does not necessarily mean that all of the things

---

90   See, for example, Albert 2005; Carretero Miramar 2010; Colectivo Situaciones 2002; Diner-
       stein 2002, 2007; Gutiérrez 2005; Hardt and Negri 2004; Klein 2003; Lewis and Klein 2004;
       Negri 2003; Trigona 2006a, 2006b, 2006c; Toronto School of Creativity & Inquiry 2007;
       Vieta 2006, 2009a, 2009b, 2010a; and Zibechi 2010, 2012.

91   Hudis 2012, p. 157.

prefigured are yet present in their full realisation and potential. Unfortunately, some of the conclusions concerning ERTs – both from supportive and critical commentators, the latter viewing ERTs as compromised experiments that do not embrace a 'pure' enough version of *autogestión* – are at times based on an oversimplified view of what led these workers to take over capitalist firms in the first place, and the intractable systemic barriers they must continue to confront as self-managed workers. Reflecting back on my own evolution as a researcher, this is most likely due to commentators reading into the phenomenon outcomes predetermined by their own personal hopes or ethico-political commitments. In reality, as I have already mentioned and as the case studies in Chapter 1 will make clear, ERT workers are, at first, not usually motivated by visions of wider social transformation or social revolution, nor even by desires to create cooperatively controlled workplaces. Rather, as Chapters 1 and 6 will show, workers are initially driven to take over firms by more pragmatic concerns: saving their jobs and livelihoods. It is only later, with time, that ERT workers come to understand the radical nature of their actions and the possibilities for a different kind of working and economic life that *autogestión* offers them.

As we will also see in the following pages, ERTs' continued tensions and challenges are fundamentally rooted in the contradictions inherent in the model of the labour-managed firm that must still tussle with the logics of free markets.[92] As with other worker-run firms and cooperatives that continue (wholly or in part) to operate within capitalist markets, ERTs' challenges, as we will particularly explore in Chapters 6–8, are heightened by competitive pressures that force them to focus on returns and survival in ways that might compromise and dilute their most promising social innovations, including egalitarian pay practices, direct democracy in the firm, and participation in community development projects. ERTs' challenges are also engrained in the Argentine state's general indifference to them and in the outright attacks on them by an insensitive state–capitalist apparatus more concerned with the rights of property and investors than with people's right to making a decent and dignified living.

Given that ERTs face myriad challenges within competitive markets while also embracing radical social innovations and prefigurative force, they can be seen to be situated in what I term a 'dual reality'.[93] Marx already alluded to this dual reality in his circumspect view of worker cooperatives. 'The cooperative factories run by workers themselves', Marx would write,

---

92   Atzeni and Vieta 2014; Jossa 2005; Marcuse 2015; McNally 1993.
93   For a similar view of cooperatives, see Diamantopolous 2012.

are, within the old form, the first examples of the emergence of a new form, even though they naturally reproduce in all cases, in their present organization, all the defects of the existing system, and must reproduce them. But the opposition between capital and labour is abolished here, even if at first only in the form that the workers in association become their own capitalist, i.e. they use the means of production to valorize their own labour. These factories show how, at a certain stage of development of the material forces of production, and of the social forms of production corresponding to them, a new mode of production develops and is formed naturally out of the old.[94]

As we will see in Chapters 4, 5, and 9, there is much to Marx's nuanced and measured support of cooperative organisations. While ERTs, like all worker cooperatives, prefigure the organisation of work by associated labour in the future, post-capitalist society, they are also delimited and challenged within the current capitalist society in having to produce for the commodity form in order to survive.

As Maurizio Atzeni and Pablo Ghigliani have convincingly shown, this is a reality that can compromise an ERT's 'sphere of collective decision' and limit 'the range of the radical changes pursued by workers after the occupations' in light of the circuits of capital that still need to be engaged with when selling their products or services.[95] Pushed to stay competitive within markets that mostly include capitalist firms that do not have a cooperative's social commitments and that have not had to traverse the same degree of micro-economic difficulties and shop floor conflicts, some ERTs, as we will see in Chapters 7 and 8, have kept aspects of old labour processes mostly intact or have returned to behaving more like capitalist firms by intensifying work processes or reviving hierarchical divisions of labour, replacing, in effect, old bosses with the top-down management of their elected workers' council. Indeed, these are tensions and challenges faced by many labour-managed firms, and highlight their propensity to 'become their own capitalist' when faced with the need to produce for the commodity form.[96]

This book aims for a nuanced view of ERTs, recognising that they exist within a dual reality. On the one hand, Argentina's ERTs are situated within a broader capitalist system and have little choice but to operate to some degree in a competitive market setting or else face closure. On the other hand, as ERTs'

---

94   Marx 1981, p. 571.
95   Atzeni and Ghigliani 2007, pp. 653, 655. For similar arguments, see Fajn and Rebón 2005.
96   Marx 1981, p. 571. See also Jossa 2005; Lebowitz 2003; McNally 1993; and Ollman 1998.

radical social innovations and recuperative moments articulate, they do indeed prefigure and actually engage in many ways in alternative economic arrangements that challenge the hegemony of free markets and capitalist modes of production. I will spend a good portion of this book disentangling and analysing ERTS' tensions between their prefigurative potential to move beyond free markets and the commodity form and the ongoing challenges they continue to face by needing to engage with the capitalist system within which they are still embedded. The hope they offer us for an alternative way of organising economic life, however, lies, as I ultimately conclude, in their sharp contrast to the previous capitalist firm they emerged from and their continued existence as socialised productive entities that strive to move beyond exploitation, alienation, and the privatisation of wealth. Despite their challenges and tensions, ERTS, I underscore in this book, make a compelling case for those struggling for the proliferation of another kind of direly needed socio-economic existence.

PART 1

The Emergence of Argentina's
Empresas Recuperadas por sus Trabajadores:
*From Workers' Lived Experiences
of Crisis to* Autogestión

∵

CHAPTER 1

'Destiny in Our Own Hands': Three Stories of Workplace Recuperations

So, one day, in a conversation with the boss, I tell him: 'Look, we're no longer your employees; we're really shareholders now, because you owe us so much in unpaid wages and because we've been working hard here with little in return'. And the guy looks at me like I'm crazy and says to me: *'Pibe, ¡vos no entendés nada!'* [Kid, you don't understand anything!].

PLÁCIDO PEÑARRIETA[1]

•••

We managed to transform this place from the bottom up. I'm talking about *everything* here ... You should've seen this place before; it was a clinic literally in ruins. And we turned it around completely ... It fills us with pride, and everything that happened after that.

ALEJANDRO TORRES[2]

•••

[W]e, the workers, can take our destiny in our own hands.

Cooperativa 'Unión Solidaria de Trabajadores'[3]

∵

Workers in Argentina who now control the once-capitalist businesses that had employed them feel they have on their side a moral imperative for having taken the actions they took in occupying and eventually self-managing their workplaces. This is in no small part due to the indifference, if not out-

---

1 Peñarrieta 2009, personal interview (co-founder and president of Cooperativa Chilavert Artes Gráficas).
2 Torres 2009, personal interview (co-founder and treasurer of Cooperativa Salud Junín).
3 Cooperativa 'Unión Solidaria de Trabajadores' 2007 (promotional pamphlet).

right hostility, towards the plight of working people on the part of Argentina's power brokers and entrepreneurial class during the neo-liberal era of the 1990s and early 2000s. And many Argentines from across the social spectrum, aware of the massive and chronic rates of unemployment and poverty that plagued the country at the time, supported (and continue to support) workers' strategies and tactics of occupying and self-managing the troubled firms that once employed them.[4] In the final pages of this book's Introduction, I called the moral legitimacy that grounds ERTs their *moral economy of work*, a moral imperative driven by a sense of overcoming injustices that guides their workers' collective struggles not only to secure their jobs, but also to regain their dignity and, ultimately, to win for themselves self-determination over their working life. Indeed, this moral economy of work infuses ERT protagonists' subversive actions of taking over and converting their place of work into a worker cooperative.[5] Moreover, the myriad stories of how these worker-run firms were founded *contest in practice* the very capitalist system from which they emerged, exposing again and again the contradictions inherent to capital–labour relations at the point of production, the ill effects of the neo-liberal turn on workers, and the system's penchant for upholding property rights and private profits over the wellbeing of workers and communities.

This chapter begins the book with three diverse ERT emergence stories. I have chosen to include these three stories at the outset because they serve to vividly illustrate – in the words, memories, and lived experiences of ERT workers – the different ways that this moral economy of work has unfolded within a neo-liberal system in crisis. The three cases of workplace recuperations we visit in this chapter are: Cooperativa de Trabajo Chilavert Artes Gráficas in the city of Buenos Aires *barrio* of Nueva Pompeya, Cooperativa de Trabajo 'Unión Solidaria de Trabajadores' (UST) in the province of Buenos Aires, and Cooperativa de Trabajo de la Salud Junín in the city of Córdoba. Their stories underscore how the crisis of the neo-liberal system in Argentina during the years spanning the turn of the millennium resonated in three particular micro-economic and micro-political conflicts at three workplaces in three different and major economic regions of the country.

---

4 For similar findings, see Instituto de Investigaciones Gino Germani 2012; Palomino 2003; Ranis 2016; Rebón 2004; Ruggeri, Mártinez, and Trinchero 2005. See also Chapters 6 and 7.

5 Recall from the Introduction that ERTs' moral economy of work undergirds what their workers *struggle against* (for example, violations of the basic tenets of the wage-labour contract when workers were pushed to work for reduced pay or without remuneration, experiences of lockouts and mass redundancies, and so on), and what they eventually *struggle for* (for example, the collective self-determination of their own working lives).

On the one hand, the three cases presented in the next pages serve to put into relief distinct situations that catalyse a collective of workers in Argentina to go down the path of occupying a troubled firm, resist subsequent repression, and attempt to self-manage the business that had formerly employed them. On the other hand, they also illustrate some of the broader commonalities in workers' lived experiences of struggle on shop floors, within the labour process, and against the strident version of neo-liberal capitalism that enveloped Argentina in the final decade of the twentieth and the first years of the twenty-first centuries (and that had returned again with *macrismo*). These common experiences include collective struggles against abusive bosses, acute exploitation, increased job insecurity and flexibilisation, and a sharp rise in precarious life conditions. As we will soon see, these struggles at the point of production that arose across the country during the late 1990s and early 2000s were heightened by mediocre union responses to the plight of workers seeking to recuperate their firms, and a dearth of support from a state that, beholden to its capitalist benefactors, would often unleash its repressive forces on occupied workplaces. While all of Argentina's struggles for workplace recuperations are specifically nuanced, they embrace common experiences that thread through each workplace occupation and conversion. Taken together, each ERT contributes to a patchwork of interconnected and relatively new experiences of workers' mobilisations and direct actions that suggest the ERT phenomenon's recompositional potential for workers' self-activity within a conjuncture marked by deindustrialisation, anti-labour policies, and an at-times divided and atomised working class absorbed by the acquisitive and individualistic temptations unleashed throughout the 1990s and early 2000s.[6] Relying on the actual testimonies of workers gathered via extended interviews and merged with my ethnographic observations and documentary research, these three case studies aspire to give voice to the struggles of ERT workers. They ground this book's analysis in subsequent chapters within, first and foremost, the lived experiences of ERT protagonists struggling to take control of their working lives in a particular moment of Argentina's political economic history.

No doubt, other stories could have been told, and perhaps even other aspects of the history of these three case studies could have been emphasised. After all, since I began this study I have heard numerous ERT emergence stories from dozens of workers in Argentina recounting myriad aspects of their struggles. The presentation of these three specific case studies is my modest attempt

---

6   Similarly, Gabriela Wyczykier has analysed the 'labour re-collectivization' processes of ERTs 'situated in scenarios in which deep processes of social, economic and political un-collectivization [were] occurring' (Wyczykier 2009b, p. 21).

at both adding voices to those ERT histories that have already been published while grounding these histories further in concrete events and circumstances. Guided by the memories and narratives of the ERT protagonists I interviewed, I have selected these testimonies because they illustrate representative moments and illuminate ERT workers' most commonly lived struggles and experiences. The presentation of the three case studies is further guided by the *political economy of the working class* approach of the book, putting into relief ERT protagonists' *moral economy of work*. The case studies get us on our way to understanding the nature of these workers' struggles and their projects of *autogestión*; what they subsequently recuperate in the process; the role of socio-economic crises in both motivating them to take over their places of work and consolidate their new cooperative workplaces; the radical social innovations they ultimately forge; and how they themselves, by taking control of their work and their workplaces, transform from managed employees to self-managed workers. In short, the following three stories help us see, via the lived experiences of the actual protagonists, the characteristics of ERTs' three-staged process of 'occupy, resist, produce' that we will revisit throughout the rest of the book.

1   Cooperativa de Trabajo Chilavert Artes Gráficas[7]

1.1   *First Approaches*
It is fitting, I realise in hindsight, that my first day at an *empresa recuperada* was 9 July 2005, Argentina's *Día de la independencia* (Independence Day). The first ERT I set foot in that day was Cooperativa de Trabajo Chilavert Artes Gráficas, Ltda. (Graphic Arts Chilavert Worker Cooperative, Ltd.). My first conversation with an ERT worker would also soon take place that evening, in my first of many long talks with Cándido González, one of the eight co-founders of the Chilavert cooperative and spokesperson at the time for one of the major ERT workers' associations and lobby groups, the Movimiento Nacional de Empresas Recuperadas (MNER, National Movement of Recuperated Enterprises).

I arrived at Chilavert late that Saturday afternoon. I rang the doorbell and María Rosa González, Cándido's wife and a person who was central in supporting the daily needs of Chilavert's workers during the long months of occupation in 2002, warmly welcomed me in: *¡Chau, Marcelo! ¿Cómo estas? Vení, pasá* [Hi, Marcelo. How are you? Come on in]. Cándido won't be long'. Upon entering

---

7 Parts of this case study were previously published in Askew and Vieta 2012a; and Vieta 2013.

FIGURE 1   Images of Cooperativa Chilavert Artes Gráficas
            PHOTOGRAPH BY AUTHOR

the print shop's foyer reception area at the front of the building, one of the first things I notice is the elaborately designed Chilavert Artes Gráficas sign above the second set of doors that lead into the main shop floor. The sign is styled in the *porteño*[8] art form called *filete*, an aesthetic of the tango bars and bordellos of early twentieth century Buenos Aires. One still sees similarly designed signage in old Buenos Aires bars and cafés and decorating the sides of city buses, and I would soon see the style greeting me at other *empresas recuperadas* such as Gráfica Patricios and Industria Metalúrgica y Plástica Argentina (IMPA, Metalurgic and Plastics Industry of Argentina).[9] There is also a prominent MNER poster on one of the two doors opening up to the shop floor that reads in bold letters *¡Autogestión ya!* (Self-management now!). The words are situated in black smoke emanating from a factory smoke-stack that is also the index finger of a stylised hand held up in a 'number 1' gesture.

---

8   *Porteño* is the demonym for the people of or something from the city of Buenos Aires.
9   IMPA was one of the first ERTs in Argentina, the first to share its space with a cultural centre, and the ERT that gave birth to MNER (see Chapters 3, and 6–8).

FIGURE 2   *'Autogestión ya'* poster at Cooperativa Chilavert Artes Gráficas
PHOTOGRAPH BY AUTHOR

Immediately to my right just off of the foyer area I notice several inter-connected and seemingly abandoned offices. I later learn that these were the offices of Horacio Gaglianone, Chilavert's last owner, and his management staff. In 2005 these offices sat mostly empty, used then only for the work-ers' regular assemblies and for storage. More recently, these offices were being used as the main space for the popular education and cooperatively organised primary school and adult *bachilleratos* (high-school equivalent programmes) that take place at the print shop every weekday afternoon and evening. To my left is a hall that leads to the communal dining room, once Boss Gaglianone's archives room. It still contains the old firm's now empty safe, left perpetually and purposefully open 'for symbolic reasons', I am later told by the workers (and because they couldn't find the key!). The spartan room also houses a long wooden table and makeshift wooden benches where Chilavert's workers now eat lunch together every day after turning off the shop lights at 12:30 p.m. This simple act of collectively eating together, I would soon learn, is another sym-bolic gesture that highlights the new, more flexible self-managed work regime now guiding the labour process at the shop.[10]

After entering the quiet shop floor, Maria Rosa turns sharply to the right and leads me up the stairs above the print shop's main supervisory office lodged within glass walls that looks out onto the shop floor. We immediately come to Chilavert's cultural centre on the mezzanine floor, ringing the shop about 15 feet above the main shop floor. Being the weekend, the print shop's offset devices, printing and binding machines, and the stacks of soon-to-be processed glossy paper and half-finished posters and books sit quietly below me on the main floor. As I look over the veranda from the mezzanine level, the miscellany of machinery and stacks of papers resembles a mini skyline, I think at the time – a haphazard metropolis of contraptions, papers, and books placed there by the pragmatic needs of the shop workers' daily workflows. Chilavert's shop floor on a Saturday afternoon gives witness to a highly productive workspace that has paused to give its resident workers time to engage in life's other activities.

From this perspective, I then think to myself, the shop is also reminiscent of an old colonial villa, with the shop floor making up the inner courtyard that was common throughout Latin America in the homes of the *penisulares* and *cri-ollo*[11] upper classes. In these villas, wealthy colonial families lived, shared family

---

10 For more on the new ways that ERT workers organise their working day in less capitalistic and more solidary ways, see Chapter 8.

11 *Peninsulares* were the Spanish-born elite of colonial Latin America. In the colonial period, *criollo* was the name given to people of Spanish descent born in Latin America. Both terms are especially used today by historians when discussing the class structure of Latin Amer-

experiences, were attended to by their servants, ate together, and held court when hosting visitors. For the colonial Europeans that ruled Latin America from the sixteenth to early nineteenth centuries, their villas were mini fortresses that shielded them from the hurly burly of colonial business outside the villa's walls, populated by the Indigenous peoples, African slaves, and mestizo *vagos* ('lazy ones', as they were derogatorily called) who lived in the surrounding countryside. This atmosphere of colonial times as I walk through Chilavert for the first time is not coincidental, I think to myself on this *Día de la independencia*. Perhaps the recuperation of Chilavert by its workers can be compared to the desire that early Argentines had for emancipation from Spain's colonial clutch. Chilavert's previous owner-boss, Gaglianone, could be analogous to the Spanish viceroys, nobility, or the old *terratenientes* (landowners) and merchants who would become Argentina's ruling elite. After all, the print shop's internal layout resembles the panoptic shape of the traditional Spanish villa, now transposed here by the shop's former boss and management to invigilate the workers inside. And perhaps the workers of Chilavert, I think, are a band of mutinous ex-servants who have now found freedom from the repression and exploitation of the former *caudillo* proprietor they once worked for.

1.2   *An ERT Punching above Its Weight*

Nestled densely amongst modest working-class homes on Calle Martiniano Chilavert 1136[12] in the working-class *barrio* of Nueva Pompeya in the southern end of the city of Buenos Aires, Cooperativa Chilavert Artes Gráficas is a small print shop that has punched well above its size since its eight remaining workers took it over in 2002. In the two decades since its last deep micro-economic crisis as an owner-controlled and -run firm reached its zenith, Cooperativa Chilavert has become one of Argentina's most emblematic ERTs. Today, inside its walls, one not only finds a self-managed print shop, but also a vibrant community arts centre known as Chilavert Recupera (Chilavert Recuperates), the ERT Documentation Centre run in partnership with researchers from the University of Buenos Aires's Programa Facultad Abierta,[13] and the already-mentioned primary and high-school equivalent popular education initiative,

---

ica's colonial period. The term *criollo* is still used in colloquial conversations in Argentina to describe the autochtonous character of something or someone.

12   As in other parts of Latin America, Argentine addresses have the street name first followed by the number of the house or establishment.

13   Indeed, much of my archival research for this book took place at Chilavert's ERT Documentation Centre. For more on the Programa Facultad Abierta, see the Introduction. For more on the ERT Documentation Centre, see Chapter 7.

which is itself run by a cooperative of teachers that emerged at the same time as the ERT phenomenon and now works closely with several worker-recuperated firms throughout greater Buenos Aires. Chilavert's workers have also been instrumental in founding the Red Gráfica Cooperativa (Graphics Network Cooperative), a second-tier coop of around 20 graphics ERTs and older print shop coops (some predating the era of ERTs) formed in mid-2006 in order to strengthen the cooperative graphics sector's market clout, make collective purchases, lobby for better national laws for self-managed print shops and other enterprises, and share customer orders and marketing needs.[14] And all of this was achieved against great odds.

Chilavert was originally known as Taller Gráfico Gaglianone, which was a family business founded in 1923 and mainly involved during its first 50 years in the design and printing of packaging for the pharmaceutical sector. By the 1980s the firm had transformed into a printing and binding shop for the prestigious art book, theatre, and government sectors under the trademark Ediciones de Arte Gaglianone. Its clients at the time included Buenos Aires's world-renowned Teatro Colón opera house, Argentina's National Museum of Fine Arts, Buenos Aires's Museum of Modern Art, and the General San Martín Municipal Theatre, as well as corporate and public sector clients such as the Casa Rosada,[15] Bank Boston, Banco Ciudad, and numerous national and international foundations. These were the firm's most lucrative years, employing around 50 workers, including graphic designers, pre-press specialists, offset printing machine operators, binding specialists, and various shop managers, administrators, and sales and marketing staff. The firm, in the midst of full expansion, had hired two-dozen or so new workers throughout the 1980s, while many of its incumbent employees at the time had been working at the firm since the late 1950s or early 1960s.

1.3   'Sleeping with the Enemy'

Micro-economic problems already began to surface at the shop in the late 1980s in the midst of the hyperinflationary crises of the era. The cooperative's president Plácido Peñarrieta (who was one of the new employees hired during the expansionary phase of the firm in the early 1980s) illustrated for me a common business practice of the time in Argentina:

---

14   Red Gráfica Cooperativa 2008, 2011. For more on the Red Gráfica and other ERT associations, see Chapter 3.

15   Literally called 'the Pink House' because of its pink ox-blood coloured stone exterior, the Casa Rosada is the colloquial name for the official offices of the President of Argentina and the seat of its national government's executive branch.

The wearing down of the workers here already began at the end of the 1980s and beginning of the 1990s, in the days of hyperinflation. That is, the problems between the workers and the boss really started years before 2001 when the owner – Horacio Gaglianone – would decide to *sometimes* pay us on time every two weeks – which was what our contract stipulated – but increasingly two or three days, even a week, late. But this wasn't because the firm wasn't making money. No, no. It was a financial game, we now realise, a trick that he was playing with us as pawns in order to make more money because, you see, during that time, the longer you delayed making payments like paying salaries, the cheaper it was for the guy paying because the peso would devalue on a daily basis. The same with paying creditors back and such. We workers had become a mere business transaction for him, a way of cheapening his costs of doing business. And we were shocked at the time because our relations with him throughout the 1980s had been good.[16]

Although the crisis of hyperinflation ended under the one-peso–one-dollar 'convertability' regime that began in 1991,[17] and while pay-cheques were again received on time for a few years thereafter (following the trend of quick economic upturns when neo-liberal policies are initially imposed), the early 1990s were to be Gráfico Gaglianone's last period of stability under owner-management. And it was to be short-lived, as owner–employee relations began to deteriorate once again as the decade wore on. By the mid-1990s, Horacio Gaglianone, capturing the neo-liberal zeitgeist of the time, decided that, rather than share growing earnings with the shop's workers, he would instead maximise profits by forcing the employees to work longer hours while not compensating them for the extra effort. 'We worked overtime and put our shoulders into our work', Plácido related to me, underscoring the workers' situation at the print shop during this period,

> but rather than raising our salaries or paying us overtime, he just told us to work harder! It was always 'for the good of the *empresa*'. And he actually told us bluntly at the time to work more but that he wasn't going to pay us more![18]

---

16   Peñarrieta 2009, personal interview.
17   For a discussion of this period, see Chapter 3.
18   Ibid.

The unbridled greed, individualism, and highly competitive fervour that marked the pace of conducting business in the early years of President Carlos Menem's regime also saturated the printing and publishing business. This fervour, it seems, began to take hold of Horacio Gaglianone as well. Seeing the possibilities of making more profits (now in US dollars with the convertability policy), Gaglianone either consciously allowed himself to be led by the spirit of individualism and acquisitiveness of the era, or else was swept up in it unwittingly. In any case, Gaglianone took advantage of the easy-to-find credit of the time, always promising with each new loan newer and better printing machines, new customers, and new books to print, while often saying that 'any day now' he would have to hire more workers. But the capitalisation plans never came to fruition, the new customers failed to materialise, and the employees of Gaglianone were working more and more hours for less and less pay as the decade wore on. Moreover, with a recently opened and deregulated national economy, the printing and publishing business began to also see a rapid inflow of foreign capital saturating local markets, the concentration of the sector in the hands of fewer and fewer paper suppliers and larger print shops and editorial firms, and, towards the end of the 1990s, the beginning of the eventual domination of the printing and publishing sector by Argentina's powerful Clarín Group.[19] In combination, all of these factors meant that small print shops like Talleres Gráfico Gaglianone could not effectively compete; 'Menem's Miracle', it seems, was only so for some.[20] 'And we had to accept this situation', Plácido continued,

> because during that period we also had to compete with foreign interests that had recently entered the printing and publishing market. Because of all of this, the workers here started demanding more compensation. We had put all of our efforts and energy into this place, so it wasn't just about money for us, but also about our *dignity*. Meantime, [Gaglianone] would tell us: 'If you don't help out, *se va todo a la mierda* [it will all go to shit]'. So we called an assembly and we decided to wait things out to see if things would improve; after all, the shop did have promise. But it never did improve! On the contrary, they froze our salaries in 1991 with

---

19   Subsecretaría de Comercio Internacional 2009.
20   One of *Time* magazine's covers and feature stories in 1992, headlined 'Menem's Miracle', praised the neo-liberalist, free market policies of Menem as an 'economic miracle'. Similar views of Argentina's 'economic miracle' were expressed by Michael Camdessus, executive director of the International Monetary Fund, on 1 October 1998, in Damill 2005, p. 215.

the Menem-Cavallo convertability plan and we only began to see our salaries rise a bit in 1996![21]

By the mid-to-late 1990s, the print shop would never again reach the profits and successes it had enjoyed in earlier decades as it followed the downward cycle of the broader Argentine economy during this period. Moreover, owner–worker conflict continued to intensify at the firm as the 1990s unravelled and as Gráfico Gaglianone's market realities began to worsen. By early 1996, there was no new business coming to the firm and management decided to focus on already existing contracts.

Throughout Gráfico Gaglianone's work-intensification conflicts of the mid-to-late 1990s, the print shop's workers began to grow more conscious. By then, they had learned full well from previous experience that increasing work intensity, not being paid adequate compensation for overtime, and other managerial shenanigans were ways for the boss to sap more profits – more surplus-value – from them, as Plácido's recounting above highlights. Increasingly, workers at the shop reacted to the increased rates of exploitation by carrying out small acts of shop floor sabotage and soldiering, and occasionally engaging in walkouts – what Plácido characterised as 'a series of personal strikes by us workers, right on the shop floor'.[22] Some of them also began to understand that Gaglianone's strategy of work intensification together with workers' uncoordinated reactions to it were actually dividing the solidarity of the shop's workers:

> Some of us were more into this direct action stuff than others, and the group of workers started to divide. We were wearing down. And the boss catches on to this and begins to give raises to some and not to others. 'Don't tell anybody', he would say to those of us that got raises. He became really skilled at dividing us.[23]

But this period also actually served to bring some of the Gráfico Gaglianone workers together, and they began to sharpen their tactics of resistance that they would deploy in more coordinated ways several years later. Furthermore, and crucially for the dramatic events that were soon to come, workers now began to feel like they co-owned part of the shop due to their increased work and lack of remuneration in return. Explained Plácido:

---

21   Peñarrieta 2009, personal interview.
22   Ibid.
23   Ibid.

And so, we felt that we were much more than employees, we were credit-ors now,[24] or actually more like shareholders. We were part owners of the shop, we felt, because we were owed so much back pay and because we had worked for so long for so little or for nothing, considering the work we had done. So, one day, in a conversation with the boss, I tell him: 'Look, we're no longer your employees, we're really shareholders now, because you owe us so much unpaid wages and because we've been working hard here with little in return'. And the guy looks at me like I'm crazy and says to me: '*Pibe, vos no entendés nada* [Kid, you don't understand any-thing]'.[25]

The beginning of the end for Horacio Gaglianone arrived when the print shop lost its lucrative Teatro Colón contract in the late 1990s. By 2000 the firms' severest troubles were well under way. 'We thought this was something normal', part of the regular ups and downs of doing business, recalled Cándido Gonzá-lez in a published interview shortly after Chilavert became a cooperative, 'but we suspected something strange when our lights got cut'.[26] Rather than exper-iencing a normal downturn in the business cycle, by the first two years of the 2000s Gráfico Gaglianone's remaining handful of workers who had not already retired, left voluntarily, or been laid off began to realise that the daily deterior-ation of the shop meant that they were in actuality living through a slow and painful dismissal. Not only were service bills and suppliers' payments in arrears, workers' wages – yet again – were not getting paid either. By 2001, for example, the González brothers, Cándido and his brother Fermín, who had both worked at the firm for over 35 years up to that time, were eventually each owed around $33,000 pesos in back pay.[27] Similarly, Plácido recalled not being paid for eight months at the time:

---

24   Plácido foreshadows for us here my detailed discussion of the effects of the neo-liberal years on small- and medium-sized firms in Argentina in Chapter 3. See in particular in that chapter Luís Caro's quote on workers becoming a firm's creditors as one of the main motivators for employees to mobilise and occupy firms during these years.

25   Peñarrieta 2009, personal interview.

26   C. González, in Lavaca 2004, p. 114.

27   F. González 2009, personal interview. Note that this was the equivalent to US$33,000 at the time, since these remuneration debts had accrued in the thick of the 1:1 peso-to-US-dollars convertability years. It is important to remember that these unpaid wages during this period were debts that were owed by bosses to employees in US dollars, when the Argentine peso was still at par with the greenback.

By the end of 2001, in the middle of the crisis, the boss already owed me eight months pay, plus unpaid vacation and four *aguinaldos*.[28] Thousands of pesos! This was the same with all of the remaining workers. And that's when our last major confrontation with the owner begins, but there was already a deep and open wound that hadn't really healed since the 1980s and our earlier struggles.[29]

And, yet again during this period of intensifying conflict, Horacio Gaglianone appealed to the goodwill of workers to put their *ombros* (shoulders) into their work to get the firm out of the crisis. But these back wages would never be paid, the remaining workers had finally realised by then, and the workers finally lost any semblance of trust they might once have had for Gaglianone. 'And again', Plácido continued,

> the guy comes and asks us to help him save the business, to wait a bit more, that he would eventually pay our wages. But we didn't believe him anymore; it was as if we were now sleeping with the enemy, you know? And that is the moment we stopped accepting his false offers.[30]

1.4   'Promising New Machines Really Meant Emptying the Firm'

Indeed, by 2000 the *vaciamiento* of the firm had turned into Horacio Gaglianone's main project.[31] By 2001, Gráfico Gaglianone had formally entered into debt restructuring proceedings, called in Argentina *concurso preventivo* (preventive hearing), the phase carried out under law before a firm officially declares *quiebra* (bankruptcy).[32] And, in what was becoming a common practice

---

28   A custom that was one of the major pragmatic victories of organised labour under the tutelage of Juán Peron, the *aguinaldo* is the extra month's pay – or 'the thirteenth month' – that has traditionally been given to employees in unionised and many non-unionised Argentine firms around Christmas. Up until the neo-liberal labour reforms of the 1990s, this was a widespread practice in Argentina. While many workplaces, especially those in the new knowledge economy and in the informal sector, have since discontinued this practice, it is still common to expect an *aguinaldo* in many blue-collar, unionised, and even in non-unionised workplaces in Argentina.

29   Peñarrieta 2009, personal interview.

30   Ibid.

31   See Chapters 6 and 7 for more on the common practice of *vaciamiento* (asset stripping of firms) throughout the late 1990s and early 2000s practised at many firms that would eventually become ERTs. It is still practised today by some business owners and still motivates some workers' collectives to carry out workplace occupations and start ERTs.

32   The *concurso preventivo* is made up of insolvency hearings and creditors' meetings with

at the time and is now a regular part of the history of many ERTs, the *vaciami-ento* continued even while the *concurso preventivo* was talking place – a flagrant but commonly practised violation of Argentine bankruptcy law that can be summed up as owner-led theft of property now belonging to a firm's creditors. When the workers went to plead to Horacio Gaglianone to not sell the firm's machines, to keep the shop open at all costs – and conveyed that they would be willing to work for free for a time in order to keep the shop open – Gaglianone glibly told them that all was under control and that production would improve again once he bought new machines, which, he told them, required the sale of the shop's most important assets, the two two-colour offset printing machines, ostensibly so that a faster and more efficient four-colour offset machine could be acquired (a line he had been delivering to the employees of the shop since the late 1990s).

But by April 2002, four months after the 'Argentine December' and *el Argentinazo* of 2001 and in the depths of Argentina's debt default crisis, it became clear to the remaining workers of Gráfico Gaglianone that the situation was vastly different than what Boss Gaglianone had painted it to be. 'The equipment that Gaglianone had sold was not in the books of the insolvency hearings', Cándido González explained to me in 2005; rather, it had all been worked out with the court trustee (who was also set to make a tidy commission from the sale of the firm).[33] The scheme was that Gaglianone would sell the remaining machines and declare bankruptcy so that, with the firm emptied of most of its fixed assets, he would be freed from the mass of outstanding debt. In return, the court trustee would get his kickback and commission on the remaining auction of the plant. This was another common business 'strategy' at the time (an illegal move that I will discuss in more detail in Chapter 6). Eventually, the workers caught on to this illegal manoeuvre and blocked the machines from leaving the shop; it was clear by then to the remaining workers that Gaglianone was actually never going to buy new machines. As Fermín González recalled after I asked him about this episode:

> *So, Gaglianone sold the two two-colour printing machines but the machines never left the shop, because you are still using the same two-colour printers he had sold, right?*[34]

---

the bankruptcy court in order to reorganise debt repayments before a firm declares bankruptcy, similar to the United States's Chapter 11. For more details, see Chapter 6.

33 C. González 2005a, personal interview.

34 From here on, italicised text immediately preceding interview quotes are my questions.

Right, that's right. He began selling the machines under our noses, and during the insolvency hearings, during the bankruptcy process! Of course, we were already very aware of what was going on, and we didn't let him leave with the machines! We took them over, protecting them, sleeping next to them, because we knew if they left we were finished, we wouldn't be able to work in this business anymore, not here at least.[35]

Plácido picked up the story of this major transformational event for the Gráfico Gaglianone workers:

Yes, we didn't let the machines leave the shop. This was our first real, joint act of resistance [leading to them becoming an ERT]. Even up until mid-2001, we were still convinced that he would bring in a new four-colour printer and that this would increase our capacity to print books. But when the end of 2001 arrives, and we are in the middle of this massive national crisis, we turned a page, so to speak. We had become much more aware of what was going on and we didn't believe [Boss Gaglianone] anymore. He had been promising new machines for years and the new machines never came. And now, we start to figure things out: We start talking amongst ourselves, especially when he then also begins to ask us to take unpaid leave days, work less for a while, maybe two shifts per week. This was all a ruse to give him space to move out the machines and empty the place. All lies! He was sweetening us with the thought of new and better equipment, but he was really going to abandon the place with nothing left in it. He was also trying to tire us out so that we wouldn't have the energy left to take him to court or to the labour tribunal. But we caught on just in time when they actually came here to take the machines away and we resisted, we didn't let them. That's when the huge struggle started that led us to what we are now.[36]

Indeed, as Cándido tersely underscored for me, '[the boss] promising new machines really meant emptying the firm'.[37]

This period was not only one of shared escalating trauma for the remaining Gráfico Gaglianone workers; it was also the immediate precursor for the collective actions to come. For the workers, the situation at the print shop

---

35   F. González 2009, personal interview.
36   Peñarrieta 2005, personal interview.
37   C. González 2005b, personal intrerview.

was mixing with the implosion of the Argentine economic system and political establishment as well as the explosion of new social movements emerging around them. Fermín succinctly summed up for me the intensity of this period and the intermingling of the problems inside the shop with the socio-political tensions outside of its walls: 'On the one hand, it was like the ice age in here' since production had stopped and the firm was in a phase of *vaciamiento*, 'while out there, on the streets', he contrasted, 'the situation was on fire!'[38]

The admixture of micro-economic duress at the point of production, socio-political and socio-economic collapse throughout Argentina, and concurrent waves of social protest growing all around the Gráfico Gaglianone workers[39] collectively coalesced in their minds and contributed to their radicalisation. At the same time, as in other ERTs, workers with past activist or community or union organising experiences were re-politicising during this conjuncture in Argentina, rekindling on shop floors their leadership capacities. Social justice issues and workers' rights activism had respectively played major parts for some time in the lives of both Plácido and Cándido, two of the main leaders of the soon-to-be Chilavert workers. Cándido, for instance, had been a shop steward for many years at Gráfico Gaglianone with the Federación Gráfica Bonaerense (FGB, Buenos Aires Graphics Federation),[40] while Plácido had been an influential housing rights activist at the *villa de emergencia*[41] where he still lives. As Cándido has stated publicly, echoing the story of many other ERT workers I have spoken with over the years, his activist past began to merge with the socio-economic and socio-political realities of the time, attuning to the new circumstances.

---

38 F. González 2005a, personal interview.

39 Social protests that were punctuated by the *piqueteros'* practices of road blockages and people's occupations of workplaces and public spaces.

40 The FGB has historically been one of Argentina's most militant unions, with a storied past in the labour struggles of the late 1960s and early 1970s, struggles that Cándido himself took part in. In passing, it is also worth mentioning that Cándido was for a time in the 1970s and 1980s close to owner Horacio Gaglianone and his family, often acting as a key intermediary between the rest of the workers and management. As Gaglianone's real intentions began to come to the light of workers by the mid-to-late 1990s, however, Cándido began to move firmly to the side of his *compañeros*. Eventually, Cándido would become not only one of the key spokespersons for the Chilavert ERT workers, but also one of the most articulate and radicalised leaders of the ERT movement more broadly. It was, of course, during this later, radicalised period that I interviewed him.

41 Literally 'town of emergency', these precarious neighbourhoods, made up mostly of migrants from the interior and surrounding countries, are also known more derogatorily in Argentina as *villas miserias* ('towns of misery', shantytowns).

Cándido and other ERT workers that I have interviewed over the years explained to me how they began to see things differently around the period of 19 and 20 December 2001. In a 2004 interview, Cándido succinctly expressed how his activism began to further radicalise during this period, when he also participated in the Pompeya Neighbourhood Assembly: 'I saw the problem with unemployment, with hunger, and I didn't want to stay still. I liked that idea of working in the neighbourhood, not only protesting'.[42] In short, this was a crucially transformative period for the workers of the print shop that would soon become Cooperativa Chilavert.

1.5   'Jumping the Hurdle': The Chilavert Workers' Turning Point

'Up to that moment', recalled Cándido in 2003, 'we just wanted to collect our pay for the year'.[43] As with the other two cases we will shortly engage with, and as has been the case with most ERTs, the Chilavert workers' original intention was not to take over the firm permanently but, rather, to prevent the firm's machines from disappearing and to force Boss Gaglianone to pay their overdue salaries. At one point in early 2002, 'out of innocence maybe', Plácido qualified, the workers had even proposed forming a cooperative with Gaglianone as a way of collaborating to save the shop from closure.[44]

But all changed for the remaining eight workers on 4 April 2002, the day the machines that had been sold were to be removed from the shop. Incredibly, Plácido remembered, it was from Gaglianone's own words that the workers finally discovered the fate that was to await them:

> We stopped Gaglianone on the 3rd of April 2002 and asked him: 'What's going to happen to the shop?' And that is when he tells us that the new machines aren't ever arriving, that it had actually never occurred to him to buy new machines. 'Don't you see what situation the country is in?' Gaglianone asked us. And that's when we tell him that he needs to pay us all he owed us in wages right then and there.[45]

---

42   C. González, in Lavaca 2004, p. 112.

43   C. González 2003.

44   Peñarrieta 2009, personal interview. This type of owner–employee collaboration is not unheard of in workplace conversions to cooperatives. A handful of ERTs in Argentina have proceeded in this manner (see, for instance, the PAUNY case in Chapter 6), while some Italian worker-buyouts have also taken up this strategy (see, for instance, Vieta et al. 2017). Québec's worker shareholder cooperatives, as well as Spain's *sociedades laborales*, also take up this model (see Chapter 2).

45   Ibid.

The following Thursday night, 4 April 2002, after convening a hastily called assembly, the remaining eight workers decided to begin to keep vigil over the shop's machines. As Cándido has expressed it, it was on that day that they 'jumped the hurdle' of deciding to 'fight' for what was rightly theirs.[46]

According to Fermín, in the following weeks Gaglianone kept coming to the shop occasionally to remove as many accounting and financial files as he could. Bankruptcy was finally declared on 10 May 2002. It was during these weeks that MNER came to assist, recommending to the workers the strategies and tactics of occupation, resistance, and eventual self-managed production that have since become par for the course for the country's ERTs. As Eduardo Murúa explained the strategy to me in a 2006 interview I was involved in when he visited Toronto, Canada: '"Occupy" the factory and don't leave[,] ... "[r]esist" because it [is] after occupation that the law ... arrive[s]', and '"produce"' as a worker cooperative, because it was at that time in Argentina (and still is) the best way

> to ensure that the factory would be able to continue to function ... because it would permit workers to self-manage their enterprise, enable decisions to be made within an assembly, and ensure that revenues would be distributed equitably [afterwards].[47]

Later on in May 2002, the eight resisting workers eventually decided to form a cooperative, calling it Cooperativa de Trabajo Chilavert Artes Gráficas after the street they were located on and which is, in turn, fittingly named in honour of a leader of the Argentine wars of independence. Their move to form a cooperative was to become for Chilavert, as for most ERTs in Argentina, a defining act that began to consolidate their self-managed production, giving them several important legal protections and helping guide the new, horizontalised labour processes I will discuss in more detail in Chapters 6–8.

But the Chilavert workers' first collective action, taking place before forming the cooperative, was to permanently occupy the plant, at first in shifts of two. This proved especially vital during the evenings because it was at night that they were at greater risk of forced eviction and the continued *vaciamiento* of the firm's assets and machinery by Gaglianone. During this period, numerous community groups and workers from other ERTs such as IMPA; members of the neighbourhood assemblies of Pompeya, Palermo Viejo, Congreso, and Parque Avellaneda; countless neighbours; and the workers' wives and families came

---

46 C. González, in Lavaca, 2004, p. 115.

47 Murúa 2006. For an analysis of the strategies and tactics of 'occupy, resist, produce' promoted by MNER and other ERT workers' organisations, see Chapter 6.

to assist the resisting workers. Their support was crucial for the resisting workers during this period of high conflict, providing food, bedding, and a larger physical presence of people to camp outside of the shop in an often-repeated strategy that was shortly after to be called by MNER 'the war of bodies', with workers and the community contesting police repression and returning owners through their very bodily presence.[48]

On 24 May 2002, in the thick of the occupation and while constituting the cooperative, the Chilavert workers received their first eviction notice. The notice arrived with a stark state presence that was to set the militant tone for the ensuing seven months of the workers' occupation of the plant: The eight occupying workers – all eventual founders of the Chilavert cooperative – were pitted against eight police cars and eight assault vehicles (one for each worker!), two ambulances, and a fire truck.[49] In response, over 300 neighbours and supporters mobilised outside of the shop, giving physical support to the workers. The workers inside went one step further, setting up a barricade of tires and scrap paper at the main doors. As Cándido is fond of relating, the resisting workers were prepared to burn the shop down rather than leave it in the hands of the state or for 'Señor Gaglianone'.[50] As Cándido emphatically recounted to me in tears while working at stacking pages of a book for cutting on Chilavert's shop floor one afternoon in late August 2005:

> We were going to go down with the shop if we couldn't work here. We had no other option. There was no work anywhere else for us and we had invested our blood and sweat into this place.[51]

The stand-off was over within 24 hours when, in the presence of the throng of supporters and closely followed by local media, the police commissioner of the city of Buenos Aires intervened to convince the judge presiding over the bankruptcy case to temporarily rescind the eviction order so as to preserve the peace and not risk shedding blood. The now *ex* Gráfico Gaglianone workers had won two major victories within the span of two months: They prevented the machines from leaving the shop, and they successfully stood down a potentially violent eviction order. And the ERT phenomenon had yet another emblematic story to spread and inspire other subsequent workplace takeovers.

---

48   Murúa 2005b, personal interview.
49   For another account of this founding story of Chilavert, see Sitrin 2005, pp. 67, 73–8.
50   C. González 2005b, personal interview. See also Sitrin 2005, 2006.
51   C. González 2005c, personal interview.

1.6 *The First Book Goes to Market through a Hole in the Wall*

Another strategy of resistance suggested to the now-cooperativised workers of Chilavert by MNER during these days was to keep on producing books and attempt to make any kind of revenue possible, both for the financial needs of the workers and for their psychological wellbeing. The Chilavert workers had now entered the 'produce' phase of the three-pronged strategy of 'occupy, resist, produce' promoted by MNER during these years. One way they restarted production was by selling scrap aluminum from the printing plates they used to the ERT metal shop IMPA, purchased by the latter in solidarity with Chilavert which the metal shop then refurbished into toothpaste and medicine tubes. And, perhaps most importantly, the Chilavert workers also continued to print books, brochures, and pamphlets, mostly for left-leaning publishers and progressive authors that have since become Chilavert's main customer base.

Perhaps the most poetic moment in the history of Chilavert is the story of the very book they were printing and binding during the first days of occupation, which also became the first book they produced as a worker cooperative – a book of collected essays by some of the most well-known progressive Argentine commentators of the period called *¿Qué son las asambleas populares?* (*What are the Popular Assemblies?*).[52] With police officers keeping guard outside of the shop over a two month period immediately after the first eviction order – ordered by the court of the city of Buenos Aires presiding over the bankruptcy to keep watch over the firm in order to, as the Lavaca journalists' collective cheekily puts it, 'impede suspicious activity from taking place inside, fundamentally [the activity] of working'[53] – the workers inside eventually took the book to market by passing copies of it through a hole they had carved out in the wall connecting the print shop to a neighbour's house. In a solidary act between ERT and neighbour that saw him risk arrest if discovered, the neighbour, in turn, placed the books in the trunk of his car and drove them past the unwitting police contingent keeping guard outside of the print shop to the publisher. This story is also now legendary throughout the ERT movement and in other Argentine social movement circles. The outline of the hole in the wall, now covered up with unpainted brick and surrounded by a sober picture frame, is still visibly on display at Chilavert. It is yet another symbol of the struggle that Chilavert's workers had to traverse on the road to *autogestión*.

Two more related victories would soon follow for the Chilavert workers, victories that would resonate with favourable consequences at other ERTS

---

52 Bielsa, Bonasso, Calloni, Feijóo, Salas Oroño, Feinmann, Le Fur, Mattini, et al. 2002. Also compare Sitrin 2005, pp. 73–8.

53 Lavaca 2004, p. 118.

throughout the ensuing years: After more mobilisations of bodies at the legislature of the city of Buenos Aires, and with the assistance again of MNER, in
October 2002 Chilavert was temporarily expropriated on behalf of its workers
by the city government, then led by centre-left leader Aníbal Ibarra, thereby
becoming one of the first ERTs to be expropriated in Argentina.[54] And on
25 November 2004, Chilavert would become one of the first groups of ERTs
in Argentina, together with more than a dozen others from the city of Buenos
Aires at the time, to become *permanently* expropriated under city of Buenos
Aires' Law 1529/04. The subsequent mayor of Buenos Aires, Mauricio Macri
(who would eventually become president of Argentina), subsequently vetoed
this expropriation law, which was set to secure the 'definitive expropriation'
of more than 20 ERTs in the city of Buenos Aires on behalf of its workers.
Prophetically, this foreshadowed the rise of expropriation vetoes and other
state-initiated blockages and challenges to ERTs by the Cambiemos coalition
government of Macri and the coalition's governors in other parts of the country.[55] Workers' struggles for ERTs' stability, as I began to suggest in the Preface
and will address in the following chapters, thus continues to this day.

1.7   'We Have Been Wakers of Consciousness'

With the exception of Cándido González (who has in recent years retired) and
his brother Fermín González (now deceased), all of the original founders still
work at the cooperative, while Chilavert had grown by the beginning of 2017 to
include 14 *socios* (associates). Moreover, Chilavert has re-hired formally retired
workers (such as Fermín González) in order to assist these *compañeros* financially and to ensure that they remain part of the more stable social security
plan of their union, the FGB, to which the cooperative still remains affiliated.[56]

---

54   Ferreyra 2002.
55   We will review the intricacies and significance of expropriation for Argentina's ERTs in
      Chapter 6.
56   While the Federación Gráfica Bonaerense (FGB) in more recent years has backed the Chil-
      avert workers and now supports the growing number of ERT and cooperativised print
      shops throughout Buenos Aires, originally the union did not support the Chilavert work-
      ers' struggle, paralleling the same dilemma that most other unions faced when confront-
      ing the emergence of an ERT: In light of not answering to a boss, most unions, particularly
      in the first period of ERTs, did not know what role they had with cooperativised rank-and-
      file members. Ironically, the FGB had been, in the past, amongst the most militant unions
      in Argentina; it is also one of the oldest, having been founded in 1857. In the late 1960s, dur-
      ing one of the most divisive periods of struggle in the organised labour movement in the
      country (see Chapter 3), the FGB, under the leadership of union boss Raimundo Ongaro,
      was an integral player in the militant and progressive breakaway CGT de los Argentinos
      (General Confederation of Labour of the Argentines), which was also led by Ongaro. Cán-

And while Chilavert's financial stability has been shaky at best over the ensuing years of *autogestión* – depending at times on subsidies from the state or customers' advances on orders to sustain the shop during downturns in production – none of the workers I spoke with at Chilavert over the years would go back to even the best days under the regime of the old boss. 'We earn less than before', Cándido stated in an interview shortly after Chilavert became a worker cooperative,

> but we are better now than we were before. We have more fun! In monetary terms and in regards to hours of work, I was better off before: one earned more before and we had fixed hours. But we compensate for this with the good work environment we have between ourselves now. We started here in 2002 earning $200 pesos a month, then $400 pesos, and now we earn $800 pesos and we have some capital on reserve in case a machine breaks down or there is some unforeseen situation.[57]

While the Chilavert workers still earn less and have more flexible hours than they did when working for Gaglianone, they have, on the other hand, managed to 'humanise' their work life, as I will detail in Chapter 8, enjoying time off during workdays in between major jobs when they need to attend to personal issues, practising more flexible work processes, and, ultimately, self-determining their working and personal lives. This is the 'good work environment' that Cándido speaks of in the above excerpt and, I will ultimately argue in Chapters 7 and 8, one of the key areas innovated by ERT protagonists in the recuperation of their work.

In early 2016, however, new challenges hit Chilavert, as they have in many other ERTs, cooperatives, and SMEs throughout Argentina with the coming to power of Macri and his Cambiemos coalition's re-hashed neo-liberal policies.

---

dido González himself was active with the FGB and the CGT de los Argentinos throughout the late 1960s and early 1970s. It was in this early union activism, Cándido has told me, that he learned about the strategies and tactics of political activism, conducting and organising workers assemblies, and general shop floor organising. A year after Chilavert was converted into a cooperative, Cándido spoke about the change in the support they now receive from the union: 'At first our union said to us that the occupation of our plant was illegal and they didn't help us in anything. Since our case emerged, our union has changed position in light of newer cases of ERTs [in our sector]. For example, our union [the FGB] now supports Gráfica Conforti and Imprenta Del Sol, today occupied by their workers, in their struggle [for securing their jobs]. Compare this to us; only now [in late 2003] is our union reaching out to us' (González 2003).

57   González 2003.

For ERTs, other cooperatives, and SMEs in general, these policies were being felt in a sharp rise in production costs and falling sales due to the inflationary pressures that had hit Argentina with force in 2016 as a consequence of *macrismo*'s economic *sinceramiento* policies.[58] Most notably for Chilavert throughout 2016, as with countless SMEs throughout the country, was the astronomic rise in the shop's production costs due to the cancellation of Kirchner-era subsidies for utility bills that formed the key part of the *macrista* policy known colloquially as *el Tarifazo*. Between February and May of 2016 alone, Chilavert's utility bills skyrocketed by over 500 percent, going from $800 pesos in February to over $8,000 pesos by May.[59] While in mid-2016 provincial and federal supreme courts had put a temporary moratorium on the increase in utility bills, after much lobbying from groups in the social and solidarity economy and arguments from opposition lawmakers that the rate hikes were unconstitutional due to the lack of public consultation, the Macri regime continued, as of this writing, to work towards finally imposing these price-gouging rates. Moreover, after Macri came to power in December 2015, there had been an increase in legislative vetoes of several expropriations of already established ERTs, while the state's permission for the sale of a handful of established ERTs to local and foreign capital and a freeze of the Ministry of Labour's support programme for self-managed firms emerged as further new challenges to the country's ERTs.[60] Overall, these challenges are risking anew the long-term viability of the country's SMEs and auguring Argentina's return to the deindustrialisation of the 1990s.

Despite these new challenges – which the Chilavert workers are determined to overcome through a struggle of solidarity with other ERTs and the country's broader union and social and solidarity economy movements[61] – Chilavert remains a living testament to what workers can do in order to control their own productive lives. The continued determination by the Chilavert workers to see their own ERT and the broader ERT movement remain influential players in the struggle against the current return of neo-liberalism and for another, more socially and economically just Argentina, is deeply rooted in the Chilavert workers' long history of battling micro-economic crises at the firm. This determination has been solidifying over the years in their collective struggles against a recalcitrant and insensitive *patrón* (boss) and a callous socio-economic system that, since at least the late 1980s, nurtured and

---

58   See Preface and Chapter 2.
59   Ruggeri 2016, p. 20.
60   For more on these new challenges faced by Arentina's ERTs, see Chapters 2, 6, and 7.
61   E. González 2017, personal interview.

coalesced into the intense solidarity of the ex-Gaglianone workers. This solidarity, in turn, would see them through the intense years of struggle against exploitation during the 1990s, and their emblematic fight for control of their place of work in the early 2000s. Since then, Chilavert has become an inspiration for other ERT experiences in Argentina and even abroad. This is in no small part due to how they have extended themselves far beyond their shop's walls. Since taking over their firm, they have, for instance: gone on to co-found the Red Gráfica network; linked up to and offered solidarity to other social movements, labour organisations, and researchers inside and outside of Argentina by housing the much-used ERT Documentation Centre; donated part of their space to a *bachillerato popular*; participated actively in numerous Argentine and regional Latin American gatherings of ERTs and cooperatives, as I will review in Chapter 7; produced a book of photographs documenting the ERT movement, a project that took two of its workers on a tour of Europe to promote it in 2008–9;[62] hosted a community recreation centre within the print shop's walls; supported in myriad ways other ERTs, especially in assisting them in production needs, in consolidating other cooperatives, and providing know-how and solidarity in numerous other occupation struggles or during moments when other ERT workers have been threatened with evictions; and have actively participated in several ERT workers' associations such as MNER, the Asociación Nacional de Trabajadores Autogestionados (ANTA, National Association of Self-Managed Workers), and the Federación Argentina de Cooperativas de Trabajadores Autogestionados (FACTA, Argentine Federation of Self-Managed Worker Cooperatives), which we will see in Chapter 3.

As Cándido evocatively suggests: '*Nosotros fuimos despertadores de conciencia* [We have been wakers (or raisers) of consciousness]'.[63] Their story is a testament to the new forms of labour organising involving the greater communities that surround these firms; the bottom-up mobilisation that is forged by ERT protagonists within a moral economy of work; the *compañerismo* (camaraderie or solidarity) that is tapped into from out of the exploitations of the capitalist labour process; and what can emerge from workers themselves within struggle. The story of the Chilavert workers is, in other words, a powerful illustration of the (re)making of the working class within struggle and of the force still present in the political economy of the working class.

---

62   E. González 2009, personal interview.
63   C. González 2003, p. 5.

FIGURE 3   Images of Cooperativa 'Unión Solidaria de Trabajadores'
PHOTOGRAPH BY AUTHOR

2   Cooperativa de Trabajo 'Unión Solidaria de Trabajadores'[64]

2.1   *First Struggle: 'To Guarantee the Continuity of Our Jobs'*

Cooperativa de Trabajo 'Unión Solidaria de Trabajadores', Ltda. (UST, 'Solidarity Union [or Gathering] of Workers' Worker Cooperative, Ltd.), is a cooperative that by late 2009 had 95 members officially involved in the business of urban solid waste treatment, waste recycling, construction, and parks maintenance. It is also an ERT deeply – and inspirationally – involved in the social and economic revitalisation of its surrounding neighbourhoods, Villa Domínico and Wilde, in the municipality of Avellaneda, located about 15 kilometres south of the country's capital in the province of Buenos Aires.

Just over a third of UST's members were originally employed by a firm called Saneamiento y Urbanización Sociedad Anónima (SYUSA, Sanitation and Urbanisation Anonymous Society), formerly owned by one of Argentina's largest multinationals, the Techint Group.[65] Between 1978 and 2003, Techint's SYUSA

---

64   Parts of this case study were previously published in Askew and Vieta 2012b.

65   The Techint Group, a multinational Italo-Argentine conglomerate based in Milan and

was contracted to manage the solid waste treatment and recycling requirements of the state-run waste management firm CEAMSE at the Villa Domínico
Disposal Centre landfill.[66] Extending out from its main interests in steel manufacturing and the oil sector, the Techint Group formed SYUSA in 1978 during
the last military dictatorship in order to capitalise on the growing practice
that was being experimented with by the military government of privatising
public services such as waste disposal.[67] And it was at SYUSA that many of
UST's current members perfected their craft of construction, managing waste,
converting landfills into parks, and maintaining green spaces. Indeed, it was
its workers, in no small part, that converted the massive Villa Domínico Disposal Centre, once a polluted 400-hectare landfill, into the sprawling 'ecological green belt' that now contains more than 40,000 trees (planted by the
SYUSA/UST workers over the years), new lakes, and vast green spaces hugging
the Rio de la Plata and spanning the waterfront of the neighbourhoods of Villa

---

Buenos Aires, is made up of more than 100 companies worldwide. While it is primarily
in the business of manufacturing seamless steel tubes for the oil and gas industries (of
which it is the largest manufacturer in the world), it is also Latin America's largest steel
manufacturer and is involved in many other important markets such as manufacturing
and installing underground cables for the telecom industry.

66 CEAMSE, or Coordinación Ecológica Area Metropolitana Sociedad del Estado (Ecological
Coordination Metropolitan Area Society of the State) is, according to Caroline Baillie and
Eric Feinblatt, 'a municipal and regional government amalgam with private affiliations,
which manages the landfill(s) that [receive] the waste of the ... greater metropolitan area
of Buenos Aires' (Baillie and Feinblatt 2010, p. 208). While there were several landfills
scattered throughout greater Buenos Aires up until the late 1990s, as of 2011 CEAMSE managed only one landfill, Norte III, northeast of the city of Buenos Aires. The other landfills,
like the Villa Domínico Disposal Centre which SYUSA formerly managed and which UST
is currently contracted to manage for CEAMSE, have been turned into 'ecoparks' or 'ecological green belts' (p. 208).

67 Although privatisations took off with force throughout the heyday of the neo-liberal
model in the 1990s, in actuality the privatisation of public services, as I map out in
Chapter 3, had its roots in Argentina in the economic practices (or, better, in the neo-
liberal rehearsals) of the last military dictatorship's self-denominated Proceso de Reorganización Nacional (National Process of Reorganisation) between 1976 and 1983. The waste
management sector was not exempt from this 'national reorganisation' and privatisation
and is still a mostly privatised service in greater Buenos Aires. According to Caroline Baillie
and Eric Feinblatt, '[g]arbage collection in Buenos Aires is almost entirely privatized. The
city government contracts five different trucking companies, each of which is assigned to
specific city districts. Each company is responsible for cleaning the streets of waste and
hauling that waste to transit points or directly to the CEAMSE landfill. In 1977 the military
government created CEAMSE in order to centralise management of urban waste and to
replace incineration practices with ... landfill disposal' (2010, p. 208).

Domínico and Wilde.[68] This is the site which UST is now contracted to manage for CEAMSE and which took years of struggle to secure for the cooperative.

At its height in the early 1990s, SYUSA employed 342 workers. By the late 1990s its workforce had been reduced to 140 employees as the neo-liberal-inspired rationalisation drives prevalent at the time, in conjunction with the more flexible labour contracts of the day facilitated by the labour reforms of the 1990s, allowed Techint to re-negotiate complex sector-wide labour contracts that had been hard-won by workers over the years. With these contract re-negotiations, by the late 1990s Techint was able to reduce SYUSA's workforce by buying out some of its workers while tempting others into early retirement.[69] By 1998, Techint had plans to completely exit the waste treatment business in greater Buenos Aires and lay off all of SYUSA's workers. By 2003, when Techint finally decided to pull out of the waste disposal business – in part excused by the strong community and media activism against the waste dump that forced its shutdown and conversion into the ecological green belt that it is today – 122 jobs were on the line.

The first struggle for UST's workers, then, according to Mario Alberto Barrios – the cooperative's president at the time of my interviews with him, one of its co-founders, a former Unón Obrera de la Construcción de la República Argentina (UOCRA, Construction Workers' Union of the Republic of Argentina) shop steward at SYUSA, and one of UST's inspirational leaders – was to preserve the jobs and source of income of fellow *compañeros* when Techint was threatening to leave the garbage business. Mario calls this the 'first struggle' to 'guarantee the continuity of our jobs'.[70] In a 2007 interview I had with him, Mario described what motivated this early struggle during the last days of SYUSA and the arguments the SYUSA workers posed to Techint at the time, which, not surprisingly, ultimately fell on deaf ears:

> Our first struggle, then, was to fight for securing our jobs. When Techint threatens to leave in the middle of the national socio-economic crisis we were in, we reacted and told them, 'No, no, we must guarantee these jobs!' We had been working here for more than 20 years up till then, and

---

68   Rolandi 2009, personal interview.

69   See Chapter 3 for a detailed discussion of the connections between Argentina's monetary policy of 'convertability' of the peso to the US dollar and this policy's facilitation of rationalisation drives at thousands of Argentine firms, the flexibilisation of labour contracts, and the erosion of collective agreements. See also Patroni 2004.

70   Barrios, in OSERA, 2010, p. 2.

we knew at the time that although the waste disposal site was shutting down, that there were years of work ahead, that the site would have to be transformed into an ecological area, which was mandated by the provincial and national governments, and that we had the expertise to do this work now and in the future. And, after all, as we also told Techint and CEAMSE at the time, 'Garbage is never going to run out!' We knew how to treat garbage, how to recycle, how to use many, many sophisticated tools and machines of the trade. And the site that we were managing for CEAMSE was vast, and we knew that there were many more years of work ahead in converting it to a greenbelt – what is called in this business the 'post-closing maintenance' of a landfill. So how was it possible, we asked Techint, for our jobs to end?[71]

2.2 Second Struggle: 'What We Knew We Had to Do was Educate Ourselves'

For this argument to not be construed as 'naïve' demands by 'unrealistic' employees, the SYUSA workers, under the leadership of Mario Barrios and other UOCRA shop stewards, began to get organised for a labour struggle while also starting an internal campaign to educate themselves regarding the future of waste recycling, waste management, and landfill conversion;[72] they began this already by 1998, when Techint started to hint that it was likely to pull out of the garbage business. During this period they also started taking stock of the skill sets of SYUSA's entire workforce. 'Already, by the late 1990s', Mario related to me in 2007,

we [the UOCRA workers at SYUSA] began to diagram several strategies for our future, ideas like becoming a cooperative, strategies at the time that appeared to some – including us! – as crazy. The thing was that by 1999 or so, the yellow lights were flashing for us, warning us that something was going to happen.[73]

Mario continued in another interview:

What we knew we had to do by then was to educate ourselves so that there would be no excuses for firing us. Another important thing we proposed then was that those of us that had not finished secondary school

---

71   Barrios 2007, personal interview.
72   Ibid.
73   Ibid.

go get their high school equivalency, and that those of us that had our high school diplomas should finish a technical [degree or certificate] in, for example, environmental issues or hydraulics.[74]

According to Barrios and other UST workers whom I have spoken with, it was this intellectual preparation, their skills upgrading, and their adroit self-organisation early on in their struggle to save their jobs that made a major difference in their future conversion into a cooperative. This drive, UST workers have told me over the years, emerged most emphatically from Mario Barrios's own style of leadership. When Barrios is in a workers' assembly or leading UST workers in a solidarity protest, one is struck by how soft-spoken he is, deeply caring about his community and *compañeros*. Barrios inspires and motivates others by leading by example rather than by giving direct orders, always arriving at meetings, conferences, assemblies, and such with much reading and study behind him. This tendency to study and learn has also been a catalyst for UST's subsequent involvement in hosting a primary school and high-school equivalent programme (connected to the *bachillerato popular* at Chilavert that I reviewed above), conducting adult education classes of all types, and organising various social and solidarity economy and cooperative administration courses for its workers with two local universities, Universidad Nacional de Quilmes and Universidad Técnologia Nacional – Facultad Nacional de Avellaneda. These leadership qualities and his knack for studying the situation at hand, his encouragement of his colleagues to get educated and upgrade their skills, as well as the community and social values which motivate him, Mario has told me, come from his family's roots in the militant Peronism of the late 1960s and early 1970s and his own subsequent community activism and union work while an employee and shop steward at SYUSA.[75]

2.3   Third Struggle: Fighting Job Flexibilisation, Outsourcing, and the Pitting of Worker against Worker

While the UST workers' struggles hit their apex in mid-2003 when Techint eventually did shut down SYUSA and pulled out of the urban waste treatment business, the years between 1999 and 2003 were already pockmarked for SYUSA's employees, as for countless other Argentine workers, by growing job insecurity. Techint's first attempt at withdrawing from the waste treatment business arrived two years before, in 2001, at first with the strategy of tempting older

---

74   Barrios, in OSERA 2010, p. 1.

75   For the connections between the ERT phenomenon, Peronism, and members' earlier experiences in labour struggles, see Chapters 3 and 8.

workers with early retirement or buy outs, which succeeded in enticing some workers to leave. But perhaps the most nefarious of Techint's schemes during this period was one that included the gradual flexibilisation of the SYUSA employees, which was sold to the workers – in a textbook case of neo-liberal practices in countless workplaces across Argentina at the time – as Techint's attempt at helping them become 'self-employed'. This 'self-employment' would, in reality, turn ex-SYUSA workers into ready-made outsourced contractors; eventually, the SYUSA workers were told, Techint would buy back the services of these ex-SYUSA now-self-employed workers by contracting back their waste management capabilities. Of course, what this was, in reality, was a way for Techint to let these workers go in order to rid the multinational of these labour costs and eliminate severance payouts while, at the same time, liberating itself from the hassles of dealing with the UOCRA union when the time came to shut down the plant. In the meantime, these workers would continue to work on Techint's projects, so the story went, but now as contracted out self-employed workers. The SYUSA workers would, in essence, become what in Argentina is known as *trabajadores terciarizados* ('tertiarised' or outsourced workers).[76] Again, this is, of course, a scheme not unheard of in the repertoire of neo-liberal business practices in Argentina and elsewhere.[77] As Ronaldo Munck has recently written, this 'informalisation' is 'just one distinguishing characteristic of working life in the South compared to the North ... also including various forms of self-employment' that in actuality are 'a subsidy to capitalist accumulation given its high levels of self-exploitation'.[78]

SYUSA's workers, however, led by the UOCRA shop stewards and armed with their years of study of the situation at hand, had figured out management's 'informalisation' strategy early on and organised various work stoppages that eventually put a premature stop to the work flexibilisation scheme. The flexibilisation drive, nevertheless, did get as far as outsourcing the services of 28 of SYUSA's truck drivers. The scheme unfolded as follows: with 'assistance' from, and out of the 'generosity' of Techint, SYUSA's truckers were guaranteed the eventual ownership of the trucks they drove within two years if they agreed

---

76 Battistini 2005.

77 This practice is a close cousin of the 'false cooperatives' phenomenon in Argentina that I will discuss in Chapter 5. Both the surge in 'false cooperativess' and outsourced or flexibilised workers were two nefarious practices by employers that grew throughout the 1990s in Argentina to weaken working-class unity and strength, lower labour costs, and increase profits. They are, in sum, in Marxist terms, forms of extreme relative surplus-value extraction that have been perfected by the neo-liberal, or post-Fordist, production model, especially in the global South.

78 Munck 2002, pp. 111–13.

to eventually 'buy' their trucks through labour credits. They could pay for the trucks by hauling at least one extra load of garbage per day, and could own them sooner if they hauled more loads than expected per day. That is, each extra haul per day would be compensated to the truckers not by extra pay per extra load but, rather, as a portion of the ostensible cost of the truck until it was 'paid' for in labour credits. Eventually, after 'buying' the trucks in this manner, the drivers, so the enticement went, would become 'self-employed' truck drivers and SYUSA would contract back their waste hauling services as 'self-employed' truckers. What seemed like a deal too good to be true for these drivers, however, ultimately was just that. In essence, and as the group of SYUSA workers led by Barrios had figured out early on, this was a move by Techint to rid themselves of the truckers, further eroding job security at the firm, dividing SYUSA's workers, and eventually increasing competition between these workers, which ultimately meant intensifying their work and increasing the profits to Techint from this work precarisation and flexibilisation scheme. The UOCRA shop stewards were thus wary of the scheme from the beginning and knew that this was the beginning of the end of their jobs, which caused deep tensions between the remaining SYUSA workers and the flexibilised and now contracted-out truckers.

Capturing important aspects of the neo-liberalisation of work at the time in Argentina, it is worth quoting Mario's recounting of this third round of struggle at some length, a struggle that now pitted the SYUSA workers against the neo-liberal strategies of job flexibilisation, job insecurity (that is, precarisation), increased competition amongst workers, and outsourcing:

> They [Techint] began to break the organisation we had been working so hard to develop by offering voluntary early retirement packages and the outsourcing of our services to our own workers. With that they began to fight us. It was very hard at the time because, in reality, *las terciarizaciones* [the outsourcing offers] were indeed tempting. They would offer our *compañeros* the actual trucks they worked with, for example, and there were several cases where the drivers actually became the owners of the trucks, which they would pay for with the work they did, plus receive a paycheque from SYUSA all along! Who would say no to that? If you said 'No', they wouldn't pay you because your *compañero* would take up the offer; if you said 'Yes', they would give you a paycheque and in two years you walked away with a truck! Saying no to that would be crazy, right? But some of us were more aware, I guess, of the ultimate risks in giving in to this scheme, generating a deep debate with us workers at the time. Fights broke out between the *compañeros*, which, after all, is what the boss always wants, right? They see that dividing workers actually works in their favour, and

this was happening all the time then, here and throughout Argentina – *en el país de los ciegos, el tuerto es el rey* [in a country of blind people, the one-eyed person is king].[79] And so, they were permanently dividing us, dividing and dividing, and that's how they were able to manage us 'better'. We started behaving how they wanted us to behave, competing against one another – getting more work out of us, and instilling fear. So, you can see that neo-liberalism was in full bloom in our country, and it saturated into our consciousness. Organised labour's credibility was zero at the time, and there was much individualism around, each worker thinking about his own pocketbook, and, well, things were no different at our firm then. It was a difficult fight for us; difficult because ... some of us saw so clearly what was about to happen, while some of our *compañeros* didn't want to see it. It was the ongoing struggle that workers within capitalism have faced for years, heads getting full of ideas from one place and us [in the union leadership] trying to change their consciousness.

So, the result was that they began to privatise even more, to outsource us. The first *terciarizaciones* went really well for Techint. Remember that these trucks were mostly already paid for [by Techint], so enticing workers to buy them for more work was a perfect strategy for the company.[80] Before the *terciarizaciones* the truckers would do three trips a day from the collection plant to the Villa Domínico Disposal area which was out back at the time, which equalled about 130 or so trips a day. When Techint outsources the trips to these new self-employed *compañeros*, they were now getting an average of around 160 or so trips a day out of the 28 truckers that took the deal, which was way more than the extra trip the truckers promised to do in order to eventually own the trucks! So you can imagine that a fierce competition began to emerge between the truck drivers to get that extra load in, and some of them would do six or seven trips per day to pay off their trucks sooner! And they would also stop maintaining the trucks, because that took time away, so things also became dangerous for public safety on the roads, as well ... So that was our next set of struggles here, the *lucha* [struggle] against the outsourcing of our jobs and dividing us workers.[81]

---

79   This is a popular Argentine saying.
80   Indeed, from the perspective of management, this was a brilliant scheme not only to get more work out of the SYUSA workers, but also to offload already depreciated fixed capital.
81   Barrios 2007, personal interview.

2.4   From Employees of a Multinational to Cooperatively Managed Workers

Several work stoppages and other direct action tactics by the UOCRA workers eventually put a monkey wrench into the Techint labour flexibilisation scheme. In any case, by late 2002 it was clear that the open pit landfill at Villa Domínico was going to be converted into an ecological greenbelt, which gave Techint the perfect excuse to leave the waste management business. The multinational eventually decided to disband SYUSA in early 2003.

The battle for the soon-to-be ex-SYUSA workers now shifted from struggling against a multinational and the outsourcing of jobs to struggling against a state-run firm when CEAMSE decided to give the Villa Domínico Disposal Centre contract to a temporary joint venture company called ESTRANS, an enterprise made up of the Argentine trucking company Nueve de Julio and a Brazilian firm called Estre. The possibility of giving a public-sector contract to this type of firm is, like the flexibilisation/outsourcing case just mapped out, illustrative of another oft-practised outsourcing scheme in Argentina that became popular in the 1990s: have two or more companies (from Argentina or elsewhere) form a joint venture firm for a limited period and for a particular contract or set of tasks and then disband the firm. This type of firm, known in Spanish as an UTE, *unión transitoria/temporaria de empresas* (transitory [or temporary] association of firms), often bid for and won the thousands of public-sector contracts available to private firms throughout the 1990s – or simply secured the contracts by paying off government officials. And the profits for these joint venture companies were astronomical at the time.[82] When both CEAMSE and ESTRANS originally refused to take on the ex-SYUSA employees after the Ministry of Labour had mandated them to do so, the workers again organised and resisted. This time they did so by adopting the road blockage strategies of the *piqueteros*, the plant occupation strategies of other ERTs that were at their peak at the time, and – with much support from the surrounding *barrios*, community groups, other ERTs, and several social justice groups – the mobilisation of hundreds of people to the ex-SYUSA workers' cause. This collective and now-community struggle would generate considerable media coverage and public sympathy for the ex-SYUSA workers.

A parallel strategy the ex-SYUSA workers decided to deploy at the same time was to form a cooperative and try to outbid ESTRANS for the CEAMSE contract. By 25 July 2003, the former SYUSA workers, now reorganised as Cooperativa de Trabajo 'Unión Solidaria de Trabajadores', made a bid for the CEAMSE con-

---

82   Liendo and Martínez 2001.

tract, arguing that what they brought to the table was 24 years of know-how in the waste management business and, in particular, managing the waste disposal site at Villa Domínico. When CEAMSE refused to give the contract to the cooperative, the now-UST workers resorted to an additional two-pronged approach: continue occupying part of the CEAMSE facilities formerly used by SYUSA, which was the *political* part of the strategy that served to attract continued media attention to their cause, while again appealing to the national Ministry of Labour for arbitration, which formed the *legal* component of the strategy.[83] UST would eventually secure the CEAMSE contract via this two-pronged approach, but it would take an additional eight months of struggle to do so.

The eight months between the founding of the UST cooperative in mid-2003 and March 2004, when UST finally managed to secure the CEAMSE contract, was perhaps the period of the ex-SYUSA/now-UST workers' most intense struggles. The UST workers would be temporarily placated during these eight months when, under the arbitration of the Ministry of Labour, CEAMSE and ESTRANS finally agreed to take on the UST workers. The proposal by the Ministry of Labour, which CEAMSE and ESTRANS agreed to, was as follows: thirty-four of the ex-SYUSA workers who were now members of the newly-founded UST cooperative would continue to be employees of ESTRANS. These 34 workers had already been hired by the joint-venture company earlier that year as a way of pacifying the ex-SYUSA workers' previous demands. Seventy-six of the ex-SYUSA/now-UST workers who had not been hired by ESTRANS would go to CEAMSE. And the rest were offered early retirement. This conciliatory phase would not last long, however. Shortly after the Ministry of Labour's mid-2003 proposal, ESTRANS' 34 UST workers were under threat of being let go again. Moreover, workers would soon again be pitched against fellow workers when CEAMSE and its plant union, the Asociación Gremial Obreros y Empleados de Ceamse (AGOEC, Association of Unionised Workers and Employees of CEAMSE) initially refused to take on the 76 ex-SYUSA workers, arguing that guaranteeing the employment of the ex-SYUSA employees was not their concern and that doing so would jeopardise the job security of the incumbent AGOEC workers at CEAMSE. To add more fuel to the fire, after CEAMSE eventually agreed to hire the workers, the five shop stewards at the ex-SYUSA plant – one of whom included Mario Barrios – were ordered to be transferred to another CEAMSE site two hours drive away and were, to add insult to injury,

---

83   Barrios 2007, personal interview. This two-pronged legal/political strategy has been used by countless ERTs, and is similar to Salud Junín's strategy, which I describe below. See also Chapters 6 and 7.

offered the night shift. The latter move by CEAMSE was the final straw for the UST workers, who understood it to be a blatant move by CEAMSE and the rival AGOEC union to cut the organisational legs from the UST workers and exhaust the motivation of the cooperative's leaders. In protest, and demanding that CEAMSE respect the decision of the Ministry of Labour and that the jobs of *all* of the ex-SYUSA workers had to be guaranteed, the five shop stewards refused the transfer, and all of the UST workers began a three-month occupation of part of the CEAMSE compound at the Villa Domínico site that SYUSA had previously worked out of. (This site is now the space controlled by UST, which includes a dining hall, a large warehouse, and an administrative building.) The escalation hit fever pitch when, during one of the negotiation meetings between the UST workers and CEAMSE, the AGOEC union deployed hired thugs to physically threaten the UST workers. This confrontation eventually escalated into a battle with sticks and fists between the UST workers and the AGOEC-hired thugs, which has now become, as with Chilavert's workers' stand-off with the state, a legendary part of UST's foundation story, told to me by many of the cooperative's members in interviews and informal conversations.[84]

2.5   'To Demonstrate That Workers Could ... Develop, Get Organised, and Manage Themselves'[85]

After yet one more intervention by the national Ministry of Labour, the CEAMSE contract to manage the now ecological green belt that was formally the Villa Domínico Disposal site was eventually offered to the UST cooperative on a one-year trial basis on 9 March 2004. A year later it was renewed for a new five-year term, and renewed again in 2009 and 2014.[86] It seems that the work of UST has proven to be better than CEAMSE ever thought it could be. The UST workers formally started self-managed production in 2004 with an agreement to use in usufruct the facilities that they had worked at formerly as SYUSA workers and which they had occupied for three months the year before. Moreover, as a sort of 'collective severance package' owed to the workers from their days at SYUSA/Techint, the cooperative began their era of *autogestión* with not only the rights to use the former dining room and warehouse installations, but also

---

84   Seeing state actors, recalcitrant owners, or even unions hiring thugs (*matones*) to intimidate workers involved in labour actions is another time-honoured tradition in Argentine labour relations, one that increased greatly during the years of crisis at the turn of the millennium.

85   Cooperativa 'Unión Solidaria de Trabajadores' 2007, p. 3.

86   Barrios 2017, personal interview.

a Mercedes Benz truck, a van, and several other items of grounds maintenance equipment that once belonged to Techint, in addition to $100,000 pesos and one hectare of land on the banks of the Rio de la Plata, land which UST has since transformed into a community recreational area for the *barrio* residents. From the initial capitalisation of $100,000 pesos, the one-year CEAMSE contract, and a contract they secured in 2004 to maintain the green spaces and parks of the municipality of Avellaneda, UST has since managed to grow exponentially over the last thirteen years, now owning a collection of tractors, excavators, backhoes, trucks of varying sizes, mowing equipment, and other heavy and light machinery, some of which the cooperative purchased as an act of solidarity from other ERTs like the PAUNY tractor factory in the province of Córdoba[87] and the Cooperar 7 de Mayo cooperative machine shop in Villa Constitución in the province of Santa Fe.

For the UST workers, having shown that they have been able to keep their word, grow, and administer the CEAMSE contract effectively and efficiently – and better than a multinational (SYUSA/Techint) or a joint venture firm (ESTRANS) – are points of deep pride. All of the workers I interviewed at UST, like most other ERT workers I have conversed with over the years (as the Salud Junín case study will shortly show), have made it a point to emphasise their collective capacity for efficiently or effectively executing their jobs, paying their bills, meeting deadlines, managing contracts, administering their firms, and satisfying customers' needs, using words like *responsabilidad* (responsibility), *compromiso* (commitment), and *crecimiento* (growth) to describe their business values.[88] For example, when in 2009 I asked Pablo Rolandi, UST's production manager, to assess the years since UST had taken on the CEAMSE contract, he responded as follows:

> Our success with the CEAMSE contract to date – witnessed in that they have renewed our contract three times now – is due to the fact that we offered them good service and work continuity, unlike the situation when we worked at SYUSA. And we have managed the contract with seriousness and commitment. We have also shown [to ourselves, the community, and CEAMSE] that we were able to get along the best we could at the beginning with the little equipment we had, then with borrowed or rented equip-

---

87   For more on PAUNY, see Chapter 6.

88   In Chapters 7 and 8, I will critically analyse the entrepreneurial discourse of business efficiency and growth taken up by some ERT workers and how this discourse is in tension with their values and practices of solidarity, cooperativism, community development, and *compañerismo*.

ment, and eventually by buying our own machines and always paying back our debts on time.

So do you think that knowing that you have to self-manage this project, and showing that you all can handle your commitments and affairs well made you all somehow work harder, or with more determination or care?

Yes! Showing that you can indeed self-manage your business – and actually doing it – is a matter of survival for us. Before you would do what you had to do to keep your job, but you weren't the owner of your own destiny. Because if the firm's numbers didn't add up – and you were just another number after all – then they could hang you out to dry. So your job security was in [your boss's] hands, until he decided to let you go. Today, here, we have the obligation to keep this going and assure its continuity. So, the commitment and responsibility we all have here to this project is definitely more intensely felt by us all.[89]

Mario Barrios expressed similar ideas to me two years before my interview with Pablo, eloquently summing up ERT workers' desires to highlight for themselves as well as for outsiders (that is, customers, suppliers, other firms they work with, banks, the state, and so on) their *commitments* and *responsibility* to their projects of *autogestión*:

For us it is satisfying to be able to say that we workers aren't only capable of working as we are told, but that we can also work to fight for our jobs. It also gives us great pride to say that we are also capable of managing ourselves, of administering our work, of having policies and practices that are friendly to the environment, to do community work. That is, that we aren't just thinking about making a profit.[90]

2.6   *From Waste Management to Community Development*

Emerging from out of these variegated struggles over the five-year period between 1999 and 2004, not only was UST's first one-year trial contract with CEAMSE extended to three more five-year contracts, but from its original 34 founding members UST has since taken on and trained another 61 cooperative members – mostly previously unemployed residents from surrounding *barrios*. It has also deeply involved itself in local community development projects, deciding in an early workers' assembly to re-direct a portion of its rev-

89   Rolandi 2009, personal interview.
90   Barrios 2007, personal interview.

enues to initiatives such as helping build 100 affordable and dignified houses for its own workers and other neighbours in need (see Figure 4), developing a youth-based community centre and sports complex for the residents of the Villa Domínico and Wilde neighbourhoods that surround UST, and spearheading a community health initiative and clinic, as well as founding a popular education high school, a waste recycling programme, a community bank that gives out credit to local projects, a multimedia centre, a community pool, and hosting a local radio show. Moreover, all of these initiatives are organised as cooperatives. Thus, UST in essence is also a second-tier multistakeholder cooperative of cooperatives, with the initial UST worker cooperative serving as its hub. In addition, the relatively new union for self-managed workers in Argentina, the Asociación Nacional de Trabajadores Autogestionados (ANTA, National Association of Self-Managed Workers), affiliated with Argentina's more progressive trade union federation the Central de Trabajadores de la Argentina (CTA, Argentine Workers' Central), was originally an initiative of UST's workers and had Mario Barrios as its general secretary at the time of my interviews with him. With these community-focused projects, UST has forged a strong alliance with progressive factions of Argentina's organised labour movement and its broader social and solidarity economy, and its workers often mobilise in solidarity with other social movements and workplaces in conflict in the country.

Ultimately, the story of UST is deeply rooted in worker-led responses to the most questionable of neo-liberal practices. It begins with private sector workers of a multinational contracted out to do public sector work reacting against the practices of job flexibilisation and outsourcing. Unlike Chilavert and most other ERT stories, which tend to be about struggles between labour and capital represented by owners of small- and medium-sized private businesses and their employees at a *micro-economic* level, what makes UST's story of workplace conflict and recuperation unique is that its workers' struggles explicitly brushed up against major parts of the *macro-economic* neo-liberal plotline of 1990s Argentina, analysed in detail in Chapter 3, to wit: the privatisation and multinationalisation of public services; practices of outsourcing and job flexibilisation; strategies of dividing workers' solidarity; increasing competition between workers at the same firm by 'entrepreneurialising' jobs; and the myriad practices deployed by management that pits worker against fellow worker by entwining them into a web of conflicting interests and fears.

And, yet again, UST's story shows that, pushed to levels of extreme exploitation and abuse when the class compromise ruptures – a compromise that usually holds together capitalist labour processes and contains class conflict in times of economic stability – opportunities for workers' self-organisation come

FIGURE 4   Townhomes for workers and the surrounding community built by Cooperativa
             'Unión Solidaria de Trabajadores'
             PHOTOGRAPH BY THE AUTHOR

to the fore as workers seek alternatives to their exploitation and begin to see
possibilities beyond working for a boss.[91] During these times, in particular, as
I will analyse further in Chapter 9, there is no stopping workers' ingenuity and
innovation for fighting for their own interests and self-managing their working
lives. A statement from a UST promotional brochure that inspired the title for
this chapter captures the sentiments and desires of many ERT protagonists:

> [What we have accomplished so far] fills us with pride, for it shows that
> we did our job well in the past, and makes us feel reassured that we can
> see the situation of our cooperative from a different angle. Because of all
> this, we say we are proud of our present and increasingly committed to
> our future, convinced that 'we, *the workers, can take our destiny in our own
> hands*'.[92]

---

91   Atzeni 2010, 2012; Atzeni and Vieta 2014.
92   Cooperativa 'Unión Solidaria de Trabajadores' 2007, p. 4 (emphasis in original).

3   Cooperativa de Trabajo de la Salud Junín[93]

3.1   *'This isn't Just Any Business, It's the Business of Delivering Health'*
'When we took over the clinic and decided to self-manage it', José López, former president, co-founder, and member of Cooperativa de Trabajo de la Salud Junín Ltda. (Junín Health Care Worker Cooperative, Ltd.), told me in my first interview with him in 2007, 'we had no idea what we were getting ourselves into. You see', he continued, eventually laughing at the thought,

> we had the particular complexity here – unlike at say a recuperated ceramics factory, say Zanón, or a recuperated textile firm like Brukman, or a car parts *recuperada* of which there are several – of dealing with health care, people's health. A sensitive issue, right? We hadn't considered this little detail when we formed our cooperative and began to self-manage this clinic![94]

The specific word José uses – *complexity* – is very appropriate for characterising the business that Salud Junín is in. Indeed, the complexity of the activities of the clinic is perhaps the main thing one notices when first walking through its main doors.

Cooperativa Salud Junín is situated on the busy and narrow downtown street Calle Deán Funes, on a short block close to one of the major avenues of Argentina's second largest city, Córdoba. When one walks through the glass doors of the clinic during certain peak hours and into the patient reception area, which takes up a good portion of the building's first floor, one is immediately struck by the human-centred bustle of this health care cooperative, populated by doctors in white overalls, nurses in light-blue uniforms, and numerous people in street clothes. At other, off-peak hours, there is a languid air to the clinic, when nurses, doctors, caretakers, or patients partake in casual conversations. Acting as a counterweight to the flow of people are the patients sitting or standing quietly, waiting to be attended to. One also notices the television hanging from the ceiling of the long rectangular reception area in one of its far corners opposite the main doors, which is usually set to a news channel with the sound off unless there is some important breaking news of some kind. One or two women are usually present behind the reception desk to one's left as one enters the receiving area. During peak hours they are juggling several things at once, often

---

93   Parts of this case study previously published in Askew and Vieta 2012c.
94   López 2007, personal interview.

FIGURE 5   Images of Cooperativa Salud Junín
PHOTOGRAPH BY AUTHOR

FIGURE 6   Medical specialties available at Cooperativa Salud Junín
PHOTOGRAPH BY AUTHOR

with a telephone receiver in one ear, while at other times when the clinic is less busy, they chat amicably with one of the nurses who has taken a pause from her busy day to converse and catch up on the latest event that has taken place at the clinic or in their personal lives.

On the wall behind the reception desk is a colourful placard in the red, white, and green colours of the cooperative that lists the names of more than 60 doctors who contract out their services to the cooperative for several hours a week and maps out the medical specialties of the clinic: pediatric care, oncology, ophthalmology, cardiology, internal medicine, hematology, neuro-logy, dentistry, urology, immunology, dermatology. When I first read this im-pressive list I noted that this is more of a hospital than a clinic; many of the most important medical specialties are represented here. To one's immediate right, across the room from the reception desk, one sees another sign with the same colour scheme that reads 'Turnos Admisión' ('Appointments Admissions') above a carefully crafted semi-circular opening in the wall with a desk on the other side of the opening and a row of medical files behind another two women admitting patients. In the middle of the reception area, rows of seats demarc-ate the patient waiting area; usually the seats are taken during peak hours, but at times there is a space for me to sit at and observe the comings and goings on the clinic's main floor until the room gets full again and I stand up to let a waiting patient sit. Surrounding this reception and waiting area are several doors, usually left open unless the clinicians are attending to a patient, leading to various examination rooms and a blood laboratory. At the very back of the reception area a small alter with neatly organised statues of saints and offeratory candles guards a hallway on one's immediate left, leading to another section of the first floor not visible from the reception area. In this section one finds an elevator, a staircase leading to the basement and the building's top three floors, and further down, the clinic's loading bay. At core times, doctors, nurses, and patients constantly come in and out of the rooms throughout the first floor, or go up or come down the stairs in what seems to be choreographed movement.

My first visits to Salud Junín were always, it seemed to me at the time, during peak hours, since I constantly needed to reschedule interviews with the clinic's members and extend my stays in Córdoba – this rescheduling happened much more often here than in other ERTs I have visited. I have since understood why this was the case: Salud Junín is a busy community health clinic and the critical nature of the work its members are involved in meant that my less critical academic querying often got relegated to the sidelines. And interviewing during non-working hours usually was not an option since many of the cooperative's nurse-members also work shifts at other private clinics or hospitals in the city. Initially, all of these false starts and rescheduling gave me a fair share of stress, especially during my first days at the clinic: 'How am I ever going to interview someone here and conduct my observations?' I would sometimes think. At other times, I felt like I was in the way, obstructing the critical work that was being conducted at the clinic. The Salud Junín workers, however, time and time again, made me feel welcome and would apologise to me – 'el investigador argentino pero que vive en Canadá' ('the Argentine researcher who lives in Canada'), or simply 'el chico canadiense' ('the Canadian kid') – for having neglected me.

Indeed, after my visits to Salud Junín between 2007 and 2009, I came to understand well what José meant when he underscored the complexity of self-managing a firm that is in the business of delivering front-line health care, differentiating the clinic from other ERTs. By the time in late August 2009 when I interviewed Alejandro Torres, another co-founder and the treasurer of the cooperative, I was better equipped to comprehend the varied nuances of the straightforward but poignant claim he made: 'This isn't just any business', he asserted, leaning forward on his chair for emphasis from behind his paper-covered desk and computer monitor, 'it's the business of delivering health, and with that comes infinite responsibility ... you just can't make a mistake here'.[95]

3.2   Neo-liberal Reforms and the Decline of Health Care

The neo-liberal rationalisation of the Argentine economy during the 1990s deeply affected its system of health care delivery. According to the official national government policy and economic discourses of the period, health care reforms in Argentina were necessary in order to increase the 'efficiency' of health care delivery and reduce the complex health system's financial wastage and mismanagement. Supported by initiatives from the World Bank, these health care reforms included: promoting the growth of private sector, frontline health care providers to take care of prevention, medical examinations, and minor surgery; the opening up of the private health insurance sector to foreign investment by multinationals; and more stringently regulating the union-controlled *obras sociales* (entities insuring and delivering health services to waged workers and funded by employer and employee contributions) which, as of 1999, delivered health care to almost nine million Argentine workers and their families. The result was increased competition for increasingly scarce resources between public, private, and union-based health service providers and insurers.[96]

The Argentine health-care system is a complex three-tiered system that has been in place since the 1940s and is made up of a public health-care delivery sector managed by the provinces, a plethora of *obras sociales* managed by Argentina's trade unions, and privatised health care. Nurtured by the neo-liberal reforms to labour, health, and social security policy throughout the 1990s and early 2000s, Argentina's health-care system would become increasingly privatised and its private health insurance agencies multinationalised, meaning that the private health-care sector grew exponentially at the expense of the public sector and the union-based *obras sociales*. Especially after the 2001 crisis and the rise of unemployment and informal work throughout the country, hundreds of thousands of workers lost their union-based *obras sociales* coverage. This eventually overburdened both the *obras sociales* and the public health care system as rising unemployment meant shrinking pools of funds from taxes and union dues for financing the public and union-based health sectors.[97]

In the province of Córdoba, these health system reforms hit hard, leading to the break-up of one of the strongest publicly funded provincial health systems

---

95   Torres 2009, personal interview.
96   Belmartino 2000; World Bank 2003.
97   Ase 2006; Burijovich and Pautassi 2005.

in Argentina via the 'municipalisation' (the Argentine term for downloading the management and financing of public hospitals, health care, and social services to cities, towns, and municipalities)[98] of many of its 512 provincial hospitals and the privatisation of myriad front-line neighbourhood health clinics.[99] As in the rest of the country, those most affected by the decline of access to good and affordable public health care were, predictably, workers and marginalised people. In addition, those who still had formal and unionised jobs had to often top up their underfunded *obras sociales* coverage with private insurance while needing to increasingly look for front-line care at private clinics. At the same time, private clinics were forced, especially in the thick of the 2001–3 crisis years, to increase 'efficiencies' in order to keep competitive by cutting down on labour costs, reducing salaries, laying off nurses and staff, and contracting fewer doctors and nurses per patient. In the middle of this dire situation, some of the owner conglomerates of private clinics in the province – often made up of doctors also affiliated to larger private hospitals and even mutual society hospitals that received funding from community organisations, the state, or *obras sociales* – also began to engage in, as in other economic sectors, shady *vaciamientos*, transferring medical equipment to more cheaply run clinics, or selling equipment at rebate prices while these owners abandoned their financially troubled private clinics. Moreover, worsening working conditions in the private and public hospital sectors meant declining health delivery standards in the province of Córdoba throughout the years spanning the turn of the millennium.[100]

Such was the conjuncture that the nurses, maintenance staff, and doctors at the private Clínica Junín found themselves living in and working through in 2001. As Alejandro explained to me when I interviewed him in August of 2009, just seven months after the cooperative finally secured temporary expropriation from the province of Córdoba after a seven-year struggle:

> This was once a prestigious private clinic here in Córdoba, started and managed for most of its existence by a group of doctors since the 1940s. At one point there were over 300 people working here. When I came here as a medical student in 2001, there were 64 of us left, and the owners at that time couldn't administer the clinic. It was in shambles. I didn't receive any salary for the first nine months that I worked here. The owners, a group of 10 doctors, were stealing money from this clinic, literally

---

98   Burijovich and Pautassi 2005.
99   Burijovich and Pautassi 2005, p. 19.
100   Ase 2006.

enriching themselves and not paying anybody else. So the clinic began to fall apart and fail, of course. This is the first job I've had administering a clinic, but I can see what had happened with the last owners; it is typical of what happened in many private clinics in Argentina, especially during the 2001 crisis. Actually, the whole health care system was falling apart along with the country: At the time, we would also receive health insurance cheques later and later – 60, 90, 120 days late. The professionals [that is, the doctors],[101] the workers, creditors, none of us were getting paid and all of us were getting screwed. In the meantime, the owners, who were getting increasingly desperate or greedy – I don't know – they started *gobbling up*[102] all the money that was left.

3.3 *The Disarticulation of Workplace Unity*

With this once thriving clinic located in the downtown core of the mostly working-class city of Córdoba[103] in shambles, and as many older workers at the clinic were being laid off or offered early retirement, a group of new workers, which included Alejandro Torres, were hired to ostensibly re-shape and 'streamline' the clinic. In reality, the clinic's owners were, as in the cases of UST and Chilavert, disarticulating workplace unity, rupturing the collective memories of the workers, and generally engaging in dividing worker solidarity and in union-busting tactics which, the workers would later find out, was all in preparation for the clinic's final *vaciamiento* and dismemberment. José López, like Alejandro, was also one of these new workers hired in 2001 to reorganise the nursing services area of the clinic. As he was led to believe at the time:

> They hired me here as chief of nursing and to reorganise the nursing area in 2001 because it was very disorganised. But when I got here I found out that there was a huge backlog in salaries owed to the workers. Soon after I got here, we started the struggle to save our jobs and reclaim our salaries. I fell right into the crisis here! And I quickly discovered that the problem

---

101 At Salud Junín, as in other medical establishments in Argentina, the term 'professionals' is used for differentiating the doctors and specialists that attend to patients from the nurses, administration, and maintenance staff.

102 The actual word Alejandro used here was *'morfando'*, which, in the Argentine slang called *lunfardo* and spoken in everyday conversations across classes, means 'to gobble up', 'devour', or 'eat voraciously'.

103 Córdoba is not only Argentina's second largest city, but also an important industrial and university centre. It was also the centre of much working-class and student discontent and protests in the late 1960s, most notably witnessed in *el Cordobazo* of late May and early June of 1969 (see Chapter 3).

wasn't so much that the workers were disorganised. The problem was that the reorganisation of the nursing services required much more profound solutions because the problems I fell into here were rooted in deep issues between the staff and the owners.[104]

The problems, as it turned out, were rooted in a combination of a collapsing health sector that was being severely affected by the deepening economic crises of 2001 and owners who found it easier to asset strip the firm, fire workers, and, in the process, carve out an exit strategy for themselves rather than protect the livelihood of the clinic's staff and the wellbeing of its patients. At first during this period of acute crisis at the clinic, and as with the Chilavert workers, Junín's employees were willing to help the owners save the clinic by working for labour credits instead of salaries, or even agreeing not to receive salaries or wages for a time. (This is, incidentally, part of the reason why the Junín and Chilavert workers continued to work for so long without receiving pay, a point I will pick up in Chapter 6 concerning the moral legitimacy workers feel they have in occupying their firms.) But the Junín workers' decision to occupy the clinic – tapping into their moral economy of work – finally came when they found that they had been lied to and abandoned by the clinic's owners and in light of what was occurring around them in the rest of the country with the collapse of the economy and the intensification of social protests by the precariously employed, the unemployed, and neighbourhood residents. Explained José:

> This period in Argentina wasn't like other periods when your job was terminated and you go and find work elsewhere. No, there simply was no work to find; everything was shutting down. So we had to find another solution. Remember that this was a period in our history with historically high unemployment; firms were closing daily. So our *lucha* here began to deepen with the institutional crisis of the time until the owners left the clinic and we were left hanging, without knowing which way to turn. We were literally abandoned; one day we came here and there were no owners to be found. We didn't know which way to turn at the time. And that is how we initiated the process of recuperating this *empresa*.[105]

---

104 López 2007, personal interview.
105 López 2009, personal interview.

3.4   'The Owners Weren't Coming Back but We Still Needed to Continue Subsisting'

On 18 December 2001, the day before the December 19 and 20 social upheavals, the remaining Junín nurses and maintenance staff discovered, without prior warning, that their firm had been sold to a conglomerate of private clinic managers, with the firm already half empty of equipment and with a skeletal staff 65 workers – a shadow of the 300 or so doctors, nurses, and support personnel that had once been employed at the clinic. The new owners, a conglomerate of entrepreneur-doctors and health-sector financiers operating in the private health-care market, consisted of the health management firm Primord and a group of doctors from one of the largest hospitals handling *obras sociales* in Córdoba, the mutual association Hospital Italiano. They arrived with new promises of job security, new equipment, and the payment of owed wages. In the five months that followed, and with the remaining staff pleading with the new owners to re-equip the clinic, the workers only saw a trickle of their owed salaries while continuing to live through a precarious existence.

The Junín workers eventually responded to this dire situation by conducting the first wave of work stoppages while appealing to the labour tribunal of the Province of Córdoba's Ministry of Labour and demanding from management their owed wages. After favourable rulings by the tribunal on behalf of the workers, this second owner-conglomerate would also abandon the firm, selling it to what turned out to be a shell company – or as José put it to me, a 'phantom firm' – called Frisias S.A., whose main 'investor' ended up being (yet again) a doctor from the Hospital Italiano.[106] After another round of hearings at the labour tribunal, this third owner also abandoned the firm in May 2002 while taking with him a small group of Junín's staff with the promise of better jobs elsewhere (a promise that was never delivered to the exiting workers). Soon, the 35 remaining Junín workers would be armed with more knowledge of direct-action tactics. Underscoring the importance of solidarity from social justice movements for Argentina's ERTs, during this period of struggle, the resisting Junín workers would receive assistance and support from various labour and social movement organisations, such as the Cordoban municipal workers' union Sindicato Unión Obreros y Empleados Municipales (SUOEM, Municipal Workers' and Employees Union of Córdoba); the Unión Obrera Gráfica Cordobesa (UOGC, Graphic Workers' Union of Córdoba); the human rights organisation HIJOS; the Partido de los Trabajadores Socialistas (PTS, Socialist Workers' Party), who shared the experiences of Brukman

---

106   Ibid.

and Zanón/FaSinPat with the Junín workers; and the progressive and storied Córdoba branch of the national electrical union Luz y Fuerza (whose
headquarters happens to be around the corner from the clinic).[107] The PTS,
Luz y Fuerza, and a handful of ERT movement lawyers, in particular, would
advise and train the Junín workers on the processes of occupying the firm,
while encouraging them to fight for expropriation and the payment of owed
wages, sue the former owners for criminal abandonment and *vaciamiento*,
and prepare to self-manage the clinic. Taking this advice and training seriously, the formal occupation of the firm by the remaining 35 workers began
on 23 May 2002, opening the clinic to patient care as a collective on 13 June
2002.[108]

The process of recuperating the clinic, then, took several months for the
workers to initiate. The idea would gradually crystallise as their collective
ire rose with each group of owners' false promises. As Edith Allende, one of
the cooperative's nurses, a co-founder, and a long-time worker at the clinic,
described it to me:

> The clinic started to slowly deteriorate in early 2001. The decline of this
> once-thriving clinic happened slowly, and we weren't prepared for the
> abandonment and owner juggling that was to follow. First pediatric care
> was shut down, then minor surgery, until you arrived one day and you
> didn't know what was open still.[109]

As with Chilavert, UST, and dozens of other ERTs, the Junín workers did not initially want to self-manage the firm. By August 2002, however, with the advice
of their lawyers and after months of contemplating the possibility, they finally
decided to form a cooperative, which they inaugurated at the end of September
2002. The occupation and resistance phase for the Junín workers, unlike Chilavert's workers' conscious occupation for the control of the print shop, would
emerge as a slow and steady escalation of actions; as the idea of self-managing
the clinic percolated collectively with the workers and as they debated what
to do, they increasingly carried out more and more aggressive direct actions
throughout 2002. In actuality, if one considers their original reasons for occupying the firm, the tactic of occupying and squatting the clinic backfired on the

---

107   Luz y Fuerza was one of the most important unions during and in the immediate years fol-
        lowing *el Cordobazo* of 1969. In more recent years, Luz y Fuerza has continued its militant
        tradition by assisting ERT workers, especially in the province of Córdoba.
108   Torletti 2017, personal interview.
109   Allende 2009, personal interview.

workers; the Junín workers had envisioned the occupation of the clinic as a tactic to force the original owners to negotiate a deal with them in order to finally receive owed salaries. Instead, they ultimately ended up gaining control of the clinic. '[Initially,] we didn't want to stay with the clinic and self-manage it forever', Alejandro underscored.

> In reality, the occupation of the firm was only a strategy on our part to generate an event that would get the original owners of the clinic to say, 'No, no, look, they are taking our clinic, let's go and negotiate with [the staff]' and, we were hoping, then collect our salaries. But the days went on and on and they never appeared.[110]

In a sense, then, the Junín workers fell into the occupation of the clinic and gradually warmed to the idea of self-managing it. Rather than pre-planning their direct action, the Junín workers would learn gradually how to occupy a firm in trouble and resist eviction from the situation at hand, as a means of survival, and from the advice of supportive ERT movement protagonists, the PTS, the Luz y Fuerza union, and other social movements that came to their assistance. As the various owners came and went during the first semester of 2002, the Junín workers simply continued working, maintaining the building and caring for the few patients that would arrive as best as they could. 'Throughout the first half of 2002, in the middle of the socio-economic meltdown that Argentina was suffering at the time', José clarified,

> we stayed here taking care of the clinic, at first because we didn't know where else to go. It was only eventually that we realised that we had to stay here and occupy the clinic in order to avoid the closure of the clinic and the loss of our jobs. By the time the third group of owners come and go – and the labour tribunal here is unable to help us because the group of owners would always delay in paying us knowing full well that they were going to eventually abandon the clinic – we realise that our struggle had to be more than just a fight to recuperate our 11 months of unpaid wages. Rather, our struggle gradually became one of defending and reactivating our source of work ... What especially inspired us at the time were the dozens of other workplaces that were being reopened by workers and managed by their own hands, and so we eventually decided to embark on that path. So, it's July, August, then September 2002, and we

---

110   Torres 2009, personal interview.

ask ourselves 'OK, what do we do?' We started to realise that the owners weren't coming back, but we still needed to continue subsisting. So that's when we decided to form a cooperative and fight for the control of the clinic.[111]

3.5 A Multidimensional Strategy of Community Support and Political and Legal Struggles as Paths out of the Crisis

'One thing that you need to understand was that this was a total *vaciamiento*', José emphatically told me in 2007, during my first interview with him. Unlike at Chilavert and most other ERTs, '[t]here was no official bankruptcy here, no insolvency hearings. It was just a plain and simple *vaciamiento* and abandonment of the firm by our former bosses'.[112] This meant that the clinic was in legal limbo for much longer than, say, at Chilavert, where its workers actually appealed to bankruptcy courts for the permission to begin production at the firm in usufruct, or at UST, where workers did not need to pursue the long road of expropriation because they were able to work out a contract and usufruct scheme with the state-run firm CEAMSE under the arbitration of the national Ministry of Labour. Junín's legal limbo, on the other hand, as with many other Argentine ERTs over the years, would become a constant worry and struggle for its workers over the ensuing years. This limbo culminated in an eviction attempt by a group of returning owners in early 2007, eventually seeing Junín's lawyers take the case to the Court of Appeals of the Province of Córdoba, which, fortunately for the workers, rescinded the eviction order after much public outcry and support. Paradoxically, this legal limbo continued while the clinic was growing exponentially every year, especially when measured in the number of patients they were caring for. Junín's legal limbo would last until December 2008 when the newly elected governor of the province of Córdoba, Juán Schiaretti, fulfilled his long-time promise to the workers made when he was deputy governor in 2003 and ensured the temporary expropriation of the firm and, finally in November 2011, the definitive (or permanent) expropriation of the clinic on behalf of its workers.[113]

Strong resonances of the community and political support that sustained the Salud Junín workers during their years of legal limbo and that began during their early days of struggle were still evident during my 2009 visits to the clinic. 'Many social organisations came to help us throughout our first days',

---

111   López 2009, personal interview.
112   Ibid.
113   Torletti 2017, personal interview.

reminisced cooperative member, co-founder, member-at-large of the cooperative's administrative council, and nurse Ana María Barrionuevo with tears in her eyes late one evening in 2009 when we talked at the clinic as her shift was ending:

> And all of this community support was very important for us at the time. We also conducted many marches on the streets of Córdoba soliciting support for our cause, once mobilising 800 people. And that was during a weekday, which was an issue because everyone has to work, right? Many, many groups from the left, neighbours from the community, and folks from other ERTs came to help us during those days ... It just takes my breath away still thinking about it![114]

Not only did the support of the community lift the morale of Junín's workers, the community also helped financially as well. 'Another memory I have of this time', Ana María continued,

> was when we started our strike fund during our first days of occupation here in 2002. And this was nothing more than a shoe box that we would pass around on the streets of Córdoba in shifts, when we sometimes blocked the inside lane of streets (so as to not prevent other workers from going to work!), or when we would set up a table at the University of Córdoba. When we took the clinic, none of us had a single cent in our pockets. And suddenly, these young people from several left political parties, social movements, and from the university would come and help us with our strike fund. It was really not much money but, at the time, it seemed like lots of money for us, do you know what I mean? From having nothing for more than a year to then having the community come in droves to help you out, to give you a hand, to give you a few pesos to help you out ... No, no, really, it is what kept us going, what gave us the energy in those early days to keep on fighting for this.[115]

It is not surprising that Ana María is still touched by this outpouring of community support. She had gone 10 months without receiving pay in 2001, for example, in addition to getting almost no pay until the end of 2002, throughout the Junín workers' year of occupation and transformation into a cooperative.

---

114   Barrionuevo 2009, personal interview.
115   Ibid.

Moreover, during this time, in a common lived experience of the neo-liberal crisis of the time by hundreds of thousands of Argentine families, Ana María's marriage would end, in no small part due to the strains on the relationship because of her experiences at the clinic. On several occasions during this period of her life, she also had to resort to pawning her jewellery and other possessions to help her get by while living for the first time in her life since her childhood with relatives and, for a while, in several rundown rentals. I heard similar stories of strained family relationships, failed marriages, and other physical stresses and psychological hardships on the path to self-managing firms in countless conversations with ERT protagonists throughout the years, bringing to light another outcome of the neo-liberal assault on Argentina's working class during this period: the precarisation of workers' everyday lives. Similar to the personal sufferings of hundreds of thousands of Argentine workers, Ana María recounted the difficulties she had lived though at the time, which was, she emphasised, a particularly tough pill to swallow for her because up to that point she had considered herself an educated and trained professional immune from structural unemployment; she underscored that she had, after all, been employed continuously in various clinics in Córdoba for more than 20 years up until the crisis years.

The community support the Junín workers received, given the gendered nature of their work, was thus particularly important for the clinic's mostly female nurses, Ana María emphasised, because many of them were also managing households with husbands who had been laid off or fired from their own jobs. 'It was a very precarious time for us all, but especially the women working here', she made a point of highlighting in our conversation, 'and this also served to bring us together as a group and to look out for each other'.[116] It also served, as Ana María continued to tell me, to educate and sensitise their male *compañeros* as to what a particularly heavy burden these trying times were for the women working at Junín. Here Ana María's story highlighted for me the many subtle and explicit ways that the crisis years at the turn of the millennium negatively affected families' wellbeing and security, especially women. This period was particularly hard on women. With husbands or partners under- or unemployed, women often had to become the major breadwinner – often by holding down two or more jobs if they could find them – while continuing to run the household and to engage in emotional work, which would often include not only caring for children or elderly parents but also the psychological needs of their spouses. Thus, a major side-effect of the crisis of the

---

116   Ibid.

neo-liberal model at the turn of the millennium was to augment the patri-
archal structures of Argentine society while increasing the amount of physical,
mental, and emotional labour that women had to tackle. As can be expected, and as Ana María will highlight for us shortly, divorce rates and family violence increased during this period, creating even more hardships for
women.

The community support received by the Junín workers at the time was
thus vital to their struggle in what was to eventually become a multidimensional strategy for securing the control of the clinic and the continuity of their
jobs. One dimension of the Junín workers' struggle consisted of, as with Chilavert and UST, the direct action tactic of occupation and resistance. The other
dimension of struggle embraced a three-pronged legal, political, and public-
support strategy. Adeptly used by Junín's workers to their long-term advantage, the details of this three-pronged strategy included: (1) tapping into the
legal tools and institutions most readily available to manoeuvre through the
Córdoban legal system; (2) engaging in political lobbying with the aim of the
expropriation of the clinic by the Córdoban provincial legislature on behalf of
the Junín workers; and (3) mobilising public sentiment and the moral legitimacy that radiated to their cause from the public support that they managed to
garner. José mapped out for me this three-pronged legal, political, and public-
support strategy as follows:

> In reality, when we establish our strategy of struggle it was at three levels:
> One area of struggle that we embarked on strategically were the many
> labour hearings and arbitrations that we had initiated at the Ministry of
> Labour for the unpaid salaries we were owed, just like any worker that
> has not been paid his or her salary would do. Another thing we did was to
> start a criminal case against the former owners for *vaciamiento*, fraudu-
> lent administration, and abandonment of the firm, all illegal in Argentina
> (although you wouldn't know it from how common this practice was at
> the time!). This criminal case, for various reasons, didn't prosper for us,
> but it did keep our cause in the media. These were all legal and political
> strategies that we mobilised. And, a third area was more of a defensive
> strategy, defending ourselves against the constant threat of eviction and
> gaining as much public support as possible. You see, when a group of the
> former owners started their eviction case against us, we knew there was a
> good chance we were going to lose it, because the system here in Argen-
> tina is rigged against workers in these cases. But, we knew that we could
> buy time by keeping our legal situation in the courts and in the media
> until we, from another angle, secured the expropriation of the building

in 2008. In reality, there wasn't a legal out for us; there was only a political out in the legislature of Córdoba, with expropriation, which we eventually got.[117]

In short, this multidimensional strategy of struggle was to become, in the language of this book, a major and *radical* social innovation for ERTS. It is, as I address at the end of this chapter, part of ERTS' first radical social innovation: *mobilising direct action strategies and workplace solidarities*. At Salud Junín, this radical social innovation saw workers innovatively develop and deploy community support, direct action tactics, political organisation, and legal tools for securing their jobs and eventually taking control of their place of work. José eloquently underlined Salud Junín's version of this radical social innovation for me like this:

> You see, [our struggle] was, after all, an entire process of permanent insistence, of consequences, of going and knocking on doors, perseverance, marches, trips here and there, waiting, pacing back and forth, talking to everyone we could wherever we could and at all levels of politics and power, of strategies of softening members of the provincial legislature, lobbying every member, debating with them ... and finally, [in 2007] we got temporary expropriation, and in December 2008, definitive expropriation! The interesting thing about our 'deal' with the government in securing our expropriation is that in our case, unlike other cases of expropriation in the country where workers have to eventually pay off the cost of the expropriation [over time] (because, after all, it is the public's money), we are partially paying back the expropriation by providing health services to state workers through their *obra social*; that is, we are paying back the state through the work that we do here [that is, through labour credits].[118]

3.6 'The Most Efficient and Fastest Growing Front-Line Medical Clinic in the Province of Córdoba'

'The problems during the first days of our cooperative was that none of us knew anything about managing a clinic or a business', admitted José. 'And so', he continued, 'we started to invite doctors sympathetic to our cause to come and help us out'.[119] Soon, after opening their doors as a cooperative clinic, they

---

117   López 2009, personal interview.
118   Ibid.
119   Ibid.

had 15 doctors assisting them in delivering front-line health care, at first on a volunteer basis and then for nominal compensation drawn from a 'solidarity fee' charged to patients. The Junín workers also voted on and agreed collectively during these first days to reserve membership to the cooperative for the founding nurses and maintenance staff that had remained to occupy the clinic, deciding to contract out the services of doctors by eventually paying them a fee for their rounds at the clinic instead of making them members of the cooperative. As several of the clinic's members I have interviewed have told me, this was a way of keeping things simple during the first days of the cooperative. It does, however, perhaps also reveal a still existent class division in the health-care sector in Argentina between health-care 'profesionales' (professionals, that is, doctors) and nurses and support staff, highlighted in part by the vast differentials in salaries and prestige in Argentina between doctors and nurses as compared to the smaller gap in salary differentials and clout between medical professions in the global North.[120] This organisational structure is still in place at Salud Junín. For now at least, Alejandro, José, and the president of the cooperative Esteban Torletti have all confirmed to me that the doctors who practice at the clinic for a few hours a week will not be included in the cooperative's membership and their services will continue to be contracted out, as has been the case since September 2002.

As of late 2009, the cooperative had 35 members made up of nurses, support staff, and maintenance specialists. Due mostly to retirements and a handful of other nurses leaving in the years since my first visits, by mid-2017 the cooperative had 25 members.[121] An innovative policy the Junín workers have taken up, showing their commitment to inter-generational solidarity, has been to continue to pay retired members a monthly salary. The roster of more than 60 doctors that conduct rounds at the clinic for several hours a week continue to be paid a fee for their services on a per-patient basis. During the clinic's first days, they charged their first group of regular patients a minor 'solidarity fee' of $3 pesos per visit. While the Junín workers initially thought of servicing Cordobans from the most marginalised sectors without health coverage, they quickly discovered that this group still mostly uses the services of the few remaining free public hospitals in the city. By 2009, the group that had emerged as one of the clinic's primary constituencies was employed (and unemployed) workers in the city of Córdoba who were not covered by union-based *obras sociales* or private health care plans, such as contract-based workers, self-

---

120   Ase 2006.
121   Torletti 2017, personal interview.

employed people, and so-called 'informal' workers and those employed '*en negro*' ('in the black') who do not work under a formal labour contract and thus are without social security. These are all important sub-sets of the working class that have expanded substantially in Argentina since the turn-of-millennium crisis years. Since the original 'solidarity fee' of $3 pesos per patient, by 2009 the Salud Junín workers had innovated their own health insurance plan for their patients without *obras sociales*, which in 2009 was an affordable $35 pesos per family per month, covering all basic services at the clinic, with an additional $15 pesos per hour for particular specialist care. In late 2009, the clinic was also providing walk-in visits for $30 pesos per visit for those patients who could not afford or decided not to be a part of the health insurance plan. By mid-2017, taking into account the devaluation of the peso in recent years, the clinic's own insurance plan and walk-in visits remained at an affordable $350 pesos per month (around US$20.00). Moreover, the clinic's insurance plan and walk-in fee serve to subsidise the cost of care for patients who are more financially challenged or on the margins of society, in effect offering a unique, clinic-based health plan for the surrounding community. The clinic has proven to be extremely popular amongst its growing list of patients, expanding astronomically from a few dozen patients by the end of 2002, to well over 4,000 patient visits per month by late 2009 and to over 10,000 visits per month by mid-2017, including patients on *obras sociales*, on the clinic's insurance plan, or from walk-ins.[122] Perhaps fittingly, Salud Junín's largest patient group is made up of working-class Cordobans who suffered – and some who continue to suffer – from the same neo-liberal policies that diminished the Junín workers' own job security, increased their life precariousness, and motivated them to begin to self-manage their clinic.

During its life as a cooperative, Salud Junín has expanded to include four fully operational floors attending to all kinds of front-line health care needs and emergencies, an operation room for minor surgeries, an oncology clinic, and a palliative care sector made up of 12 beds. Furthermore, in 2009 the clinic opened a cataract surgery centre on its third floor funded entirely by the joint Cuban and Venezuelan international ophthalmology project known as Operación Milagro (Operation Miracle), which, until the initiative moved to its own clinic recently, offered free cataract operations to people in need, as in several countries throughout Latin American and the Caribbean.[123] Telling of

---

122   Torres 2009, personal interview; Torletti 2017, personal interview.
123   Operación Milagro, also known as Misión Milagro (Miracle Mission), is discussed by Steve Brouwer in his book *Revolutionary Doctors: How Venezuela and Cuba are Changing the World's Conception of Health Care* (2011). There he points out that the mission was ini-

the impact and diffusion that the ERT phenomenon has had within Latin America's social justice movements and the transnational networks of solidarity that have been developing throughout the region in recent years (see Chapter 7), it was specifically because Salud Junín was an ERT that Operación Milagro first approached the clinic's workers and offered to open the ophthalmology centre there. The programme also invited a group of Salud Junín's nurses to travel to Cuba to train for the cataract procedures, while also bringing to the cooperative a Cuban delegation of specialists to help set up the clinic with state-of-the-art German eye surgery equipment donated by the Cuban government.

Echoing the words of UST's Pablo Rolandi and Chilavert's Cándido González, Salud Junín's Alejandro Torres made sure that I left my interview with him with the understanding that ERT workers are indeed capable of efficiently and effectively self-managing their workplaces and jobs. In this spirit, Alejandro concluded our talk in August 2009 with much evident pride by underscoring to me that

> the clinic, if measured by how our patient list has expanded over the years, has grown by an astounding 80 per cent per year under our management. We have shown that we have what it takes to take this project forward, *unlike the previous owners*.[124]

When an independent health-sector consultant visited the clinic in 2008, Alejandro continued,

> she tells us that Cooperativa Junín is the most efficient and fastest growing front-line medical clinic in the province of Córdoba! I don't know what other proof there is that we are more than capable of self-managing our business here.

To make sure I left with a clear idea of the cooperative members' capacities for administering their clinic and innovating in the delivery of health care, he ended the interview with the following statement:

---

tially funded by the Venezuelan government, with the technical support and expertise of the Cuban medical system, and that free eye surgery has been provided 'to more than one and a half million people in Latin America and the Caribbean' (Brouwer 2011, pp. 43–4). See also Operación Milagro 2016.

124　Torres 2009, personal interview.

If you leave here with one idea, I would like it to be this: We managed to transform this place from the bottom up. I'm talking about *everything* here. In what we produce – affordable health care delivery. In how we deliver health to those without *obras sociales* or private health insurance. In how we re-capitalised this clinic with our own revenues. In how we fixed it up aesthetically to look the way it does today … Right from the first days when we recuperated this clinic, we have been innovating here. Before, this was a clinic literally in ruins, and we turned it around completely. If we look back it is incredible to see how we have grown. It fills us with pride, especially with everything that happened after that. The clinic did not end in oblivion. We recuperated salaries for all the workers, we provide good quality health care, and at the same time the clinic continues to grow. For example, take our affordable health plan. We don't overcharge for coming to our clinic. A lot of people think that because you pay more, you get better service. This is not correct. Charging more and privatising health is really about making a profit, it is not really about caring for patients … We have shown that you can offer health service at an economic rate, an accessible rate, and that everybody has a right to health. You understand?

4 Mobilising Direct Action Strategies and Workplace Solidarity

Through the words of ERT workers in three stories of workplace recuperations, this chapter has laid the experiential ground for this study's historical materialist and class-struggle analysis of Argentina's ERTs. ERT workers' own stories as told to me in formal interviews and informal conversations begin to map out for us unique situations of workplace conflicts in Argentina that lead to the transformation of troubled capitalist firms into cooperative ERTs. They draw attention to how macro-economic and socio-political crises within a particular conjucture of the neo-liberal model in recent years have influenced the point of production and service delivery, how these moments of crises overflowed into workers' personal and collective lives, and how workers took destiny into their own hands in order to secure their livelihoods. These three stories of recuperation particularly bring together for us workers' motivations for collaboratively resisting situations of heightened exploitation within the labour process that eventually have them embarking on more ethical projects of *auto-gestión*. These motivations are undergirded by what I have been calling ERT protagonists' *moral economy of work*. In short, ERT protagonists' own words and recollections lucidly nuance their lived experiences of crises as well as put into relief their reasons for occupying and subsequently self-managing the firms that had been employing them.

Starting out this book with these three exemplary stories of occupation, resistance, and self-managed production in Argentina sets out for us the key empirical themes that will be explored in more detail in Chapters 6 through 8: the varied dimensions of ERTs' strategies and tactics of occupying, resisting, and producing (Chapter 6); the tensions and challenges of converting troubled capitalist firms into cooperatives and self-managing them (Chapters 6 and 7); workers' transformations and innovations of an ERT's labour process (Chapters 7 and 8); how they informally learn cooperative values and practices (Chapter 8); and how and why these firms open up their workplaces to the communities that surround them (Chapter 8). At the same time, the case studies presented here allude to, implicitly, what ERT workers begin to essentially recuperate when they take over and self-manage their firms, bridging the critical historical and theoretical discussion of Chapters 4 and 5 with the political economy of the working-class approach of the book. In sum, in presenting the three case studies here, in the book's first pages, I begin to lay out the particular nuances of the struggles ERT workers have had to face with recalcitrant or returning owners, the state, and even their unions on the road to taking over their firms and converting them to worker cooperatives.

On the whole, we saw in this chapter that in ERT protagonists' very actions of occupations and in their multifaceted and emergent resistances to the multidimensional onslaughts of the production regime under the neo-liberal mantle, ERT workers tap into the solidarity previously forged on shop floors, a solidarity that is subsequently strengthened by the very struggles they have had to collectively traverse. As Marx's third thesis on Feuerbach foreshadows, and as I will further address in Chapter 4, these workers gradually transform themselves by reinventing their working lives under the rubrics of self-determination and *autogestión* as they collectively struggle to change their circumstances; that is, they transform from managed employees to self-managed workers as they immanently endeavour to change the material conditions of their working lives.

In the process of ERT workers themselves recuperating their workplaces they, in essence, take back control of their work, skills, and creative capacities via bottom-up and direct actions, unmediated, on the whole, by political vanguardism, the traditional labour movement, or the state. Chapter 9 will return to this theme, suggesting ERT protagonists' direct action strategies and tactics serve to, at bottom, recuperate not only jobs and a workplace, but, more fundamentally, workers' very dignity and self-control over their labouring capacities – that is, over their labour-power. They underscore for us ERT protagonists' *first radical social innovation*:

> *The mobilisation of direct action strategies and the re-forging of workplace solidarity in order for workers to keep their jobs and safeguard their places of work via the occupation of the firms that had been employing them and their subsequent pursuit of self-managed production.*

This first radical social innovation grounds the particular experiences of ERT protagonists with the three-staged process of occupation, resistance, and subsequent self-managed production that I will explore in more detail in Chapters 6–8. In those chapters, I will return to a broader, macro perspective by looking at general trends in the ERT phenomenon as a whole, highlighting how ERTs are new forms of labour organisations and worker cooperatives. Chapter 8 will explicitly link the particularities of ERTs' new labour processes to the three case studies introduced in this chapter. And Chapters 4 and 5 will help us begin to theoretically and historically interpret ERTs' practices of 'occupy, resist, produce' with the broader history of working-class self-activity (Chapter 4) and theories of *autogestión* and cooperativism (Chapter 5).

But first, to begin to grasp the significance of Argentina's ERTs and answer the two broad questions driving Part 1 of this book – why did ERTs emerge in Argentina, and why did they emerge when they did? – in the next chapter we turn to a macro-sociological analysis of the emergence of the ERT phenomenon, while in Chapter 3 we will more explicitly link Argentina's ERTs to their historical heritage and political economic contexts.

Empresas Recuparadas pos sus Trabajadores: Why, Where, What, and How

For the first time in the 1990s, with the emergence of neo-liberalism, workers fully embraced the cooperative world, not because they came from
it but as a necessity to give life to a social economic enterprise in order
to preserve jobs, giving rise to a form of productive organisation and of
struggle as class politics. This happened because, when a company fails,
the conventional mechanisms developed by the trade union movement
no longer have a *raison d'être* – there is no negotiation because there
are no owners. So it is necessary to appropriate the means of production, generate wealth, and distribute it equally. This experience gave a
new consciousness to the workers. It was hard [for us workers] because
they repressed us, but soon after [ERTs emerged] they impacted society
because the factory closures were happening day after day ... It was not
[initially] an offensive, we were defending ourselves from misery. We did
not ask for [social] plans and packages, we wanted jobs and we were willing to do what the bosses and the state would not do: lift the shutters from
the factories.

> JOSÉ ABELLI[1]

∴

1   Section 1: The Emergence of Argentina's *Empresas Recuperadas*
     (with Andrés Ruggeri)

1.1   *Why in Argentina?*
Not surprisingly, ERTs started to become visible to most Argentines and increasingly to the rest of the world during the days, weeks, and months following
el Argentinazo of 19 and 20 December 2001, as one of the many social justice

---

1   ERT worker-activist and former president of the Movimiento Nacional de Empresas Recuper-
     adas (MNER), in Battisacco 2016, para. 4.

movements that arose in a constellation of bottom-up responses to the crisis on the part of the country's growing population of the marginalised, the dispossessed, the exploited, the underemployed, and the unemployed. With a dearth of options left for working people on the brink of structural unemployment, between circa 1995 and 2003 – and especially between the years 2001–03 – Argentina's deep class divisions crystallised into the radicalisation of countless marginalised groups. Throughout these years, a contagion of bottom-up popular resistance spread across many popular sectors, witnessed in the widespread direct action tactics of property occupations and squatting, the now-famous road blockages of the *piqueteros*,[2] and myriad other initiatives and mobilisations such as the mushrooming of *clubes de trueque* (barter clubs), *asambleas barriales* (neighbourhood assemblies), and neighbourhood-based food security and provisioning projects.[3] What spilled over from these grass-roots initiatives onto all forms of popular struggle in the country at the time was a renewed sense of collective purpose against a callous, exploitative, and socially alienating system; a growing ethos of direct participatory democracy from below expressed in extremely flat – or horizontal – organising structures[4] and, overall, a massive 'reactivation' of 'communitarian social experience'.[5] During this period, as Antonio Negri has observed, the responses of groups such as the *piqueteros*, the *asambleas barriales*, and ERTs to the neo-liberalisation of the national economy and its ensuing crisis bore witness to a new 'energy ... [of] conviction, and ... egalitarian social recomposition' emerging from the urban *barrios* and industrialised towns of the country.[6] By the early years of the 2000s, much cross-pollination was taking place between these grass roots

---

2 Literally 'picketers', *los piqueteros* is the colloquial name for the diverse movement of unemployed workers more formally known as Movimiento de Trabajadores Desocupados (MTD, Movement of Unemployed Workers) that emerged circa 1995–96. Without workplaces to strike or unions to represent them and to express their various demands for dignified work and the re-organisation of Argentina's political economy, the *piqueteros'* main mode of protest and resistance consisted of blocking major roadways – the economic lifeline of the country.

3 For more on these mobilisations, see Chapter 3. For other accounts of contemporaneous Argentine social movements that surged during the years spanning the turn of the millennium, see especially Adamovsky 2007; Almeyra 2004; Belmartino 2005; Colectivo Situaciones 2002; Dinerstein 2002, 2012; Jelin 2003; La Serna 2004; Sartelli 2005; Sitrin 2006, 2012; Sitrin and Azzellini 2014; Svampa and Pereyra 2004.

4 Colectivo Situaciones 2004. On horizontalism in Argentina during these years, see also Sitrin 2006; Sitrin and Azzellini 2014.

5 Svampa and Pereyra 2004, p. 233.

6 Negri 2003, para. 2.

initiatives, reflected in the diverse composition of those engaging in neighbourhood organisations, radical actions, workplace occupations, and myriad
protests and rebellions across Argentina.[7]

At the same time, this contagion of bottom-up initiatives and movements
intermingled with the collective memory[8] of popular struggle, historical labour
militancy, and workers' self-activity. Moreover, a shared imaginary of Argentina's 'golden years' of the 1940s, 1950s, and 1960s took hold amongst working
people, which, depending on one's political convictions, included a united and
politically influential labour movement, a developmentalist state with pro-
labour inclinations, a relatively prosperous working class, and a mostly nationalised and self-sustaining economy underscored by the import substitution
industrialisation (ISI) model. For a growing number of Argentina's workers, this
contagion and collective memory also nurtured, as we have already assessed,
a 'moral economy of work'. In Argentina, this has historically embodied workers' shared convictions, traditions, values, and practices of working life defended by their collective actions and organising, especially when they perceive
injustices to long-held labour rights and privileges. In the case of Argentina's
ERTs, mobilising and organising around this moral economy of work manifested as workers' collective actions to reclaim threatened workplaces, save jobs,
and secure a dignified livelihood.[9]

In part inspiring and motivating the collective actions of ERT protagonists,
then, the moral economy of work that resurfaced during this period, imbued
with collective memories of past struggles, gave impetus to a resurgence of
working-class self-activity that, at times, has not only resisted employers, their
rationalisation drives, and state economic restructuring programmes, but also
Argentina's traditional corporatist bureaucratic unionism.[10] For instance, two
ways in which the Argentine working class has historically self-organised on
shop floors have included *comisiones internas* (shop floor workers' commissions, or factory committees) and *cuerpos de delegados* (shop-stewards' committees or plenaries). Their practices have embraced holding ongoing workers'
assemblies where workers debate both broader union and specific labour pro-

---

7   Almeyra 2004; Sartelli 2005; Svampa and Pereyra 2004; Zibechi 2012.

8   The term *collective memory* emphasises how shared recollections of the past shapes indi-
        vidual and group identities and consciousness (Halbwachs 1980). Collective memories
        help make sense of group members' present, moulding social practices and co-creating
        shared identities that may also envision alternative futures (Fentress and Wickham 1992;
        Koselleck 2004; Ricoeur 2004).

9   See also Fajn and Rebón 2005; Ruggeri 2009; Vieta 2012.

10   Atzeni 2010; Godio 2000; Smith 1991. See also Chapter 3.

cess issues.[11] At the same time, a long tradition of strong sector-wide collective agreements[12] has commingled uncomfortably with spontaneous workers' agitation such as wildcat strikes, walkouts, sit-ins, and factory occupations that have often by-passed official union protocols. During key historical moments, these bottom-up worker resistances and actions – fluctuating between mobilising against the state, capital, and the brand of hierarchical and bureaucratic Argentine unionism encouraged by Juán Domingo Perón during his years in exile (1955–73) and called *verticalismo* (verticalism) – have emerged spontaneously over the past 70 or so years in Argentina and have spurred working-class actions such as sit-ins, workplace takeovers, and democratic organising of shop floors.

Some of the most powerful historical moments that highlight this working-class self-activity before Argentina's turn-of-millennium economic crisis were rooted in bottom-up, worker-led actions that have had lasting legacies for Argentina's working class. These moments include: the mostly spontaneous mass mobilisations of workers on 17 October 1945 that would eventually see Perón released from prison and surge to electoral victory a few months later;[13] the student and worker takeover of the city of Córdoba at the end of May 1969 known as *el Cordobazo* (together with a wave of worker and student rebellions in other cities across Argentina that same year); and various periods marked by extensive workplace occupations during key moments of intense labour conflicts throughout the second half of the twentieth century (for instance, in the early 1950s, 1958–9, 1962–3, 1964, 1969, 1970–71, 1973, 1975, 1982, 1985, 1988, and 1989).[14] Two of the most memorable of these historical periods were the mass strikes and workplace takeovers inspired by the occupation of the Lisandro de la Torre meatpacking plant in the city of Buenos Aires by its 9,000 workers against the privatisation of the nationalised plant, and the worker-driven general strikes against the unpopular government of Isabel Perón (the third wife of Juán Perón) in June and July 1975, which included the brief period of the *coordinadores interfabriles*, inter-factory coordinating bodies that collect-

---

11   Munck, Falcón, and Galitelli 1987. For more on these traditional shop floor practices, see Chapter 3.

12   In no small part, as will be reviewed in Chapter 3, as a result of Perón's reshaping and centralisation of union politics and his empowering of the Confederación General del Trabajo de la República Argentina (CGT, General Confederation of Labour of the Republic of Argentina) during his first two presidenices (1946–55).

13   Commemorated to this day as '*Día de la lealtad*' (Loyalty Day) by Peronists and made into a national holiday during the Kirchner years.

14   Hernandez 2013, pp. 34–5. See also Llorens and Ferroni 2017; Munck et al. 1987; Petras and Veltmeyer 2002; and Wyczykier 2009a.

ively organised worker mobilisations and workplace issues at a district level. In sum, as we will see in Chapter 3, the occupation of workplaces, street mobilisations, and collective resistances to repression – strategies and tactics mastered by ERT protagonists – are part of a long tradition of workers' self-activity and bottom-up mobilisation in Argentina.[15]

As a result of these cross-pollinations, collective memories, and socio-political conjunctures, up until at least 2005 and the relative recovery of Argentina's economy during the first Kirchner government[16] much of the routines of daily life in urban Argentina were peppered by constant street protests, the occupation of land by the dispossessed, road blockages, and workplace takeovers by a recomposing working class experimenting with new *and* reclaimed forms of collective actions. These actions were not only driven by demands for better living and working conditions, but also began to actually forge new forms of grassroots-based economic and political organising and institutions deeply ensconced within neighbourhoods and engaged in solidarity-based economic activity run by and benefiting the people most affected by the enclosures of the neo-liberal years.[17] At the same time that these experiments were resisting neo-liberalism, in other words, people also began to co-create community-based solutions that looked beyond the mediation of competitive markets, austerity, and cumbersome state or union bureaucracies.[18]

These are the most direct roots of Argentina's wave of workplace recuperations that slowly began in the early 1990s and surged during the first years of the new century. ERT workers' tactics of workplace occupations and their subsequent practices of *autogestión* – with their connections to workers' collective memories of past labour struggles – were also being modelled after the new social transformations and grassroots social and economic organisations that were taking shape around them at the time. On the other hand, and simultaneously, workplace occupations and recuperations were themselves influencing other social and cultural expressions of self-determination throughout the country. Moreover, Argentina's bottom-up social experiments were also encouraged by myriad popular forms of resistance and directly democratic organising that were surging across Latin America at the same time, such as

---

15   Atzeni 2010; Godio 2000; Petras and Veltmeyer 2002; Werner and Aguirre 2007.

16   Which, it should be said, as we will discuss later in this chapter and in more depth in Chapters 3, 5, and 7, eventually included the Kirchner administrations' co-optation of some of these grassroots social justice groups via policies of social containment and '*asistencialismo*' (assistentialism).

17   Sitrin 2006; Sitrin and Azzellini 2012; Vieta 2010a.

18   Coraggio 2003, 2004; La Serna 2004; Pastore 2010; Svampa and Pereyra 2004; Vieta 2010a.

Bolivia's water and gas struggles, Brazil's landless peasants' and workers' move-ments, Indigenous uprisings like Mexico's Zapatistas, and other popular move-ments from below.

Since those harrowing days of uncertainty and economic hardship span-ning the turn of the millennium, ERTs have been offering hope and inspiration for workers in hard times in Argentina and throughout the world. This is wit-nessed in similar workplace occupations in other countries of the region, as in Venezuela, Brazil, Bolivia, Mexico, and Uruguay; overseas as in France, Italy, and Spain; and, since the financial crises of 2008, in other places as diverse as the United States, the UK, South Korea, and, in more recent years, in Greece and Turkey.[19] As we will see in the second section of this chapter, the prac-tice of employees taking over workplaces in trouble and subsequently convert-ing them into cooperatives, while not necessarily new in the history of Latin America[20] or in other parts of the world,[21] has spread anew over the past two decades as direct responses by workers in places undergoing similar struggles against neo-liberal austerity, crises, and heightened exploitation and precari-ousness.[22]

1.2   *Argentine ERTs' Historical Periods*

As Figure 7 illustrates, the contemporary ERT phenomenon in Argentina began with workplace recuperations in the early-to-mid 1990s as businesses began to face trouble in the convertability years. The apex of new ERTs unfolded at the height of the country's years of deep socio-economic crisis between 2001 and 2003, when Argentine firms were closing at record rates and unemploy-ment and underemployment were at their highest historical levels. However, Argentina's ERTs have a longer historical pedigree. For instance, almost two-thirds of ERTs that exist today have roots in firms that were first founded as capitalist enterprises between the early decades of the twentieth century to the early 1970s, as was the case with Chilavert and Salud Junín in Chapter 1.[23]

---

19   Jensen 2011, 2012; Vieta 2010a, 2013; Vieta et al. 2017; Zevi et al. 2011.

20   See, for example, Allegrone, Partenio, and Fernández Álvarez 2004; Bayat 1991; Escobedo and Deux Marzi 2005; Petras and Veltmeyer 2002; and Ruggeri 2009.

21   See, for example, Bayat 1991; Ness 2009; Ness and Azzellini 2011; and Plys 2016.

22   See, for example, Dangl 2009; Martí, Bertullo, Soria, Barrios, Silveira, Camilletti et al. 2004; Ness 2009; Ness and Azzellini 2011; Novaes 2007; Carpintero and Hernández 2002; Piñiero Harnecker 2007; and Trigona 2010.

23   It should also be noted that the two oldest worker cooperatives that consider themselves ERTs today – COGTAL (Gráfica Talleres Argentinos) in the municipality of Avellaneda in the province of Buenos Aires, and Obrera de Transporte La Calera in the province of Cór-doba – converted to cooperatives in the late 1950s during a previous period of political

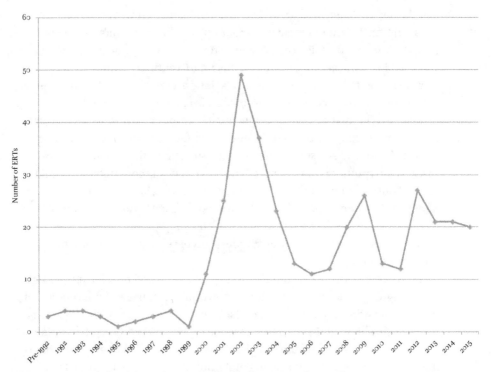

FIGURE 7   Founding of ERTs by year for those still active, as of December 2015
            Note: N=367 active ERTs as of first quarter of 2016.
            SOURCE: RUGGERI 2016, P. 11

The remaining ERTs in existence today arose from capitalist firms that had originally opened during or after the mid-1970s. Thus, as Peter Ranis suggests, the
majority of today's ERTs emerged from previous capitalist firms that were foun-

---

economic crisis and labour militancy that included worker occupations of workplaces.
They were both founded as worker cooperatives in 1958 and emerged during a previous
wave of factory occupations of the late 1950s that included the events surrounding the
occupation of the Lisandro de la Torre meatpacking plant (see Chapter 3). A small number of firms at the time managed to convert to worker cooperatives, and COGTAL and La
Calera are the two surviving conversions of this period. They are both included in the
universe of contemporary ERTs because their workers consider their self-managed experiences as such; because they have taken on new members in recent years as a consequence
of the neo-liberal crisis of the 1990s and early 2000s; and because they work with other
ERTs and community groups in the same spirit as many ERTs that have emerged over
the past two decades. For more on why these older conversions to worker cooperatives
consider themselves part of today's ERT phenomenon, see Palomino, Bleynat, Garro, and
Giacomuzzi 2010.

ded during the 'halcyon days of Argentine industrial growth';[24] it was the era of ISI and the height of organised labour's power in Argentina's version of the Fordist 'class-compromise' that, as will be touched on in the next chapter, characterised its political economy during the mid-twentieth century.

While it is telling of how the ERT solution continues to be compelling for Argentine workers, Figure 7 also shows that ERTs continued to emerge throughout the first decade of the new millennium and into its second decade. Between 2005–8, the rate of new ERTs fell compared to their apex in 2001–3. As we will see shortly, this was in part due to the economic recovery of the country during these years; the reappearance of more traditional union-centred outlets for labour demands; and more favourable state policies for the under- and unemployed. However, from 2009 on, a fairly consistent rate of ERT growth returned as responses to the new challenges brought on by the 2008 global recession and the inflationary pressures of recent years in the Argentine political economy.

Together with the other conjunctural factors discussed thus far, it is important to highlight that macro-economic downturns influence the formation of ERTs in Argentina, especially in manufacturing-based sectors with a high density of SMEs. This is similar to trends in workplace conversions in other national contexts, as supported by the broader literature on the emergence of labour-managed firms.[25] For instance, a simple non-linear comparison in Figure 8 between the rate of growth and decline of Argentina's GDP and the curve of new ERT cases shows a clear, inversely symmetrical relationship: the greater the decline in GDP, the more ERTs emerge; the greater the economic stability and GDP growth, the fewer new ERTs. Thus, the largest wave of new ERT cases in Argentina at the height of the economic crisis between 2001–3 concurrently witnessed the lowest GDP rates in recent Argentine history. As the macro-economic situation stabilised in the country, the curve of new ERTs diminished, levelling out at around 10 new cases per year between 2004 and 2007. With the US sub-prime crisis in 2007–8 and its negative effects on the Argentine economy, the GDP rate dipped to less than one percent growth for the first time in Argentina's post-convertability period[26] and, at the same time,

24   Ranis 2016, p. 54.

25   See, for instance, Ben-Ner 1988; Birchall 2003; Birchall and Hammond Ketilson 2009; Dow 2003; Ruggeri 2009; Ruggeri, Novaes, and Sardá de Faria 2014; Ruggeri and Vieta 2015; Sanchez Bajo and Roelants 2011; Smith and Rothbaum 2014; Vieta et al. 2017; and Zevi et al. 2011.

26   Amongst Argentine political economists, sociologists, historians, and other analysts, the neo-liberal years under the presidencies of Carlos Menem (1989–99) and Fernando de la Rúa (1999–2001) are also known as 'the years of covertability', or 'the era of convertabil-

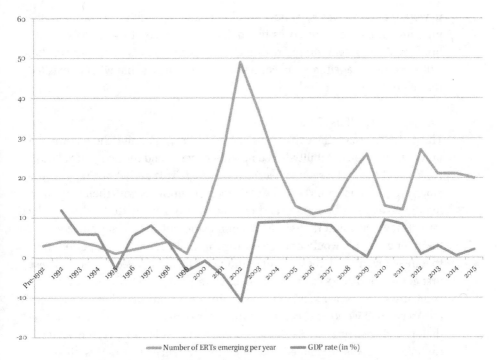

FIGURE 8   Relationship between the Argentine GDP rate and business recuperations per
year (1992–2015)
Note: *N*=367 active ERTs as of first quarter of 2016.
SOURCES: RUGGERI AND VIETA 2015; RUGGERI 2016, P. 12; WORLD BANK
2016B

the curve of new ERTs began to rise again. And recent drops in GDP with the
growing rate of inflation and other sector-specific micro-economic challenges
since 2012 has, again, meant a rise in new ERTs in recent years, with an average of 22 new ERTs per year between 2012 and 2015. Similarly, a recent study of
Italy's worker buyout-generated ERTs has shown an analogous inverse relationship between the country's GDP rate and the growth in new worker-recuperated
firms in that country, linked to its ongoing economic recession brought on by
lingering effects of the 2007–8 crisis years.[27]
   What the continued growth of ERTs in Argentina over the past two decades
suggests is that the working-class action of company takeovers and conversions

---

ity', since many of their economic policies were linked to the one-to-one fixed exchange
rate between the Argentine peso and the US dollar. For more on these policies during this
period, see Chapter 3.

27   Vieta et al. 2017.

to worker cooperatives is, by now, a well-engrained possibility for workers' living through moments of crises in troubled workplaces. In what follows, we briefly review contemporary Argentine ERTs' four major historical periods that will serve to better situate the contextual particularities that will be revisited throughout the rest of the book.

1.2.1   ERTS' 'First Period'

The period between the early 1990s and early 2004, spanning the rise and fall of Argentina's convertability-based neo-liberal years and the first years of post-convertability, can be seen as ERT's 'first period'. This period begins with the emergence of the first ERTs in the early 1990s, continuing with their surge during the crisis years of 2001–3, and ending in early 2004 with the drop in the rate of new ERTS and the relative recomposition of the Argentine economy. Just over 200 ERTs would emerge during this first contemporary period, with the great majority of these recuperations occurring between 2001–3. These first contemporary ERTs began to highlight a particularly vibrant and highly combative form of workers' self-activity during a politically charged moment for Argentina's working class. It is during this period – and especially during their peak between 2001–3 – that the process of creating an ERT from a failing capitalist firm was articulated and when the presence of ERTs was disseminated widely in Argentina and to the rest of the world. During these years, the strategies and tactics of '*ocupar, resistir, producir*' (occupy, resist, produce) – the guiding slogan of one of the ERT phenomenon's first umbrella associations of self-managed workers, the Movimiento Nacional de Empresas Recuperadas (MNER, National Movement of Recuperated Enterprises)[28] – would gradually become yet one more set of tools for resistance and survival available for workers' struggles in Argentina.

In the final years of this period, ERT protagonists and their most important political organisations and lobby groups of the time – MNER and the Movimiento Nacional de Fábricas Recuperadas por los Trabajadores (MNFRT, National Movement of Worker-Recuperated Factories) – would prioritise political mobilisation, embrace projects to legitimate workplace takeovers with the political-judicial system and the broader Argentine public, and, as was especially the case with MNER, engage in solidarity actions with other social justice movements and community groups.[29] The last years of ERTs' first period were also when expropriations of bankrupted firms as 'public goods' ceded to workers began to take place, in no small part due to the political and lobbying efforts

---

28   For more on these self-managed workers' associations, see Chapters 3, 6–8.
29   Ranis 2006, 2010, 2016.

of MNER, MNFRT, and other ERT workers and advocates.[30] In sum, it was during ERTs' first period that former employees across Argentina began to demonstrate to themselves and the Argentine public how workers can recuperate and safeguard their jobs and workplaces and, in the process and most fundamentally, self-manage their places of work and self-control their own productive lives.

1.2.2   ERTs' 'Second Period'

ERTs would continue to emerge in subsequent years, although at a lesser rate as Argentina's economy improved due to the combination of rising world commodity prices in the mid-to-late 2000s and Presidents Néstor Kirchner's (2003–7) and Cristina Fernández de Kirchner's (2007–15) more heterodox nationalist-developmentalist economic policies.[31] The first Kirchner administration's policies, designed to both steady Argentina's economy and directly redress the anti-labour and deindustrialisation initiatives of the convertability years, included: a renewed focus on human rights issues, a strengthening of social assistance plans, a raising of the minimum wage, the privileging of Argentine industry over foreign direct investment, and the renegotiation of sectoral collective agreements that had been neglected or eradicated during the convertability years. Some critical analysts have argued that these were also, if not primarily, left-populist policies linked to a political strategy of assimilating the demands of popular sectors and social movements in order to contain social protest and strengthen *kirchnerismo*'s power-base.[32] While there is certainly merit to this perspective, as we will see in later chapters, *kirchnerismo*'s left-nationalist and developmentalist policies did also encourage the consolidation of community associations and cooperatives and expanded outlets for workers' demands, including reinvigorating the country's traditional labour movement. This was reflected in the sharp rise in new worker cooperatives, revised collective agreements across a variety of sectors, and even in the rise of traditional labour actions such as strikes over working conditions, wages, and other bread-and-butter issues.[33] In this more stable economic period in Argentina – what we call ERTs' 'second period' (circa 2004–9) – new *empresas recuperadas* tended to come onto the scene specifically as worker-led responses to *micro-economic* crises at the point of production.

---

30   Ranis 2006; Rebón 2007; Vieta 2010a.

31   Arroyo 2006; Felder and Patroni 2011; Levy Yeyati and Valenzuela 2013; Piva 2015.

32   See, for instance, Dinerstein 2007; Mercatante 2015; Piva 2015; Schuster 2008.

33   Atzeni and Ghigliani 2008; Mercatante 2015; Vuotto 2011, 2014a. For more on the political economy of the Kirchner years, see Chapters 3, 6, and 7.

Overall, ERTs' second period is characterised by the consolidation of the processes of business takeovers and *autogestión* innovated by ERT protagonists during the first period. Most noticeably, second-period ERTs contrasted with those that were founded during the first period in that they were less visibly suffused with workers' indignation towards the severe macro-economic crises of the late 1990s and early 2000s and the neo-liberal system that had undergirded it. Whereas ERTs' first period was marked by the politically infused tactics of workplace occupations, workers' resistances to repression and eviction, and the lobbying of state institutions such as provincial and municipal legislatures and bankruptcy courts in order to secure these firms legally for their workers, the second period was characterised more by the increased 'institutionalisation' of the process of creating ERTs.[34] This institutionalisation included the broadening recognition of the process of converting failing capitalist firms into the legal form of worker cooperatives; the increasing use of national, provincial and, in the case of the autonomously governed city of Buenos Aires, municipal expropriation legislation; proposals for a more worker-friendly Ley de Concursos y Quiebras (Argentina's national bankruptcy law); and initiatives that proposed more robust self-managed workers' rights and social security legislation in line with the guarantees enjoyed by other private and public sector employees. This growing institutionalisation that began to be consolidated during ERTs' second period (and that was led in no small part by the increasing political and lobbying efforts of ERT umbrella organisations and some of the movement's most politicised workers), meant that, increasingly, policy makers, national and provincial government ministries and departments, the legal establishment, organised labour, and other workers in Argentina began to recognise ERTs more and more as viable alternatives to lost jobs, permanent business closures, underemployment, and unemployment.[35]

---

34   Here, the 'institutionalisation' of the creation of ERTs means the consolidation and regularisation of the social, political, and legal mechanisms, processes, and practices of converting failing firms into cooperatives. Undoubtedly, ERTs had (and still have) many challenges, and some policymakers and bankruptcy courts, judges, and trustees during the second period (as today) continued to contest the legitimacy and even legality of ERTs because, it was mainly argued, they violated Argentine property laws. Increasingly, however, and beginning during the second period, ERTs have been seen by the state and the legal system as permissable solutions to business closures. We will more fully explore the tensions and paradoxes inherent to the institutionalisation of ERTs in Chapters 6 and 7.

35   Palomino et al. 2010.

During the second period, worker-protagonists in new ERTs would learn about the processes of workplace recuperations and conversions from the pioneering struggles and support of first-period ERTs. By the time the second period began, strategies for workplace recuperations and the ins-and-outs of *autogestión* were being discussed widely amongst workers, social and political movements and parties of the left, social justice groups, cooperative associations and federations, organised labour, and researchers. These discussions would migrate into workplaces in trouble across the country. Finally, ERTs continued to garner much public support during the second period because workers were seen to be saving jobs and the country's productive capacity rather than relying on social assistance or informal work.[36]

1.2.3 ERTs' 'Third Period'

ERTs' 'third period', between 2010 and the end of 2015, witnessed a revived wave of new ERTs. These newer ERTs emerged as the impact of the subprime and financial crises of 2007–8 and its subsequent recessionary effects hit Argentina's economy and as workers' already-established solution for saving jobs in troubled workplaces under threat of closure. Already by the second period and throughout the third period, however, as ERTs consolidated their production processes as worker cooperatives, they would consistently face a set of new challenges not uncommon to other SMEs and cooperatives in post-convertability Argentina. These challenges were less a result of macroeconomic crises and more about ongoing micro-economic difficulties in specific workplaces. Many of these issues are still present and are being struggled over today in ERT workplaces. They include: securing organisational stability; gaining market share; fixing or replacing depreciated machinery; reskilling workers; replacing retired workers; recuperating workers' social security benefits lost with the failure of the previous firms; educating ERT workers in the values of cooperativism; and lobbying for the continued reforms of bankruptcy, expropriation, social security, and cooperative legislation that could improve the competitive advantage of these firms and, more generally, the long-term wellbeing of its workers.

In contrast to the first period's more combative and politically motivated ERT workers' associations (that is, MNER and MNFRT), during the second and third periods broader labour coalitions and associations would be created that focused on common issues and challenges to the working conditions and life needs of self-managed workers. These newer self-managed workers' associ-

---

ations, reviewed in detail in Chapter 3, also reached out to traditional unions, the larger cooperative movement, older and newer ERTs, and other self-managed workers' and community collectives. Three of the most important of these newer self-managed workers' associations included: the Asociación Nacional de Trabajadores Autogestionados (ANTA, National Association of Self-Managed Workers), the Federación Argentina de Cooperativas de Trabajo Autogestionado (FACTA, Argentine Federation of Self-Managed Worker Cooperatives), and the Confederación Nacional de Cooperativas de Trabajo (CNCT, National Confederation of Worker Cooperatives). The issues and struggles taken up by these newer self-managed workers' associations also directly engaged the state and often included proposals for the reform of applicable laws and easier access to financing and grants. ANTA, for instance, had been active throughout the second and third periods in the project of reforming national cooperative law that would have workers' pension plans and other social security guarantees carry over into a new ERT worker cooperative. This is a struggle which still continues today and has been taken up most recently by the Confederación de Trabajadores de la Economía Popular (CTEP, Confederation of Workers of the Popular Economy), which embraces older para-union organisations of former *piquetero* groups and "informal sector" workers such as Barrios de Pie and the Corriente Clasista y Combativa (CCC, Classist and Combative Current), and other social, solidarity, and popular economy organisations. These self-managed workers' associations have also increasingly worked collaboratively. For example, CNCT, FACTA, and other ERT protagonists were central in organising lobbying efforts, public mobilisations, and consultations and proposals in the lead-up to the 2011 reforms of the Ley de Concursos y Quiebras (the national bankruptcy law). Discussed in detail in Chapter 6, this reform promises guarantees to employees desiring to take over failing firms (but not without some paradoxical results for the ERT movement, as will be discussed there).

1.2.4   ERTs' 'Fourth Period'

As of this writing, the ERT phenomenon has entered its 'fourth period', which had its start with the new administration of President Mauricio Macri's Cambiemos coalition that took power in December 2015. While ERTs continued to emerge throughout the four years of the Cambiemos government, challenges that had been partly overcome during the years of *kirchnerismo* have returned for ERT workers. These challenges have been linked to Macri's renewed neoliberal economic policies of *'sinceramiento'*, his administration's neologism for returning the economy to its 'true' state (or, from another perspective, for unleashing unencumbered market forces again) in response to the more protectionist and nationalist economic policies of the 12 previous years of *kirchnerismo*.[37] So far, *macrismo*'s policies of *sinceramiento* have proven to be an echo of the years of *menemismo*. With an ostensible desire to curtail the inflationary pressures of the last years of Fernández de Kirchner's administration and re-animate investment, the Cambiemos government's policies of *sinceramiento* included: the promotion of new rationalisation initiatives for local businesses;[38] a new wave of layoffs of so-called 'superfluous' jobs in both the public and private sectors that once again threatens to drive up the rates of unemployment and precarious work throughout the country;[39] a new courting of foreign financial interests by promising to ratify international free trade deals; the reduction or elimination of various trade tariffs; cutbacks to subsidies and programmes benefitting working people, community organisations, cooperatives, and marginalised social groups; and a massive increase in consumer and business sector utility rates (the so-called *Tarifazo*) as the Macri regime dropped the Kirchner-era subsidies on water, gas, and electricity prices.[40] These policies were all throwbacks to the neo-liberal agenda of 1990s Argentina, justified as necessary for economic stability and to return the country to the global economic stage.[41]

For the country's SMEs, which include ERTs and Argentina's extensive cooperative movement, these drastic changes in national economic policy – and especially the introduction of utility rate hikes as we saw with the case of Chilavert in Chapter 1 – were being felt in substantive increases in production costs and falling sales, putting at risk their long-term viability. In addition, soon after Macri came to power in December 2015, state programmes that privileged public procurement contracts for ERTs, cooperatives, and other micro-enterprise were frozen.[42] There had also been a concerning increase in cases of repressive eviction attempts[43] and legislative vetoes of several expropriations of already established ERTs,[44] while the actual or threatened sale of a handful of established ERTs to local and foreign 'investors', as the Cam-

---

37   Radio Nacional 2016.
38   FACTA 2016a.
39   By July 2016, there had already been 167,000 public and private sector layoffs throughout Argentina (Dillon 2016; Vales 2016; Télam 2016).
40   Boorstin 2016; Lewkowicz 2016; Reuters 2016; Ruggeri 2016; Ruoco 2016.
41   Devita 2016.
42   Ruggeri 2016. See also Chapter 7.
43   Such as the case of the new ERT newspaper, *El Tiempo Argentino* (del Pont 2016; Tiempo Argentino 2016).
44   Ruggeri 2016.

biemos government called them, emerged as yet another new challenge.[45] All in all, Argentina's sharp-right (re)turn to an explicitly neo-liberal project had contributed new trials and tribulations for the security of the country's SMEs and myriad social and solidarity economy initiatives (including ERTs) and suggests a possible revival of the deindustrialisation of Argentina that was so acutely felt in the 1990s and that was thought to have been overcome with the more heterodox and nationalist-developmentalist policies of the Kirchner years.[46] We will dig deeper into these and other challenges to the ERT movement in Chapters 6 and 7.

More than two decades after ERTs first made their mark in Argentina under less-than-favourable political and economic circumstances, its worker protagonists are by now fairly well organised and better prepared to tackle these new challenges and resist the new neo-liberal turn. After all, many ERTs originally emerged out of neo-liberal crises and struggles against nefarious business management and anti-labour policies introduced by the contentious Washington Consensus-inspired regimes of turn-of-millennium Argentina. In many ways, ERT protagonists, especially ERTs' veteran workers, are well versed in dealing with threats to the movement's existence by reactionary capitalist and state actors. The long-term survival of the ERT movement, however, will hinge on how effectively their worker-protagonists will be able to come together in a united and organised front in collaboration with sympathetic unions and other social justice groups against the new neo-liberalism.

Such an organised front of ERTs and their umbrella associations, groups from the social and solidarity economy, and various neighbourhood and precarious workers' associations is already afoot in light of the new threats of the Macri regime.[47] Throughout 2016–18, for instance, a growing number of social, solidarity, and popular economy organisations were leading the fight against the *Tarifazo* and other potentially damaging *macrista* social and economic policies, including the CTEP, Barrios de Pie, and the CCC; many of Argentina's unions and union centrals, including its two national confederations, the CGT and CTA; associations representing the country's SMEs; and many ERTs and their umbrella associations. Various public acts and mass protests coordinated by these and other organisations had taken place throughout 2016 culminating in the 18 November mass rally of over 200,000 workers and members of social and solidarity economy organisations in front of the National

---

45   Ruggeri 2016.
46   Ruggeri 2016; Vales 2016.
47   See, for instance, CNCT 2016; FACTA 2016b; and Página/12 2016c.

Congress in support of the Ley de Emergencia Social (Law of Social Emergency).[48] These escalating social protests and organised resistances to *macrismo*, echoes of the months leading up to *el Argentinazo* of December 2001, guaranteed that Macri's Cambiemos coalition was not able to fully introduce their proposed utility rate hikes and sundry anti-labour policies without further confrontations or continued dialogues with the broad coalition of the country's social and solidarity economy protagonists and working people.

1.3 An Overview of the Emergence and Development of Argentina's ERTS[49]

As we see in Figure 9, the most widely accepted survey research on Argentina's ERTs, conducted by the Programa Facultad Abierta of the University of Buenos Aires,[50] indicates that over 400 ERTs have existed at some point in Argentina between the early 1990s to the first months of 2016. Showing an astonishing survival rate of almost 90 percent, only 43 firms that became fully operational as ERT worker cooperatives had closed as of the first quarter of 2016. This high survival rate is testament to the capacity of ERT workers to self-manage their workplaces, contrary to the assumptions of orthodox economic thinking or business media pundits that assume that workers are not capable of administering business interests and that 'entrepreneurial' and 'risk-taking' owners and managers are needed to lead them. This is also remarkable given that most ERT workers have had to restart production in formerly depleted workplaces. We will return to a discussion of ERTs' high rates of survival and the possible reasons why 43 ERTs had eventually closed in the final discussion of this sub-section.

As Figures 9 and 10 illustrate, the Argentine ERT phenomenon has grown consistently since the first contemporary ERTs came onto the scene as direct responses to the neo-liberal model's precarisation of working life in the 1990s.

---

48 Página/12 2016c. In a unified effort between sympathetic national legislators; social, solidarity, and popular economy organisations; and the CGT (a coalition which has become a powerful oppositional force to *macrismo*), the national Ley de Emergencia Social proposes the creation of one million new jobs, crucial updates to the Asignación Universal por Hijo (a form of guaranteed income social assistance programme that provisions monthly payments to families experiencing unemployment or precarious employment, with incomes less than the minimum wage, and calculated per child), and the creation of a 'complementary social salary' for all workers in the 'popular economy' (CTEP 2016).

49 Parts of this sub-section first appeared in Ruggeri and Vieta 2015. All data sourced from Ruggeri, Martínez, and Trinchero 2005; Ruggeri, Polti, Clark, Antivero, Delegdisch, et al. 2010; Ruggeri, Antivero, Elena, Polti, et al. 2014; and Ruggeri 2016.

50 For more on this research team working with Argentina's ERTs, see Introduction and Chapter 7.

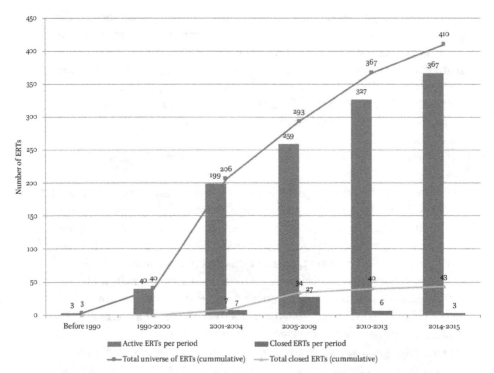

Emergence of ERTs by active firms, closed firms, and total firms by indicated
period
Note: *N*=410 ERTs. Figures as of December 2016. The line indicating the 'total universe of ERTs' includes all active and closed ERTs for each indicated period plus
the sum of all closed ERTs up to and including each period, making up a total
number of ERTs that have existed up to the period of time indicated.
SOURCE: RUGGERI 2016, PP. 9, 13

Throughout the decade of the 1990s, around 40 firms became ERTs, employing
almost 2,100 workers. By 2001–4 – the years including the height of expansion
of the ERT phenomenon in the country during the peak crisis years of its neo-
liberal model and the last years of what we have called ERTs' first period –
206 ERTs employing over 8,300 workers had existed, with only seven eventual
closures by the end of 2004. By 2005–9, which we earmarked as ERTs' second
period, 293 ERTs had existed, 259 survived the period, and 27 had closed during the period, while by the end of 2009 they employed over 11,200 workers. The
years 2005–9 also proved to be the span of time with the most ERT closures, as
Figure 9 shows, due mostly to the return of macro-economic difficulties in the
recessionary years around 2008 and the failure of some earlier ERTs to consolidate fully as worker cooperatives. Between 2010–13, during ERTs' third period,
367 ERTs had existed, 327 survived employing over 13,600 workers, while only

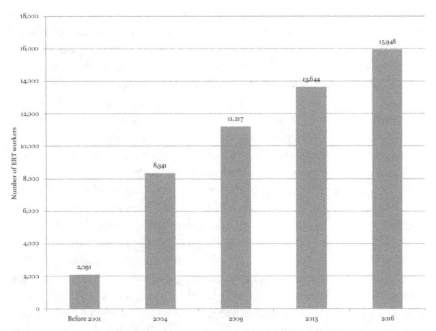

FIGURE 10 Number of ERT workers by indicated year, up to first quarter of 2016
SOURCE: PROGRAMA FACULTAD ABIERTA 2016

six ERTs closed during these years. And between 2014 and the end of ERTs' third period in December 2015, 410 ERTs had existed, 367 ERTs survived, and only 3 ERTs closed, with almost 16,000 workers self-managing their working lives throughout Argentina's urban-based economy and across its national territory.

The panorama at the beginning of 2016 showed that Argentina's ERTs were still primarily, and as with earlier periods, SMEs by number of workers per firm. In some sectors, such as in meatpacking, transportation, and footwear, ERTs tend to be larger medium-sized firms with upwards of 80–100 employees (see Table 1). However, while the mean number of workers per ERT varies by economic sector and province, ERTs in Argentina as of early 2016 had on average 43.4 workers per firm, a consistent size throughout the history of Argentina's contemporary ERTs.[51] Suggesting an adequate size for worker-recuperated firms, this is in line with the size of ERTs elsewhere, such as in Brazil and Italy.[52] This corresponds to one of the three conditions for the formation of worker-led conversions to cooperatives that include, as the literature

51   Ruggeri 2016, p. 8.
52   Chedid Henriques 2014; Vieta et al. 2017. The size of Argentine ERTs is comparable, for instance, with Italy's average of almost 40 workers per ERT (Vieta et al. 2017).

suggests: (1) firm size (that is, conversions tend to occur with SMEs); (2) their propensity to be located in labour-intensive and highly skilled sectors; and (3) their likelihood of emergence during conjunctures of economic downturn.[53] Argentina's ERTs seem to challenge the second condition, however, since a large number of them also emerge in capital-intensive sectors.

In a testament to the extent of the neo-liberal assault on Argentina's national economy during the 1990s and over the years spanning the turn of the millennium, and also to the ongoing relevance of ERTs for saving jobs and firms in subsequent years, from Table 1 we see that ERTs are found throughout the country's urban-based economy in sectors as diverse as metallurgy (that is, steel-based or metal work industries), printing and publishing, foodstuffs, construction, textiles, tourism, education, media and newspapers, and health provisioning. Some ERTs have even emerged in heavier, capital-intensive industries such as shipbuilding, meatpacking, chemicals, pulp and paper, and fuel and hydrocarbons.[54] Historically, as Table 1 also shows, the ERT phenomenon in Argentina has been predominantly a manufacturing and industrial one, with a still-sizable but smaller number of firms in the services sectors. This is also similar to ERTs in other national contexts, such as in Italy, Spain, France, and Brazil.[55]

The aggregation of economic sectors in Figure 11 illustrates that, even though most ERTs are industrial, a change in the composition of the ERT phenomenon has taken place in recent years, transforming it into one that is less industrial than it originally was during its first and second periods. By ERTs' third period starting around 2010, proportionally more new ERTs were entering in other major urban economic sectors. While Figure 11 shows us that up until the

---

53   See Ben-Ner 1988; Dickstein 1991; Dow 2003; Estrin 1989; Estrin, Jones, and Svejnar 1987; Jensen 2012; Quarter and Brown 1992; Ruggeri and Vieta, 2015; Vieta 2010a, 2013, 2014a; and Vieta et al. 2017.

54   For similar findings, see Fajn 2003; Howarth 2007; Lavaca 2004; Palomino et al. 2010; Ranis 2006, 2016; and Rebon 2004, 2007.

55   Chedid Henriques 2014; Jensen 2012; Martí et al. 2004; Novaes 2007; Vieta et al. 2017; Zevi et al. 2011. In Italy, for instance, around 70 percent of its ERTs that form primarily via worker buyouts are found in the manufacuring sector (Vieta et al. 2017, p. 51). On the whole, however, Italian ERTs differ somewhat from Argentina's ERTs in that most of them are in labour-intensive, relatively low-capital manufacturing sectors made up of highly skilled workers. The reasons that ERTs in Italy have developed along these lines in comparison to Argentina's more heterogenous ERT phneomenon include: a wider array of alternative organised labour outlets; long-standing and effective regional development policies; a more cohesive cooperative movement; more robust government supports for starting new cooperatives and worker buyouts linked to its Legge Marcora (Marcora Law) framework; and the ability to use unemployment insurance for capitalising worker buyouts (Vieta et al. 2017; see also the second section of this chapter).

TABLE 1   Total active ERTs and number of workers per economic sector, up to first quarter of 2016

Sector	ERTS	Workers	% of ERTS	% of Workers
Metallurgical Products	72	3,196	19.62%	20.04%
Foodstuffs	50	1,445	13.62%	9.06%
Printing and Graphics	38	1,519	10.35%	9.52%
Textiles	28	1,196	7.63%	7.50%
Restaurants / Gastronomy	25	487	6.81%	3.05%
Meatpacking	25	2,092	6.81%	13.12%
Construction	18	1,033	4.90%	6.48%
Health	12	572	3.27%	3.59%
Wood Products and Sawmills	10	318	2.72%	1.99%
Education	9	250	2.45%	1.57%
Leather Products	9	520	2.45%	3.26%
Chemicals	8	186	2.18%	1.17%
Transportation	8	778	2.18%	4.88%
Media and Newspapers	8	394	2.18%	2.47%
Glass products	7	478	1.91%	3,00%
Retail	6	232	1.63%	1.45%
Plastics	6	117	1.63%	0.73%
Hotel	5	232	1.36%	1.45%
Fuel and Hydrocarbons	5	88	1.36%	0.55%
Maintenance and Logistics	5	143	1.36%	0.90%
Footware	4	401	1.09%	2.51%
Pulp and Paper	3	102	0.82%	0.64%
Shipbuilding	2	62	0.54%	0.39%
Mining	2	83	0.54%	0.52%
Rubber	1	13	0.27%	0.08%
Editorial	1	11	0.27%	0.07%
Total	367	15,948	100.00%	100.00%

Note: N=367 ERTs still active as of the first quarter of 2016.
SOURCE: RUGGERI 2016, P. 7

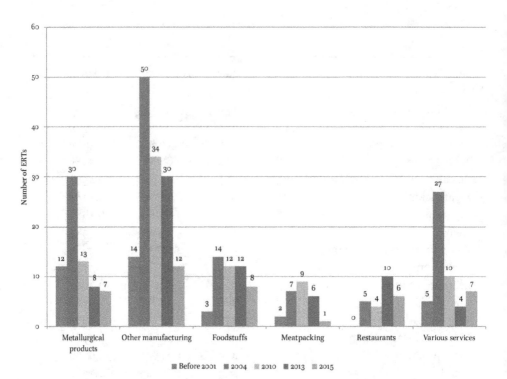

FIGURE 11   Changes in ERTs' economic sectors by year indicated
            Note: *N*=362 ERTs that known to be active as of the third quarter of 2015.
            SOURCE: PROGRAMA FACULTAD ABIERTA 2016

beginning of 2016 ERTs were continuing to emerge in all sectors, an increasing relative number can now be seen in various other manufacturing sectors besides metallurgy, such as in textiles, foodstuffs, and especially in the services sectors, such as restaurants, health provisioning, and education. Shortly we will discuss how the rise in ERTs in these newer sectors and the comparative drop in new ERTs in other industrial sectors since 2010 are linked to two phenomena: an increase in economic difficulties in historically low-wage jobs (such as those found in textiles and gastronomy) and more union-based outlets for meeting workers' demands in recent years in sectors that have historically predominated during the ERT phenomenon's earlier periods (such as metallurgy and printing and publishing).

ERTs have also extended out further throughout the national territory in recent years when compared to the first and second ERT periods, and have also, at the same time, continued to concentrate in traditional ERT regions such as in the city of Buenos Aires and its greater conurbation. As Table 2 shows, by the beginning of 2016, ERTs were present in 19 out of 23 provinces, as well as

TABLE 2   Breakdown of ERTs and number of workers by province, up to first quarter of
            2016

Provinceª	ERTS	Workers	% of ERTS by province	% of workers by province
GBAᵇ	119	5,524	32.43%	34.64%
CABAᶜ	70	2,257	19.07%	14.15%
Rest of Province of Buenos Airesᵈ	54	1,744	14.71%	10.94%
Santa Fe	26	1,064	7.08%	6.67%
Córdoba	15	1,270	4.09%	7.96%
Rio Negro	12	496	3.27%	3.11%
Chaco	9	343	2.45%	2.15%
Mendoza	8	212	2.18%	1.33%
Misiones	7	242	1.91%	1.52%
Entre Rios	6	386	1.63%	2.42%
La Pampa	6	163	1.63%	1.02%
Neuquén	6	922	1.63%	5.78%
San Luis	6	257	1.63%	1.61%
Corrientes	5	454	1.36%	2.85%
La Rioja	5	140	1.36%	0.88%
Chubut	4	80	1.09%	0.50%
Tucumán	3	25	0.82%	0.16%
San Juan	2	39	0,54%	0.24%
Jujuy	2	80	0.54%	0.50%
Santiago del Estero	1	70	0.27%	0.44%
Tierra del Fuego	1	180	0.27%	1.13%
Total	367	15,948	100.00%	100.00%

a   Including the Autonomous City of Buenos Aires (CABA) and Greater Buenos Aires (GBA).
b   Gran Buenos Aires (Greater Buenos Aires).
c   Ciudad Autónoma de Buenos Aires (Autonomous City of Buenos Aires).
d   Not including GBA and CABA.
Note: N=367 ERTs that were still active as of the first quarter of 2016.
SOURCE: RUGGERI 2016, P. 5

TABLE 3   Total distribution of ERTs by region and number of workers, up to first quarter of
           2016

Region	ERTS	Workers	% of ERTs by region	% of workers by region
AMBA[a]	189	7,781	51.50%	48.79%
Pampas[b]	110	4,828	29.97%	30.27%
Northeast[c]	28	1,190	7.63%	7.46%
Northwest[d]	2	80	0.54%	0.50%
Cuyo[e]	15	391	4.09%	2.45%
Patagonia[f]	23	1,678	6.27%	10.52%
Total	367	15,948	100.00%	100.00%

a   Area Metropolitana de Buenos Aires (Metropolitan Area of Buenos Aires), including the City
    of Buenos Aires and surrounding municipalities in the Province of Buenos Aires.
b   Province of Buenos Aires (beyond AMBA), and provinces of La Pampa, Santa Fe, Entre Ríos,
    and Córdoba.
c   Provinces of Misiones, Corrientes, and Chaco (while the province of Formosa is part of the
    northeast region of the country, there are no known ERTs in this province).
d   Provinces of Jujuy, Salta, Catamarca, Tucumán, and Santiago del Estero.
e   Provinces of San Juan, San Luis, and Mendoza.
f   Provinces of Neuquén, Río Negro, Chubut, and Tierra del Fuego (while the province of Santa
    Cruz is part of the Patagonia region of the country, there are no known ERTs in this province).
Note: N=367 ERTs that were still active as of the first quarter of 2016.
SOURCE: RUGGERI 2016, P. 6

in the Ciudad Autónoma de Buenos Aires (CABA, Autonomous City of Buenos Aires).[56] Their concentration continues to be the highest in CABA and in Gran Buenos Aires (GBA, Greater Buenos Aires),[57] as has been the case since the first ERTs emerged and coinciding with the historical importance of Buenos Aires and its environs as the economic and industrial engine of the country.

When we group the geographic distribution of Argentina's ERTs into main regions, as we do in Table 3, we observe a clear concentration of ERTs in the Area Metropolitana de Buenos Aires (AMBA, Metropolitan Area of Buenos Aires, including CABA and GBA) and, secondly, in the region of the Pampas (the rest of the province of Buenos Aires outside of AMBA plus the provinces of Sante Fe, Córdoba, Entre Rios, and La Pampa). If we group AMBA and the

56   The Autonomous City of Buenos Aires, the country's capital region, is a non-provincial,
      autonomous political entity within the Argentine federal system.
57   The sprawling Province of Buenos Aires municipalities surrounding CABA.

Pampa region, we find that it is home to almost 81.5 percent of the nation's ERTs, again mapping onto the historical centres of the country's urban-based industrial economy.

1.3.1   Argentina's Newer ERTs (2010–16[58])

If we focus solely on ERTs that emerged between 2010 and the first quarter of 2016, we discover that new dimensions arose in the ERT phenomenon during its third period: by then there was a greater level of regional and economic-sector diversity when compared to earlier periods. Our analysis here divides the emergence of Argentina's newer ERTs between two sub-periods, 2010 and 2013 and 2014 and 2016, finding that an increasing number of them – especially with those that formed in the 2010–13 sub-period – were found in more heterogeneous and non-industrial economic sectors than had historically been the case.

Of the 367 active ERTs at the start of 2016, 116 cases emerged during ERTs' third period between 2010 and the first quarter of 2016. Witnessing a new high-point of ERT formation since the height of ERT entries between 2001 and 2004 and the smaller spike in ERTs in 2009 (see Figure 7), the 116 third-period ERTs contradict the commonly held assumption that the ERT movement in Argentina was limited to the crisis of 2001 and the years immediately following it. If we disaggregate ERTs' third period, we especially note an important growth of new ERTs between 2010 and 2013 with 73 new cases, and 43 new cases between 2014 and the start of 2016. That is, these two sub-periods within ERTs' third period witnessed the creation of almost 20 percent and 12 percent respectively of all active ERTs, collectively encompassing almost 32 percent of the 367 ERTs that were active by the first quarter of 2016. We also notice, returning to Figure 7, that 2012 was a particularly vibrant year for new, third-period ERTs with 27 new cases, which is comparable to the prior peak of ERT entry in 2009 (26 new cases). Not surprisingly, both 2009 and 2012 coincide with two recent economic troughs in Argentina, specifically: the outbreak of the Great Recession around 2008 and its subsequent reverberations in Argentina; and the expansion of the recession, especially in the European Union, in 2012, felt in Argentina as a concomitant drop in economic productivity and a steady increase in the rate of inflation.[59] The 2009 and 2012 spikes in ERT creation also map inversely, the reader will recall, to the declining GDP during these two years, as we saw in Figure 8. Moreover, with continued inflationary challenges after 2012 and the subsequent drops in consumer demand (especially affecting the services sectors), the attendant rise in the cost of production inputs, and the stagnant GDP

---

58   As of the first quarter of 2016.
59   Kulfas 2016; Mercatante 2015.

growth rate, between 2012 and the beginning of 2016 we witness a heightened level of new ERT entry. Indeed, between 2012–15 alone, during the last years of Cristina Fernández de Kirchner's administration, 89 new ERTs entered the scene. In order to see similarly elevated numbers of ERT entries within a four-year timeframe, we have to go back to the turn-of-millennium crisis years at the end of ERTs' first period.

As we reported in an article published in 2015 focusing on ERTs that emerged in the first four years of the phenomenon's third period (2010–13),[60] there began to emerge during these four years a more even distribution of ERTs across the national territory than in previous periods. We observed then that, for the first time since the beginning of the ERT movement, there was an increased presence of ERTs outside of CABA and GBA, the historical hub of ERT development. That is, while ERTs still continued to be highly concentrated in the city of Buenos Aires and its metropolitan area as a result of the historical economic and industrial development of Argentina, proportionally between 2010 and 2013 the growth rate in new ERT cases in the rest of the country was more significant than in previous periods. As evidence of the continued expansion of the movement, between 2010 and 2013, for instance, there was a substantive growth of new ERTs in regions that, until then, had had low numbers of ERTs, like the northeast (especially the provinces of Chaco and Misiones) and in the Patagonia region (especially in the provinces of Neuquén, Rio Negro, and Chubut). Significant surges in new ERTs were also noted in provinces outside of AMBA and the rest of the province of Buenos Aires, such as in Sante Fe and Córdoba. This wider distribution of new ERTs thus increased the numerical weight of the phenomenon outside of its traditional AMBA and Pampas strongholds identified in earlier surveys.[61] We connected this trend in new ERTs emerging beyond the historical centre of the phenomenon to the broadening macro-economic difficulties felt throughout the country post-2008 and to the continued diffusion of the ERT solution for business closure across the national territory. On the other hand, of the 43 newest ERTs that we tracked between 2014 and the first quarter of 2016, we began to see a return of the metropolitan area of Buenos Aires as the hub of ERT development, with almost 56 percent of ERTs emerging during this timeframe doing so in CABA or its conurbation, indicative of the continued presence of economic stagnation in Argentina's economic and industrial centre.

Besides the increase in new ERTs, especially since 2012, and the phenomenon's relatively more even distribution across the country in recent years,

---

60   Ruggeri and Vieta 2015.

61   For instance, Ruggeri et al. 2005; Ruggeri et al. 2010.

another aspect that changed by ERTs' third period was the mix of firms by economic sector, as we graphically highlighted in Figure 11. As already mentioned, new ERTs are now not as concentrated in industrial sectors as they were during its first and second periods and now include a more heterogeneous mix of firms, becoming more representative of Argentina's urban-based economy. Focusing solely on the newer cases of ERTs that we have tracked (that is, the 43 ERTs that emerged between 2014 and the first quarter of 2016), the percentage of ERTs that are industrial enterprises, for example, shrinks relative to the historical universe of ERTs. We particularly find that, while the metallurgical sector has historically had the largest concentration of ERTs in relation to the entire group of Argentine ERTs (historically at almost 20 percent in Table 1), new ERTs in the metallurgical sector declined slightly between 2014 and 2016, making up by the beginning of 2016 18.6 percent of the country's newest ERTs. This drop in the numerical importance of the metallurgical sector was already a trend identified by the Programa Facultad Abierta team in 2010.[62] On the other hand, ERTs in the foodstuffs sector increased substantially during these years when compared to their historical numbers, making up 18.6 percent of new ERTs (compared to almost 14 percent of ERTs historically), while those in the restaurant sector increased to almost 14 percent of new ERTs (compared historically to almost 7 percent of all ERTs). Print shops and graphics ERTs have also seen a solid increase in new ERTs, making up over 16 percent of new ERTs (compared to the historical figure of almost 10.5 percent of all ERTs). Interestingly, while ERTs in the textiles sector increased largely between 2010 and 2013, making up almost 14.5 percent of new ERTs then,[63] only one new textile ERT had come onto the scene between 2014 and 2016, suggesting improving conditions and more union-based outlets for meeting workers' needs in the textiles sector since 2014. Overall, by ERTs' third period, we observe a greater diversification of its economic sectors, with particular growth in foodstuffs, textiles, restaurants, and other service sectors.

To summarise, we can see a tangible change in the character of Argentina's ERT phenomenon between 2010 and the beginning of 2016. In contrast to the historical characteristic of ERTs as primarily made up of industrial firms, newer ERTs have emerged increasingly in the services sector and in new manufacturing and processing sectors. We can explain this change in the ERT phenomenon during its third period by taking into account key aspects of the Argentine political economy in recent years. For instance, the decline in the percentage of ERTs in the metallurgical industry and other manufacturing sectors was in part due to the process of re-industrialisation that took place in Argentina during

---

62   Ruggeri et al. 2010.
63   Ruggeri and Vieta 2015.

the Kirchner period between 2004 and 2015. In addition, the general strengthening of the national metalworkers union, Unión Obrera Metalúrgica (UOM), and the reconsolidation of the gastronomic and print workers' unions during the same period – nurtured by the return of the overall bargaining power of organised labour during these years – afforded workers in these sectors other outlets for protecting jobs besides taking over their firms. These union-based outlets, which had been greatly diminished during the convertability years of the 1990s and early 2000s, had regained their strength and power-base during the era of *kirchnerismo*. Conversely, the rise of ERTs in other sectors in recent years, such as restaurants, food processing, and textiles, correlates with the deterioration of working conditions and economic circumstances in those sectors, where unsavoury business practices, outsourcing, and labour precariousness are still the order of the day. Hence, it is precisely in these sectors that we currently find a heightened number of new ERTs. In other economic sectors, such as in printing and graphics, growth in ERTs is related to the influence of new union policies and attitudes towards self-managed workers that seek to support the formation of new worker cooperatives and that promote the ERT solution as a way to keep workers in the union. In short, this new attitude of unions towards ERTs has also supported the growth of the phenomenon in recent years, but with some continued challenges.

1.3.2   Recent Changes in the Relationship between ERTs and Argentina's Trade Unions

While many Argentine unions in recent years have begun to look more favourably on ERTs, on the whole different unions continue to take varying positions on the phenemonon. These include: support and assistance for workers during the recuperation process; outright opposition to workplace takeovers; complicity with management; and the undermining of workers' own struggles against owner asset stripping, for instance, or during workers' periods of workplace occupation. The degree of support of different unions towards ERTs connects to their particular history, the kinds of activity traditionally engaged in by the union, the composition and characteristic of its leadership, and the particular operational policies in place. These factors also affect the relationships that are established between unions and an ERT's workers once the cooperative is established. Sectors in which unions have had a mostly positive role to play in supporting ERT workers include those that have been historically more militant and inclusive of rank-and-file participation. Tellingly, these unions are to be found in sectors with the greatest number of ERTs, including printing and graphics, metallurgy, construction, and, in recent years, in the textile and restaurant sectors.

Printing and graphics ERTs, for instance, especially in the city of Buenos Aires, have enjoyed a particularly strong union presence. Despite not originally supporting workers' recuperations of firms during ERTs' first period, as we saw with the Chilavert case study in Chapter 1, the Federación Gráfica Bonaerense (FGB) has been a union that has gradually changed its position towards ERTs, becoming in recent years one of the principal promoters of ERTs and providing important assistance and legal advice to their workers during occupations and the early days of self-managed production. Moreover, since ERTs' second period, there has been a strong relationship between the FGB and the Red Gráfica Cooperativa (Graphics Network Cooperative), the second-tier cooperative made up of ERTs and non-ERT cooperative print shops. The Unión Obrera Gráfica Cordobesa (UOGC, Print Workers' Union of the Province of Cordoba) has also been active in supporting ERT workers during periods of occupation in the province of Córdoba. And UOM, the Argentine metalworkers union, as we have already touched on, has also been a strong promoter of ERTs since the phenomenon's early days, especially in some of its local branches such as in the greater Buenos Aires municipality of Quilmes. All of these unions, it is also important to note, have also participated in recent years in solidarity marches and in lobbying bankruptcy courts and legislatures during sittings where ERT expropriation cases were being deliberated. Further, these unions have maintained full rights for ERT workers, including continuing to recognise health insurance benefits even when workers are unable to pay union dues.

Textile-sector ERTs have also witnessed support from that sector's various unions, although with more mixed results. The presence of various unions within each textile-based ERT follows the broader and historical pattern of the development of this sector in Argentina. Textile unions that are active in ERTs include the Sindicato Obrero de la Industria del Vestido y Afines (SOIVA, Workers' Union of Clothing and Related Industries), the Sindicato de Empleados Textiles de la Industria y Afines (SETIA, Union of Employees of Textile and Related Industries), and the Asociación Obrera Textil de la República Argentina (AOTRA, Textile Workers' Association of the Republic of Argentina). The Programa Facultad Abierta researchers have observed that different positions have been taken by each of these textile unions – some more supportive, some less so – regarding workers' conflicts with management and owners, during moments of occupation, and in the actual conversion of the enterprise.[64]

Finally, it is also worth noting the strong role that the Unión de Trabajadores del Turismo, Hoteleros y Gastronómicos (UTHGRA, Union of Tourism,

---

64   Ruggeri and Vieta 2015.

Hotel, and Gastronomy Workers) has had in the recent wave of new restaurant ERTs; this union has played an important part in the recent recuperation of six restaurants in the City of Buenos Aires. The surge in these and other restaurant ERTs in recent years (where the influence of the chain of five worker-recuperated restaurants in the city of Buenos Aires is notable) parallels the growing recuperation of service sector firms by workers. Interestingly, while five of these new ERT restaurants originally belonged to the same business group, their workers created separate cooperatives for each establishment in order to maximise their autonomy while retaining important solidarity relationships with each other.[65]

But this union support of ERTs is still far from uniform across sectors. This reality, as we will see in the final pages of Chapter 3, had given impetus in the early 2000s to the formation of cross-sectoral self-managed workers' associations. Overall, the traditional union model of representing workers collectively has been challenged by worker-recuperated and controlled businesses since ERTs can be seen to directly question unions' very *raison d'être*.[66] Traditionally, of course, unions have represented wage labourers who are in a dependent relationship to employers, focusing on struggles directly affected by this relationship such as bargaining for salaries, benefits, and improvements in working conditions. During ERTs' first period Argentine unions that had historically played a strong role not only in sector-wide bargaining in the country, but also in the working lives and culture of the country's working class and on shop floors, simply did not know what to do with cases of ERTs where *el patrón* (the boss) was removed from the equation. This conundrum continued to be the case with a number of ERTs until very recently. While 43 percent of ERTs in 2013, during ERTs' third period, reported that their unions had had a strong role to play in the recuperation of the firm, 22 percent still reported that they had experienced general 'indifference' from their unions concerning the recuperation of the firm while 14 percent said that their unions 'opposed' outright the recuperation process.[67]

Thus, from one perspective, the existence of ERTs can be seen to question the traditional role of unions, particularly when workers have moved beyond the employer–employee relationship and decide collectively how to run and manage their shop and divvy up surpluses. Indeed, in an ERT, the boss disap-

---

65   Some of these most recent restaurant-sector ERTs include Alé Alé and Los Chanchitos, both recuperated in 2013 and found in the Villa Crespo *barrio* of Buenos Aires, and La Casona, recuperated in 2016 and found in the Microcentro *barrio* of Buenos Aires.

66   Clark and Antivero 2009; Dávolos and Perelman 2004.

67   Ruggeri et al. 2014, pp. 47–9.

pears while the worker-subject – employees' identities as *workers* – remains. This makes for a paradoxical relationship between many ERT workers and their unions: As we will see in later chapters, while a fair number of the country's unions still distance themselves from or are indifferent to ERTS, most ERT workers nevertheless continue to identify with their unions via their working-class identities.[68]

But from another perspective, the broad take-up of workers' self-management in Argentina over the past two decades has begun to transform the traditional labour movement itself. Indeed, more and more unions in recent years have shown support for ERT workers, in no small part due to the efforts of ERT workers themselves as they have often mobilised to bring their unions more fully into an ERT's shop floor. In addition, the increased proliferation of ERTS throughout the national territory, their relative longevity as a phenomenon, their high survival rates, and the impact they have had on the country's workers within and outside of the ERT movement have all contributed to notable changes of attitude towards ERTS in Argentina's traditional labour movement. These factors have pushed some unions with members that are actively engaged in ERTS to rethink their responses and attitudes towards the ERT phenomena. Moreover, new discussions have been taking place in recent years between the broader labour movement's leaders (including the CGT and the CTA), ERTS, and other cooperatives concerning how to collectively respond to new threats to workers' rights given *macrismo*'s resurgent neo-liberalism.[69] This more positive ERT–union relationship was already palpable by late 2013, for instance, when 64 percent of new ERTS reported favourable involvement on the part of their unions in their self-management projects, 47 percent of ERTS had kept the relations with their unions intact as before the recuperation, and 33 percent had at least continued contributing to their union-based social security plans.[70]

This more favourable relationship between ERTS and traditional unions today, then, driven in no small part by the very efforts of ERT workers and their continued identification as members of the working class, is the predominant reality today. By ERTS' third period, the involvement of unions in ERTS had considerably changed from the first period, reflected in the increasing participation of traditional unions in the process of creating new ERTS and in helping ERT workers secure pensions and other benefits lost during the struggle to create a new worker cooperative.

---

68   On ERT workers' continued working-class identities, see Chapters 6 and 8.

69   See, for instance, FACTA 2016c, 2016d.

70   Ruggeri et al. 2014, p. 47. Multiple answers were permitted.

1.3.3   A Summary of ERTs' Emergence and Development

Subsequent chapters will work out the qualitative details latent in this chapter's quantitative analysis of ERTs. For example, Chapters 7 and 8 will look at how the breadth of the ERT phenomenon, cutting across most of Argentina's economic sectors, suggests that worker cooperatives, at least upon the conversion of a capitalist business into a labour-managed firm when most of its assets are still usable to some extent, *can* indeed function in diverse types of economic activity, including in capital-intensive sectors. Indeed, Argentina's ERTs begin to cast a different light on the common assumption in the economic literature that labour-managed firms are most adequate for labour-intensive and low-capital production.[71]

Overall, it is noteworthy that the economic sectors with the heaviest conglomeration of ERTs have consistently been those that have traditionally had militant union histories, suggesting, as the case studies in Chapter 1 highlighted and the political economic analysis in Chapter 3 will show further, the connections between ERTs and the country's history of working-class self-activity. Recalling Table 1, it is no coincidence, then, that almost 70 percent of Argentina's ERTs are found in the metallurgical, printing and graphics, meatpacking, construction, restaurants, textiles, and foodstuffs sectors, represented historically by some of the most militant unions in Argentina. In addition, the revived importance and militancy of several unions in recent years; the improved relations between ERTs and their unions; and the widespread knowledge, legitimacy, and take-up of the ERT solution to the closing of firms by the second and third periods of the phenomenon, have also contributed to the emergence of new ERTs in sectors where they were previously under-represented, such as in gastronomy and textiles.

As Chapters 6 and 8 will further discuss (and as the Chilavert and UST case studies underscored in Chapter 1), some of the more radicalised ERT workers and leaders with past community advocacy or union organising experiences are often key players in an ERTs' founding collective, and some of these workers subsequently go on to become leaders of their worker cooperative. Their formation as radicalised workers, as we saw in Chapter 1, often takes place within former union settings as shop stewards, or from having taken part in past strikes, other forms of union-based organising, or in community activism. Many ERT workers also first learn the ins-and-outs of activism from family members with histories of participation in union actions or other kinds of community activism. Lastly, it is also not coincidental that, as we saw in

---

71   See, for instance, the review of this literature in Dow 2003; and Drèze 1993.

Table 2, over 77 percent of currently active ERTs are to be found in the city of Buenos Aires, the capital's conurbation, in concentrated pockets of the interior of the province of Buenos Aires, and in the provinces of Santa Fe and Córdoba. These happen to be the country's five major industrial areas with the greatest union density. Not surprisingly, they are also the places where much of Argentina's working-class struggles have taken place over the past 130 years or so.[72]

Argentine ERTs' high rates of survival, as we pointed out earlier in this chapter, are also notable and worthy of additional reflection, especially since most of these firms were in very precarious conditions when workers began to self-manage them as worker cooperatives. Moreover, that almost 90 percent of the 410 contemporary ERTs that have existed since they first began to emerge in the early 1990s have survived as of early 2016 (and some of them doing so for over three decades or more) is strong evidence that the ERT movement's worker-protagonists have been very capable of self-managing their working lives and their businesses.[73] While research into the specific characteristics and conditions of the 43 ERTs that had closed up to the beginning of 2016 is at its early stages,[74] the Programa Facultad Abierta team has uncovered preliminary data suggesting that these firms did *not* close because of workers' inability to collectively manage them; they closed, rather, due to circumstances beyond their workers' full control. Encompassing some of the challenges faced by ERTs that will be discussed in later chapters, some of the major reasons for these closures include: inheriting extremely difficult micro-economic circumstances

---

72   Godio 1990; Munck et al. 1987; Murmis and Portantiero 1971.

73   Early research suggests that this survival rate is comparable to or better than workplace conversions in other conjunctures. A study of Italian worker buyout-based ERTs, for instance, found that in the 257 Italian worker-recuperated firms that it tracked and that emerged between 1979–2014, 57 percent survived up to the end of 2014 (Vieta et al. 2017). The survival rate of Argentine ERTs can also be interpreted inversely: the death rate of Argentine ERTs is roughly one out of every 10 firms. In a review of labour-managed firm (LMF) formations in earlier historical conjunctures of crises, Avner Ben-Ner (1988) reported that the annual death rates of European LMFs in the 1970s and 1980s were: 6.9 percent for French LMFs; 28.6 per cent for Dutch LMFs; 9.3 percent for Italian LMFs; 6.3 percent for UK LMFs; and 29.5 percent for Swedish LMFs. The strong caveat in comparing Argentine ERTs' death rates to these other cases is that our research of Argentine ERTs considers the survivability and mortality rates of the entire universe of ERTs over close to a thirty-year period, while these other studies cited by Ben-Ner have focused on year-by-year mortality rates within a much smaller timeframe of a few years.

74   For obvious reasons such as the unavailability of workers or hard-to-access or non-existent documentation, it has been difficult to track, after the fact, most historical attempts at ERTs that were not successful. This is an area that remains to be researched.

from the previous firm that workers had not been able to overcome; successful evictions; completed auctioning of a firm's assets by bankruptcy courts; and sundry legal or market difficulties that workers were not able to overcome. Tellingly, only one of the closed ERTs that the research team tracked closed due to internal worker conflicts, while another was sold to new private investors.[75] The latter point, however, was a trend that threatened to rise with the new neo-liberal policies of *macrismo* and will have to be monitored in the coming years.

In order to further contextualise Argentina's ERTs, the next section situates ERTs within the varied practices and policies of workplace conversions to labour-managed firms around the world, and begins to develop a worker-led definition of *empresas recuperadas por sus trabajadores*. We will then move on to situate Argentina's ERTs with other contemporary worker-recuperated firms in other national contexts in the final pages of this chapter.

2   Section 2: ERT Types and Experiences of Workplace Conversions around the World[76]

Workers' occupations, takeovers, or conversions of the workplaces that employ them into some form of self-managed entity are certainly not new from a world-historical perspective.[77] Such experiences have appeared at different historical conjunctures involving socio-economic crises or political upheaval. For example, we can think of the European revolutions of 1848; the Paris Commune of 1871; the Russian Revolutions of 1905 and 1917, especially during the first months of the Bolshevik Revolution starting in October 1917; Italy's *biennio rosso* of 1919–20; the wave of union-led factory occupations during the Great Depression in the US in the 1930s; workers' control of private and public businesses in regions of revolutionary Spain in 1936; worker-led experiments in Hungary in 1956, in post-colonial Algeria in 1962, during Czechoslovakia's Prague Spring, and in various other revolts and uprisings around the world in 1968; and state- or union-sanctioned factory occupations and takeovers in France, Italy, Spain, and the United Kingdom in the 1970s and 1980s.[78]

---

75   Ruggeri et al. 2014; Ruggeri 2016.
76   Portions of this section were first published in Vieta 2015 and Vieta et al. 2017. All of the text in this section has been written by this book's author.
77   Bayat 1991; Plys 2016.
78   Bayat 1991; Chase 1987; Horvat 1982; Ness and Azzellini 2011; Petras and Veltmeyer 2002; Plys 2016; Vieta 2010a, 2013, 2014a.

Workers' occupations, takeovers, or conversions of workplaces to workers' self-management are also not new in Latin America.[79] The most salient historical examples before the 1990s and 2000s include: the factory occupations of failing firms in Chile in the late 1960s and the 100 or so factories that were nationalised under workers' control as '*empresas de trabajadores*' (workers' enterprises) in Salvador Allende's Chile between 1970 and 1973;[80] the nationalisation and co-management of mines and rural enterprises during Bolivia's National Revolutionary Movement of the 1950s and again during J.J. Torres's left-wing dictatorship of the early 1970s; the surge in cooperativised 'industrial communities' in General Velasco Alvarado's leftist military regime in Peru during the late 1960s and early 1970s; and the situations of union-instigated and temporary workplace takeovers in Argentina in the late 1950s, throughout the 1960s, in the first half of the 1970s, and in the mid-1980s.[81]

Today, workplace conversions to labour-managed firms (LMFs) mostly arise due to the deleterious effects of globalising markets, deregulation, austerity, and deindustrialisation on working people and communities. For workplace conversions to become widespread and even institutionalised as solutions to business closures, economic downturns, or market failure, broader amenable conditions need to be in place. These amenable conditions tend to emerge in national contexts of declining economic circumstances merging with a country's historical and material particularities, including traditions of cooperativism, long-held practices of shop floor labour organising and workers' self-activity, and various forms (to a greater or lesser extent) of institutionalised support mechanisms. In these conjunctures, to which Johnston Birchall alludes, workers have 'set up worker cooperatives that took over failing firms or parts of firms that were still viable'.[82] The combination of these conjunctural factors reduces the barriers and opportunity costs for workers contemplating starting an LMF from a process of business conversion. Avner Ben-Ner's comprehensive study comparing the conversion of capitalist firms (CFs) to worker-owned firms (WOFs) in different national contexts serves to synthesise for us the conjunctural realities for the emergence of ERTs:

Declining economic conditions ... reduce the obstacles present to WOF formation ... The buyout of a CF entails particularly low formation obsta-

---

79   Bayat 1991; Munck et al. 1987; Petras and Veltmeyer 2002; Plys 2016.
80   Horvat 1982, p. 163.
81   See Chapter 3 for a recounting of these earlier experiences of workers' occupations and
      self-management of firms in Argentina.
82   Birchall 2003, p. 48.

cles because the firm is already in existence and because the cost of purchasing capital that lacks alternative uses is lower. Thus industrial decline
and recessions simultaneously increase the demand for WOFs and lower
the obstacles to their entry, increasing the probability of WOF formation.
Governments and other organizations may accentuate the trend of WOF
formation if they realize that WOFs constitute a comparatively inexpens-
ive measure to combat loss of employment and unemployment ... As relatively large numbers of WOFs are established they become more widely
known, and the recurrence of recessions or decline of industries prompts
even larger waves of WOF formation.[83]

Argentina's *empresas recuperadas por sus trabajadores* and other ERT-type
experiences in other parts of the world as we have known them over the past
20 or so years can be seen as a particular subset of workplace conversions
to LMFs.[84] ERT-type conversions today tend to explicitly arise out of *workers' own initiatives* to *recuperate* their livelihoods, their dignity, and a dying
firm from *the socio-economic ills* wrought by the crisis-ridden neo-liberal capitalist model within national contexts containing the amenable conditions
just mentioned. Around the world, ERTs are also known variously as worker-
recuperated, worker-recovered, or worker-occupied companies, businesses,
factories, firms, or enterprises.

While most contemporary ERTs arise out of shop floor conflicts over the
assets of the former business and its ex-employees' rights to continue to work in
the firm in question under their own control, it should be noted that not all conversions to LMFs emerge out of explicilty conflictual situations. For instance,
negotiated agreements using the mechanism of worker buyouts (WBOs) (described shortly) are the predominate way that conversions of troubled firms to
LMFs take place in the global North, especially in Italy, Spain, and France, but
also in the United States, Canada, and in smaller pockets in the UK and other
European jurisdictions.[85] A handful of Argentina's ERTs have also emerged
from WBO processes, such as the case of ERT newspaper *Comercio y Justicia*
in the city of Córdoba.[86]

The state can also be the impetus for conversions of productive entities
to LMFs. Since these conversions, however, tend not to have some of the

---

83   Ben-Ner 1988, p. 23.
84   Workplace conversions to LMFs are also termed business transfers to workers/employees,
        or business conversions to worker/employee ownership.
85   Vieta et al. 2017.
86   Vieta 2014b. For more on *Comercio y Justicia*, see Chapters 6 and 8.

most important worker-led or radicalised characteristics of Argentina's ERTs, whether or not they should be considered *worker-recuperated* firms remains an open question. In addition, while workers may become involved in some form of participation or administration of the subsequent LMF, workers in these state-initiated cases might not recuperate the firm under their full and autonomous control. For instance, formerly state-owned enterprises (SOEs) can also be converted to worker cooperatives or other forms of LMFs in order to deliver public services at arms-length from government, or even to privatise economic activity formerly under governemnt jurisdiction. The latter is arguably the case with Cuba's new non-agricultural cooperatives stemming from the Communist Party's economic reforms of 2011–12.[87] We could also mention nationalisation schemes that form workers' self- or co-managed farms or industrial plants. Historically, we can think of the *kolkhozy* in the former USSR, China's nationalised industry in the 1940s and 1950s and township and village enterprises (TVEs) beginning in the 1980s, self-managed firms in the former Yugoslavia, or Bolivarian Venezuela's *unidades/empresas de producción socialista/social* (SPEs, socialist or social production enterprises).[88]

In contrast, today's *empreseas recuperadas por sus trabajadores* have workers *initiating* the recuperation of the firm while also fully converting it to workers' collective *ownership* and *administration*, both important for the radical concept of *autogestión* that will be developed in Chapters 4 and 5. Rising in numbers in recent years in national contexts afflicted by neo-liberal crises, ERTs tend to specifically arise as worker-led responses to the imminent or full closure or bankruptcy of the firm that has employed them or from out of conflicts between employees and the firm's owners or managers. At times they can also emerge from succession issues of an otherwise healthy firm when new

---

87   There has been a new wave of non-agricultural cooperatives in Cuba since 2012 in sectors such as tourism, public transport, logistics, light manufacturing, services, and construction. 77 percent of them have emerged from the conversion of state enterprises to worker cooperatives. This has been an initiative encouraged by the 2011–12 economic reforms of the Sixth Congress of the Communist Party and the passage of a new law of cooperatives in late 2012. For more, see Giovannini and Vieta 2017; Piñeiro Harnecker 2013, 2016; and Vieta 2018a.

88   Bayat 1990; Chun 2006; Azzellini 2011; El Universal 2012; Larrabure, Vieta, and Schugurensky 2011; Vieta, Larrabure, and Schugurensky 2012; Weitzman and Chenggang 1994. Less clear here is the Italian state's confiscation or expropriation of mafia-owned properties and conversion to worker cooperatives. Once confiscated or expropriated, these properties are handed over to worker or community ownership and administration. These experiments could thus be considered state-initiated ERTS (Vieta et al. 2017). While in these conversion processes workers do eventually fully control and administer the firm, most often, however, workers do not initiate the conversion.

investors cannot be found to continue the business after owner-retirement or exit. Most commonly, ERT worker-protagonists recuperate a formerly capitalist firm.[89] While less common, ERTs can also be formed from the conversion of established cooperatives to new cooperatives, usually when the former cooperative has entered a period of crisis putting at risk its continuity or when the administrative council or board of the former cooperative has lost the confidence of the broader assembly of members. This was the case, for instance, in one of Argentina's first ERTs, Industria Metalúrgicas y Plásticas Argentina (IMPA).[90] Equally uncommon, ERTs can also arise from worker-initiated takeovers and conversions of branch-plants of multinationals, as we saw with the case of UST in Chapter 1 and as we will see with France's Fralib shortly.

In sum, as Andrés Ruggeri reminds us, what distinguishes ERTs is not so much the type of firm they emerge from nor the legal form they take once workers have recuperated them; what distinguishes them, rather, is that the employees who were formerly employed in the previous firm *initiate* its conversion and become *co-owners* and *co-administrators* of the subsequent workplace. In other words, what primarily differentiates ERTs from other kinds of conversions to LMFs is that the workers themselves transform a business into one that is collectively managed and owned by the same employees of the former firm under the auspices of *autogestión*.[91] Most importantly, this definition of ERTs is guided by ERT worker-protagonists' own conceptualisations of their self-managed projects. As many ERT workers have told me over the years, what differentiates ERTs from other businesses (including other forms of cooperatives and labour-managed entities) is that they, the ex-employees of the former business, took the initiative – usually during situations of crisis or collective duress that threatened the loss of their jobs – to convert the firm to worker-ownership and -control under the guidance of *autogestión*.

2.1   *Types of* Empressas Recuperadas *Today*

Most broadly, we can identify two common types of ERTs today: The 'labour-conflict' ERT and the 'negotiated' ERT.

Recent years have witnessed a rise in the 'labour-conflict' ERT, especially in countries and communities hardest hit by the fallout of market failures, firm closures, and economic crises driven by neo-liberal policies. It is no coincidence, therefore, that these conflict-driven ERTs are mainly to be found in Latin

---

89   Investor-owned, sole proprietary, partnerships, or other capitalist business forms.
90   For more on IMPA, see Chapters 6 and 7.
91   Ruggeri et al. 2010; Ruggeri and Vieta 2015.

America and in other regions where urban economic sectors have particularly suffered from crises and austerity, such as in southern Europe. Labour-conflict ERTs emerge in situations with some degree of conflict between workers and owners, management, and/or local and regional authorities, as has happened for instance in Argentina, Brazil, and Uruguay and with new ERTs in southern Europe today. Often, ERTs emerging out of labour conflicts also involve community activists, local unions, or social movement groups assisting workers in their struggle to save the firm and their jobs. Part of the resolution of these conflicts and the eventual conversion of firms to workers' control includes transitioning them legally into worker cooperatives or other forms of worker ownership. In these scenarios, as has occurred in Latin America and more recently in Greece, Turkey, Spain, France, and Italy, the conversion process happens after the employee collective's occupation of the business, which can sometimes last weeks or months.[92] Also, part of the resolution of the conflict involves the collective of workers coming to some agreement with bankruptcy courts and/or local or regional authorities over the control or final purchase of the firm's assets.

Recent years have also seen the rise of what can be termed the 'negotiated' ERT, a form especially prevalent in southern Europe and North America, but also in some cases in Argentina and in other Latin American countries. These ERTs are most often created via WBOs, where the purchase and eventual conversion of the firm by workers is negotiated with exiting owners or management, often with the mediation and assistance of local, regional, or national authorities.[93] In the negotiated ERT, workers sometimes establish what is called a 'newco' or trust, a separate legal entity entrusted to manage the funds that will be used to purchase or, in some cases, lease all or parts of the 'target company' on behalf of the employee group. As with Italy's WBO model under its Legge Marcora (Marcora Law) framework (detailed below), the

---

92   As with ERTs in Argentina, Brazil, and Uruguay, or the cases of Fralib in France, Ri-Maflow and Officine Zero in Italy, VioMe in Greece, Kazova in Turkey, and Musicop and Profinox in Spain, all reviewed shortly.

93   WBOs are scenarios where workers purchase some or all of the assets of the firm as business rescues or succession initiatives. These asset purchases (or sometimes leases) often occur as negotiations between workers, former owners, and at times the state, and are, in jurisdictions where they are prevelent, guided by established legal frameworks (Jensen, 2012; Quarter and Brown 1992; Vieta et al. 2017). WBOs can develop through employees buying out wholesale the property, machines, trademarks and patents, and customer lists and restarting the entire business as a worker-owned firm, or employees can purchase parts of the business and start production elsewhere as a new, or '*de novo*', worker-owned firm (Ben-Ner 1988; Quarter 1995).

creation of negotiated ERTs is further facilitated by clear legislation for such buyouts and involves various stakeholders such as local business experts, lawyers, the cooperative sector, or unions, as well as local, regional, or national authorities.[94] In some instances, such as with Québec's worker-shareholder cooperatives, Spain's *sociedades laborales* (SALs, labour societies), France's *société coopérative ouvrières de production* (SCOPs, society of workers' cooperatives of production), and as with Argentina's PAUNY tractor factory,[95] employees of an existing company may form a worker cooperative or labour-managed firm and purchase or be granted a portion of the stock of the target company, entering into a co-ownership agreement with the target company's other shareholders.[96] In this scenario, which can be characterised as a partial ERT, the worker cooperative may or may not also participate directly in the management of the firm, depending on the agreement reached with the target company's original owners and administrators. Other examples of negotiated ERTs include business succession plans supported by retiring or exiting owners whereby they cede or sell the business to the firm's employees.[97]

We should also briefly address a third possible model – the employee share ownership plan (ESOP). As with nationalisation schemes that include some form of workers' control, or co-ownership agreements between a worker cooperative and other shareholders, ESOPs tend to be partial recuperations or conversions. Because ESOPs tend to not include administration rights for workers, they are not, in the main, ERTs. It is nevertheless worth mentioning ESOPS as an unrealised third model for ERT creation since some (albeit very few) ESOP initiatives have included conversions to full workers' control. This would be the case when ESOPs take on 100 percent employee ownership and practice extensive worker participation in the running of the firm, an example of which is Colorado's New Belgium Brewing Company.[98]

Legislated formally in the United States in the 1970s with the reforms of its pension laws, the ESOP model originated in that country in the 1950s when Louis Kelso permitted the employees of Peninsula Newspapers to purchase the company using share ownership.[99] Growing in numbers throughout the 1970s

---

94   Vieta et al. 2017.
95   On PAUNY, see Chapter 6.
96   Jensen 2011; Soulage 2011; Vieta et al. 2017.
97   Business successions to employees are long-held practices in Canada, the United States, and the UK, for instance. Two of the most famous succession initiatives are David Erdal's ceding of his family firm to employees (Erdal 2011) and the Scott Bader Commonwealth (Hoe 1978), both in the UK.
98   Palmer 2015.
99   Kelso and Adler 1958; Narvaez 1991.

and 1980s, ESOPs have re-emerged in recent years in the US, Canada, and the UK in particular.[100] ESOPs enable employees to purchase shares of the company where they work, usually via a trust, and ownership of the company is then shared between employees and other types of more traditional shareholders.[101] In many cases, the ESOP purchase is financed through workers' pension plans, but can also be financed by employees' personal savings or via loans. Today in the United States over 7,000 firms have ESOPs involving over 13.5 million employees, including companies such as Publix Supermarkets, Price Chopper, W.L. Gore, and Austin Industries.[102] In Canada, WestJet has incorporated an ESOP model, while United Airlines attempted an ESOP model, unsuccessfully, in the 1990s.[103]

ESOPs, it must be emphasised again, in almost all cases do not become *worker-recuperated* firms since workers tend not to initiate or lead the process, and nor does the firm transfer to their complete ownership and control.[104] In ESOPs, rather, workers' participation in the firm is usually limited to a partial ownership stake via shares, and management in most cases retains administrative control. Moreover, the vast majority of ESOPs are primarily incentivised by offering tax credits to the firms' original owners.[105] More problematic for the radical alternatives that interest us in this book, ESOPs may be considered an example of the doctrine of a 'people's capitalism',[106] or even a capitalism with a human face, doing little to address the fundamental contradictions inherent to the social relations of capitalist production. Hence for Peter Ranis, ESOPs are not ERTs nor do they offer radical alternatives for the working class since they do not include employees' direct control of the company's assets or management rights and are most often deployed as tax-saving schemes by owners rather than for the benefit of workers.[107] More concerning, as Ranis underscores, the 'marginal wage differentials' created by ESOP schemes serve to purchase labour peace for bosses, effectively 'mollifying any potential worker confrontation with their paternalistic job environment' while further conditioning workers to 'the arbitrary decisions foisted upon them in the workplace'.[108] Overall, we can thus agree that the ESOP model certainly does not, in practice,

---

100   NCEO 2014.
101   Kruse, Freeman, and Blasi 2010; Vieta, Quarter, Spear, and Moskovskaya 2016.
102   NCEO 2014.
103   Manjoo 2002.
104   Ellerman 1985.
105   Curl 2009.
106   Phillips 2003, p. 29.
107   Ranis 2016, p. 35.
108   Ibid.

promise the radical social innovations for workers' control as do labour conflict or even negotiated ERTS, which most often do include workers' full ownership *and* administrative control of the firm.

2.2   *ERT Experiences from around the World*

Spikes in recent years in the number of new 'labour conflict' and 'negotiated' ERTS in jurisdictions hardest hit by the most recent economic crisis are not coincidental. Besides in Latin America, there has been, throughout the past four decades of neo-liberal global capitalism – and especially since the 2008 crisis – a growth in new worker cooperatives emanating from workers taking over the troubled companies that had been employing them. As we shall shortly see in the following pages, conversions that we could also call ERTS have emerged in France, Spain, Italy, and to a lesser degree in other national contexts.[109] While they are perhaps less well-known than their South American cousins, other ERT experiences around the world are, as in Argentina, proving to be equally promising for saving jobs, businesses, and even local communities from further depletion, especially in the wake of continued struggles with crisis and austerity.[110]

A discussion of Argentina's ERTS in the context of and as responses to the ongoing crises of the neo-liberal paradigm would not be complete without at least briefly mentioning other contemporary ERT-type experiences in other countries in Latin America and their presence elsewhere. In what follows, we will take an approach that is illustrative (rather than exhaustive) and wide-angled (rather than partisan). We will not limit our overview of ERTS here to those that have been specifically influenced by non-statist, autonomist, or other leftist political approaches, as some commentators of ERTS do today, but instead focus in on national contexts where various types of non-institution-alised and institutionalised forms of workplace conversions to cooperatives or other forms of labour-managed firms are present and that, in some way, involve workers responding to the crisis of the neo-liberal model. Hence, most of the examples we will draw on in the remaining pages of this chapter concentrate on instances where workers themselves have been, to some extent, the principal drivers of workplace occupations and conversions.

---

109   Jensen, 2011, 2012; Soulage, 2011; Vieta 2013, 2014a; Vieta et al. 2017; Zanotti, 2011.
110   Vieta et al. 2017.

2.2.1   Other Latin American Experiences

Besides in Argentina, there are ERT-type experiences throughout Latin America in Bolivia, Brazil, Colombia, Ecuador, Mexico, Peru, Venezuela, Uruguay, and in very small pockets in a few other countries. Next to Argentina's experiences, however, and for reasons we will elaborate on in the next few pages, Brazil's and Uruguay's are the most developed in Latin America, while Venezuela's potential for a large ERT sector was subdued by the late 2000s when the government of then-president Hugo Chávez favoured other 'co-management' and workers' control under nationalisation initiatives. Additionally, a recent decree by the Bolivian government of Evo Morales supporting workplace recuperations shows much promise for the creation of new ERTs in that country.[111] Colombia, Ecuador, and Mexico have only a few cases of ERTs mobilised by workers and local unions in a few specific cases of workplace conflict.[112] And in Peru, a handful of ERT-type worker cooperatives share the scene with hundreds of smaller self-managed agricultural and housing initiatives, which could more rightly be called self-managed community-based social enterprises.[113] Because of the relative embryonic nature of ERTs in Colombia, Peru, Mexico, and Ecuador, closer economic and political comparisons to Argentina can be made from an assessment of Brazilian, Uruguayan, Venezuelan, and Bolivian experiences.

Brazil. In Brazil, *empresas recuperadas por trabalhadores* (worker-recuperated enterprises) (also called *empresas autogeridas*, self-managed enterprises) began to emerge in the 1980s and especially in the early 1990s as a consequence of the rise in bankruptcies and unemployment catalysed by a plethora of neo-liberal policies overseen by the national governments of Fernando Collor de Melo (1990–2), Itamar Franco (1992–5), and Fernando Cardoso (1995–2002).[114] As with Argentina, many of Brazil's 67 recorded ERTs, which employ 10–12,000 workers, take on the organisational structure of worker cooperat-

---

111   Fidler 2013.

112   For instance, see Cuninghame 2016; Huertas, Ladron de Guevara, and Castillo 2010; Ministerio de Coordinación y Desarrollo Social 2010. Of these experiences, Mexico's two well-documented cases of ERTs are worth noting for their resilience over the years and their influence in the country's broader labour movement and struggles: the tire manufacturer Tradoc (taken over and restarted as a cooperative by its workers in 2001) and the older beverage manufacturer Sociedad Cooperativa Trabajadores de Pascual (formed as a cooperative in 1985) (La Coperacha 2016). Their presence, however, has not yet translated into a broader ERT movement in Mexico.

113   Babilón Poma 2005; Peredo and Chrisman 2006.

114   Chedid Henriques, Moreira Sígolo, Rufino, Santos Araújo, Nepomuceno et al. 2013; Novaes 2007; Paulucci 2013; Sardá de Faria and Novaes 2011.

ives,[115] although it is now also possible to organise self-managed firms as 'limited [liability] companies or corporations'.[116]

While Brazil's early ERTs, as in Argentina, experienced resistance from the broader union movement, ERT workers' demands for recognition would soon result in the support of workplace recuperation initiatives by many of the country's unions. Over the years, Brazilian ERTs have also enjoyed the solid presence of self-managed workers' associations linked to the country's union and solidarity economy movements, such as the União e Solidariedade das Cooperativas de São Paulo (UNISOL São Paulo, Union and Solidarity of Cooperatives of Sao Paulo), founded in 1999 by cooperatives in the metallurgical sector in the state of Sao Paulo and the metallurgical union, later growing nationally to become the Central de Cooperativas e Empreendimentos Solidários de Economia Social do Brasil (UNISOL Brasil, Central of Cooperatives and Solidarity Enterprises of the Social Economy of Brazil) which as of 2010 embraced around 280 cooperatives, including 25 *empresas autogeridas*.[117] In 1999 the Central Única dos Trabalhadores (CUT, Unified Workers' Central) also created the Agência de Desenvolvimento Solidário (ADS/CUT, Agency of Solidary Development), which 'provides credit and technical assistance for groups wishing to set up cooperatives'.[118] Hence, for much longer than in Argentina, unions in Brazil have been actively involved in assisting workers in processes of company takeovers and the challenges of self-management.

ERT-specific umbrella organisations have also played an important part in the development of the phenomenon in Brazil. For instance, the Associação Nacional dos Trabalhadores em Empresas de Autogestão e Participação Acionária (ANTEAG, National Association of Workers of Self-Managed and Participatory Share Enterprises), Brazil's first ERT-specific umbrella association, was founded in 1994 with the creation of the first ERTs in the country, including the Markeli shoe company in the state of Sao Paulo, the Coperminas mining firm in the state of Santa Catarina, and the Catende Harmonia Project sugar mill in the state of Pernambuco.[119] ANTEAG assists member *autogeridas* with

---

115   Some studies have estimated that somewhere around 260 ERTs might have existed in Brazil, while most studies agree that around 70 experiences with workplace conversions in the country are definitely ERTs of the type found in Argentina (Chedid Henriques et al. 2013). Calculating the exact number of ERTs in Brazil is complicated by the fact that the country's official government databases lump ERTs together with other cooperatives and solidarity economy inititives.

116   Sardá de Faria and Novaes 2011, p. 407. See also Chedid Henriques 2014.

117   Sardá de Faria and Novaes 2011, p. 404.

118   Ibid.

119   Sardá de Faria and Novaes 2011, p. 403.

their technological and administrative needs, brings them together with other solidarity economy organisations, facilitates the market insertion of ERTs, and generally liaises with the state. Moreover, the Brazilian state had considered ERTs – although not without tensions and contradictions – as integral players in its burgeoning (and formally recognised) solidarity economy and, subsequently, they had enjoyed some of the attention of the Worker's Party and national government via the auspices of the National Secretary of the Solidarity Economy overseen by the Ministry of Labour. Consequently, some Brazilian self-managed workers have not had to traverse as many political and economic hurdles as their Argentine counterparts in terms of access to soft loans, government grants, and technical assistance,[120] while others have experienced similar and ongoing challenges to their self-management projects, including isolation from other ERTs and difficulties in attaining loans or state subsidies.[121]

Uruguay. As in Argentina, ERT-like experiences have existed in Uruguay since at least the mid-twentieth century.[122] Uruguay's circa 50 contemporary ERTs,[123] again similar to Argentina's contemporary ERTs, began to emerge around the late 1990s as responses to growing unemployment and firm bankruptcies in a country with an economy heavily intertwined with Argentina's and Brazil's.[124] The subsequent institutional experiences of Uruguay's ERTs, however, differ from Argentina's in that they, like Brazil's ERTs, were supported early on by the country's union federation, the Plenario Intersindical de Trabajadores–Convención Nacional de Trabajadores (PIT–CNT, Inter-Union Assembly of Workers–National Workers' Central). Uruguay's ERTs have thus on the whole enjoyed more economic stability when compared to Argentina's. In addition, Martí et al. (2004) contend that because in Uruguay, in contrast to Argentina, there has been historically a tighter and more amiable relationship

---

120   Ghibaudi 2004.
121   Sardá de Faria and Novaes 2011.
122   Martí, Thul, and Cancela 2013.
123   There is a lack of clarity in the literature regarding how many ERTs actually exist in Uruguay; figures range from 20 to 50 or more enterprises. This lack of clarity is due to several factors, including how the 'recuperation' of companies is defined in the country, and the fact that some worker cooperatives in Uruguay that consider themselves worker-recuperated firms did not have the majority of its workers emerging from a previous capitalist firm. Consequently, there is an ongoing discussion between social and solidarity economy associations, unions, the state, and academics in Uruguay concerning what exactly characterises a self-managed ERT in that country (see Guerra 2013, p. 29).
124   As in Argentina, there were several earlier ERT-type experiences in Uruguay that responded to the crisis of deindustrialisation in the 1970s and 1980s but that failed to prosper long-term due to the depleted conditions of the firms and the lack of supports (Guerra 2013, p. 23).

between working-class organisations and the traditional cooperative sector, the Federación de Cooperativas de Producción del Uruguay (FCPU, Federation of Producer Cooperatives of Uruguay) has played a major role in supporting and helping to articulate the methods for converting formerly owner-managed or otherwise capitalist workspaces into worker cooperatives. The FCPU has also done much to secure start-up funds for new ERTs as well as offering them various forms of technical, educational, and administrative assistance.[125] The ERT-specific umbrella organisation Asociación Nacional de Empresas Recuperadas por sus Trabajadores (ANERT, National Association of Worker-Recuperated Enterprises) and new technical assistance programmes offered by the Universidad de la República have also risen in importance in recent years, and both work closely with the FCPU in joint initiatives geared at assisting with the technical needs of the country's ERTs.[126] And, while Uruguay does not have a formal process of expropriation for ERTs as does Argentina, the government of leftist president José Mujica had in the early 2010s set aside a fund entitled Fondo para el Desarollo (FONDES, Development Fund) of US$110 million for securing national policies and mechanisms aimed at self-managed organisations and consisting of soft loans (administered by the National Bank of Uruguay), capacity building, and to provide for the educational needs of self-managed workers.[127]

Venezuela. By the mid-2000s, the Venezuelan government of now-deceased president Hugo Chávez was inspired by the ERT experiences in Argentina, Brazil, and Uruguay and contributed to Chávez's vision of blending self-managed workspaces with his project of nationalising industrial plants via *cogestión* (co-management).[128] In contrast to the Argentine, Brazilian, and Uruguayan ERT movements, where only a handful of ERTs have advocated for nationalisation solutions,[129] the concept of *cogestión* in Venezuela fully embraces

---

125   Camilletti, Guidini, Herrera, Rodríguez, Martí, et al. 2005; Guerra 2013; Martí et al. 2004; Vitabar 2005.

126   Paulucci 2013.

127   Dellatorre 2013; Rieiro 2017.

128   Lebowitz 2005. For more on Venezuela's contribution to the concept of *cogestión*, see Chapter 5.

129   In Brazil, a handful of ERTs have been advocating nationalisation solutions (Sardá de Faria and Novaes 2011), while in Argentina, the famed Zanón/FaSinPat ceramics manufacturer in the province of Neuquén and the city of Buenos Aires textile cooperative Brukman have both demanded nationalisation of ERTs (Aiziczón 2009; Lavaca 2004; Picchetti 2002). However, in both Brazil and Argentina, the nationalisation solution for ERTs has not taken off practically or politically. In Uragay, ERTs have not sought nationalisation solutions given the stronger supports ERTs there have received from the state and the labour and cooperative sectors (Paulucci 2013). For more on the decision of the early Argentine ERT

nationalisation and has affinities with the former Yugoslavia's model of state-sponsored worker self-managed factories working within a mixed market and planned economy. There were signs that an expansive worker-led ERT phenomenon was developing in Venezuela by the middle of the 2000s; indeed, in mid-2005 the Chávez government was proposing expropriating hundreds of troubled firms and converting them to worker-controlled firms.[130] Nevertheless, ERTs as found in other parts of Latin America have been slower to emerge in Venezuela. According to Marie Trigona, while by late 2006 the Venezuelan government had indicated that around 1,200 capitalist companies had (as in Argentina, Brazil, and Uruguay) declared bankruptcy, been abandoned by their owners, occupied by their workers, or otherwise deemed to be suitable for conversions, only 'some 20 companies [had] been formally nationalized and function[ed] under worker co-management or control' by the end of that year.[131] As of early 2016, according to the Venezuelan government news agency AVN, around 85 firms had been converted to worker cooperatives, almost all via processes of nationalisation under workers' control.[132] Other workers from closed or troubled firms that did not become worker-initiated ERTs would go on to work at the *unidades/empresas de producción socialista/social* (SPES)[133] or in the burgeoning cooperative sector that had been expanding in recent years.

One explanation for the stunted nature of worker-initiated ERTs in Venezuela has to do with the government's active support of the creation of cooperatives in the early 2000s via the Special Law of Cooperative Associations and the Vuelvan Caras cooperative development initiatives; both of these initiatives incentivised under- and unemployed workers to create *de novo* cooperatives rather than convert firms. By 2006, the mostly micro-cooperatives that emerged from these initiatives numbered almost 159,000[134] and by 2009 they included over 286,000 cooperatives.[135] In addition, other workers have been absorbed into the more than 3,000 SPES and other co-managed enterprises that span the country.[136] It can be argued that these government-sanctioned initiatives have directly addressed the immediate needs of otherwise under-

---

protagonists to choose the cooperative path rather than nationalisation, see Chapters 6 and 7. For more on Zanón/FaSinPat, see Chapter 6.

130   Venezuelanalysis.com 2005.
131   Trigona 2006d, para. 2.
132   Agencia Venezolana de Notícias 2016.
133   State-owned and worker-managed enterprises (Vieta, Larrabure, and Schugurensky 2011; Larrabure, Vieta, and Schugurensky 2012).
134   Piñeiro Harnecker 2007.
135   Vieta et al. 2012.
136   Vieta et al. 2012.

or unemployed workers in recent years and have thus curbed workers' own impetus for converting failing firms that had employed them into ERTs. In other words, while occupations of failing capitalist firms were inspired and even openly encouraged by Chávez's vision of a worker-led Bolivarian Revolution in the mid-2000s – which would have seen strong state support of arguably hundreds of incipient Venezuelan ERTs, and could have become an ERT movement larger than Argentina's – the Venezuelan state has had a prominent role in articulating another vision for workers' control. Indeed, Venezuela's version of *cogestión* – articulated in its 'triangle' of the 'popular economy'[137] – has attempted to go beyond the need for workers to go through the uncertain process of creating ERTs.[138]

As a response to Venezuela's nationalisation-centred plan for the formation of ERTS, a grassroots, worker-based umbrella group called the Frente Revoloucionario de Trabajadores de Empresas en Cogestión y Ocupadas (FRETECO, Revolutionary Front of Enterprises Co-managed and Occupied by Workers) was formed in mid-2006 by workers of the nationalised and worker-managed industrial valve manufacturing plant INVEVAL in order to 'strategize how the worker occupied factory movement can multiply industry under genuine worker control'.[139] Despite FRETECO's subsequent energetic interventions in national economic policy and its continued push for the recuperation and workers' self-management of failing capitalist firms, it had met challenges regarding any quickening of the pace of Chávez's and, more recently, President Nicolás Maduro's nationalisation plans in light of other solutions favoured for the country's popular economy, such as *cogestión*, communal councils and communes, socialist or 'communal social property' enterprises, and cooperatives.[140]

Bolivia. In Bolivia, cooperatives and grassroots occupations of property are most readily found in the primary resource sectors such as mining, agriculture, and water provisioning.[141] In addition to the already-mentioned nationalisation and co-management projects of the 1950s and 1970s, a radical wave of

---

137 Reviewed in detail in Chapter 5, Venezuela's socialist triangle of production includes 'social ownership of the means of production, social production organised by workers, and production for social needs and purposes' (Vieta et al. 2012, p. 145; see also Azzellini 2011, 2017; and Lebowitz 2005). It purposefully constrasts with the capitalist economic triangle of private ownership of the means of production, hierarchical control of production, and privatised profit.

138 Campos 2007.

139 Trigona 2006d, para. 3. See also Azzellini 2011.

140 Azzellini 2011, 2017.

141 Ceceña 2005; Bocangel 2001.

temporary factory occupations and bossnappings by workers also occurred in La Paz and Sucre in 1985 as workers' direct responses to rising economic difficulties.[142] But if we stick to our definition of ERTs – troubled capitalist firms that are subsequently taken over by former employees and transformed into some type of labour-managed enterprise – the ERT experience in Bolivia comes into better focus. Up until 2013, for instance, only a few small-scale mining cooperatives could have been called ERTs, while the majority of related initiatives were in reality community-led cooperatives (at times also supported by unions or other social justice movements) that responded to privatisation schemes and other neo-liberal encroachments.

Evo Morales' recent governmental decree allowing for workers in troubled or bankrupted firms to set up 'social enterprises' has been a promising new turn. In October 2013, at a gathering attended by hundreds of union members as part of the 62nd anniversary celebrations of the founding of the Confederación General de Trabajadores Fabriles de Bolivia (CGTFB, General Confederation of Industrial Workers of Bolivia), Morales and Labour Minister Daniel Santalla foresaw the growth of new worker-recuperated firms with Decree 1754 under the auspices of Article 54 of the 2009 constitution. The Bolivian government now explicitly supports the formation of what it calls 'empresas sociales' (social enterprises, which are, in effect, worker-run businesses) from the conversion of capitalist or public-sector firms that have closed due to fraudulent business practices or bankruptcy.[143] By 2014, a handful of social enterprise ERTs, all in the La Paz metropolitan area, had been established under the provisions of Article 54 in the textile sector, such as Enatex, Instrabol, and Traboltex,[144] with others having emerged in subsequent years including the textile social enterprises Punto Blanco and Polar, and the ceramics social enterprise Victoria. It remains to be seen how widespread ERTs will become in Bolivia as a result of this new legal framework. While these new ERTs have experienced continued difficulties due to unfavourable debt burdens from the previous firm (including debts based on unpaid taxes owed by former owners), the CGTGB has been working with the Bolivian state to find a legal solution to these issues.[145] On the whole, the new institutional soil and the strong support of the CGTGB seem to be pointing to the possibility of more ERTs emerging in Bolivia in the coming years.

---

142   Ottawa Citizen 1985.
143   Callejas 2014; Quispe 2013.
144   Fidler 2013.
145   Chávez 2016.

2.2.2   European Experiences

'Labour-conflict' ERTs similar to Argentina's have been an increasing trend since the Great Recession of 2008 in Europe, in countries such as Italy, France, Spain, Greece, and Turkey. A much larger number of 'negotiated' ERTs, however, has existed on the European continent for several decades. In a handful of European jurisdictions, specific legislation has facilitated the conversions of businesses into worker cooperatives, other forms of labour-managed firms, or employee share-ownership arrangements. In Spain, for instance, the emergence of some strictly labour-conflict ERTs and, more commonly, WBOs has been facilitated by its *pago único* (sole contribution) scheme,[146] its SAL model of LMF, as well as various regional initiatives for conversions to worker cooperatives. In France, its SCOP worker cooperative model, favourable national legislation, and cooperative movement support have also converged to promote new WBOs. The negotiated, mostly WBO solutions found in France and Spain emulate Italy's Legge Marcora framework for creating new worker cooperatives; as we will see, this framework is perhaps Europe's most advanced form of negotiated ERT-creation mechanism.[147] And employee share-ownership provisions have existed for several decades in the United Kingdom. The UK also has older experiences with ERTs dating back to its workplace occupations and Industrial Common Ownership Movement (ICOM) of the 1970s, and ERT-type experiences continue to emerge to this day, with a modest but promising number still in existence in England, Wales, and Scotland.

In recent years, European Union policy proposals and cooperative sector consultants and social researchers in a handful of member states have been seriously considering strengthening initiatives for 'business transfers' to workers, the European term for the creation of new worker cooperatives from conversions of troubled businesses or firms with succession issues. Over the past 15 or so years, there has been a surge of policy reports, opinion papers, and resolutions at the level of the European Union that have attempted to deal with broader proposals and recommendations for business transfers to employees.[148] In addition, CECOP–CICOPA Europe (the European confederation of industrial and service cooperatives) has been heavily involved in lobbying the EU in order to influence policy seeking to fast-track business transfers to employees across the continent.[149]

---

146   Reviewed shortly, the *pago único* is, in brief, a programme allowing employees to tap into unemployment benefits for capitalising cooperative start-ups and buyouts.

147   Vieta et al. 2017.

148   For a thorough review of European business transfer policy initiatives, see Vieta et al. 2017, pp. 16–30.

149   CECOP–CICOPA Europe 2012a, 2012b, 2013.

Italy. Worker-led occupations of firms have been occurring in Italy since the early part of the twentieth century, such as the massive occupations of factories in Turin during the *biennio rosso* of 1919–20.[150] They would re-emerge again during Italy's reconstruction after World War II and during the years of social and labour strife in the 1970s. Throughout the 1970s, the Italian cooperative federation Lega Nazionale delle Cooperative e Mutue (Legacoop, National League of Cooperatives and Mutuals), historically representing the largest number of worker cooperative affiliates in the country, assisted in the conversion of over 100 failing firms to worker cooperatives.[151] Italy's contemporary phenomenon of mostly WBO-based, negotiated ERTs would take off in the early-to-mid 1980s during a period of persistent economic difficulties and, particularly, with the passing of supportive legislation and the creation of new forms of financial support mechanisms.[152]

As with most cases of ERTs around the world, contemporary Italian ERTs have had a pattern of development following closely the country's microeconomic ebbs and flows, including, as we saw with Argentina's ERTs, stubbornly high unemployment and downward trends in GDP.[153] Contemporary Italian ERTs began to emerge as workers' responses to the rise in unemployment caused by the business downsizings, restructurings, and closures of large parts of its industrial sector during the 1970s and 1980s. Much of this economic upheaval and restructuring was also due to the recessions caused by the oil price shocks of 1970s as well as the increased competition that Italy's traditional manufacturing sector has faced from developing countries, with cheaper labour markets, more lax labour laws and practices, or more productive labour processes.[154]

Italian ERTs would particularly take off after the passing of Law 49/1985 on 27 February 1985, commonly known as Legge Marcora (Marcora Law) after the Minister of Industry who sponsored it, Giovanni Marcora.[155] The number of new Italian ERTs has recently surged again due to the after-effects of the 2008 financial crisis and the influence of additional complementary cooperative and business legislation and further reforms to Legge Marcora in recent years. As of the beginning of 2015, there were 131 known active ERTs in Italy, while approximately 300 or so have existed since the 1980s, with the vast major-

---

150   Earle 1986; Forgacs 2000.
151   Earle 1986.
152   Vieta et al. 2017.
153   Vieta 2015; Vieta et al. 2017.
154   Morone and Testa 2008; Whitford 2001.
155   Dandolo 2009.

ity of them being SMEs consisting of between 10 and 50 workers.[156] Almost 70 percent of Italy's ERTs are found in the manufacturing sector, including woodworking, metallurgy, footwear, textiles, food processing, and in some heavier industries such as shipbuilding. The highest concentrations of ERTs are located in the administrative regions of Toscana, Emilia Romagna, Veneto, Umbria, Le Marche, and Lazio.[157] These are regions renowned for their interlinked, multi-firm, and SME-based production processes of specialty-made goods in what is commonly called the 'Third Italy' or the 'Made in Italy' manufacturing regions.[158] In recent years Legge Marcora provisions have also been used for a growing number of state-led conversions of mafia-run businesses that are ceded to employees.[159]

Most Italian ERTs are of the 'negotiated' variety, with the vast majority consisting of WBO solutions emerging from collaborations between workers and their union representatives, the cooperative movement, and the Italian state. As in Argentina after its 2011 reforms to its bankruptcy laws,[160] Italian employees of firms in liquidation or in bankruptcy proceedings have a right-of-first refusal in bidding for and taking over the firm. Unlike in Argentina but as in Spain, Italian employees contemplating a WBO may also request an advance of their unused unemployment insurance and severance pay in order to finance the conversion of the firm into a worker cooperative or for starting a *de novo* worker cooperative. Employees involved in a WBO project most often will also eventually work with one of the Italian cooperative confederations, such as Legacoop or the Confederazione Cooperative Italiane (Confcooperative, Italian Cooperative Confederation). The members of the new worker cooperative can access technical assistance and know-how and secure share-capital or debt-capital financing from the confederations' portion of the cooperative movement's *fondo mutualistico* (mutualistic fund). The *fondo mutualistico*, the national fund for cooperative development, is capitalised by three percent of

---

156   The exact number of Italian ERT experiences is not known, since there is no formal designation for conversions in Italy and since no universal database of these experiences exists. The only known attempt at systematically documenting known Italian ERTs emerging in the years since the passing of Legge Marcora has been carried out by a team led by this book's author and working out of the European Research Institute of Cooperative and Social Enterprises (EURICSE). For more on this research, see Vieta et al. 2017.

157   Vieta et al. 2017.

158   Bagnasco 1977; Becattini and Ottati 2006; Piore and Sabel 1984; Triglia and Burroni 2009; Vieta, et al. 2017.

159   Vieta et al. 2017.

160   See Chapter 6.

all Italian cooperatives' yearly net income that, by legislation, must be contributed to the fund on an annual basis, and also from the remaining proceeds of
dissolved Italian cooperatives. Complemented by numerous laws and provisions guiding Italian cooperative societies, the Italian state, via Legge Marcora
provisions and the law's subsequent reforms, has made available two additional funds for the start-up, development, or consolidation of work-generating
cooperatives in order to promote and secure levels of employment in times of
crisis and for the conversion of businesses in crisis into cooperatives: a rotating
fund consisting of soft loans known as Foncooper, and a 'Special Fund' consisting of risk-capital financing. Much of the Legge Marcora process for WBOs
has been managed by two national institutional investors: Cooperazione Finanza Imprese (CFI) and, to a much lesser extent, Società Finanza Cooperazione
(SOFICOOP).[161] Both CFI and SOFICOOP have been mandated by the Italian
state, via the auspices of the Ministry of Economic Development, to coordinate
and facilitate within the Legge Marcora framework the financing of cooperative
start-ups, the consolidation of established work-generating cooperatives, and
WBOs.

In addition to the institutionalised process of ERT formation via its Legge
Marcora framework (which in 2015 included the worker buyout of the famed
Communist newspaper *Il manifesto*), in the last few years there have been what
has been called 'non-institutional workplace takeovers emerging from company crisis, conflict, and workers' occupation of the property', which are akin
to Argentina's *empresas recuperadas*.[162] These 'non-institutionalised' Italian
ERTs are more anti-systemic and critical of both the state-based paths to WBO-
based conversions and Italy's traditional cooperative movemement, which
its protagonists view as being in the sevice of neo-liberal capitalist interests.
'Non-institutionalised' Italian ERTs thus do not tap into the Legge Marcora
framework and have histories of intensive struggles and occupations characterised by shop floor conflict and property takeovers by workers and community
members.[163] Two such cases that have garnered growing media, academic,

---

161   CFI, the larger of the two institutional investors and at the vanguard of financing and sup-
      porting Italy's WBOs, is a limited liability second-tier cooperative formed in 1986 as an
      initiative of Italy's three largest cooperative federations (Legacoop, Confcooperative, and
      AGCI), together with Italy's three major union federations (CGIL, CSIL, and UIL). To date,
      CFI has intervened in over three-quarters of the 257 Italian WBOs tracked by Vieta et al.
      (2017).
162   Vieta et al. 2017, pp. 149–53.
163   Ibid.

and activist attention in recent years include Ri-Maflow in Milan[164] and Officine Zero in Rome.[165]

Ri-Maflow emerged in 2013 from a former car-parts manufacturing company that went into bankruptcy. Its workers physically occupied the plant and
directly faced off with its former owners and the Milanese bankruptcy court,
managing to radically transform the firm into a new community-oriented productive space that also serves as a site for social and cultural initiatives. Adopting the slogan of *'Redito, Lavoro, Dignità, Autogestione'* ('Income, Work, Dignity, Self-Management'), the cooperative is now a vital centre of community
and cultural production in Italy's northwest and actively promotes and practices what it terms 'the other' social and solidarity-based economy, co-managed
cooperatively by a broad multistakeholder assembly and housing various community micro-enterprises. RiMaflow also initiated the Fuorimercato (meaning
both 'out of' and 'out with' the market) alternative economy network. Affiliated with the Via Campesina movement and Brazil's MST, Fuorimercato brings
together self-managed organic agriculture and urban cooperatives and communal experiments from across Italy by fostering solidarity exchanges and
alternative production initiatives. Moreover, in April 2019, RiMaflow hosted
the third gathering of the 'Euromediterranean' region of the 'Workers' Economy' conferences, where other European ERTs, activists, academics, cooperative sector protagonists, pro-self-management labour unions, and even policymakers joined Latin American ERTs and labour scholars in three days of
discussions. In the process of conversion, and via its myriad experiments in
autogestión, the Ri-Maflow workers have tapped into the spirit of Italy's older
autonomist and anarchist social centre movement[166] as well as being inspired
by experiments with workers' control and self-management in Argentina.[167]
Giving witness to the increased cross-pollination between ERT workers' experiments from around the world and the importance that the Argentine ERT
movement has had for these forms of workers' struggles today, the Ri-Maflow
workers have especially embraced the Argentine notion of *'la fábrica abierta'*
('the open factory'),[168] which they often use to describe their community-
oriented self-management project.

---

164   See, for instance, Azzellini and Ressler 2014; La Repubblica 2014; and Vieta et al. 2017.
165   See, for instance, Azzellini and Ressler 2015; and Vieta et al. 2017.
166   Pusey 2010.
167   Azzellini and Ressler 2014.
168   For more on Argentine ERTs' concept of *'la fábrica abierta'* and their networking with
       other experiences from around the world, see Chapters 7 and 8.

At the same time that the Ri-Maflow workers were organising and struggling to reclaim their workplace, the experiment known today as Officine Zero (that is, 'zero exploitation, zero bosses, zero contamination')[169] emerged in Rome's Casalbertone neighbourhood, a few blocks from the Tiburtina railway station. Officine Zero was born out of the closure of Officine RSI (Rail Service International, SpA) when a collective of ex-RSI workers and local community stakeholders decided – in the wake of the ongoing financial crisis and a dearth of alternative job prospects – to occupy the space of the RSI rail yard and restart a community-based production project. Uniquely, Officine Zero formed from a collective recuperation process that included a group of ex-employees of RSI, a larger group of community activists led by the neighbouring social centre Strike, and other precarious workers from across Rome. In the ensuing years, Officine Zero has become, like Ri-Maflow, a diverse and hybrid community production and work-integration experiment consisting of multiple participants and initiatives. The protagonists of Officine Zero originally spearheaded the idea that the skills relevant to rail maintenance could be re-deployed in provisioning socially useful goods. Since taking over the rail yard, Officine Zero has transformed into a community-managed facility that has taken on a multipurpose production model, including craft-based metal, textile, and woodworking shops; an electronics recycling initiative; a co-working space for self-employed knowledge economy workers, known as CowOz; a free and self-managed student housing complex called Mushrooms; a community kitchen; and a public meeting space that often hosts numerous community-based how-to workshops, conferences, and gatherings. Moreover, Officine Zero is also the headquarters of the newly formed union for precarious, contingent, and self-employed workers called the Camere del Lavoro Autonomo e Precario (CLAP, Chamber of Autonomous and Precarious Work).[170] And, like Ri-Maflow, Officine Zero was inspired by the experiences of Argentina's ERTs, the concept of *la fábrica abierta*, and the emergence and promotion of an alternative, solidarity-based economy.

France. In France today, ERTs, as in Italy, tend to also be in the main negotiated WBOs, with most conversions taking on the *société coopérative ouvrières de production* (SCOPs) worker cooperative model.[171] WBOs in France are particularly distinguished for their use in business succession cases of otherwise healthy firms.[172] By 2010, there were close to 1,600 SCOPs in France, with 12

169 Portal de Economía Solidaria 2014.
170 Ciccarelli 2015.
171 Pérotin 2006; Soulage 2011.
172 Soulage 2011.

percent emerging from the conversion of 'sound companies' and nine percent from the recuperation of 'ailing businesses'.[173] Moreover, mutual funds called *FCPE de reprise* were introduced in 2006 and can be used to finance new WBOS and *de novo* SCOPS.[174]

WBOS in France have also recently been bolstered by the country's Social and Solidarity Economy Law, passed in 2014 by the National Assembly, whereby employees of troubled firms are now granted the right to be informed in advance if their employer's business is to be sold or closed in order to give them the option of either converting the firm to a cooperative or of starting a new cooperative project. The law also has provisions for the creation of 'seed' transition cooperatives (termed *SCOP d'amorçage*), through which employees desiring to take over their firms without the required starting capital can bring into the buy out process temporary external investors, similar to the institutional investors afforded by Italy's Legge Marcora framework.[175] Promising social and solidarity economy initiatives for WBO creation in France have also included projects led by regional SCOP federations. In addition, an innovative 'transregional' working group with EU funding was set up in 2009 between France's CG-SCOP (its national confederation of SCOPS), Italy's Legacoop confederation, and Spain's COCETA (its worker cooperative confederation) and CONFESAL (its confederation of SALS), becoming a transnational support and research initiative to study and further develop business transfers to worker ownership.[176]

One recent French ERT experiment similar to Argentina's ERTs and Italy's Ri-Maflow and Officine Zero is Fralib, an historical tea and herb processing and packaging factory located in Gémenos near Marseille that had specialised in the storied Elephant brand of teas. More recently, it was a former branch plant of the chemical and agri-food multinational Unilever. After Unilever decided to close the plant in 2010 and, in a typical move by globalised capital, after a five-year process of moving production of its Lipton tea brand from the Marseille plant to Poland's cheaper labour market, the 182 remaining workers decided to fight for owed severance. In May 2014, after 1,336 days of protest, lobbying, and sit-ins, the Fralib workers received €5 million from the greater Marseille authority to buy the plant in order to save its jobs and managed to secure an additional €20 million of owed severance and €1.5 million of start-up capital from Unilever. This gave its remaining workers the legal and financial path

173   Soulage 2011, p. 157.
174   Intercentar, n.d.
175   ICA 2014.
176   Corcoran and Wilson 2010, p. 41.

to buy out the plant and restart production as a SCOP worker cooperative.[177] Since then, the Fralib workers, renaming themselves Scop-Ti, have managed to convert their tea and herb production to an entirely organic process, secured distribution deals with France's supermarkets under a fair trade label, and have been working with local French producers of linden to restart the flailing linden orchards of Provence. Fralib was also host in February 2014 to the first gathering of the 'Euromediterranean' region of the 'Workers' Economy' conferences, in which, as with the third gathering hosted by Italy's RiMaflow, other European and Latin American ERTs, supporting labour unions, and activists engaged in workshops and panels right on the factory floor.[178]

Spain. In addition to the strong presence of workers' control in revolutionary Spain in 1936, especially in Catalonia,[179] and the emergence of the Mondragón cooperatives founded by a local priest, engineers, and workers as replies to the socio-economic difficulties and nationalist sentiments for self-reliance in the Basque country in the 1950s,[180] in Spain business takeovers and conversions to labour-managed firms have been a reality since at least the early 1970s. According to Anthony Jensen, they emerged with vigour in that decade 'when workers took over factories to save their jobs' in the wake of economic stagnation and crises.[181] Most of these early ERTs took on the form of SALs. Studies have estimated that by the mid-1980s there were around 1,300, mostly state-funded, workplace conversions using the SAL model.[182] Today SALs are still a vehicle for workplace conversions and adapt, on the whole, a negotiated WBO model.

In addition, as a collaborative response between the state, the cooperative movement, and labour unions to the growing economic difficulties in Spain in recent years, Spanish legislation, similar to Italy's Legge Marcora framework, now affords the *pago único* model through which redundant workers can use their unemployment insurance for buying out their employers' firms or for creating new worker cooperatives or SALs. An unemployment benefits capitalisation model, Spain's *pago único* solution includes the ability for employees to claim advanced lump-sum payments of up to three years of unemployment

---

177   Henley, Kassam, Letsch, and Goñi 2015.
178   Portal de Economía Solidaria 2014; Karyotis 2014a. For more on the 'Workers' Economy' conferences, started in 2007 in Argentina by the University of Buenos Aires's Programa Facultad Abierta and various Argentine ERT umbrela organisations, see Chapter 7.
179   Mintz 2006.
180   MacLeod 1997.
181   Jensen 2011, p. 703.
182   Jensen 2011; Paton 1989.

insurance for joining or creating worker cooperatives or SALs.[183] Spanish workers can also come to agreements with owners to form partnerships, in which the SAL or cooperative co-owns the firm with other investors, as with the Cuin Factory in Vilanova i la Geltrú, Barcelona.[184] Moreover, regional programmes in Spain, such as the Aracoop initiative between the Autonomous Community of Catalonia, Catalonia's confederation of cooperatives, and its federation of worker cooperatives, have also assisted in the successful transfer of numerous conventional businesses to cooperatives.[185]

In addition to Spain's negotiated ERTs, by 2012 around 75 labour-conflict ERTs had emerged in the country as direct responses by workers to soaring unemployment and the country's severe austerity measures.[186] Some of the most promising examples include: Conservatorio Histórico de Santiago de Compostela, a music conservatory created in 2005 and self-managed as a cooperative by five music teachers; another music school, Musicop, a worker cooperative of music teachers created by 35 redundant employees of the Escuela de Música de Mataró in Barcelona; Profinox, a stainless steel manufacturing plant in the Autonomous Community of Murcia founded in 2012 after its workers received the company's assets as severance; and the national online daily *Más Público*, converted by its journalists and production staff from out of the closure of the *Público* newspaper in 2012.[187]

United Kingdom. The UK has also had historical experiences with workplace occupations and worker-recuperated firms. As worker-led responses to the business restructuring, deindustrialisation, and rising unemployment of the late 1960s and early 1970s, Glasgow's Upper Clyde Shipyards work-ins in 1971 inspired a wave of occupations of over 260 firms throughout the 1970s. Many of these became worker cooperatives or firms run under workers' control or workers' councils and were supported by their unions and, for a time, by the Labour and Conservative governments of the decade.[188] In addition, in 1976 the British Parliament passed legislation in support of the creation of worker cooperatives that became the Industrial Common Ownership Movement (ICOM); by 2001, the ICOM movement had created over 2,000 cooperat-

---

183   CECOP–CICOPA Europe 2013; El Economista 2018.
184   Cúneo 2014.
185   Corcoran and Wilson 2010, p. 39; Aracoop 2016.
186   Cúneo 2014.
187   Alfieri 2014; Gallego 2014.
188   Tuckman 2012. Many of these included firms in complex, capital-intensive sectors, such as Triumph motorcycles, the Fisher Bendix motor components firm, Lucas Aerospace, and the Sexton, Son and Everard shoe manufacturer.

ives.[189] Today, transfers of businesses to cooperatives in the UK are also present but less common than in other European jurisdictions. Instead, in the UK the ESOP model is more widespread, with employees' ownership shares held in trusts (as with the John Lewis model) or in a combination of direct and trust-held share ownership. While the former Conservative-led coalition government of David Cameron (2010–16) passed additional legislation to favour employee-shareholder provisions,[190] this legislation had mixed results in promoting new ESOPs and labour-managed firms.[191] Most recently, former Labour Party leader Ed Miliband had been explicitly advocating for the UK government's increased support of worker buyout solutions,[192] while, under Jeremy Corbyn's leadership, the Labour Party in early 2016 and again in their 2017 election manifesto announced a policy platform that included the facilitation of WBOs and workers' shares in company ownership.[193]

Other European experiences. A number of new worker-run firms and ERT-type experiences have emerged in recent decades in other parts of Europe as solutions to the growing rate of unemployment and economic crises. This occurred, for instance, in Finland in the 1990s with the noticeable expansion in worker and labour cooperatives, the latter a unique form of work-integration social enterprise (WISE) that hires out labour services to other firms. Their growth in Finland was stimulated by the *de rigueur* deregulation of the times, and particularly in the wake of the economic disruption of the country caused by the break-up of the Soviet Union.[194]

During the Soviet Union's years of *perestroika* at the end of the 1980s and the first post-Communist years of the early 1990s, a wave of mostly short-lived cooperatives emerged with the dismantling and privatisation of its state-run industries.[195] Cases of labour-conflict ERTs have also existed in Russia. In the late 1990s, for example, workers of the Vyborg pulp and paper mill in Sovietsky on the Finnish border and the Yasnogorsk machine plant in Tula Oblast occupied and eventually ran their factories as self-managed workplaces in situations similar to what motivated many first-period ERTs in Argentina: macroeconomic crises and micro-economic blight; long occupations by workers after the threatened closure of the plants (in the case of Vyborg, due to the buying

189   Vieta et al. 2016.
190   Pushkar 2012.
191   Ribgy 2013.
192   Rigby, Bounds, and Massoudi 2015.
193   Labour Party 2017; R. Mason 2016.
194   Birchall 2003.
195   Kotkin 1991.

and selling of the firm by various multinational interests); asset stripping by former owners; workers' risk of permanent unemployment; mass support of the occupying workers by the local community; and several violent attempts at eviction by owner-hired thugs and militias.[196]

The Balkan countries have also had experiences with ERTs in recent years. While state-supported workers' self-management was a key feature of the socialist economic model of the former Yugoslavia, virtually none of these firms survived the civil wars and virulent form of predatory capitalism that engulfed the region in the 1990s as self-managed companies. At least three con-temporary experiments with ERTs, however, have emerged in the Balkans in recent years: ITAS-Prvomajska precision tools manufacturer in Ivanec, Croa-tia;[197] the Jugoremedija pharmaceutical firm in Zrenjanin, Serbia;[198] and the Dita detergent factory in Tuzla, Bosnia and Herzegovina.[199] With aspects of the former Yugoslavia's self-management model still in the collective memory of its worker protagonists, all three ERT experiments have managed to deploy a hybrid worker–community or worker–state shareholding model. ITAS-Prvo-majska was founded in the former Yugoslavia, was privatised in the 1990s, and was then taken over by its 220 workers in 2005 when the plant experienced fin-ancial difficulties. The ITAS-Prvomajska workers now employ a collective share-holding arrangement between current and retired workers where no worker may own more than 10 percent shares in the firm. Its workers have also created a social enterprise that supports the technological development of the plant. In late 2006 and early 2007, the majority worker-shareholders of the Jugoremedija pharmaceutical factory, after a nine-month occupation of the plant and a two-and-a-half year strike, managed to restore its 58 percent control of the company in a model similar to Spain's SALs or Québec's worker-shareholder cooperative model of co-ownership. The Jugoremedija workers did so after its capitalist co-owner attempted to illegally reclaim full control of the business using the police and government militias to try and violently evict the workers. In the ensu-ing years, the remaining 42 percent of the firm owned by the previous owner was purchased by the Serbian state, while the workers retain full administrat-ive control of the plant. Since then, the Jugoremedija workers have gone on to

---

196   A-Infos Anarchist News Service 1999; Mandel 2001; Volkov 2000. David Mandel has argued that the Vyborg workers' experiment ultimately failed due to the lack of coordination amongst workers and due to a hostile state (Mandel 2001), essentially making late 1990s Russia not amenable to the emergence of an ERT movement.

197   Vlaisavljevic 2016.

198   Workerscontrol.net 2012.

199   Jukic 2015.

create an additional spin-off worker-run business manufacturing penicillin.[200] And Dita became an ERT in June 2015 when 70 of the 760 former workers of the factory, also privatised in the 1990s, revived the firm from its 2013 bankruptcy and restored its machines and remaining stock of supplies. The Dita workers have since negotiated marketing agreements with several supermarkets to restock the popular Dita brand of detergents.

More recently, as a consequence of the lingering effects of the 2008 crisis, the continuation of austerity policies, and the lingering reality of falling job security and increasing unemployment, instances of workplace occupations or full takeovers by workers have also occurred in countries such as Ireland, Greece, and Turkey. While Ireland's two recent experiences with workplace occupations by workers did not become ERTs after arriving at union-negotiated settlement deals with owners, the eight-month worker occupation and sit-in of Waterford Crystals in 2008–9[201] and the occupation of the foam packing plant Vita Cortex in 2011–12 provide tantalising possibilities for worker-driven ERTs to emerge in that country.[202] On the other hand, workplace occupations in Turkey and Greece as workers' direct responses to abuse by bosses, potential plant closures, and dwindling job prospects have led to a number of full conversions to worker cooperatives. ERT cases in Turkey and Greece are labour-conflict ERTs with affinities to Argentina's ERTs, France's Fralib, and Italy's Ri-Maflow and Officine Zero.

Turkey's most notable ERT experience is the worker takeover of Istanbul's Kazova Textile Factory, which produced luxury clothing for an assortment of Europe's top brands. Similar to the experiences of many Argentine ERTs, a group of Kazova's workers occuped the plant in early 2013 after the nefarious financial practices, asset stripping, and eventual closure of the firm by its former family owners left its 94 employees out of work and with unpaid wages. Their plight became widely known during the Taksim Square and Gezi Park uprisings and the remaining Kazova workers received support from the Taksim/Gezi protesters and the surrounding community, resulting in the eventual takeover of the firm by its resisting workers in 2015. After the workers eventually agreed to receive the remaining machinery in light of due wages, two new Kazova enterprises formed: Free Kazova (Özgür Kazova) and Resist! Kazova (Diren! Kazova–DİH). The emergence of two Kazova ERTs occurred after Devrimci İşçi Hareketi (DİH, Revolutionary Workers' Movement) – which provided legal support to the Kazova workers during the initial resistance and takeover –

---

200   Indymedia UK 2007; Workerscontrol.net 2012.
201   Gillespie and Boyd 2009.
202   James 2011.

started selling Kazova's clothing at their DİH storefront using the Diren! Kazova brand. A number of the workers saw DİH as benefiting from Kazova's name, which had became known nationally and internationally at the time, without adequately recompensing the original workers. As a result, the Resist! Kazova workers, now manufacturing their own clothing line, formed a cooperative, while the Free Kazova workers, continuing to manufacture clothing under the Kazova brand, did not formally constitute a cooperative but restarted production democratically under cooperative principles. Both Kazovas have been supported by numerous social justice groups in Turkey and from abroad. As of 2016, Free Kazova was also selling their clothing in solidarity markets throughout Turkey and exporting textiles to various European countries.[203]

Greece's most celebrated ERT, Vio.Me, emerged in similar circumstances. Vio.Me was created by its workers' recuperation of a Greek industrial adhesives manufacturer in Thessaloniki, eventually reopening the firm as a worker cooperative in April 2014 after a three-year struggle with state authorities and the former employers. With the added support of the local community and numerous social movements, and with inspiration from and contacts with Argentina's ERT movement, especially the Zanón/FaSinPat workers and other ERTs associated with the 'Workers' Economy' conferences,[204] Vio.Me has become one of Europe's most emblematic ERT. Today, Vio.Me produces environmentally sound cleaning products under the administration of a workers' assembly and an innovative, multistakeholder community model that includes a 'community assembly' of over 1,000 'solidarity supporters' consisting of 'any individual who commits to consuming a certain quantity of the factory's products yearly',[205] as well as a solidarity and holistic medicine workers' medical centre located inside of the factory. Although Vio.Me's legal struggles against eviction by the state and former owners' attempts at getting back control of the firm was still in play as of the last months of 2016, its workers continue to resist and have followed in the footsteps of France's Fralib by organising the second gathering of the 'Euromediterranean' region of the 'Workers' Economy' conference that took place in the Vio.Me facilities in October 2016.

2.2.3   Other Experiences
The spread of neo-liberalism on a world-scale, the recurrent crises of globalised capital, the lingering wake of the 2008 recession, and newly emergent troubles wrought by austerity and deindustrialisation have meant the rise of new ERTS

---

203   Leverink 2015; Salı 2015.
204   Ranis 2016, p. 68.
205   Karyotis 2014b, para. 6.

in places where they had not previously existed. Recent years, for example, have seen instances of ERTs in South Korea in sectors such as transportation, furniture manufacturing, and media.[206] And, in India, while a handful of tea plantations and jute mills in the Communist-run state of West Bengal either had its workers convert them to a worker cooperative or occupy the establishment and run them cooperatively in the 1970s, 1980s, and 1990s,[207] more recently new workplace occupations and WBO conversions have taken place in Delhi's industrial south and, most notably, with the Kannan Devan tea plantation in the state of Kerala.

More historically, the United States and Canada have been two additional places where workers have occupied and converted workplaces to cooperatives. In the United States, demands for increased workers' control of industry have had historical expression in the numerous worker cooperative initiatives of the Knights of Labour in the late 1800s and early 1900s and in the manifestos and initiatives of the Industrial Workers of the World (IWW) in the early years of the twentieth century. The idea of establishing workers' control would return in unionised industry during the wave of factory occupations and sit-down strikes of the 1930s, especially driven by unions such as the United Steelworkers (USW); United Automobile Workers (UAW); and United Electrical, Radio and Machine Workers of America (UE).[208] Specific conversions of plants to worker cooperatives took place in the plywood industry during the 1950s and 1960s in the Pacific Northwest.[209] And, although not usually leading to outright workers' control, the ESOP model, as we have already discussed, has also become an option for worker ownership in the United States, taking off in the 1970s.

In recent decades in the US, employee ownership, conversions to cooperatives via succession, and worker buyouts have been supported by initiatives such as that of the ICA Group, led by a collective of academics and activists;[210] the US Federation of Worker Cooperatives (USFWC);[211] and Kent State University's Ohio Employee Ownership Center (OEOC)[212] and other employee ownership centres in New York, Vermont, Michigan, and in other states.[213] In 2009, the USW and the OEOC developed an agreement with the Basque

---

206   Ho and Jang 2015; Kim and Jang 2015.
207   Sen 2011.
208   Ness 2011.
209   Curl 2009; Dow 2003.
210   ICA Group 2016.
211   USFWC 2016.
212   OEOC 2016.
213   ICA Group 2016.

country's Corporación Mondragón worker cooperative to promote the creation of new US worker cooperatives in what has been called 'The Union Co-op Model'.[214] This revived takeup of worker cooperatives in the United States, in a collaborative approach between workers, the cooperative sector, and national and local unions, has the aim of securing fair wages and other workers' rights in worker cooperatives. The Union Co-op Model has already fostered several new cooperative projects, including: the Cincinnati Union Cooperative Initiative and the Our Harvest Cooperative, the latter involving local food growing, distribution, and retailing; union–cooperative projects in Pittsburgh, Denver, and Seattle; and, perhaps most famously, Cleveland's public procurement and work provisioning Evergreen Cooperatives that, while not specifically a Union Co-op initiative, has used Mondragón as a model for organising various worker cooperatives in that city.[215] Overall, The Union Co-op Model, while still nascent, holds much promise for creating a wave of new cooperatives from conversions in the depleted rust belt and across the United States more widely.[216]

The most storied ERT case in the United States is Chicago's New Era Windows Cooperative, formed in 2012 from the closing of Republic Windows and Doors after decades of being in business. The workers' struggles began when the factory laid off its entire staff of 279 unionised workers and 21 managers in late 2008 during the height of the financial crisis. After a six-day sit-in centred on securing owed severance pay facilitated by its union, UE Local 1110, that garnered wide media attention at the time (with support even coming from documentary filmmaker and author Michael Moore and then president-elect Barack Obama), a West Coast green energy company named Serious Energy eventually bought out the firm and operated it until it too closed. By 2012, a group of remaining workers, with the assistance of the UE, Chicago's Center for Workplace Democracy, and US$ 665,000 start-up capital raised by The Working World (a New York-based non-profit, cooperative-funding organisation),[217] reopened the firm under worker-ownership and rebranded it New Era Windows Cooperative. Central to the conversion of the firm into one of the United States's most inspirational and well-known ERTs has been the assistance of the UE, the start-up and administrative support of The Working World, and

---

214   Witherell, Cooper, and Peck 2012.
215   Clay 2013.
216   Clay 2013; Truthout 2013.
217   The Working World also has deep connections with Argentina's ERTs, as we will see in Chapter 7.

the leadership of three former Republic Windows workers.[218] As Project Equity has stated, '[a]gainst tremendous odds, New Era has been able to transform a massive, unforeseen lay-off into an opportunity to build secure jobs and a company that is responsive first and foremost to its workers'.[219] And, like Greece's Vio.Me, Italy's RiMaflow, and France's Fralib, in recent years New Era's workers have had fruitful exchanges with Latin America's ERTs, helping to contribute to a burgeoning transnational network of ERTs.[220]

In Canada, worker-led buyouts and conversions have also been a reality, although few in numbers, since at least the 1970s. One early case involved the creation of Tembec, a WBO initiative that unfolded as a partnership between workers, private investors, the local community, and the provincial and federal governments after the closing of Canadian International Paper in Temiscaming, Québec. Notably, the buyout was preceded by and relied on the mobilisation and activism of the community together with the support of the Canadian Paperworkers Union (CPU).[221] Throughout the 1970s, 1980s, and 1990s, other WBOs would emerge on occasion, including several plywood companies in British Columbia, a brewery in Saskatchewan, the conversion of smaller firms in Manitoba with the support of the social democratic New Democratic Party (NDP) provincial government, and several buyouts in Ontario, including Canada's largest WBO to date, the Algoma steel plant in Sault Ste. Marie in 1995 involving 6,000 workers under the leadership of the USW.[222] By 1990, there were 39 WBO-initiated firms throughout Canada,[223] while some health and social services sector worker cooperatives have formed in recent years from workplace conversions, such as Nova Scotia's Careforce.[224] The Canadian Worker

---

218 Project Equity 2015; Ranis 2016.
219 Project Equity 2015, p. 66. Other similar conversions to cooperatives that have formed ERTs in the United States include Amherst, Massachusetts' Collective Copies (also assisted by the UE) and Oakland, California's Taste of Denmark bakery (Project Equity 2015, p. 55 ff.).
220 In 2015, for instance, New Era's Armando Robles (who is also UE shop steward at the firm) attended the fifth international conference of the 'Workers' Economy' in Venezuela with the support of the University of Toronto's Centre for Learning, Social Economy & Work (CLSEW), while in 2016 Robles also participated in the North American regional conference of the 'Workers' Economy' in Mexico City, also with the support of CLSEW. This book's author was a part of the international committee that organised both conferences, helping to secure Robles' participation in both. For more on this growing transnational network of ERTs, see Chapter 7.
221 Quarter 1995.
222 Quarter 1995.
223 Quarter and Brown 1992.
224 Careforce 2016.

Co-operative Federation (CWCF), together with Canada's third-tier cooperative federation, Co-operatives and Mutuals Canada (CMC), and other research centres and social economy organisations in Québec have also recently taken up the cause of worker buyouts and conversions, providing literature and how-to manuals, forming a research network, and lobbying the Canadian government for better legislation to facilitate the creation of worker cooperatives from conversions. Moreover, some Canadian credit unions, such as Desjardins and VanCity, have also facilitated the financing of conversions to worker cooperatives.

Since the 1990s, the province of Québec has been the centre of conversions to cooperatives in Canada, becoming a particularly conducive jurisdiction for converting both healthy and troubled workplaces to worker cooperatives or its multistakeholder model of *coopératives de solidarité* (solidarity cooperatives). Factors contributing to Québec's leadership with conversions in Canada include: union assistance in workplace conversions, especially with the support of Québec's Confédération des Sindicats Nationaux (CSN, National Confederation of Unions), union and social economy consulting entities, and the use of labour-run solidarity funds; tight links with and additional supports from the province's broader social and solidarity economy movement; various technical and financial supports made available by the provincial government, regional jurisdictions, and municipalities; and the province's long tradition of cooperatives and cooperative development. Additionally, Québec's worker-shareholder cooperative model, in which employees form a cooperative and co-own the business with other traditional shareholders, has also been a vehicle for workplace rescues and workers' participation.[225] Through these institutionalised vehicles for conversions in Québec, over the past two decades a notable number of conversions have taken place, for instance, in the province's forestry and ambulance services sectors.[226]

Overall, however, and as in the United States, most workplace occupations in Canada have not led to the formation of ERTs. Rather, they have been struggles for sectoral labour rights or better collective agreements via the pressure of temporary workplace takeovers, such as the Telecommunication Workers Union-led occupation and work-in at BCTel in 1981;[227] the workers' occu-

---

225   More a model of workers' participation in the running of a business than an ERT, Daniel Coté has estimated that 60 such cooperatives existed in Québec by the late 2000s (Coté 2007, p. 107).

226   Coté 2007.

227   Bernard 2011.

pation and temporary running of Molson Breweries in Ontario in 1999[228] and Alcan in Jonquière, Québec in early 2004;[229] and the occupations and sit-ins of the Aradco and Aramco auto parts plants by workers represented by the Canadian Auto Workers (CAW) in 2009,[230] matching similar sit-ins in the automotive sector the UK that same year.[231]

3   The Emergence and Characteristics of *Empresas Recuperadas*: A Summation

ERTs, then, are not unique to Argentina, although they have particularly taken off there for reasons that have already been touched on and that will be explored in some depth throughout the rest of the book. As we have reviewed in this chapter, ERTs are also present, although in smaller numbers, across Latin America and in other parts of the world that have traversed similar political economic conditions. In recent decades, workers' direct actions – including occupations, sit-ins, work-ins, and takeovers and buyouts leading to full conversions of formerly capitalist firms to workers' control – have been responses by workers to recurrent crises in the neo-liberal model linked to policies of austerity and deindustrialisation, financial downturns, and broader socio-economic difficulties. ERTs can especially emerge, although with variations and in differing degrees, in countries with some form of semi- or full industrialisation; with histories of militant working-class self-activity; with traditions of strong or activist labour unions; often with an already established cooperative sector; with some degree of state or juridical support, or both; and with some form of institutionalised supports for cooperatives, social and solidarity economy organisations, or specifically for business conversions.

While the nature of conversions to LMFs differ depending on the national context, ERTs generally form either from conflictual situations of struggle on shop floors between workers and owners or managers, or out of worker buyouts in more institutionalised contexts. Overall, ERTs tend to arise from out of troubled capitalist firms – investor owned or privately owned – that are taken over and revived by employees facing job loss after either risky occupations or confrontations with former owners or the state over the legal standing of the business, or as a negotiated procedure such as a buyout. At first, takeovers or

---

228   Parsons 1999.
229   Phebus 2004.
230   Eley 2009.
231   Hopkins, Milmo, and MacDonald 2009.

buyouts are often impelled by workers' fears at having to face the closure of their workplaces and of becoming structurally unemployed given the dearth of alternative jobs. Most usually, ERTs that last beyond the takeover or buyout phase overwhelmingly become some form of labour-managed firm, such as a worker cooperative, and are to some degree redesigned by workers along the lines of democratic administrative structures via workers' councils and workers' assemblies.

Latin America has been a particularly vibrant place for ERT development over the past two decades due to a strong confluence of these factors, and especially as a consequence of the starkly negative outcomes of the neo-liberal model for working people across the region. One estimate from the late 2000s numbered the region's ERTs at over 500, embracing circa 40,000 workers.[232] The few comparative studies of ERTs between different countries in Latin America that exist to date show that the strategies and tactics of ERT worker cooperatives and other forms of self-management, particularly in Argentina, Brazil, and Uruguay, are enjoying surprising longevity despite their ongoing challenges.[233] These studies also assert that the rise of worker-recuperated enterprises in recent years in the region is proving the ERT form to be a viable grassroots answer for workers facing structural unemployment and the dismantling of national economies by speculative global capital and neo-liberal market policies. This chapter's comparative examination of Argentina's ERT experiences with the emergence of ERTs in other national contexts over the past 20 years or so shows how similar self-directed strategies of workplace occupations and conversions to LMFs have been developing around the world as workers' direct responses to the ill effects of neo-liberal policies on their lives. But differences between Argentina's ERTs and ERTs in other conjunctures were also noted – for instance, in the relative lack of consistent institutional or state support for ERTs in Argentina when compared to ERTs in Italy, France, or Spain, or in the more chequered relationship between Argentine ERTs and the country's union movement when contrasted to ERT-type experiences in other national contexts. Indeed, the relative longevity of ERTs in Argentina and throughout Latin America is a testimony to the resilience, agency, and innovative capacities of workers despite the continued presence of some degree of neo-liberal policies on the part of most of the recent centre-left governments of Latin America.

---

232   Trigona 2010.
233   See, for instance, Camilletti et al. 2005; Chedid Henriques 2014; Ghibaudi 2004; Paulucci 2013; Ruggeri 2009; Ruggeri et al. 2010, 2014; and Vieta and Ruggeri 2009.

Chapters 6–8 will review some of the founding and organisational particularities of Argentina's ERTs that, Chapter 9 will argue, distinguish them in
ways from other ERT experiments to date. One way that Argentine ERTs differentiate themselves, for instance, is in how many of them practice egalitarian remuneration schemes despite variations in worker seniority or skill
sets. Another is in how the majority of Argentine ERTs practice some form
of solidarity-based community engagement or development. In this regard,
Argentine ERT protagonists have been showing how – in almost two-thirds
of ERTs – socialised economic practices are being forged that extend beyond
the walls of the cooperative via non-marketised socio-economic relations with
the surrounding communities they touch and with other ERTs and social and
solidarity economy organisations.[234] Practising the International Co-operative
Alliance's sixth and seventh principles of cooperativism – respectively, 'cooperation between cooperatives' and 'concern for community'[235] – competitive
markets, while certainly not eradicated, are beginning to be challenged and
even replaced in some ways by practices that have a fair number of Argentina's
ERTs in similar or related sectors sharing in production and customer orders;
opening up their shops to community centres, free health clinics, and popular
education initiatives; and even investing portions of their surpluses in community economic development.

It is true that the almost 16,000 self-managed workers who were employed
in 367 active ERTs in early 2016 constitute just 0.13 percent of Argentina's
approximately 12.5 million 'economically active population'.[236] Nevertheless,
Argentina's ERT workers have extended their influence far beyond their numbers and economic influence. As we saw in the case studies in Chapter 1 and in
the more macro-level overview of this chapter, and as we will continue to see
throughout the rest of this book, ERT worker-protagonists have been crafting
promising – and *workable* – solutions for overcoming micro-economic hardship at the point of production and in the everyday lives of workers more

---

234   Ranis 2016; Ruggeri et al. 2010; Ruggeri et al. 2014.
235   ICA 2016. See also Chapters 5 and 7.
236   INDEC 2016, p. 6. According to INDEC, Argentina's national statistical organ, the country's
      formally registered and employed workers (*asalariados*) are part of the 'economically act-
      ive population', which encompasses all employed and unemployed people actively seek-
      ing work (La Nación 2015; INDEC 2016). It also includes people who are actively employed
      and actively looking for other work, and the underemployed. Argentina's economically
      active population, however, does not officially include around 4.5 million Argentines
      engaged in informal and non-registered economic activity (so-called '*trabajo en negro*')
      (La Nación 2015), which in reality makes the number of economically active people in the
      Argentine economy much higher than official numbers indicate.

broadly. In short, ERTs bear witness to workers' continued capacities to self-determine their own working lives, as we will continue to explore, while at the same time responding to ongoing situations of socio-economic crises in ways that both contest them *and* begin to move beyond intransigent capitalist and competitive logics.

The Political Economy of Argentina's Working Class: Historical Underpinnings of the *Empresas Recuperadas*

[Argentina's *empresas recuperadas*] reverberate with infrequently used words, charged with old political content: *solidaridad, autonomía, auto-gestión* ... The experiences that originate this conceptual resurrection so contrary to neo-liberalism surge more from a creative and combative response to necessity rather than from a theoretical understanding of world history and workers' own past because there was nobody – much less after the killings of the last Argentine dictatorship – to transmit and care for this historical memory. But the very fact that thousands of workers in different parts of Argentina and in other countries simultaneously relied on the same methods and ideas reveals the existence of a profound and hidden subterranean historical conscience.

GUILLERMO ALMEYRA[1]

∴

As the voices of the workers in Chapter 1 highlighted, and as our overview of the main characteristics of ERTs made clear in the previous chapter, Argentina's *empresas recuperadas* did not emerge in a vacuum. For sure, each group of workers that founds an ERT lives through unique experiences and challenges. Indeed, ERTs do represent new forms of labour struggles and organising that arose as worker-led resistances to a particularly virulent form of neo-liberal capitalism that marked Argentina's political economy throughout the 1990s and early 2000s. These new forms of labour struggles have been tailored to respond to micro-economic and localised workplace crises that, in most instances, are the reverberations of neo-liberalism's ill effects in the lives of working people. But ERTs are at the same time also intimately linked to older forms of labour militancy and workers' self-activity that re-emerged with

---

1 Almeyra 2004, p. 182 (*La protesta social en la Argentina, 1990–2004*).

force in recent years within a particularly conflictive moment in capital–labour relations in Argentina. During the 1990s and early 2000s, for instance, Argentine workers engaged increasingly in time-honoured working-class practices such as street marches, road blockages, soldiering, sabotage, wildcat strikes, company occupations, workplace takeovers, and ultimately self-management. These practices are deeply rooted in long-held Argentine working-class responses to the ebbs and flows of the country's turbulent political economic history and workers' on-going experiences of exploitation and repression on shop floors. They are practices that, in varying combinations and degrees, shape the foundation stories of all ERT experiences in Argentina.

This chapter elaborates on the historical roots of Argentina's ERTs, especially the political economic and social conditions from out of which they emerged. It situates the ERT phenomenon within the country's long history of workers' bottom-up militancy and democratic practices. These are practices that at key historical moments have overflowed from workplace conflicts onto the country's streets and plazas, intersecting with other radical movements for social change. Ultimately, the historical analysis presented in this chapter links the country's ERTs and their practices of *autogestión* with the broader history and political economy of Argentina's working class.

The first section of the chapter begins our understanding of the political economy of Argentina's working class starting circa 1900, especially during the years immediately preceding the coming to power of Juán Domingo Perón. It then focuses on the rise of an influential labour movement mainly infused, especially after 1943, with the populist and developmentalist ideals that have broadly come to be known as *peronismo*. These ideals, however, would eventually express themselves in the minds of the rank and file and on shop floors in directly democratic values and practices that the union bureaucracy and Perón himself had not intended for the labour movement. I then argue that the experiences and struggles of workers during the years demarcated by the rise, fall, exile, return, and death of Perón (1943–74); the brief and unstable presidency of his widow, Isabel Perón (1974–76); and the genocidal rule of Argentina's last military dictatorship and its euphemistically self-labelled Proceso de Reorganización Nacional (National Process of Reorganisation) (1976–83) were crucial for laying the groundwork for workers' and popular sectors' subsequent resistances, protests, and actions during the neo-liberal era of the 1990s. In this section I also map out some of the historical tensions between bottom-up working-class practices during the last half of the twentieth century and the variegated and contentious history of the ultimately failed 'class compromise' between organised labour, capital, and the country's authoritarian political regimes, especially during the years spanning the mid-1950s to the mid-1970s.

Throughout these years, workers would come face to face with and often resist the repression and violence that the state would frequently deploy to maintain this class compromise. Ultimately, the first section of this chapter serves to situate ERTs as contemporary extensions of these historical workers' struggles against capital in Argentina, expressed in the continued influence of the Peronist imaginary of a self-sustaining national economy and the 'dignity' of work for the working class, and kept alive in the collective memories of key historical events such as *el Cordobazo* of 1969; the *coordinadoras interfabriles* (coordinating bodies of factory and workers' commissions by district) of 1974–5; the disappearance of unionised workers during the last dictatorship; and earlier experiences of factory occupations of the late 1950s and throughout the 1960s, 1970s, and 1980s.

The chapter's next section moves to an account of the rise and (incomplete) fall of the neo-liberal model between 1976–2003 – the most immediate macroeconomic and macro-political conjuncture that gave rise to ERTs – and the transformation of organised labour during these years with the partial diminishment of the role of Argentina's Peronist-influenced union central, the Confederación General del Trabajo de la República Argentina (CGT, General Confederation of Labour of the Republic of Argentina). This transformation, on the other hand, also included by the 1990s the emergence of alternative union centrals and new working-class organisations that arose in opposition to neo-liberal policies and the mainline CGT's support of *menemismo*, such as the Central de Trabajadores de la Argentina (CTA, Argentine Workers' Central), the Movimiento de los Trabajadores Argentinos (MTA, Movement of Argentine Workers), and the Corriente Clasista y Combativa (CCC, Classist and Combative Current).

The chapter's last section reviews the surge of ERTs in the last years of the 1990s and early years of the 2000s around the notions of *autogestión* and *horizontalidad* (horizontality). Elaborated on theoretically and historically in Chapters 4 and 5, this section highlights how these concepts came to their own with the self-management practices of ERTs intermingling with the directly democratic and militant practices of the *piquetero* movement and other expressions of bottom-up working-class self-activity responding to the crisis of neo-liberalism throughout the late 1990s and early 2000s. Finally, the last pages of the chapter give a broad overview of the new forms of labour organisations and self-managed workers' associations that have arisen in recent years, which I claim are part of a new social movement- and community-based unionism driven by the concept of *autogestión*.

Implicitly weaving this chapter together are the concepts of the *composition, decomposition,* and *recomposition* of the working class that I borrow from the autonomist and Open Marxist strands of 'class-struggle Marxism'. I believe these concepts are useful for understanding the significance of working-class struggles in Argentina in light of ongoing state repression, neo-liberalism's economic forms of repression of the 1990s, and workers' bottom-up responses to this onslaught. They allow us to see that throughout this violent history, Argentina's workers did not sit by compliantly nor did they ultimately succumb to these economic and outright violent attempts at breaking working-class unity. What I argue in this chapter, instead, is that the history and political economy of Argentina's working class is both etched with attempts at class compromise between mostly authoritarian governments, the representatives of capital, and bureaucratic unionism, and the recalcitrance and self-activity of workers on shop floors and on the streets. The neo-liberal assault on labour and workers' responses to this assault, especially during the crisis years at the turn of the millennium, was yet another chapter in this long history. In no small way, the neo-liberal project of privatising profits and socialising risk was, in Argentina, part of an evolving methodology deployed by its IMF-backed, pro-market state and capitalist classes in order to ultimately decompose the working class (or, at minimum, de-claw it) and recompose it as cheaper and cheaper forms of labour-power. In contrast, the subsequent direct-action strategies and self-directed organisational activities of workers – exemplified by ERT protagonists – that began to move beyond the anti-labour climate of the neo-liberal years show that the working class had (and continues to have) other visions for its own (re)composition – on shop floors and within the broader socio-political milieu.

1   Section 1: The Rise and Consolidation of Argentina's Working Class (1900–89)

> I have spoken to many workers in the Federal Capital and in the interior, and each one says, 'Now I am something, I am someone'.
> ENRIQUE DICKMANN[2]

Argentina's myriad social justice groups; community kitchens and neighbourhood free clinics and cultural centres; community-led initiatives for dignified and affordable housing; popular education programmes; growing Indigenous struggles for recognition and the recuperation of traditional lands; the oldest

---

2 Leader and militant of the Socialist Party in the mid-twentieth century, paraphrasing a common expression by workers shortly after the 1943 rise of Perón, in James 1988, p. 37.

and still expanding cooperative sector in Latin America; worker-recuperated enterprises ... These are just a handful of examples of what is known in Argentina and other countries in Latin America as *the social and solidarity economy*: a vast array of alternative economic practices and community-based organisations that privilege social objectives over private gain and that have been in the ascension over the past three or so decades, in response to the cyclical economic crises and social dead ends spawned by the neo-liberal model.[3] But their roots connect to a long tradition of spontaneous and organised popular and working-class struggles dating back decades.

The genealogy of Argentina's ERT movement can be traced back to a long history of militant working-class activism, often acting as counterweight to constituted forms of state power, remnants of colonial institutions, and capitalist privileges. Argentine working-class activism has historically included not only struggles over working conditions and wages, but also initiatives for stabilising livelihoods and returning control to workers via practices of shop floor democracy and consistent protests and acts of revolt carried out in the factory, on the street, and in the public plaza.[4] At times, these struggles have been union-led. At other times, they have been linked to grassroots initiatives aligned with broader popular struggles against the authoritarian state and even union bureaucracy.

Throughout this history, four working-class forms of organising stand out, underscoring the tenacity of Argentine workers' self-activity and the often directly democratic structures that have composed them: *comisiones internas* (shop floor workers' commissions, or factory committees); *cuerpos de delegados* (shop-stewards' committees or plenaries); *coordinadores interfabriles* or *obreras* (interfactory or worker coordinating bodies); and recurring experiments with workplace occupations. These working-class forms of organising are the historical cousins of Argentina's ERTs. Their roots begin with Argentina's late nineteenth- and early twentieth-century socialist, communist, anarchist, and syndicalist unions and labour organisations; they continued to grow with the consolidation of the country's labour movement promoted and in part inspired by Argentina's mid-twentieth-century populist and nationalist-developmentalist president, Juán Domingo Perón; and they began to flower with the very self-determination and self-activity of the country's workers as they reinterpreted and reconfigured the political strategies and tactics of organised labour and the socio-economic policies of *peronismo*.

---

3   For a fuller definition and analysis of the social and solidarity economy, see Chapter 5.
4   James 1988, p. 37.

Although seemingly obvious, it is still important to point out upfront that Argentina's labour movement did not begin with Perón, as committed aficionados of the colonel's storied rise to power are (erroneously) wont to believe.[5] In truth, by the time Perón came to power Argentina already had a long history of workers' mutuals, friendly societies, and cooperatives; anarchist, syndicalist, socialist, and communist unions and union centrals; and experiences with general strikes and bottom-up working-class self-activity dating back to at least the 1880s with the rise of its early industries rooted in the agro-export sectors, the country's early urbanisation, and waves of European immigration.[6] But up until the rise of Perón in the mid-1940s, the labour movement was, on the whole, fragmented into a plethora of trade and industrial unions and union centrals and any semblance of an organised national labour movement under-represented the working class. Perón was the first national Argentine leader to successfully inspire and encourage the broad consolidation of the working class into a national labour movement, opportunistically capitalising on an already existing yet loose coalition of syndicalist, anarchist, communist, and socialist labour organisations and growing working-class self-identity. Indeed, as Miguel Murmis and Juán Carlos Portantiero, Hugo Del Campo, Juan Carlos Torre,[7] and other Argentine labour historians have forcefully shown, it was an ascendant working class under a loose fabric of established trade and increasingly industrial unions (many of which had already been promoting a nationalist and anti-imperialist vision for Argentina's working people) that had an important part to play in the rise of Perón starting in 1943, first as Secretary of Labour and Social Provision in the military governments of Pedro Ramírez and Edelmiro Farrell between 1943–5, then as Farrell's vice president in 1944, and finally as president in 1946. At the same time, Perón would prove to be the national leader who helped articulate a vision for a new, self-sustaining Argentina organised in no small part around a consolidated and centralised labour movement. While throughout the conservative 1930s and early 1940s the working class had already been engaged in increasingly frequent organised strikes and the growth of industrial (rather than strictly trade-based) unions, gaining some important victories in its struggle for better pay and working conditions, *peronismo*, as Daniel James points out, would assist in giving a national voice to the long-stifled desires of working people for more rights, recognition, and

---

5   For explicit critiques of this position, see Del Campo 2005; James 1998; Munck, Falcón, and Galitelli 1987; Murmis and Portantiero 1971; and Torre 2012.

6   Del Campo 2005; James 1988; Munck et al. 1987.

7   Del Campo 2005; Murmis and Portantiero 1971; Torre 2012.

respect.[8] The labour movement saw in *peronismo* an opening for both fulfilling these working-class desires and for claiming the movement's perceived rightful place in national political life. At the same time, Perón provided the vision – an avowedly non-Communist yet also anti-imperialist and nationalist-corporatist one based on a state-managed social justice platform – that would see the working class and its organised labour movement experience a concrete and 'fundamental "remaking"'.[9] As a consequence, the consolidated labour movement under the helmsmanship of Perón would, for the first time, go on to have a strong influence in national politics and the processes of national wealth redistribution.

What Perón did for the working class, then, was to help consolidate it into a real protagonist in national Argentine politics while granting it myriad new citizenship rights, social protections, and political say. And, in turn, what the working class did for Perón was help bring him to power and articulate his version of the 'third way' – *'ni comunismo, ni capitalismo'* ('neither communism nor capitalism') – also known as *justicialismo* (or more commonly, *peronismo*), with its three main principles of political sovereignty, economic independence, and social justice.[10] After Perón's first two presidencies (1946–55) and his ouster in a prolonged and bloody *coup d'état* led by oppositional conservative forces, the organised labour movement would become in key moments a counterforce to authoritarian governments and the capitalist establishment that propped them up in the following decades. James sums up this synchronic relationship between Peronism and the working class concisely:

> [While] Peronism marked a critical conjuncture in the emergence and formation of the modern Argentine working class[,] ... [a] two-way process of interaction was clearly involved and if the [modern] working class was partly constituted by Peronism then Peronism was itself also in part a creation of the working class.[11]

ERT workers' notion of the 'dignity of work', central to their 'moral economy of work' that I have already introduced, is rooted in part in how they have interpreted Argentina's historical working-class practices and, for many of them, the long-held promises of *peronismo* – promises that continue to saturate Argentina's working-class discourses to this day. Thus, to begin to understand how

---

8   James 1988, p. 36.
9   Munck et al. 1987, p. 106.
10   Godio 2000; James 1988; Munck et al. 1987.
11   James 1988, pp. 37–8.

and why ERTs emerged when they did (two of the main questions driving this book), we must first come to terms with this history.

1.1   Perón, the Consolidation of the Labour Movement, and 'the Dignity of Work' (1930–55)

By the 1930s, the capitalist elite of the period held on tenaciously to political and economic power via a back-and-forth contest between military regimes and corruptly elected conservative governments that lasted until the early 1940s. This period has thus come to be known as *la década infame* (the infamous decade). With the real possibility of war in Europe and growing nationalist sentiments at home, the homegrown Argentine capitalist establishment of the 1930s increasingly promoted heterodox economic policies geared towards repatriating its foreign-owned (largely British) industry. By the middle of the decade, a model of development rooted in import-substitution industrialisation (ISI) would be firmly entrenched, propping up local industry and promoting a growing internal market for consumer durables.[12] Since, by then, the great waves of immigration from Europe of the last two decades of the nineteenth and the first two of the twentieth century had subsided, the developing industrial sectors of Argentina increasingly sought labour-power from its vast and mostly underdeveloped interior provinces. This speed-up of industrialisation in the 1930s – motivated also by global economic depression, the subsequent fall in exports of prime materials, and the need felt by the Argentine establishment to become more economically sovereign[13] – was 'largely labour-intensive and based on the extraction of absolute surplus-value'.[14] Towards the end of the 1930s, the growing urban-based working class, in response to the harsh conditions of work in new industries, increasingly engaged in strikes and work stoppages for basic rights still denied to many of its members, such as shorter workdays, Sundays off, and better working conditions, which would later all be definitively entrenched in labour legislation and sector-wide collective agreements under Perón. With its growing numerical weight and voice, by the end of the 1930s the Argentine working class was undeniably a rising national force, with active leadership and labour organisations (although still, on the whole, segmented between various political tendencies) that would soon have a vital role to play in the rise of Perón.[15]

---

12   Ferrer 1967; James 1988; Smith 1991.
13   Della Paolera and Taylor 2003.
14   Munck et al. 1987, p. 123.
15   Del Campo 2005; Murmis and Portantiero 1971.

During this period, a growing migration of labourers from Argentina's rural hinterland desiring to avoid poverty and unemployment flowed into the country's cities. Responding to the growing labour demand from new urban industries, this migration effectively expanded the country's working class with new semi-skilled workers. Gaining significantly in strength during these years, the working class's objective transformation was thus linked to growing urbanisation and industrialisation. Contrary to earlier theories of Perón's rise that postulated a sharp break between the 'old' pre-Perón and a 'new' Perón-era working class, there is no doubt that the growing importance of the working class was already a reality well before Perón came onto the political scene.[16] But up until 1943 the working class, while able at times to organise for better wages and working conditions since at least the beginning of the twentieth century, had generally failed to win the broader sectoral and social demands it had been seeking, fragmented as it was between several union centrals aligned along varying political sympathies and differing views on the role of the general strike, whether or not to seek the overthrow of the capitalist system or seek a class compromise within it, and so on.[17]

There was also by the 1930s a clear gulf emerging between the growing rank and file, a majority of whose members still remained outside of the pur-

---

16   Revisionist historians and sociologists in the 1970s and 1980s, led by the work of Murmis and Portantiero (1971), began to question the explanation, spearheaded by Italo-Argentine sociologist Gino Germani, that the rise of Perón was primarily connected to the support he received from a 'new' yet fragmented working class that was ripe for Perón's nationalist-developmentalist project and that contrasted to the immigrant-based, European origins of the 'pre-Perón' working class. This new working class, according to Germani's orthodox assessment, grew with the waves of internal migration from the country and small towns to the cities during the period of intensifying urbanisation and industrialisation of the 1930s and early 1940s (see, for instance, Germani and de Yujnovsky 1973). The reality for the role of the working class in Perón's rise lies somewhere in between the orthodox and revisionist explanations. For Munck et al., while – in agreement with the revisionists – '[t]here was no clear-cut division between an anti-Peronist established working class and a "new" Peronist working class' (Munck et al. 1987, p. 122), there is also 'little doubt' – in a tip of the hat to Germani's position – 'about the objective change in the composition of the working class in the 1930s. There was a massive process of urbanisation and industrialisation along with a reversal of the previous dominance of overseas migrants within the Argentine working class' (Munck et al. 1987, p. 108). This emerging socio-economic dynamic, according to Munck et al., favoured both the consolidating labour movement and Perón's political ambitions.

17   According to Munck et al., this fragmentation was the case in part due to the 'lack of representativity' of the union movement over the first three decades of 1900s, which was in turn linked to the disgreements between the varying political forces from the left that were claiming to be its representatives (Munck et al. 1987, p. 108).

view of collective agreements or even union representation, and the various anti-statist or pro-statist, class-compromise or class-struggle visions of the syndicalist, communist, and socialist leadership of the various unions and union centrals. That is, although official union membership was consistently rising between the mid-1930s and the early 1940s,[18] it was still comparatively low by the standards to be set in the coming decades.[19] Moreover, the labour movement of the period continued to be disintegrated, a situation noted by the dearth of collective agreements, relatively weak and divided unions contending for different objectives, and a handful of union centrals vying for the allegiances and control of labour.[20] The political differences characterising the representatives of the labour movement up until the late 1930s and early 1940s thus prevented the working class from establishing a unified front for demanding more equitable distribution of the nation's wealth, although after 1940, according to David Rock, 'the primary issue' for labour increasingly became 'fringe benefits' (that is, vacation, insurance, paid sick days) and 'the amelioration of acceptable conditions'.[21]

From out of this reality of a growing urban working class, its rising demands for better working and life conditions, fragmented labour organisations, and an expanding and industrialising national economy, the Argentina of the early 1940s was ripe for the consolidation of labour into a more unified national movement. Guaranteeing the proper level of purchasing power and social benefits to the rank and file of this new labour movement would also spur on a national consumer market for new durable goods being manufactured in the country. As secretary of labour in 1943, Perón, through his anti-imperialist and anti-oligarchic public rhetoric and pro-labour policies, would closely align himself to the fate of this growing urban working class. The Peronist vision would be crystallised for workers in the myth promulgated by Perón and his enigmatic wife and political partner, Eva (Evita) Perón of Argentina's *descamisados* (the shirtless ones) – a catch-all term deployed by Perón and Evita that served to differentiate and give identity to this new urban working class. On the other hand, the labour movement leadership, increasingly being consolidated under the mantle of the CGT (which had brought together socialist, syndicalist, and a group of communist unions in 1930), sought to align itself with the secretary of labour's political ambitions, seeing its interests at the national level best

---

18   Rock 1987; Murmis and Portantiero 1971.
19   Matsushita 1983.
20   Rock 1987, pp. 254–7. See also Godio 2000; and Munck et al. 2007.
21   Rock 1987, p. 256.

carried out through the path Perón was paving.[22] The new urban-based industrial workers and their union leaders would help seal Perón's immediate future when they mobilised *en masse* and marched from Buenos Aires's industrial suburbs to the Plaza de Mayo on 17 October 1945, forcing the then-military government that Perón had been a part of to not only free him from his recent imprisonment,[23] but also to call elections for February 1946. Winning these elections comfortably under the short-lived Partido Laborista (Labour Party) ticket, Perón would soon go on to empower the CGT to become the main union central in the country, entrenching the legal right of unions under its purview *personería gremial* – legal recognition for the most representative union of each sector to negotiate sector-wide collective agreements. The CGT and the country's unions, via the auspices of the Ministry of Labour, would eventually oversee much of the state's broad national social benefits and welfare regime that included workers' recreation and vacation facilities, subsidised housing, and universal health coverage linked to unions' *obras sociales*. This proved to be the beginning of what his since been called in Argentina *verticalismo*, the moniker used to define the bureaucratic-corporatist and statist unionism that has had lasting impacts on Argentina's official labour movement over the past seven decades.

While Perón centralised organised labour's power in the CGT, and even included union leaders in his national government, he also understood that sustaining a growing national economy required a more affluent working class. To this end, Perón began to enunciate a tenuous class compromise between organised labour's bureaucracy (as primary representative of the interests of rank-and-file workers), the agro-export sector, industry, and the urban entrepreneurial class, a compromise that has ebbed, flowed, ruptured, and recomposed itself throughout Argentina's political economic history ever since.[24] To guarantee this class compromise, Perón perfected a political posture that included the state's appeasement of workers' demands for better living and working conditions on the one hand, while assuring national employers of the continuation of the capitalist system on the other. Via this 'third way', in a made-in-Argentina version of the developmentalist state, Perón entrenched in law improved labour rights, developed social security benefits (including a large extension of the national pension system and a minimum wage), and introduced paid vacations and sick leave, union- and cooperative-run family

---

22   Del Campo 2005.
23   Perón had been jailed a few days before due to his increasing political threat to the military
       government.
24   Smith 1991.

recreation and vacation facilities throughout the country, the institutionalisation of the *aguinaldo* system,[25] severance pay, regulations of work hazards, workers' compensation, maternity leave, and a policy of provisioning affordable and dignified housing.[26] He executed these new policies mainly through the Ministry of Labour – which had become, next to the office of the presidency, the centre of power of the national executive branch – while personifying them through the popular imaginary of Evita Perón and, between 1948 and 1955, the social work carried out via the foundation that carried her name.

This exponential growth of labour rights and organised labour's newfound standing in national politics, however, was always in tension with Perón's overall bid to hold on to power by centrally controlling the labour movement from the presidency. While workers were no doubt enjoying better living conditions and a greater share of national wealth under Perón, the union movement would increasingly come under state control. This situation was further confounded in that, at the same time that workers were experiencing increased wealth, they were also demanding more say on shop floors. Perón's vision for *justicialismo*, however, did not include increased shop floor democracy as the rank and file were increasingly envisioning. Rather, for Perón, workers' power had distinctive corporatist hues; for him, it was about vertical integration of the working class in a representative and hierarchical system that would delegate power to shop stewards. From shop stewards, power would then flow to regional union leaders, on up to the higher echelons of the CGT, then to the Ministry of Labour, and on to the executive branch of government and the office of the president.[27] In turn, most of the social welfare system was to be delivered through the CGT, while workers' agitation and potential anti-managerial and anti-employer shop floor democracy was to be contained (it was hoped) via the social benefits workers enjoyed and the bureaucratic union system. Indeed, Perón had already mapped out his state-centred corporatist ideals and his vision for the role of the unions early in his rise to power, assuring the country's employers as Secretary of Labour in 1944 that

> [i]t is a grave error to think that workers' unions are detrimental to the boss. In no way is this so. On the contrary, it is the best way to avoid the boss having to fight with his workers ... It is the means to reach an agreement, not a struggle. Thus strikes and stoppages are suppressed, though, undoubtedly, the working masses obtain the right to discuss their own

---

25   The 'thirteenth month' of salary at the end of the year.
26   Munck et al. 1987, p. 134.
27   James 1988; Munck et al. 1987.

interests at the same level as the employers' organizations, which, on ana-
lyzing it, is absolutely just ... That is why we're promoting trade unions,
a truly professional trade unionism. You do not want unions which are
divided and political factions, because the dangerous thing is, incidentally, political trade unionism.[28]

But, contrary to Perón's and the employers' desires, unions *did* become politicised and shop floors more democratic under *peronismo*. Perón's vision for the
'dignity of work', a notion that has maintained its relevance for Argentina's
working class until today, had the real effect of actually touching the labour
process on shop floors in ways unintended by his version of 'professional trade
unionism'. Especially taking off in 1944, according to Munck et al., 'a sophisticated system of direct democracy ... developed in ... factories', wherein sections of workshops would elect delegates via open assemblies.[29] 'The delegates
[in turn] constituted the *cuerpo de delegados* (shop-stewards plenary) which
in turn elected a *comisión interna* (factory committee) which negotiated with
management'.[30] During Perón's first two presidencies and thereafter, the result
was the creation of '[a] strong shop-stewards' organisation ... which gave the
Argentine labour movement an unrivalled level of participation and activism
in its best periods'.[31] Moreover, the authors go on, the factory committees and
shop-stewards' plenaries would take on an increasingly

> major role in pushing back the 'frontiers of control', as workers took away
> more and more of management's prerogatives. For the first time in Argen-
> tina, workers could meet legally during working hours and elect shop
> stewards – often after a vigorous political debate – and these could go
> on to defend workers' rights while being paid by the firm. The *comisiones
> internas* [thus] became important organs of self-defense which helped
> enforce the social gains made by the working class at the national level.[32]

These bodies of workplace democracy, in the Gramscian sense I will explore
further in Chapters 4 and 5, were not only spaces where issues such as dis-
missals, unjust managerial control, and production disputes were discussed
and debated, they were also 'political schools in which workers debated the

---

28   Perón, in Munck et al. 1987, p. 132.
29   Munck et al. 1987, p. 134.
30   Ibid.
31   Ibid.
32   Ibid.

major issues of the day, learned to organize, and to strike'.[33] Such were the unintended consequences of *peronismo*, which, in the imaginary and experiences of workers, would spawn decades-long desires and practices of organised, sophisticated, and directly democratic workers' institutions on shop floors. As Munck et al. sum up:

> Workers would henceforth associate [these social and political] gains of the Peronist period with the growth of the *comisiones internas*. These would sometimes become bureaucratised, but at their best they functioned as genuine organs of workers' democracy or 'workers' parliaments'.[34]

Perón's genius was to try to balance and hold in check the demands of employers with the desires of workers, bringing the interests of workers and employers together under a nationalist and populist agenda of a corporatist 'good society'. The flipside of *peronismo* would witness ongoing tensions between workers' participation and democracy, bureaucratic unionism, and employers' interests – tensions that would remain a recurring theme in the future history of Argentina's political economy.[35] These tensions would forever complicate a tenuously balanced class compromise in a power tug-of-war between a centralising and authoritarian state, an emboldened union bureaucracy, the growing demands of participation from workers on shop floors, and the recalcitrance of the country's entrepreneurial class.[36]

1.2 *Working-Class Self-Activity, Labour Resistance, and the Ebbs and Flows of Workers' Participation (1955–89)*

The ouster of Perón in 1955 further catalysed and redirected the resistive nature of Argentina's working class. This did not reduce the hold of *verticalismo* on the unions but, instead, saw the CGT mobilise on and off over the next decade and a half through, amongst other tactics, intermittent shop floor agitation in order to express its national political ambitions which had been, together with Peronism itself, proscribed by the military and civilian governments of the mid-to-late 1950s and throughout the 1960s. Now, mobilised in part by the struggle for the return of Perón by both the rank-and-file and the CGT leadership, a more revolutionary strand of labour activity emerged, helping to spawn by the end

---

33   Munck et al. 1987, pp. 134–5.
34   Munck et al. 1987, p. 135.
35   James 1988; Sidicaro 1999; Smith 1991.
36   Feinmann 2010.

of the 1960s 'clandestine Peronist bodies',[37] in addition to Maoist, Guevarist, Trotskyist, and other leftist urban and rural guerrilla groups.[38] Often, these clandestine bodies joined with or were supported by the *comisiones internas*. As Munck et al. assert, 'labour resistance during this period [in the years immediately after the ouster of Perón] was not contained by the government's repressive measures'.[39] Often, clandestine workers' assemblies would be organised in workplaces tightly controlled by union bureaucracies or intervened by the government of the day. At other times, planned and spontaneous strikes would be called. All of these bottom-up working-class initiatives would act as centres of counterpower to the authoritarian governments and the union *verticalismo* to come.[40]

As subsequent alternating military and civilian governments throughout the late 1950s and into the 1960s began to put in place economic policies based on growing foreign investment and rationalisation drives,[41] coupled with continued anti-labour policies and intermittent state repression, workers would (if periodically) increase their militancy. The first of a series of storied moments of mass labour resistance against anti-labour and pro-employer state policies during this era occurred in January 1959, when plans to privatise the state-owned Lisandro de la Torre meatpacking plant in the Mataderos *barrio* of Buenos Aires came to light. In response, 9,000 workers occupied the plant and even set it to work for a time with the additional support of tens of thousands of workers from surrounding *barrios* and municipalities taking over their plants, occupying streets, and setting up barricades.[42] While the revolt was eventually broken via state violence, the Lisandro de la Torre episode would prove to be a key moment in Argentine working-class militancy, a militancy that began the articulation of the strategy of occupying factories in defence of labour rights.[43]

---

37   Munck et al. 1987, p. 149.
38   Not all of these later 1960s groups were Peronist or militating for the return of Perón. The most leftist groups were by the end of this decade, rather, agitating for the revolutionary transformation of Argentina in various visions of a liberated workers' or communist society. What I mean to point out here, however, is that the socio-political tumult of the 1960s, much of it radiating out from shop floors, spawned the formation and expansion of a number of revolutionary parties and urban and rural guerrilla organisations that, as with for instance the Montoneros, also included those that saw the return of Perón as central to a new Argentina.
39   Munck et al. 1987, p. 149.
40   Munck et al. 1987, pp. 149–59. See also Feinmann 2010.
41   That is, mechanising or restructuring in order to save on labour costs.
42   Petit 2009.
43   Godio 2000; Wyczykier 2009a. Unlike the contemporary ERT phenomenon, most of the

With Perón still in exile, the late 1950s and early-to-mid 1960s witnessed a gradual increase in labour militancy via strikes and more factory occupations. This period would even see the CGT take up at times a specifically anti-imperialist and anti-capitalist agenda which posited demands for workers' control of the state and production, for unity amongst Latin America's working class, and a counter-hegemonic position for the labour movement, specifically against capitalist interests and in support of the redistribution of the nation's wealth and workers' control of national resources. These were positions that were to be adopted later by the dissident unions of the late 1960s and early 1970s and again during the 1990s in specific opposition to neo-liberalism. Suggestive of Gramsci's position regarding the educative role of workers' organisations for a counter-hegemonic working class, 'the official labour movement probably never intended to apply this radical program, but it is indicative of the mood of the period, and had a certain educative role [for workers' self-organising] over the years'.[44]

Moreover, as employers sought to implement their rationalisation drives throughout the 1960s, shop-stewards' plenaries, *comisiones internas*, strikes, and the tactic of factory occupations would increasingly have a centre-stage role in the Argentine political economy. As Munck et al. underscore, 'the spreading of factory occupations after 1960', in particular, 'provided a new element of concern to employers, who saw the sacred rights of private property being threatened'.[45] For instance, in 1962 and again in 1964 and 1965, a series of plant occupations took place, with rank-and-file participation guided by strike committees, mass meetings, and factory-wide participation in assemblies. This 'workers' plan' was coupled, under Augusto Vandor's leadership of the CGT, by a *plan de lucha* (plan of struggle) evocatively framed around the often-used Argentine labour strategy of *golpear y negociar* (hit and negotiate).[46] Thus, even during this era of deep 'verticalist' unionism in what would come to be known as *vandorismo*, the entrenchment of top-down union bureaucracy was coun-

---

factory occupations of the late 1950s were union-led tactics of resistance against rationalisation drives and pro-market policies of the *de facto* military government of President Aramburu (1955–58) and the elected government of President Frondizi (1958–60) and did not include the conversion of the majority of these experiences into worker cooperatives. Two experiences that did convert to worker cooperatives during this period, COGTAL and Obrera de Transporte La Calera, still survive and today consider themselves ERTs. See Chapter 2 for more on these two experiences.

44   Munck et al. 1987, p. 150.
45   Munck et al. 1987, p. 155.
46   Munck et al. 1987, p. 156.

terbalanced by vibrant grassroots workers' organisations that developed into a broad network of factory committees and union locals, in no small way led by rank-and-file workers' organisations and delegates.[47] According to Munck et al., then, the conventional historical literature's emphasis on the phenomena of union thugs (*matones*) used during this period under Vandor to 'control meetings and discipline wayward elements, tends to neglect the extent of [increasing] rank-and-file participation'[48] and the actual counter-hegemonic political force of workers' collective persistence and self-activity.

A case in point here is the factory occupations of 1964. While carefully coordinated by the CGT leadership, the *plan de lucha*'s apogee in 1964 included the occupation of 11,000 factories (or 10 percent of the country's industrial establishments) by almost four million workers in a seemingly paradoxical move by the CGT to '"cancel out rank and file action, to continue wearing them down, and at the same time to create the appropriate climate for a coup d'état"' against the elected government of President Illia.[49] Despite the intentions of the CGT leadership, the 1964 *plan de lucha* occupations proved to be a vital educational moment for the rank and file and for the future of militant workers' actions. Foreshadowing the rise of ERTs four decades later, over a quarter of these occupations occurred in the metallurgic sector, with important participation from textile, food processing, meatpacking, and construction sectors; not coincidentally, all of these sectors would subsequently play important protagonistic roles in the futue ERT phenomenon. Again hearkening back to Gramsci's insights, these mobilisations were, according to Munck et al., 'a tremendously important experience for the working class' and '[t]he power, organisation and combativity demonstrated in the factory occupations by the labour movement [during this period] were undeniable'.[50] 'To a certain extent', the authors continue, 'the [union bureaucracy of the CGT at the time] was in practice outflanked by rank-and-file activists who impressed a more radical

47   James 1988, p. 190; Munck et al. 1987, p. 156. While the CGT during this period was far from proposing the overthrow of capital, according to Daniel James it was central in promoting a new 'social function of capital' in a programme some factions of the CGT (such as the group that came to be known as the 62 Organisations) termed *cogestión* (James 1988, p. 190). As Munck et al. clarify, this programme included worker participation in production, the nationalisation of 'key sectors of the economy ...[, the] abolish[ment of] commercial secrecy ... [the] control [of] commercial associations and [the planning of] production efforts' (Munck et al. 1987, p. 156).

48   Munck et al. 1987, p. 157.

49   Echagüe, in Munck et al. 1987, p. 158. See also James 1978, 1988; and Wyczykier 2009a.

50   Munck et al., 1987, pp. 158.

stamp on what was originally conceived of as a carefully controlled "revolutionary gymnastics" (*gimnasia revolucionaria*)' by the exiled Perón and the CGT leadership.[51]

By the late 1960s, the labour movement would take on characteristics that brought to the fore even more radical and bottom-up dimensions to Argentina's working-class militancy. Despite the troubled state of the class compromise in the 1960s, the working class had continued to gain considerable purchasing power by the end of the decade. Furthermore, relatively new industrial sectors gained in economic force by the end of the 1960s, bringing to the labour movement a new generation of educated and radicalised workers in, for instance, the automobile and aeronautics industries in new industrial centres such as Córdoba and Rosario.

The new generation of rank-and-file workers of this era was increasingly made up of workers from the provinces without former links to the established union and CGT hierarchies, which were mostly located in the city and suburbs of Buenos Aires. Additionally, there was an increase in demands for higher education from Argentine youth by the end of the 1960s as the children of the first generation of workers from the Peronist years of the 1940s and 1950s sought upward mobility. Students' aspirations during this period would merge with broader societal demands for increased social justice and more democratic institutions. They would also merge with the demands being made by the new generation of workers for better working conditions, more control over the labour process, less union and state authoritarianism, and even an increased demand from some sectors for a democratic socialist country, including amongst radical Peronists and other non-Peronist leftist unions and political groups. On the other hand, a recalcitrant authoritarian state increased its assault on the working class during this period by attempting to roll back further union gains of the past, promoting plant unions and collective agreements at the level of the firm (rather than sector-wide agreements), and encouraging industrial rationalisation.[52] These were some of the now familiar ways that the military government of General Juan Carlos Onganía (1966–70) would attempt to counter the CGT's influence while, more fundamentally, attempting to exhaust workers' unity and militancy on shop floors.

The killing of a student on 29 May 1969 by state security forces in the city of Córdoba during a planned mass strike was the final trigger for what would turn out to be a year of workers' and students' revolts throughout the country.

---

51   Munck et al., 1987, pp. 158–9.
52   Godio 2000; James 1988; Munck et al. 1987.

El Cordobazo, in particular, the largest and most explosive of these uprisings, was to be etched forever in the minds of Argentine workers, foreshadowing the events of *el Argentinazo* of December 2001. The countrywide CGT-organised general strike planned for 30 May 1969 was anticipated by Córdoba's militant unions as a *paro activo* (active work stoppage) on 29 May, soon joined by the city's university students' takeover of the Universidad Nacional de Córdoba. Street fighting soon broke out later that day as workers and students faced off against 4,000 police and, in the following days, 5,000 armed soldiers. During these last days of May, the entire city centre of Córdoba would be behind barricades as students, white-collar workers, and especially the new metalworkers of the automobile sector (mostly belonging to UOM, SMATA,[53] and the electrical workers of Luz y Fuerza) supported by the residents of the *barrios* they occupied marched in columns, guarded the barricades, engaged in riots, deployed Molotov cocktails and other makeshift weapons, and even exchanged gunfire with the Argentine military and the city's police.[54]

These more militant, more spontaneous, politically more radical and direct action-infused tactics of street violence and workplace occupations, often bypassing the apex of the country's organised labour hierarchy, would increasingly become regular methods of struggle for Argentine workers in the ensuing years.[55] In March 1971 in a related event known as *el Viborazo*, the city of Córdoba would again experience several days of workers' and students' occupation and the barricading of large swaths of the city, this time including mass factory occupations by the city's FIAT workers and those from other related sectors. Together with more stringent anti-capitalist, anti-imperialist, and pronationalist views that strongly identified with a subversive working class (and even aspiring in the minds of some militants toward the eventual founding of a workers' state), this new radicalised faction of the labour movement would come to be known as *clasismo*. Large strikes, work stoppages, and factory occupations such as occurred during *el Viborazo* would take place more frequently throughout the first years of the 1970s, forcing the military dictatorships of the time to eventually permit the return of Perón from exile, leading to his brief and tumultuous third presidency in 1973.

With the return of Perón, bureaucratic unionism would also revive but would live uncomfortably with the new rank-and-file protagonism that had

---

53 Sindicato de Mecánicos y Afines del Transporte Automotor de la República Argentina (Union of Mechanics and Allied Automotive Transport Workers of the Republic of Argentina).

54 Munck et al. 1987, pp. 171–2.

55 Munck et al. 1987; Svampa and Pereyra 2004; Wyckzkier 2009a.

been on the rise by the late 1960s and early 1970s. The third Peronist government restored the system of *personería gremial* and instituted a new Ley de Contracto de Trabajo (Law of Labour Contracts), strengthening once again the labour rights lost during the years when Peronism was proscribed. But these would also be years of deep social divisions, confrontations, and violence throughout Argentine social sectors, witnessed most famously in the rise of urban and rural guerrilla activity, kidnappings, insecurity, increasingly violent state repression, and the first disappearances of suspected guerrilla activists by state-sanctioned paramilitary death squads such as the Alianza Anticomunista Argentina (Argentine Anticommunist Alliance, also known as *'la triple A'*). With the death of Perón in 1974 and the subsequent troubled presidency of his third wife, María Estela (Isabel) Martínez de Perón (1974–6), economic crises, hyperinflation, and a new wave of wage-control legislation laid bare a new strand of *peronismo* that overtly turned on workers for the first time as the government of Isabel Perón cancelled new collective contracts (in a foreshadowing of Menem's neo-liberal version of *peronismo* that would arrive again within two decades).

Workers reacted spontaneously to this new assault via street protests, a new surge of workplace occupations, and eventually a new wave of strikes uncontrolled by the union bureaucracy.[56] As Elizabeth Jelin recalls of these days:

> [s]pontaneous protests ... dominated the scene as workers from one plant would start a street demonstration and soon the workers from neighbouring plants would join in. Within minutes, thousands of workers would be marching through the streets [of Argentina's major industrial centres].[57]

These demonstrations were as much about the freezing of salaries and the 'cancellation of free collective bargaining without government intervention' as they were about workers' intensifying frustrations and disappointments with the anti-labour turn Peronism had taken after Juán Perón's death.[58]

A novel strategy of workers' organised self-activity during this period that would channel otherwise spontaneous grassroots workers' protests were the *coordinadoras interfabriles*, emulating Chile's earlier *coordinadores industriales* of the Allende years.[59] Participants in this new brand of workers' organisation that, according to Munck et al., were 'a new type of rank-and-file organisation

---

56   Ruggeri 2009, pp. 37–8.
57   Jelin, in Munck et al. 1987, p. 199.
58   Munck et al. 1987, p. 199.
59   Bayat 1991.

... [of] ... coordinating bodies of factory activists and workers' commissions on a district level' included local union branches, shop-steward committees, and worker activists.[60] The *coordinadoras interfabriles* would eventually play a central role in coordinating the massive general strikes of June and July 1975. The *coordinadoras*, Munck et al. conclude, became a potential alternative power centre to both the union bureaucracy and the state, highlighting a crisis in Peronism, organised labour, and the Argentine political economy in general at the time.[61]

The coup that overthrew Isabel Perón's government in March 1976 would bring with it a military dictatorship that, yet again, proscribed the Peronist party and intervened in the CGT, most unions, and the most radicalised workplaces. But this time the form of military intervention was particularly bloody; the new military dictatorship literally disembowelled the labour movement. Labelled the Proceso de Reorganización Nacional (National Process of Reorganisation) by the military, the major groups that would be 'reorganised' (a euphemism for economic restructuring and the waves of imprisonments and disappearances that would soon take place during these years) were union leaders and politicised workers. This would prove to be a watershed moment in modern Argentine history, a moment that has deeply marked not only the labour movement but also all of Argentine society ever since. In addition to the genocide, throughout the 1976–83 dictatorship (known also in shorthand as the period of *el Proceso*) the ratio of shop stewards per worker was massively reduced, the Ministry of Labour was gutted, strikes were made illegal, wages were frozen, and the neo-liberal order began to take shape in the midst of massive human rights violations[62] in order to, in no small way, restore the class privileges of the capitalist elite.[63] But even this form of extreme state repression did not completely cancel out the militancy of Argentine workers. Organised labour would eventually get its footing back with the demise of the legitimacy of the military dictatorship during a new series of strikes by the start of the 1980s that, in addition to the disaster of the Falklands War in 1982, would lead to the eventual return of representative democracy in 1983.

With democracy's return in December 1983 and President Raul Alfonsín's UCR party in government (1983–9), a new moment of working-class recomposition emerged. With the Peronist party relegated to the opposition and, together with the CGT hierarchy, in a general state of shock after the failures of the last

---

60 Munck et al. 1987, p. 199. See also Slatman, Rodriguez, and Lascano 2009.

61 Munck et al. 1987, p. 200. See also Smith 1991; and Werner and Aguire 2007.

62 Suriano 2005b.

63 Harvey 2005; Smith 1991.

Peronist government of Isabel Perón and the working class's decimation during the years of *el Proceso*, a new series of debates took hold during these years concerning how to reorganise unions and reconstitute the shop floor workers' institutions that had been proscribed during the dictatorship years.[64] However, in the midst of rising inflation, workers' disappointments with the failed promises for labour renewal, and a new yet tenuous social pact imposed by the Alfonsín government, 13 general strikes would unfold throughout the 1980s. Moreover, a new acme of workers' self-activity arose in 1984 and 1985 with a wave of work stoppages and occupations responding to the worsening economic situation. In July of 1985, for instance, an 18-day factory occupation at the Pacheco Ford plant by almost 1,500 workers protesting against lay-offs had them set the factory to work under self-management,[65] while in the mid-to-late 1980s several metal shops in the southern Buenos Aires suburbs were also occupied and set to produce under workers' control.[66] These were the years that would immediately precede the rise of the ERT phenomenon in the 1990s, years that saw the very first contemporary recuperations of failing capitalist enterprises in Argentina and their conversions into worker cooperatives as a way of saving jobs.

While the occupations and workers' self-management experiences of the 1980s can be seen to be cases of ERTs, all of these work sites have since closed or, as in the case of Ford Pacheco, long returned to private hands.[67] In reality, early workplace occupations in Argentina – that is, during the late 1950s, early-to-mid 1960s, late 1960s, and early 1970s; the Ford Pacheco takeover; and the occupations and conversions of the mid-to-late 1980s – were different from today's ERTs in that they were mostly about particular shop floor conflicts, union demands, and broader struggles for union power against state authoritarianism or inaction. Once jobs were restored or wages reset, most of these workplace occupations ended, at times with the firm's eventual closure and workers seeking employment elsewhere. Today's ERTs, as we have seen in the case studies in Chapter 1 and our analysis in Chapter 2, are fundamentally different from these earlier forms of takeovers because they actually attempt to work out, in practice, long-term projects of *autogestión* and thus go beyond the usual bread and butter issues or demands for bettering the conditions of work that guide union-based actions.

---

64   Godio 2000.
65   Aguilar 2015.
66   Ruggeri 2009, p. 38.
67   Ruggeri 2009, p. 39.

1.3   *The Legacy of the Peronist Imaginary for Argentina's Workers*

The notions of the 'dignity of work' and the right for workers to be central players in the Argentine political economy – so strongly articulated by Perón and the Peronist-controlled union movement under the auspices of the CGT in the 1940s, 1950s, and 1960s – are perhaps the two central ideas that remain ensconced in the cultural and collective memories of Argentina's working class.[68] Moreover, as Maurizio Atzeni frames it, Peronism and the centralised, nationalist unionism it propagated brought with them new forms of 'citizenship around workers' rights' as unions became de facto state organs 'responsible for the administration of substantive financial resources' such as with health and social security delivery.[69] All this would bring to the CGT, in particular, 'tangible power' in the Argentine political economy.[70] Indeed, as Atzeni further underscores, after Perón's rearticulation of the national political economy, 'the unions' would become 'a key intermediary in Argentina's equivalent of a welfare state'.[71] In short, as James has also pointed out, one of the major and enduring legacies of *peronismo* for Argentina's working class has been to extend the guarantee of citizenship rights to workers via their union representation.[72]

These Peronist-tinged imaginaries around the dignity of work and citizenship rooted in workers' rights have, not surprisingly, overflowed into the ERT phenomenon's cultural, political, and discursive milieus via its worker-protagonists' collective memories and past experiences, which can be heard in the language used by the leaders of ERT umbrella organisations and the phenomenon's most militant protagonists. For instance, many ERT leaders and advocates, such as Eduardo Murúa, former president of the Movimiento Nacional de Empresas Recuperadas (MNER); Mario Barrios, former president of UST and general secretary of the Asociación Nacional de Trabajadores Auto-gestionados (ANTA); and Chilavert's Plácido Peñarrieta and brothers Cándido and Fermín González – five of this study's key informants whom we already met in Chapter 1 – have come from some of the most militant sectors of Peronist and *clasista* trade unionism. Murúa, for example, learned his militancy in the ranks of the steelworkers and in his involvement with the 1980s' Montonero movement. The González brothers (especially Cándido) were active for a time in the graphic workers' union under dissident CGT leader Raimundo Ongaro in

---

68   Munck et al. 1987, pp. 133, 238, 240. See also Del Campo 2005; Feinmann 2010; James 1988; and Vieta 2010a.

69   Atzeni 2010, p. 55.

70   Ibid.

71   Ibid.

72   James 1988.

the late 1960s, while, Peñarrieta, as we saw in Chapter 1, has been a long-time social housing activist. And UST's Mario Barrios, son of a Peronist union activist, emerged from the construction workers' union and has shared with me vivid memories of his presence with his father in the crowds that had gathered for the fateful and definitive return of Perón from exile at the Buenos Aires international airport of Ezeiza in June 1973. Not surprisingly, the sectors that these five protagonists work in make up together around 35 percent of all of Argentina's ERTs.[73]

In addition, some of the particular events that still colour the imaginary of ERT protagonists I have spoken with include: the massive worker mobilisations that brought Perón to power on 17 October 1945; the occupations of factories during the 1960s, 1970s, and 1980s; the worker-led sieges of the cities of Córdoba (*el Cordobazo*) and Rosario (*el Rosariazo*) in May and September of 1969 respectively; and the countless general strikes, popular revolts, and myriad forms of workers' activism and resistances that have taken place over the last several decades, including, of course, *el Argentinazo* of 19 and 20 December 2001. I have also especially witnessed a Peronist imaginary in the social gatherings of ERT workers I have been privy to since 2005, at which time workers will often bring up the ideals of the 'golden years' of the labour movement of the mid-to-late 1940s, 1960s, and early 1970s when unemployment was low, salaries high, and working class militancy and labour protections strong. Moreover, during these social gatherings, the discursive images of Perón and Evita are often positioned as the propagators and symbols of workers' rights, protections, and the 'just society', and of a time when the working class could aspire to a life of economic wellbeing and secure jobs.[74] For these workers, working life is one of the most central parts of Argentine life; work is not only a 'right', but it also defines much of one's human dignity. These are views that, within the context

---

73   See Table 1 in Chapter 2.

74   Of course, not all ERT workers outwardly express or share Peronist sympathies, although most of them, as with all Argentine workers, have been influenced in one way or another by *peronismo*. I have had informal discussions with a handful of ERT workers who actually distanced themselves from or have critiqued the centralist or 'verticalist' tendencies of *peronismo* and even the potential of Argentina's ERTs for an alternative socio-economic and political reality for Argentina. This was, for instance, the position of one self-described Trotskyist worker (and former urban guerrilla activist in the 1960s) from the city of Córdoba's *Comercio y Jusitica* worker-recuperated newspaper, as he explained to me in a 2009 interview. Moreover, other ERTs have been influenced by other political tendencies, such as the early desires of the leadership of the Zanón/FaSinPat workers for nationalisation of Argentina's ERT, a leadership inspired by the Trotskyist political views of a group of its founders affiliated with the Partido de los Trabajadores Socialistas (PTS, Socialist Workers' Party).

of the Argentine working class, Juán and Evita Perón persuasively and memorably articulated at a national level. They are also notions that contribute to the moral economy of work driving workers' justifications for the recuperation of firms and ERTS' six recuperative moments that we will be assessing in the next chapter.

But equally present in the minds of Argentina's working class is the dismantling of the 'just society' that began to unfold with the brutal repressions of the 1976–83 dictatorships. And, paradoxically, the Argentina of the 1990s under the tutelage of Peronist president Carlos Menem (1989–99) also witnessed an intensification of the severing of the strong ties that *peronismo* had traditionally enjoyed since the 1940s with the country's popular sectors and its working class. Indeed, the Peronist party's vestiges of a vision of social justice for all Argentines and an economically self-reliant Argentina temporarily dissolved with Menem's zealous neo-liberalist policies, as the dissolution of Perón's nationalist and developmentalist state throughout the 1990s relegated hundreds of thousands of working-class people – the traditional grassroots supporters of *peronismo* – to the ranks of the unemployed and the desperate.[75] Additionally, the strong collective agreements that were formalised in the 1940s, 1950s, 1960s, and 1970s, coupled with national economic policies guided by mostly ISI initiatives in the 1930s, 1940s, and early 1950s, were slowly dismantled throughout the 1960s, 1970s, 1980s, and 1990s with the gradual but steady introduction of a neo-liberalised economic model and its inherent discourse of less meddlesome government, more entrepreneurialism, and leaner businesses.[76] In response, by the late 1990s, thousands of those who were part of this later urban working class began to take to the streets and highways of the nation in the only form of protest that remained for the unemployed, the underemployed, and the flexibilised: occupying and squatting roads, highways, and – for those who still had jobs – workplaces. With these tactics, organised groups of the underemployed and structurally unemployed managed to directly cut off for short periods of time the economic veins of the country,[77] eventually contributing to the end of *menemismo*; the surge of social and solidarity economy initiatives around the crisis years at the turn of the millennium; and the rise of a more traditional, yet also uniquely contemporary version of Peronism articulated throughout the 12 years of *kirchnerismo* beginning in 2003.

---

75   Gambina and Campione 2002; Svampa and Pereyra 2004.
76   Patroni 2004.
77   Svampa and Pereyra 2004, pp. 54–7.

As this section's historical overview has hopefully made clear, taking over workspaces to gain labour victories, together with vibrant shop floor demo-cratic institutions, are worker-led practices with deep roots in Argentina. These practices, often emerging as the spontaneous and bottom-up collective actions of workers, have acutely marked the history of Argentina's working class and its struggles in the seven decades since the first Peronist period.[78] The upsurge of self-managed enterprises in Argentina, motivated at first by conjunctures of economic precariousness and dire necessity, is thus rooted in a long tradition of workers' militancy and workplace democratic institutions within the country's broader labour movement. It is also linked to the repercussions of Argentina's intense social mobilisations that began circa 1995–6 with the multidimensional Movimiento de Trabajadores Desocupados (MTD, Movement of Unemployed Workers) – popularly known as *los piqueteros* – and other, grassroots-based popular struggles against the neo-liberal order that engulfed the country dur-ing the 1990s. I turn to these more recent historical themes in the next section and the remaining pages of this chapter.

1.4   *A Few Words on the Use of State-Sanctioned Violence and Repression in Argentina*

Before I go on, I would be remiss if I did not specifically underscore how the recurrent use of repression and outright violence has been a consistent tool deployed in the Argentine state's 'regimes of ruling'[79] against the working class and its bottom-up initiatives. A specific comment on state-sanctioned violence and repression is warranted since it has pockmarked the history of Argentina's political economy and the collective memory of its working people. Violence and repression also played an important part in the difficult transition to post-convertability during the years spanning the turn of the millennium, including the state's often-violent responses to workers' occupations and conversions of firms to worker cooperatives, especially during ERTS' first period.

Indeed, dating back at least to the mid-nineteenth century, with the first signs of industrialisation in Argentina in the meatpacking sector, the state and capitalist actors have used repressive tactics on working people in order to entrench a dominative position over the growing working class. Most often, repressive measures and outright violence have been reasoned by the state and the capitalist class as either a way of re-establishing 'social order' when workers protested against unfair treatment (as witnessed most vividly in the

---

78   Atzeni 2010; James 1988; Munck et al. 1987; Palomino 2005a, 2005b; Wyczykier 2009a.

79   Smith 2005, pp. 7–10.

Semana Trágica of 1919 or the Patagonia Rebelde episode of the early 1920s), or as authoritarian responses to strikes, factory takeovers, and general working-class militancy (as, for example, in the Lisandro de la Torre factory occupation and subsequent mass workers' revolts of 1959 or during *el Cordobazo* and *el Viborazo*). The last half of the twentieth century witnessed an Argentine state increasingly turn to extreme forms of violence and repression for reformulating or restoring the country's class compromise.[80] More brutally and notoriously, of course, were the strategies and tactics of the last military dictatorship's so-called National Process of Reorganisation between 1976–83 that unleashed massive waves of fear, human rights violations, and the systematic killings and disappearances of mostly workers and union leaders. This brutal period of 'reorganisation' fundamentally served to introduce to Argentina what would later come to be known as neo-liberalism and forcefully phased out the ISI model that had predominated its political economy in the previous four decades.[81] State-sanctioned repression was also present throughout the 1990s, and especially during the crisis years of 1999–2003, remembered by many for the killing of more than two dozen protesters during the 19 and 20 December mass protests and Eduardo Duhalde's caretaker government's implication in the killing of two young *piqueteros*, Maximiliano Kosteki and Darío Santillán, on 26 June 2002, which would hasten the early elections that saw Néstor Kirchner win the presidency in 2003.

In sum, the use of repression and violence to quash social unrest, protests, or labour activism has been a central *modus operandi* of the Argentine state for decades. Repression and violence certainly did not go unused in dealing with ERTs, especially during the phenomenon's first period, as the cases in Chapter 1 made clear. Indeed, while state repression was not unheard of even during the three Kirchner presidencies, the governments of Néstor Kirchner and his successor, Cristina Fernández de Kirchner, had distinguished themselves from previous governments by, at least in their policies and in their public discourses, distancing themselves from state violence and campaigning on platforms of and actually carrying out numerous projects focused on human rights, social justice, and workers' issues. With the coming to power of Mauricio Macri, however, old ways returned. Hearkening back to usual modes of relating to the country's popular sectors and social movements, repression as an instrument of control, as I will return to in Chapters 6 and 7, had resurfaced with *macrismo*. This was already witnessed within Macri's first

---

80   Smith 1991.
81   Smith 1991.

months in power in several confrontations with social movement leaders, such as in the province of Jujuy, and with the new ERT newspaper *El Tiempo Argentino*.[82]

2   Section 2: Argentina's Neo-liberal Turn and the After-Effects of Socio-economic Crisis (1990–2016)

> This period in Argentina wasn't like other periods where your job was terminated and you go and find work elsewhere. No, there simply was no work to find; everything was shutting down.
>
> JOSÉ LÓPEZ[83]

There is little doubt today that the economic decisions that had, in real material terms, immiserated the Argentine working class in the last decades of the twentieth century have roots in the orthodox economic policies of the military dictatorship of 1976–83.[84] *El Proceso* was, amongst other things, a bloody attempt at breaking working-class unity and union power via fear and genocide. It would prove to be *the* test-bed in Argentina for the neo-liberal assault on the working class throughout the 1990s.[85] With human rights violations becoming more and more obvious as the years of the last dictatorship wore on, and with increasing pressure from local and international human rights groups (in no small part via the fearless work of the Madres de la Plaza de Mayo), this sort of decomposition of labour was unsustainable in the long-term. But the neo-liberal experiment that began with *el Proceso* would continue to consolidate itself long after the military regime's demise. The ill effects of neo-liberalism on Argentina's working people were accelerated via ongoing reforms to labour legislation and the deregulation of social security that in essence entrenched precarious working conditions and, in the long-term, transformed shop floors and labour processes across economic sectors.[86] Moreover, as business owners became emboldened by this increased privileging of entrepreneurial prerogatives, throughout the late 1980s and into the 1990s employers

---

82   Ámbito.com 2016a; El Destape 2016; López 2016.

83   López 2009, personal interview (co-founder and former president of Cooperativa Salud Junín).

84   Damill 2005; Piva 2015; Recalde 2012; Sitrin 2012; Suriano 2005a, 2005b; Svampa and Pereyra 2004.

85   Harvey 2005; Saad-Filho, Iannini, and Molinari 2007.

86   Olmedo and Murray 2002.

began demanding higher productivity from workers as they increased ration-alisation drives and chipped away at salaries. At the same time, workers' began to lower their salary expectations, union-based solidarity and democratic insti-tutions on shop floors weakened, and the role of organised labour via the lead-ership of the CGT – since the mid-1940s the central player and key mediator for securing the class compromise so adeptly crafted by Perón – would dramatic-ally transform under the presidency of Carlos Menem.[87]

Within the *menemista* political economic model, the mainline CGT would split into factions supportive of the regime's neo-liberal policies and those opposed to them.[88] In addition, a plethora of new forms of alternative labour organising would emerge in the 1990s as a counterforce to the neo-liberal model and the co-opted factions of the CGT. What I will soon characterise as a new social movement and community unionism would initially bring dispar-ate social actors together in order to resist the state's unwavering adoption of the neo-liberal model, and the mainline CGT's support of it.

The leadership of the CGT's support of Menem's neo-liberal policies even-tually motivated several splits of the confederation by the early-to-mid 1990s and to the founding of the breakaway Movimiento de Trabajadores Argentinos (MTA, Movement of Argentine Workers). It also saw the rise of alternative union organisations such as the Central de Trabajadores de la Argentina (CTA, Argen-tine Workers Central), a new union confederation that emerged from break-away former-CGT unions, workers, and organisers, especially from the teachers' and state employees' unions; the Corriente Clasista y Combativa (CCC, Classist and Combative Current), a new multi-sectoral organisation of disaffected and left-leaning Peronist and socialist workers' organisations with roots in 1970s res-istance groups representing employed, unemployed, and retired workers; and myriad other smaller but equally combative groups of the unemployed, the underemployed, and the marginalised.

The other major new form of labour organising of the period that would fore-shadow and influence the mass street protests of *el Argentinazo*, the takeovers of private and public spaces, workplace occupations, and the *asambleas bar-riales*, was the Movimiento de Trabajadores Desocupados (MTD, Movement of Unemployed Workers), known informally as *los piqueteros* (literally, 'the picketers'). The *piqueteros* were a vast and diverse movement of unemployed workers that emerged circa 1996 in the wake of the Menem administration's mass public-sector privatisations and the private sector's subsequent downsiz-

---

87   Damill 2005; Palomino 2005a; Recalde 2012.
88   Olivera 2007.

ings and restructurings.[89] Without workplaces to strike or unions to represent them, the *piqueteros'* main mode of protest entailed blocking major roadways throughout the country as a strategy of strangling the economic lifeline of the country. At first, the *piqueteros* consisted mainly of the burgeoning population of unemployed state workers, especially from the oil sector in the provinces of Neuquén and Salta.[90] The MTD would eventually include a broad cross-section of structurally unemployed Argentine workers composed of numerous organisations spanning the spectrum of political views, from those unemployed workers led by ethico-political commitments to autonomy from the state or organised labour bureaucracies, to those espousing various Marxist or anarchist perspectives, to several organisations that were eventually assimilated into various municipal, provincial, or national factions of parties of the left or of the Peronist party. By the mid-2000s, many *piquetero* groups took on hierarchical structures and their leadership became intermediaries for the distribution of welfare to members linked to the social assistance programmes initiated by the Kirchner governments.[91]

These protagonists of Argentina's new and alternative labour organisations that began to emerge in the early 1990s would, by the middle of that decade, merge the strategy of the general strike with a diversity of groups and associations embracing affinity relationships between the unemployed, human rights groups, pensioners' organisations, and various other social justice initiatives.[92] Together, these alternative labour movements and organisations of the period embraced the common goal of directly opposing both Menem's Washington Consensus model as well as the mainline CGT's *sindicalismo de negociación* (unionism of negotiation), which saw its leaders either take on a policy of negotiating with the Menem regime or a posture of self-preservation in light of the regime's anti-labour policies.[93] They also commonly proposed an array of alternative socio-economic solutions embracing aspects of *autogestión*.[94] The rise of the ERTs can be seen as part of this community- and social movement-based labour organising and activism that emerged most directly in opposition to the effects of the neo-liberal model at the point of produc-

---

89   Pozzi 1998.
90   Svampa and Pereyra 2004.
91   Adamovsky 2007; Dinerstein 2002; Svampa and Pereyra 2004.
92   The CTA, for instance, would introduce a policy of direct worker affiliation without the need for a workplace's union itself to be affiliated to the confederation, while it also reached out actively to all workers, including the employed, the unemployed, and those seeking employment and to numerous social movement organisations.
93   Godio 2000.
94   Dinerstein 2015; Sartelli 2005; Svampa and Pereyra 2004.

tion and in the lives of working people throughout the 1990s. We will return to outlining the characteristics of these alternative labour organisations that encompass ERTs in the last section of this chapter.

2.1 The Lived Experiences of Neo-liberalism in Argentina (1990–2003)

The first years of the 1990s brought with them a consensus that cut across socio-economic sectors and introduced a new form of class compromise based not on the 'benevolent' or nationalist-developmentalist state model of earlier years, but rather on discourses of economic growth, consumerism, easy credit, individualism, and entrepreneurial values. This new national consensus especially gained momentum with the neo-liberal policies of Menem's influential economics minister, Domingo Cavallo. But by the late 1990s, many in Argentina's working class began to see through the empty promises of upward socio-economic mobility for all. The ultimately unsustainable neo-liberal experiment in Argentina came to a temporary break with the forced resignation of Menem's successor, Fernando de la Rúa (1999–2001) amidst the massive popular uprisings of December 2001. In particular, the surge of today's ERT phenomenon was a direct response to the drastic increases in business closures, unemployment, poverty, and indigence that resulted from the policies and market liberalisations of this period. As Murúa expressively explained to me in a interview in 2005:

> The number of recuperated enterprises began to grow until 2001, a year which culminated in the severe crisis of the convertibility model. The state fails to collect its revenues, the sector of the dominant classes ... are no longer profitable, and there is a crisis of the system from above and a high degree of conflict from below, with the maximum expression of our people being the struggles of work stoppages and mass picketing. The combination of the experiences of the working class in these work stoppages, plus the experiences that were generated within the mobilisations of the *piqueteros*, made the system reflect on itself and say, 'We can no longer continue on this path'. This was at the time a country in flames![95]

Argentina's neo-liberal experiment of the 1990s primarily consisted of the privatisation of much of the country's national assets and public enterprises, the multinationalisation of a great portion of its once domestically oriented industrial and economic base, the opening up of the nation's economy to spec-

---

95   Murúa 2005a, personal interview.

ulative foreign capital, the 'dollarisation' of the peso, and persistent and broad cuts in social spending.[96] Encouraged throughout the 1980s and 1990s by the structural adjustments imposed on the country by the IMF and other international financial institutions, these policies resulted in the eventual deindustrialisation of an economy that had been, between the mid-1940s and mid-1970s, sustained to a great degree by the class compromise upheld by ISI policies and high salaries that encouraged a strong national consumer market.[97] But rather than bring to Argentina the 'economic miracle' that many mainstream media outlets and financial pundits were predicting throughout the early-to-mid 1990s, its neo-liberal venture served to, on the one hand, enrich the affluent and the politically connected and assist in the capital accumulation projects of foreign investors while simultaneously impoverishing a large swath of Argentina's working people.

Argentina's neo-liberal economic policies of the 1990s took shape with the fixed-rate exchange policy known as the Plan de Convertibilidad (Convertability Plan), introduced by Cavallo via the Ley de Convertibilidad (Convertability Law) in the first trimester of 1991.[98] The Convertability Plan was openly meant to be a strong pro-market price stabilisation programme implemented to stem acute macro-economic instability and, most of all, the persistent tides of inflation and hyperinflation that plagued much of Raúl Alfonsín's government throughout the 1980s.[99] While in the first years of the 1990s, soon after the Plan's implementation, inflation was curtailed, price stability took root, GDP rose, and exports began to increase, eventually an overvalued peso meant that Argentine goods became exceedingly costly compared to imports. Already by the mid-1990s, the Plan de Convertibilidad was setting the stage for the socio-economic misery that was to unfold in the lives of countless Argentines in the last years of the 1990s and early 2000s.[100] The Plan de Convertibilidad played such a central role in Argentina's political economy of the era that the neo-liberal years of the 1990s and early 2000s have come to be known as *la época de la convertibilidad* (the convertability era).[101]

As a result of these convertability based neo-liberal policies, with no restrictions on the flow of capital out of Argentina by the multinationals that had

---

96   Aroskind 2001; Belmartino 2005; Lo Vuolo and Barbeito 1998; Piva 2015; Romero 2003; Schvarzer 1998.
97   Elgue 2007; Kosacoff 2007; Lewis 2001; Romero 2003.
98   Gambina and Campione 2002; Kosacoff 2007; Patroni 2004.
99   Damill 2005; Velde and Veracierto 2000.
100   Schvarzer 1998.
101   Mercatante 2015; Piva 2015.

bought up a great portion of its economy, with easily available consumer credit, and with cheaper imports saturating local markets, a chronic trade deficit took hold by the middle of the decade.[102] The Plan de Convertibilidad also took away much of the lending flexibility and monetary autonomy of the country's central bank, the Banco Central de la República Argentina (BCRA), which was required under the IMF-sanctioned convertability model to back fully the dollarised peso with foreign reserves. The result was that Argentina lost the monetary sovereignty that could have responded to the eventual trade deficit.

In this macro-economic environment, many local companies – and SME firms in particular – discovered that they were unable to conduct business, losing their competitive advantage to more stable or predatory foreign companies subsidised in part by Argentina's favourable tax rates and anti-labour policies and the free reign these foreign firms were given to do business across most economic sectors. As Viviana Patroni explains, 'many [Argentine] firms could not adjust to the new conditions created under trade liberalisation, in many cases because they did not have access to the financing required to increase their efficiency' and to stay competitive.[103] SMEs were especially overburdened in this macro-economic reality, Patroni further explains, because an overvalued peso, and thus overvalued Argentine products, 'in combination with trade liberalisation, proved to be a deadly formula for several economic sectors in Argentina which could simply not compete with the volume of imports domestic policies were undervaluing'.[104] Dwindling national and international markets and the increased cost of doing business in the country, including having to pay for wages in dollars, meant that an escalating number of once-profitable SMEs began to court bankruptcy by the mid-1990s.[105] By 2001, the national month-over-month business bankruptcy rate had reached its highest point in modern history: During the Menem/de la Rúa years, bankruptcies soared from an average of 772 per month in 1991 to over 2,600 per month by 2001.[106] The most notable result of this sharp rise in bankruptcies for Argentina's workers was that, already by 1995, jobs were beginning to disappear in Argentina at unprecedented speed (see Figure 12). In sum, the fixed exchange rate, relatively high interest rates, and the increasing prices for goods and services in the private sector meant 'wages and other labour costs became practically the main variables

---

102   Díaz-Bonilla, Díaz-Bonilla, Piñiero, and Robinson 2004.
103   Patroni 2004, p. 103.
104   Ibid.
105   Palomino 2003, 2005a, 2005b.
106   Magnani 2003, p. 37.

available to reduce production costs'.[107] As Patroni concludes, the neo-liberal policy of convertability was thus *the* major macro-economic backdrop for the rising tide of unemployment, increased exploitation at the point of production, and the ultimate immiseration of the working class throughout the mid-to-late 1990s. For the first time in Argentina's modern history, economic growth (as measured by increases in national productivity) also meant increased unemployment and poverty.

Another audacious move by the Menem regime in the first years of the 1990s was the selling of almost all of Argentina's national public services (telecommunications, transportation, gas, electricity, hydro, sanitation, and so on), which included the privatisation of its petrochemical and oil sectors; the mining industry; the country's national airline; passenger rail and subway services; its postal service; many municipal and provincial government services such as maintenance and waste management; and even portions of its health and education sectors. The Menem administration's rationale for the sell-offs was ostensibly to recompose the national economy by paying down Argentina's exponentially swelling national debt and to stimulate foreign investments.[108] In reality, the eventual privatisation of more than 150 national firms served to grease the skids of what proved to be a cheap and profitable auction-block for foreign investors and multinationals; the consequence of this massive sell-off was nothing less than a foreign takeover of much of the country's industrial base by dozens of foreign multinationals and the dismissal of 40 percent of its state employees.[109] Not only did these policies deepen the deindustrialisation and foreign economic takeover of the country, they would also, of course, influence the redundancies of hundreds of thousands of private and public sector workers.[110]

As Figure 12 illustrates, the socio-economic ruptures caused by these neoliberal economic policies were showing already by the mid-1990s. That ERTs have emerged within the past two decades as worker-led responses to macroeconomic fluctuations in Argentina can be clearly inferred from Figure 12, which parallels the surge of ERTs with other socio-economic trends such as the rising tides of underemployment, unemployment, poverty, indigence, and business closure rates throughout the 1990s and early 2000s.[111] Tellingly, for

---

107   Patroni 2004, p. 113.
108   Borón and Thwaites Rey 2004, p. 114.
109   Galiani, Gertler, Shargrodksy, and Sturzenegger 2003, p. 5.
110   Gambina and Campione 2002; Levy Yeyati and Valenzuela 2013.
111   These indicators have a similar symmetrical relationship that we saw in Chapter 2 with the rise of ERTs and the GDP rate in Figure 8.

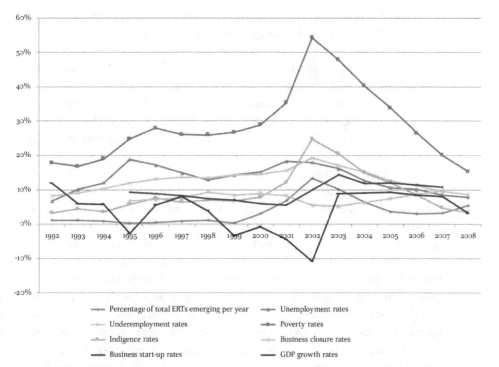

FIGURE 12   ERT recuperations per year compared to key socio-economic indicators in Argentina, 1991–2008
SOURCES: 'PERCENTAGE OF TOTAL ERTS EMERGING PER YEAR' (MINISTERIO DE TRABAJO 2008A; RUGGERI 2016; RUGGERI, MARTÍNEZ, AND TRINCHERO 2005; RUGGERI, POLTI, CLARK, ANTIVERO, DELEGDISCH, ET AL. 2010; RUGGERI, ANTIVERO, ELENA, POLTI, ET AL. 2014; RUGGERI AND VIETA 2015); 'UNEMPLOYMENT RATES' AND 'UNDEREMPLOYMENT RATES' (NUMBERS ARE FOR LAST SEMESTER OF EACH YEAR) (MINISTERIO DE TRABAJO 2007; WORLD BANK 2016A); 'POVERTY RATES' AND 'INDIGENCE RATES' (CLARÍN 2005, 2009; INDEC 2011); 'BUSINESS CLOSURE RATES' AND 'BUSINESS START-UP RATES' (MINISTERIO DE TRABAJO 2008B); 'GDP GROWTH RATES' (WORLD BANK 2016B)

example, Figure 12 shows that the period between 1998 and 2002 in particular was consistently marked by more business closures than start-ups, ominously presaging the final implosion of the neo-liberal model that was felt with force across all of Argentina's economic sectors between late 2001 and mid-2003. Within this macro-economic quagmire, and after suffering months and sometimes years of being owed back-pay and lost benefits, of decreased job security, and sometimes after layoffs or legally questionable lockouts, some workers of the most affected SMEs from a broad cross-section of Argentina's urban-based economy decided to take action and occupy their failing or failed firms.

Between 1995 and 1998, the seams of Menem's extreme free market policies and the underlying Plan de Convertibilidad began to gradually tear open as the country edged closer to its eventual default on its foreign debt in the dying days of 2001.[112] Argentina's default on circa $US 82 billion of this debt was, until Greece's 2012 default, the largest sovereign debt default in history.[113] Concurrently, between 1998 and 2001, more and more people from Argentina's once-strong working class were getting relegated to the ranks of the underemployed, the unemployed, and the poor. In real material terms, Argentina's Washington Consensus-inspired 'progressive' neo-liberal policies spurred on a national unemployment rate that, at its peak during the crisis years of 2001–2, was over 20 percent, going as high as 40 to 60 percent in some of greater Buenos Aires's working-class suburbs.[114] These unemployment rates, a tragedy in any country, were perhaps even more pronounced in Argentina when one considers that in the early-to-mid 1970s, during the end of the country's 'golden years' of working-class strength and industrialisation, its official unemployment rate hovered at between two percent and four percent,[115] levels which economists consider technically to be full employment. The gradual evaporation of jobs that paralleled the increasing entrenchment of neo-liberalism can clearly be seen when one looks at 22-year trends in unemployment between 1980 and 2002, the same span of years that saw the national debt balloon by 240 percent. According to Argentina's Ministry of Labour, the official unemployment rate in 1980 was 1.9 percent. By 1989, at the height of the hyperinflation crisis, it had risen to 7.6 per cent. By 1994 it hit the two-digit mark, coming in at 11.5

---

112 It is important to note that the national debt also soared during roughly the same time-frame that saw the entrenchment of neo-liberalism and the unfolding of the *convertibilidad* years, from US$ 6 billion at the beginning of the military government of 1976 to US$ 45 billion in early 1984 when Raúl Alfonsín took power to $ 60 billion during the first full year of Menem's regime in 1990 to well over $ 150 billion in both private and public debt by the time of the de la Rúa administration's fall in late 2001. As Baer, Margot, and Montes-Rojas succinctly summarise: 'On December 24th [2001] the service payments of a significant part of the public debt were suspended (it initially affected 61.8 billion dollars in public bonds and 8 in other debt instruments). It did not include debt contracted with multilateral institutions (such as the IMF, the World Bank and the Inter-American Development Bank) of about 32.4 billion dollars and recently issued guaranteed loans (42.3 billion). This turned out to be the largest default in Latin American economic history, as the foreign private debt amounted to US$ 82 billion out of US$ 153 billion' (Baer, Margot, and Montes-Rojas 2011, sec. 4).

113 Huang 2014; Scott 2010; Walsh 2011.

114 Petras and Veltmeyer 2004, pp. 5–54.

115 Damill 2005, p. 220.

per cent. Between 1995 and 2001, it was averaging 15.6 percent. And by 2002, the official unemployment rate had hit 19.7 percent of Argentina's working population, although unofficial statistics pegged it at the time at well over 20 percent.[116]

Not surprisingly, with the rise of unemployment the poverty rate rose as well. By the early months of 2002, the most chaotic year of the economic crisis, it was estimated that 18.2 million Argentines, or 51.4 percent of the population, had fallen below the line of poverty. By October 2002, the poverty rate in the nation's urban centres had crept up to 57.5 percent, affecting in one way or another 70 percent of the country's population, while, at the same time, 27.5 percent of its urban population was considered indigent.[117] These were the largest poverty and indigence rates in Argentina's modern history. The drastic descent into pauperisation that plagued many Argentines became starkly visible in the early months of 2002. Between January and May of that year, 3.2 million Argentines fell for the first time below the poverty line. Put another way, in the first five months of 2002, almost 800,000 people per month – 25,000 people per day – were becoming poor.[118] While it is true that this downward spiral of immiseration had stabilised somewhat by 2005, and certainly by the time of this writing, poverty and indigence still remained at historical highs by the middle of the first decade of the 2000s. As of September of 2005, 38.5 percent of Argentines (15 million people) were considered poor, while 13.6 percent of Argentines were indigent (five million people).[119]

Another lingering carryover from the neo-liberal years is the continued presence of informal or precarious work, or *trabajo en negro* (literally, work in the black), a type of work that became a chronic problem for many in the 1990s and throughout the entire decade of the 2000s.[120] Workers in this situation, according to national government sources, are considered to be 'non-registered' workers who do not work under a formal labour contract and do not receive the social benefits required by Argentine labour law. By mid-2010, *trabajo en negro* was still the reality for 36.5 percent of the economically active population of the country, impacting 4.3 million working people.[121] And by mid-2014, *trabajo en negro* was still affecting 32.8 percent of the country's economically active

116   Ministerio de Trabajo 2007.
117   Lozano 2005; Petras and Veltmeyer 2004; Rofman 2005.
118   Petras and Veltmeyer 2004.
119   Clarín 2005.
120   Kulfas 2016; Levy Yeyati and Valenzuela 2013; Olmedo and Murray 2002; Patroni 2004.
121   Página/12 2010.

population, representing more than 3 million workers.[122] Thus, it can safely be said that since at least the mid-1990s, to be structurally unemployed, underemployed, or informally employed in Argentina means for too many entrance into the ranks of the precarious, the poor, or the indigent, all of whom continue to feel the after-effects of the dismantling of Argentina's union-based social safety nets during the Menem years.

By the mid-to-late 1990s, then, the results of Argentina's radical free-market economics were clearly anything but miraculous, and the immiseration of millions of Argentines was palpably being felt throughout society. This state of impoverishment was especially visible in the cities with their growing populations of homeless people, the increased visibility of *cartoneros* (cardboard and waste recyclers) on the streets of the country's urban centres (mostly made up of the newly unemployed and working poor), and the chronic growth of the infamous *villas miserias* (shantytowns or, literally, 'towns of misery') that rim the peripheries of Argentina's cities and towns with migrants looking for an elusively better life.

But not all Argentines were suffering under the country's neo-liberal market reforms, of course – the rich were getting richer. In 1974, Argentina's top ten percent of income earners officially monopolised 28 percent of the national income. In 1992, at the height of Menem's market liberalisations, they monopolised 34 percent of the national income. By 2001, more than 37 percent of the nations' earnings officially remained within the top ten percent of the population. In contrast, the poorest ten percent of the population received 2.2 percent of the nation's wealth in 1974; by 2001, just before the massive increases in unemployment, the poorest decile received a paltry 1.3 percent.[123] Given that the wealthiest classes in Argentina tend to under-report their income, James Petras and Henry Veltmeyer point out that the Argentine government estimated this wealth disparity to be even more marked than the official numbers indicated at the time.[124]

While an inordinate number of people in Argentina's working class were falling down this sinkhole of immiseration and informalisation throughout the mid-to-late 1990s, many owners of SMEs were incurring unwieldy debt-loads in order to stay afloat amidst drying up national and export markets. The particularly negative impact of these years on the country's SMEs and their workers was vividly related to us by the experiences suffered by this book's ERT case study protagonists in Chapter 1. As Peter Ranis underscores, the years of

---

122   Diario Popular 2014.
123   Petras and Veltmeyer 2004, pp. 7–12.
124   Ibid.

convertibilidad encouraged SME owners to react to dwindling competitiveness and rising indebtedness by engaging in practices such as labour flexibilisation schemes (as the UST workers faced); rationalisation drives, downsizing, and de-capitalisation (as in the cases of Chilavert and Salud Junín); the holding back of salaries; reducing or negating severance packages;[125] layoffs or permanent firings; or, increasingly as the years of *convertibilidad* wore on, declaring bankruptcy.[126]

While some of the ensuing business bankruptcies of these years were legitimate, others would strain even the most liberal notions of legality as many business owners, encouraged by the political economic climate of the time, were willing to incur questionable debt or speculate away their business assets in risky investment schemes.[127] When these schemes faltered or business debts became unwieldy, some owners would resort to embezzlement or corruption to stay solvent. A common practice by business owners at the time (and a continuing practice in the country even today) was to attempt to (illegally) sell off business assets while the firm was still in the process of bankruptcy proceedings. This was, as we saw in Chapter 1, the intention of Boss Gaglianone that finally motivated the Chilavert workers to occupy the plant and start their ERT. With this manoeuvre, owners would attempt to empty (*vaciar*) the firm of its assets in order to either sell off the machines, land, inventory, buildings, and such that should have gone to repay creditors, or to start production somewhere else with cheaper labour. In addition, owners would often turn to simple bribery – a time-honoured tradition amongst Argentina's moneyed classes – to gain protection from the courts, pay off corrupt court trustees or politicians, or seek out other disreputable forms of protection from creditors.[128] Thus, even as annual business bankruptcies soared between 1991 and 2001, many in the entrepreneurial and ruling classes continued to benefit from Argentina's neoliberal free-for-all.

---

125 Which was permitted by the labour policies of the time if owners could prove to the Ministry of Labour that the firm's productivity was at risk (Ranis 2016).

126 Ranis 2016, pp. 50–1. For details of some of these business practices, see also Chapters 6 and 7.

127 Ruggeri 2005, personal interview.

128 Magnani 2003; Palomino 2003; Ruggeri, Martínez, and Trinchero 2005. Understanding why these illegal practices were allowed to take place and how they, in part, motivated the emergence of ERTs requires one to unravel the quagmires of Argentina's nefarious political and business spheres, the two colluding sectors of society that have been blamed for most of Argentina's steady economic meltdown that culminated in the crisis years of 2001–2. We will look into some of the unsavoury practices carried on by Argentina's political and business elites and employers during these years in Chapters 6 and 7.

In most cases of bankruptcies or owner-abandonment, employees also became creditors because bonuses, benefits, and paycheques (usually in that order) made up considerable parts of the growing debt load that negligent owners never had the intention of paying back to workers. The major difference between workers' transformations into creditors and the firm's other creditors, as the case studies in Chapter 1 underscored, is that workers had little choice in the matter: The implicit ultimatum given to workers by their bosses – an ultimatum that is well understood by employees – is to either work for vastly reduced wages, pay vouchers, or with no benefits or overtime pay, or have their positions terminated.[129] As many ERT protagonists have explained to me over the years, workers were often amongst the largest group of creditors in many failing companies because it was relatively easy for owners to convince workers to make personal sacrifices for the firm since owners knew the reputation of the Argentine worker: hard working, loyal, and committed. Using similes of football culture which often colour the daily conversations of Argentines, owners would often ask employees during the firm's most difficult moments to 'put on the jersey of the *empresa*' for the greater cause of 'the team'. As employees would quickly learn, however, putting on the 'team's jersey' often meant being relegated to the substitutes bench with no chance of coming back onto the 'pitch' of the shop floor again.

These extremely exploitative practices on shop floors put into sharp relief the tendencies of a capitalist system in deep crisis. Indeed, such practices clearly illustrate Karl Marx's account of the capitalist's desire, especially in times of business and economic crises, to minimise the cost of 'necessary labour' as much as business owners can get away with by reducing the cost of labour inputs via mechanisation (or rationalisation drives), layoffs, or redundancies, while, at the same time, extracting as much 'relative surplus-labour' as possible from the workers who are left.[130] In an interview from the early 2000s, conducted in the thick of economic crisis, one of the ERT movement's early leaders, Luís Caro (who went on to found and lead the ERT umbrella organisation Movimiento Nacional de Fábricas Recuperadas por los Trabajadores, or MNFRT), clearly described the resultant transformation of many of Argentina's workers from employees to creditors during the years of *convertibilidad* and socio-economic crisis of the 1990s and early 2000s; it is similar to stories

---

129   Magnani 2003.

130   Marx, 1967, pp. 216–17, 241. See, in particular, Marx's (1967) analysis of these capitalist tendencies in Chapter 9, 'The Rate of Surplus-Value', Section 1, 'The Degree of Exploitation of Labour-Power' (pp. 212–20), and Chapter 10, 'The Working Day', Section 2, 'The Greed for Surplus-Labour: Manufacturer and Boyard' (pp. 235–43).

I heard time and time again in the conversations I have had with ERT workers and activists, as their own words made clear for us in Chapter 1:

> Business owners' debts would actually begin with their employees ... This would eventually produce a deterioration in workers themselves because [workers were often owed months of back pay], ... bonuses, vacation pay, and retirement contributions. In the [lead-up to imminent bankruptcy,] workers would transform into owners' financiers. Instead of taking on more debt from outside sources, owners would not pay their workers. What was lived in Argentina [during the years of *convertibildad* and crisis] was to push its workers to one side and the labouring subject – that is, workers – began to get conditioned. Even the unions couldn't take actions [to protect workers] because of their deep interrelations with the impresarios.[131]

In sum, the Menem and de la Rúa regimes and their neo-liberal policies upheld by the Plan de Convertibilidad of the 1990s were deeply ensconced in this downward spiral of national impoverishment and greed. Under their administrations, the state and the country's economic elites chose to appease the minions of globalisation and its free-market advocates instead of protecting the interests of their own people. Furthermore, their pro-market, anti-labour policies in effect placed the long-term security of Argentina's own people at risk for short-term gains and set the tone for a culture of individualism and avarice that would take hold throughout the 1990s. In short, in a rehashing of the predictable narrative of the ongoing neo-liberal script, in yet one more national economic conjuncture, the privatisation of wealth and profit in 1990s Argentina was ensured by the socialisation of risk via the cheapening of the cost of variable capital – that is, drops in wages, heightened exploitation, and rising redundancies – and the dismantling of all types of workers' social securities.

In other words, as Argentina's neo-liberal version of the regime of regulation of production that kept workers producing value for capital in the 1990s – that is, that kept workers working throughout the 1990s despite the drop in labour protections and relative wages – reached a crisis point and ultimately ruptured, the increasing tearing of the macro-economic system echoing in the lives of working people in heightened micro-economic conflicts between capital and labour at the level of the labour process on shop floors. The re-emergent forms of non-conventional labour mobilisations, such as the upsurge of work-

---

131   Caro, in Magnani 2003, p. 54.

place occupations and ERTs, intermingled with the rise of other new and re-emergent labour actions and forms of organising outside of the supervision of the CGT and its affiliate unions, which had been temporarily debilitated and questioned by a growing number of workers throughout the 1990s with *menemismo*'s co-optation of many of its leaders. To recap, these new labour actions and organisations included: the increasing protests and road blockages of the *piqueteros*; the rise and organising of the *cartonero* workers and other informalised workers; an increase in mobilisations around living conditions, affordable housing, and human rights issues; and the emergence of progressive alternative union centrals such as the CTA and MTA.

The massive loss of jobs throughout the mid-to-late 1990s, the growing rate of immiseration, a national currency crisis, a trade deficit, eroding national consumer markets, an unpayable national debt, exorbitant debt-servicing and structural adjustment demands insisted upon by the IMF and carried out by the Menem and de la Rúa governments, and the subsequently infamous *corralito*[132] instated to stem the inevitable run on the banks that began in early December 2001 – all wedded to the political and economic establishments' greed, impotence, or ineptitude – culminated in the social upheaval of 19 and 20 December 2001. While radical academics, social activists, and the otherwise fractured parties of the left were temporarily emboldened by the force of popular rebellion of *el Argentinazo* of December 2001 – inflated by the fury of a momentarily radicalised middle class that was denied its access to savings and credit – the 'multitude' failed, however, to sustain itself on a massive scale once private bank accounts were reopened and middle-class consumerism was allowed to find its footing again.[133]

---

132   *Corralito* is the Spanish diminutive for 'corral' or 'enclosure'. It was the nickname given to the national government's policy put in place in late 2001 to prevent a massive run at the banks. Passed into law in the first days of December 2001, the *corralito* in effect legally barred Argentine's from withdrawing more than $250 pesos a week from their bank accounts when the Law of Convertability was rescinded and the peso was allowed to float once again (and thus devalued) against the US dollar after more than ten years of being pegged to it. The passing of this law had much to do with flaming the massive popular uprisings during the days of 19 and 20 December 2001.

133   As I have already touched on in the Introduction, some radical academics theorised during this time that *el Argentinazo* of December 19 and 20 was evidence of the emergence of the 'multitude' and the force of 'constituent power' from below in Argentina. For such accounts, see Dinerstein 2002; Colectivo Situaciones 2002; Gutierrez 2005; and Hardt and Negri 2004, pp. 216–17.

2.2   The Post-convertability Era: The kirchnerista Response and macrismo's Return to Neo-liberalism (2004–17)

To be clear, the production regime – that is, the 'regimes of regulation' affecting 'the point of production'[134] – that guided Argentina's economic, political, and ideological arrangements of capitalist accumulation only temporarily came apart on shop floors across the country during the neo-liberal model's brief collapse at the turn of the millennium.[135] Moreover, this was a gradual unravelling that unfolded throughout the mid-to-late 1990s and that came to a head during the 'Argentine December' of 2001 and the years immediately subsequent to it, reflected in the surge of business closures, unemployment and indigence rates, and the growth in informal work, as well as in the number of new ERTS that emerged during this period. As reflected in the drop in new ERTS by 2005 in Figure 7 in Chapter 2, by 2004 Argentina experienced a return to a more domestically focused regime of production and capitalist accumulation in the nationalist-developmentalist turn of Néstor Kirchner's presidency (2003–7) and his successor, Crístina Férnandez de Kirchner (2007–15), under their left-Peronist Frente para la Victoria coalition.

The new nationalist-developmentalist approach of *kirchnerismo*, especially during Néstor Kirchner's presidency, was underscored by a resurgent national economy bolstered in part by high international commodity prices and new pro-labour policies and social assistance programmes that would, for both pragmatic and political purposes, take up the demands of popular sectors and working-class groups such as the *piqueteros*, the *cartoneros*, ERTS, and the traditional union movement. The main tenets and policies of *kirchnerismo*, then, contrasted with the state's stance of confrontation towards popular sectors and the working class during the years of *convertibilidad*. This contrast was most palpable in *kirchnerismo*'s embrace of a new political economic vision that revived left-nationalist and neo-populist Peronist ruling discourses and policies by appeasing, to some degree, the demands of popular sectors, workers, and organised labour.[136] Indeed, over the 12 years spanning the three Kirchner

---

134   Burawoy 1985, pp. 17, 83–6.
135   Kulfas 2016; Mercatante 2015; Piva 2015.
136   The Kirchner era political economic project has also been called a 'neo-developmentalist' or 'productivist-developmentalist' regime of capitalist accumulation by Argentine political commentators and heterodox economists in recent years since it echoed, but did not completely emulate, the political economic policies guided by ISI and the approach advocated by the first two administrations of Juán Perón between 1946–55 (see, for instance, Rougier and Schorr 2012; Mercatante 2015; Piva 2015; Wainfeld 2016; and Wylde 2011).

administrations a renewed and demonstrable pro-labour posture was taken up by the Frente para la Victoria governments. Moreover, a shift in the centre of power in the executive branch during these years would see the disempowering of the Ministry of the Economy and more political power ceded to the Ministries of Labour and Social Development. This shift drove the creation of new policies that involved concessions to the demands of community organisations, coalitions of the poor and the unemployed, and organised labour, while yielding renewed political room for the reconsolidation of unions and a return to labour organising around basic bread and butter issues such as increases in salaries and the minimum wage, new collective agreements, and the re-entrenchment of social security and unemployment insurance.

The renewed voice of the traditional labour movement during the Kirchner years, witnessed in the sharp increase in labour conflicts by 2005 (that is, strikes, walkouts, occupations, and other types of labour protests), as Figure 13 illustrates, has been understood by commentators as a sign of the revived vitality of traditional organised labour actions in contrast to the downturn of organised labour activities throughout the 1990s and early 2000s.[137] As Maurizio Atzeni and Pablo Ghagliani state, a rise in the number of labour conflicts is one (although imperfect) indicator of the level of union power and growing working-class protagonism.[138] Figure 13 also maps out the rough inverse trend between new ERTs and other forms of labour actions as outlets for meeting working-class demands, as was discussed in Chapter 2 and as I will address in more detail shortly. For instance, note how, with the downward trend in new ERTs during and after 2005 in Figure 13, we also see a steep increase in other, more traditional forms of labour actions, while with the new waves of ERTs post-2009 we also see a concomitant relative drop or stabilisation of other forms of labour actions.

Despite the revived political space for organised labour and other popular sectors to voice their concerns and issues, it is also undeniable that one of the major motivations of the nationalist-developmentalist project of the Kirchner years was to secure anew the hegemony and legitimacy of the political establishment that had been severely weakened after the 'que se vayan todos' of 2001. Kirchnerismo pursued this in part through the following nationalist-developmentalist agenda: the re-nationalisation of once-privatised assets and

---

137   For further analyses of patterns of organised labour activities during these years, see
        Atzeni and Ghigliani 2008; Eckstein 2006; Etchemendy and Berins Collier 2007; Levitsky
        2003; Pozzi and Nigra 2015; Schuster 2008; Svampa and Pereyra 2004; and Wylde 2011.
138   Atzeni and Ghigliani 2008.

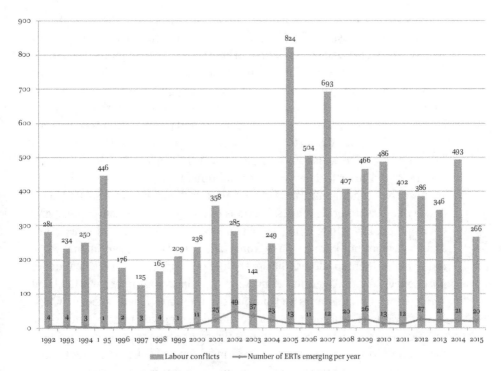

FIGURE 13   Labour conflicts per year in Argentina and the emergence of ERTs, 1992–2015
Note: 'Labour conflicts' include strikes, walkouts, sit-ins, workplace occuptions,
and other types of labour protests.
SOURCES: ATZENI AND GHAGLIANI 2008; NUEVA MAYORIA 2016; RUGGERI
2016

resources; explicit policies supporting national productivity, economic growth,
and re-industrialisation, much of which focused on the country's SMEs; new
tariffs on imports and commodity exports; and an attempt to de-link the country from the influence of international financial institutions through the renegotiation and repayment of portions of its national debt.[139] The Kirchner
years would also see the return of a wide assortment of social policies focused
on addressing the demands of popular sectors and workers, which included
consistent raises to the minimum wage, renewed sector-wide collective agreements, social assistance plans for families linked to their size, as well as welfare
plans connected to the creation of new public maintenance-oriented worker
cooperatives.

---

139   Kulfas 2016; Piva 2015.

These social policies, it has been pointed out, also had the goal of containing social unrest.[140] The Kirchner governments in effect created a new social compact between capital, the working class, and popular sectors, affording a new regime of capitalist production and accumulation that was, while more responsive to the demands of workers and popular sectors, also a way of smoothing national markets and consumer demand. Thus, at the same time, both as a way to contain mass dissent, discord, and protest (what we will come to know as *kirchnerismo*'s strategy of 'social containment' in Chapters 6 and 7), and as a way to expand economic activity, Néstor Kirchner's administration managed to articulate the new conditions for securing political power, stabilise the economy, and appease and address the demands of social groups and workers, countering the disaffections of the 1990s with a left-populist and developmentalist 'Argentina first' political-economic discourse. This discourse and its policies both drew energy from traditional Peronist sentiments while modernising them to address the new political economic and social realities of post-convertability Argentina. A posture of social containment – articulated via new social programmes and subsidies to the poor (for instance, new welfare programmes and social assistance linked to dignified housing and access to clean water), a new focus on human rights, pro-labour policies, new funds for community groups and cooperatives, and so on – also served to 'internalise' social struggles and 'translated [for the new political regime] potentially antagonistic and disruptive social demands into a reformist logic via the granting of concessions'.[141]

In this way, the first Kirchner administration would succeed in returning Argentina to a form of class compromise it had experienced in moments up until the mid-1970s, reconstructing a national consensus that served, at the same time, as a platform for some degree of working-class recomposition and for recomposing the state's political power. On the other hand, as Ana Dinerstein, Esteban Mercatante, Adrián Piva, Maristella Svampa and Sebastián Pereyra,[142] and others have noted, and as I will also argue in Chapters 6 and 7, this 'institutionalisation' of popular groups and social movements – such as some political factions of the *piqueteros*, bottom-up experiences of *autogestión* such as the ERT phenomenon, and groups of informal workers such as the *cartoneros* – would also to some degree de-politicise the most promising and socially transformative potential of the turn-of-the-millennium social movements for forging another socio-economic reality in Argentina.[143]

---

140   Mercatante 2015.
141   Piva 2015, p. 96.
142   Dinerstein 2007; Mercatante 2015; Piva 2015; Svampa and Pereyra 2004.
143   Svampa and Pereyra 2004, pp. 202–24. The potential of the ERT phenomenon for suggest-

Overall, the Kirchner years have been seen to be a part of the broader tendency of the 'pink tide' of left-leaning, 'neo-developmentalist', and anti-Washington Consensus governments across Latin America that emerged throughout the first decade of the 2000s.[144] In countries such as Argentina, Bolivia, Brazil, Ecuador, Venezuela, and Uruguay, the centrist and centre-right governments of the 1990s, partially spent due to the intensity with which the neo-liberal project was practised during that decade, gave way to nationally and regionally focused left-populist governments. According to Piva, these new left approaches to the region's national political economies – including Argentina's – would take on, in varying degrees, a twenty-first century version of Keynesianism, including dedication of public funds for shoring up domestic industries and for public works projects, subsidised job creation plans, regular re-negotiations of country-wide wage increases and price subsidies, improved supports for social and solidarity economy initiatives, and a clearing of the road for the re-politicisation and empowerment of labour unions. In effect, these new approaches would underscore a 'recomposed state-based political power and the conditions for capitalist accumulation', shifting from the arena of financialisation to one of re-industrialising national economies 'on the foundation of incorporating the demands and the political inclusion of the social movements that had been leading the social mobilisations' against previous neo-liberal national governments.[145]

Facilitating this new left turn under *kirchnerismo* was a more favourable post-convertability economic climate at the international level for primary resource exporting countries like Argentina, which lasted until the new international crisis spawned by the Great Recession of 2008 had firmly touched down in the country by 2009. The Kirchner administrations would also secure their hold on political power via an approach that relied, to a great extent, on yielding concessions to popular sectors and organised labour. For Argentina's labour movement, the Kirchner years would include a post-convertability regime of production that facilitated the relative recomposition and stabilisation of shop floor labour processes and a recomposed autonomy for the country's unions that, in essence, collectively underpinned a new class compromise. This approach contrasted sharply with the anti-labour climate of the Menem–de la Rúa years, was developed within a more heterodox political economic milieu, and gave political legitimacy to the Kirchnerist neo-developmentalist

---

ing another form of productive reality, however, was not completely co-opted into the Kirchnerist project, as we will see in Part 3.

144   Rougier and Schorr 2012; Piva 2015; Wylde 2011.
145   Piva 2015, p. 161.

project. However, already by the first years of Cristina Fernández de Kirchner's first administration (2007–11), aspects of the Kirchnerist compromise would begin to unravel. This was due to several global and local realities, including: a new world-economic situation of recession, a renewed activism and opposition to the heterodoxy of *kirchnerismo*'s economic and political direction by the country's business classes and its rural oligarchical elites (energetically taking off with the rural oligarchy's opposition to export taxes on commodities in 2008), and increasing inflationary pressures and monetary instability by the first years of the second decade of the 2000s.[146]

The Kirchners' nationalist-developmentalist project began to be systematically dismantled throughout Mauricio Macri's centre-right and neo-liberal Cambiemos administration (2015–19). Termed by the Macri administration as economic '*sinceramiento*', as we saw in Chapter 2, a neologism for returning Argentina's economy to a 'truer' (read 'neo-liberal') path in contrast to the political-economic direction of the Kirchner years,[147] these policies had brought with them a return of rising unemployment,[148] poverty,[149] and social insecurity;[150] continued inflationary pressures on consumer goods and production inputs;[151] and overall drops in national productivity.[152] By April 2016, the Cambiemos administration's pro-market policies included sharp increases to consumer and business utility rates (dubbed '*el Tarifazo*' by progressive media outlets and opposition political groups), overturning the Kirchner governments' price controls on what utility companies could charge for gas, water, and electricity as well as limiting utility rate subsidies for cooperative and community organisations.[153] For the country's SMEs, including ERTs and other cooperatives, these policies have led to drastic increases in their cost of production and falling demand for their products and services. Already by the first months of Macri's Cambiemos government, these policies were directly threatening the expansive fabric of the country's broad social and solidarity economy.

While ERTs continued to emerge during the first three years of the Cambiemos administration, new challenges have confronted ERTs, the broader labour movement, and other cooperatives and community organisations.

146   Kulfas 2016.
147   See Chapter 2, 3, and 6.
148   Dillon 2016; Télam 2016.
149   Ámbito.com 2016b; Página/12 2017a.
150   Urien 2016.
151   Lewkowicz 2016; Ruggeri 2016; Reuters 2016.
152   INDEC 2016.
153   Lewkowicz 2016; Ruggeri 2016.

While collectively overcoming political and economic challenges in the past has, as we will soon discover, fundamentally defined the working-class movement of self-managed firms, new political challenges to the until-now legal methods of saving closing firms via ERT solutions will no doubt require ERT protagonists to redeploy older strategies of struggle and combine them with renewed conviction and tactics against the inevitable confrontations that continued to come from the Macri administration and any future antagonistic regimes. We can anticipate what these coming struggles will be if we recall Macri's opposition to the expropriation of ERTs from the city of Buenos Aires during his leadership of the city government between 2007–15. Indeed, Macri and the Cambiemos governor of the province of Buenos Aires, María Eugenia Vidal, had vetoed several legislative decisions to expropriate ERTs on behalf of workers, as we will see in later chapters. Other indicators of the imminent challenges for social groups and the labour movement under *macrismo* – including for ERTs – were: new austerity policies; *macrismos'* quick moves soon after taking power to regain favourable relations with its G20 counterparts by re-settling outstanding loans from US vulture funds; its policy of promoting leaner public and private sector workplaces by beginning its tenure with a massive wave of layoffs; its privileging of private property rights over the right to work, witnessed in new eviction attempts in some ERTs and other social movements occupying lands; its avowed faith in individualist entrepreneurialism and free-trade, expressed in the appointment of pro-business ministers across the executive branch of government; and the introduction of sharp increases in consumer and business utility fees (that is, '*el Tarifazo*').

For the ERT movement, however, the future still remains hopeful. ERTs, after all, emerged from situations of deep micro-economic crises and struggles against nefarious business management and reticent governments in the late 1990s. Surviving the challenges of constituted power and neo-liberal-induced crises is in the DNA of ERTs. As I will explore in Part 3 of the book, because of this history ERT protagonists today are in many ways better prepared for and well-versed in dealing with any threats to the movements' existence by the inevitable return to more neo-liberal policies that the next years will bring. Their protagonism in creating new forms of self-managed workers' associations is one immediate way that ERTs have organised around their common struggles and concerns.

3   Section 3: Working-Class Recomposition and New Forms of
         Self-Managed Workers' Organisations (2001–17)

> It is true that ... [while] in every organisation *autogestión* is inscribed with
> different strategic proposals, without doubt, and beyond the differences,
> the fact that this is the most visible mark [of the social organisations]
> clearly conveys its place in the 'new politics'.
> MARISTELLA SVAMPA and SEBASTIÁN PEREYRA[154]

While the 1990s in Argentina are remembered for the tenacity with which neo-liberalism was implemented, the decade, as we have seen, also brought with it new forms of working-class struggles and self-directed activities that both responded to the neo-liberal juggernaut and attempted to move beyond it. In the Introduction and Chapter 2, I highlighted how the response of the country's marginalised to the radical liberalisation and subsequent crises of the national economy – via myriad neighbourhood grassroots social initiatives, tactics of occupying and squatting public and private spaces, horizontal forms of organising, and so on – was, in part, evidence of a surging communitarian conviction and an energetic social recomposition emanating at once from the streets, neighbourhoods, factories, and squares of the country.[155] These collective attempts at directly addressing social exclusion and economic suffering bore witness to a recomposed combativeness amongst workers and the dispossessed; they would prove to be a contagion that symbiotically impelled thousands of grassroots activists and popular groups to self-organise organically under the rubric of *autogestión*. And they would be administered by people's assemblies working within the principles of direct participatory democracy that served as sharp contrasts to the hierarchical institutions of the state, capital, and bureaucratic unions. In light of this historical confluence, for many workers in Argentina participation in direct action to recuperate their workspaces, both modelled after and also influencing the new social transformations that were taking shape around them, seemed to be the only viable alternative left in the face of a retreating and ineffectual state committed to the neo-liberal model and to acquiescing to the whims of international finance capital.

Moreover, with traditional unions initially proving mostly un-receptive to the plight of workers in troubled firms, as we saw in Chapters 1 and 2, ERT prot-

---

154   Svampa and Pereyra 2004, p. 201 (*Entre la ruta y el barrio: La experiencia de las organiza-
       ciones piqueteras*).
155   Svampa and Pereyra 2004, p. 233.

agonists would forge new networks and connections between ERTs, with their communities, and with other social movements. Here, ERTs are illustrative of one of the ways the Argentine working class recomposed itself at the turn of the millennium and in the years that followed via alternative forms of organising rooted in community–workplace and social movement–labour alliances.

3.1 Social Movement and Community Unionism

As Alejandro Portes and Kelly Hoffman have shown, community-based popular mobilisations increased across Latin America during the heyday of the neo-liberal years.[156] In places such as Argentina, Bolivia, Brazil, Ecuador, Mexico, and Venezuela, the impulses of popular groups most affected by the neo-liberal model, such as the under- and unemployed, Indigenous peoples, the poor, and the marginalised, would often see them draw together and combine forces with groups from the traditional labour movement. What brought them together, according to Portes and Hoffman, was 'a common fate of poverty and deprivation that includes both formal and informal proletarians, provid[ing] the basis for collective action'.[157] What Patroni has called Argentina's 'new union alternatives' encompass new labour struggles throughout the country that began to move beyond the monopoly of the CGT and that responded directly to the fundamental transformations in labour protections instigated by the neo-liberal model throughout the 1990s.[158] Increasingly over the past three or so decades, social movement and labour studies theorists and researchers have been conceptualising this coming together of formal labour organisations with popular movements and community groups as *social movement* or *community unionism*.

With some variations based on its contexts, social movement/community unionism has been contrasted to the traditional bureaucratic union model.[159] Social movement/community union models have emerged over the past three decades in Latin America and in other regions of the global South (and increasingly in pockets of the global North) as direct responses by workers and the marginalised to the worst effects of neo-liberal policy on the conditions of working and living wrought by austerity, business restructuring, direct foreign investment, and state downsizing. Social movement/community unionism is fundamentally different from 'big labour' in that it focuses primarily on bottom-up organising beyond the shop floor and bread-and-butter issues and

---

156   Portes and Hoffman 2003.
157   Portes and Hoffman 2003, p. 76.
158   Patroni 2014, p. 114.
159   McBride and Greenwood 2009.

includes solidarity with local community struggles and people's wellbeing. In this vein, Peter Evans and Chris Tilly define community unionism as

> an elastic term denoting a set of forms and strategies that extend union-ism's terrain beyond a particular workplace or multi-workplace employer to organize workers on a territorial basis ... [and] ... go beyond employer-employee relationships to take on community issues.[160]

Moreover, it tends to promote democratic participation by all members, forges affinities with broader social justice movements, and is inclusive of new scenes of workers' struggles such as those taking place in flexibilised or informalised work situations and due to the disaffections of globalised divisions of labour.[161]

The new self-managed workers' associations, networks of solidarity, ERT umbrella groups, and worker cooperative federations that have arisen in Argentina since the late 1990s begin to outline this new form of social movement/community unionism. They arose not only as direct responses to the worst effects of neo-liberalism, but also as solutions to the co-optation of mainstream unions by the state and organised labour's overall reluctance to fully assist with the needs of, or take on issues related to, self-managed workers, especially during the crisis years at the turn of the millennium. On the other hand, as we examined in Chapter 2, ERT workers continue to identify with their working-class roots and have also tended to remain affiliated to their traditional sectoral unions for pragmatic reasons. This means that ERT workers most often belong to both their traditional unions and to newer self-managed workers' associations. In the remaining pages of this chapter, I first summarise Argentine ERTs' mixed relationship to traditional unions that we looked at in some detail in Chapter 2, and then review the most important organisations and associations that have emerged in support of ERTs and other self-managed workers.

3.2 Revisiting the Relationship between Argentina's ERTs and Traditional Unions

Historically, traditional union support of ERTs has been patchy, as we have already seen. Indeed, with the exception of a few supportive union locals, such as the Quilmes branch of the steelworkers union, the Argentine labour movement has historically on the whole been either tentatively supportive,

---

160   Evans and Tilly 2016, p. 660.
161   Evans and Tilly 2016; McBride and Greenwood 2009; Moody 1997; Munck 2002; Pozzi and Nigra 2015; Seidman 1994; Serdar 2015; Waterman 1999, 2001; Webster 1988.

indifferent, or even hostile to the plight of ERT workers. This mixed union–ERT landscape in Argentina is in contrast to the involvement of unions with worker buyouts and business conversions to worker cooperatives in other conjunctures today. In Chapter 2, for instance, we reviewed the more consistent involvement of Brazil's and Uruguay's unions with their respective ERT movements. We also saw how Italy's unions have been, in the main, supportive of worker buyout solutions and have had a strong role to play in the creation of its Legge Marcora worker buyout model and in joint initiatives with the country's cooperative sector in funding business conversions to cooperatives.[162] In the Canadian province of Québec, as we also saw in Chapter 2, the labour movement has also played a strong role in working with the cooperative and state sectors in the creation of new conversion-based worker cooperatives.[163] And recently in the United States, new initiatives for union–cooperative partnerships have been initiated, most famously by the Mondragón–US Steelworkers partnership signed in 2009, while the role of the United Electrical, Radio and Machine Workers of America (UE) in the emergence of the New Era Windows Cooperative in Chicago is another example of strong union support for an ERT.[164]

But Argentina's ERTs' more chequered relationship with unions has to do in part with how intensely the traditional labour movement was co-opted into the neo-liberal project of the 1990s. Since the traditional labour movement, led by the CGT, embraced *menemismo*'s neo-liberal reinvention of the country's economy and its complementary re-design of the Peronist party, it was no coincidence that ERTs received little support from most unions during its first period (1990s–2004). Ensconced within the neo-liberal consensus that permeated even Argentina's official representatives of its working class, and with widespread bafflement amongst traditional union leaders as to how to deal with workers who no longer reported to bosses, most unions in this period chose instead to focus their efforts on employees who continued to work in conventional firms. As a result – and with the exception of the important support ERTs received from some political parties of the left, some union locals, and many neighbours, sympathetic social activists, academ-

---

162   Vieta, Depedri and Carrano 2017.

163   Vieta, Quarter, Spear, and Moskovsaya 2016.

164   OEOC 2016; Ranis 2014, 2016; Webb and Cheney 2014. Indeed, the role of unions in creating and supporting worker cooperatives has historical precedence, as well, as I discussed in Chapter 2. Recall, for example, that in North America the Knights of Labour were active in promoting worker cooperatives in the decades spanning the late nineteenth and early twentieth century.

ics, and social movement organisations – ERT protagonists during the phenomenon's first period were mostly left to fend for their own destinies in a sea
of neo-liberal values and practices that effectively denied them much-needed
union advocacy.[165]

Given this historically tenuous relationship with traditional unionism, it is
perhaps initially surprising to discover that most ERT workers remain affiliated to their sectoral unions. Indeed, the presence of unions in ERT shops has
remained consistent throughout the years. The Programa Facultad Abierta's
third survey of Argentina's ERTs in 2010 found that, by the end of ERT's second
period, union penetration in both the pre-existing firm and in the subsequent
ERT was high.[166] The survey showed that a union was present in 90 percent
of all ERTs and that most of Argentina's ERTs emerged from unionised workplaces. These figures continue to characterise ERTs' affiliations with traditional
unions today.[167] As we saw in Chapter 2, this high penetration of unionisation in
ERTs is due both to ERT workers' continued identification with their working-
class roots and for pragmatic reasons in order for ERT workers to continue to tap
into their basic union benefits such as health insurance linked to unions' *obras
sociales*. In the case of the most supportive unions, such as the metalworkers
union, the print graphics unions, the gastronomic union, and others, ERT workers have been able to tap into these benefits even when they are unable to pay
their union dues.[168]

3.3 *Organising ERTs via Self-Managed Workers' Associations*

Notwithstanding the increasing support of ERTs from some of Argentina's
traditional unions today, the historical apathy and sometimes outright dis-
dain towards the struggles of self-managed workers among sections of Argentina's traditional labour movement – especially prevalent during ERTs' first
period – disappointed many in the ERT movement.[169] Faced with the possibility of taking a leadership role in a new chapter of Argentina's labour history,
the country's traditional unions, many ERT protagonists have argued, initially
squandered the chance of making a real difference in the lives of Argentine
workers.

---

165   Recall, for instance, the struggles of USTs' workers with their unions in Chapter 1.
166   Ruggeri et al. 2010.
167   Ruggeri and Vieta 2015.
168   Recall from Chapter 1's review of the Salud Junín case study that Argentine unions man-
       age health care benefits for their workers, a role for Argentina's unions, as we saw in Part 1
       of this chapter, originally secured by Perón in the 1940s.
169   Barrios 2007, personal interview; Murúa 2005b, personal interview.

Partly in response to the challenges with Argentina's traditional labour movement, new cross-sectoral and community-based representative organisations of ERTs and self-managed workers emerged by the early 2000s.[170] In addition, numerous regional and provincial networks of ERTs have formed in order to meet ERTs' and other self-managed firms' most direct organisational and local business needs. Essentially, these representative organisations of self-managed workers have developed over the years into new forms of workers' organisations rooted in *autogestión*, with strong links to other social justice struggles and surrounding communities, and with more sensitivity to the plight of not only ERT workers, but also the unemployed and contingently and informally employed non-unionised workers.

On the one hand, these new self-managed workers' associations can be viewed as union-like because of their advocacy in improving working conditions in worker cooperatives and supporting ERTs in the struggle for recognition of self-managed workers' pensions, previous social security plans, and so on. But they also extend their advocacy beyond the basic bread-and-butter issues that drive more traditional unions. While self-managed workers' associations usually advise workers from potential or existing ERTs to continue their affiliations with their sector's traditional unions, they have also helped workers form new relations with other social movements, social justice groups, and even with non-ERT cooperatives to collectively make demands of the state for reforms of cooperative, bankruptcy, expropriation, and other related labour legislation. Viewing the state as *la nueva patronal* (the new boss) for workplaces that do not otherwise report to bosses on shop floors, these self-managed workers' associations also lobby the state and have successfully proposed new legislation to better reflect and respond to the needs of a new form of worker: *el trabajador autogestionado* (the self-managed worker).

Unlike traditional unions, however, ERT workers' associations are more analogous to workers' mutual aid organisations, while some of them are in actuality federations of ERTs or confederations of ERT and other self-managed workers' associations. Their primary goal, for instance, is not to negotiate working conditions or wage-based issues directly with employers, who are, after all, no longer present in the workplace. Nor are they political parties or even business associations. Rather, ERT workers' associations tend to be cooperatively-run support organisations or federations for self-managed workers that began to emerge organically after the first ERTs appeared in the late 1990s and early 2000s. They serve to represent the interests of the protagonists of Argentina's

---

170   Hirtz and Giacone 2013; Vieta and Ruggeri 2009; Ranis 2016.

ERTs in numerous ways, providing management, governance, organisational, and legal advice; organising plenary sessions, conferences, workers' assemblies, educational outlets, and spaces for voicing the concerns of self-managed workers' groups; and offering support and political lobbying on behalf of workers when a workplace's employees are considering occupying or self-managing the companies that had been employing them or when an already established ERT is seeking the expropriation path from local legislatures.

I have already introduced in previous pages some of the most important ERT workers' associations involved in assisting in the recuperation of workspaces that emerged during the ERTs' first period. These include the Movimiento Nacional de Empresas Recuperadas (MNER, National Movement of Recuperated Enterprises), the Movimiento Nacional de Fábricas Recuperadas por los Trabajadores (MNFRT, National Movement of Worker-Recuperated Factories), and the Federación de Cooperativas de Trabajo de la República Argentina (FECOOTRA, Federation of Work Cooperatives of the Republic of Argentina). During ERTs' second and third periods, as the ERT phenomenon matured, more pragmatically oriented inter-ERT networks of solidarity and assistance formed as the need for political lobbying or for learning the strategies and tactics of 'occupy' and 'resist' gave way to the need for more and more ERTs to consolidate and regularise their administration, labour processes, and technical infrastructures. Inter-ERT organisations that have formed in more recent years include, amongst others: the Associación Nacional de Trabajadores Autogestionados (ANTA, National Association of Self-Managed Workers), Red Gráfica Cooperativa (Graphics Network Cooperative), Diaros y Periódicos Regionales Argentinos (DyPRA, Regional Argentine Newspapers and Periodicals), Federación Asociativa de Diarios y Comunicadores Cooperativos de la República Argentina (FADICCRA, Associational Federation of Cooperative Newspapers and Communicators of the Republic of Argentina), the Federación Argentina de Cooperativas de Trabajadores Autogestionados (FACTA, Argentine Federation of Self-Managed Worker Cooperatives), the Confederación Nacional de Cooperativas de Trabajo (CNCT, National Confederation of Worker Cooperatives), and the Federación Autogestión, Cooperativismo y Trabajo (ACTRA, Federation of Self-Management, Cooperativism and Work). For reasons I will discuss shortly, these more recent ERT associations tend to be second- and third-tier cooperatives made up of worker cooperatives and self-managed firms that include, but are not limited to, ERTs.

During ERTs' first period, MNER and MNFRT represented by far the two most influential ERT workers' associations.[171] Founded by the workers of Indústrias

---

171   Ruggeri et al. 2005.

Metalúrgicas y Plásticas Argentina (IMPA), one of the first contemporary ERTs that emerged in the late 1990s, MNER was the ERT lobby-group and umbrella organisation that between late 2001 and early 2004 constituted the most politically significant, largest, and most written-about ERT organisation. Beginning in late 2005, however, MNER began experiencing a period of acute fragmentation. Even though, via the relentless early work of its first presidents, José Abelli and then Eduardo Murúa, as well as other worker-activists, MNER had done much to articulate the processes and tactics of workplace occupation and the concept of '*recuperar*' (to recuperate or to recover) troubled firms, the eventual fragmentation of MNER was foreshadowed by its bifurcation in 2003. This split would go on to form MNFRT under the tight leadership of Luís Caro, the centre-right lawyer we heard from earlier in this chapter. The split between MNER that was to form MNFRT in 2003 was due to internal conflicts at MNER that revolved around various practical and ideological differences.

These conflicts would characterise the differences between these two organisations and set the tone for the two main political and economic directions that the ERT phenomenon was to take in the immediate post-convertability years. MNER, for instance, has always advocated for the basic autonomy of each ERT, while MNFRT on the other hand has since its inception taken on a more pragmatic – if not hands-on and to some extent even more authoritarian – approach in dealing with the ERTs it represents. Another point of difference between these two organisations is their positions on whether or not ERTs should open up community centres or get involved with community work and solidarity activism with other social movements. On the one hand, MNER has always been a strong advocate for ERTs' solidarity work as a way of giving back to the communities that have supported them and as a self-protection strategy that complicates attempts at eviction by the state and bankruptcy courts. MNFRT, on the other hand, has argued that engaging in community work takes precious energy and resources away from consolidating production in an ERT and negatively impacts their competitiveness. Moreover, MNER has tended to operate more autonomously as an organisation, and consequently also more chaotically, than MNFRT. The roster of ERT workers who would participate in MNER meetings and activist work would change regularly, for example, while MNFRT has taken a more centralist and hierarchical approach to managing itself, with Caro firmly at the helm. MNER also aligned itself closely with various global social justice movements such as the World Social Forum (WSF), while MNFRT has not.

These two organisations also differed on how to deal with the state. MNER has maintained a 'hit-and-negotiate' posture with the state and, following the tradition of Argentine labour militancy from the 1960s and 1970s that we saw in Section 1 of this chapter, attempted to balance a distancing from the state as much as it practically could while, at the same time, aggressively lobbying it for strategic subsidies and workers' benefits (for example, in securing pensions for ERT workers, funds for technical upgrading, funding for cultural centres, and so on). This aggressive lobbying strategy proved successful during ERTs' first period when, for instance, MNER deployed the tactic of occupying local legislatures that were in session as a way to persuade incumbent politicians to vote in favour of expropriating an ERT on behalf of workers. It also used public marches and street blockades to gain media attention to the plight of ERTS. MNFRT, on the other hand, has taken a more conciliatory tone of negotiating with the state for legal reforms of relevant laws and subsidies and has had, as a result, a central role in reforming certain laws that would ease an ERT's legal burdens. MNFRT, for example, was a central player in the struggle for amending Argentina's bankruptcy law to favour worker takeovers of failing firms so that they would not have to face the financial burdens left by former owners.[172]

In the Programa Facultad Abierta's second quantitative investigation of ERTs in existence as of December 2004,[173] the research team was able to determine a numerical parity of ERTs belonging to either MNER and MNFRT during the phenomenon's first period; by early 2005, each organisation represented roughly 34 percent of ERTs that existed at the time.[174] At the same time, they were also able to identify a fairly large lack of commitment on the part of most ERT workers with regards to these two umbrella organisations. What they were also able to distinguish was a more pronounced identification with these organisations amongst ERTs that found themselves in the midst of their most conflict-filled first days, and the widest gap in identifying with these organisations amongst those ERTs that perceived themselves to be already consolidated and regularised as a self-sustaining worker cooperative. Another reason for the tendency of some ERTs to be non-committal to the workers' associations that attempt to represent them lies in the perception amongst some ERT workers that their struggles are, indeed, *their struggles* and that, at the end of the day, it is only themselves, their families, friends, and neighbours that truly risk their lives for the fight to open up their workspaces as self-managed entities.

The Programa Facultad Abierta researchers also found that ERTs affiliated with MNER have been more non-committal to the organisation than those affiliated with MNFRT. This is due, in part, to the fact that the latter organisation's

---

172   See Chapters 6 and 7.
173   Ruggeri et al. 2005.
174   Ruggeri et al. 2005, p. 94.

structure and ways of relating with its affiliate ERTs have been, in practice, more akin to the practices of a classic bureaucratic union rather than a looser affinity-based organisation which has characterised MNER. This is also reflected in the tighter political control MNFRT has exerted over its member ERTs as compared to MNER. Also, unlike MNER's Murúa, Caro has institutionalised within MNFRT the practice of taking a percentage cut of the revenues of each ERT for MNFRT and, it has been reported, for himself as a consultant's fee, thus linking himself tightly to the administrative organisation of the ERTs affiliated with MNFRT.[175]

In recent years, while MNFRT has continued to consolidate itself with the ERTs it represents, it has not grown substantially beyond the membership base it had by the mid-to-late 2000s. MNER, on the other hand, although still in existence and involved in the lobbying efforts of a handful of older and some new ERTs, is, at the time of this writing, a shadow of what it was up until 2005, mostly due to internal differences and leadership ambitions of its most vocal activists and leaders. These differences have involved divergent opinions amongst its leadership regarding what kind of role MNER is to play since the national economy stabilised after the crisis years of 2001–2. While Murúa, for example, continues to believe in an antagonistically combative posture towards the state and advocates 'fighting for a different Argentina, an Argentina without exploitation',[176] others within MNER felt that a more conciliatory role towards the state was acceptable, especially given the increased supports ERTs received during Cristina Fernández de Kirchner's administration. Only time will tell whether or not MNER will revive its former protagonism with Argentina's ERTs after the return of a more antagonistic state actor with Mauricio Macri's Cambiemos coalition.[177]

---

175 Ruggeri 2006, personal interview.
176 Murúa 2005a, personal interview.
177 It is also important to note that between 2003 and May 2006, MNER and MNFRT did not work together. Since parting from MNER, Caro's MNFRT was still in conflict with MNER, a dispute lasting until what turned out to be a temporary truce on 15 May 2006. Consequently, Caro had until then almost completely disassociated MNFRT from all events and programmes spearheaded by MNER, such as the first organised meeting of worker-recuperated enterprises from across Latin America in Caracas, Venezuela held in October 2005 and organised to a great extent by MNER's Murúa. In May 2006, however, the two organisations came together for the first time in an internal battle for control of one of the oldest and most emblematic ERTs, IMPA, between three internal factions of its workers. In the battle, Murúa and Caro created an alliance in order to gather more votes than the third faction of workers who desired to sell IMPA to private investors. This alliance, however, was short-lived after the third faction won the internal leadership elections by

In light of the organisational vacuum created by MNER's effective disintegration, coupled with MNFRT's tightening control of its core ERT-base, new attempts at organising ERTs around their cooperative structures and organisational needs soon emerged. By mid-2006, ERT workers from several city and province of Buenos Aires ERTs, including the Hotel BAUEN, the balloon manufacturer Global/La Nueva Esperanza, the print shop Gráfica Patricios, the plastics manufacture Viniplast, and a dozen or so other ERTs met to begin to organise a new umbrella organisation that aspired to be less hierarchical and more democratic than both MNER and MNFRT.[178] This new organisation, it was envisioned, would collectively lobby and coordinate funds from the state and forge alliances with universities and non-governmental organisations (NGOS) for assistance with technical and administrative upgrading, job creation, improvements in ERTs' revenue potential and market share, and the restitution of lost retirement benefits and medical and health coverage for ERT workers.[179] These meetings would prove to be the first, led by ERT workers, to begin to articulate both a political and productivity based platform along a new, more inclusive organisational model during ERTs' second period. These talks would foreshadow subsequent self-managed workers' associations that have formed in recent years as second- and third-tier federations of ERT and non-ERT cooperatives organised in order to assist with the production, marketing, and financial needs of self-managed firms.

By late 2006, these meetings would form the Federación Argentina de Cooperativas de Trabajadores Autogestionados (FACTA, Argentine Federation of Self-Managed Worker Cooperatives), since led by workers from ERTs from the city of Buenos Aires such as Federico Tonarelli from the Hotel BAUEN, Fabio Resino from the dairy ERT La Ciudad, and José Abelli (formerly involved with MNER). Taking up the broad platform that had been discussed in the 2006 meetings, FACTA has articulated close links between ERTs from the city and province of Buenos Aires and the interior of the country. Further, in a move that underlines the direction that ERTs pragmatically took in the recomposed economic, political, and social reality of Argentina throughout ERTs' second

---

a small majority and, for about a year after, took control of IMPA. Since then, MNER and MNFRT have remained divided, IMPA has returned to workers' control, and the current iteration of MNER (and Murúa) is based out of this ERT.

178   Castiglioni 2006.

179   Luisina Castiglioni has suggested that during these meetings this new association was considered being called the Asociación de Cooperativas Argentinas Sin Patrón (Association of Argentine Cooperatives without a Boss) (Castiglioni 2006, para. 12). This name was never formally used.

and third periods, FACTA has, in particular, made an effort to incorporate other cooperatives into the federation that have not been, strictly speaking, recuperated.[180]

Since its founding, FACTA has become one of the most recognisable and influential self-managed workers' associations in Argentina. Soon after its establishment, it was involved in a long political and media campaign against then-leader of the government of the city of Buenos Aires[181] (and, as of this writing, now Argentine president) Mauricio Macri's vetoes of the definitive expropriation of almost two-dozen of the city's ERTs, originally passed by the city legislature in 2004.[182] Together with MNFRT and a more recent and more broadly-based third-tier coalition of the country's worker cooperative federations known as the Confederación Nacional de Cooperativas de Trabajo (CNCT, National Confederation of Worker Cooperatives), in 2011 FACTA was also decisive in lobbying for and actually assisting in further reforming Argentina's bankruptcy law for facilitating the conversion of failing firms into worker cooperatives, which we will explore in detail in Chapter 6. Over the years, FACTA has been central in supporting the consolidation of numerous ERTs throughout the country, while contributing to the ongoing education and capacity building of self-managed workers;[183] the struggle for permanent expropriation of the Hotel BAUEN via solidarity events and initiating worldwide signature campaigns (for instance, in 2015 and early 2017);[184] and playing a key role in the 2016 mobilisations of ERTs, worker cooperatives, and other social and solidarity economy organisations against the Macri government's drastic increases in utility prices (*el Tarifazo*).[185] In 2014, FACTA became a member of Argentina's second union central, the CTA, and by September 2016 it had entered into formal discussions to also collaborate with Argentina's re-unified main union central, the CGT.[186]

FACTA was also instrumental in the founding of the already mentioned CNCT in May 2009. The CNCT is a third-tier, cooperatively run confederation of

---

180   EnRedAndo 2006, 2007.
181   Since the city of Buenos Aires is a unique and autonomous entity within the Argentine federal system, it does not have a mayor, but rather a government leader.
182   For more on Macri's expropriation vetoes, see the Chilavert case study in Chapter 1.
183   In this regard, for instance, FACTA facilitates numerous gatherings of self-managed workers and has a consulting division that works actively with ERTs and other worker cooperatives (see, for instance, FACTA 2016b, 2016c, 2016d, 2017).
184   For more on the Hotel BAUEN, see Chapter 6.
185   Página/12 2016a; FACTA 2016b.
186   FACTA 2016d.

worker cooperatives that was formed to represent the interests of Argentina's burgeoning worker cooperative movement, encompassing ERT workers' associations and other social and solidarity economy federations of self-managed workers from across the country. With 30 federations currently making up the CNCT's membership, its main goal is to act as a 'union central' for self-managed workers from across the country, and it has increasingly played a leadership role in proposing and lobbying the state for policies and laws that are better attuned to the needs of self-managed and cooperativised workers. In this regard, with FACTA and other self-managed workers' associations, it managed to help articulate and successfully lobby for the passing of the bankruptcy law reforms of 2011;[187] continues to push for reforms to Argentina's legislation on cooperatives;[188] supports in various ways new ERT worker cooperatives emerging from the Plan Argentina Trabaja initiative introduced by Fernández de Kirchner's government in the late 2000s;[189] and mobilises media campaigns and political actions in order to push for more favourable treatment of self-managed workers' initiatives, such as actively participating with FACTA and other social justice groups in the 2016 protests against the Cambiemos coalition government's utility rate increases.

Another promising solidarity initiative has been spearheaded by the Quilmes branch of the UOM steelworkers union in the southern suburbs of greater Buenos Aires. The UOM Quilmes cooperative–ERT–union consortium, originally assisting 13 member ERTs in the Quilmes region, now includes over 30 metalurgical and non-metalurgical sector ERTs in the municipalities of Quilmes, Berazategui, and Florencio Varela and has managed over the years to negotiate agreements with several European agencies[190] and with the National

---

187   See Chapter 6.
188   For example, to have worker cooperative members recognised as 'workers' rather than self-employed entrepreneurs (*trabajadores autónomos*), thus securing the social benefits and labour rights guaranteed to Argentine employees (see Chapters 6 and 7).
189   See Chapters 6 and 7.
190   Showing the growing tendency for international solidarity between ERTs and other cooperative and labour movement initiatives from around the world (which I will pick up again in Chapter 7), in 2006 ERTs affiliated with UOM Quilmes, its NGO Fundación Fundemos (2017), and the Mesa de Empresas Recuperadas de la Provincia de Buenos Aires (MERPBA, Committee of Recuperated Enterprises of the Province of Buenos Aires) received financial and capacity-building support from the European Union and Italy's cooperative movement, including Cooperazione por lo Svillupo de Paesi Emergenti (COSPE, Cooperation for the Development of Emerging Countries), Legacoop Bologna, and Legacoop Marche. This formed an initiative called Redes de Empresas, Redes de Personas (Networks of Enterprises, Networks of People), also known as Proyecto Redes (NUDOS 2006a, 2006b). As a side note, that both FACTA and UOM Quilmes have had to

University of Quilmes to provide its member ERTs with access to technical assistance and professional consulting services.[191] Under the leadership of Francisco 'Barba' Gutiérrez, who would eventually become mayor of the municipality of Quilmes, UOM Quilmes was also central in founding the Mesa de Empresas Recuperadas de la Provincia de Buenos Aires (MERPBA, Committee of Recuperated Enterprises of the Province of Buenos Aires), a regional ERT workers' association that had in the mid-2000s worked mostly with ERTs in greater Buenos Aires conurbation and that had also emerged from the fragmentation of MNER.

Since 2006, ERTs working in the graphics sector under the second-tier Red Gráfica Cooperativa (Graphics Network Cooperative) have formalised an effective economic solidarity network of ERTs and non-ERT cooperative print shops throughout the city of Buenos Aires and its greater metropolitan area. The Red Gráfica has been able to successfully pool resources between its member cooperatives, seeing them sharing production and customers, working closely with the Buenos Aires printers' union (FGB) to ensure its workers' well-being and lobbying the state for better supports for cooperatives in the printing and graphics sector, and collectively tackling the various challenges cooperatives in this sector face in a highly concentrated and competitive Argentine printing and publishing market.[192] Similar associations of self-managed workplaces in the printing and publishing sector representing cooperative and independent newspapers and print shops across Argentina have also emerged in recent years, such as the already mentioned FADICCRA and DyPRA.[193]

Yet another small group of ERTs continue to be linked to the Federación de Cooperativas de Trabajo de la República Argentina (FECOOTRA, Federation of Worker Cooperatives of the Republic of Argentina), including those forming a part of the UOM Quilmes network. Founded in 1988 before the rise of today's ERT movement, FECOOTRA is a cooperative federation that includes a broad coalition of different cooperatives and which eventually also took on representing the interests of ERTs, especially in the Avellaneda suburb of Buenos Aires in the late 1990s and early 2000s.[194] Other second-tier cooperative asso-

---

rely on European funding and technical assistance also alludes to the Argentine federal government's mixed track record in supporting ERTs (see Chapter 7).

191 NUDOS 2006a.

192 For more on the Red Gráfica, see Chapters 6 and 7 and the Chilavert case study in Chapter 1.

193 Self-defined as 'the first cooperative entity created for defending graphics communication media, SMEs, and cooperatives in Argentina', DyPRA is also involved in provisioning cheaper paper products for its members than those offered by the monopolistic Clarín Group (DyPRA 2011).

194 FECOOTRA 2017.

ciations that have formed more recently, that highlight the production and organisational aspects of *autogestión*, and that incorporate ERTs and non-ERT cooperatives, include (amongst many others): the Grupo de Empresas Sociales y Trabajadores Autogestionados de la República Argentina (GESTARA, Group of Social Enterprises and Self-Managed Workers of the Republic of Argentina), the Federación de Cooperativas Autogestionadas de Buenos Aires (FEDECABA, Federation of Self-Managed Cooperatives of Buenos Aires), and the Federación Autogestión, Cooperativismo y Trabajo (ACTRA, Federation of Self-Management, Cooperativism and Work), the latter formed in 2016 from some members of FACTA and other ERTs and non-ERT cooperatives mainly from the province of Santa Fe but also including experiences from various parts of Argentina.

This complex and still fragmented landscape of ERT-related self-managed workers associations is further layered with yet another experience, that of the workers of the iconic ceramics ERT cooperative Zanón/FaSinPat (Fábrica Sin Patrón, or Factory Without a Boss) in the province of Neuquén, perhaps the strongest example of a contemporary social movement/community union model emerging from the ERT movement to date.[195] Since its founding in 2001, the Zanón/FaSinPat workers have maintained strong ties with many of Argentina's ERTs and various ERT associations while at the same time remaining at arms length from them. This posture of autonomy, a concept actively used by the Zanón/FaSinPat workers and influenced by the various political affiliations of its leaders, which includes the Trotskyist Partido de los Trabajadores Socialistas (PTS, Socialist Workers' Party), has boded well for them and for keeping their vision of nationalising the plant under workers' control in the national and international spotlight. In part because of this posture of non-affiliation, Zanón/FaSinPat – only expropriated by the province of Neuquén on behalf of its workers in August 2009 after many years of legal and political struggle – has received some healthy financial contributions from several state institutes that other ERTs have not managed to secure, such as with the Instituto Nacional de Tecnología Industrial (INTI, National Institute of Industrial Technology).[196] Moreover, their workers' initial strategy of taking over their local ceramics union, the Sindicato de Obreros y Empleados Ceramistas de Neuquén (SOECN, Union of Ceramics Workers and Employees of Neuquén) before recuperating the plant in 2001, while also tightly ingraining itself in mobilising local community development projects, has been a unique case in

---

195   See Ranis 2016.
196   INTI is a support and research institute for Argentina's industrial sectors.

the Argentine universe of ERTs that highlights yet another model of new social movement/community unionism.[197]

Besides the CNCT, two other groups that have formed in recent years with the specific intent of organising ERTs and other self-managed collectives and worker cooperatives along the lines of a union model have been the Asociación Nacional de Trabajadores Autogestionados (ANTA, National Association of Self-Managed Workers) and the Unión Productiva de Empresas Autogestionadas (UPEA, Productive Union of Self-Managed Enterprises). Situated within the progressive CTA union central, ANTA has been closely connected with UST (one of the case studies in Chapter 1), and was founded in late 2005 by sympathetic activists within the CTA and several UST members who also had past experiences as shop stewards and with other forms of union organising.[198] Envisioned as a union of self-managed firms, ANTA specifically formed as a response to the state's and the traditional union movement's general indifference or outright hostility to the plight of the self-managed, the underemployed, and the unemployed. Initially made up of 83 organisations of ERTs, self-managed micro-enterprises, and other workers' collectives, ANTA, with UST's Mario Barrios as its general secretary, has been lobbying the state to recognise the labour rights of self-managed workers in their struggle to secure pensions, stabilise sector-wide wages, create a national health and workers' compensation plan for self-managed workers, and provide self-managed firms with favourable and just loans.[199]

Similarly, UPEA was formed circa 2010–11 by a group of 25 founding ERTs, cooperatives, and self-managed micro-enterprises as a space to collectively advocate for the interests of self-managed firms and its workers. UPEA specifically represents, in the words of its founding principles, those firms that 'counterpose' themselves to purely capitalist firms and to other forms of micro-enterprises 'centred on the perverse model of state subsidies'.[200] As with ANTA, UPEA's main aims have centred on the recognition of Argentina's two million self-managed workers (according to its own estimates) as 'complete workers' that should have the same rights and privileges as fully unionised and dependent employees. UPEA has also proposed initiatives such as ensuring access to fair loans for self-managed firms and for the state to guarantee at least 30 percent of its procurements to the social and solidarity economy sector.[201]

---

197 Aiziczón 2009; Ranis 2016.
198 Vales 2005.
199 Barrios 2007, personal interview.
200 Kasparian 2012, p. 1.
201 Kasparian 2012, pp. 1, 3.

While ANTA and UPEA have been promising initiatives organised around the principles of regional councils, horizontality, and direct democracy, there are, to date, only a handful of ERTs that associate themselves with these still-nascent attempts at unionising self-managed workers. The majority of ANTA's and UPEA's members are cooperatives and micro-enterprises associated with Argentina's social and solidarity economy that did not originate from owner-managed firms.[202] While relatively small associations, over the years both ANTA and UPEA have proven to be important advocates for *autogestión* and promising models for creating community-based unions of self-managed workers.

Collectively, Argentina's self-managed workers' associations are, I argue, rich examples of new forms of labour organisations containing aspects of what we can characterise as social movement/community unionism. Not only do they point towards new, cross-sectoral modes of organising labour centred on the notion of *autogestión*, but also serve to underscore, in practice, the sixth and seventh cooperative principles of the ICA, namely, cooperatives cooperating and concern for community, as I will further explore in Chapters 5 and 9.

3.4   *New Ways of Associating Self-Managed Workers: Taking Stock*

As this brief historical map of Argentina's new self-managed workers' associations has demonstrated, attempts at organising ERTs are not primarily based on their sectoral commonalities as with traditional trade or industrial unions, nor on political commitments to official parties, but rather on their common experiences in struggling for the recuperation of workspaces guided by *autogestión*. Indeed, most attempts to date at organising ERTs along some common political or traditional union lines rather than along their practical experiences with *autogestión* have met with difficulties. And telling of the characteristic of the ERT phenomenon in its second and third periods, recent organising initiatives such as FACTA, CNCT, ANTA, as well as the Zanón/FaSinPat workers' approach, have consciously striven to build bridges of solidarity between ERTs and other cooperative or self-managed entities; social movements; social and solidarity economy organisations such as with the Confederación de Trabajadores de la Economía Popular (CTEP, Confederation of Workers of the Popular Economy); community groups and neighbourhood associations; and sympathetic unions such as UOM Quilmes and the Federación de Trabajadores de la Energía de la República Argentina (FETERA, Federation of Energy Workers of the Republic of Argentina). On the other hand, perhaps because of each ERT's particular historical situation or the unique technological, financial and market

---

202   ANTA 2007; Kasparian 2012.

challenges that most worker-recuperated firms must confront once production restarts,[203] the attempts by ANTA, UPEA, and the CNCT at organising ERTs along union lines has been limited and should still be considered a work-in-progress.

The character of self-managed workers' associations and second- and third-tier cooperative organisations of ERTs has transformed since the earlier days of the ERT phenomenon. The early and implosive socio-economic years between the mid-to-late 1990s and early 2004 – the first period of ERTs – required MNER and subsequently MNFRT to primarily focus on articulating and assisting ERTs' political struggles and direct action tactics as well as initiate the struggle – quite effectively, as it eventually turned out – for a national political voice for its worker protagonists and for securing legal status for ERTs. By the end of second and beginning of the third period of the ERT phenomenon around 2010, the need for more politically minded entities such as an MNER or an MNFRT had diminished substantially given the recomposed socio-economic climate of Argentina at the time. By ERTs' third period, self-managed workers' associations that also took up issues of production and other economic dimensions of cooperatives stepped in to meet the new challenges faced by already established ERTs within a reconsolidated and more stable Argentine economy. These associations included ANTA and UPEA; those that specifically worked with ERTs to improve and consolidate their cooperative organisational structures, such as FACTA, CNCT, and FECOOTRA; and many other smaller regional entities. Rather than direct action tactics and occupations, the main concerns of these newer ERT associations have tended to focus on the viability and long-term sustainability of self-managed firms within a relatively more stable economy and intensifying market competition. In other words, rather than needing to organise numerically for lobbying the state and struggle for occupations and workers' control of firms via the 'war of bodies', as Eduardo Murúa characterises it for us in Chapters 1 and 6, the major needs that have been facing ERTs in recent years have tended to be securing sources of financing, improving technological infrastructure, winning back customers, and generally securing market share. Towards these goals, these more recent organisations aspire to facilitate inter-ERT relations of cooperation and mutual aid while building bridges to other self-managed workspaces and national and international sources of financing and grants. Not as revolutionary in vision as MNER was, nor as authoritative and paternal as MNFRT still is, the focus of these new organisations are more respectful of the autonomy of each ERT, and more pragmatic, concrete, and realistic of their needs, reflecting more the macro-

---

203   See Chapter 7.

economically stabilised conjuncture that the ERT phenomenon on the whole found itself in by its third period.

With the reappearance of more explicit neo-liberal policies arising out of Mauricio Macri's Cambiemos coalition since December 2015, however, signs are emerging that ERT workers' associations are returning to the militancy, political actions, and lobbying efforts that defined them during the crisis years spanning the turn of the millennium. New collective efforts between ERT workers' associations and other social and solidarity economy organisations throughout the Cambiemos administration – which have so far included media campaigns; political lobbying efforts at the national Ministries of Labour, Energy, and Social Development; and mass protests against *macrismo*'s austerity and pro-investor policies – are pointing to what we can characterise as a new phase of social movement-based militancy and organising across sectors of groups practising *autogestión*. Poignantly, this return to collective organising and militancy is drawing on the strategies and tactics of resistance learned during the previous crisis of the neo-liberal model. How effectively they will sway the posture and policies of Argentina's new neo-liberal government in order to secure the long-term sustainability of self-managed workers in Argentina remains to be seen. In no small part due to the lobbying efforts and political mobilisations of self-managed workers' associations such as FACTA and CNCT, some positive results from these collective efforts can already be seen in, for instance, the temporary freezing of rising utility rates as the Supreme Court deliberates on the constitutionality of the stark rise in gas, water, and electricity bills, and the Ministry of Labour's promise to reinstitute subsidies to self-managed workplaces.[204]

4 ERTs and the Political Economy of the Working Class in Argentina: A Summation

The rise of neo-liberalism in Argentina that began soon after the military *coup d'état* of 26 March 1976 (but that in some ways had been already occurring with the courting of foreign capital and rationalisation drives since perhaps the late 1950s) was in no small part a strategy by the country's capitalist elites to fragment union power, curtail the economic and political clout of the working class, and force workers into docility and compliance on shop floors. Between the mid-1940s and mid-1970s, the composition of Argentina's working class

---

204   FACTA 2016b; Página/12 2016a. See also Chapters 6 and 7.

and organised labour's strength was in part achieved by a combination of the class compromise that Perón had forged between the state, big capital, small business owners, and the union bureaucracy led by the CGT as well as via workers' own self-activity and grassroots organising initiatives. Undoubtedly, within this Peronist class compromise, Argentina's working class would begin to enjoy a large part of the national economic pie and even national political power. The new confidence that Perón's pro-labour polices gave to the working class throughout the 1940s and early 1950s would also motivate and continue to develop a vibrant democratic ethos on shop floors that would extend beyond Perón's intentions for social containment and economic peace.[205]

This mid-twentieth-century working-class composition, however, would change in no small way with the attempt at its bloody decomposition that began in the last months of Isabel Perón's presidency and was unleashed with genocidal ferocity during the 1976–83 military dictatorship's ominously self-proclaimed Proceso de Reorganización Nacional, in effect decimating much of Argentina's union leadership and many of its most politically active workers. While *el Proceso* would ultimately implode under the weight of international pressure and workers' renewed resistance, its socio-economic effects would resonate well into the 1990s. Its orthodox economic policies opened up a mostly unencumbered path for President Carlos Menem's eventual enthusiastic uptake of the tenets of the Washington Consensus.

By the mid-1990s, with the effects of Menem's neo-liberal policies immiserating more and more workers, and unemployment and underemployment rates soaring, the working class would begin a new cycle of recomposition, becoming especially visible in the new forms of occupation-based protests, in diverse affinity projects between different social groups struggling for social justice, and in the new worker organisations that arose at the time, such as the *piqueteros*, the new form of militant shop floor organising concerned with workplace-specific struggles, the emergence of social movement and community unionism and complementary forms of new self-managed workers' associations, the rise of the progressive CTA and the CCC, and the appearance of myriad new groups rooted in multiple alternative left politics, including a revived and militant grassroots Peronism and even autonomist- and anarchist-based tendencies. Many of these new groups were made up primarily of the unemployed, the underemployed, students, and marginalised sectors. All of these new groups have undeniably helped recompose Argentina's working class in recent years, with parts of the working class going in new directions

---

205   Munck et al. 1987; James 1988; Smith 1991.

rooted in social and economic justice issues that extended beyond the traditional and bureaucratic union movement. What especially made them *new* was their two-pronged approach to this recomposition: Their forms of organising were both *direct responses, reactions*, and *resistances* to the worst abuses of neo-liberalism that came to a head in the social upheavals in the months leading up to and the years following *el Argentinazo* of 19 and 20 December 2001, while also *proposing and offering novel ways of reconstituting the production and distribution of goods and services* via *self-managed shop floor and worker- and community-centric methods of organising the labour process.* These recompositions and reorganisations of the working class, which continued to unfold under the more sympathetic neo-populist social and economic policies of *kirchnerismo*, were principally grounded in new and bottom-up democratic institutions and made-in-Argentina solutions to particular socio-economic needs.

With the recent resurgence of neo-liberalist policies under Macri's Cambiemos coalition government, a new stage of growing militancy seems to be emerging amongst Argentina's self-managed workers' associations. Today, this growing militancy is bringing together social movements and self-managed workers' associations with sectors of the traditional union movement and new coalitions of working-class associations in a continuation, now along more activist lines, of the social movement/community unionism that has been coalescing over the past 15 years.

Before returning to the lived experience of these new forms of labour organisations, self-managed labour processes, and the collective production of social wealth prefigured and actually practised by ERTs in Chapters 6–8 (which we first witnessed in the three case studies in Chapter 1), we will need to theoretically and historically situate the concepts of workers' self-activity, association, and self-determination; the political economy of the working class; and *auto-gestión* that have until now only been touched upon. I turn to these tasks in the next two chapters.

PART 2

Theorising and Historicising Autogestión

∵

The Stream of Self-Determination: Freedom, Cooperation, and the Recuperations of Living Labour

But there was in store a still greater victory of the political economy of labour over the political economy of property. We speak of the co-operative movement, especially the co-operative factories raised by the unassisted efforts of a few bold 'hands'. The value of these great social experiments cannot be over-rated. By deed, instead of by argument, they have shown that production on a large scale, and in accord with the behests of modern science, may be carried on without the existence of a class of masters employing a class of hands; that to bear fruit, the means of labour need not be monopolised as a means of dominion over, and of extortion against, the labouring man himself; and that, like slave labour, like serf labour, hired labour is but a transitory and inferior form, destined to disappear before associated labour plying its toil with a willing hand, a ready mind, and a joyous heart.

KARL MARX[1]

∴

Part 1 began the book with ERT protagonists' lived experiences of struggle, workplace recuperation, and *autogestión*. In Chapter 1 we relied on the voices of the worker-protagonists of three exemplar Argentine ERTs to highlight the various processes and challenges of taking over troubled firms and restarting them as worker cooperatives. Chapter 2 provided an empirical overview of Argentina's ERT phenomenon and located it amongst other ERT-type experiments in the world today. Chapter 3 then situated the emergence of Argentina's ERTs in the country's long history of working-class militancy and self-activity, influenced by political economic conjunctures fluctuating between authoritarian,

---

1 Marx 1978a, pp. 517–18 ('Inaugural Address of the Working Men's International Association').

populist, and, by the mid-1970s, neo-liberal regimes of ruling in a constant ebb and flow of growth and crises.

Part 2 now pauses from the empirical exploration of Argentina's ERTs and sets out to situate the book's critical theoretical and conceptual framework. This chapter theoretically locates practices of *autogestión* within an inheritance of workers' self-activity linked to the long-held desire of working people to self-determine their lives; it is an inheritance with a genealogy that both predates capitalism and parallels its evolution.[2] The next chapter continues this genealogy by tracing out the evolution of the concept of *autogestión* from the nineteenth to the twenty-first centuries in Europe and in Latin America. What we learn in Part 2 will be useful later on for unpacking the common characteristics and challenges of ERTs and their worker-protagonists' experiments with *autogestión*, as well as for helping us understand ERTs' recuperative moments, radical social innovations, and their potential for delineating an alternative to capitalist modes of production.

This chapter first looks at the most salient theoretical roots of workers' cooperation and *autogestión* in what I call modern socialism's *stream of self-determination* – the historical recognition of working people's continued capacities for resistance and self-activity. Here the chapter also outlines the complementary perspectives of class-struggle Marxism and the political economy of the working class, which help us to focus in further on how workers are able to collectively resist exploitation, overcome crises, and innovate cooperatively in ways that prefigure socialised and non-capitalist modes of production. The chapter then disentangles the two-fold character of labour and technology in the capitalist system of production, positing that capitalist production and its underlying norms, practices, and technologies are exploitative and alienating *yet also* bring workers together in solidarity and cooperation in ways that catalyse the potential for their collective self-determination. Understanding this two-fold character of labour and technology in capitalism, I argue, is key for coming to grips with workers' inherent and historical capacities to resist and begin to move beyond capitalist enclosures and, more specifically, 'value-production'.[3] In the chapter's last section I work out the six *recuperative moments* that thread through ERTs' practices of *autogestión*, encompassed in the slogan we will pick up in detail in Chapter 6: *'ocupar, resistir, producir'*. That is, in occupying, taking over, and subsequently self-managing the firms

---

2   By *genealogy* I mean, as it does for Michael Burawoy, a historical and theoretical 'tracing [of] how we got to where we are' (Burawoy 2000, p. 5).

3   Hudis 2012, pp. 6–8.

that formerly employed them, ERT workers also begin to recuperate *from capitalist control* and *for themselves*: (1) their labour-power, (2) their surpluses, (3) their capacities to voluntarily associate and cooperate in production, (4) the labour process in general, (5) the division of labour, and (6) the social production of social wealth. This chapter thus continues and deepens our journey of coming to know what ERT protagonists are fighting against (exploitative and alienating capitalist labour practices and the socio-economic ills inherent to neo-liberalism), what they are struggling for (self-determination and *autogestión*), and what they are recuperating in the process (control over their own living labour and working lives).

1   Section 1: The Stream of Self-Determination and Modern Socialist
         Thought

There is a central idea, a primary motif piercing through modern socialist thought: People must free themselves from exploitation, especially when a small group of the population has most of its needs and wants met on the backs of a vastly larger group that goes with many of its needs unmet and desires unfulfilled. Modern socialist thought suggests that this reality is dependent on a class-based social hierarchy that relies on the labours of the latter group – workers – for its existence. For modern socialism(s), the emancipated society is one in which the realm of necessity of *all* would be met without the exploitation of *any*. As we will soon see, the concept and practices of cooperation – and implicitly, *autogestión* – figure prominently in socialist visions of the liberated future society free from exploitation. Variations on Morelly's, Saint-Simon's, and Louis Blanc's maxim, equally shared by utopian socialist reformers, social anarchists, and Marxists, resonate with this central idea: 'From each according to his [or her] abilities, to each according to his [or her] needs'.[4]

Nineteenth-century socialist thinkers who were living through the late-adolescent stage of capitalism already presaged the consequences of this system's exploitative tendencies. In different circumstances, and at different times throughout the nineteenth century, these critics astutely dissected the practices and ideologies of a system built around the ostensibly self-interested 'propensity of human nature' to 'truck, barter, and exchange'.[5] Robert Owen, Charles Fourier, Friedrich Engels, and Karl Marx,[6] for instance, meticulously

---

4   Laidler 1938, pp. 57, 65, 77–8.
5   Smith 1976, p. 17.
6   Owen 1991b; Fourier 1971; Engels 1968; Marx 1967, 1973, 1976.

exposed the causes of the harsh working conditions of labourers, most convincingly, I would argue, with Marx's unmasking of capital–labour relations in the 'hidden abode' of production in the *Grundrisse*[7] and the first volume of *Capital*.[8] Classical social anarchists,[9] such as Pierre-Joseph Proudhon, Mikhail Bakunin, and Peter Kropotkin,[10] would also level severe critiques at the capitalist system while underscoring the role of the state in upholding this unjust system.[11] On the whole, all of these nineteenth-century socialist theorists, experimenters, reformers, and revolutionaries had something poignant and foreboding to say about the negative aspects of the capitalist system for workers. Their critiques were most forceful when lambasting the misery irradiating from the modes of production of an increasingly global capitalism onto the lives of the growing working class. But nineteenth-century socialist thinkers also theorised or even experimented with alternative economic arrangements, driven by the pursuit of a different organisation of production and exchange rooted in mutual self-help and cooperative association.

In no small way, inspiration for these socialist alternatives were drawn from history. Indeed, people's experiences with bottom-up cooperative association and practices of self-help have long preceded the capitalist era.[12] Pre-modern examples of such experiences include the life of 'the commons';[13] social practices of mutual aid;[14] organisations of craft-based production;[15] and traditional and Indigenous communities' economies of reciprocity, redistribution, and

---

7   Marx 1973.

8   Marx 1967, 1976.

9   Encompassing variants of anarchism such as 'mutualism', 'anarcho-communisim' (or 'communist anarchism'), 'socialist anarchism', 'anarcho-syndicalism', and strands of 'libertarian socialism', 'social anarchism' is the anarchist tradition that considers the struggle for personal freedom to be deeply entwined with social struggle against oppression and for mutual aid via collective action (Berkman 1972; Kropotkin 1989). While social anarchists are deeply critical of the state and its institutions, as with more individualist-inclined anarchists, believing that they are 'destructive to individual liberty and social harmony' (Berkman 1972, p. xxii), social anarchists take pains to also critique the role played by the capitalist system, its wage-based coercive apparatuses, and the privately owned mode of production that upholds modernity's hierarchies of control, inequality, and exploitation. Moreover, social anarchists contemplate, aspire towards, and struggle for 'ownership in common and joint use' of the technological, productive, and distributive components of the economy (Berkman 1972, p. 197).

10   Proudhon 1989; Bakunin 1990; Kropotkin 1995.

11   Marshall 1992.

12   Heilbronner and Milberg 1998; Kropotkin 1989; Laidler 1938; Polanyi 2001.

13   De Angelis 2007; De Angelis and Harvie 2014; Thompson 1993.

14   Kropotkin 1989.

15   Horvat 1982; Tierney 1999.

house-holding.[16] In addition, accounts of the rise of capitalism must also not forget working people's continued self-directed economic activities, as well as their tenacious resistances to dispossession. A more complete history of capitalism thus also includes: rural people's ongoing challenges to the privatisation of common lands and the erosion of traditional ways of life, motivating movements such as the Levellers, the Diggers, and others;[17] the expansion of maroon and *quilombo* communities of escaped slaves across the Americas;[18] sailors' resistances to the deplorable working conditions in colonial shipping and navy fleets, including buccaneer and pirate communities and their often horizontal modes of organising;[19] the recurrence of poor riots due to the rising cost of bread and grain in the eighteenth century;[20] the Luddites' struggles against the deep transformations of working life wrought by the rise of industrialism;[21] and early working-class struggles for better working and living conditions.[22]

By the late eighteenth and throughout the nineteenth century, friendly societies, mutual associations, cooperatives, trade unions, and other forms of workers' combinations were developing throughout Europe and its colonies, most often as bottom-up responses to the callous exploitation of emergent industrial capitalism.[23] Experiments in or proposals for alternative economic organisations that developed specifically because of the stark inequalities of the new economic order include: early organised cooperatives, such as Scotland's Fenwick Weaver's Society of the mid-eighteenth century;[24] the utopian socialists' initiatives for communalising work, led by Owen's worker-centred revival of the New Lanark mill in the first decades of the nineteenth century and Fourier's contemporaneous proposals for 'attractive labour' and collective work;[25] the London Cooperative Society of 1824; the consumer cooperative 'union shops' of the 1820s; and the Rochdale Society of Equitable Pioneers in the 1840s.[26]

Already by the early nineteenth century, utopian socialists were campaigning for a more equitable society for workers in the midst of a rapidly industrialising Europe. To get there, they envisioned a socialised economy of cooper-

16   Polanyi 2001. See also Curl 2009, pp. 15–27.
17   Bookchin 1990; De Angelis and Harvie 2014.
18   Price 1996.
19   Linebaugh and Rediker 2000.
20   Hill 1986; Thompson 1993.
21   Noble 1993; Sale 1996.
22   Hobsbawm 1964; Laidler 1938; Thompson 1993.
23   McNally 1993.
24   Carrell 2007. On early cooperatives, see also Infield 1947.
25   Claeys 1991; Fourier 1971; Garnett 1972; Owen 1991a.
26   Fairbairn 1994; Quarter 2000.

ative communities, which would some decades later be conceptualised as a cooperative commonwealth.[27] For classical social anarchists such as Proudhon, Bakunin, and Kropotkin, cooperatives, as locally rooted and collectively owned productive entities organised within federated associations, were also vital for building the alternative to the capitalist-state system.[28] And Marx, too, had favourable views of 'workers' cooperative factories'[29] that, for him, proved to be, together with the ten-hour workday, one of the most promising victories for the struggle of workers' against capital and central to the 'political economy of the working class'.[30]

By the third decade of the nineteenth century, Owen and other socialist contemporaries, such as John Francis Bray, Thomas Hodgskin, John Gray, and William Thompson,[31] were conceptualising 'communities of mutual cooperation'[32] and 'labour exchanges',[33] the latter to allow workers to buy and sell goods more fairly based on products directly valued by labour-time and exchanged via labour-note currency.[34] A few experiments in market reform along these lines were even attempted, such as Owen's short-lived National Equitable Labour Exchange in London, England in 1832–4.[35] Another early Owenite, physician and philanthropist William King, advocated especially for a cooperative movement and started the early 'union shops' (the precursors to Rochdale) in Brighton, England, and the paper *The Co-operator* (published between 1828–30), in which many of the first theories and histories of cooperativism were printed.[36] By the second half of the nineteenth century, reformers and revolutionaries also became inspired by Proudhon's condemnation of property relations and his subsequent proposals for mutualism and equal exchange between small producers working in socialised production arrangements.[37]

For modern socialist theorists, then, an alternative to the capitalist order – whatever that was to look like – or, at minimum, a reform of it, was direly needed. The *ends*, then, often broadly align in modern socialist thinking, espe-

---

27   Birchall 1994, 2004; Curl 2010.

28   Marshall 1992.

29   Marx 1981, p. 512.

30   Marx 1978a, p. 517.

31   Bray 1839; Gray 1825, 1831; Hodgskin 1825; Thompson 1824, 1827.

32   Ranis 2016, pp. 11.

33   Fay 1947, p. 196.

34   For Marxist-based critiques of these utopian and Ricardian socialists' labour-theory of value, see Hudis 2012, pp. 96–7; and McNally 1993, pp. 104–38.

35   Dowd 2012; Fay 1947.

36   Birchall 1994; Infield 1956.

37   Proudhon 1970, 1972, 1989. See also Marshall 1992 and especially McNally 1993, p. 142.

cially, as I will show shortly, in regards to the role of cooperation and self-determination in a new social order grounded in associated forms of labour. It is the *means* of getting there that tend to differ.[38]

Let me pause for a moment to say straight out that my intent here is not to efface the well-documented differences and debates between the various currents of modern socialist thought.[39] Instead, in this and the next chapter, as part of the political economy of the working class approach that undergirds what I term 'a genealogy of *autogestión*', my intention is to look at the common ground shared by modern socialisms in their search for another path to human development that sharply contrasts with the one offered by capitalism and its institutional forms. That is, I appeal to the overlaps in socialist visions that delineate the future, non-exploitative and non-alienated society and the potential for alternatives opened by the resistances and experiments of workers and the marginalised. Thus, even Marx and Engels were prone at times to envision and theorise the future liberated society.[40] True, they did so while, at the same time, reproving the utopian socialists and anarchists for desiring social transformation without properly understanding the intricacies of capital's processes of valorisation;[41] of desiring to 'emancipate ... all humanity at once' and to 'evolve' a new system 'out of the human brain' without adequately considering broader historical materialist conditions;[42] or for 'writing receipts ... for the cook-shops of the future'.[43] Social anarchists, in turn, would ultimately distance themselves from the vanguardist and statist conclusions arrived at by Marxists.[44] Despite the differences between these socialist critics of capitalism,

---

38   Buber 1996, p. 13.

39   Briefly, the major divergences between socialisms tend to focus on how they answer the following questions: Are workers to liberate themselves or should their representatives – the party, the vanguard, intellectuals, secret revolutionary societies, and so on – lead the way? How does the transition from capitalist society to the socialist society unfold, via reform or revolution? What should the role of the state be in this transition and in the new society? Is the state even needed, or should it be taken over by the working class? Or should the state be allowed to wither and be replaced by another form of decentralised federation? If so, when should the takeover of the state or its dissolution occur? Is the main culprit responsible for the domination of people capital(ism), the state, or both working together to make the entire world a standing reserve of raw materials for the global production machine? And, how should we compensate those who work more, or who have more abilities, while protecting the more vulnerable members of society?

40   See, for instance, Marx 1978a, 1978b, 1978c; and Marx and Engels 1998.

41   Marx and Engels 1998.

42   Engels 1978, pp. 685, 687.

43   Marx 1967, p. 17.

44   Anarchist FAQ Collective 2009, sec. H.

it is undeniable that all of them, writing in the thick of a new capitalist order overtaking the world, had profound and at times complementary views on the un-free life being lived by workers. In short, the primary continuity between modern socialisms on which I focus here is to be found in their support of and faith in (with varying degrees of emphasis) the emancipative potential inherent in the self-activity of working people.[45] For this book, these socialist visions of a liberated future forged via the self-activity of working people help us understand the other socio-economic reality prefigured by ERTs and their practices of *autogestión*.

In beginning to ground my genealogy of *autogestión* for this study, then, I would like to home in on two common notions I see streaming through modern socialist thought:

(1)   That the struggle for freedom from the exploitative society is the struggle for the self-governing society, where working people would be, in some way, co-responsible for the economic realm (that is, producing and distributing resources otherwise in short supply) as well as in their own reproduction as human beings.[46]

(2)   That there are experiences of workers in the present already sketching out prefiguratively, in degrees of opacity and clarity, aspects of the future emancipated society.[47]

It is my contention that modern socialist thought recognises that these two notions meet, in particular, in the *lived experiences of labouring people*. They also resonate with the historically consistent desire and struggle of workers *to self-determine* their productive and creative lives. This historical struggle and desire, although of course predating the era of industrialisation, parallels

---

45   Modern socialisms' faith in the self-activity of working people is, one can also argue, connected to their implicit or explicit utopian impulses. For instance, while Martin Buber identifies the differences between socialist traditions and, particularly, Marx and Engels' critiques of utopian socialism and anarchism on various fronts, for him even Marx and Engels do not escape an implicit utopianism in their writings. Buber quotes Paul Tillich to drive the point home: '"Marxism has never, despite its animosity to Utopias, been able to clear itself of the suspicion of a hidden belief in Utopia"' (Tillich, in Buber 1996, p. 11). Similarly, Norman Geras has argued that 'despite Marx and Engels' attempt ... to take their distance from utopia as mere abstraction or speculation[,] ... it remains true that from the outset socialism was utopian. It was a distant land, another moral universe. It was radically other vis-à-vis the order of things it aspired to replace. And that is what it still is. A society beyond exploitation in the realm of the ideal' (Geras 2000, p. 42).

46   Horvat 1982, pp. 497–513.

47   Buber 1996.

the historical rise of capitalism and its underlying liberal ideologies of self-interest, competition, 'free markets', and 'free enterprise'.[48] It marks 'the other side' of the development of capitalism,[49] the side that sees workers resisting the encroachments of capital on life. These two commonalities meet and intermingle in modern socialist thought in a radical current that I call *the stream of self-determination*.

1.1   *The Human Desire for Freedom and the Stream of Self-Determination*

The notion of the stream of self-determination is rooted in modern social-isms' longing for *human freedom*,[50] which was itself inspired in part by the Enlightenment's call for freedom from autocratic rule, religion, and myth.[51] The stream of self-determination also draws inspiration from historical account-ings of working people's self-activity and key moments of resistance that I have already begun to map out. A critical theory of freedom, however, is not just about the emancipation of the individual from age-old habits, ways of think-ing, tradition, and myth, as encapsulated in the Enlightenment project or in the French Revolution's slogan of *Liberté, égalité, fraternité*. Certainly, modern socialisms consider these kinds of freedoms too. A critical theory of freedom is not only a *freedom from* socio-political and socio-economic constraints – a 'negative freedom'.[52] Rather than the emancipation of individuals in order to more 'freely' operate in the liberal system that upholds capitalist 'free' markets, modern socialisms' stream of self-determination advocates for a negative free-dom from *all* dominative logics and practices, perhaps most concisely summed up in Herbert Marcuse's concern for liberating humanity from all forms of 'toil, aggressiveness, misery, and injustice'.[53] More importantly, this negative *free-dom from* should ultimately lead, for modern socialist traditions, to a positive *freedom for* the full enjoyment of 'human development' as multidimensional

---

48   Wood 2002; Polanyi 2001.
49   Lebowitz 2009.
50   What David McNally has called 'the dream of freedom' (McNally 1997, sec. 1).
51   Adorno and Horkheimer 2002; Horkheimer 1947, 2002; Horvat 1982; Lichtheim 1970.
52   Berlin 1969; Fromm 1968.
53   Marcuse 1964, p. 5. Socialists of various stripes also agree that, with the expansion of capitalism, the real problem of late modernity is not necessarily the need to engage in some work or the restraining of some individual and social freedoms to meet the realm of necessity. The real problem rests with the way capitalism restrains human freedoms and propagates a compulsion to work – that is, in requiring people to rely on the sys-tem that dominates them in order to meet their needs and wants (Fromm 1968; Marcuse 1964).

social beings.[54] This kind of freedom, as Paulo Freire summarises, is 'the indispensable condition for the quest for human completion'.[55]

What the stream of self-determination recognises is that historically, as Assef Bayat insists, the 'uniquely human' characteristic has been 'the desire for freedom and the struggle against domination'.[56] Similarly, Branko Horvat contends in his sweeping book *The Political Economy of Socialism* that 'the highest as well as the purely and exclusive human [need] is the need for self-determination'.[57] This is, for Horvat, 'identical with an authentic human existence'.[58] A *freedom for* leads to 'full self-actualization', Horvat continues, or 'to be conscious' of one's situation and the possibilities to creatively change one's environment and oneself, determining 'one's [own] position in the world'.[59] Ultimately, Horvat maintains, the freedom to self-actualise – for the full 'development of [human] faculties', as Saint-Simon termed it,[60] or 'the free development of individualities' to quote Marx[61] – merges *freedom from* with *freedom for*, the negative and the positive sides of freedom, into something beyond them:

> The essential precondition for [self-actualisation] is freedom. In fact, it is so essential that the totality of freedom – as distinct from various partial freedoms, such as freedom of action and of will, formal and effective freedom, etc. – can meaningfully be described only as *self-determination*. In particular, the traditional distinction between negative and positive freedom – freedom *from* and freedom *for* – disappears [in the socialist society], and the two freedoms coalesce in to *one single freedom of self-determination*.[62]

In sum, this desire for '*freedom of self-determination*' courses through modern socialist thought. The stream of self-determination draws inspiration from workers' ongoing and historical desires for freedom witnessed in the diversity of their responses to the rise of capitalism.[63] The concept highlights how workers, the people most affected by the traumatic social transformations character-

---

54   Marx and Engels 1970. See also Burkett 2005; McNally 1993; and Lebowitz 2008, 2011.
55   Freire 1970, p. 47.
56   Bayat 1991, p. 2.
57   Horvat 1982, p. 497.
58   Ibid.
59   Ibid.
60   Saint-Simon, in Lebowitz 2008, par. 8.
61   Marx 1973, p. 706.
62   Horvat 1982, p. 497 (emphasis added).
63   Vieta 2014a.

ising the evolution of capitalism, have not merely been victims of its dominative logics, but have also refused these very logics, resisting and struggling against capital's myriad enclosures throughout its history. This has been true, for instance, of the massive population movements from country to town in the dying days of feudalism through to the 'formal' and then on to the 'real subsumption' of labour in the early days of capitalism,[64] to the rise of industrial capitalism, and on to the emergence of advanced Fordism and the various iterations of so-called 'post-Fordism' that we are currently living through. In Marxist terms, this is the other side of the capital totality,[65] the side that has living labour resisting its valorisations of capital in the class struggle. In short, the stream of self-determination recognises labour as both the vital force that catalyses capital and as the antithesis of capital's incessant drive to 'accumulate, accumulate'.[66]

The desire for freedom of self-determination, as I aim to show throughout the book, courses throughout ERT protagonists' projects of *autogestión* and their radical social innovations. It does so, however, in varying degrees of completion and in a constant unfolding state of 'becoming other than capital',[67] as we will see in later chapters in the ongoing tensions and challenges ERT projects face from having to continue to exist in a capitalist system and produce within competitive markets.

1.2 Self-Determination, Cooperation, and Modern Socialist Thought

Modern socialisms realised early on that the struggle for self-determination in a capitalist-controlled world was to be first contested in the economic realm. Because economic considerations have such a privileged position in the project

---

64 On the distinction between 'formal' and 'real subsumption' (or 'subjection') of labour under capital, see Marx 1976b, pp. 1019–49. In a nutshell, for Marx the transition from the formal subsumption of labour (the extraction of 'absolute surplus-value') to the real subsumption of labour (the extraction of 'relative surplus-value') underscored the historical socio-economic and socio-political processes that eventually enabled the expanding capitalist system of production to tap into the 'social productive forces of labour' working in cooperation (Marx 1976b, p. 1024). This transition represents the evolution of the 'forms' of production that enabled the capitalist valorisation process via the extraction of surplus-value from surplus-labour (p. 1025). In short, the transition from the formal to the real subsumption of labour under capital was the principal historical process through which workers were brought into the capitalist mode of production (first from country to town, then from craft workshops to the factory) and made to cooperate in increasingly detailed divisions of labour 'under one roof' (Marx 1967, p. 473).

65 Burawoy 1985; Lebowitz 2003.

66 Marx 1976b, p. 742.

67 De Angelis 2007, p. 229.

of modernity, it is in this sphere – in the economic arrangements of society – where the struggle for eventually winning the freedom to self-determine the rest of life begins.[68] Put another way, in a society where provisioning for most of life's needs and wants is mediated through market relations, and where the means of production are the property of a few, liberating the economic realm is the prerequisite for winning other social and political freedoms. At core, this is a struggle to recuperate from the grip of capitalist control the trans-historical human capacities for cooperation, combination, and association for confronting the realm of necessity.

Owen, for example, by his middle writings in the late 1810s and early 1820s, proposed a 'social system' that would displace the worst aspects of the growing industrial society that was immiserating workers from their capacities to fully develop as human beings. He called his 'Plan' for a new society 'socialism'[69] and, after experimenting with his new work complexes in the New Lanark mill he managed for almost 20 years, envisioned a new social and economic system rooted in associated labour guided by 'the principle of union and mutual co-operation'.[70] Central to his vision for an emancipated social reality was overcoming 'the principle of individual interest'[71] by repurposing the new inventions of production within small, cooperative-like 'villages of union'. There, the community would co-manage the means of production and work in common for the 'mutual and combined interest' of all.[72] For Owen, working people's freedom of self-determination and broader social justice were tightly enmeshed

---

68   See, for instance, Rocker 1978. This position would also be explicitly taken up in the mid-twentieth century by liberation movements in the global South and cooperative movements in the global North, such as the first years of the Basque's Mondragón cooperatives and Maritime Canada's Antigonish adult education and cooperative movement. One of the founders of the Antigonish Movement, Father Moses Coady, for instance, thought that education for the emancipation of workers – a vital aspect of working-class consciousness, as I will address shortly – should start with knowledge of their material conditions: 'The question ... is where this process of education should begin[,] ...' Coady would write, 'the correct point of departure ... We consider it good pedagogy and good psychology to begin with the economic phase. We put our first emphasis on the material and the economic that we may more readily attain the spiritual and cultural towards which all our efforts are directed ...' (Coady 1939, p. 112).

69   Claeys 1991, p. xiii.

70   Owen 1991c, p. 276.

71   Ibid.

72   Owen, in Claeys, 1991, p. xiii. As Owen would write: 'Yet when they shall know themselves, and discover the wonderful effects which combination and union can produce, they will acknowledge that the present arrangement of society is the most antisocial, impolitic, and irrational, that can be devised ... In short, if there be one closet doctrine more contrary to truth than another, it is the notion that individual interest ... is a more advantageous prin-

with the transformation of workers' material 'circumstances', work in common, and the provision of education for all. While it is true that his Plan was to be paternalistically driven by a reformed and altruistic industrialist class, it did prove to be the first articulation of modern cooperative values that would soon inspire an entire movement.[73]

Similarly inspired was Fourier's minutely detailed (albeit similarly paternalistic) vision for a new society.[74] Fourier envisaged this new society to be organised as small, self-sustaining productive communities of people working for their mutual wellbeing in communal complexes he called *phalanstères*. As Fourier proposed, his communal work complexes would engage men and women in a new productive society grounded in 'attractive labour', job rotation, and shared and adequate incomes for all.[75]

Classical social anarchists, in turn, would bring together the search for freedom from the capitalist-state apparatus with economic self-determination, perhaps being the first socialist thinkers to begin to conceptualise (if not using the term themselves) the concept of *autogestión*. They too, as with Owen and Fourier, envisioned economic freedom to be rooted in some form of cooperative organisation co-managed by the direct producers themselves. For them, economic arrangements were closely tied to the political realm as well; cooperative societies were to be the bulwark from which a greater regional federation of producer cooperatives and communes would replace the nation-state.[76] Moreover, these cooperatives, communes, and federations were to take on less hierarchical structural forms by remaining rooted in the needs of local communities.[77] On shop floors, workers were to control decision-making mutually and horizontally. In the greater community, political entities such as communes and townships were to be the sites where councils of workers and peasants would co-manage production, distribution, and political life.[78]

Proudhon, for example, drew inspiration for such a social system from his own craft background and from the self-activity of working people such as those in the craft trades, factory workers, and peasants. He used these experiences as his model for *mutuellisme* (mutualism) and its proposals for equit-

---

        ciple on which to found the social system, for the benefit of all, or of any, than the principle
        of union and mutual cooperation' (Owen 1991c, p. 276).

73   Craig 1993; Quarter 2000.
74   Fourier 1971.
75   Beecher 1986; Fourier 1971.
76   Marshall 1992; Woodcock 2004.
77   Bookchin 1971, 1990.
78   Marshall 1992.

able exchange, popular banks, private possessions over personal property, and 'social ownership' via federated, 'democratically organized workers' associations' (that is, worker cooperatives).[79] Proudhon's *mutuellisme* was to be grounded in something similar to Owenite labour exchanges, where labour time, via labour notes managed by 'people's banks', would be the currency in circulation.[80] These were to be his keys to a more economically just society.[81]

While he viewed large associations such as nationalisation schemes, trading blocs, large state apparatuses, or other hierarchical forms of economic institutions to be constraints on individual liberties and the free society (that is, to decentralised and autonomous forms of organising),[82] Proudhon did favour grassroots-based economic associations such as worker/producer cooperatives, what later anarchist writers would variably call a 'syndicate', 'collective', 'producers' commune', or an 'association of producers'.[83] These were, in essence, what we would today call worker cooperatives, which were beginning to emerge during Proudhon's most intellectually fruitful years in France.[84] Proudhon would eventually conceptualise his ideal economic system as an 'agro-industrial federation' whereby the political functions of the state would be reduced to broader policy initiatives and making economic and industrial proposals.[85]

Proudhon's arguably contradictory propositions for centralisation of all policy and economic planning in the form of a reduced form of state entity on the one hand, and his search for the autonomy of the individual and collectives on the other, however, as well as his individualist labour theory of value, made his project of *mutuellisme* unworkable in practice.[86] Moreover, an unresolved

---

79   Proudhon 2011, pp. 30–1.
80   Woodcock 2004, p. 110.
81   Horvat 1982, pp. 117–19. See also Proudhon 1979.
82   In Proudhon's final work, 'Political Capacity of the Working Classes', he affirms the following: 'What necessitates, in politics, that idea of *mutuality* that is the economic program of the working classes, is that, in the political order as well, all things, all ideas, all interests can be reduced to equality, to the common right, to justice, to balancing, to the free play of forces, to the free manifestation of ambitions, to the free activity of individuals and groups, in a word, to *autonomy*' (Proudhon 2014, par. 56).
83   Anarchist FAQ Collective 2009, sec. I.3.1.
84   Gide 1905; Vuotto 2011.
85   Proudhon 1979, pp. 67 ff.
86   In contrast to Marx's laws of value, where commodities are valued based on socially necessary and abstracted labour times (addressed later on in this chapter), in Proudhon's *mutuellisme* goods and services were to be exchanged based on proportional ammounts of concrete individual labour that went into producing each commodity. Additionally, the ultimate inoperability of his 'peoples' bank' during his tenure in the revolutionary legis-

tension between individual freedom/competition and collective responsibil-
ity/community is consistently present in Proudhon's writings. Whether or not a
state, however small and federated, could be reduced to only making economic
decisions, how centralised this system had to be, or whether the economic can
ever be decoupled from the political, remain points of contention in Proudhon's vision for the future society. And while Proudhon's politics disdained
outright revolutionary uprising, preferring social transformation via gradual
change, Proudhon's proposals for alternative organisational arrangements beyond capital were amongst the first in modern socialist thought to both critique
capitalism and the state mechanisms that upheld it and offer worker-led alternatives to it.[87] Undoubtedly, Proudhon's ideas would henceforth be important
for conceptualising the struggle for workers' self-management. His visions for
an alternative economics grounded in workers' autonomy and notions of *autogestión* are strong early articulations for a society rooted in human freedom
from exploitation and the re-embedding of economic life back into the social
sphere. There is also no doubt that a more economically just and more humane
reality for working people was vital for Proudhon.[88]

Drawing inspiration from Proudhon, Bakunin also viewed the struggle for
the liberation and self-determination of otherwise oppressed people – workers, peasants, and the poor and dispossessed – as central for a truly free society.
For him, the full development of human beings and their capacities to self-
organise and act cooperatively were crucial to his revolutionary visions for a
just society; economic justice, equality amongst all, and cooperative work fit
hand-in-hand with his post-revolutionary society. 'Man [sic] is truly free', Bakunin would write, 'only among equally free men'.[89] Foreshadowing the notion
of the post-scarcity society that would be proposed a century later by Herbert Marcuse, Ivan Illich, Murray Bookchin, and others, Bakunin believed that
human beings, with the imaginative and technological capacities at their dis-

---

lature of 1848 is indicative of the issues with his individualist labour theory of value, and
with what was later to be conceived of as 'market socialism' (McNally 1993).

87   Price 2012, Ch. 1.
88   While Proudhon's politics were really reformist rather than revolutionary, and his treatment of women, labour unions, and most large associations in his writings leave much to
be desired, I believe, his original views of federated socialism justifies including him in any
genealogy of workers' self-determination and *autogestión* worth its salt. As Wayne Price
writes: 'Proudhon opposed labour unions and strikes, let alone working-class revolution.
But, Proudhon worked out a concept of decentralised-federalist socialism, which was contrary to Marx's centralist statism. Proudhon's concept was important in the development
of revolutionary anarchism' (Price 2012, Ch. 1).
89   Bakunin 1974, p. 65.

posal, 'can only free themselves from the yoke of external nature through collective labour'.[90] For him, as with Marx and Kropotkin, freedom consisted of 'the full development of our potential'.[91] Ultimately for Bakunin, paralleling Marx's measured views of cooperatives, while 'cooperative associations' were susceptible to being co-opted 'under the existing conditions of the social economy' controlled by the capitalist–state system and thus 'cannot liberate the worker masses', '[c]ooperation in all its forms' was also 'undeniably a rational and just mode of future production'[92] that carried 'within itself the germ of the future economic order'.[93]

Anticipating a theme that was to be picked up later by Kropotkin, Antonio Gramsci's considerations of workers' associations, and even V.I. Lenin's later writings on cooperation,[94] cooperatives were also for Bakunin important sites of learning for the working class's organisation of the future society, offering 'the benefit ... of accustoming the workers to unite, organize, and independently manage their own affairs'.[95] Here, Bakunin was also close to Proudhon's hopes for 'workmen's unions' as 'the open school, both theoretical and practical, where the workman [sic] learns the science of the production and distribution of wealth, where he studies, without masters and without books, by his own experience solely, the laws of ... industrial organization'.[96] In this regard, both Proudhon and Bakunin prefigured the early and mid-twentieth-century anarcho-syndicalist, guild socialist, and council communist ideas of canalising social change through 'industrial action',[97] and even the cooperative movement's (albeit more reformist) fifth Rochdale principle of 'Education, training, and information'.[98] They both also prefigured one of the key aspects of ERTS – and worker cooperatives overall – as sites for the further development

---

90   Marshall 1992, p. 291.
91   Marshall 1992, p. 39.
92   Bakunin 1990, p. 201.
93   Bakunin 1953, p. 385.
94   Gramsci 2000; Lenin 1965.
95   Bakunin 1990, pp. 201–2.
96   Proudhon 1989, p. 78.
97   Woodcock 2004, p. 100. See also Cole 1920; Mattick 1969; Pannekoek 2003; and Rocker 1989. Rocker synthesised the anarcho-syndicalist and (indirectly) the guild socialist and council communist perspective on workers' self-managmenet when he wrote that 'by taking the land and the industrial plants under their own management [workers] have taken the first and most important step on the road to Socialism. Above all, they have proved *that the workers, even without the capitalists, are able to carry on production and to do it better than a lot of profit-hungry entrepreneurs'* (Rocker 1989, p. 104, emphasis in original).
98   ICA 2016.

of workers' solidarity, consciousness raising, and rich and collaborative forms of transformative and informal learning, which I will explore in Chapter 8.

Kropotkin, in turn, also viewed cooperatives, 'village community institutions' such as the Russian *artel* (cooperative association) and the *mir* (rural village commune),[99] the Swiss cantons, professional guilds and early workers' combinations, labour unions,[100] friendly societies and social clubs,[101] and other forms of 'federated' human associations[102] and economic and social collaborations, as continuations of the evolutionary nature of human beings' inherent ability to cooperate. For him, 'mutual aid' rather than competition and the capitalist perversions of the division of labour were essential human practices that could be traced back throughout human history and pre-history. For Kropotkin, human beings naturally gravitate toward and always already privilege cooperation over competition. If, for Marx, human beings are at core *homo faber*,[103] for Kropotkin they are at core *homo reciprocans*.[104] And while Kropotkin also held Marx's and Bakunin's measured views on cooperatives, realising that there was the possibility for members to be seized by a 'co-operative egotism', Kropotkin ultimately held faith in the cooperative movement's 'essentially mutual aid character' and that 'co-operation' could lead humanity 'to a higher harmonic state of economical relations'.[105] Indeed, the mutual aid character infused and catalysed, for him, all forms of cooperation. In Kropotkin's view, 'the strongholds of co-operation in the North [of Britain,] ... Holland, Denmark ... [and] ... Germany' were rooted in 'broader ideals of general welfare and of the producers' solidarity' and were thus prime examples of the self-help nature of people that compelled them to come together into cooperative relations.[106] Indeed, the mutual aid character of human beings prefigured for Kropotkin the truly free modern society – 'Communism'.[107] In Kropotkin's vision of communism, Martin Buber points to a 'double inter-communal bond' between 'the federation of regional communes and trade communes variously intercrossing and supporting one another' via voluntary membership.[108] Further, 'the fullest

---

99   Kropotkin 1989, pp. 238, 271–3.
100   Kropotkin 1989, p. 262.
101   Kropotkin 1989, p. 274.
102   Kropotkin 1989, p. 238.
103   Marx 1967, pp. 39–40, 44, 178–179, 189, 508. See also Arendt 1998, p. 136.
104   While I am not aware of Kropotkin using this term, his treatise of mutual aid and its implications for human society could be synthesised as such. See Kropotkin 1989.
105   Kropotkin 1989, p. 271.
106   Kropotkin 1989, pp. 271–2.
107   Buber 1996, p. 43.
108   Buber 1996, p. 42.

development of individuality', Kropotkin wrote when conceptualising his vision of a decentralised and federated communism, would combine

> with the highest development of *voluntary association* in all its aspects,
> in all possible degrees and for all conceivable purposes: an ever changing
> association bearing in itself the elements of its own duration and taking on the forms which at any moment best correspond to the manifold
> endeavours of all ... creat[ing] regional and autonomous life in the smallest of its units – the street, the house-block, the district, the parish.[109]

Marx and Engels also saw the future communist society as merging social and economic cooperation with human freedom. But they were to extend this analysis, as I will shortly show, to point out the two-fold nature of capitalist production, a production that both controlled and restrained workers in a technological system run by capitalist masters *while also* suggesting the possibilities for real human development and an easing of the pursuit of meeting life's basic needs via the level and scale of technical invention mobilised by the capitalist system. For Marx, for instance, 'the true realm of freedom' was made possible by the 'civilizing aspects of capital', in which the unleashing of productive forces had the potential of lessening labour-time and unshackling humanity from its age-old surrender to the 'realm of necessity'.[110] But, captured as labouring people were within capitalist logics, the unleashing of the social productive forces and, ultimately, *time* into what Marx termed 'disposable time'[111] for the benefit of all would only occur once the means of production and the supporting state apparatus was seized by the associated producers guided by the values and practices of cooperation beyond capital. '[T]he realm of freedom really begins', Marx asserted in *Capital Vol. III*,

> only where labour determined by necessity and external expediency
> ends; it lies by its very nature beyond the sphere of material production
> proper ... Freedom, in this sphere, can consist only in this, that *socialized
> man* [sic], *the associated producers*, govern the human metabolism with
> nature in a rational way, bringing it under their collective control instead

---

109   Kropotkin, in Buber 1996, p. 43 (emphasis added).

110   Marx 1981, pp. 958–9.

111   '[F]ree time, *disposable time*', was for Marx 'wealth itself'. In disposable time Marx saw the
       possibility for human self-development, 'partly for the enjoyment of the product, partly
       for free activity which – unlike labour – is not dominated by the pressure of an extraneous
       purpose which must be fulfilled' (Marx 1969, p. 860; see also Marx 1973, pp. 706, 708).

of being dominated by it as a blind power; accomplishing it with *the least expenditure of energy and in conditions most worthy and appropriate for their human nature* [that is, beyond capitalist modes of production].[112]

Hence, the coming communist society for Marx and Engels would be rooted in 'an *association*, in which the free development of each is the condition for the free development of all'.[113] Crucially, for Marx, cooperation by 'the association of free and equal producers' would be one of the vital requisites for realising this free development in the communist society. Indeed, the model of the worker/producer cooperative – which for Marx embodied 'labour in common or directly associated labour'[114] – was, for him, one clear and already existing organisational form that could potentially coordinate for workers (rather than for capitalists) 'the general productive power'[115] of socialised production. This was a productive power that had already been assembled by capitalists and that could be re-appropriated by workers themselves for their own ends via a cooperative mode of production.[116] In order for cooperatives not to remain 'dwarfish forms' within 'capitalist society', however, broader social changes in political struggle would be required, such as workers seizing state power from 'capitalists and landlords'.[117] Within these broader social transformations, cooperatives could unfurl the potential for the associated producers to collectively organise and decide when, how, and what to produce.[118] Indeed, Marx linked the 'co-operative movement' of his day with one of the 'transforming forces of the present society based upon class antagonism' whose 'great merit is to practically show, that ... the *subordination of labour* to capital can be superseded by the republican and beneficent system of *the association of free and equal producers*'.[119] Alluding to how worker/producer cooperatives both immanently critique the capitalist economic system *and* prefiguratively suggest a key aspect of the coming communist society, cooperative work organisations mapped for Marx a viable worker-centred mode of production of 'free individuals, carrying on their work with the means of production in common'.[120] Marx would thus call on the First International to 'recommend to the

---

112   Marx 1981, pp. 958–9 (emphasis added).
113   Marx and Engels 1998, p. 27 (emphasis added).
114   Marx 1967, p. 77.
115   Marx 1973, p. 705.
116   Compare with Marx 1978a, p. 518; and Marx 1981, pp. 571, 959.
117   Marx 1985, p. 190.
118   Marx 1978b.
119   Marx 1985, p. 190 (emphasis in original).
120   Marx 1967, p. 78.

working men to embark in *co-operative production* rather than in *co-operative stores*. The latter touch but the surface of the present economical system, the former attacks its groundwork'.[121]

Although Marx was undoubtedly also aware of the deficiencies of cooperatives as 'dwarfish forms' given that cooperators become 'their own capitalist' within an economic system centred on the commodity form,[122] in general Marx had auspicious views of 'workers' cooperative factories'.[123] Certainly for Marx some form of cooperative arrangement of the means of production and economic activity was vital for attaining real human freedom in the communist society. As with Bakunin and, later on, Kropotkin and Gramsci, cooperation and cooperative organisations could play a key role in the communist society. Worker/producer cooperatives embodied for Marx the potential to organise freely associated labour.[124] Since Marx believed 'a realm of necessity' would still remain in the free communist society, 'the development of human energy' in the 'true realm of freedom' that lay beyond the realm of necessity could be fairly and non-exploitatively controlled by cooperative work, or work in common.[125] 'If the material conditions of production are the co-operative property of the workers themselves', he wrote in 'The Critique of the Gotha Program', 'then there likewise results a distribution of the means of consumption different from the present one'[126] – that is, potentially free from commodities valued by abstract labour-times and the exploitation of labour.[127] Cooperative societies thus had an important part to play in Marx's vision for a new social order 'based on the common ownership of the means of production'.[128] Cooperatives, in short and as I explore below, were a core element of his 'political economy of labour over the political economy of property'[129] – or the political economy of the working class.

1.3   *Prefiguring Another Mode of Productive Life*

The notion of *prefiguring* another reality for socio-economic life undergirds the stream of self-determination and the agentic capacities of living labour, point-

---

121   Marx 1985, p. 190 (emphasis in original).
122   Marx 1981, p. 571. This is an issue I will take up in Chapters 7 and 8 in relation to ERTS.
123   Marx 1981, p. 512. See also Jossa 2005, 2017.
124   Marx 1978a, 1978b, 1981.
125   Marx 1981, pp. 958–9.
126   Marx 1978b, p. 532.
127   See this second section of this chapter.
128   Marx 1978b, p. 529.
129   Marx 1978a, p. 517.

ing to the recuperative moments unleashed by ERTs.[130] It is thus opportune to further explore the concept of prefiguration.

Prefigurative practices, as I first reviewed in the Introduction, foreshadow another type of world *in the now*. For those seeking alternatives to our capitalist reality, prefigurative practices chart aspects of a post-capitalist world 'by experimenting with alternatives that develop the seeds of the future in the present society, creating the new inside of the old'.[131] Today, theories of prefiguration have been taken up by contemporary social anarchist, post-anarchist, autonomist Marxist, and other libertarian socialist thinkers.[132] Taking their cue from the alter-globalisation movements of the late 1990s and early 2000s, these theorists have been exploring the prefigurative potential of radical alternative socio-economic practices and ethico-political commitments that begin to move beyond capitalist logics, hierarchical power relations, and institutions that systematise oppressions.

From the perspective of contemporary social anarchist theory, Benjamin Franks, for instance, has theorised prefigurative social practices as those guided by value orientations that model the ends sought by 'reflect[ing], as far as possible, the desired goals' in the present.[133] Importantly for Franks, the methods must strive to not reproduce the 'economic or political hierarchies, or [generate] new, detrimental power relations'.[134] Simon Critchley[135] and David Graeber[136] deploy similar perspectives in order to bridge the ethical-philosophical underpinnings of a 'post-anarchist' politics with the desires and struggles of contemporary radical politics and social movements. Richard Day[137] and Uri Gordon[138] have also explicitly drawn on the practices and desires of the 'newest social movements' against the neo-liberalism of recent years and merged them with classical and contemporary anarchist and poststructuralist theory in order to conceptualise prefigurative ethico-political social practice.[139] The connection made by Harry Cleaver between anarchism and autonomist Marx-

---

130 Explored in the last pages of this chapter.
131 Larrabure, Vieta, and Schugurensky 2011, p. 183. See also Allman 2001; Bakunin 1990; and Boggs 1977.
132 See, for instance, Day 2005; Franks 2006; 2010; Gordon 2008; Graeber 2004, 2009; van de Sande 2015; and Vieta 2014a; 2017.
133 Franks 2010, p. 102.
134 Ibid.
135 Critchley 2007.
136 Graeber 2004, 2009.
137 Day 2005.
138 Gordon 2008.
139 Day 2005.

ism helps us arrive at a succinct definition of prefiguration that begins to map out ways of 'transcending capitalism'; for him, this is about 'the search for the future in the present, and the identification of already existing activities which embody new, alternative forms of social cooperation and ways of being'.[140] As Day affirms, this recent take-up of a theory of prefiguration thus owes as much to anarchism as it does to strands of libertarian and autonomist Marxist thought.[141] I would take it further: The theory of prefiguration imbuing altern- ative socio-economic practices opposed to neo-liberal logics is more broadly and historically present in the stream of self-determination of modern social- ism.[142]

In particular, for classical social anarchists and even in moments in Marx's and Gramsci's writings, a theory of prefiguration can be intuited from their understanding of the role of workers' and people's associations for learning about and rehearsing how to organise the desired alternative society. That is, worker- and community-based organisations have long been viewed as spaces not only to resist the status quo, but also to experiment with self-managed alternatives. In short, they have been seen as spaces for learning about how to self-organise alternative forms of economic and social arrangements that embody the desired post-capitalist society.

For Proudhon, for instance, social transformation would emerge from 'the labouring classes[,] ... generating from the bowels of the people, from the depths of labour, a greater authority, a more potent fact, which shall envelop capital and the State and subjugate them'.[143] And specifically pointing to 'work- ingmen's societies' and 'workmen's unions', he would ask: 'Do [they] not ... at this moment serve as the cradle for the social revolution?'[144] Similarly, for Bak- unin:

> the organization of the trade sections and their representation in the Chambers of Labour creates a great academy in which all the workers can and must study economic sciences; these sections also bear in them- selves the living seeds of the new society which is to replace the old world. They are creating not only the ideas, but also the facts of the future itself.[145]

---

140   Cleaver 1992b, para. 35.
141   Day 2005.
142   See also Buber 1996.
143   Proudhon 2011, p. 226.
144   Proudhon 1989, p. 78.
145   Bakunin 2005, pp. 93–4.

For Marx, in a moment of agreement with Bakunin, the Paris Commune of 1871 prefigured the future communist society directed by 'free and associ-ated labour'.[146] 'Yes, gentlemen', Marx would exhort, 'the Commune intended to abolish that class-property which makes the labour of many the wealth of the few. It aimed at the expropriation of the expropriators ... But this is Com-munism, "impossible" Communism!'[147] Moreover, 'co-operative production', for Marx, served what can be seen as a prefigurative function for the working class, the seeds of a '"possible" Communism'.[148] Worker cooperatives for Marx ultimately underscored a possible organisational form for freely associated labour in the future communist society, while at the same time putting into relief the superfluousness and arbitrariness of capitalist managerial control:

> Cooperative factories provide proof that the capitalist has become just as superfluous as a functionary in production as he himself, from his superior vantage point, finds the landlord ... In the case of the cooperat-ive factory, the antithetical character of the supervisory work disappears, since the manager is paid by the workers instead of representing capital in opposition to them.[149]

And Gramsci, drawing on this long tradition of prefigurative theory of working-class organisations, viewed factory councils, socialist clubs, peasant communit-ies, and other workers' associations as harbingers of workers' democracy on a society-wide level. In the thick of the general strikes and factory occupations of the *biennio rosso* of 1919–20, Gramsci would write that

> the social life of the working class is rich in the very institutions and activ-ities which need to be developed, fully organized and coordinated into a broad and flexible system that is capable of absorbing and disciplining the entire working class.[150]

Furthermore, with an aim to 'stimulate thought and action',[151] for Gramsci the prefigurative moments of this working-class 'social life', the workers' councils of

---

146   Marx 1978c, p. 635.
147   Ibid.
148   Ibid. Indeed, his famous quote on cooperatives in *Capital, Vol. III* that we first visited in this book's Introduction also clearly highlights the prefigurative nature of cooperatives for Marx (see Marx 1981, p. 571).
149   Marx 1981, pp. 511–12.
150   Gramsci 2000, p. 80.
151   Gramsci 2000, p. 79.

the *biennio rosso*, and other working-class organisations, were spaces of learning for the unleashing of workers' democracy under the workers' state. They
would make him ask, in a posture of prefiguration: 'How can the present be
welded to the future, so that while satisfying the urgent necessities of the one
we may work effectively to create and "anticipate" the other?'.[152]

In short, prefiguration foreshadows the other world's new socio-economic
practices and ethico-political commitments in the present one, affirming that
workers' self-directed resistances to capital and their self-activity and organisations have a delineating and educative force for shaping a different socio-
economic reality for the future in the present. Prefiguration in the actual practices of the oppressed, the exploited, and the marginalised is thus an additional historical undercurrent in modern socialist thought's stream of self-
determination and, by implication, *autogestión*.

1.4   *The Self-Determination of the Working Class*

1.4.1   Class-Struggle Marxism

A branch of modern socialisms' stream of self-determination – together with
its prefigurative theoretical moments – has fed into what has been called
'"class-struggle" Marxism'.[153] Much of the critical work of theorists within the
class-struggle Marxist tradition, extending throughout the twentieth and into
the twenty-first centuries, analyses working-class agency and working people's
potential to struggle against and move beyond the technological rationalities
and dominative logics of capitalism.[154] Specifically looking at the ways workers struggle against the valorisation process,[155] it is a Marxism that 'traces the
conflict between exploiters and exploited'[156] and is linked intimately to Marx's
notion of the political economy of the working class.[157]

---

152   Ibid.
153   Dyer-Witheford 1999, p. 62. For a similar approach, see also So 1991; So and Hikam 1989;
       and Meiksins 1987.
154   Hudis (2012) categorises class-struggle Marxism as subjective Marxism, in comparison to
       more orthodox objective Marxisms.
155   Harvie 2005.
156   Dyer-Witheford 1999, p. 62.
157   Class-struggle Marxism begins with passages from Marx and Engels (some of which I
       cite in this chapter), taking hold in the early twentieth century in various alternative
       Marxisms (alternatives, that is, to Leninist-Bolshevist-*étatist* or other strictly economistic
       Marxist perspectives, and also to reform-minded social democratic tendencies). An illus-
       trative, if incomplete, sketch of class-struggle Marxism could include: Rosa Luxemburg's
       defence of working-class spontaneity and bottom-up organising and revolution; certain
       moments in Gramscian analysis focusing on the role of workers' organisations for devel-

Class struggle Marxism tends to eschew a strictly 'economic analysis of cap-italism'[158] – that is, the primary orthodox Marxist focus on capital and prop-erty theory. Such 'one-sided' Marxisms[159] are inclined to minimise or forget the dynamism, agency, and resistances of 'living labour' in the capital-labour relation. Furthermore, one-sided Marxisms' neglect of 'the counteractivities of workers' in their strict critique of the structures of capital tends towards interpreting contemporary capitalist society as 'the unfolding of pregiven, inev-itable, and objective laws'.[160] For class-struggle Marxism, on the other hand, 'such "laws,"' writes Dyer-Witheford,

> are no more than the outcome of two intersecting vectors – exploitation and its refusal in the constantly recurrent eruptions of fight and flight by which rebellious subjects seek a way beyond work, wage, and profit.[161]

---

oping working-class consciousness and as organs of revolution; the early Lukács's class consciousness and cultural theory critiques; strains of syndicalism; moments in the first generation of the Frankfurt School, such as with Walter Benjamin's cultural theory and in the work of Herbert Marcuse and Erich Fromm; the Johnson-Forest Tendency headed by C.L.R. James, Raya Dunayevskaya, and Grace Lee Boggs; the French group Socialisme ou Barbarie; and the Italian traditions of *operaismo* ('workerism') in the 1960s and *auto-nomia* ('autonomism') from the 1970s onward. These alternative Marxisms also continued to evolve alongside scientific, objectivist, and structuralist Marxisms throughout the mid-twentieth century in the writings of, to name only a few, Anton Pannekoek's theories of council communism; André Gorz's 1960s writings on workers' control; Herbert Mar-cuse's liberational hopes for the capitalist technological inheritance; Paulo Freire's the-ories and radical education practices centred on the notion of *conscientização*; and the radical, bottom-up labour histories of E.P. Thompson, Eric Hobsbawm, and Christopher Hill. Today, the most prominent thinkers espousing a class-struggle Marxist approach include the group of theorists inspired by and making up the Italian autonomist tradi-tion, such as Antonio Negri, Franco Berardi, Harry Cleaver, Maurizio Lazzarato, Mariarosa Dalla Costa, Silvia Federici, and Nick Dyer-Witheford; the related tradition of 'Open Marx-ism' (see, for instance, Bonefeld, Gunn, Holloway, and Psychopedis 1995); Massimo De Angelis's analysis of the commons, commoning, and 'value' as class struggle (De Angelis 1995, 2007); the 'political economy of the working class' approach of David McNally (1993) and Michael Lebowitz (2003, 2008); Ellen Meiksins Wood's analysis of class struggle (Wood 1982, 1986, 1983, 1988); moments in the work of second generation labour pro-cess theorists such as Michael Burawoy (1979, 1985) and Andrew Freidman (1977); and the critical theory of technology as, for example, espoused by Andrew Feenberg (1999, 2002).

158   Feenberg 2002, p. 41.
159   Lebowitz 2003, pp. viii.
160   Dyer-Witheford 1999, p. 62.
161   Ibid.

In short, class-struggle Marxism differentiates itself from objectivist, 'one-sided' Marxisms in hypothesising that the laws of capital remain mutable and constantly influenced and challenged by the ongoing resistances of working people.

Class-struggle Marxists, then, rather than remaining fixed on how workers are acted upon by capital, most broadly home in on the potentiality for another world that resides in workers' continued autonomy. Here *autonomy* is a condition of agency through praxis in situated and 'historically located modes of activity' where one 'could have done otherwise', to cite Anthony Giddens.[162] From the perspective of class-struggle analysis, workers' continued autonomy in 'historically located modes of activity' delineated by capital–labour relations means that workers remain more than wage-labour (that is, more than simply the bearers of the commodity labour-power) and as such are able to push back against capitalist control. This is because workers overflow the limits placed on them by the wage-labour contract and also live – if partially – outside of the capitalist valorisation process.[163] At a minimum, the concept of autonomy points to the fact that workers can and often do – in their cooperation, combinations, unionisations, sabotages, refusals, and resistances – struggle against and resist the valorisation process, even while still being within it.[164] Workers' autonomy means that some form of agency akin to Marx's 'anthropogenesis', as Martin Jay writes – or 'man's [sic] ability to create himself anew'[165] – inevitably remains with living labour despite capitalism's totalising tendencies. Marxist thinkers such as E.P. Thompson, Ellen Meiksins Wood, Paula Allman, and Laurence Cox and Alf Gunvald Nilsen[166] (amongst many others) conceptualise this as the ongoing capacities for people to be their own agents of history rather than being passively affected by it.

In sum, class-struggle Marxists see continued hopes for human agency and rationality despite capitalism's preponderance. This critical theoretical tribu-

---

162   Giddens 1979, p. 56.

163   Lebowitz 2003, pp. 91–2.

164   Camila Piñeiro Harnecker has recently reminded us, however, that autonomy is never absolute: 'no social organisation anywhere in the world is completely autonomous since its options are always conditioned in one way or another by its social context' (Piñeiro Harnecker 2011, p. 8). Moreover, in an assessment of Castoriadis's theory of autonomy, Anthony Elliott reminds us that it is also open-ended and ambivalent: 'This open-ended process of engagement with the autonomy of the self and the Other is situated in the context of ambivalence, uncertainty and the realm of conflicting scenarios' (Elliott 2002, p. 388).

165   Jay 1973, p. 57.

166   Allman 2001, 2007; Cox and Nilsen 2014; Thompson 1963; Wood 1982, 1986.

tary has redirected the focus of Marxist analysis onto the possibilities for the working class's self-directed liberation from exploitation and alienation, witnessed historically in workers' reinventions of the capitalist technological and productive inheritance, their acts of self-activity on shop floors, and – particularly relevant to the study of ERTs – in the experiences of cooperation, workers' control, and self-management.

1.4.2   The Political Economy of the Working Class

Class-struggle Marxists have been contributing to and re-theorising Marx's writings and public statements in which he offered explicit views of the working class's potential for self-determination and alternatives to the capitalist organisation of society.[167] In works such as the 'The Inaugural Address of the Working Men's International Association', in parts of the *Grundrisse*, and in the 'Critique of the Gotha Program' and 'The Civil War in France', for instance, Marx, despite a widely held assumption that he refused to contemplate the future post-capitalist society, began, if only in sketch form, to do just that.[168] In these writings Marx starts to work out what a future, post-capitalist alternative might entail from the perspective of a historical materialist lens both deeply critical of capital and also sensitive to the resistances and alternative economic practices and organisations already available to workers for owning and controlling the means of production in common.[169]

Class-struggle Marxists thus consider how workers' subjectivities transform within the praxis of their struggles against capital. Marx termed this approach 'the political economy of the working class'.[170] Two historical moments within Marx's own time that illustrated for him the political economy of the working class was the struggle for the 'Ten Hours' Bill' (legislation that secured the 10-hour workday in Britain) and the emergence of 'co-operative factories', or what we today term worker cooperatives. Marx specifically characterised these two moments as evidence of 'the political economy of labour over the political economy of property'.[171] Especially pertinent to our study of ERTs, for Marx worker cooperatives not only revealed in practice the suprfluousness of capitalist own-

167   See, for instance, Marx 1973, pp. 690–712; Marx 1978a, 1978b, 1978c, 1985, 1988, 2007; and Marx and Engels 1998.

168   Marx 1978a, 1978b, 1978c, 1973. For compelling reinterpretations of Marx's proposals for alternatives to capitalism, see also Hudis 2012; Jossa 2005, 2017; Lebowitz 2003, 2011; and Mészáros 1995.

169   Marx 1978b, p. 529; Hobsbawm 2011, p. 8.

170   Marx 1978a, p. 517. See also Marx 1973, 1978b, 1978c; 1981.

171   Marx 1978a, pp. 517–18.

ership and management, but most crucially the gratuitousness of capital as mediator in social production and for meeting people's material needs.[172] As Lebowitz reminds us here, paraphrasing Marx:

> The very existence of co-operative factories, then, was a practical demonstration that capital was not necessary as a mediator in social production. This 'victory of the political economy of labour over the political economy of property' was an *ideological* victory [for the working class].[173]

Moreover, the alternatives that a political economy of the working class approach is attentive to centre on what Marx characterised as 'social production' under 'freely associated' labour, where the priorities of productive life are not about control and exploitation of labour's capacities to create surplus-value. The priorities, rather, are: socialised and cooperatively managed production and distribution,[174] the eventual abolition of the wage-based system of labour and the market for labour-power,[175] the eradication of market logics,[176] the maximisation of workers' free time (that is, 'disposable time') in order to permit the 'free development' of individuals' talents and passions,[177] the redeployment of technologies of production in order to reduce and eventually do away with socially necessary labour-time,[178] and, ultimately, the proliferation of 'co-operative societies based on the common ownership of the means of production'.[179] In other words, a political economy of the working class approach focuses on 'the ongoing struggles of workers *against their exploitation and alienation*', as well as the '*crafting of better, alternative forms of social life*'.[180]

In sum, focusing on the conditions of possibility of workers' ongoing struggles *and* the conditions of possibility for alternative forms of productive life that these struggles may forge is what I mean when I refer to the political economy of the working class. While continuing to unravel capitalist logics by exposing the real source of capital's valorisation, the political economy of the

---

172   Marx 1981, pp. 511–12.
173   Lebowitz 2003, p. 89 (emphasis in original).
174   Marx 1978a, 1978b.
175   Marx 1967, 1973, 1978b.
176   McNally 1993.
177   Marx 1973, pp. 704–6. See also Marcuse 1966.
178   Marcuse 1964; Marx 1973.
179   Marx 1978b, p. 529.
180   Cleaver 2000, p. 9.

working class approach that I take up in this book also keeps in view workers' continued capacities to not only resist, subvert, and refuse coercive work,
but also their ability to *innovate* and *invent* at the point of production and beyond it despite capitalism's tendencies to constantly deploy new strategies for
controlling and co-opting workers and extending exploitation and commodification into every nook and cranny of life. ERTs, I contend, are contemporary
instances of this worker-centred political economy.

1.4.3   Class-in-the-Making

The political economy of the working class approach taken up by class-struggle
Marxists, then, considers at core how workers' subjectivities transform in praxis
through their struggles, both within and against capital.[181] Rather than being
a structurally fixed category in a 'static class structure map' characterised by
taxonomic social categories,[182] 'class', as E.P. Thompson reminds us, 'happens'
within social relations and in the thick of struggle and action when people 'live
[out] their own history' as a class-in-the-making.[183] Thompson clarifies this
process as follows:

> *Making*, because [class] is ... an active process, which owes as much to
> agency as to conditioning. The working class did not rise like the sun at an
> appointed time. It was present at its own making ... By class I understand
> an historical phenomenon, unifying a number of disparate and seemingly
> unconnected events, both in the raw material of experience and in con-
> sciousness. I emphasise that it is an *historical* phenomenon. I do not see
> class as a 'structure', nor even as a 'category', but as something which in
> fact happens (and can be shown to have happened) in human relation-
> ships.[184]

In short, a class-struggle analysis understands class as rooted in a complex historical materialist dynamic situated in multifarious social relations whereby
people are made by *and also* make history. Marx suggests this two-fold historical materialist conceptualisation of a class-in-the-making in the third thesis on
Feuerbach: 'The coincidence of the changing of circumstances and of human
activity or self-change can be conceived and rationally understood only as

---

181   Lebowitz 2003, 2008; Thompson 1963.
182   So 1991, p. 39.
183   Thompson 1963, pp. 9, 11.
184   Ibid.

revolutionary practice'.[185] For Marx, as Cox and Nilsen remind us, human activity is potentially transformative and critical consciousness rests with people being praxically situated in

> a constant process of ... *becoming* human beings, or *making themselves*, through reflecting on their social experience, developing their needs and capacities, and finding new ways of socially organising their needs and capacities and thus transforming their worlds.[186]

We are made, in other words, by our historical material conditions and circumstances *and* our acts and our doings. And these acts and doings can foster radical and revolutionary change as subordinated people critically reflect on and learn from the confluence of their needs, experiences, and collective practices, concurrently pushing against and reconceptualising and transforming their circumstances in the process. In short, in becoming human beings we can remake our current circumstances and our futures within a constant process of critically engaging with the world that in moments manifests as revolutionary praxis and struggle. As such, a class-in-the-making is always already latent with potential transformative and revolutionary force.[187]

The experiences of Argentina's ERT workers, I argue, also delineate how such a collective, historical materialist, and relational working-class consciousness can arise via initially spontaneous struggle, without vanguard leadership, in an unfinished and multilayered state of becoming, and within the tensions inherent to the 'labour-capital *social relation of production*'.[188] In short, a critical theoretical lens on working-class consciousness shows that it is both conjuncturally shaped *and* praxically formed by workers' collective desires, actions, and projects that seek to overcome exploitation and crises. Thus, the formation of a working-class consciousness and self-identity amongst ERT workers is not, hearkening back to Maurice Merleau-Ponty's words in the *Phenomenology of Perception*, predetermined by an 'idea' of what 'the working class' should be,[189] nor by the visions of enlightened vanguards, representative union leadership, or 'the Party'. Rather and as we will see, ERT workers' collective identities

---

185   Marx 1976a, p. 4.
186   Cox and Nilsen 2014, p. 7.
187   For a rigorous class-struggle Marxist treatment of human beings' self-making and the role of critical and revolutionary praxis, see Allman 2001, 2007. Also see Paulo Freire's writings on *conscientização* (concientisation) in Freire 1970.
188   Allman 2007, p. 74 (emphasis in original).
189   Merleau-Ponty 1962, p. 444.

as working-class protagonists and their eventual and related practices of resistance and *autogestión* emerge *intersubjectively* from the entanglement and ruptures of ERT workers' circumstances and from subjectivities that

> co-exist in the same situation and feel alike, not in virtue of some comparison, as if each one of [them] lived primarily within [themselves], but on the basis of [their shared] tasks and gestures.[190]

That is, ERT protagonists' working-class consciousness, self-identity, and alternative projects of *autogestión* are forged intersubjectively by individuals whose lives are 'synchronised' and that 'share a common lot'[191] within the socioeconomic and micro-economic crises that have pockmarked Argentina's political economy over the past decades.[192] And what are the commonly shared lived-experiences – this 'common lot' – that peaked in Argentina during the implosion of the neo-liberal model and that brought together some of its workers through their direct actions of occupying firms and eventually selfmanaging them? Shared feelings of frustration and even fear as thousands of firms were closing and declaring bankruptcy or were idle. Collectively felt anxieties at being relegated to the growing ranks of the underemployed, the unemployed, and the poor. Common experiences of helplessness and the loss of dignity as job security eroded. Shared anger and indignation at the intensification of rates of exploitation in the wake of dwindling salaries and benefits. And countless stories of domestic crises and the breakdown of families as a result of increased life precarisation.

But in the collective actions of ERT protagonists living out their lives within a particular conjuncture of systemic capitalist crises, they also begin to move beyond their shared predicament and to recuperate what appeared to be, especially within neo-liberal discourses, 'lost causes', to borrow from E.P. Thompson.[193] These 'lost causes' – lost only if we continue to view them through neo-liberal ideological lenses – are in reality the antithesis of the creation of surplus-value determined by socially necessary labour-time and are rooted in practices of cooperation (not competition) that catalyse new articulations of work in free association in order to cooperatively produce social wealth. Historically, as E.P. Thompson reminds us, in productive scenarios that were mostly

---

190   Ibid.
191   Ibid.
192   Recall my discussion of the historical roots of ERTs in Chapter 3. See also my concluding comments in Chapter 9.
193   Thompson 2001, p. 6.

exempt from market logics and capitalist accumulation, the 'lost causes' that working people tended to privilege were 'egalitarian and democratic values' and 'communitarian ideals',[194] values and ideals in direct opposition to self-interest, competition, and resignation to the whims of capitalist logics. ERTs, I argue throughout this book, are part of this oft-forgotten vein of working people's self-activity coursing through the history of the pre-capitalist and capitalist era. In this light, in their workers living out their own history, ERTs are, in particular, prefigurative of a mode of production that re-embeds the economic back into the social needs of human beings and communities. ERTs thus offer hope for workers equally pummelled by global neo-liberal capital in other conjunctures. They teach us how resistance from the standpoint of living labour *can* emerge from within capital and even move beyond the dross of an economic and productive system in perpetual crisis – a form of crisis that is, as current events are showing us, part and parcel of our globalised neo-liberal reality.

2 Section 2: Critical Theories of Labour and Capitalist Technology

To better understand what ERT workers specifically recuperate, the radical social innovations they subsequently forge, and their broader desire for *autogestión*, we must first grasp that workers' struggles for self-determination are fundamentally struggles against the capitalist process of value-production (that is, valorisation). ERTs are yet one more historical experience of workers' struggles against capitalist valorisation in a long history paralleling the rise, consolidation, and expansion of capitalism. A critical theoretical perspective helps us understand workers' normative bases and continued potential for both struggling against capitalist value-production and for creating alternative, self-directed projects of *autogestión*.

This section explores workers' normative foundation to and potential for their struggles against value and for *autogestión* by unpacking the two-fold character of labour and capitalist technology. It does so from the class-struggle Marxist understanding that workers' living in capitalism are situated in an exploitation–resistance nexus. That is, workers are both exploited by capital and its related technologies *and* simultaneously engaged in struggle against it. Workers subsequently participate in a reshaping of the capitalist technological inheritance that opens up possibilities for self-determining their own

---

194   Ibid.

working lives, both as direct responses to capitalism's dominative logics from within (given that labour is 'value creating' for capital) *and* despite these logics as workers struggle to move beyond capitalist imperatives and reaffirm their own destiny beyond exploitation.[195]

2.1 The Two-Fold Character of Labour in Capitalism

The quintessential capitalist contradiction deeply embedded in its economic system, and what Marx shows most fundamentally in Part 1 of *Capital* Volume I is to be found in the inner workings of the commodity form. Central to the very process of valorising commodities are the abstractions of social relations and, ultimately, the human being. These abstractions are at the root of the capitalist system's exploitation, alienation, and thus diminishment of *labour* – the very force that paradoxically valorises things exchanged on the market.[196] To begin to understand what exactly it is that workers recuperate when taking over and converting their places of employment into worker cooperatives, and what normatively justifies this recuperation, we must start from the same place that Marx did when he set out to unpack the capitalist system: the contradictory process of valorising commodities.

As Marx showed in the first pages of *Capital* Volume I, in order to buy and sell commodities within capitalist markets and subsequently trigger the accumulation process, the exerted labour that is embodied within them must be equalised as value. The capitalist system does this through the abstraction and simplification of the myriad forms of labour that produce the vast array of commodities and their social use-values, defined as 'social labour in the abstract'.[197] To be exchangeable at the societal scale required by a capitalist economy, commodities must be *compared* in a common way, or 'must be capable of being expressed in terms of something common to them all'.[198] What is common to all commodities – and what makes them comparable and thus exchangeable within markets – is not use-value, because the use-value of any one thing will always be different depending on the individual and socio-

---

195 Bonefeld 2004, pp. 47. Not intending at all to reify capital nor treat labour as separate or apart from capital as its dichotomous opposite, in this section, instead, I am appealing to Open Marxism's understanding of the labour–capital relation. For these heterodox Marxist theorists, labour today does not exist outside of capital but rather 'in and against capital, while capital ... exists only in and through labour' (p. 47). This is why we can say that labour is constitutive of capital in a way that capital is not so of labour (Bonefeld 1994; Cleaver 1992a; Vieta 2018b).

196 Colletti 1972.

197 Fine and Saad-Filho 2004, p. 20.

198 Marx 1967, p. 37.

cultural circumstances. When the mutable use-values and the physical shape and chemical composition of commodities are left out, Marx explains, the only thing common to commodities are that they are the 'products of labour' and that certain amounts of 'labour-time' go into producing them. Moreover, for this comparison to happen at the social scale required for the capitalist system to function, all commodities must be reducible to quantifiable 'human labour in the abstract'. In other words, taken to a societal level, commodities are exchangeable in capitalist markets because the entire process of production and exchange relies on 'homogeneous human labour' that averages out (or abstracts) all of the 'labour-power expended' in producing them.[199] This averaging out of concrete labour deployed to produce commodities and exchange them at a societal scale – and, thus, '[t]he labour that forms the substance of value' – Marx called '[t]he labour-time socially necessary', or the labour-time 'required to produce an article under the normal conditions of production, and with the average degree of skill and intensity prevalent at the time'.[200]

In the process of abstracting out the individual efforts of living labour, capitalist logics efface the social relations embedded in commodities – the social relations between the flesh-and-blood workers who create them and the owners of the means of production, and between the people who exchange them. Moreover, in this abstraction, the myriad skills and capacities of workers are also elided. In short (and paradoxically), the valorisation process at once needs *and* dehumanises labour.[201] From the point of view of capital, this dehumanisation transforms workers themselves into commodities or, at most, into possessors and sellers of only one thing – the commodity *labour-power*. This theory of dehumanisation is essentially a more advanced analysis of Marx's earlier theory of alienation[202] and is central to his value-theory of labour.

Marx's value-theory of labour – and what differentiated him from classical political economy's ahistoricised labour theories of value – fundamentally exposited that the 'labour contained in commodities', and thus the process of labour valuing commodities, has a 'two-fold nature'.[203] In capitalist circuits of production and exchange, the labour-power that is embodied in commodities is two-fold because it is both concrete labour – labour that is reflected in multiplicities of human skills needed to produce things and that create and satisfy multiplicities of human needs and use-values – *and* abstract labour – deskilled,

199   Marx 1967, p. 38.
200   Marx 1967, p. 39.
201   Colletti 1972.
202   Marx 2007, pp. 67–83. See also Marx 1967, pp. 184–5.
203   Marx 1967, p. 41.

averaged-out, and homogenised labour that enables exchange-value.[204] The former contains qualitatively different kinds of labour that embrace the myriad human capacities necessary for making useful things. The latter is quantitatively measured labour that necessarily abstracts out the qualitative differences between the capacities of diverse labourers, and even abstracts the varied capacities possessed by the same worker.[205] This averaged-out, abstracted, or equalised labour is necessary in a capitalist system in order to meet the 'labour-time socially required' to produce things ready for market exchange.[206] In sum, capitalist circuits of exchange within commodity markets need comparable values between otherwise diverse products – values afforded by abstracted labour – in order for: (1) exchange to happen at the scale required to satisfy capitalist accumulation; (2) for the reproduction of labour-power (as the key input in the production process); and, ultimately, (3) to *valorise* capital as such. The result? In the abstraction process of capital, all social relations between people – in workplaces and within circuits of exchange – are ultimately reduced to relations between things.[207] Moreover, workers' concrete labour transmogrifies, from the point of view of capital, into a mere input factor of production, a certain quantity of some 'thing' – 'labour-power', or the commodity that promises to produce more value than it costs to the buyer and that is bought and sold on the market for labour-power.[208]

What is the outcome of the capitalist's seizure of workers' abounding capacities to make useful things when purchasing labour-power on the wage-labour market? The answer, according to Lucio Colletti, gets us to 'Marx's essential thesis' in *Capital* Volume I: To abstract the diverse skills of workers into 'simple average labour' is to 'equalise', or reduce, otherwise diverse people to one characteristic.[209] It is a reduction of workers' multifaceted skills into one socially commensurable type of labour. One of the results of this reduction, linked as

---

204   Marx 1967, pp. 44–6; Marx 1976b, pp. 992–4. For Marx, while labour and nature were the
       two sources of wealth (Marx 1978b, p. 525) and both could create use-value, in the cap-
       italist process of production labour was specifically the source of exchange-value and,
       ultimately, value. More specifically, expended labour, while not 'itself value' (Marx 1967,
       p. 51), is the source of, or 'creates', both the use-value and exchange-value of commodities
       (Marx 1967, pp. 41, 200–1; see also McLellan, 1973, p. 345).

205   Marx 1967, pp. 41–6. In a footnote at the end of Part 1, Section 2 of *Capital* Volume I,
       Engels adds that concrete useful labour 'which creates Use-Value and counts qualitatively
       is *Work*, as distinguished from Labour; that which creates Value and counts quantitatively
       is *Labour*, as distinguished from Work' (Engels, in Marx 1967, p. 47).

206   Marx 1967, p. 317.

207   Marx 1967, p. 72.

208   Marx 1967, pp. 177–85.

209   Colletti 1972, p. 83.

it is to the wage-labour contract, is the loss of any rights that workers have not only to the products of their labour, but also to the very control of their labour-power. What are the consequences of this abstraction of labour? 'In abstracting from the object or concrete material of their labour', Colletti continues, '[capital] also *ipso facto* abstract[s] from that which serves to differentiate their labours',[210] in effect putting 'out of sight'[211] both the multiplicity of each individual workers' physical and intellectual capacities and the 'concrete forms of labour' that distinguish workers as people.[212] As Colletti further points out most poignantly, this homogenisation is nothing less than the capitalists' '*expropriation* of *human subjectivity*'[213] from workers' own productive capacities and the products of their labour – *ergo*, alienation. In the capitalist workshop, as Marx dissects in grim detail in Chapters 10 and 15 of *Capital* Volume I,[214] this expropriation transforms the labourer from an active agent of his or her work into a fungible input of production – 'variable capital'.[215]

Thus, the values of commodities are, in reality and despite capitalist ideology, not something intrinsic to them outside of the social and historical realities that created them, nor are they something merely accidental, arbitrary, or neutral. They only *appear* to be so when relegated to the 'invisible hand' of the market. Despite capitalism's fetishisation of the immateriality of the value of commodities, on the one hand virtually all commodities exist, Marx asserted, because of 'the result of a special sort of productive activity, the nature of which is determined by its aim, mode of operation, subject, means, and result'; that is, 'concrete useful labour' producing use-value.[216] On the other hand, this useful labour deployed in a capitalist system – as the 'productive activity' that creates commodities *and* value – is executed by wage-labour in action, or, more precisely, expended labour-power.[217] In a nutshell, the valorisation of commodities in a capitalist system is the result of this wage-labour employed by the purchaser of labour-power (that is, capitalists) for the explicit production of surplus-value.

Arguably the most crucial contribution Marx makes in exposing the actual dynamics of the labour–value relationship in *Capital* Volume I is to *re-humanise labour*. He does so most fundamentally by clarifying that the two aspects

---

210   Ibid.
211   Marx 1967, p. 38.
212   Ibid.
213   Colletti 1972, p. 87 (emphasis in original).
214   Respectively, in the chapters on 'The Working Day' and 'Machinery and Modern Industry'.
215   Marx 1967, pp. 199–211.
216   Marx 1967, p. 41.
217   Marx 1967, p. 197.

of labour that are 'embodied' in commodities – *concrete labour* and *abstract labour* – are both, despite capitalist pretensions to its own inventiveness and self-proclaimed ingenuity, indebted first and foremost to *workers' boundless capacities for making useful things and cooperating in the process of creating social wealth* – that is, to 'living labour'. This value-creating capacity is expropriated from living labour in the unequal exchange between the sellers and buyers of labour-power, since the wage is never able to justly compensate workers for the ultimate value they create. Normatively, Marx suggests implicitly in the *Grundrisse* and *Capital* Volume I, the capitalist labour process and the means of production should rightfully belong to *the real producers*, those who actually create things with both use-values for people and value for capital via the 'form-giving fire' of their living labour. The implication is that the labour process and the means of production are thus theirs – the workers' – to rightfully take back.[218]

2.2 The Two-Fold Character of Capitalist Technology

A critical theory of capitalist production also hinges on a two-fold theory of technology, similar to Marx's two-fold theory of labour. Indeed, critical philosopher of technology Andrew Feenberg suggests that Marx was the first critical theorist of technology as Marx took into account technology's two-fold character in what Feenberg calls Marx's 'design critique' of technology.[219] According to Feenberg's reading of Marx's design theory, 'capitalism's technology is', on the one hand, 'shaped by the same bias that governs other aspects of capitalist production, such as management'.[220] That is, capitalist technology *is* designed for control in as much as it 'condense[s] ... social and technical functions' shaped by 'the power of ruling groups'[221] and is aimed at securing surplus-value extraction. On the other hand, technology can also 'achieve advances of general utility' in, for instance, reducing labour-time.[222] This is because technology, Feenberg clarifies, is also imbued with 'ambivalent potentialities' whereby 'technical features determined by social functions are subject to social change'.[223] Here, Feenberg goes on to expand on Marx's design theory of technology by merging it with more recent social theories of technology to develop

---

218   Marx 1967, p. 183; 1973, p. 361. For a similar conclusion, see Braverman 1974, pp. 445–6.
219   Feenberg 2002, pp. 47–53.
220   Feenberg 2002, p. 48.
221   Feenberg 2002, p. 64.
222   Feenberg 2002, p. 47.
223   Feenberg 2002, p. 64.

a broader 'theory of [technological] ambivalence'.[224] Feenberg summarises this two-fold and ambivalent character of technology as follows: '[T]he design critique relates the values embodied in technology to social hegemony. But what depends on a social force can be changed by another social force: technology is not destiny'.[225] Hence, capitalist technologies of production, while central to the capitalist project of maximising surplus-value, also have the *potential* of efficiently organising and provisioning for the need to overcome scarcity while affording time outside of work for the self-development of people. At is most revolutionary, then, workers' control of the means of production that includes the democratic appropriation of technology implies the creation of a new society that would end superfluous and compulsive work, eliminate exploitation and alienation, and ensure that working people's desires for and projects of self-actualisation and human becoming are privileged.[226]

To be clear, the theory of technological ambivalence is not a theory of neutrality. To consider technology as being neutral is to link technology, as economistic Marxisms or Marxist control theorists such as Harry Braverman seem to do, to a property theory of technology – that simply transferring ownership of the means of production to workers while retaining technologies intact will lead to labours' liberation from capitalist processes of production. Feenberg, on the other hand, drawing critically on the work of Marx, Martin Heidegger, Herbert Marcuse, Jürgen Habermas, Michel Foucault, Gilbert Simondon, Michael Burawoy, and other critical and social theorists of technology, has shown that modern technologies are not neutral but are, rather, both inscribed with the technical codes etched into them by their designers and implementers *and also* re-inscribed by users within their social contexts. For Feenberg, technical systems are thus *ambivalent* in that they are perched between a multitude of possibilities whereby both their initial designs and ultimate uses are interwoven with the socially contextualised values stamped onto them. Technical activities thus operate in a tension between the intended outcomes of planners', managers', and capitalists' 'operational autonomy' and the reinterpretations of these technical domains within the 'margin of manoeuvre' available to users ensconced within socio-technological spheres.[227] Since these spheres – or in more social phenomenological terms, lifeworlds – remain open to the diversity of practices that can still be taken up by even the dominated, and since it is impossible to predict and control how these practices will unfold in the lived

---

224   Feenberg 2002, pp. 63–88.
225   Ibid.
226   Feenberg 2002, pp. 47–8.
227   Feenberg 2002, pp. 63–88.

experiences of users (despite the attempts by technologists and technocrats to do so), technologies are always already embedded ambivalently within users' margin of manoeuvrability that are also the 'germs of a new society'.[228]

For Feenberg, then, emancipating practices such as workers' control and bottom-up and horizontal reorganisations of workplaces are possible because of the 'ambivalent potentialities' of our technological inheritance situated in socio-political spheres of class struggle.[229] In Feenberg's critical theoretical language, the technologically mediated spheres of life are a 'scene of struggle' and a 'social battlefield'[230] where the social relations of 'class and power' determine 'which of the ambivalent potentialities of the [technical] heritage will be realized'.[231] Hence, capitalist machines of production, labour processes, and divisions of labour are not deterministically exploitative and alienating in a strong sense, but are rather always already ensconced in class struggle. Consequently, as Feenberg argues, technologies are suspended within a multitude of possibilities, having within them the potentiality to unfold in diverse ways, and can be 'creatively appropriated'[232] or 'reshaped as machines developed under capitalism are employed to produce a new generation of machines adapted to socialist purposes'.[233] Ultimately, for Feenberg, 'the theory of ambivalence ... asserts the possibility of *bootstrapping* from capitalism to socialism'.[234]

The ambivalence theory of technology, I suggest, also shows how capitalist modes of production and labour processes bring workers together; after all, capitalism needs their cooperative capacities to realise the valorisation process.[235] But in bringing workers together, even within workspaces controlled by capitalist technologies of production and subdivided into detailed tasks, solidarity between workers is also being forged as they cooperate in a common purpose. However minimal or weak these solidarities might be within capitalist labour processes operating in times of relative labour peace, they are, as

---

228 Feenberg 2002, p. 87. As I will discuss in Chapter 5, transferring the means of production over to the control of workers while still retaining the capitalist processes of production, the technological designs that uphold them, and the buying and selling of the products of production on open markets is only one step to a more complete workers' control promised by *autogestión*. Rather, technologies of production, the labour process, the divisions of labour, and the market system of exchange must also ultimately be *transformed* under the auspices of other rationalities and values that begin to move beyond capitalist logics.

229 Feenberg 2002, pp. 50, 87.

230 Feenberg 2002, p. 15.

231 Feenberg 2002, p. 53.

232 Feenberg 1999, pp. 120–9.

233 Feenberg 2002, p. 53.

234 Ibid.

235 Lebowitz 2003.

Maurizio Atzeni points out, ripe for other, more radical forms of solidarity and collective actions that arise when the actual exploitative nature of the labour process under capital comes to the surface for workers.[236] This exploitative nature, and the actual differences that exist between the interests of employers and employees, can especially come to the surface during moments of macro-economic crises, as occurred in Argentina during the years spanning the turn of the millennium, or, from the perspective of the shop floor, when employers resort to rationalisation drives or redundancy strategies in order to force more surplus-value extraction, often in order to address micro-economic downturns. As we will empirically see in Chapters 6–8, ERT protagonists' strategies and tactics of 'occupy, resist, produce' show that the same socio-political realities compelling workers to organise, join unions, agitate for better wages, and bargain for improvements on shop floors can also extend struggle to other areas of life beyond the labour process.[237]

Hence, capitalist workplaces also bring with them new vantage points and possibilities for those working within the always-porous boundaries of technologically rationalised systems. Marcuse,[238] for example, also drawing from Marx's ambivalence theory – mostly from the section of the *Grundrisse* that would later be called 'The Fragment on Machines' by autonomist Marxists[239] – proposes that the very production apparatus that controls labour under a capitalist technological rationality of perpetual growth and competition has within it the potentiality to actually reduce labour-time to a minimum.[240] If, Marcuse then conjectures, this technological inheritance were to be guided by a *new regime of rationality* under more communal and humane values and less exploitative and alienating means and ends, a new world could be opened up. This new world could be centred on values that aspire to reduce the need for compulsive work, relegating necessary and alienating work more and more to machines while maximising the moments for self-development and self-actualisation for all in the process.[241] A re-conceptualisation of modern technology rooted in another form of rationality, then, could afford the 'civilizational change' that would rest fundamentally with not only 'technological progress' itself,[242] but also with the 'radical reconstruction' of technology's means

---

236 Atzeni 2010.

237 Atzeni 2010.

238 Marcuse 1964, 1968.

239 Marx, 1973, pp. 690–712. See also Marcuse 1964, pp. 35–36; 1968, p. xviii.

240 Marcuse 1964, 1966.

241 Vieta 2016a, 2017.

242 Marcuse, 1969, p. 19. 'Freedom', writes Marcuse most directly in his book *An Essay on Lib-*

with a view towards different, more human-centred ends.[243] With automation, writes Marcuse, 'appears the chance of the transformation of quantity into quality, the leap into a qualitatively different stage [of human existence]'.[244] 'Behind all the inhuman aspects of automation as it is organized under capitalism', Marcuse continues,

> its real possibilities appear: the genesis of a technological world in which man [sic] can finally withdraw from, evacuate, and oversee the apparatus of his labour – in order to experiment freely with it.[245]

Most fundamentally for Marcuse, the move beyond exploitation and alienation was to be rooted in a new radical subjectivity seized by a different, non-instrumentalised *rationality* that could underpin new forms of technological mediations.[246] Revealing the stream of self-determination present in Marcuse's writings, for him nothing less than *freedom* was at stake in this re-rationalised technological project.

Similarly for autonomist Marxists, in close affinity with Marcuse's and Feenberg's theories of technological ambivalence, capitalism in particular works within deep tensional relations between the opposing poles of the exploitation of labour and workers' resistance as framed by an 'interweaving of technology and power'.[247] While autonomist Marxist theorists agree with classical Marxism that capitalism has a strong tendency to use technical innovations as a means of securing and maximising relative surplus-value (that is, exploitation) by increasing workers' dependence on capital (that is, alienation), they also emphasise how capitalists' propensities to increase 'the proportion of dead or "constant" capital as against living or "variable" capital' are efforts to specifically

---

eration, 'indeed depends largely on technical progress, on the advancement of science' (Ibid).

243   Feenberg 2005, p. 19; Vieta 2016a, 2017. 'If the completion of the technological project involves a break with the prevailing technological rationality', writes Marcuse, 'the break in turn depends on the continued existence of the technical base itself. For it is this base which has rendered possible the satisfaction of needs and the reduction of toil – it remains the very base of all forms of human freedom. The qualitative change rather lies in the *reconstruction of this base* – that is, *in its development with a view of different ends* ... The new ends, as technical ends, would then operate in the project and in the construction of the machinery, and not only in its utilization' (Marcuse, 1964, pp. 231–32, emphasis added).

244   Marcuse 1968 p. xviii.

245   Marcuse 1968 p. xix.

246   Vieta 2016a, 2017.

247   Dyer-Witheford 1999, p. 69. See also Panzieri 1980; and Vieta 2016a.

quell workers' resistances and insurgencies.[248] For these theorists, it is, most necessarily, capital that needs living labour for its valorisation and existence. Living labour, on the other hand, is not similarly reliant on capital. That is, it is labour, not capital, which can be seen as being *a priori* in the capital–labour relation.[249] This, for autonomist Marxists, points to the 'self-valorising' capacities of workers.[250]

Homing in on the self-valorisation of labour – the capacity for workers to not only resist capital but to also innovate social and economic life beyond it in their own name – autonomist Marxists particularly emphasise the insurrectionary and creative capacities of workers in their social research on workers' self-activity in workplaces; the role of domestic (that is, non-waged, mostly female) work for reproducing the capitalist valorisation process; in non-traditional and non-factory work; in the new conditions of work emerging in post-Fordist production regimes; and, increasingly, in the rise of contractual, flexibilised, and precarious work of the 'the creative industries' and the 'knowledge economy'.[251] In this way, autonomists refocus the critical analysis

---

248 Dyer-Witheford 1999, pp. 69–70. For an example of this logic in Marx's analysis of machinery in modern industry, see Marx 1967, p. 403.

249 'Capital', wrote Marx, 'is dead labour, that, vampire-like, only lives by sucking living labour, and lives the more, the more labour it sucks' (Marx 1967, p. 233).

250 Cleaver 1992a, 2000.

251 For some autonomist Marxists (for example, Berardi 2003; de Peuter 2010; and Dyer-Witheford 1999), a new 'virtual' class emerged with the rise of post-Fordism. By the late 1960s, forms of labour in the global North started to become more flexible with the perfection of automation, which, instead of freeing up labour-time, totalised capitalism's need for labour-power even more through the techniques of deskilling, reskilling, outsourcing, and, thus, the flexibilisation of labour. Because of rising unemployement in industrial sectors due to the profit-squeeze crises of the late 1960s and factory downsizings throughout the 1970s and 1980s (Harvey 1990, 2005), a new class of 'knowledge-based' workers of the 'network society' emerged with the introduction of digital technologies such as the personal computer, cellular phones, and the internet (Castells 2000; Huws 2014; P. Mason 2016; Dyer-Witheford 1999, 2015, Weeks 2011). With this new class of labour, the new tools and elements of work, these theorists argue, became 'immaterial', rooted in knowledge, information, and creative mental skills rather than hammers and wrenches. In addition, labour's capacity to work perpetually flexible hours began to be exploited with the development of the computer. Now the knowledge worker, or 'cognitive-based' working class, tends to consider the home, the park, or cafés their workspaces, or works in open-concept, downtown office spaces where work merges with play – not to make work more libidinal, as Marcuse called for, but to make alienated labour seem that much more attractive, obscuring the alienated plight of these workers even further. Now, 'the cognitariate' (Berardi 2003) is seduced by work that is 'entrepreneurial' or 'play' and by flexible hours, is incentivised through stock options and gadgets as bonuses, and is enticed by the idea that it works in creative, 'fun', trendy, or socially influential jobs. Paradoxically, however, as the

of capital onto the autonomy still present with those who work and toil within contemporary capitalism, showing how working people are not merely help- less pawns of capitalist technological rationality but are, instead, also active agents capable of usurping to some degree capitalists' increasingly automated and socialised forms of control.[252] Beyond more traditional organised worker agitation, insurgencies in contemporary 'post-Fordist' capitalism can occur, for example, in acts of sabotage, in the 'refusal' to work,[253] and with living labour's sheer 'inventive power – the creative capacity on which capital depends for its incessant innovation – in order to re-appropriate technology'.[254] For autonom- ist theorists, then, as with Marcuse and Feenberg, these resistive tendencies of workers and the inherent ambivalences of technology that open up spaces for them to self-valorise show promising routes for workers themselves to reinvent the interplay of work and life, re-appropriate the technological inheritance, and perhaps forge paths beyond the compulsions of wage-based work.

2.3   Re-appropriating Technologies of Work for Living Labour

While it is true, then, that capitalist technology is designed under the patron- age of a utilitarian project of control and with the ultimate goal of obscuring and securing surplus-value from workers,[255] technology is nevertheless not as deterministic a variable as when it is primarily looked at through econom- istic and technologically deterministic lenses. There is no doubt that capit- alist technological rationality absorbs what is inherent to 'living labour' into the very techniques of production and automation ('dead labour'). There is also no doubt that, in capitalist production regimes, the processes of produc- tion are 'owned' by capitalists. But it is also equally true, as Harry Cleaver pointedly writes, that the most crucial technological and social innovations in capitalist labour processes derive 'not from capital but from the working class'.[256] 'It is', he concludes, in the final analysis 'only labor that is creative and

---

autonomists have pointed out, in tune with the ambivalence theory of technology, their very knowledge-base in computer literacy and their connectivity and access to digital net- works also empower the cognitariate to tap into the potential to re-appropriate and carry out counter-hegemonic, resistive practices that can contest the high-tech capitalist sys- tem from within their very sites of work in something similar to what Feenberg (2002) has in mind in his theory of 'democratic appropriation'. For compelling accounts of this ambivalence theory of contemporary digital technologies, see Dyer-Witheford 1999, 2015; Huws 2014; and P. Mason 2016.

252   Negri 1991.
253   Weeks 2005, 2011.
254   Dyer-Witheford 1999, pp. 70–1.
255   Burawoy 1985.
256   Cleaver n.d., sec. 5. For Marx, 'the labourer alone is productive', although labourers' pro-

innovative'.[257] Rather than *innovate*, then, the capitalist can be said to *appropriate* what is innovated through the capacities of workers to cooperate and create useful things.[258] Indeed, as Marx shows throughout *Capital* Volume I, shop floor innovations, surplus-value, and the capitalist's resultant profit are *enabled* by labour, not by the capitalist's ingenuity, the vagaries of competition, the 'invisible hand' of the marketplace, or the axioms of technological progress.[259] Ambivalence theory underscores and helps us understand how capitalist technology, organisations, divisions of labour, and labour processes are rather 'dependent variable[s] in the social system', both shaped by the goals of the hegemonic capitalist class while always already 'subject to reshaping to new purposes' under a new rationality geared towards different ends.[260] The ambivalent and two-fold nature of capitalist technologies of production helps us see the possibilities still available to workers for self-determining their lives, and how and why it is that ERT workers are compelled to take over their former capitalist places of work and restart them as worker cooperatives. It is this that the practices of 'occupy, resist, produce' prefigure for the working class, captured in ERT protagonists' recuperative moments unleashed in the process of taking over and converting capitalist workplaces to cooperatives.

---

ductiveness in capitalist labour processes is appropriated by the capitalist in order to produce 'surplus-value for the capitalist' (Marx 1967, p. 509).

257 Cleaver n.d., sec. 5. While Marx shows how capital revolutionises processes of production in 'the epoch of mechanical industry' (Marx 1967, p. 379), he also emphasises how the 'dead labour' that is embodied in machine production is created and valorised by the very living labourers that produced those machines in the first place (see in particular Marx 1967, pp. 371–507). Thus, the introduction of automated processes of production was, for Marx, the imposition of appropriated and congealed creative efforts of previously expended labour-power for the creation of future value and the management of new labour-power in mechanised labour processes. Marx goes on to explain how these innovations of automation are ultimately introduced into the labour process by capitalists for two purposes: (1) to *increase productivity* in order to increase 'relative surplus-value' while decreasing inputs such as 'variable capital' (that is, the cost of labour-power) by shortening labours' 'necessary' labour-time (that is, the cost of labour-power equivalent to the cost of labourers' means of subsistence); and (2) as capitalist *reactions* against increased worker resistance to the intensification of work brought on by the quest for increased productivity via machinery. See, for instance, Marx 1967, pp. 312–21, 359–68, 508–18.

258 Marx 1967, p. 508.

259 The appropriation of the inventiveness of labour by capital is nowhere more clearly stated by Marx than in Section 2 of Chapter 10 of *Capital* on the working day: 'Capital has not invented surplus-labour' (Marx 1967, p. 235).

260 Feenberg 2002, p. 48.

3   Section 3: ERTS' Six Recuperative Moments

3.1   *The Recuperation of Workers' Labour-Power*

Implicit throughout this book and threading through ERT protagonists' radical social innovations[261] is the assertion that *the most fundamental thing that
ERT workers begin to recuperate is control over their own labour-power* – workers' capacities to invent, collaborate, and produce socially useful things. In
this most elemental recuperation, ERT workers, at core, begin to de-alienate
themselves from their work and reclaim their once-expropriated subjectivity
from the capital–labour relation for themselves as creative and cooperative
beings. By taking back their workplaces and beginning to self-manage their
labour-time and the processes of production, ERT workers – like all voluntarily
associated workers potentially do – begin to cooperatively take back control
over their capacities to be creative, to make things that they first set out in
their imagination to make, and to re-combine their abilities to conceive with
their abilities to manually engage with the things of the world, in order to craft
something that is socially useful. These are crucial human qualities that workers legally renounce in the standard employment agreement when, in return
for a wage, workers sell their labouring capacities for a time (that is, 'the working day') to employers (that is, capitalist purchasers of labour-power).[262]

3.2   *The Renouncement of Surplus-Value, the Recuperation of Workers'*
Own Surpluses

As Marx also reminds us, the capitalist valorisation process[263] is essentially the
creation and extraction of *surplus-value* from workers' surplus-labour, or labour
expended beyond its value (that is, beyond the cost of wages). Writes Marx:
'Capitalist production is not merely the production of commodities, it is essentially the production of surplus-value'.[264] Under the auspices of wage-labour,

---

261   See Chapters 1 and 6–8.
262   Braverman 1974; Vosko 2006.
263   Marx 1976b, p. 302.
264   Marx 1967, p. 509. '[T]o lay bare [this] essential character of [the capitalist method of val-
        orisation]', according to Engels 'which was still a secret [before Marx]', was one of Marx's
        main contributions to political economy (Engels 1978, p. 700). '[T]his was done', Engels
        continues, 'through the discovery of *surplus value*. It was shown that the appropriation of
        unpaid labour is the basis of the capitalist mode of production and of the exploitation of
        the worker that occurs under it; that even if the capitalist buys the labour-power of his
        labourer at its full value as a commodity on the market, he yet extracts more value from it
        than he paid for, and that in the ultimate analysis this surplus value forms those sums of

the labourer produces, not for himself, but for capital. It no longer suffices, therefore, that he [sic] must simply produce. He must produce surplus-value. That labourer alone is productive, who produces surplus-value for the capitalist, and thus works for the self-expansion of capital.[265]

This is why the capitalist valorisation process is quintessentially what the working class struggles against; indeed, *the class struggle is the struggle against the valorisation process*.[266]

For Marx, therefore, as we already saw in his assessment of worker/producer cooperatives, the revolutionary transformation of capitalist society rested firmly in the eradication of surplus-value. 'It is clear', as Marx writes in *Capital* Volume I, 'that in any given economic formation of society, where not the exchange-value but the use-value of the product predominates, surplus-labour will be limited'.[267] Moreover, where 'the chief parts of the product is destined for direct use by the community itself' outside of market relations (that is, relations and exchange between people mediated by things), the products of this collective labour 'does not take the form of a commodity'.[268] And Marx further writes in the last pages of *Capital* Volume I: 'So long, therefore, as the labourer can accumulate for himself – and this he can do so long as he *remains possessor of his means of production* – capitalist accumulation and the capitalist mode of production are impossible'.[269] Implicitly alluded to in passages such as these scattered throughout Marx's middle and later works, in short, is his unbridled support of full workers' control of the means of production.

As I review in later chapters, the social and solidarity economies that ERTs and other self-managed collectives are creating are contemporary examples of scenarios where surplus-labour and surplus-value are being limited and at times eradicated, prefiguring other relations of production and exchange in which the social is privileged over the economic.[270] Another recuperative

---

value from which are heaped up the constantly increasing masses of capital in the hands of the possessing classes' (Ibid).

265   Marx 1967 p. 509.
266   Harvie 2005.
267   Marx 1967, p. 235.
268   Marx 1967, p. 357.
269   Marx 1967, p. 767 (emphasis added). For Harry Braverman, unearthing this reality for the emancipation of workers themselves was the very crux of Marx's *raison d'être* for writing *Capital* Volume I. As Braverman asserts: 'Marx's entire discussion of the capitalist mode of production in [*Capital* Volume I] is permeated by a revolutionary conception, which is the return of the process of production itself to the control of workers in the fullest and most direct way' (Braverman 1974, pp. 445–6).
270   As I first presented in the Preface and describe in more detail in Chapter 5, *the social and*

moment for ERTs, then, is *the reclamation of workers' surpluses for themselves via their own control of the means of production.*

3.3   A Return to 'Labour in Common or Directly Associated Labour' in Voluntary Cooperation

Greig de Peuter and Nick Dyer-Witheford have recently called workers' collective and voluntary control of a productive entity and the redistribution of economic surpluses between and by workers themselves a type of 'labour commons'.[271] For them, the prefigurative force of worker cooperatives rests in their role in 'the circulation of the common' in contrast to conventional capitalist firms' role in the 'circulation of capital'.[272] For de Peuter and Dyer-Witheford, the interplay of three major areas of the commons are crucial for this alternative circulation: the 'eco-social commons', such as fisheries and nature reserves, protected watersheds, and commonly controlled forestry practices; the 'networked commons', such as 'non-rivalrous' digital goods, online resource pooling, and copyleft practices; and, most relevant for this book, the 'democratized organization of productive and reproductive work' or the 'labour commons', most readily visible in worker cooperatives and other labour-managed firms.[273] De Peuter and Dyer-Witheford illustrate how a new circulation of the common could unfold by reconfiguring Marx's circulation of capital formula:

> C represents not a Commodity but Commons, and the transformation is not into Money but Association [A]. The basic formula is therefore: A – C – A'. This can then be elaborated into A – C ... P ... C' – A' ...[274]

As a 'labour commons',[275] worker cooperatives are socialised productive entities. As I will elaborate on in the next chapter, in a worker cooperative it is labour (the direct producers) that *hires* capital, not the other way around as in capitalist businesses, permitting worker-members to control the labour process and distribution of surpluses.[276] And so long as worker cooperatives

---

solidarity economy is a broad concept that takes into account all organisations and economic practices in which the social dimensions and requisites of life are privileged over, or guide, the economic.

271   de Peuter and Dyer-Witheford 2010, pp. 37–9.
272   de Peuter and Dyer-Witheford 2010, p. 45.
273   Ibid.
274   Ibid.
275   de Peuter and Dyer-Witheford 2010, pp. 37–9.
276   Craig 1993, p. 94.

do not hire waged-workers as non-members of the cooperative, and so long as they redistribute earnings equitably amongst all members, surplus-labour too begins to be eliminated in these spaces. Indeed, in a cooperative society, production *and* surpluses are *socialised*.[277] In sum, a labour commons transforms the workplace into 'an *organizational commons*, the labour performed ... [into] a *commoning practice*, and the surplus generated, [into] a *commonwealth*'.[278]

Yet another moment of recuperation for ERTs, then, is their *workers' return to directly associated labour in voluntary cooperation* – that is, to combine their capacities and increase their productive power in a 'labour commons'. Voluntary cooperation within a labour commons is indeed what Marx means by 'labour in common or directly associated labour',[279] which was for him central for the future communist society beyond capital.[280] By *associated labour* I follow Marx here to mean the *voluntary* coming together 'of free and equal producers'[281] disengaged from the power of capital as mediator of wage-labour, a power that within the capital–labour relation extracts value from labour-power 'in each moment of the circuit of capital' for the capitalist.[282] As Michael Lebowitz puts it, when members of worker cooperatives voluntarily associate, they are reclaiming the trans-historical cooperative tendencies of workers that are subsumed by capital within its modes of production.[283] Association under the rubric of a worker cooperative thus means that workers begin to disentangle themselves from capitalist social relations of the wage-labour contract wherein 'each wage labourer is an individual, isolated owner of labour-power'.[284] Rather, as members of a worker cooperative, each worker's labour-power is *recombined socially* for the benefit of the entire collective of workers, in effect taking power away from capital and putting it back in the hands of the collective of workers associated within a cooperative.

While it is true that worker cooperatives and other labour-managed arrangements working within a broader capitalist market system are forced to compromise the full potential of associated labour, challenging its workers' collective autonomy from the commodity form (an issue that I will bring up

---

277   De Martino 2003; Gibson-Graham 2006.
278   de Peuter and Dyer-Witheford 2010, p. 45 (emphasis in original).
279   Marx 1967, pp. 77–8.
280   See the first part of this chapter.
281   Marx, in Lebowitz 2003, p. 89.
282   Lebowitz 2003, p. 88.
283   Lebowitz 2003; See also Marx 1967, pp. 322–35, 530.
284   Lebowitz 2003 p. 88.

later in my discussion of ERT's 'dual reality'), they continue to prefiguratively suggest, nevertheless, a non-capitalist labour commons recombined socially to produce a social product.[285]

3.4   The Recuperation of the Labour Process in General

As I have already noted, ERT protagonists consistently deploy the concept of *autogestión* in speaking about the reorganisation of their places of work. Theoretically, we can interpret *autogestión* to be ERT workers' lived experiences of their cooperative self-direction of the *labour process*.

The labour process for this study is informed by Marx's historical materialist definition, which is intimately associated with his notion of 'labour in common or directly associated labour'. At core for Marx, the labour process is not unique to capitalist production.[286] Rather, it most fundamentally refers to human beings' historical practices of cooperatively and socially organising work. The labour process is thus not exclusive to any particular production regime (and thus not an invention of capitalism), as Michael Burawoy's classical Marxist analysis of the labour process reminds us.[287] It is, rather, present whenever human beings come together and enter into social relations 'in order to produce useful things'.[288] To underscore this, Marx begins his discussion of the labour process in *Capital* Volume I with the general concept of 'the labour-process pure and simple',[289] a 'nature-imposed condition of human existence'[290] that requires human beings to work collaboratively and with nature to survive. At this most 'elementary' level, the labour process for Marx includes three aspects: (1) the human activities of work, or the *act of labouring* itself; (2) the *subject of the work*, or the materials which are worked upon and transformed by workers to produce useful things; and (3) *the tools, or instruments, of work* that mediate this transformation, which themselves are already-made products honed by human hands or nature and which bear use-value.[291]

---

285   As Marx clearly underscored early on in *Capital* Volume I, the products of labour are 'a social product' rather than commodities when they are created by 'a community of free individuals ... carrying on their work with the means of production in common, in which the labour-power of all the different individuals is consciously applied as the combined labour-power of the community' producing for its own needs (Marx 1967, p. 78).

286   Marx 1967.

287   Burawoy 1985.

288   Burawoy 1985, p. 13.

289   Marx 1967, p. 189.

290   Marx 1967, p. 184.

291   Marx 1967, p. 178.

Taken together, these three 'elementary factors' of the labour process are, in other words, *a priori* for all human making and survival.[292]

Marx further distinguishes the 'process of production' from the labour process *per se*. The labour process is enfolded within particular production processes (or production regimes.)[293] Historically, the process of production, which encompasses the labour process, can include all forms of value creation by human beings. 'The process of production', writes Marx, 'considered on the one hand as the unity of the labour process and the process of creating value, is production of commodities'.[294] Further, 'from the point of view of ... the product' in the labour process, the 'subject of labour' and the 'instruments' are the 'means of production' and 'the labour itself productive labour'.[295] Of course, Marx reminds us, the production of commodities took place in pre-capitalist epochs as well. The 'capitalist production process', however, is historically distinguished from other production processes – ideologically, politically, and economically[296] – in that it specifically creates surplus-value. What differentiates the capitalist production process from others, he continues, is not necessarily the production of commodities *per se*, but rather 'the *unity* of the labour process and the process of *producing surplus-value*', which is quintessentially 'the capitalist production of commodities'.[297]

For Marx, then, as Burawoy explains, at issue with the labour process under capitalist production (that is, the capitalist production regime) is the nature of its social relations in producing surplus-value, which are inherently exploitative and alienating.[298] Rather than Braverman's thesis that the main purpose

---

292 Ibid.

293 A 'production regime', as Burawoy explains, constitutes the 'regimes of regulation [that impact] the point of production' and encompasses the ideological, political, and economic dimensions that meet in the labour process on shop floors in a given historical conjuncture (Burawoy 1985, pp. 17, 83–6).

294 Marx 1967 p. 197; Marx 1976b, p. 995.

295 Marx 1967, p. 181.

296 Burawoy 1985.

297 Marx 1967, p. 197 (emphasis added). Given Marx's distinction between the labour process and the production process as I explain above, one should technically refer to 'the labour process under capitalist production'. However, for the sake of simplicity and stylistic issues, throughout this book I at times use the term 'the capitalist labour process' to mean the same thing. Also, when I use the term 'the capitalist production process', I specifically mean to refer to 'the unity of the labour process and the process of producing surplus-value' (Ibid).

298 These social relations are propped up by contractual commitments between employer and employee. Essentially, under the wage-labour contract the owners of the means of

of the labour process under capitalism is the *control* of workers,[299] the crucial motivator driving the capitalist labour process is, in actuality, *the production and maximisation of surplus-value*. While various degrees of managerial control, of course, do play an important part in ensuring the extraction of surplus-value, Fordist and post-Fordist capitalist production regimes would eventually discover that workers' *consent*, rather than the intensification of direct control, is more effective for the continued extraction of surplus-value.

Most fundamentally, then, the labour process under capitalist production regimes, as Burawoy, drawing from Gramsci, convincingly argued, is about the manufacturing of workers' consent to waged-labour and to the capitalist socio-economic system more broadly, both on the shop floor and in the reproduction of the worker during off-work hours in the domestic realm of consumption.[300] To manufacture this consent, the capitalist system has learned to invest the worker with the profit-maximising interests of employers by enmeshing them deeply – cognitively, emotionally, and bodily – with the goals, success, and growth of the firms that employ them. After all, in the capitalist economic system, workers' subsistence, purchasing power, and reproduction depend on the very profit-making capacities of the firms that also exploit their labour-power. Capitalism's production regimes, however, also bury the exploitative reality of the valorisation process within the abstractive tendencies I discussed earlier.

More precisely, then, the labour process under capitalist production regimes is about the '*obscuring* and *securing* of surplus-value',[301] or the veiling from the actual producers of the role of their labour in valorising capital. For Burawoy,[302] this consent and worker investment in the interests of the employer on shop floors at the point of production most clearly play out when workers 'accommodate' to capital. Such accommodation happens, for example, in the socio-political and cultural discourses that uphold ideologies of competition, individual effort, the work ethic, and respect of authority and the rule of law. This worker accommodation can also be seen in the competition that exists on shop floors between workers or work teams in the practices that Burawoy calls 'playing games' and 'making out';[303] in how unions set limits to benefit and wage demands 'for the good of the workers and the company'; when workers'

---

       production (capitalists) have the legal right to extract surplus-value from the expended labour-power of workers.

299   Braverman 1974.

300   Buroway 1979; Gramsci 1971b.

301   Burawoy 1985, p. 32 (emphasis added).

302   Burawoy 1979, 1985.

303   Burawoy 1984 pp. 134–43. See also Burawoy 1979, 1985.

agree to pay cuts or rationalisation drives; in workers' sense of betrayal when laid off; and, most broadly, in the continued compulsion to work for wages.

Taking back and restructuring the labour process and placing it within workers' own control is, then, one more major recuperative moment of ERTs. In taking over the private firms that formally employed them and restructuring the labour process along cooperative lines, ERT workers also break from the former consent they gave as wage-labourers within the capitalist labour process. They begin to extricate themselves from the compromises that kept them from self-determining their working lives and the consent they furnished for enabling the production of surplus-value. The labour process for this book, then, is the prime concept which delineates what is organisationally and technically reconstituted at an ERT within the new project of *autogestión* and what ERT workers continue to struggle to develop and remould as they face their many challenges as a worker cooperative. Critically, in analysing the transition from a capitalist labour process to a self-managed labour process (as I began to do through the actual voices of ERT protagonists in Chapter 1 and as I pick up again in more analytical detail in Chapters 6–8), we begin to understand how ERTs' new, self-managed social relations of production are, in many ways, fundamentally different from the social relations of production experienced when they were employees of the former firm.

3.5   *The Recuperation of the Division of Labour*

For Marx, the division of labour and the labour process are intimately connected. Similar to the labour process, Marx differentiates between the historical division of labour, practised by all human societies working in collaboration to attend to the realm of necessity, and the capitalist division of labour as such. As E.K. Hunt asserts, on the one hand 'the division of labour is simply another name for human social and economic interdependence'.[304] As Braverman puts it, 'the social division of labor is apparently inherent in the species character of human labor as soon as it becomes social labor'.[305] On the other hand, the *capitalist* division of labour – what Braverman has termed 'the detailed division of labour'[306] – *is* different in crucial ways from the social divisions of labour practised by traditional agricultural, tribal, feudal, or craft-based societies. Explains Braverman: 'no society before capitalism systematically subdivided the work of each productive specialty into limited operations'.[307] In capitalist modes of

---

304   Hunt 1986, p. 102. See also Marx, 1967, pp. 41–4.
305   Braverman 1974, p. 72.
306   Braverman 1974, pp. 72–3.
307   Braverman 1974, p. 70.

production, unlike the crafts, we tend to see particular and incrementally smaller parts of the labour process 'assigned to different workers' rather than to one worker engaging in many tasks.[308] The capitalist subdivision of work into limited operations thus 'divides the crafts and destroys traditional occupations',[309] condemning the worker, as Marx points out, to becoming less 'attracted by the nature of his [sic] work' and 'the less, therefore, he enjoys it as something which gives play to his bodily and mental powers'.[310] Eventually, in the real subsumption of labour within more advanced forms of capitalism, the increased detailed division of labour into more fragmented tasks would, according to Braverman, decouple 'the hand and brain' of the worker,[311] or separate 'conception from execution'.[312]

In practice, then, capitalist divisions of labour tend to fragment workers' very subjectivities by rupturing the unity of their mental and manual labouring capacities, as well as dividing workers from each other and separating them from the products of their labour. Hence, the division of labour under capitalism is at the heart of Marx's concept of worker alienation. While capital's real subsumption of labour does bring workers together 'under one roof',[313] it also, contradictorily, serves to *separate* workers from each other by increasing worker competition, degrading workers by engaging them in monotonous and detailed work, and, ultimately, decomposing class unity.[314] This is why, for Bayat, 'the detailed division of labour' is nothing less than 'the antithesis of workers' control'.[315] Ultimately, the detailed divisions of labour under capitalist production regimes – closely aligned with the pursuit of relative surplus-value via mechanisation, or, in more contemporary industrial relations language, 'rationalisation drives' – is essentially about increasing profits by cheapening

---

308   Braverman 1974, p. 77.

309   Bayat 1991, p. 181.

310   Marx 1967, p. 178.

311   Braverman 1974, p. 126.

312   Braverman 1974, p. 114. While this separation of conception from execution is key to Braverman's analysis of the capitalist labour process, the totalising nature of Braverman's conclusions is what Burawoy explicitly argues against in his more nuanced assessment of the labour process under capitalist production regimes and the role of workers' consent (rather than Braverman's overtheorising of control) in its enablement (see, for instance, Burawoy 1985).

313   Marx 1967, p. 473.

314   Writes Braverman: 'The ideal towards which capitalism strives is the domination of dead labor over living labour ... by the incessant drive to enlarge and perfect machinery on the one hand, and diminish the worker on the other' (Braverman 1974, pp. 227–8).

315   Bayat 1991, p. 181.

the cost of labour for the capitalist.[316] '[T]he splitting up of handicrafts', Marx writes, 'lowers the cost of forming the workman [sic], and thereby lowers his value'.[317] Again, contrary to Braverman's overarching focus on control, however, the real drive to cheapen labour's value is to maximise profits. If profits can be maximised by, for example, increasing workers' participation in directing production on shop floors (and thus afford the worker some level of conceptualisation), or by instituting profit-sharing schemes like ESOPs, the capitalist will not hesitate to deploy such strategies. Exploitation, however, in these situations does not cease. The all-out pursuit of surplus-value extraction is all that matters to the astute capitalist, and self-managed work teams, post-Fordist empowerment plans, and employee share-ownership schemes can still get the capitalist there.[318]

As I will expand on historically and theoretically in the next chapter and relate specifically to ERTs in Chapter 8, one of the breakthroughs of *autogestión*, in which workers actually control the means of production *and* their own surpluses and begin to practice non-marketised forms of social wealth creation, is to open up the divisions of labour to less hierarchical and less exploitative modes of social production whereby workers' capacities, desires, and overall wellbeing are taken into account and the pace of work is controlled by workers themselves. *The transformation of the division of labour* within horizontalised and cooperative workspaces, then, is also a major recuperative moment of ERTs. While this will have contradictions, as we shall see in subsequent chapters, in ERTs that must still operate within competitive markets (in what I will term ERTs' 'dual reality'), the horizontalisation and loosening of the divisions of labour within an ERT – from within a workspace that was formerly privately owned and strictly capitalist – does nevertheless point to the emancipative possibilities and viability of workers controlling the means of production.

3.6   The Recuperation of Social Production and Social Wealth

As ERT workers begin to engage in associated and cooperative production within a democratised labour process and humanised division of labour, they also mobilise *social production for social wealth generation*. Here we come to yet another of their recuperative moments. ERT workers begin to recuperate social production for social (rather than private) wealth generation when they

---

316   Braverman 1974.
317   Marx 1967, p. 367.
318   This is, in part, where critics of self-management from the left begin their arguments, as I will touch on in Chapter 5.

repurpose portions of their surpluses for the further production and distribution of goods and services in non-commodified, non-marketised ways and for
the benefit of the wider communities they are located within.[319]

Also related to the concept of associated labour, *social production* means
both the capacity for workers *to be productive in association* and for *workers
to be able to choose how to allocate their productive capacities and final products*
free from the internal coercions of capitalist work organisation or the external
coercions of the market or the state. Social production under associated labour
begins to also allude to de-alienated forms of work. For McNally, in a close reading of Marx, the social production suggested by worker cooperatives prefigures
a new economic model under principles 'which are antithetical to the imperatives of capitalism', such as economic planning with 'social foresight' and
under the rubric of 'associated' rather than 'waged' labour. Moreover, *associated* social production, unlike working under the confines of the wage contract
and capital–labour relations, is driven by and 'necessitates [directly] democratic control' by the direct producers, while also requiring 'the involvement
of the [direct] producers in determining how their labour will contribute to
the satisfaction of freely determined social needs ... through conscious interac-
tion among the producers themselves' rather than 'through interactions among
things'.[320] When ERTs create and distribute social wealth in collaborative and
non-market mediated ways via their engagements in community development
work, as I will show in Chapter 8, this social production begins to take on
characteristics of social and solidarity economies that prefigure alternatives to
capital-mediated economic arrangements.

4 Cooperative Self-Determination, Recuperation, and Argentina's ERTs: Looking Forward

Ultimately, for modern socialist thought, the freedom for workers' self-determination and self-development rests in securing the socialisation of the economic realm via cooperation and association by freely (that is, voluntarily)
associated labour – both for meeting the realm of necessity *and* moving beyond it. As I will further clarify in Chapter 5, this is part of the historical and
conceptual DNA of Argentina's ERTs and other experiments with *autogestión*
and social and solidarity economies. As I argue throughout this book, I contend

---

319 See Chapters 1 and 8.
320 McNally 1993, pp. 186–7. Ibid. On the 'social product', see Marx 1967, p. 78. On 'social pro-
      duction', see Marx 1967, p. 329; and Marx 1978a, pp. 517–18.

that ERTs prefigure the self-determining society – in their workers' practices of taking over the proprietary firms that formerly employed them; in converting these firms into cooperatives; in their loosening of the intensity of work and democratising the labour process; in their overall concern for the wellbeing of all members of the ERT and surrounding communities; and in the forms of associated labour and solidarity economies they begin to practice.

As we shall also see in subsequent chapters, evidence from Argentina's ERTs can contest arguments that worker cooperatives are heavily challenged – and ultimately failures – on the path beyond capitalist societies, an argument from the left put forward, for example, by Bayat.[321] ERTs, I will instead argue, underscore Marx's more nuanced perspective for cooperatively associated labour; for Marx, workers organising production along cooperative lines, while able to effectively operate within capitalist markets (as collective capitalists), also begin to point forward to *new* 'material conditions of production' via the 'cooperative property of the workers themselves'.[322] As the experiences of ERT protagonists will continue to teach us in Chapters 6–8 (already alluded to in the case studies in Chapter 1), the struggle for the self-determination of workers' own lives rests with the struggle to *recuperate* – that is, *recover* and *take back control of* – their productive capacities and outcomes.[323] It depends on workers securing the 'possession in common'[324] of *their* labour-power, of *their* labour process, of *their* means of production, of the products of *their* labour, *their* surpluses, *their* labour-time, *their* free time, *their* skills, *their* cooperation and work in association ... in sum, of *their* living labour.

The social possibilities that open up for ERT workers, then, through their resistances, technological reshapings and re-appropriations, and sheer inventiveness when taking over the firms that had once employed them and when they collaboratively forge their projects of *autogestión*, create for them potential paths where new economic and productive relations can unfold. These social possibilities, I argue in this book, are encompassed in ERTs' recuperative moments, radical social innovations, and the moral economy of work of their worker-protagonists. I will continue to work out these themes throughout the rest of the book and return to them explicitly in Chapter 9.

From socialist, historical materialist, and critical theoretical perspectives, this chapter has, most fundamentally, sought to lay the theoretical and histor-

---

321   Bayat 1991, pp. 154–6. For a more nuanced critical perspective from the left, see Horvat 1982, pp. 457–61.
322   Marx 1978b, pp. 531–2.
323   See Chapter 9 for concluding definitions of 'recuperate' and 'recuperation'.
324   Marx 1967, p. 357.

ical groundwork that I rely on in the rest of the book in order to: (1) understand the implications of ERT workers' processes of taking over their former capitalist places of work; (2) better grasp their continued challenges; and (3) come to know more deeply the radical social innovations they forge and the recuperations they unleash. The next chapter connects with this one in that it historicises and theorises where ERTs fit into the broader and historical struggles of workers against capital and, in particular, in their periodic struggles for more autonomy at work and for control of their workplaces through the values and practices of *autogestión*, the very concept used by ERT workers themselves to self-define their recuperated and cooperativised workplaces and their community development projects. In the next chapter, then, I work towards developing a theoretical and historical genealogy of *autogestión*. There I will also work through and define key terms that fall under the umbrella concept of *autogestión*, such as workers' control, workers' participation, workplace democracy, cooperation, worker cooperatives, horizontalism, and the social and solidarity economy.

CHAPTER 5

A Genealogy of *Autogestión*

> [*A*]*utogestión* ... is a moment in a process of struggle, a process that is not determined mechanically nor blindly, nor is it wholly economistic. Rather, it is open to uncertainty and the dialectic of chance and necessity as internal components of the totality in conflict ... *Autogestión* signifies the conscious capacity of the self-organised to not only administer their present but also, above all, to prepare to navigate the waves of possibilities and uncertainties, of present and future dangers ... Self-determination [in *autogestión*] thus appears as a litmus test that sooner or later must be confronted by those individuals or collectives that rise to their emancipation.
>
> IÑAKI GIL DE SAN VICENTE[1]

∴

ERT workers themselves use the concept of *autogestión* in their discourses and everyday conversations to describe the collective struggles that led them to re-appropriate their workplaces and their projects of remaking them as cooperatives. Javier De Pascuale, former president and one of the founders of the city of Córdoba newspaper ERT *Comercio y Justicia*, concisely introduced the concept to us in the first pages of this book. While not all ERT workers articulate the concept at the theoretical level that De Pascuale did for us, my interviews and conversations with them show that they intuitively know through praxis the broader implications and possibilities *autogestión* encapsulates for both their own lives and the future of workers in Argentina and elsewhere. Some ERT workers, such as De Pascuale, use the concept to articulate succinctly to each other and those outside of the ERT movement how the (re)invention and (re)construction of their labour processes and their social relations of production can take place under more humane values than those offered by the capitalist system of work organisation that so uncaringly left them behind. Continuing to ground ERTs in a longer history of workers' self-determination

---

1 Gil de San Vicente 2013, pp. 3, 132 (*Cooperativismo obrero, consejismo y autogestión socialista*).

that I began in Chapter 4, this chapter traces out in more detail one possible genealogy of the concept of *autogestión*.[2]

1   Section 1: *Autogestión* and the Self-Determination of Productive
        Life

The Spanish word *autogestión*[3] has a Greek and Latin etymology. The word *auto* comes from the Greek '*autós* (self, same)', while *gestión* comes from the Latin '*gestio* (managing)', which in turn comes from '*gerere* (to bear, carry, manage)'.[4] More evocatively and literally, one can conceptualise *autogestión* as 'self-gestation' – to self-create, self-control, and self-provision; in other words, to be *self-reliant* and *self-determining*. Tellingly, the English words 'gestate' and 'gestation' evolved from the word *gestión*. Taken together, *auto-gestión* alludes to a processual movement of self-creation, self-conception, and self-definition, and is pregnant with socio-political relevance in its implicit notion of *potentiality* – an evolution into something other than what one is in the now. Here, there are deep connections with the proposals for the self-determination of working lives that, as I argued in Chapter 4, cuts across modern socialist thought. When practised by a collective of people living in capitalist economic conjunctures, *autogestión* points – prefiguratively – to a future possibility of becoming something other than waged-workers relegated to spending life producing for others within the capital–labour relation. Together, the words *auto* and *gestión* yield the perhaps inadequate English term 'self-management'.

Michael Lebowitz, in his capacity as one-time advisor to the Venezuelan government of former president Hugo Chávez, has called for a re-assessment of the English term 'self-management' specifically because of the over-determining focus on the individual in the term 'self'. In contrast specifically to the Yugoslavian model of self-management,[5] Lebowitz instead proposes the concept

---

2   For this chapter, a 'genealogical approach' looks for historical moments and conjunctures and the theoretical threads that trace a *possible path* for the emergence of *autogestión* without trying to find *the* 'authoritative' history of its 'origins' (Day 2004, p. 720; see also Burawoy 2000).

3   In French, *autogestion*; in Portuguese, *autogestão*; in Italian, *autogestione*.

4   Farmer 1979, p. 59.

5   It has been well documented, as Lebowitz points out, that workers in the Yugoslavian model of self-management, in which workers controlled workplaces under state ownership, in practical daily matters of production and consumption tended to look out 'primarily for ... their own ... and their collective self-interest' in the factory, downplaying the social implications of their firms (Lebowitz 2005, par. 13; see also Flaherty 1992).

used in Chávez's Bolivarian Venezuela: *cogestión* (co-management).[6] In Bolivarian Venezuela's extensive and historically new cooperative and social enterprise movements,[7] *cogestión* considers, according to Lebowitz, 'a sense of solidarity' between the firm and 'society as a whole'.[8] In particular, *cogestión* highlights '[t]he development of worker decision-making, the process of combining thinking and doing', and suggests the possibility for workers and society at large to develop 'their capacities and potential' for provisioning for the realm of necessity *and* the realms of individual and collective self-development.[9] What Lebowitz has in mind here for *cogestión* is a form of social production in a 'partnership between workers as producers and society'.[10] Furthermore, in contrast to the self-interested motivations and dictates of capitalist production, *cogestión* is centred on collective autonomy from capital in order to 'change the purpose of productive activity' itself into more community-centred and social economic production.[11] In the case of Bolivarian Venezuela, the concept of *cogestión* also includes state-ownership of enterprises with workers' control of production, wherein the state serves as steward of society's interests via 'social property'. In Bolivarian Venezuela, *cogestión*, specifically under the auspices of the Ministerio del Poder Popular para las Comunas y los Movimientos Sociales (Ministery of Popular Power for the Communes and Social Movements, originally the Ministry of Popular Economy), which oversees the country's cooperatives and its *unidades de producción socialista* (socialist production enterprises),[12] is positioned conceptually within 'the elementary triangle of socialism': social ownership of production, social production organised by workers, and production for social needs.[13] The triangle of socialism, at the same time, is contrasted specifically to capitalism's triangle of private property, exploitation, and for-profit production.[14]

---

6   Lebowitz 2005, par. 14.
7   As Larrabure, Vieta, and Schugurensky (2011) report, after Chávez's assumption of power in 1999 there was a substantive expansion of Venezuela's cooperative movement, from 877 cooperatives in 1998 to 158,917 by 2006. Encouraged by the 2001 Special Law of Cooperative Associations and the Vuelvan Caras cooperative development programme, the cooperative sector in Venezuela was by the early 2010s the largest in Latin America and one of the largest sectors in the world (see also Azzellini 2011, 2016; and Piñeiro Harnecker 2013).
8   Lebowitz 2005, par. 15.
9   Lebowitz 2005, par. 10.
10   Lebowitz 2005, par. 27.
11   Lebowitz 2005, par. 14.
12   Larrabure, Vieta, and Schugurensky 2011.
13   Lebowitz 2005, par. 3.
14   Ibid. See also Azzellini 2011, 2016; and Larrabure et al. 2011.

But while the term *cogestión* has taken on conceptual importance in Venezuela's Bolivarian project of the popular economy, the term *self-management* remains the principal English translation for *autogestión*. For lack of a better English term, perhaps, workers' control theorists, unlike Lebowitz, have tended to take broader views of the term self-management. Most radical definitions of self-management in English de-emphasise the individualist connotations and assume, when using the term, a social or collective project akin to Lebowitz's definition of co-management. Hans Seibel and Ukandi Damachi, for example, view self-management as a concept that, in practice, predates the modern era and encapsulates all forms of collective control of the economic sphere in contrast to its private ownership and that is imbued with values analogous to Kropotkin's notion of mutual aid. In the context of (re)structuring contemporary economic organisations, they specifically define self-management 'as a system designed to utilise fully the potential of every individual participating in an organization'.[15]

Asef Bayat takes an even broader approach in defining self-management. Also inspired to move beyond how it was actually practised in Yugoslavia, for Bayat the term embraces the collective management of society as a whole, referring 'to the democratic control of the economy and society by the working people'.[16] Because of its close connection to the Yugoslavian model, however, Bayat has preferred to subsume the term self-management within what he views to be the more specific concepts of *workers' participation* and *workers' control*. For Bayat, *workers' participation* is the umbrella concept, delineating the broad spectrum of participation workers may take on within a firm. This participation spectrum spans from, on one end, nominal participation schemes such as a feedback box, to sharing in the running of the firm with management, all the way to, on the other end of the spectrum, the running of the firm entirely by workers either in a nationalised co-management model (as is currently proposed in Venezuela), or even to the co-ownership and co-administration of the firm between workers within a capitalist market system (as with most worker cooperatives) or within a socialist system. *Workers' control*, in turn, signifies for Bayat 'a general organization of *work* within an individual enterprise ... or a sector of the economy in which employees exert a certain degree of control over the labour process'.[17] Thus, for Bayat, '"workers' participation" [denotes] the general problematic of the participation of the

---

15   Seibel and Damachi 1982, p. 235.
16   Bayat 1991, pp. 13.
17   Bayat 1991, p. 13 (emphasis in original).

workers in decision-making within enterprises', including 'arrangements with various degree of power conferred upon workers, such as self-management, workers' control, co-determination or job-enrichment'.[18] In turn, 'by "workers' control"' he means to account for an instance of workers' participation whereby workers take 'control ... over the process ... and ... administration of production'.[19]

Seibel and Damachi's and Bayat's conceptualisations of self-management and Bayat's further definitions of workers' participation and workers' control, however, while broad and aiming to be inclusive, remain potentially vague politically. Indeed, the possibilities for workers' involvement in production encapsulated by these broad definitions, as I will show in the following pages, are equally amenable to post-Fordist neo-liberal management schemes of 'job enrichment', 'quality circles', or 'autonomous work teams' (such as in the Toyota production model) or to more radicalised forms of economic organisation that outwardly shun most aspects of capitalist work regimes and the notion of wage-labour, such as with anarchist communes, contemporary autonomous social centres, and many eco-villages and intentional communities.

Defining the socio-political dimension of self-management, workers' control, or workers' participation thus remains in tension in the literature and has been long debated in conceptualising what exactly the terms entail for workers and society or how radical and socially transformative their practices might be.[20] First, do workers actually *control* the labour process, and, if so, how? This is a question of *management* and is related to who manages the actual producers (workers themselves or administrators?), and to how this management is organised (horizontally or vertically?). Second, do workers themselves *own* the means of production? This is a question of *property relations* related to rights over assets and the dispersal of earnings, and to whether ownership remains private (for instance, in a sole-proprietorship or a partnership of entrepreneurs, or shared between private investors, or between workers and private investors or entrepreneurs) or becomes collective (for instance, shared amongst workers themselves, or even between workers and the community or workers and the state). Both questions also force us to further ask, as Paul Bernstein has suggested, *to what degree* and *at what level of the firm* do workers participate in and decide organisational and production issues, such as what is to be worked on, when the work is to take place, how much work is to be done, how the labour

---

18   Bayat 1991, pp. 13–14.
19   Bayat 1991, p. 14.
20   Bernstein 2012; Rothschild-Whitt 1979.

process and the division of labour is to be arranged, and so on?[21] When workers' control and self-management are questions of how much *participation* workers have in *managing* the firm while the means of production continues to be owned by private investors or the state, their conceptualisations tend to fall within the liberal democratic or state socialist camps. Here, in other words, the degree to which workers can self- or co-manage their work extends only to issues concerning the degree of participation they have been allowed or afforded by the owners of the means of production. Moreover, within liberal democratic perspectives, workers' control and self-management are usually considered and constituted within a broader capitalist system of private property and free markets rather than as an alternative economic system. When, on the other hand, workers' control and self-management are also considered as issues of workers' *ownership* of the means of production, private property relations are directly addressed while the direct or indirect management of the means of production by workers themselves is assumed. This latter scenario is the usual case with those that advocate for an expansion of worker cooperatives and even in state-socialist models of co-management that, as in Bolivarian Venezuela and socialist Yugoslavia, at least theoretically consider productive entities as 'social property'.[22]

Workers' control and self-management in this latter model, however, as we shall soon see, encounter further problems and tensions when workers co-own and co-manage the means of production yet still produce for competitive capitalist markets. Here, as Marx already foresaw, workers' cooperatively managing enterprises in order to produce commodities for markets risk becoming 'their own capitalist'[23] engaging in self-exploitative work practices readily accommodative to capitalist production. This position, regularly taken up by leftist critics of workers' control and self-management, was bolstered by influential Marxist critiques, such as Rosa Luxemburg's critical stance regarding the stunted role of worker cooperatives as working-class revolutionary organisations,[24] or Amadeo Bordiga's contention that '[s]ocialism resides entirely in the revolutionary negation of the enterprise, not in granting the enterprise to the factory workers'.[25] This position was also influenced by Beatrice Potter's negative assessments of workers' ultimate capacities to self-manage their cooperative

---

21   Bernstein 2012.
22   Horvat 1982; Lebowitz 2005.
23   Marx 1981, p. 571.
24   Luxemburg 2006.
25   Bordiga, in Thoburn 2003, p. 110.

workplaces in her analysis of the UK cooperative movement of the nineteenth and early twentieth centuries.[26]

Extending Luxemburg's and Bordiga's critiques, some libertarian Marxist theorists writing in the aftermath of 1968 disparage the role of workers' self-management of enterprises for their reformist tendencies, falling far short, these libertarian Marxists argue, in their revolutionary potential for abolishing the capitalist system of production.[27] From Mario Tronti's perspective of *operaismo*, as Nicholas Thoburn has succinctly summarised, workers' self-management within an extant capitalist system at best merely upholds the 'socialist affirmation of work' while not recognising that it is work itself, as 'always already capital', that must be overcome for a more profound revolutionary transformation.[28] The collective of contributors to the journal *Négation* arrive at similar conclusions in their critical assessment of the French worker-recuperated LIP watch factory that had emerged in 1973 with much fanfare from the post '68 radical left.[29] For critical libertarian Marxists, workers' self-management as the 'other' of capitalism borders on an impossibility because all labour in a system that privileges work without negating it 'equals exploitation' and 'embodies the class relation' predicated by the capitalist labour process.[30] In addition, workers' self-management of the production of commodities that will ultimately be sold in competitive markets is still the 'management' of labour and leads to workers' self-exploitation as collective capitalists.[31] For these critics of workers' self-management, real freedom towards self-determination and self-actualisation rests with the 'refusal of work', including 'exodus' from the compulsion to work and the presumably puritan notion that any 'dignity' might reside in work.[32] The specifics of the alternative economic arrangements that would still need to undergird a system rooted in the refusal of work, however, remain vague in contemporary libertarian and autonomist Marxist thought.[33]

---

26   Potter 1904. For a review of these early socialist critiques of cooperatives, see Hudis 2012, pp. 177–81; Marcuse 2015; Ratner 2015; and Sandoval 2016.
27   See, for instance, Négation 1975.
28   Tronti, in Thoburn 2003, p. 109. Also see Tronti 2007.
29   Négation, in Thoburn 2003, p. 110.
30   Tronti, in Thoburn 2003, pp. 110, 111.
31   On these themes, see also Chapter 4 and McNally 1993.
32   See, for instance, Negri 1988, 2005; and Weeks 2005, 2011.
33   It deserves to be pointed out here, if only in passing, that libertarian socialists such as autonomist Marxists and social anarchists decidedly agree on what a liberational self-management is *not*. As I will review shortly, the adoption of workplace participation schemes by *laissez faire* human resource management (HRM) programmes with roots in

While recognising these cautions, I do not espouse these radical-left critics' *tout court* dismissal of workers' self-management, which are rooted in the
argument that these experiments exalt the notion of work and are thus 'not
revolutionary enough'. Instead, as I argue, while worker-led experiments with
autogestión such as Argentina's ERTs face many challenges on the path to full
autonomy from capital; while they must be pragmatic at times in how they
engage with the state, markets, and other institutions of capital; and even
though their radical social innovations might be still incomplete, they nevertheless continue to prefigure in many ways a world beyond capital for the
reasons I theorised in Chapter 4 and that I will further elaborate on in Part 3 of
the book.[34] As Marx also foresaw, and as I assessed in Chapter 4, socially owned
and co-managed workers' associations and cooperatives do point to the possibility for another form of production without the need for supervisors or private
owners. Moreover, they already in many ways practice, despite the continued
existence of the capitalist system, a new form of 'labour commons' rooted in
associated labour, social production, and the creation of non-marketised forms
of social wealth, as de Peuter and Dyer-Witheford proposed for us in Chapter 4.
Such is also the case with Argentina's ERTs, as I will argue in later chapters, and
why I view them as prefigurative of an alternative to capitalist or state-socialist
production models and as key way-stations on the path beyond capitalism.

To think more praxically, then, both control (management) *and* ownership
(property relations) of the means of production must be taken into account
when considering both the conjunctural characteristics of a particular form
of workers' control or self-management model and when contemplating their
prefigurative possibilities for another, non-capitalist mode of work organisation. I am convinced that *autogestión*, as it has been historically conceptualised and as currently practised by many Argentine ERTs and other Latin
American social movements, is a term that takes into account – implicitly and
at times explicitly – both of these issues for envisaging a radical alternative
organisational and economic project. That is, the contemporary Latin American concept of *autogestión* considers, at once, the actual control that workers
can possess in the labour process *and* the extent to which workers can collect-

---

the Human Relations School (HRS) of the 1930s, for instance, underscore the criticisms
levelled at self-management by some on the radical libertarian left.

34   For a similar argument, see Hudis 2012. As will be made evident in later chapters of this
book, many of the continued challenges faced by Argentina's ERTs can be accounted for
due to both the market realities they must still operate within and the various political
and state-based barriers that block their full flourishing. These challenges do not, however,
counter their prefigurative potential.

ively co-own and guide the means of production and the broader economic system.[35] In its application by those that define their projects as one of *autogestión* – again, as with the protagonists of Argentina's ERTs and other contemporary social movements in Argentina and throughout Latin America – or in its conceptualisations by scholars on the left who view it favourably and who have theorised its prefigurative potential, the term has been applied in a much more radical way than merely *workers' participation* in co-managing an otherwise proprietary or investor-owned capitalist firm. These more radical and prefigurative notions recognise that *autogestión* already always taps into the desires of workers to more fully self-determine their working lives, as witnessed in moments of the history of the worker cooperative movement or in the positive ways that, as I discussed in Chapter 4 and as I will discuss further shortly, socialist theorists such as Antonio Gramsci, Anton Pannekoek, Michael Bakunin, Peter Kropotkin, and Marx himself viewed workers' organisations such as cooperatives or factory councils. After all, the concept of *autogestión* emerges from the actual collective practices of working people and is deeply ensconced in their historical desires for freedom from exploitation and for self-actualisation.

1.1   *Theorising* Autogestión

While this book argues that today's ERTs are a new outlet for working-class struggle that directly responds to the particular dynamics of the neo-liberal model in the lives of working people, ERTs undeniably also form part of the long-tradition of workers' collective struggles for more control of their socio-economic lives. As I argued in Chapter 4, and as Brazilian social theorists Mauricio Sardá de Faria and Henrique Novaes also remind us, workers' experiments in *autogestión* have emerged from time to time over the past two centuries of global capitalism,

> either in the context of revolutionary outbreak or in the intensification of class conflict ... bringing together the two sides of the associative principle: resistance and the production of the means of life.[36]

Historically, practices of *autogestión* long predate its conceptualisation.[37] The term, however, was first used widely in France in the 1950s (particularly

---

35   Arvon 1980; Lorenzo 2011; Peixoto de Albaquerque 2004.
36   Sardá de Faria and Novaes 2011, p. 401.
37   Arvon 1980. This is similar to what has been observed of the concept of the social and solidarity economy (see below).

amongst the contributors of the journal *Socialisme ou Barbarie*), and subsequently in the 1960s by social theorists in the context of the Yugoslav model as
an alternative to the capitalist and other state-socialist systems and to describe
Algeria's independence movement and the first months of the social and economic reorganisation of its post-colonial economy in 1962.[38] It would also be
used to name historical events that saw workers take on both the control and
co-ownership of economic and political life, such as during the Paris Commune
of 1871 and the communes and anarchist collectives of Catalonia and other
parts of Spain during the civil war.[39] Thereafter, the term was especially adopted by protagonists and theorists of the emergent and post '68 social movements to circumscribe their main demands and desires for a post-capitalist
society.[40] The term has had similarly radical connotations for social transformation as the turn-of-millennium Argentine social movements have adopted it.
Autogestión, then, from its first usage, has tended to have a more radical meaning than the English term self-management.

The Franco-German historian of ideas Henri Arvon,[41] for example, whose
book on self-management was translated into Spanish in 1980 as *La autogestión*
and which has been widely read by Latin American historians and theorists
of workers' control,[42] posits that the practices of and desire for *autogestión*
long predate the 1960s social movements. For him, the term parallels the ways
that more traditional communities have autonomously controlled their own
productive and social affairs. For Arvon, however, as with the related definition of the social and solidarity economy that I will engage with shortly, the
conscious demand for *autogestión* from workers, underscoring its roots in the
emergence of the stream of self-determination, only arises with the formal
subsumption of labour within capitalist paradigms. As traditional, more self-
determined, and locally rooted ways of economic life like the commons and
craft-based production began to disappear from Europe with the advent of
capitalism, more and more workers began to demand greater participation
in economic and productive life and indeed increasingly, as witnessed in the
rise of worker cooperatives after the 1820s, began to demand autonomy from
capital and to search for alternatives to waged work. Here we find, according to Arvon, the first modern struggles for and experiments with *autogestión*.

---

38 Bayat 1991; Brenner and Elden 2009; Hudson 2010. See also CNT–AIT n.d., p. 6.
39 Arvon 1980; Jainchill and Moyn 2004; Rosanvallon 1979.
40 Arvon 1980; Gorz 1973; Hunnius, Garson, and Case 1973; Lefebvre 2009; Rosanvallon 1979.
41 Arvon 1980.
42 See, for instance, Arango Jaramillo 2005; Hudson 2010; Iturraspe 1986; and Wyczykier
    2009b.

Arvon's conceptualisation of *autogestión*, in fact, could also be conceived using E.P. Thompson's notion of the moral economy undergirding the drive of working people and the marginalised to self-determine their own economic and social lives and retain traditional and communal ways of provisioning for life's needs in the wake of the increased encroachment of capitalism. As Argentine sociologist Gabriela Wyczykier puts it, commenting on Arvon's analysis, the struggle for *autogestión* 'reflects a permanent hope for the human being'[43] for self-determining socio-economic life. Here we see conceptual links to Bayat's and Horvat's claims for self-determination,[44] reviewed in Chapter 4. Most fundamentally, then, extending out from Arvon's notion, the desire for *autogestión* is the historical human drive and demand to be free from exploitation and to collectively determine the direction of the socio-economic spheres of life.

Together with Arvon, another French theorist who has had a role to play in theorising *autogestión* in Latin America[45] is Pierre Rosanvallon. For Rosanvallon, *autogestión* is saturated in praxis and is the umbrella concept that encapsulates the socio-economic transformation of society at large from capitalist concentration or state-capitalist centralisation to more horizontal, bottom-up, and directly democratic practices. For Rosanvallon, these practices at the local level, both in the sphere of production and beyond (and in tune with anarchist and Gramscian views of workers' democracy), can potentially radiate out onto all socio-economic institutions. While for Rosanvallon the practice is not limited to workplace or industrial democracy, certainly workplaces would need to be democratised too in an emancipated society. Before it became a demand and desire of the New Left, Rosanvallon claims, in line with Arvon, that *autogestión* had already long been a socio-economic practice[46] embodied in institutions such as cooperatives and in bottom-up workers' movements such as the 1871 Paris Commune, the early soviets of the 1905 Russian Revolution, and the Catalonian communes in 1930s revolutionary Spain. And in the practices and demands infusing the movements of '68, he underscores, in contrast to the centralist and *étatist* positions of the French Communist Party and the French CGT union central at the time, *autogestión* promised a 'socialism of liberty'. *Autogestión* has thus always been, for Rosanvallon, a prefigurative concept infused with 'promises and hopes' for a different political and economic reality.[47] Here, Rosanvallon coincides with Henri Lefebvre's socio-

---

43   Wyczykier 2009b, p. 30.
44   Bayat 1991; Horvat 1982.
45   See Arango Jaramillo 2005; Hudson 2010; Iturraspe 1986; Wyczykier 2009b.
46   Rosanvallon 1979, p. 12.
47   Ibid.

political and territorial vision for *autogestión* (similarly inspired for Lefebvre by the movements of '68) as holding potential for a withering away of the state in a grassroots-driven, decentralised, and radically socialist and democratic political and economic arrangement 'of material and intellectual production'.[48]

For Rosanvallon, however, akin to Lefebvre's measured assessment of the concept, the demands for *autogestión* after 1968 in practice turned out to be a disappointment. By the time Rosanvallon was reflecting on *autogestión* in the aftermath of the movements of '68, the concept encapsulated for him 'what could have been' rather than what *autogestión* had actually become.[49] Nevertheless, the concept continued for him to implicitly suggest what can still be. For Rosanvallon, *autogestión* is charged with five themes carrying prefigurative promise for social change, which can still unleash people's direct participation in the socio-economic and political dimensions of society. In this vein, *autogestión* is, for Rosanvallon:

(1) 'a new political idea' where power is returned to people rather than to their representatives;

(2) 'a democratic realism' where the inadequacies of representative democracy from above are put into question and solutions to them are sought from below via directly democratic means;

(3) the transformation of society, as a whole, beyond only appropriating the means of production;

(4) a 'strategy and an objective' that moves beyond the dichotomies of 'reform or revolution' and instead 'defends a political problematic of social experimentation'; and

(5) in the economic realm, 'an autonomous mode of production' without authority from above and organised via directly democratic decision-making organs.[50]

More recent conceptualisations of *autogestión*, while not discarding its potential for societal transformation advocated by Arvon, Rosanvallon, and Lefebvre post '68, tend to focus on the implications for transforming the economic realm and, more specifically, the firm as first steps to possible longer term and broader social changes. Basque social economy theorists Antxon Mendizábal and Anjel Errasti, for instance, argue that *autogestión* is a dynamic concept rooted in libertarian strands of workers' self-activity,[51] also suggesting for us its conceptual roots in the stream of self-determination. As with Lebowitz's description of

---

48 Lefebvre 2009, p. 120.
49 Rosanvallon 1979, p. 20.
50 Rosanvallon 1979, pp. 20–1.
51 Mendizábal and Errasti 2008.

the Venezuelan model of *cogestión*, Mendizábal and Errasti position *autoges-tión* on two planes, taking into account practices of 'cooperative production' at the level of the enterprise and 'social and participative democracy' at the 'territorial level'.[52] For Mendizábal and Errasti, historical experiences of *auto-gestión* within the economic realm have been about 'processes which look for the transformation of relations of production' and 'a process that articulates the different workers' collectives to be coordinated and realized within product-ive structures of cooperation and solidarity'.[53] More specifically for Mendizábal and Errasti, *autogestión* entails:

(1)   the organisational nature of productive entities as social(ised) property;
(2)   the collective and directly democratic participation in the coordination of this productive activity by workers and, ideally, by all people affected in what they term 'common solidarity';
(3)   respect for the differences and autonomy of each productive entity and the people that work therein; and
(4)   the social(ised) organisation of such a system by some sort of federated political entity that, via a recallable delegate model, configures the way production is to unfold socially.[54]

As with Arvon and Rosanvallon, Mendizábal and Errasti's model of *autogestión* shows its theoretical roots in the forms of cooperative and collective produc-tion practised in parts of revolutionary Spain in the 1930s[55] as well as resonating with anarcho-syndicalist and council communist proposals (see below). With Mendizábal and Errasti, we also begin to see links to how the concept has been taken up in Latin America throughout the 1990s and the 2000s.

Contemporary Latin American theorists of *autogestión* suggest that the term most immediately invokes the bottom-up democratisation of the economic realm at the micro-level of the productive entity, such as with worker-recuperated firms, rural producer collectives and cooperatives, family-based micro-enterprises, and neighbourhood collectives.[56] From out of these micro-economic experiments, often at least loosely federated territorially in some way, the state can be lobbied to support them and then, it is hoped, trans-formed into an entity responsive to the needs of worker-led firms and local community development. Such has been the approach taken up in Brazil in recent years, for example, with the close ties developed between the rural and

---

52   Mendizábal and Errasti 2008, p. 1.
53   Mendizábal and Errasti 2008, p. 3.
54   Ibid.
55   Broué and Témine 1962; Rama 1962.
56   Cattani 2004.

urban cooperative movements that gradually emerged after the proliferation of experiments like the landless peasant and worker movements, many of the country's unions, and the state via the National Secretary of the Solidarity Economy established by the national government of the Partido dos Trabalhadores (PT, Workers' Party) in 2004.[57] Eventually, this bottom-up approach, it is thought, could see the further proliferation of a people-centred solidarity or popular economy rooted in economic justice and participative democracy.[58] The Brazilian sociologist Paulo Peixoto de Albuquerque,[59] for instance, suggests this gradual encroachment approach to social transformation in his four-pronged definition of *autogestión*. For him, *autogestión* has:

(1)   a *social character*, where people within all social strata are engaged in the development of a new societal order grounded in self-determination and participation;

(2)   an *economic character*, where the social implications of production are taken into account and where work would be privileged over capital, as in the case of worker cooperatives;

(3)   a *political character*, where, as with Porto Alegre's participatory budgeting practices, all people affected would have a say in decision-making and collectively constructing some sort of popular power;[60] and

(4)   a *technical character*, which points to the (re)design and (re)deployment of non-exploitative and re-rationalised divisions of labour and production processes.[61]

Whereas Rosanvallon refuses to specifically centre on the economic realm and the firm when conceptualising *autogestión*, preferring to remain at the level of sociological theorisation and have the emancipated, self-managed society worked out immanently by those living it, Peixoto de Albuquerque and other contemporary Latin American theorists of *autogestión* such as José Luís Coraggio, Paul Singer, and Luiz Inácio Gaiger[62] have reversed the theorisation, working outwards from the myriad experiments of the social and solidarity economies across the region that have been responding to and moving beyond neo-liberal enclosures in recent years.

---

57   Gaiger and Dos Anjos 2013; Singer and Souza 2000.
58   Coraggio 1999, 2004; Pastore 2010; Sarria Icaza and Tiribia 2004.
59   Peixoto de Albuquerque 2004.
60   That is, in a version of 'the principle of affected interests', whereby 'people should have a say in decisions in rough proportion to the degree to which they are affected by them' (Malleson 2014, p. 205).
61   Peixoto de Albuquerque 2004, pp. 31–8 (emphasis added).
62   Coraggio 1999, 2003, 2004; Gaiger 2003; Singer 2004.

1.2   *Three Justifications for* Autogestión

The conceptualisations of *autogestión* that I have been sketching out up to now can be seen to implicitly take into account three broad considerations: (1) the *effectiveness* and *viability* (or, in other words, the *efficacy*) of associated forms of social production for provisioning for life's needs and producing social wealth; (2) the normative basis for extending economic justice in some form of *democratic organisation* of productive entities; and (3) the *collective* or *social ownership* of the means of production. These loosely parallel Bayat's contention that, on the whole, the literature's justifications for workers' participation, which includes workers' control and self-management, fall within three themes: (1) the principle of *efficiency*, with a focus on economic and productivity gains; (2) the *sociopolitical* argument, which considers 'workers' participation as a means by which democracy is extended'; and (3) *ethical-moral* appeals, whereby workers' participation is taken up with a view to 'ideas of justice and freedom'.[63] We now turn to these three justifications for *autogestión*.

1.2.1   'Efficient' Production

One common conclusion arrived at by liberal economic theorists of the firm when assessing employee participation and LMFs[64] is that, where democracy in the workplace is increased, efficiency will necessarily suffer. Another conclusion is that investors (read: capitalists) are best positioned to exercise control over firms and that 'alternative' firm arrangements, such as worker cooperatives and workers' control, arise in sub-optimal economic conditions when there are inordinate barriers to conventional entrepreneurial investment and control. And yet another conclusion, known as the 'under-capitalisation' thesis, is that members of LMFs will tend to under-invest in their firms due to their risk averseness and their incentivisation for short-term net income maximisation at the expense of reinvesting in the long-term sustainability of the firm, including taking on new members. Collectively, these factors, amongst others, have been mobilised by liberal economists to explain the relative 'rarity' of LMFs when compared to conventional, investor-owned businesses.[65] As I will also show with regard to ERTs in Chapters 7 and 8, a growing group of heterodox

---

63   Bayat 1991, pp. 24–7.
64   In this sub-section, the notion of the labor-managed firm (LMF), commonly used in the heterodox economic literature, will serve as a proxy for *autogestión* at the level of the firm.
65   See, for instance, Furubotn and Pejovich 1970, 1974; Hansmann 1988, 1996; Jensen and Meckling 1976, 1979; and Ward 1958. For critical overviews of this argument, see Dow 2003; Howard 2000; Jensen 2012; and Jossa 2015.

economists and progressive or radical researchers of LMFs has been showing that empirical evidence casts doubts on these conclusions. Rather, heterodox theorists and researchers of cooperatives and other forms of LMFs have shown that worker-managed firms can be as – if not more – efficacious, productive, and efficient as strictly capitalist firms.[66] Amongst the reasons for this, these theorists underscore, are that workers in LMFs hold deep commitments to and emotional investments in their cooperative projects, as well as foster strong ties of solidarity that are forged when worker-owners share in the responsibilities of running firms.

As I will show in subsequent chapters, these characteristics are also present in ERTs. As ERTs also teach us, under-production and inefficiencies in LMFs when in competition with conventional capitalistic firms usually arise from lack of start-up or loan capital from a financial system averse to workers' own equity (including 'labour capital'), or politically from states that do not have adequate policies for the development of cooperatives or workplace conversions to LMFs, or from a general lack of sufficient institutional supports for LMFs via start-up grants or favourable public procurement policies that could privilege these firms. On the whole, contemporary conjunctures wherein LMFs are on the rise and also benefit from adequate supports from the state (as in Québec, Italy, and, until recently, Venezuela and Brazil)[67] or from the cooperative sector and credit unions or cooperative banks (as in Italy, France, and Spain)[68] show the adequateness of the model for productivity gains, firm

---

66   See, for instance, Altman 2014; Ben-Ner and Jones 1995; Birchall and Kettilson 2009; Bonin, Jones, and Putterman 1993; Borzaga and Tortia 2007; Borzaga, Depedri, and Tortia 2009; Bowles and Gintis 1993b; Craig 1993; Dow 2003; Drèze 1976, 1993; Estrin, Jones, and Svejnar 1987; Fakhfakh, Pérotin, and Gago 2012; Howard 2000; Jensen 2011, 2012; Jones and Svejnar 1984; Jossa 2005, 2014, 2017; Kruse and Blasi 1995; Melman 1975; Münkner 1995; Novkovic and Webb 2014; Pérotin 2006, 2014; Smith and Rothbaum 2014; Sauser 2009; Vanek 1975, 1977; Zevi, Zanotti, Soulage, and Zelaia 2011. Even Marx made indirect reference to this in a footnote in the chapter on cooperation in *Capital* Volume I, suggesting that such views, common in his time (especially the democracy-productivity dichotomy), were actually about justifying liberal political economy's ideological standpoints on private property, free markets, and competition. 'That Philistine paper, the *Spectator*[,]' writes Marx, 'finds that the main defect in the Rochdale cooperative experiments is this: "They showed that associations of workmen could manage shops, mills, and almost all forms of industry with success, and they immediately improved the condition of the men but then they did not leave a clear place for masters." *Quelle horreur!*' (Marx 1967, p. 331).

67   Bowman and Stone 2006; Coté 2007; Gaiger and Dos Anjos 2013; Piñeiro Harnecker 2007. See also Chapter 2.

68   Corcoran and Wilson 2010; Vieta, Depedri, and Carrano 2017; Zevi et al. 2011. See also Chapter 2.

longevity, and workers' perceptions of wellbeing.[69] The flip side to this is evid-
enced in the challenges that Argentina's ERTs face in light of inadequate state
supports and the preponderance of competitive markets. However, despite
Argentina's ERTs' multiple challenges – as the case studies in Chapter 1 underscored, and as I will assess in depth in Chapters 6 and 7 – their longevity and
workers' overwhelming successes at restarting production of formerly depleted
firms in the country over the past two decades bears additional witness to
the efficacy of solidary-based, worker-led production and cooperative organisation.

Moreover, radical theorists and economists sensitive to the LMF contend
that labour-managed production is 'tantamount to the liberation and thus
advancement of the productive forces, wealth and prosperity'.[70] In this vein,
Mike Cooley,[71] for instance, has argued that, at minimum, workers' participation in the running of firms is better than top-down control by managers
for improving or stimulating productivity because it brings workers into the
decision-making and labour process as active agents of change. According to
Cooley, by relying on the strength of workers' initiatives, workers' participation mobilises their knowledge in the intricacies of production in their areas
of specialty. Here, Cooley's position is similar to Braverman's and Burawoy's
calls to re-unite workers' capacities for conceptualisation with their capacities
for execution.[72] In his book, *Architect or Bee? The Human/Technology Relationship*,[73] Cooley uses the case of Lucas Aerospace in the United Kingdom in the
1970s as an example of the efficacy of workers' participation. The Lucas Corporate Plan, as it was called, was an experiment in workers' management of
the firm and for developing worker-led and community-centred innovations
of new 'socially useful' products, in part as a solution to the threat of massive
layoffs at the firm. Through a joint worker–union council called the Combined Shop Stewards' Committee, the incorporation of the Lucas Aerospace
Company's skilled and semi-skilled workers into the management, decision-
making, and product proposal and design areas of the company for a brief
time was, by all accounts, a success.[74] Cooley shows how the Lucas Aerospace
workers immediately began to deploy their skills and knowledge for propos-

69   Ben-Ner 1984, 1988; Becchetti, Castriota, and Depedri 2010; Borzaga, Depedri, and Tortia
      2010; Erdal 2011, 2012; Pérotin 2006, 2014; Vieta et al. 2017.
70   Bayat 1991, p. 25.
71   Cooley 1980.
72   Braverman 1974; Burawoy 1985.
73   Cooley 1980.
74   Bayat 1991; Cooley 1980; Noble 1984.

ing and producing new, technologically sophisticated products in collaboration with the communities (rather than markets) that would benefit most from such technologies. Through worker innovation and community collaboration, Lucas went from producing jet turbines to co-inventing and producing energy-saving domestic products, medical machines, and versatile power generation devices. The relative success of the Lucas Plan inspired other experiments in 'socially useful production' such as the Greater London Enterprise Board and the London Innovation Network under the political leadership of then-London councillor Ken Livingstone. All were, however, perhaps too successful for the capitalist system to bear, eventually being shut down by the Thatcher government by 1985.[75]

More liberal theorists of workers' participation that hold on to the capitalist system and free markets have also recognised since at least the 1930s the efficaciousness of workers' participation for increasing productivity and profits. Scholars from within the human relations school (HRS), the human resource management (HRM) tradition, and industrial relations, for instance, have considered and advocated for workers' participation as responses to the resistances by workers to Taylorism and scientific management, for improving workers' motivation, and for actually increasing productivity.[76] Moreover, proponents of HRM have recognised the efficaciousness of aspects of workers' participation for appeasing unions' demands for 'healthier', more 'participative', and more 'open' workplaces. Here, of course, the ends are not about deploying workers' participation in order to give workers more autonomy *per se* or for ethical reasons that aim to lessen exploitation and alienation in the workplace. Rather, these relatively recent strategies taken up in otherwise capitalist workplace are about increasing productivity via a more limited employee autonomy and self-direction in order to tap into workers' expansive capacities to cooperate and find creative solutions to production issues. Far short of reducing exploitation in the workplace, of course, these reactionary workers' participation and self-management schemes have generally succeeded in investing workers more and more into the broader capitalist system and the workplaces that employ them and, thus, paradoxically, have served to extract more relative surplus-value from them while lessening the costly application and need of direct supervision.[77] These workers' participation schemes have also ultimately served, in the hands

---

75 For an historical assessment of the Lucas Plan, see also Bayat, 1991, pp. 198–9.
76 Bayat 1991; Bratton et al. 2004; Grint 2005.
77 Bratton, Helms Mills, Pyrch, and Sawchuk 2004; Burawoy 1985; Rinehart, Huxley, and Robertson 1997; Shukaitis 2010.

of savvy capitalists, to cheapen the cost of variable capital in a way that Marx perhaps could not have foreseen.

By the late 1960s and early 1970s, HRM and other industrial relations programmes started to actively research and assist in deploying forms of workers' participation as 'a modernizing form of industrial democracy ... in which administrative councils of workers, technicians, and managers engage in cooperative decision-making, over-seeing [more and more] aspects of industrial life'.[78] Called 'responsible autonomy' by Andrew Friedman,[79] recent historical examples of this strategy that come to mind include experiences with self-managed work teams in industrial settings (such as Toyota's *kaizen* system), total quality management (TQM), quality work circles, humanised work, 'new public management' (NPM) programmes in the public sector, flexible work schedules, working from home, and European co-determination plans and 'works councils' whereby workers co-determine production with managers and are afforded limited seats on boards of companies.

Since the 1970s, these initiatives have been, on the one hand, responses by capital to pressures from below emerging from workers and unions demanding greater autonomy, more control of production, better working conditions, and more fulfilling work. They have become relatively new ways for capital to re-subsume labour into emerging post-Fordist production regimes since the profit squeeze and energy crises of the early 1970s.[80] On the other hand, they point to workers' capacities to innovate and care for the production of socially useful products without the need for managerial control, which was perhaps an unintended consequence of the participation schemes of HRM and industrial relations. This is a tension – part of *autogestión*'s 'dual reality', as I will argue in Chapters 7 and 8 – that perhaps all self-managed work projects and LMFs that still operate within capitalist markets must contend with, ERTs being no exception. These capitalist adaptations to and co-optations of workers' participation and self-management schemes and the overall tensions with broader practices of *autogestión* existing within contemporary capitalist economic conjunctures are issues that will re-emerge in varying ways in the case of Argentina's ERTs when we return to our empirical analysis in Part 3.

1.2.2 Democratising Workplaces

Social, political, and economic theorists who support workers' control and self-management and who ground their arguments in normative theories of par-

---

78 *New Republic*, in Farmer 1979, p. 59.
79 Friedman 1977.
80 Boltanski and Chiapello 2005; Harvey 2005.

ticipatory democracy and economic justice have advocated for *more workers' participation in production*, and some for the *democratisation of the workplace* on a broader level.

Heterodox economists, such as Bruno Jossa, Samuel Bowles, and Herbert Gintis, and political and social theorists such as Robert Dahl, Tom Malleson, Ronald Mason, Carole Pateman, David Schweickart, and Michael Walzer,[81] have justified workers' control and self-management by treating the workplace as an extension of the political sphere that demands less authoritarianism and more participation and democracy. The workplace, for these theorists, resembles something akin to the state, or is, at minimum, an integral part of society.[82] Because the workplace in contemporary social and liberal democracies, for these theorists, remains one of the last bastions of autocratic rule, they advocate for the need to increase democracy at work by extending into the factory, the shop floor, and the office representative democratic forms[83] or more participative forms of democracy struggled for in society at large.[84] 'If democracy is justified in governing the state', writes Dahl, 'then it is justified in governing economic enterprises'.[85] Walzer goes a step further, specifically calling for disassociating the 'authoritarian command' of productive activity framing the private firm from property ownership by arguing that the nature of the activity of production within firms, as 'common enterprises', needs workers to be included in their democratic stewardship.[86] Moreover, participative justice in the workplace would not only encourage broader economic or industrial democracy reforms, but would help to further extend democratic consciousness and practices out to civil society and everyday life, as Pateman has forcefully reasoned.[87] Theorists who argue along these lines ultimately contend that decreasing exploitation and exclusion in the workplace and increasing participation in society begins by increasing democracy and inclusion in the workplace and, ultimately, eliminating 'industrial authoritarianism'.[88]

Mason and Pateman have specifically argued that the nature of democracy within the workplace should be participative rather than representative.[89]

---

81   Bowles and Gintis 1993a, 1993b; Dahl 1985; Jossa 2005, 2014, 2016, 2017; Malleson 2014; Mason 1982; Pateman 1970; Schweickart 1996, 2011; Walzer 1983.
82   Dahl 1985; Malleson 2014.
83   Walzer 1983.
84   Malleson 2014; Pateman 1970.
85   Dahl 1985, p. 135.
86   Walzer 1983, p. 298.
87   Pateman 1970.
88   Jones and Seabrook 1969, p. 29.
89   Mason 1982; Pateman 1970.

Mason defines the participative democracy that should be incorporated into firms as 'community rule in which the process of decision-making generally entails widespread and effective participation of community members'.[90] For both Mason and Pateman, moreover, more participation in the workplace converts the latter into learning spaces for more participation in the greater polity. Drawing from the work of J.-J. Rousseau, J.S. Mill, and G.D.H. Cole, Pateman contends that 'participation [in all levels of society, including the workplace] develops and fosters the very qualities necessary for it; the more individuals participate the better able they become to do so'.[91] Gregory Dow summarises these greater hopes for participative democracy in the workplace when he writes that 'Pateman and Mason agree that participation [at work] is good because it creates a better kind of human being ... [and that] ... these benefits go beyond the acquisition of democratic skills, and extend to attitudinal changes'.[92] As I review in Chapter 8, evidence from my own empirical work on the attitudinal and practical changes that ERT workers undergo, the connections between their participation in the ERT and their personal and collective transformations into cooperators and into individuals more sensitive to the plight of their surrounding communities coincides with Mason and Pateman's assertions.[93]

In Argentina, notions of directly democratic participation in alternative economic endeavours in the social movements that emerged at the end of the 1990s and that surged especially during and immediately after the 2001–2 crisis have tended to go hand-in-hand with the strong view of participative workplace democracy, particularly resonating in how *autogestión* has been conceived of and practised in recent years.[94] In many of Argentina's alternative social and solidarity economy projects and movements, such as ERTs, community-driven economic and social initiatives, neighbourhood assemblies, human rights groups, associations of *cartoneros*, and the *piquetero* movement of the 1990s and early 2000s, the concept and practices of *horizontalidad* (horizontalism) as a more just way of organising productive life has streamed through their practices of *autogestión*.[95] *Horizontalidad* is a concept that has historical roots in the practices of European and Latin American anarchist

90   Mason, in Dow 2003, p. 30.
91   Pateman 1970, p. 42.
92   Dow 2003, p. 31.
93   See also Larrabure, Vieta, and Schugurensky 2013; Vieta 2014a, 2014b; and Vieta, Larrabure, and Schugurensky 2012.
94   Sitrin 2006, 2012; Zibechi 2012.
95   Almeyra 2004; Sitrin 2006, 2012; Svampa and Pereyra 2004.

and autonomist collectives and in Latin American Indigenous groups. Over the past three or so decades, *horizontalidad* has been explicitly taken up and practised by numerous contemporary Latin American groups engaging in solidarity economics and bottom-up community development emerging around social justice issues, such as the Zapatistas, the Brazilian participatory budgeting movement, Brazil's landless workers' and peasants' movements, and also in many aspects of Argentina's ERT phenomenon.[96] Most prominently, *horizontalidad* espouses an egalitarian (re)distribution of economic *and* political power. More specifically, it is both a theory and a practice, immanently mapping out within the realm of the everyday – rather than in a predetermined way 'from above' – how the ongoing participation of all individuals in the decision-making of a particular collective and between collectives can be facilitated. Moreover, *horizontalidad* points to the conscious attempt by a collective to lessen the coercive force of obligation or representative politics by rallying around a more inclusive force of mutual commitments and consensus.[97] As I will bring up shortly, this last point, again, deeply connects *autogestión* with social and solidarity economy initiatives.

1.2.3   The Ethical-Moral Position

Ethical-moral positions justifying workers' control and self-management often begin with critical theories and assessments of capitalist modes of organising the economy and the workplace, which I covered at length in Chapter 4. Contemporary theorists and proponents of workers' control and self-management who start from the ethical-moral position, often taking up Marxist or social anarchist perspectives, ground their views on the ethical legitimacy of workers' control and self-management for minimising and eventually eradicating exploitation and alienation and maximising the self-determination and self-actualisation of associated forms of labour.

By the last half of the nineteenth century, early notions of *autogestión* would merge with movements for worker cooperatives and democratised workplaces and were important for envisioning the post-capitalist society. This can be witnessed in, for example, the First International's qualified endorsement of worker/producer cooperatives.[98] The possibilities seen in the short-lived worker takeover of factories and shops during the Paris Commune of 1871 also did much to inspire socialist and anarchist visions of the post-capitalist society, equally impressing Marx, Bakunin, and Kropotkin. Moreover, in the

---

96   Holloway 2002; Schugurensky 2001; Sitrin 2006, 2012.
97   Sitrin 2006, 2012.
98   Horvat 1982, pp. 126–8.

United States and Canada during the last quarter of the nineteenth century and the first decades of the twentieth century, the expansion of unionism, workplace and grassroots democracy, and cooperative experiments were early expressions of the labour movement with the Knights of Labour and the Industrial Workers of the World (IWW).[99] Within the anarchist labour movement, anarcho-syndicalism became the predominant early French union position, which viewed the general strike and workers' takeover of factories as the first steps to the transformation of society.[100] The more reformist British shop-stewards' movement of the early twentieth century would also centre social transformation on the shop floor, embodying 'the resentment of the craft unions against certain encroachments of power by capitalists'.[101] Conceptualised politically as 'guild socialism' in Britain in the 1910s, primarily via the writings of G.D.H. Cole,[102] workers' guilds, it was envisioned, would lead 'an alternative to capitalist industrial control' by highly skilled workers who had lost power to capital.[103] Here, the proposal was for workers' guilds to control the means of production, which would ultimately be owned by the state, in order to 'transform capitalism to industrial unionism'.[104] And in Argentina, too, its early twentieth-century trade-union movement dominated by anarchist, socialist, and syndicalist unions also supported worker and consumer cooperatives in various ways.[105] For all of these early labour movements and proposals, organising workers into associations of labourers at the point of production was seen as central for raising working-class consciousness and as the key point of struggle. In other words, transforming the 'social relations at the point of production' could be the first step towards transforming society.[106]

For a time in the years following World War I, a broad European movement of bottom-up shop floor organisations including factory committees, workers' councils, and soviets proliferated in countries such as Italy, Russia, Hungary, Poland, Germany, and Bulgaria. At first, they tended to emerge as direct reactions on the part of workers and their representatives to the deplorable post-war socio-economic conditions. Some of these workers' actions and organisations in places such as Russia, Hungary, and Germany would subsequently expand into broader political movements bringing together parties

---

99   Curl 2009, pp. 86–110, 125–8. See also Curl 2010.
100   Darlington 2013.
101   Bayat 1991, p. 17.
102   Cole 1920.
103   Bayat 1991, p. 17. See also Hutchinson and Burkitt 2005.
104   Cole, in Bayat 1991, p. 18.
105   Wyczykier 2009a, 2009b.
106   Hinton, in Bayat 1991, p. 15.

of the left with workers' control movements. The 1917 Russian Revolution's roots in directly democratic workers' committees is often overlooked or underplayed in official histories of the rise of the Soviet Union, for instance.[107] Factory seizures and the creation of workers' councils also followed general strikes in Germany in January through February 1918, while the seizure of industry by workers in Northern Italy in 1919–20 during the *biennio rosso* included up to 200,000 workers occupying and running factories, mostly focused in Turin.[108] Indeed, established trade unions' and leftist political parties' general failure to respond to or support long-term these bottom-up workers' movements created political and leadership vacuums and situations of dual power that, in places like Italy and Russia, would see the working class acting independently for a time.[109]

These examples of worker-led and workplace-centred collective actions and the promotion of a bottom-up revolutionary path, often by class-struggle and libertarian Marxist advocates, have come to be known as the 'aggressive encroachment approach' to workers' control.[110] Most broadly, such an approach involves situations of dual power emerging, whereby alternative centres of power form in workplaces that contest the state's authority via democratised workers' control and takeovers of factories and shops. Aggressive encroachment theorists see such forms of workers' control as the first step towards the post-revolutionary workers' state. According to Bayat, for example, John Street appeals to a strong moral-ethical position for justifying workers' control when he suggests that socialists do not have to resort to the other two justifications for it – namely, to efficiency or expanding democratic workplaces.[111] Instead, those seeking socialist transformation should resort specifically to the strong moral argument for workers' control suggested by actions such as workplace takeovers, embracing 'ideas about the value of human life and what it is good for human beings to do'.[112] Aggressive encroachment theorists argue that it is workers, after all, who create surplus-value through their labour in capitalist modes of production and should therefore reap the most from them. In the final analysis, for aggressive encroachment advocates, workers themselves, either directly or via a workers' state, should own the means of production. The work of council communists such as Anton Pannekoek and Paul Mattick and

---

107   Brinton 1970; Chase 1987; Fitzpatrick 2008; Horvat 1982.
108   Forgacs 2000; Horvat 1982.
109   Bayat 1991.
110   Bayat 1991, p. 33.
111   Bayat 1991, pp. 26–7.
112   Street 1983, p. 530.

anarcho-syndicalists such as Rudolf Rocker[113] explicitly argue for workers' control as a bottom-up political movement that could ground 'the revolutionary self-organization of the working class'.[114] In contrast to the centralist, vanguardist, and *étatist* proposals of the Bolsheviks and their takeover of the workers', peasants', and soldiers' soviets by early 1918,[115] councilists believe that through workers' councils the working class can prepare and self-direct the eventual takeover of the state, transforming it into, unlike the Soviet Union, a true workers' state.

Ernest Mandel, from a Trostkyist perspective, held even stronger views, pointing out the impossibility of true, tranformational workers' control when it is limited to mere workers' participation in enterprises while also arguing how it is, nevertheless, a valuable 'transitional demand' on the path to the postcapitalist and communist society.[116] Through aggressive encroachment rather than, for example, guild socialism's gradualist encroachment approach, the establishment of workers' councils in factories, according to Mandel, must go hand-in-hand with broader 'practical proposals' for workers' involvement in controlling the economy. Only then will workers' control become an *offensive measure* by workers on the path towards 'triggering struggles that go beyond the framework of the capitalist system'.[117] Here, Mandel seeks to show how a more profound form of workers' control could counter the shortcomings of dual power by extending the notion from the factory out to other spheres of the economy; history, after all, has shown that situations of temporary dual power, such as in 1917–18 Soviet Russia and 1919–20 Italy, most often fail due to the state's repression of workers, their co-optation by vanguardist parties, or *coup d'états* and capitalist strikes, often coordinated by the bourgeois political establishment.

Also part of the aggressive encroachment approach, but in some contrast to Mandel's hard position on workers' control or the more pessimistic views of Luxemburg and other radical left critics discussed earlier in this chapter, Antonio Gramsci considered workers' democracy overseen by workers' or factory councils to be central for the struggle towards the future communist society.[118] For Gramsci, workers' councils, as an early stage of full workers' control, were learning experiences for the proletarian struggle. They were spaces where the

---

113   Pannekoek 2003; Mattick 1969; Rocker 1989.
114   Bayat 1991, p. 38.
115   Chase 1987; Fitzpatrick 2008; Horvat 1982.
116   Mandel 1973, p. 345.
117   Mandel 1973, p. 367.
118   Gramsci 2000.

working class could learn how to 'exert power' and 'through struggle ... consolidate their self-rule in a post-revolutionary era'.[119] For Gramsci, in essence,
workers' democracy within capitalism was preparation for the socialist state
and the workers' economy to come. As he wrote during the factory occupations
of 1919–20:

> the social life of the working class is rich in the very institutions and activ-
> ities which need to be developed, fully organized and co-ordinated into
> a broad and flexible system that is capable of absorbing and disciplining
> the entire working class.[120]

Workers' councils were amongst the most powerful of these institutions for
Gramsci. Similar to the council communist proposals, democratically-elected
workers' and peasants' councils could catalyse social transformation in the rest
of society from the factories and the fields, unifying this transformation under a
mass workers' and peasants' movement.[121] While for Gramsci workers' control
was not posited as an alternative to the organising role of the vanguard Party
or the state, workers' control could nevertheless be a way, Gramsci believed,
for the working class to gain much valuable experience and break capitalist-
aligned state power in both the economy and society at large, ultimately establishing a 'hegemony' of the working class.

For most proponents of ethical-moral justifications for workers' control and
autogestión, the struggle for workers' democracy – whether on large industrial
shop floors, in offices, in fields, or in small shops – is generally the ground
from which to learn how to democratically reorganise society, prepare for the
seizure of power, and extend this bottom-up power out to the rest of society in
order to eventually create the workers' economy. For them, workplace democracy can transform movements of the self-governing firm to broader political
movements for the self-governing society. Indeed, according to Horvat, only a
social system rooted in equality of opportunity and solidarity, expansive democratic institutions inclusive of workplaces, and the distribution of goods and
services according to the needs of all will ultimately lead to the emancipated
self-governing society and 'economic freedom'.[122]

---

119   Bayat 1991, p. 39. See also Clark 1977.
120   Gramsci 2000, p. 80.
121   Gramsci 2000. See particularly, Gramsci 1919.
122   Horvat 1982, pp. 498–500.

2   Section 2: Cooperatives, the Social and Solidarity Economy, and
         Autogestión

From the discussion thus far, it is hopefully clear that notions of workers' participation and self-management can be either accommodative to capital or take
more radical directions. This was an ambivalence that Marx, for example, suggested regarding worker/producer cooperatives.[123] For distinguishing between
more accommodative perspectives of workers' participation and self-management and more radical notions of workers' control and *autogestión*, it is useful
to briefly look at how cooperatives have emerged and, in recent years, how the
social and solidarity economy has been conceptualised.

     In considering the socio-political implications of alternative economic ar-
rangements such as cooperatives, social economy theorists have positioned
the various practices of alternative organisations within a spectrum or a continuum that places them somewhere either towards reformist or social democratic designs for a kinder capitalist market system, at the one extreme, or
towards more utopian visions for a radically different form of economic life
free of inequalities, at the other.[124] The following discussion takes such an
approach.

2.1   *The Rise of the World Cooperative Movement*
Broadly, the historical emergence of the cooperative movement has espoused
some of the main hopes and desires present in our genealogy of *autogestión*
that I reviewed in the first section of this chapter, including increased economic
equality and justice, more workers' participation in economic life, more just
ways of redistributing social wealth, and so on.[125] In the main, however, with
perhaps the exception of certain moments in the history of worker cooperatives, historically the cooperative movement has tended to be more reformist
than revolutionary.[126] While credit unions and cooperative banks and consumer, service, and marketing cooperatives, for example, can be understood to
be alternative economic arrangements that show in practice how life's needs
may be provisioned more equitably, they have emerged as direct responses
to strictly capitalist arrangements while, at the same time, working within
the already existing capitalist economy. On the whole, they have proposed a
reformed market system.[127] In such a reformed system, while production, dis-

---

123   See Chapter 4.
124   See, for example, Amin 2009; Fontan and Shragge 2000; McMurtry 2010; Melnyk 1985.
125   See also Zamagni and Zamagni 2010.
126   Craig 1993; Melnyk 1985.
127   Howard 2000; Restakis 2010.

tribution, and consumption may be socialised through some form of collective, cooperative, or even state control, markets still do the allocation via price
indicators.[128]

Influenced by Robert Owen's reformist visions, early social democratic and
liberal theorists argued that cooperatives – as economic organisational forms
made up of, in the words of John Stuart Mill, 'the association of the labourers themselves'[129] – represented the height of human economic development.
For these theorists, cooperatives were seen as associations that could reform
and even perfect the capitalist market system. As more humane '[c]ommun-
istic' economic arrangements, as the nineteenth- and early twentieth-century
cooperative historian and promoter George Holyoake would put it,[130] these
theorists argued that cooperative forms of economics should be reaffirmed and
practised in order to soften the harsh effects of capitalism and, ultimately, begin
to assert a more inclusive, mutually beneficial, and less exploitative economic
model.[131] J.S. Mill, for instance, viewed associated labourers' 'collectively owning the capital with which they carry on their operations, and working under
managers elected and removable by themselves' as the pinnacle of economic
development, although he would continue to advocate for competition as a
motivating economic force contra the revolutionary proposals of 'the Socialist
writers' of his time.[132]

These early liberal theorists of cooperation also justified the need for more
equitable markets, more just forms of distributing wealth, and more benign
forms of production from the understanding that cooperation between people
in producing to meet life's needs long predated the industrialised society and
was still worthy of guiding economic activity.[133] As Holyoake would write in
1875:

> From the commencement of human society Co-operation has been com-
> mon in the sense of two or more persons uniting to attain an end which
> each was unable to effect singly ... The new Co-operation, of which I here
> write, begins in mutual help, with a view to end in a common competence.
> A cooperative society commences in persuasion, proceeds by consent,

---

128   Borzaga and Tortia 2007.
129   Mill 1909, sec. IV.7.21.
130   Holyoake, in Gurney 1988, p. 71.
131   Zamagni 2014.
132   Mill 1909, sec. IV.7.63. See also similar views on cooperatives and cooperation by one of
      the founders of modern economics, Alfred Marshall, in Dévadhar 1971.
133   Polanyi 2001.

seeks success by common efforts, incurs risks, and shares losses, intending that all its members shall proportionately share whatever benefits are secured.[134]

By 1895, the widespread growth of consumer cooperatives throughout Europe and its contemporary or former colonies motivated the founding of the International Co-operative Alliance (ICA), which began consolidating the growing world cooperative movement by 'coordinating the activities of affiliated cooperative federations'.[135] Adopting the cooperative principles of the earlier Rochdale pioneers, the ICA would eventually arrive at a definition of cooperativism similar to but more specific than Owen's, King's, and Holyoake's earlier reformist conceptualisations.[136] While, as Argentina's ERTs will show us, the socio-economic practices of *autogestión* are certainly not limited to the definition of cooperativism provided by the ICA, it does nevertheless offer some viable guiding concepts from which to begin to think about more radical forms of the cooperative firm and of *autogestión* more broadly. At the same time, the liberal democratic and reformist roots of the cooperative movement are still palpably present in the ICA's definition, which does not take a direct stance against the capitalist or state-socialist systems of organising production, distribution, and consumption.

According to the ICA, a cooperative is 'an autonomous association of persons united voluntarily to meet their common economic, social, and cultural needs and aspirations through a jointly owned and democratically controlled enterprise'.[137] The values of cooperation guiding cooperative economic enterprises should be, according to the ICA, rooted in 'self-help, self-responsibility, democracy, equality, equity and solidarity' (par. 2). And, as I will bring up periodically throughout the rest of this book, the principles that all formal cooperatives are asked to adopt by the ICA, expanding on and rewriting the original Rochdale principles at key moments throughout the twentieth century, include: (1) voluntary and open membership; (2) democratic member control; (3) member economic participation; (4) autonomy and independence; (5) education, training, and information; (6) cooperation among cooperatives; and (7) concern for community.[138]

---

134   Holyoake 1875, p. 4.
135   Craig 1993, p. 33.
136   See Chapter 4.
137   ICA 2016, par. 1.
138   ICA 2016, pars. 3–10. For the original Rochdale principles, see Fairbairn 1994. For a history of the ICA, see Birchall 1997.

Many progressive collectives or cooperative-based experiments or move-ments espousing or practising associated forms of labour and alternative eco-nomic arrangements have taken up (directly or indirectly) some or most of these principles as foundations for alleviating or moving beyond capitalist market logics and values of individualism and competition.[139] Historically, to recap our discussion in Chapters 2 and 3, some of these have included, to name only a few: Argentina's nineteenth-century urban mutual societies and rural cooperatives and its burgeoning late twentieth and twenty-first century worker cooperative movement, including earlier workplace conversions and the current ERT movement; Nova Scotia's Antigonish community development movement of consumer and worker cooperatives in the mid-twentieth cen-tury; Catalonia's self-management movement during the years of the Span-ish Civil War, including the cooperativisation and collectivisation of agricul-ture and industry in the mid-1930s; Yugoslavia's self-managed factories; post-colonial Algeria's originally spontaneous self-management movement; fact-ory takeovers in France in May 1968 and in the ensuing years, including the emblematic LIP watch factory takeover in the early 1970s; Chile's cooperat-ive agricultural experiments and factory takeovers just before and during the presidency of Salvador Allende; and the conversion of private, investor-owned firms into worker cooperatives in the United Kingdom, France, Spain, and Italy beginning in the 1970s and emerging again in recent years.[140]

But increasingly throughout the twentieth century, other worker cooperat-ive and self-management experiences accommodated to or were co-opted by centrally planned economies, monopoly capitalism, or the global post-Fordist system. Examples here include the outsourcing of production to the global South by the Mondragón Cooperative Corporation (MCC)[141] or the demutual-isation of agricultural, marketing, insurance, and consumer cooperatives throughout the global North and in pockets of the global South.[142] These accommodations and co-optations were also witnessed in state takeovers or control of traditional collectives and cooperatives, such as in the collectivisa-tion drives of agricultural cooperatives in Stalin's Soviet Union, the collectiv-isation of agriculture in Mao's China in the 1960s and Julius Nyerere's Tanzania in the 1970s, and the state's increased control over self-managed firms in Ben Bella's Algeria post-1962.[143] Argentina's state-sponsored worker cooperatives

139   Vieta 2010b.
140   Bayat 1991; Craig 1993; Dow 2003; Horvat 1982; Melnyk 1985; Ness and Azzellini 2011.
141   Webb and Cheney 2014.
142   Giovanni and Vieta 2017.
143   Bayat 1991.

that have been formed in recent years in order to deliver social assistance to the underemployed, the unemployed, and other marginalised communities is yet another form of co-opted cooperativism, as I discuss further in the following paragraphs and again in Chapter 7. Indeed, cooperativism's durability within and accommodation to capitalism or even state-socialism, as well as the lack of evidence in the eyes of some radical commentators of their usefulness for establishing an enduring model that moves beyond capitalism or centralised economies, have been upheld as proof that cooperatives are too easily co-opted or controlled by the hegemonic economic system to proliferate a sustainable alternative social and economic project.[144]

The co-optation critique, however, blinds this perspective to the countless cooperative projects that actually have in practice returned control over economic and productive life to workers and communities.[145] Other progressive commentators have been more sympathetic to the potential of cooperatives for guiding an alternative socio-economic project. John Craig and Suren Saxena, for instance, writing in the 1980s when cooperative studies scholars and community development researchers were increasingly advocating for cooperatives as ideal organisations for bottom-up community development initiatives, emphasise the more radical potential of cooperatives.[146] Inspired by the solidarity-based cooperatives they studied in the global South, Craig and Saxena highlight how associated production in cooperative organisations possesses the foundation for minimising profiting from others while maximising equity and collective control. Their definition of cooperation, I believe, proves useful for beginning to conceptualise more radical forms of cooperatives, particularly with the explicit connections they make to building solidarity relationships between cooperatives and other member-based, democratically run, and community focused initiatives:

> Cooperation is the free and voluntary association of people to create an organization which they democratically control, providing themselves with goods, services and/or a livelihood rather than profiting from others, with an equitable contribution of capital and acceptance of a fair share of risks and benefits generated by the joint activity. To sustain their endeav-

---

144   For critical commentary on these themes, see Atzeni and Vieta 2014; Gasper 2014; Gindin 2016; Luxemburg 2006; and Ratner 2015.

145   See, for instance, Craig and Saxena 1986; Jossa 2005, 2014, 2016, 2017; Sandoval 2016; Vieta 2010b.

146   Craig and Saxena 1986.

our they must develop individuals and build a solidarity relationship with other cooperators and like-minded people.[147]

Beginning in the last years of the twentieth century and extending into the first two decades of the twenty-first, conceptualisations of the worker cooperative, in particular, have been taking into account more explicitly the three positions that, as I suggested earlier, are most important for a more radical notion of *autogestión*, to wit: (1) the efficacy of social production for provisioning for life's needs; (2) economic justice via the directly democratic organisation of the firm by workers; and (3) normative considerations for the collective ownership of the means of production.[148] Taking up these three positions for *autogestión* specifically from the perspective of the labour-managed and labour-owned firm and consolidating it with the ICA's, Craig and Saxena's, and others' conceptualisations of cooperatives and cooperation, the definition of worker cooperatives for understanding Argentina's ERTs that will be assumed in the rest of this book is the following:

> Worker cooperatives are productive entities whereby 'labour hires capital',[149] where 'work' is the common contribution of each member,[150] where 'control is linked to work' rather than financial investment,[151] and where revenues are the common property of the cooperative's members.[152] Furthermore, they are voluntary associations of workers collaborating democratically, wherein each worker has an 'equal say' in the running of the firm[153] via workers' boards or councils elected from its membership base.[154]

Worker cooperatives, the growing empirical evidence suggests, are particularly suited for tackling economic downturns, often proving to be more robust than

---

147   Craig and Saxena 1986, p. 67.
148   See, for instance Cheney and Webb 2014; DuRand 2016; Jossa 2014, 2016; Lionais and Vieta 2017; Malleson 2014; Novkovic and Webb 2014; Quarter 1992; Sanchez Bajo and Roellants 2011; Vieta 2014; Vieta and Lionais 2015; Wolff 2012.
149   Smith, Chivers, and Goodfellow 1988, p. 25.
150   INAES 2007.
151   Oakeshott 1990, p. 27.
152   Quarter, Mook, and Armstrong 2009.
153   Mathews 1999, p. 198.
154   Quarter 1992, p. 27. Arguably, a further distinguishing feature of worker cooperatives could be added to this definition: As Gregory Dow (2003) points out, labour-managed firms, which of course include worker cooperatives, engage in 'membership-markets' when taking on new members, rather than in wage-labour markets.

conventional investor-owned firms[155] and experiencing far fewer job losses during economic troughs.[156] The resilience of worker cooperatives is especially connected to the intrinsic motivations of worker-members (that is, job satisfaction, good work environments, worker wellbeing, and so on), as well as the positive externalities they bring to local communities.[157] Factors that contribute to their robustness as business models are often linked to the democratic decision-making responsibilities of members, in how worker-members take on flexible work hours and adjust salaries rather than reduce jobs during market downturns, how members will often decide to look for other business opportunities to redeploy the firm's capabilities for local needs, and in how they are businesses often committed to the wellbeing of members and other social objectives rather than the sole pursuit of profits.[158]

Worker cooperatives, as with ERTs, can emerge in differing ways, too. The most common is a start-up of a new enterprise via some form of what has been called social or collective entrepreneurship, which includes collective risk sharing and workers' pooling of start-up funds and resources.[159] Increasingly in recent years, as I have already reviewed in Chapter 2, one source for the recent growth in worker cooperatives has been via the conversion of troubled conventional capitalist businesses by employees, especially after the crises of the neo-liberal model of the 1990s in Latin America and the impact of the 2008 financial crisis in southern Europe.

As the cooperative economics literature suggests, challenges for worker cooperatives, as with those emerging from ERT processes, tend to include: start-up financing; ongoing capitalisation; and, as for small businesses in general, surviving the early years in competitive markets with non-cooperative competitors and drawing a decent income for worker-members.[160] The literature also suggests that worker cooperatives that start as ERTs are usually more precarious during their initial start-up period when compared to planned cooperative

155   Bentivogli and Viviano 2012; Borda-Rodriguez and Vicari 2016; Smith and Rothbaum 2014; Zanotti 2011.

156   Pérotin 2006, 2014; Zevi et al. 2011.

157   Fakhfakh et al. 2012; Oakeshott 2000; Theorell 2003.

158   Artz and Kim 2011; Burdín and Dean 2009; CECOP–CICOPA Europe 2012a, 2012b, 2013; Pérotin 2014; Sanchez Bajo and Roellants 2011; Zevi et al. 2011.

159   On the concept of social (or collective) entrepreneurship, see, among others, Brouard and Larivet 2011; Defourny and Nyssens 2010; Duguid, Tarhan, and Vieta 2015; Lundgaard Andersen, Gawell, and Spear 2016; Webb and Cheney 2014.

160   Ben-Ner and Jones 1995; Craig 1993; Dow 2003; Pérotin 2006, 2014; Vieta et al. 2017; Vieta, Quarter, Spear, and Moskovskaya 2016; Webb and Cheney 2014.

start-ups, especially if no external sources of funding and supports exist.[161] This is because, it is argued, an ERT often emerges from a troubled firm and, as with Argentina's ERTs, workers often have to go through long periods of struggle to take over the firm, make wage sacrifices, and replace depleted machinery.[162] Even given these challenges, however, as I suggested earlier, worker cooperatives, including ERTs, can eventually become as productive and even outperform conventional firms, especially during economic downturns.[163]

Argentina's ERTs, as we will soon see, have been showing that new worker cooperatives can overcome these challenges via the solidarity and initiative that is forged from having gone through moments of crisis together. This initial solidarity, as well as the support these firms garner from the broder community, other ERTs, some unions, and new forms of self-managed workers' associations, contribute to strengthening the worker cooperative initiatiated via an ERT process and serve to counter difficulties experienced in the conversion process.[164]

2.2   The Ebbs and Flows of Argentina's Cooperative Movement

It is perhaps no surprise that the early debates of the ERT protagonists, which would settle on the worker cooperative model that will be looked at in detail in the next chapter, emerged in a country with a long history of cooperativism. Indeed, according to Jack Schaffer, the Argentine cooperative movement was the 'first to begin in a country outside the industrialised countries of Europe, Australia, Canada, Japan, and the United States'.[165] Already by the middle of the nineteenth century, a growing urban working class in Argentina was engaged in projects containing the seeds of today's experiments with *autogestión*, forming mutual associations, benevolent societies, renters' associations, and, by the mid-1870s, the first cooperatives. Historically, cooperatives in Argentina were linked to the country's ties to Europe through the waves of immigrants from Spain, Italy, and other countries that arrived beginning in the last quarter of the nineteenth century with new ideas of how to organise social, economic, and working life.[166] During the late nineteenth and early twentieth centuries, consumer and eventually worker and producer cooperatives would be pro-

---

161   CECOP–CICOPA Europe 2013; Quarter and Brown 1992; Quarter 1995; Vieta et al. 2017.
162   McCain 1999; Paton 1989; Quarter 1995; Ruggeri and Vieta 2015.
163   See also Altman 2014; Birchall and Kettilson 2009; Fakhfakh et al. 2012; Sauser 2009; Pérotin and Robinson 2004; and Smith and Rothbaum 2014.
164   For more on these themes, see Chapters 2, 3, and 6–8.
165   Shaffer 1999, p. 139.
166   Montes and Ressel 2003; Shaffer 1999.

moted by most of Argentina's emerging anarchist, syndicalist, socialist, and communist unions as organisations that more closely responded to the needs of the growing working-class population in lieu of absent state assistance and lack of effective collective agreements.[167] Argentina's first national regulation for cooperatives was passed in 1905, with a more robust legislative framework coming into effect as Ley 11.388 in 1926. This law was updated by the third government of Juán Perón as Law 20.337 in 1973 and is still in effect today.[168]

Over the years, Argentina has developed a rich and diverse cooperative movement. Its agricultural cooperative sector emerged in the late nineteenth century, for instance, as responses by local farmers to the *latifundio* model of land ownership and corporate monopolies. Today, its agricultural cooperative sector includes some of the largest cooperatives in Argentina, such as the SanCor dairy cooperative. Consumer cooperatives are also numerous, with one of the most storied, El Hogar Obrero (the Workers' House), founded in 1905 as an initiative of the Socialist Party. El Hogar Obrero accompanied the emergence of the working class throughout the twentieth century, provisioning the first countrywide tourism and recreational facilities for workers, and offering social housing, grocery stores, and consumer credit-granting facilities to working people.[169] The first formal worker cooperative in Argentina was founded in 1928 by a small group of construction workers.[170] Perhaps because of the historically strong role of unions and the relatively early introduction of national social security under the auspices of the labour movement in the 1940s and 1950s during Perón's first two presidencies, worker cooperatives have had a slower initial uptake in Argentina as compared to agricultural or consumer cooperatives. Nevertheless, new worker cooperatives would emerge during Perón's first two administrations, and cooperatives (officially at least) were the preferred form of the firm in Perón's socio-political framework of *justicialismo*, touted as the 'basic enterprise for the social economy'.[171] By 1954, Perón himself would support the founding of the first worker cooperative federation within the CGT, the Asociación de Cooperativas de Trabajo de la República Argentina (Worker Cooperative Association of the Republic of Argentina).[172] Today, there are around 20 million cooperative members in Argentina belonging to almost 29,000 producer, consumer, credit, insurance, housing, and worker cooperat-

---

167 Wyczykier 2009b.
168 Shaffer 1999.
169 Ronchi 2012.
170 Vuotto 2012.
171 Elgue and Cieza 2007, p. 12.
172 Ibid.

ives; the latter (which we will shortly address in some detail) is amongst the largest sectors in the world, with almost 23,000 worker cooperatives.[173] Argentina's contemporary cooperative movement also includes a broad network of cooperative federations (175 as of 2012), cooperative education and training institutes (such as the Centro Cultural de la Cooperación), and even a reputable cooperative-movement publishing house (InterCoop Editora). Merging the cooperative sector with the broader social and solidarity economy and founded in the late 1990s, the Instituto Nacional de la Economía Social (INAES, National Institute for Associationalism and the Social Economy), overseen by the Ministry of Social Development, is the body that officially regulates cooperatives in the country.

From its original focus on the needs of local people seeking socio-economic redress and autonomy, Argentina's cooperative movement would soon find itself tussling with the state's variegated and often-changing socio-economic policies that have fluctuated between representing the needs of workers and communities and deregulating the economy and favouring multinational and corporate interests. Since the 1990s, Argentina's cooperative movement has experienced additional and profound changes. On the one hand, cooperative enterprises were threatened by the neo-liberal turn under *menemismo*, threats that had returned with *macrismo*. On the other hand, partially in response to the weakening of labour rights, the increased closures of conventional businesses, and more and more workers facing under- or unemployment, by the mid-to-late 1990s the number of new worker cooperatives began to rise,[174] proliferating in numbers during the Kirchner years in no small part because they also became an instrument for the delivery of welfare programmes. In the period after the 2001–2 socio-economic crisis, this rise in worker cooperatives would turn into a surge, spurred slightly by the rise of ERTs but to a much larger degree by worker cooperatives linked to the delivery of social assistance programmes.[175] These recent changes in Argentina's cooperative movement, engrained in the ebbs and flows of the country's neo-liberal political economy of recent decades, are thus worth reviewing, if briefly, since it significantly bears on the emergence of the country's ERTs.

As Table 4 shows, there was, on the one hand, a marked increase in the number of cooperatives between 1985 and 2002. In the former year, there were a total of 4,204 cooperatives in Argentina, jumping to 8,142 by 1991 and 16,008 by 2002. While this represents almost a threefold increase in the number of

173   ICA 2013; Vuotto 2014a, 2014b.
174   INAES 2008; Levin and Verbeke 1997.
175   Vuotto 2012, 2014b. See also Chapter 7.

TABLE 4   Number of Argentine cooperatives and cooperative members per year, 1985–2002

Year	Total cooperatives per year	Total cooperative members per year
1985	4,204	10,592,359
1991	8,142	9,103,269
2002	16,008	6,874,064

SOURCE: INAES 2008; MONTES AND RESSEL 2003, PP. 18–19; SHAFFER 1999, P. 149

registered cooperatives in Argentina in less than two decades, combined membership in cooperatives, on the other hand, dropped almost twofold in the same 17-year period: In 1985 there were over 10.5 million cooperative members in the country; in 1991, over 9.1 million members; and by 2002, the number of total cooperators in the country had fallen to less than 6.9 million members.[176] Recent studies hypothesise that this paradoxical inversion of growth in the number of cooperatives with a concomitant decline in membership had to do with the rise of neo-liberalist policies between the 1970s and 1990s. While the neo-liberal model was strengthening its hold on the Argentine economy throughout this period, labour flexibilisation, centralisation, and privatisation schemes were also exerting strong blows to cooperatives, especially on those that operated within sectors most affected by Menem's unregulated free market policies, such as in agriculture, transportation, social services, utilities, and savings and credit. In particular, by the 1990s, the establishment of an unregulated free market system and the entrenchment of international financial interests in Argentina were also intensifying competition in the cooperative sector, destroying established national networks of production and distribution, and encouraging the merger or demutualisation of cooperatives (especially in the agricultural and utility sectors, and the once-diverse credit union sector).[177] As Alberto Muñoz has written: 'In the privatisation process of the mid-1990s, the cooperative movement was not only denied the possibility of participating as an alternative, it was effectively excluded'.[178]

---

176   Montes and Ressel 2003.

177   Basañes 1999. Savings and credit cooperatives also have a long history in Argentina and were mainstays in small towns and cities throughout the country until the arrival of neo-liberal policies beginning in the 1970s that put most of them out of business. Banco Credicoop emerged in the late 1970s from the merger of 44 credit unions during the military dictatorship and still remains the major cooperative presence in the country's banking sector as the country's only nation-wide cooperative bank (Martí 2006).

178   Muñoz 2005, p. 107.

Some have theorised that this inverse relationship between the growth in cooperatives and the drop in members up until 2002 might have to do with the rise in what in Argentina are called 'false cooperatives' – cooperatives that were formed by the outsourced workers of larger firms and multinationals that were downsizing during the 1990s in order for these corporations to unburden themselves of 'high labour costs' (similar to what happened to UST's workers before they became an ERT in Chapter 1). 'Assisting' former workers and entire workplaces to become 'cooperatives' that the same downsizing firms were then ostensibly to do business with were, in reality, practices of labour flexibilisation and union busting. Fundamentally, the practice served to deaden the inevitable reactions by organised labour to what in essence were job cuts. As Mario Mittelman suggests, these downsizing businesses facilitated the creation of 'false cooperatives' in order to appear to be supporting an alternative to the loss of jobs; for Mittelman, these practices were countermoves to a problem that presents itself periodically in Argentina – labour strife in the midst of downturning economies and rising unemployment.[179] Indeed, the rise in worker cooperatives in Argentina, from almost 10 percent of total cooperatives in 1984 to over 40 percent by 2002 (Table 5), while the number of cooperators dropped almost twofold over the same period (Table 4), can in part be explained by the surge of these 'false cooperatives' and the closure of older coops.

But another dramatic shift impacted Argentina's cooperative movement after 2002, bolstered by the state's subsidisation of new worker cooperatives as a method of channelling and downloading social services delivery to the social and solidarity economy. These policies, taken up with much enthusiasm during the three Kirchner administrations, have contributed to the dramatic surge in the number of cooperatives throughout the country over the past 15 years and to the increase in cooperative members more broadly since the mid-to-late 2000s.[180] For instance, as Table 5 shows, while in 1984 there were only 404 worker cooperatives in Argentina accounting for 9.9 percent of all coops in the country at the time, by 1994 there were 2,632 worker coops accounting for 34.8 percent of all cooperatives. By 1997, this number had risen to 4,264 worker cooperatives, making up 34.7 percent of all coops. By 2002, there were already 6,549 worker cooperatives (41 percent of all coops), while by 2008 a full 67.4 percent of all cooperatives in Argentina (11,371 coops) were worker cooperatives, and by 2014 worker coops made up 78 percent of the universe of cooperatives (22,516 coops).

---

179   Mittelman 2005.
180   ICA 2013; Vuotto 2014a.

TABLE 5   Development of Argentine cooperatives, 1984–2014

Sector	1984		1994		1997		2002		2008		2014	
	No	%	No.	%	No.	%	No.	%	No.	%	No.	%
Agriculture	1,282	31.5	1,305	17.3	1,921	15.6	2,190	13.7	1,064	6.3	1,297	4.5
Consumer	209	5.1	106	1.4	206	1.7	243	1.5	95	0.6	195	0.7
Credit	287	7	200	2.6	375	3	311	1.9	259	1.5	290	1
Provisioning	342	8.4	631	8.3	1,106	9	1,512	9.4	1,265	7.5	1,582	5.5
Insurance	57	1.4	55	0.7	105	0.9	50	0.3	17	0.1	19	0.1
Public Services	1,100	27.1	1,270	16.8	1,800	14.6	1,868	11.7	1,019	6	1,167	4
Worker Coops	404	9.9	2,632	34.8	4,264	34.7	6,549	41	11,371	67.4	22,516	78
Housing and Construction	392	9.6	1,365	18.1	2,526	20.5	2,966	18.5	1,607	9.5	1,787	6.2
Others	NA	NA	NA	NA	NA	NA	319	2	172	1	NA	NA
Total	4,073	100	7,564	100	12,303	100	16,008	100	16,869	100	28,853	100

SOURCES: INAES 2008; LEVIN AND VERBEKE 1997; MONTES AND RESSEL, 2003; SHAFFER 1999; VUOTTO 2014A

Perhaps with the exception of Italy, Spain, and France, where worker cooperatives have had a long history or have benefited from healthy state funding and support, as we saw in Chapter 2,[181] Argentina currently witnesses an exceptionally large number of worker cooperatives, especially when compared to cooperative movements in other parts of the global North.[182] Why, then, is Argentina's worker cooperative sector so large? Before answering this question, we must underscore that this meteoric growth in worker coops in Argentina is not due to Argentina's ERTs. Representation of Argentina's ERTs within the total universe of worker cooperatives has continued to remain small and has not contributed substantively to the broader increase in worker coops in recent years; the 367 ERTs that existed in early 2016 represented just over 1.6 percent of all worker cooperatives in the country. To put it another way, slightly more than 98.4 percent of Argentina's worker coops that existed in early 2016 *did not* originate from workers' taking over failed capitalist firms.[183]

---

181   See also Craddock and Kennedy 2006; and Vieta et al. 2017.

182   In Canada in 2004, for example, there were around 360 worker cooperatives in existence, making up six percent of the country's non-financial cooperatives at the time (Quarter et al. 2009, p. 64; see also Hough, Wilson, and Corcoran 2010). The United Kingdom's 632 worker cooperatives as of 2017 made up 7.5 percent of its universe of cooperatives (Co-operatives UK 2017), while in the United States, a mere 0.63 percent (or around 300) of its 48,000 cooperatives were worker coops in 2008 (Curl 2009, p. 2).

183   As Table 5 also indicates, a large number of Argentina's non-worker cooperatives today

The great majority of worker cooperatives in existence in Argentina today are, rather, cooperatives that emerged since the late 1990s and early 2000s and that are linked to the state's social assistance initiatives for the still-sizable population of unemployed and underemployed that began to be implemented during the crisis years at the turn of the millennium. During the administrations of Néstor Kirchner and Cristina Fernández de Kirchner (2003–15), these social assistance initiatives expanded into municipal infrastructure maintenance programmes, such as Manos a la Obra (Hands to Work), Plan Agua Más Trabajo (Water Plus Work Plan), and the more recent Plan Argentina Trabaja (Argentina Works Plan), all overseen by the Ministerio de Desarollo Social (Ministry of Social Development).[184] Crucially, these programmes have included the promotion of beneficiary-run 'social, pre-cooperative, mutualistic, and cooperative' enterprises, a policy taken up more explicitly with the Plan Argentina Trabaja programme initiated by Fernández de Kirchner's administration in 2009.[185] Undoubtedly, such initiatives have accounted for much of the stratospheric surge in worker cooperatives in Argentina over the past two decades, creating, for instance, more than 7,300 new worker cooperatives between the inception of the Plan Argentina Trabaja programme in 2009 and March 2011.[186] Tellingly, almost 16,000 of the 22,516 worker cooperatives that existed in 2014 emerged from these social assistance plans. Critical commentators, as we will see in more detail in Chapter 7, have called these 'assistentialist' uses of cooperatives that create further dependency on the state for its beneficiary populations.[187] Some have also called coops emerging from these plans

---

belong to the rural, housing, insurance, consumer, public/social services, and credit sectors, rather than to the economic sectors where most ERTs are to be found. Recall that, to date, most ERTs have come from urban economic sectors most affected by the implosion of the neo-liberal model of the 1990s, which include urban industrial sectors or service sectors that deal with intermediary production (that is, graphics, metal works, food processing, and so forth) or final consumption (that is, editorial houses, schools, tourism, and so on).

184   Piva 2015, p. 100. See also Guimenez 2011; INAES 2009; Somoza Zanuy 2011; and Vuotto 2011, 2014a, 2014b. Other social assistance programmes linked to the creation of worker cooperatives have included, amongst others: the Centros Integradores Comunitarios (Integrating Community Centres), Capacitación con Obra (Training with Work), and Obra Pública Provincial y/o Municipal (Provincial and/or Municipal Public Works) (Vuotto 2014a, 2014b).

185   Vuotto 2011, p. 35.

186   Vuotto 2012.

187   These social welfare policies, commonly known in Argentina as policies of *contención social* (social welfare, or literally, 'social containment'), have been viewed by critical commentators as strategies of *asistencialismo* (assistentialism) linked to containing social

'false cooperatives' because they are, it is argued, in reality work-for-welfare programmes delivered by a downsizing state that has insufficiently attempted to organise local groups of under- and unemployed social assistance recipients via top-down and hastily put together cooperatives. Moreover, critics have further argued, the creation of these new worker cooperatives is not really about local community empowerment or development but an excuse to dole out welfare plans in ways that actually weakens local empowerment since recipients of these plans are not supported in learning about the intricacies of self-management or cooperative values and practice.[188] Notwithstanding these persuasive critiques, there is also evidence that some of these new worker cooperatives have developed into viable labour-managed and community-focused social businesses. These new worker cooperatives and their related social assistance policies also underscore that, to some degree, there had been a willingness by the state under the Kirchner administrations to take a deeper interest in local development, job creation, and social inclusion,[189] policy positions that were increasingly at risk with President Mauricio Macri's administration, as we will explore later.

While ERTs too emerged within this general wave of new worker cooperatives in Argentina, they are different from the state-sponsored work-for-welfare version. As I have already indicated, ERTs did not emerge from or as a by-product of programmes of social assistance or work-for-welfare plans, nor have they been sustained or accompanied by any substantial state supports. Rather, ERTs have emerged and have been sustained, to a great extent, by the outcomes of working-class struggles and workers' own self-determination and bottom-up initiatives. ERT workers' practices of *autogestión*, then, as we will continue to see in the next chapters, are not in the main rooted in either Argentina's traditional cooperative movement nor in state-sanctioned programmes. Rather, as I have suggested in earlier chapters, they have emerged from out of a long history of bottom-up workers' struggles and grassroots labour militancy merging with new forms of social protest that arose against neo-liberalism at the end of the 1990s and throughout the early 2000s. And it is the political and organisational tools that they learn and adopt from these sources, and not the traditional cooperative movement, that have allowed thousands of

---

unrest while building a political coalition for the party in power by addressing the demands of popular sectors via co-optive strategies linked to work creation and welfare delivery. I discuss in more detail *asistencialismo* and *contención social* as they relate to these social welfare policies and ERTs in Chapter 7.

188   Dinerstein 2007; Ruggeri 2009; Vieta and Ruggeri 2009; Vuotto 2011.
189   Vuotto 2011, 2014b.

Argentine workers to begin subsequently to experiment with horizontalised and self-managed workplaces.

2.3 The Emergence of the Social and Solidarity Economy

As with notions and practices of workers' participation, workers' control, and cooperatives, the transformative potential of the social and solidarity economy and its myriad organisations and practices also span a political continuum, with reformist designs for a kinder capitalist market system on one end to more ambitious visions for radical economic transformations on the other.[190] Our current epoch's neo-liberal order and the associated tensions for working people inherent to globalisation, the global division of labour, and the decline of the welfare state have opened up new proposals for alternative socio-economic arrangements, made possible by the social and solidarity economy.[191] Ash Amin has recently asserted, for example, that '[t]his new interest joins traditional fringe interest in the social economy as real evidence of post-capitalist possibility based on social participation and an explicit ethic of care' emerging in myriad communities the world over.[192] Led by communities of the marginalised, social justice groups, and in some cases progressive governments, this new interest has also inspired new theorisations of the social and solidarity economy in the wake of the emergence of actual alternative economic models that directly respond to and begin to move beyond the worst injustices of the global neo-liberal status quo. Conceptually engaging with the social and solidarity economy here can thus help us further grasp what *autogestión* means today in Argentina, while also helping us to better understand later on some of the alternative economic and organisational practices engaged with by the country's ERTs.

Practices of the 'social economy' as it is known in the global North,[193] or the *la economía popular* (the popular economy) or *la economía social/solidaria y popular* (the social/solidarity and popular economy) as it is alternatively referred to in Latin America,[194] have increasingly been capturing the interest of academics, policy makers, and progressive governments in the past two or so decades.[195] Conceptualisations of this broad and complex sector of economic

---

190 Amin 2009; Fontan and Shragge 2000; McMurtry 2010.

191 Amin 2009; Gibson-Graham 2006; Miller 2004.

192 Amin 2009, p. 5.

193 McMurtry 2010; Quarter et al. 2009.

194 Elgue 2015.

195 While the Canadian anglophone and increasingly UK and US literatures primarily use the term 'social economy', I prefer the Latin American and francophone term 'social and solid-

activity consider that a large part of life unfolds within practices and organisations where the social takes priority over or drives the economic, rather than
the other way around as with liberal conceptions of economic life. As such,
the social and solidarity economy embraces practices and organisational forms
that lie beyond strictly state-based or strictly capitalist/market-based transactions and where the social production of social wealth – that is, fairly distributed wealth for multiple social stakeholders rather than for private gain – is
the goal. As with Arvon's and Rosanvallon's assertions concerning the concept
of *autogestión*, socialised economic practices have been understood to predate
markets and capitalist economics by millennia.[196] Indeed, it is increasingly less
controversial today to assert that the social dimensions of economic life, rather
than the Smithian self-interested individual, grounded pre-capitalist societies.[197] As Jean-Marc Fontan and Eric Shragge assert, the social economy has
been around for as long as humans have been cooperating and sharing in the
'results of their [collective] labour' in order to meet their life needs.[198] But
ascertaining an all-embracing definition of the social and solidarity economy
has proven to be much more difficult than emphasising its long history.

Currently, the concept of the social and solidarity economy is a contested
one amongst academics, policy makers, and even practitioners, who argue
about how to conceptualise it and what practices it encompasses, despite its
recognised multi-billion dollar force throughout the world today.[199] Understanding it depends both on the particular theoretical or political perspective
from which one views it and on the regional or national conjuncture one homes
in on.[200] For instance, in the United States, commentators, researchers, and
policymakers tend to recognise the 'third sector' of the economy, a sector in
which tertiary activities not viable for commercialisation or market exchanges
predominate and in which non-profits and voluntary associations proliferate.[201] In Western Europe, Anglophone Canada, and Québec, 'the social eco-

---

arity economy' for the greater inclusiveness of alternative organisational forms, practices,
and values it implies. I will retain the use of the term 'social economy' when directly citing
or discussing sources that deploy it in this sub-section of the chapter, while using the term
'social and solidarity economy' throughout the rest of the book.

196   McMurtry 2010; Polanyi 2001.
197   Heilbroner and Milberg 2008; McMurtry 2010; Polanyi 2001.
198   Fontan and Shragge 2000, p. 3.
199   McMurtry 2010.
200   Ash 2009; McMurtry 2010.
201   Salomon 1999. The concepts of the 'third sector' and the 'non-profit sector', however, tend
       to be limited to organisations and practices that do not generate profit and tend to act
       outside of markets. This, of course, excludes cooperatives and other forms of social enter-

nomy' categorically encompasses a wider array of organisations which might participate both within and outside of markets, including cooperatives, social enterprises, mutual associations, community initiatives, charities, civil society non-profits, and even quasi-public sector entities.[202] In Latin America, 'the social and solidarity economy' (SSE) encompasses a similarly inclusive array of activities and organisations, but with the difference that the term tends to often embrace a more explicitly political character that delineates a socio-economic space that contrasts to, or is the antithesis of, neo-liberal capitalist economic activity.[203] Some common definitional trends that cross-cut academic traditions and regional and national boundaries can, nevertheless, be discerned.

First, the social and solidarity economy is a concept that takes into account *organisations* that are: (1) autonomously managed by members or community stakeholders, (2) neither directly state-owned or -controlled (although they might be wholly or partially state-funded), nor (3) owned or controlled by private investors, that (4) do not seek profit-making as their guiding aim (although they might make some profit or surpluses within markets), and that (5) serve the mutual needs of members and broader community stakeholders via clear social objectives.[204]

Second, the social and solidarity economy also embraces *a set of activities* motivated by 'the production, distribution, and consumption of goods otherwise in short supply'[205] *and* the collective desires or needs by a group of people to overcome the economic gaps and social inequalities brought about by markets, governments, or economic crises. As Jack Quarter, Laurie Mook, and Ann Armstrong suggest, social economy activities tend to have four primary characteristics: (1) social objectives: (2) social ownership: (3) volunteer/social participation; and (4) civic engagement.[206] Together, these *activities* and *organisations* are overlaid by *values* of mutual aid rather than gain, solidarity rather than individualism, community interests rather than self-interest, and common ownership and democratic self-determination rather than investor ownership and hierarchical control.

In Latin America, especially with the entrenchment of neo-liberalism over the past four decades, solidary economic practices and values that both chal-

---

      prises that do indeed to some degree participate in markets and, again to some degree, engage in revenue generating activities that support their social objectives.

202   Ash 2009; Quarter et al. 2009.

203   Cattani 2004; Coraggio 2003, 2004; Elgue 2015; Singer 2004.

204   Amin 2009; Coraggio 2003; Elgue 2007, 2015; Fontan and Shragge 2000; Laville, Lévesque, and Mendell 2007; McMurtry 2010; Quarter et al. 2009; Pearce 2009.

205   McMurtry 2010, p. 8.

206   Quarter et al. 2009, p. 12.

lenge the neo-liberal capitalist status quo *and* create alternatives to it have returned with dynamism in recent years. At times I specifically call these social and solidarity economic practices *new* because, while rooted in age-old social and economic practices such as community-led or worker-led decision-making processes, worker-run and -organised labour processes, and bottom-up community development, they also directly resist and move beyond neo-liberal capitalism – the main economic paradigm of our age. That is, to borrow a notion from Karl Polanyi,[207] organisations of the social and solidarity economy are part of a contemporary *double movement*. As neo-liberalism expands, changes, and reasserts itself in light of recent crises, social and solidarity economy practices both emerge within its permeable economic structures and also move against it in a different direction. That is, neo-liberalism creates the conditions and needs for the social and solidarty economy and social and solidarity economic practices at the same time reaffirm people's needs and desires for control and say over economic decisions, advocating for and influencing broader social transformations in opposition to neo-liberal propositions.[208] In Latin America, this double-movement sees new social and solidarity economy organisations emerging throughout the region (including Argentina's ERTs) in ways that respond to the pervading, status quo neo-liberal economic model *and* move beyond it by reinventing or adopting modes of economic practices and social relations that run counter to the individualist and hyper-competitive directions of contemporary neo-liberal capital. Moreover, I view the two-pronged resistive (negative) and proactive (positive) movements of organisations of the social and solidarity economy as new forms of economic practices *from below*, led by those most negatively affected by neo-liberal reforms and that at the same time most directly benefit from controlling their own economic destinies. Thus, this *new* social and solidarity economy has *prefigurative characteristics* – prefigurative because these new forms of socially infused economic practices contain the seeds of a new society, foreshadowing different, less exploitative, and less alienating forms of economic organisation as compared to the neo-liberal capitalist order they contest. They contain within them, in other words, a set of future-oriented possibilities or preliminary sketches of another alternative economic, productive, cultural, and social reality in the present *and* for tomorrow.

The new social and solidarity economies of Latin America have gradually emerged over time in the region, driven by and responding to the socio-

---

207   Polanyi 2001.
208   Diamantopolous 2012; Vieta 2010b.

economic realities of recent decades. Before Latin America's neo-liberal experiments began to take off in the mid-1970s, the voices of its working and marginalised classes, mediated by strong labour movements, helped forge a version of
the developmentalist state that served in many countries in the region to guarantee some sort of redistribution of substantial portions of wealth.[209] During
the 1980s and early 1990s, with the widespread return of democracy and the
concomitant rise of neo-liberal ideology and policies in the region, discourses
of an equitable redistribution of wealth and self-sustaining economies grounding a developmentalist socio-economic model gave way to the discourses of
possessive individualism and globalisation.[210] In political economic terms, this
ideological shift, in practice, meant the outsourcing of the state's role in securing some sort of social safety net to a broadly conceived 'social economy'.
By the 1990s, the notion of the social economy in countries such as Mexico,
Venezuela, Argentina, Brazil, Chile, and Uruguay became a catch-all concept
for an eclectic and loose fabric of NGOs (some foreign), union-controlled benefits programmes, ad hoc community organisations (soup kitchens, garbage col-
lectors and recyclers, affordable housing initiatives, community centres, free
medical clinics, and so on), and precarious enterprises (community baker-
ies, food dispensaries, service-oriented entities, and so forth). Throughout the
region, this uncoordinated mix of entities essentially served to eventually
replace much of the state-funded social safety net. The neo-liberal discourse
of the time positioned this new, 'autonomous' social economy as a more 'efficient' means of service delivery in comparison to the 'cumbersome' apparatus
of state or, as in Argentina, state and union welfare provisioning. In actuality,
versions of the social economy during the 1990s became, in the eyes of many
observers, an 'economy of the poor' held together by policies of 'social containment' as clientelistic and assistentialist work-for-welfare schemes tied to social
service delivery rendered certain community groups more 'worthy' of assistance than others, while leaving many without any basic social protections.[211]

---

209 Portes 1985; Portes and Hoffman 2003; Saad-Filho 2005.
210 Saad-Filho 2005.
211 Dinerstein 2015; Elgue 2007, 2015; Ruggeri 2009. State-based policies and proposals for
     a 'social economy' are, thus, not without their contradictions. Proposals for social eco-
     nomies that are spearheaded by states tend to rely on subsidies that at times co-opt and
     contain grassroots entities from experimenting with more autonomous practices of self-
     management. Such proposals also paradoxically risk reproducing and legitimising the
     very neo-liberal system that led to people's socio-economic hardship and submission to
     the whims of the system in the first place. As Ruggeri (2009) points out in regards to
     state-based proposals for the social economy during the years of crisis at the turn of the
     millennium: 'A social economy, in addition to being spearheaded by international finan-

Rather than a top-down, clientelist, assistentialist, or under-serviced and under-funded 'social economy of the poor' in the service of government outsourcing, the arrival of Latin America's new social and solidarity economies has seen this sector, since the mid-to-late 1990s, increasingly rooted in locally focused, community-led, democratically driven, and self-managed economic activity.[212] At core, a social economy of *solidarity* is fundamentally differentiated from the neo-liberal system's version of poor-aid (or 'assistentialist') schemes[213] or offering conditional handouts to structurally marginalised communities by, instead, being grounded in practices of self-reliance, self-direction, self-control, and directly democratic decision-making structures and peoples' assemblies (that is, horizontalism)[214] made up of individuals from those communities directly engaged in the actual production of goods and services. While not doing away with efforts to reform the system or lobby the state for more recognition and assistance, however, many organisations in Latin America today operating within social and solidarity economies focus first on the equitable redistribution of surpluses amongst the direct producers (workers) and the otherwise marginalised. These social and solidarity economy groups, in other words, anchor themselves in what José-Luis Coraggio has termed an 'economy of work' rather than an economy of capital.[215] Moreover, across Latin America, social and solidarity economies also include aspects of explicitly non-capitalist economic practices such as bartering, householding and domestic production, participative democracy, mutual aid, and camaraderie (what ERT protagonists call *compañerismo*, as I will show in coming chapters). Furthermore, organisations of the social and solidarity economy are satur-

---

cial organisms as a way of alleviating the inevitable effects of neo-liberal reforms, is often spearheaded by NGOs and sometimes by the state itself as a wall of containment against further social breakdown; this was finally realised in the case of Argentina. At the same time, [social economic strategies] end up entrenching the most neglected sectors of society within a condition of overdependence on the state or NGO subsidies and donations that, in the long-run, [tend to co-opt] these vulnerable sectors and impede their struggle for a stable [self-managed] structure of productiveness' (p. 2). In the case of Argentina's ERTs, as I will critically evaluate in Chapter 7, the pursuit of a social and solidarity economy is, to date, multifold and informal. On the whole, ERTs in Argentina choose to engage in non-hierarchical forms of economic solidarity formations with each other while accepting some state assistance if available. That is, most ERTs have sought some degree of state subsidies or NGO support as they accept, on pragmatic grounds, the reality of needing to work for the near future with the state and within traditional capitalist marketplaces.

212   Dinerstein 2015; Giovannini and Vieta 2017; Sitrin 2012; Zibechi 2012.
213   See Chapters 6 and 7.
214   Sitrin 2005.
215   Coraggio 2004, pp. 151–63.

ated by values oriented towards viable yet sustainable exodus from conditions of perpetual marginality and social exclusion. Organisations operating within economies of solidarity do this by creating and engaging in economic practices that are consciously not a central part of the state-capitalist system, that emerge despite and in many ways apart from the continued presence of competitive markets, and that prefigure other modes of non-commodified economic and productive life.[216] As I will show, especially in Chapter 8, Argentina's ERTs in many ways fall within this broad Latin American movement of the social and solidarity economy.

3   *Autogestión* and the Continuing Stream of Self-Determination

This chapter has traced out a genealogy of *autogestión*, the key notion that drives the values and practices that undergird Argentina's ERTs. It is a concept that is most broadly grounded in the desire of working people to self-determine their own lives, encapsulated in the historical stream of self-determination, the political economy of the working class, and the agency of living labour explored in Chapter 4. While always in tension with the broader state apparatus and the capitalist system, modern practices of *autogestión*, as we assessed in this chapter, such as experiments in workers' control, worker cooperatives, and other forms of community collectives and solidarity-based economic initiatives, often emerge as direct responses to and solutions that move beyond the injustices and exclusions of their specific socio-economic contexts.

Autogestión, then, is this book's umbrella concept. It encompasses within it radical notions of workers' control, cooperation, and the social and solidarity economy that begin to directly contest – praxically – capitalist logics of production, exchange, and individual gain. The book in essence follows the use of the term by ERT workers themselves as they self-describe their new collective projects of production in the formerly capitalist firms they have taken over. *Autogestión* addresses how ERT workers begin to control their labour-power and labour process when they co-own the means of production within the legal rubric of a worker cooperative. It also points to how ERT workers pragmatically come to cooperativism, as we will continue to explore in Chapters 6–8. As we will see in those chapters, they learn cooperative values and practices of *autogestión* immanently, or '*sobre la marcha*' ('on the path of doing'), as one ERT member put it to me. As we will also see by Chapter 8, ERT protagonists'

---

take-up of *autogestión* also points to their emergent consciousness raising as participants of the working class in-the-(re)making.

From the discussion brought together in this and the previous chapter, then, *autogestión* means most fundamentally: *to collectively and democratically self-constitute, self-organise, and self-direct the productive, social, cultural, or economic spheres of life by the very people and communities that most directly benefit from or are affected by these activities, while attempting to minimise the intrusive mediation of markets, hierarchical organisation, or the state.* That is, *autogestión* is the desire and lived experience of a collective's striving to self-determine its own socio-economic destiny. Specifically, it encompasses, as more and more social justice groups and social movements are discovering across Latina America, the collection of *organisational forms*, *practices*, and *values* of horizontal and solidarity-based production or service delivery whereby workers, and at times also the communities that they interact with, directly and democratically collaborate in conceptualising, mobilising, organising, planning, managing, and executing the production and delivery of social wealth.[217]

In sum, *autogestión* means that the collective control of a productive entity takes on multiple social dimensions, merging workers' interest with the interests of the local community and society at large. Here, the community outside of the walls of a firm may be represented in part by state-ownership while workers control the daily operations of the firm, as in Venezuelan *cogestión*, or may be represented by workers' control and worker-ownership of the firm without state ownership but with community involvement in the productive entity, as in the case of Argentina's ERTs. Prefiguratively infused, in short, *autogestión* is equivalent to *the collective control of production under social ownership and participation* by a collective of workers *and* by those within the broader community who are directly affected by or benefit from the productive activity of the firm.

Theoretically and historically situating and defining *autogestión* in Chapters 4 and 5 before engaging with the ethnographic and sociological analysis of Chapters 6–8 has been important because we are now better placed to understand the intricacies that ERT protagonists face in self-managing a formerly capitalist enterprise within the Argentine conjuncture of recent decades. We will return to many of the themes covered in this chapter and the previous chapter in the book's subsequent pages. In Parts 3 and 4, we will revisit the praxical relevance of ERTs' recuperative moments for labour struggles today; con-

---

217   See also Garcia 2005; Araus 2004; Peixoto de Albuquerque 2004; Vieta 2010b; Wyczykier 2009b.

tinue to delineate their radical social innovations; explore their common experiences, possibilities, and challenges; delve into how their worker-protagonists begin to transform the labour process; and, by the concluding chapter, review why ERTs emerged in Argentina, what other struggles for *autogestión* can learn from them, and summarise what makes ERTs both a continuation of and also unique experiences in the history of workers' self-activity.

PART 3

The Consolidation of Argentina's Empresas Recuperadas: *Common Experiences, Challenges, and Social Transformations*

∴

'Occupy, Resist, Produce': Commonalities in the Lived Experiences of Recuperating Workplaces in Argentina (with Andrés Ruggeri)

> This new form of struggle ... no longer is limited to the common type of union demands for increased wages or for better work conditions. Rather, it was a struggle to occupy the factory in order to operate it ourselves – as a response to the neo-liberal model ... [W]e made solidarity our central theme. We began our practice of rallying around our *compañeros* in conflict, and we [adopted] a slogan that communicated what we wanted to do: *ocupar, resistir, producir*. It has to do with occupation as a founding practice. When we spoke with our *compañeros* who were engaged in conflict, the first thing we would say was: 'Occupy the factory and do not leave!' Then we would say: 'Resist' ... [and] put the factory back into operation.
>
> EDUARDO MURÚA[1]

∴

The case studies in Chapter 1 introduced the stories of three diverse recuperated firms in Argentina from the standpoint of the lived experiences of its worker protagonists. They detailed some of the ways that the crisis of the neo-liberal model at the turn of the millennium in Argentina was *lived* and *felt* existentially by workers within specific workplaces, how this macro-economic crisis heightened exploitation on shop floors, and how these shared experiences catalysed workers in some failing small- and medium-sized firms throughout the country and in different economic sectors to take over and eventually self-manage their workplaces.

This chapter sets out to further contextualise these three case studies specifically and Argentina's ERT phenomenon more broadly by bringing together

---

1 Murúa 2005a, personal interview (co-founder and former president of Movimiento Nacional de Empresas Recuperadas).

some of the most common characteristics of these workplaces' conflicts, founding struggles, and ongoing development while connecting them to wider political economic and historical trends. The chapter's first section sketches out the most common motivators that compel an ERT's founding members to engage in direct action, occupying the troubled firms that had been employing them – sometimes for lengthy periods of time and under threat of violent evictions and repression. During ERTs' 'first period' (early 1990s to around 2004), these motivators were intimately connected to how the turn-of-millennium macro-economic crisis of Argentina's neo-liberal political economy resonated at the point of production or point of service delivery. These resonances helped mobilise the self-directed actions of some employees involved in micro-economic conflicts on shop floors to take over their troubled places of work. During ERTS' 'second period' (circa 2004 to the end of 2009) and 'third period' (2010 to the end of 2015), motivations for workplace takeovers somewhat changed, from occupations coloured by specific anti-systemic resistances against broader macro-economic circumstances to more localised, shop floor-based actions by employees struggling to reclaim unpaid salaries, lost benefits and rights, and against threats of firm closure. Eventually, as shop floor struggles against employers unfold and as workers begin to embark on their projects of *autogestión*, they convert these firms into worker cooperatives while often facing off against returning former owners and the established legal and political system for recognition of their cooperative.

The second section of this chapter, in turn, homes in on the general trends in the processes of workplace takeovers and ERTS' ensuing conflicts, situating these processes within the three-staged progression of recuperating workplaces in Argentina encapsulated in the slogan embraced by many ERT protagonists: 'occupy, resist, produce'. Here, the chapter pays particular attention to ERT workers' responses to their initial conflicts, the legal challenges they face, and how they have re-appropriated and transformed bankruptcy and expropriation laws to favour workplace takeovers.

1   Section 1: From Workplace Conflicts to *Autogestión*

1.1   *From Micro-economic Crises to 'Struggling for the Other'*
As Salud Junín's José López, Alejandro Torres, and Ana María Barrionuevo, and Chilavert's Plácido Peñarrieta and Cándido González articulated for us in Chapter 1, one major experience that stands out from the three ERT case studies is that workers' initial acts of workplace occupations – called *ocupaciones* or *tomas* (takes) by ERT workers in Argentina – are not *initially* about permanently

taking over a factory, clinic, or shop, or about owning the firm's property or even kicking out abusive bosses. In none of the three cases – again, *initially* – did the collective of workers premeditate their *tomas* with visions of self-managing their places of employment. Rather, as was made clear in the case studies, the *tomas* and *recuperaciones* of troubled workplaces in Argentina by a group of its employees tend to almost always be primarily about – again, at least at the beginning of each struggle – securing the salaries each worker is due in back pay, guaranteeing fair severance packages, or saving their jobs in light of the absence of work elsewhere. Recall what Alejandro Torres, for example, said of the Salud Junín workers' initial reasons for occupying the failing clinic during the height of their struggle with their fleeing bosses:

> We didn't want to stay with the clinic and self-manage it forever. In reality, the occupation of the firm was only a strategy on our part to generate an event that would get the original owners of the clinic to [negotiate with us] and, we were hoping, then collect our salaries.[2]

Indeed, according to Andrés Ruggeri, this has been the case in most workplace recuperations to date in Argentina:

> It is significant that, among other things, the surge of ERTs at the height of the socio-economic crisis in Argentina, especially within say 1999 and 2002 [within ERTs' first period], is directly connected to the massive closure of industries and the consequent unemployment of millions of workers. Within these conditions, the first ERTs – and for many worker collectives still who are thinking about occupying a firm – usually emerge from desperate reactions by workers who were, first and foremost, looking to conserve their places of work via whatever means that would permit them to escape the social marginality and rising unemployment that had become very real possibilities for their own future.[3]

Ruggeri's assessment was discernable in the stories of ERT protagonists in Chapter 1, especially workers' fear of being left without work. The catalyst for a group of employees to take over troubled firms tends to also be rooted in their collectively shared experiences and feelings of deception and loss of dignity due to the mistreatment and abuses they suffered at the hands of managers

---

2   Torres 2009, personal interview.
3   Ruggeri 2006, personal interview.

and bosses. During ERTs' first period this was all compounded by indifference or outright hostility to their plight on the part of some unions and the state.

Additionally, as ERT workers in Chapter 1 also made clear, these collective experiences of suffering at specific workplaces, especially during the years of macro-economic crises at the turn of the millennium, intermingled with what workers were seeing occurring at the time in the work situations of their family members, friends, and neighbours who were also suffering abuses at work or facing unemployment or poverty. These collective experiences were also being reflected in the daily media images workers were consuming that constantly depicted street protests by the country's marginalised and other factory occupations, and in news reports on the corruption of the ruling establishment and the collapsing social order.

On the whole, the abuses that are suffered by workers in shops that eventually become ERTs – or, in Marxian terms, the increased rate of exploitation of the capitalist labour process taken to unbearable levels – are most often related by workers to outright violations of their labour contracts, placing into sharp relief for them (perhaps for the first time in their lives) the exploitative nature of the relationship between capital – embodied for workers in '*el patron*' ('the boss') – and labour – that is, workers themselves. This emergent and growing realisation, grounded in intensifying forms of exploitation and shared moments of heightened work uncertainty, as we will continue to see in Chapters 7 and 8, are intimately tied to Maurice Merleau-Ponty's and E.P. Thompson's conceptions of a class-in-the-making, an emergent working-class consciousness, and the moral economy of work that was first reviewed in the Introduction and theorised further in Chapter 4.

Most ERT protagonists, then, are driven to embark on the risky project of taking over their workplaces – despite the ensuing struggles that this decision entails – due to the *existentially felt* and *lived experiences* of fear, deception, and foreboding shared with their workmates – Merleau-Ponty's 'synchronized' experiences and feelings within a 'common lot',[4] as we saw in Chapter 4. These lived experiences and feelings of fear and deception were especially common on shop floors throughout Argentina during ERTs' first period and included: increased job precariousness and heightened life uncertainty within a socio-political and socio-economic system perceived to be unfair; the unjust treatment workers felt they received from their managers or bosses; and the widespread apprehension of imminent unemployment experienced in common with others from their immediate and broader social networks.

---

4   Merleau-Ponty 1962, p. 444.

One not only palpably senses some of the nuances of these intersubjectively lived experiences of fear and insecurity in the interview excerpts from Chapter 1, but also the solidarity amongst workers that the collective overcoming of these experiences eventually fosters. These shared experiences ultimately serve to solidify ERT workers' projects of *autogestión*, as we will return to in Chapter 8. Recall, for example, when Salud Junín's José López recounted the clinic's workers' shared feelings of uncertainty for their future and the future of the clinic, the tenuousness of their collective actions during their first weeks and months of occupation, and the common precarious life situations that brought them together in solidarity: '[W]e stayed here taking care of the clinic, at first because *we didn't know where else to go*', José related in Chapter 1, '[i]t was only eventually that we realised that we had to stay here and occupy the clinic in order to avoid [its closure]'.[5] Salud Junín's Ana María Barrionuevo further highlighted how this shared sense of precariousness served to bring the collective together in a spirit of mutual aid when she states that: '[i]t was a *very precarious time for us all* ... and this also *served to bring us together as a group*, to look out for each other'.[6]

Many other ERT workers we have spoken with in numerous ERTs over the years have also underscored the importance of these collectively lived experiences of micro-economic crises for building workers' sense of solidarity with each other and, ultimately, carrying out the worker collective's eventual projects of *autogestión*. Javier De Pascuale, for example, former president of the ERT newspaper *Comercio y Justicia* and in 2009 its editorial director,[7] emphasised the importance of these commonly lived experiences for the cooperative members' eventual '*compromiso*' (a high level of commitment) to the cooperative project and to each other.[8] This *compromiso* to the cooperative project and to struggling for the ongoing wellbeing of '*el otro*' (the other), Javier stressed,

---

5   López 2009, personal interview.

6   Barrionuevo 2008, personal interview.

7   *Comercio y Justicia*, a worker-recuperated newspaper covering business and legal issues that now also includes a multipurpose print shop in the city of Córdoba, was founded as an ERT in 2001 after its Brazilian owners abandoned the plant just before Argentina's default on its national debt. It was the first newspaper to be recuperated in Argentina and was the first case of an ERT emerging from a worker buyout when the workers managed to buy back the firm from bankruptcy. It was also recuperated without much conflict, as the workers (knowledgable in legal business matters given the focus of the newspaper) negotiated their own workplace conversion to worker management with the local bankruptcy courts rather than seeking the expropriation solution. As of 2016, *Comercio y Justicia* had 78 *socios*, many of them younger journalists and print shop workers who joined the firm after it was converted to a worker cooperative.

8   De Pascuale 2009, personal interview.

strengthens the solidarity between *compañeros* and interlaces their destinies. Javier made clear how the acquisition of this shared *compromiso* is intimately connected both to working out immanently and collectively the nuances of their cooperative project and to the past activist and community work of some of the founding members. Both are necessary, he told me, in order for their self-management project to last and prosper:

> I believe that what one incorporates from a past of social and political activism and shared struggles are values and methodologies of working together, democratic participation, and so on. Most importantly, I think, is that one incorporates *un compromiso* [a commitment, a sense of ethics], *una lucha por el otro* [a struggle for the other]. One doesn't learn to be a cooperator until one lives it because, in a sense, one's level of commitment in a cooperative [to a common project and to the other] is maximum, not like the commitment you have when you are an activist, which is temporary or for a little while. In a cooperative you live it daily and you are a *compañero* for life ... Your destiny is linked to the other, not on a temporary basis to, say, fight for a better society with someone you meet on the street, but rather your very existence, your destiny, is linked to the other all the time in a cooperative, it's a kind of twenty-four-hour militancy, right?[9]

A number of this book's key ERT informants, including workers at all three case studies, also used the word '*compromiso*' and phrases such as '*la lucha por el otro*' ('the struggle for the other') when describing the heightened sense of '*responsabilidad*' ('responsibility') needed by an ERT's worker collective in order to make the cooperative work and prosper. Javier's quote also alludes to the ethical position of '*esto es de todos*' ('this belongs to all of us') that infuses, either implicitly or explicitly, all of the ERT key informants' discussions of their collectives' past and ongoing struggles, the events that mobilised their direct actions, and what is needed to ensure the ongoing unity and continued stability of their projects of *autogestión*. In Chapter 8, we will link the practices and values of *compromiso*, *la lucha por el otro*, and *esto es de todos* to what we will come to know as a broader 'ethics of the other' that emerges from out of ERT protagonists' common struggles. Often, this study's key informants would implicitly link these values of solidarity, mutual aid, and shared commitment and responsibility (that is, their ethics of the other) to: (1) their stories of how

---

9   Ibid.

the worker collective had to surmount various challenges in the process of securing the firm; (2) their recounting of how the struggles of occupying the firm, resisting repression, and starting to self-manage an ERT helped gel the worker collective; (3) individual members' histories of militancy, community involvement, or political work; and (4) how the collective's challenges often brought an ERT's members closer together later when they finally formed a fully functioning worker cooperative. Indeed, these shared values and commitments that emerge immanently from intersubjective experiences of struggle and that are necessary for consolidating and securing the subsequent project of *autogestión* in the worker cooperative are some of this book's most important findings.[10]

In sum, all of these shared memories, narratives, and lived experiences of struggles and challenges – common travails at work from the abuses of bosses and managers, and similar stories of domestic suffering at home from the indifference of a callous neo-liberal system that shed itself of much of the costs of labour protections and social safety nets (all especially common in Argentina during the crisis years at the turn of the millennium) – serve to heighten the collective anger of workers and entrench their solidarity during moments of micro-economic crisis on shop floors. These commonly shared narratives and recollections of intersubjectively lived experiences, evident in the three ERT case studies in Chapter 1, subsequently serve to catalyse workers in troubled firms to carry out the direct-action tactics of occupation and resistance that characterise the Argentine ERT phenomenon. In turn, these *struggles in common* deeply infuse the motivating factors[11] that compel workers at troubled firms in Argentina to take over and self-manage them. Chapters 8 and 9 will further analyse these shared experiential dimensions in light of the critical theories that frame this book.

1.2 Common Motivations for Workplace Takeovers in Argentina

The *conflictive origins* of Argentina's ERTs is the characteristic that has garnered the most media, political, and research attention, making this the best-known aspect of the process of forming an ERT.[12] This has some merit. It is worthwhile to underscore that every workplace recuperation process means some sort of

---

10   These findings are analysed in further in Chapters 8 and 9.

11   Or, as suggested earlier, the 'mobilising grievances' and the 'moral economy of work'. For an assessment of the various ways that the literature on ERTs has interpreted the motivating factors impelling workers to form ERTs, see Gracia and Cavaliere 2007.

12   Vieta and Ruggeri 2009; Ruggeri 2009; Ruggeri, Antivero, Elena, Polti, et al. 2014; Vieta 2010a, 2012, 2013.

conflict between workers and owners, and often also with management, bankruptcy court officials and judges or other state actors. Some sort of conflict is also present when workers do not physically occupy the firm in the process of conversion. Indeed, and unlike other conversion experiences in other countries today, with Argentina's ERTs it is conflict that most often mediates the transformation of a troubled capitalist firm into a worker self-managed workplace, thus characterising them as 'labour conflict ERTs'.[13] In the transitional stage between the former capitalist firm and the worker cooperative, as we explicitly saw in the three recuperation stories in Chapter 1, an inevitable tipping point emerges when workers realise that their jobs are at risk. It is then that the preservation of livelihoods becomes the key point of struggle. Moreover, the transition of firms from capitalist to collective management, even with the few Argentine ERTs that emerge in more favourable and less conflictive scenarios,[14] continues to create concerns and uncertainty amongst workers regarding the security of their jobs or their ultimate ability to self-manage a business. After all, workers must inevitably change their mindset from being wage-labourers (employees) to self-managed workers, which includes the not so clear task of figuring out how to collectively manage a business that used to operate in a strictly capitalist manner under owner-management or 'specialist' administrators/managers and that are often inherited in poor operational conditions. These anxieties are exacerbated when the transition to *autogestión* is preceded by unmistakable signs heralding the closure of a firm, most usually taking shape in Argentina when previous owners begin to have problems paying wages, when businesses start to experience a decrease in the rate and volume of work, with the gradual disappearance or lack of maintenance of machines, or other signs that the business is in crisis.

The five main reasons that most often initially motivate workers to take over their places of work, as self-reported by ERT workers themselves, has been identified by the Programa Facultad Abierta team to include: (1) workers' perceived sense of the inevitability of the firm's *vaciamiento* (asset stripping, or literally 'emptying') of the plant by its owners; (2) the impending or already declared bankruptcy of the firm; (3) a chronic situation of workers not being paid wages, not receiving compensation for overtime, or cutbacks in the employer's portion of social security contributions or other benefits; (4) the actual laying off of fellow workers; and (5) other related factors such as assorted experi-

---

13   See Chapter 2.
14   For example, in cases where workers managed to negotiate the conversion of the firm
      without the need for an occupation, such as the case of the ERT newspaper *Comercio y
      Justicia*.

ences of mistreatment at the hands of managers or bosses, the anticipation of future conflict at the firm, and so on.[15] As the Programa Facultad Abierta team assert, for ERTs emerging during the first period (1990s–2004) during the turn-of-millennium years of crisis, these self-reported motivators for workplace takeovers by 'those [workers] that were victims' of Argentina's neo-liberal collapse, were 'consistent with the [socio-economic] context of the loss of productive entities that characterised the decade of the 1990s and the process of deindustrialisation [in Argentina], coming to a head in the crisis of 2001'.[16] In other words, here we see the tight connections between macro-economic crisis and the responses to this crisis by Argentine workers in some troubled firms that surged in the first years of the twenty-first century.

The self-reported reasons motivating workers to take over and eventually self-manage their firms have remained quite consistent over time, as the Programa Facultad Abierta's fourth survey during ERTs' third period revealed.[17] This points out both the constancy of what workers must still struggle against in Argentina, and the broad recognition by Argentine society of workers' takeovers of firms as legitimate methods of resistance against and restitution for overt exploitation. With more recent ERTs, overdue wages or the total absence of pay over an extended period of time in the former firm continue to be central motivators for founding an ERT, reported in more than 80 percent of the sample of new ERT cases surveyed by the Programa Facultad Abierta in 2014. The issue of *vaciamiento* has also remained a core motivator, with 60 percent of the new ERT cases in 2014 having faced this dilemma in the previous firm.[18] Other motivators for founding an ERT that have remained consistent over time include the neglect or actual or imminent sale of machinery and facilities, or the impending bankruptcy of the firm. Moreover, and also consistent throughout the history of contemporary Argentine ERTs, workers' motivators for taking over a firm have usually included a combination of factors.

Nevertheless, there are some variations in workers' motivations for creating ERTs when comparing more recent cases to those emerging during ERTs' first two periods. In ERT's third period (2010–15), relatively few workers were actually fired or locked out prior to the takeover, two circumstances which were especially common in ERTs' first period. Additionally, the Programa Facultad

---

15   Ruggeri, Martínez, and Trinchero 2005, p. 66.
16   Ibid. For a clear picture of the 'loss of productive entities' in the 1990s, see Figure 12 and the related discussion of this period in Argentine history in Chapters 2 and 3.
17   Ruggeri et al. 2014.
18   Multiple answers were permitted in the fourth survey for this question.

Abierta's fourth survey of third period ERTs[19] found that all of the self-reported responses by ERTs regarding the motivators for their emergence were fairly evenly dispersed. In their second survey (up to December 2004),[20] on the other hand, still within the aftermath of the 2001–2 crisis and resonating with record numbers of SME closures during these years, the lack of payment of wages was mentioned less often than in subsequent surveys, while mistreatment of workers and threats of or actual firings and lockouts were mentioned more often. On the whole, however, and despite some variations over time, Argentina's ERTs are workplace conversion processes particularly ensconced in prolonged and by now predictable labour conflicts.

Overall, and cutting across ERTs' historical periods, the self-reported reasons initially provoking workers' direct actions of occupying their workplaces can be synthesised into two overarching experiential motivators, contributing to some of the major distinguishing characteristics of Argentina's ERTs: (1) workers' *anger* or *indignation* at suffering maltreatment from bosses and managers, and (2) *deep worries* about becoming structurally unemployed, a life situation that Argentine workers term '*muerte en vida*' ('death in life').[21] The first overarching motivator is focused on the conditions of work on shop floors. The second, on broader macro-economic and socio-political realities as they resonate in workers' lives. Both key motivators are further nuanced by the fact that the average ERT worker, as will be expanded on in the following chapter, is mid-career (around 40 to 50 years of age), while many others are near retirement. This age-based factor further concretises in workers' minds the decision to engage in an ERT project, especially given the fact that finding a new job for anyone over 35 in Argentina is a challenge in its ageist job market in the best of times. In other words, ERTs originate first as direct and immanent responses to their worker-protagonists' lived experiences of deep conflict on shop floors and their emerging precarious life situations in light of the paucity of other alternatives for work. Ruggeri explained how this situation was particularly augmented during the years of crisis at the turn of the millennium in a long conversation we had in 2006:

> The precarious conditions of life for the unemployed served as visible threats for those workers that still had jobs. This motivated them to develop *new labour survival strategies* that could replace old union methods that didn't seem to be useful any longer. Remember that traditional

---

19   Ruggeri et al. 2014.
20   Ruggeri et al. 2005.
21   Vieta and Ruggeri 2009, p. 202.

unions [during the height of the crisis of the neo-liberal model in Argentina] had lost most of their abilities to apply pressure to business. In addition, workers faced a situation where there was a massive demand for work but little supply. Our society was one where jobs became a scarce commodity for an enormous army of reserve labour.[22]

Theorising these motivators linked to socio-political and micro-economic contexts and ERT workers' lived experience, Argentine labour sociologist Hector Palomino[23] has identified three stages in the emergence of an ERT:

(1) a *worker collective's recognition and genesis of conflict* with former bosses and/or the state,

(2) the *transformation of workers' perceptions of their capacity to change their situation* and *shift the terrain of conflict* from their workspaces onto the streets and the houses of power,[24] and

(3) the struggle to *regulate and normalise their work* once again as self-managed firms.

In a similar vein, the Movimiento Nacional de Empresas Recuperadas (MNER)[25] evocatively captured ERTs' three-staged struggle towards *autogestión* in the following slogan they popularised, borrowed from Brazil's Movimiento dos Trabalhadores Rurais Sem Terra (MTS, Movement of Landless Rural Workers) and still used by many ERT protagonists to poignantly and efficiently communicate to themselves, to new ERTs, and to others the three main stages of their struggle: '*ocupar, resistir, producir*' ('occupy, resist, produce'). Complementing Palomino's three stages and Ruggeri's quote above, Eduardo Murúa, president of MNER at the time of the interview, explained the meaning behind this slogan as follows:

> This new form of struggle – or, let's say, the *necessity* for a new form of struggle – now appears; a new method of workers' struggle. It marked a new form of struggle that no longer is limited to the common type of union demands for increased wages or for better work conditions. Rather, it was a struggle to *occupy* the factory in order to operate it *ourselves* – as a

---

22   Ruggeri 2006, personal interview.

23   Palomino 2003.

24   Particularly as ERT workers seek legal recognition and protections for their self-management projects from the state. See, for example, the discussion of the strategy of seeking out state-sanctioned expropriations of their firms and lobbying lawmakers to reform Argentina's bankruptcy procedures later on in this chapter.

25   For more on MNER and other ERT and self-managed workers' associations, see Chapter 3.

response to the neo-liberal model. This was, in the beginning, a *defensive struggle*. This [was the case] when the first recuperations start appearing, and this is also when IMPA is recuperated.[26]

It was then that we made *solidarity* our central theme. We began our practice of rallying around our *compañeros* in conflict, and we [adopted] a slogan that communicated what we wanted to do: *ocupar, resistir, producir*. It has to do with *occupation* as a founding practice. When we spoke with our *compañeros* who were engaged in conflict, the first thing we would say was: 'Occupy the factory and do not leave!' Then we would say: 'Resist', because it was after occupation that the law would arrive. While the workers are being swindled, left out on the streets, and not getting paid, 'the law' – and I say this in scare quotes – fails to show up. The reason for the word 'resist' is because what the justice system orders is the clearing out of the plant in order to liquidate it. It is then that we have to resist with our bodies, and with the solidarity of our people, so that the police cannot move on the juridical decision [to close the plant and evict the resisting workers]. It is this resistance that [eventually] convinces judges or politicians to seek a solution that will put the factory back into operation.[27]

Pragmatically, then, the slogan 'occupy, resist, produce' serves to concisely capture the three distinctive stages most ERT worker protagonists must go through on their way towards *autogestión*. Some of the nuances of the principal struggles that tend to preoccupy workers in the first two stages of an emer-

---

26   IMPA, Industria Metalúrgica y Plástica Argentina, was one of the first ERTs, recuperated in 1997–8. Still existing as an ERT, this large aluminium manufacturing plant is located on the border of the central Buenos Aires *barrios* of Caballito and Almagro. Already a cooperative by the time it was taken over by a group of its worker-members (it had been nationalised by Juán Perón during his second presidency, and then turned into a cooperative in 1961), IMPA became an ERT in 1998 when a group of its *socios* (members) took it over from the old cooperative's administrative council when it declared bankruptcy and threatened to close the plant. Murúa had been one of the shop stewards at the plant and, together with another early MNER activist, Guillermo Robledo, led the takeover of IMPA. Since then, IMPA has become one of the most emblematic ERTs. It was, for instance, one of the first ERTs to open up its space to community projects. Since its reopening as an ERT cooperative, IMPA has dedicated a large part of its space to an art school, silkscreen shop, theatre, cultural centre, free medical clinic, and for popular education programmes under a broad project called La Fábrica Ciudad Cultural (The Factory Cultural City) (see Chapter 8). In the early days of IMPA, Murúa continued his union and workers' rights activism and consolidated his organising work by co-founding MNER at this ERT.

27   Murúa 2005a, personal interview.

gent ERT – the 'occupy' and 'resist' stages – were particularly illustrated in the three case studies in Chapter 1.[28] They follow the tactics of physically occupying workplaces, coupled by street mobilisations and public protests that, as the case studies showed, often see hundreds of supporters from the local neighbourhood, the broader community, other ERTs, and civil society and social movement groups mobilising for the cause of an emerging ERT in what Murúa has evocatively termed 'the war of bodies'.[29] In the remaining pages of this chapter, we highlight ERT workers' most common experiences during the first two stages of struggle and the initial reasons for specifically forming a worker cooperative in the third stage ('produce'). An indepth analysis of the intricacies of ERTs' cooperative production will be taken up, in turn, in Chapters 7 and 8.

2 Section 2: The Strategies and Tactics of 'Occupy, Resist, Produce'[30]

2.1 'Occupy, ...'

Chapter 1's cases illustrated some of the ways that Argentina's 'production regime'[31] ruptured on the shop floors of SMEs across the country at the height of the years of crisis at the turn of the millennium. The articulation of the strategies and tactics of workplace takeovers and occupations would thus emerge within a conjuncture of a de-legitimated neo-liberal model and the rise of new forms of bottom-up labour militancy and social movements that were directly responding to the crisis throughout the late 1990s and early 2000s. Some of the circumstances for occupying firms during the years of crisis are still present to this day, while the strategies and tactics innovated by workers at that time continue to be deployed and perfected. As with the motivators for founding an ERT, however, new circumstances and situations of struggle have also emerged over the years, adding further characteristics to the ERT phenomenon.

---

28 Avi Lewis and Naomi Klein's film *The Take: Occupy, Resist, Produce* (Lewis and Klein 2004), Isaac Isitan and Carole Poliquin's *The Women of Brukman* (Isitan 2007), Darío Doria and Luis Camardella's *Grissinopoli: El país de los grisines* (Doria and Camardella 2005), and Ricardo Díaz Iacoponi's feature film *Industria Argentina: La fábrica es para los que trabajan* (Iacopini and Sánchez Sotelo 2012) also vividly capture ERTs' early stages of occupation, resistance, initial legal battles, and their workers' struggles to restart production runs under self-management.

29 Murúa 2005b, personal interview.

30 Portions of this section first appeared in Ruggeri and Vieta 2015.

31 As we reviewed in Chapter 4, 'production regimes' are characterised by the 'regimes of regulation [affecting] the point of production' (Burawoy 1985, pp. 17, 83–6).

As discussed in the first section of this chapter, workplace occupations tend to often be at the start desperate responses by workers to the *vaciamiento* of a near-bankrupt firm's machinery and assets, as we saw with Chilavert and Salud Junín in Chapter 1. They also occur with the imminence of job flexibilisation, firings, or plant closures, as with UST. Almost all occupations are driven by workers' ultimate fear of losing their jobs. As we also saw in the case studies, the 'occupy' stage of ERTs has workers facing down either returning owners wishing to reclaim their abandoned firms (at times with the assistance of hired thugs), or in some cases even unions colluding with business owners, as was the case with UST, or, as with Chilavert, confronting police batons and assault vehicles as local bankruptcy or commercial court judges preside over eviction orders which at times turn to violent eviction attempts. As was also the case with Chilavert, *vaciamiento* attempts or forced evictions often occur under the stealth of night and tend to be surrounded by onerous circumstances. This was especially part of the recuperation story of many ERTs during the phenomenon's first period (early 1990s to around 2004), including also, amongst many others, the ceramics factory Zanón/FaSinPat in the province of Neuquén,[32] and the Global/La Nueva Esperanza balloon factory[33] and the Brukman textile plant[34] in the city of Buenos Aires.

Hence, with the very real possibility of the disappearance of machinery and inventory, imminent or actual bankruptcy often under onerous circumstances, and, ultimately, the loss of jobs, workers will first mobilise either by: physically occupying the firm, as is most frequently the case; camping outside of the doors of the firm when locked out; or other types of collective mobilisations such as street protests or street blockages, lobbying local courts or legislatures, or other public acts of resistance.[35] During ERT's third period, the number of ERT experiences that have had to resort to the direct occupations of firms or

---

32   Aiziczón 2009.

33   Monteagudo 2008.

34   As with Chilavert, UST, and Salud Junín, Brukman's textile workers (almost all female) also originally took the factory – ominously, as with Salud Junín, on 18 December 2001, the day before the massive social protests of 19 and 20 December – as a tactic to force the owners to preserve their jobs. The fleeing owners failed to acquiesce to the demands and the Brukman workers began to eventually produce again as a cooperatively run firm, resisting several eviction orders that turned violent as numerous community groups and hundreds of ERT workers from across the country, including the Zanán/FaSinPat workers, offered them support over the following two years. Brukman has since been the topic of several documentaries and has, as with Zanón, Chilavert, IMPA, and the Hotel BAUEN, become one of the most emblematic and well-known ERTs (see, for example, Grupo de Boedo Films 2002; and Isitan and Poliquin 2007).

35   Ruggeri, Polti, Clark, Antivero, Delegdisch, et al. 2010, p. 16.

other forms of direct actions by employees remained almost unchanged from the second period. In the Programa Facultad Abierta's fourth survey covering third period ERTs, 61 percent of ERTs reported that they had resorted to occupations or protests of different kinds, compared to 62 percent in Programa's third survey covering ERTs' second period.[36] Of the 61 percent of ERT respondents to the fourth survey that said they had engaged in some form of occupation or protest, nearly 60 percent had engaged in actual occupations of the firm, and the rest had carried out other forms of direct action including encampments at the front doors of the firm, community rallies, solidarity marches, strikes, or a combination of these measures.

It is perhaps not surprising to learn that a high percentage of ERT cases, especially with those that emerged in the years of macro-economic crisis, had experienced repressive situations either from state authorities or from private interests associated with returning owners.[37] Of the 205 ERTs that were surveyed by the Programa Facultad Abierta research team in their third survey (up to December 2009), 50 percent reported having experienced 'repression or orders of forced eviction' from the state, usually during the worker collective's first days, weeks, or months of occupation.[38] By the Programa Facultad Abierta's fourth survey (up to December 2013), this had gone down to 37 percent of reporting ERTs, indicating that newer ERTs by 2014 were not on the whole experiencing state-sanctioned repression.[39] Part of the reason for this drop is that threats of or actual repression, generally instigated by judicial eviction orders, often do not succeed in actually evicting occupying workers, due most usually to the pressure exerted on state authorities or local police by supporting local community groups, social movement protagonists, workers from other ERTs, or from intensive media coverage. Additionally, national and regional governments and local judges, soon recognising the bad publicity they were receiving in light of the chronically high rates of unemployment that weighed down the country's economy throughout ERTs' first period and into the first years of its second period, had been, by the end of the third period in late 2015, much more reticent to invoke draconian measures against workplace occupations.[40]

---

36   Ruggeri et al. 2014, p. 22.
37   As reviewed in Chapter 3, repression as both methods of social control and as a weapon used by capital–state alliances to control working-class resistance has a long history in Argentina.
38   Ruggeri et al. 2010, p. 17.
39   Ruggeri et al. 2014, p. 22.
40   It is important to note that while the state repression that tended to follow factory seizures in the early days of the ERT phenomenon had substantially abated with newer cases of

A further 20 percent of experiences with repression with newer ERTs are 'private' eviction attempts or other forms of intimidation by returning owners, including verbal threats or physical violence by private security personnel or from hired and armed thugs (*matones*) who try to expel or threaten workers, at times paid by the owners or other parties who stand to benefit from the auctioning of the business's assets. The increase in these repressive situations by private interests in recent years, however, which the Programa Facultad Abierta researchers had already noted in their 2010 report, continues to raise the alarm about ERT workers' ongoing difficulties, the ongoing risks they face in creating an ERT, and the continued lack of robust institutional protections for workers, even during the more pro-labour Kirchner years. And, as was discussed in Chapter 3, there is evidence that cases of repression against ERT workers from private interests – again, usually from thugs hired by returning owners – sharply increased with the recent return to neo-liberal policies under the presidency of Mauricio Macri, as with the recently recuperated newspaper *El Tiempo Argentino*.[41]

Because repression and orders of forced eviction continue to be a reality for ERT protagonists, the support of the local community, universities, and social movement groups – such as the long-term support of ERTs by the Programa Facultad Abierta and the Madres de la Plaza de Mayo – remains crucial for the survival of particular ERTs and the broader ERT movement. This support is particularly vital during a collective of workers' first stages of occupation. As Chilavert's Fermín González clearly articulated in 2005:

> During the days when Chilavert was under siege by police and our moments of occupation, the community support we received was key for us. We couldn't have kept this place open or resisted repression without the community, without the support we received from the ERT movement, from the neighbourhood assemblies, from students, from our families. Their support in so many ways – bringing us food, helping us stand off against police, coming to visit us, making this place relevant – is one of the most important parts of our history.[42]

ERTs by the second and third periods, acts of state repression did still occur. In 2009, for example, then new ERTs such as Textil Quilmes, the print shop Indugraf, the chocolate manufacturer Arufat, and the continued struggles of the Hotel BAUEN workers to have their hotel legally recognised have all included threats of forced eviction and threats of or actual repression by state agents.

41   Ámbito.com 2016a; del Pont 2016; Tiempo Argentino 2016.
42   F. González 2005b, personal interview.

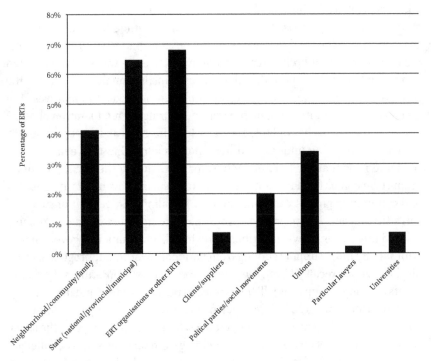

FIGURE 14   Support received by ERTs during the recuperation process
            Note: *N*=85 ERTs, multiple answers permitted.
            SOURCE: RUGGERI ET AL. 2010, P. 19

Indeed, as Figure 14 explicitly shows, by ERTs' second period almost 70 percent of ERTs received support during the recuperation process from ERT umbrella organisations and associations such as MNER, FACTA, or MNFRT; from other ERTs; or from other cooperatives, while more than 41 percent also received support from neighbours, the community, or family members during this time. Moreover, 34 percent also received support from their unions,[43] and 20 percent of ERTs were supported by political parties or other social movement groups during the recuperation process.

That 65 percent of ERTs existing in 2009 claimed to have also received support from the state during the recuperation process (municipal, provincial, or federal governments and related ministries) was a reflection of the state's change in attitude towards ERTs during the post-convertability Kirchner years,

---

43   As we have already covered, by 2010 there was a growing awareness and support for ERTs
     from unions when compared to 2005 numbers, when only 19 percent of ERTs claimed to
     have received support from them (Ruggeri et al. 2005, p. 62).

which also relates to the overall drop in state-sanctioned repression during the second and third periods. This more supportive attitude towards ERTs from the state during the Kirchner years – due in no small part to the ongoing lobbying efforts of ERT umbrella organisations and activists – was witnessed, when compared to ERTs' first period, in the increased institutional acceptance of the processes of converting workplaces in trouble into worker cooperatives,[44] in greater support for ERTs by state programmes during the recuperation phase,[45] and in modest gains in available state subsidies for ERTs after recuperation.[46]

What needs to be underscored here, however, 'reading between the bars' of Figure 14, is that the bulk of support for ERTs during the occupy/recuperation stage comes from other ERTs, supportive social movements, neighbours and community groups, and some unions. The almost 65 percent of surveyed ERTs that received some support from the state in Figure 14 can be roughly divided into thirds between national, provincial, and municipal governments, with slightly more support coming from national government programs. Overall, the supports received from the state, however (mostly one-time subsidies or grants as salary top-ups), as will be clarified in the next section and in Chapter 7, still have a long way to go in Argentina in order to more thoroughly facilitate the conversion of failing firms into cooperatives, for assisting in meeting the social security needs of ERT workers, and for helping overcome the sundry challenges of self-managing depleted firms. Moreover, as we will also see in Chapter 7, many of these state supports had been frozen by Mauricio Macri's first year in power in 2016 and have yet to be reinstated as of this writing. In short, the solidary accompaniment of emerging ERTs by the community, social movement groups, other ERTs, and social and solidarity economy organisations – rather than state supports – is vitally important for an emerging ERT during its

---

44   See next section and Chapters 2 and 7.

45   This more pro-ERT attitude that was gradually embraced by the three Kirchner administrations and various provincial and municipal governments across Argentina can be further grasped when we compare the Programa Facultad Abierta's 2009 data with its earlier 2004 survey. By the end of 2004, 59 percent of ERTs existing at that time claimed to have received some form of state support for the recuperation of the ERT from the national government, the provincial government, or municipalities (Ruggeri et al. 2005, p. 62). Chapter 7 will analyse this further.

46   Over the years, these state supports for ERTs after recuperation (that is, once they have been established as worker cooperatives), as we will see in more detail in Chapter 7, had expanded substantially from less than five percent of ERTs receiving some form of state assistance in 2001 to more than 60 percent of ERTs claiming to have received some form of state support by 2013. These supports, however, had fallen in recent years, from a high of 85 percent of ERTs reporting that they had received post-recuperation state support as of 2009 (Ruggeri et al. 2010, p. 75; Ruggeri et al. 2014, p. 59).

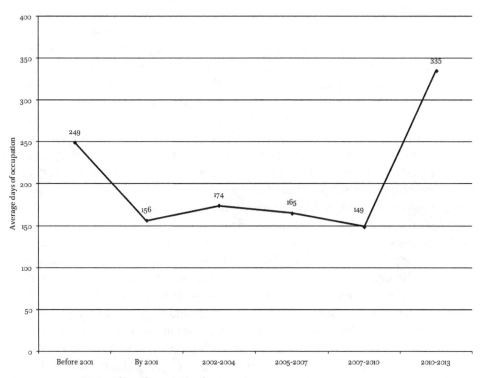

FIGURE 15   Average days of occupation for emerging ERTs
Note: *N*=311 ERTS.
SOURCE: RUGGERI ET AL. 2014, P. 24

'occupy' stage. This community-based accompaniment not only offers moral support to workers squatting a plant, but is also important for pragmatic reasons, helping protect ERT protagonists against possible repression as a strategy linked to what Murúa described for us earlier on as the 'war of bodies'.

Already in the first years of the 2010s, however, with the more unstable economic reality of post-2008 Argentina and rising inflation taking hold in the country, and with new legal hurdles faced by workers desiring to take over firms, the scenario was changing for new ERTs. Figure 15 illustrates one of the most surprising findings regarding ERTs that emerged during the third-period: the considerable increase in the number of days that workers had to endure occupying the firm in order to recuperate it. Counting from the beginning of the occupation of the firm to the beginning of full workers' control of the ERT, the number of days of occupation during the second period had actually decreased in relation to the average days of occupation before 2001 during the years and months leading to the financial collapse, which was around eight months. Between 2001 and 2010, the length of time of these conflicts had stabilised to around four or five months. Between 2010 and 2013, however, the average period of workplace occupation needed to finally win control over an ERT had doubled from the previous period, almost equalling one year.

A telling socio-political reality implicitly suggested by comparing Figures 14, 15, and 16 is the ambiguous if not perplexed position of the state with regard to worker takeovers over the years. The paucity of legal options available to ERTs during their first period, together with the bottleneck situation of their cases in bankruptcy courts for workers that were occupying their plants during this period, is reflected in the extensive number of average days they would need to occupy a plant before they could reopen it. As we have analysed in earlier chapters, during ERTs' first period, the state in the main failed or chose not to see the connection between its desire to promote more business activity during the lows of Argentina's economic crisis years at the turn of the millennium and the opportunity the ERT model offered for the preservation of jobs and productive entities in the midst of massive rates of unemployment and poverty at the time. Tellingly, during the most acute years of socio-economic crisis, the state, via the decisions of bankruptcy courts and the paucity of legal outlets for workers willing to reopen shuttered firms, would most often side with business owners and the capitalist class by privileging property rights over the right to work, attempting forced evictions against a majority of ERTs during these years, or trying to exhaust workers occupying firms by delaying legal decisions. As the state came to see ERTs as viable solutions for economic recovery during the years immediately following the end of convertability, and as ERTs gained public and legal legitimacy during these years, the period of conflict during the occupation stage of ERTs decreased while the state took a more supportive position towards ERTs and substantially decreased legal bottlenecks, repression, and eviction attempts.

The more recent situation of heightened conflict with new ERTs, measured by the dramatic increase in the number of days needed on average to occupy a firm before full self-management can begin, has brought back some of the challenges ERT workers believed they had overcome. The extended duration of occupations and conflict for workers struggling to create an ERT in recent years has forced an intensification of the resoluteness required by a workers' collective desiring to save their workplace, while also, not surprisingly, adding to the challenges that must be traversed to found an ERT. First, the workplace remains closed during the period of occupation and continued conflict. On occasion workers do manage to start some kind of informal activity during the period of occupation, but this is usually a far cry from the levels of work activity that they were accustomed to during the best days of the previous firm. More concretely for the lives of workers in struggle, this extended period of occupation and conflict draws out the time in which workers do not receive regular income and compounds the hardships that they and their families face. Second, extended periods of occupation and conflict means that it is increasingly hard for workers to restart production when and if they regain control of the business, making it particularly difficult to gather necessary resources and continue to mobilise support. Third, the extension of periods of occupation increases the challenges faced by more technologically complex industrial plants, especially since machines remain unused and their maintenance is neglected. Fourth, it is even harder during these conflictual periods to rebuild value chains, retain or secure new customers and suppliers, or reintegrate competitively into the market. In sum, rather than a 'heroic struggle' from the point of view of working-class militancy, pragmatically the excessive duration of conflicts and days of occupation is a serious hurdle for the successful recuperation and conversion of a business, adding significantly to the difficulties that worker-recuperated businesses already bring with them. An average of 11 months of conflict for the newest ERTs is no small detail to overcome and can become a strong disincentive for ERT formation and the future of workers' self-management.

If we connect the challenges involved in starting an ERT with others related to their ongoing legal issues, we find several clues as to why this extended situation of conflict has been occurring with Argentina's newest ERTs. We next address the legal reasons that have been extending the periods of conflict and occupations with newer ERTs, especially – and paradoxically – as related to the new national bankruptcy law introduced in 2011; a legislative reform which was intended to facilitate the process of workplace recuperations but which, in practice, has served to exacerbate an emerging ERTs' challenges.

2.2   '... Resist, ...'

After the turmoil of the initial period of shop floor crisis, the realisation by a firm's employees that their jobs are at risk, and the subsequent occupation of the troubled firm, the collective of workers that decide to stay and struggle enter the 'resist' phase of an ERT. The 'occupation' phase, in reality, blends into the 'resist' phase. During this phase, workers ensure that they are present within the shop at all times or, if they have been locked out, that they camp outside of it on an ongoing basis. They do so in shifts, often with the solidarity of neighbours and *compañeros* from other ERTs who bring them food, bedding, and other supplies. In some cases during this period, as was the case with Chilavert and Salud Junín, the occupying workers begin to run machines, produce in small batches, or deliver some services, as the case may be, sometimes even using the help of supportive neighbours or other community groups to bring their

products to market, as we saw with Chilavert. In most cases, substantial production runs must wait until the resisting worker collective's numerous legal
issues are resolved, which can take several more months or even years, as we
saw with Salud Junín in particular.

The resistance phase of the struggle is exhausting for the already psycholo-
gically and emotionally drained ERT workers. After having experienced trau-
mas related to the deteriorating conditions of work during the last months of
employment and the initial takeover of the plant, resisting workers more often
than not must tackle yet another precarious stage of their lives characterised
by little or no income, legal instability, and the constant threat of eviction or
even repression. ERTs' sources of income during the 'resist' phase, if they have
been able to secure any, tend to come from community solidarity funds, financial support from family, strike funds from unions that decide to support ERT
workers, or whatever they can manage to earn from initial sales of goods or services or from recycling or selling remaining inventory or raw materials on hand
from the previous firm.

Challenges at the resistance stage are compounded by inconsistent or inadequate state support for emerging ERTs, support that would go a long way
towards easing workers' struggles during this period, as well as speeding up the
resumption of production or service delivery. Moreover, unlike ERTs in Brazil,
Uruguay, and in Southern Europe, as we saw in Chapter 2, where workplace
conversions enjoy wider support from the state, in Argentina – more than 20
years after the first ERTs appeared – there is still a dearth of comprehensive
or consistent national policies in place for assisting workers in the process of
converting firms to cooperatives. As will be explored in Chapter 7, the Néstor
Kirchner and Cristina Fernández de Kirchner governments, as well as several
provincial and municipal governments, had begun to take a much more sympathetic approach to ERTs. Assistance programmes for ERTs from the state in
recent years (again, instigated in no small way because of the lobbying efforts
of ERT umbrella organisations) have included some technical renovation programmes, start-up grants, and subsidies from the national labour, social development, and economy ministries, as well as from provincial ministries such as
the province of Buenos Aires's Ministry of Production.

Situations of legal limbo have particularly intensified the challenges faced by
workers in new ERTs, especially during the period of resistance. On the whole,
and since the first contemporary ERTs emerged, national cooperative, labour,
and (until June 2011)[47] bankruptcy laws have remained unclear or counterpro-

---

47   As we will see shortly, a promising new reform of Argentina's bankruptcy law has been

ductive with regard to their legal status and organisational needs. Most extant laws affecting ERTs, for example, do not detail the exact legal and bureaucratic steps needed to transition a firm in trouble from private ownership to cooperative management. They also do not adequately address the continued social security needs of self-managed workers who risk losing, for instance, pension contributions and workers' compensation benefits since they are inadequately considered 'autonomous' (that is, 'self-employed') workers under Argentine labour and business law. Nor are there sufficient nation-wide grants and subsidies for the ongoing capitalisation needs of self-managed firms.

One of the consequences of this lack of a comprehensive set of policies or legal frameworks for ERTs is that each new conversion case is subject to the legal interpretations of bankruptcy court judges or the whims of court trustees appointed by these judges to oversee the administration of the troubled firm's assets. While Chapter 7 will address the consequences of this legal situation for ERTs, and the proposals to ameliorate them that have been innovated and championed by ERT workers and their legal and political supporters, we here review some of the more pertinent legal challenges faced by ERTs during the 'resist' stage of their emergence. They underscore some of the reasons why this stage often involves the most precarious days for an ERT's collective of workers.

2.2.1   The Struggle for ERTs' Moral and Legal Legitimacy during the 'Resist' Stage

With most new ERTs, self-managed production can only begin when the resisting workers have secured certain legal recognitions and guarantees concerning their rights to use the firm's assets and control the business. Such legal assurances can bring considerable stability and protections from otherwise countless eviction orders, creditors' claims on the firm, or future legal challenges from former owners. In short, some of the legal issues that ERT workers have had to deal with and address during the 'resist' stage of the recuperation process include: (1) how private property laws are to be interpreted by the legal system; (2) the process of transferring control of the firm from previous owners or creditors to the worker collective; (3) how outstanding debts from the days when the firm was under owner-control are to be handled; and (4) the legal business entity the worker controlled firm is to take.[48]

---

ratified in May and June of 2011 by Argentina's Senate and Chamber of Deputies, with the intention of facilitating the transition of a firm in financial trouble to its employees when they form into a worker cooperative (CNCT 2011; Feser and Lazarini 2011).

48   Fajn 2003; Magnani 2003; Palomino 2003; Rebón 2007; Ruggeri 2009; Ruggeri et al. 2010.

ERT protagonists, including workers, ERT lawyers, and ERT umbrella organisations such as MNER, MNFRT, FACTA, and CNCT,[49] have thus had to be innovative when arguing in courts and with power blocs in regional legislatures for the moral and legal legitimacy of workers taking over private businesses. The ERT movement's innovations in the political and legal spheres have emerged over the years from out of their efforts in lobbying the political and legal establishments to adapt or reform extant law. In essence, to transpose Andrew Feenberg's[50] term from his critical theory of technology to the legal-political realm, the ERT movement has had to 'creatively appropriate' already existing commercial, cooperative, expropriation, and bankruptcy laws. As Esteban Magnani, journalist and author of one of the first book-length analyses of Argentina's ERTs, writes:

> [W]ithin the existing system, [ERTs'] lawyers try to find the path that will permit them to reach their objective in the best way possible, although they recognise that this might not be necessarily the best path imaginable. The result is that, up till now, [ERT protagonists have taken on] an *adaptive politics* that take into account the legal resources at their disposal.[51]

These 'adaptive politics' that appropriate the 'legal resources at their disposal' are most fundamentally rooted in a set of consistent moral arguments that ERT advocates have been bringing to the legal and political table over the past two decades, which generally unfolds along the following logic:

> These workers are justified in taking over their firms because they (1) experienced clear violations of their labour contracts while working for their former employers, (2) were not properly remunerated for the work they had completed (often for lengthy periods of time), and (3) are thus legitimate creditors of the failing firm. Further, (4) in light of the high rates of business closures, under- and unemployment, and poverty in Argentina (especially during the crisis years of the neo-liberal system), and (5) in light of the fact that workers initially merely wanted to stay employed and that they are now keenly interested and able to keep the firm afloat and thus save jobs, the remaining worker collective thus (6) merits controlling recuperated workplaces and the legal right to self-manage the

---

49   For more on these organisations, see Chapter 3.
50   Feenberg 1995, 1999.
51   Magnani 2003, p. 92 (emphasis added).

firm. Moreover, (7) because workers are not unduly burdening the state by entering into unemployment, and because they are keeping a productive entity afloat, thus contributing to the national economy, (8) they should also have access to credit at favourable rates, government grants or subsidies, and privileged access to state contracts in order to (9) start production as quickly as possible.

Grounded in what we have been calling 'the moral economy of work', these moral arguments put forward by ERT advocates in bankruptcy courts, local legislatures, and in the public sphere via the mass media and other communicative modalities such as leafleting and word of mouth, essentially address two major political and jurisprudential areas that ERT protagonists believe could facilitate the creation and consolidation of an ERT and have its workers begin production as soon as possible: (1) the moral legitimacy of the direct action tactics deployed by ERT workers; and (2) the need for legal and political reforms in Argentina (at best), or new interpretations of existing business and property laws by judges, politicians, and bureaucrats (at minimum).

There is no doubt, as has been argued in different places throughout this book, that the strategies and tactics of occupation, resistance, and self-managed production of once privately owned firms within a capitalist market system are progressive in praxis, transformative in potential, and prefigurative of another socio-economic reality.[52] Indeed, there is an implicit challenge to the current system's privileging of capital over labour and property over the rights and wellbeing of workers when Mario Barrios, then president of UST, emphatically related in a 2009 interview that 'our struggles and our practices of *autogestión*, given Argentina's current legal, economic, and political system, forces us to emerge from and work in illegality'.[53] But the 'legal weapons', as Magnani terms it, that ERT workers have been creatively appropriating and arming themselves with from within extant Argentine legislation has also been legitimising and gradually institutionalising their otherwise illegal actions.[54] ERTs' legitimising force is not only suggested by the gradual changes that have been taking place in the normative dimensions of labour relations in Argentina via the example of *autogestión*, but is also witnessed in the literal reform and transformation of labour and business laws that ERT protagonists them-

---

52 For my justification of these claims, see this book's Introduction and Chapters 4, 5 and 9.

53 Barrios 2009, personal interview.

54 Magnani 2003, p. 91.

selves have been championing through their political lobbying efforts. Recalling labour sociologist Hector Palomino's claim, mentioned earlier in this book, that ERTS are fundamentally showing 'new institutional relations' for Argentina and its workers,[55] the jurisprudential and macro-political spheres are two key areas where the ERT movement has been punching above its weight. Suggesting the socio-political reach of ERT protagonists' moral economy of work that extends well beyond their conflicts with bosses at the point of production, Gabriel Fajn articulates the key debate that the mere presence of ERTs has been engendering in Argentina:

> The debate generated from out of the conflicts unlocked by [ERT] workers poses a confrontation between the concepts of legality and legitimacy. The occupation of firms directly challenges the right to property but, at the same time, demands within the framework of legitimacy, the right to work.[56]

For both Fajn and Magnani, there is thus a pragmatic side to these debates, a *material necessity* for ERT workers to first seek out legitimacy within existing legal frameworks in order to provide an ERT the initial stability it needs to get the firm producing as quickly as possible and meet the first desire of its workers: to earn a dignified living. At the same time, however, this legitimacy is also grounded in the moral logic that was laid out above, within ERTs' moral economy of work. That is, the struggles for legal recognition during the 'resist' stage of an ERT are infused with a moral legitimacy that pushes Argentine commercial, labour, and property law to reconsider certain foundational tenets, and at the same time challenge ERT workers to think pragmatically and use these laws to secure their livelihoods and the self-management of their places of work. As Magnani explains:

> The challenge [for ERTS] is not only the creation of a force for physical resistance ... It is also necessary [for ERTS] to find a legal framework that can permit them to function not only within a position of moral legitimacy, but also from one of legal legitimacy that can allow workers to throw their energies [, especially in the vital first months of *autogestión*,] into production rather than having to dedicate them all to resistance.[57]

---

55   Palomino 2003, p. 71.
56   Fajn 2003, p. 100.
57   Magnani 2003, p. 91.

In this light, ERT protagonists' struggles for legitimacy can be seen as emerging, at one level, from what Marx calls the clash of 'rights' in the struggle between 'the class of capitalists' and 'collective labour, i.e., the working-class' over concrete issues such as the length of 'the working day',[58] or, in the case of ERTs, the right to a job, to work with dignity, to receive 'just' remuneration, and for the overall legal recognition of their projects of *autogestión*. From out of this battle of normative values as such, ERTs, as will be expanded on shortly, are pragmatically influencing the real transformations of existing labour, commercial, cooperative, and bankruptcy laws. But, as argued earlier, these debates and struggles over legitimacy and the rights of property versus work are actually and more fundamentally rooted in the contradictions inherent to the capitalist labour process and the rupture of the production regime that had held sway in Argentina up until the neo-liberal years. Thus, and from another more critical theoretical angle using Marx's terms, 'the driving motive' of ERTs' moral economy of work is rooted in the clash between the 'self-valorisation of capital to the greatest possible extent, i.e., the greatest possible production of surplus-value, hence the greatest possible exploitation of labor-power by the capitalist',[59] and the already-always present desires of living labourers to not only resist this exploitation, but also struggle for their own self-determination and self-development.[60] We will return to these theoretical themes related to what ERTs recuperate for workers in Chapter 9. For now, however, we will focus on the pragmatic side to the pursuit and creative appropriation of the 'legal weapons' that ERT protagonists discovered were already at hand for securing their self-management projects.

The vast majority of ERTs reconstitute themselves within the organisational framework of a worker cooperative at some point during the stage of resistance for the legal and pragmatic reasons that will be explained in more detail in this chapter's last section. After constituting the cooperative, the next matter that an ERT's members must tackle during their stage of resistance is the issue of how to transfer the rights to use the business installations, machinery, trademarks, and property to the newly formed worker cooperative – especially given that, for some observers, judges, and politicians, the occupation of a business by its workers is potentially a criminal act of 'usurpation' of private property.[61] Hence, the conversion of a troubled private firm into a worker cooperative is

---

58   Marx 1967, p. 235.
59   Marx, 1976, p. 449.
60   For similar arguments concerning the rights of capital versus workers, see Atzeni 2010; Cleaver 1992a; Dyer-Witheford 1999; Lebowitz 2003; and Pusey 2010.
61   Magnani 2003.

intimately related to the application of Argentine bankruptcy law and, as ERT protagonists have innovatively shown, its national and regional laws of expropriation.

The next pages will deal with the use of expropriation laws for securing the creation of an ERT, then discuss the potential of and challenges entailed by the recent reform of the country's bankruptcy law, and finally analyse how the use of these laws have had promising but mixed results in securing the legal status of Argentina's ERTs.

2.2.2   Re-appropriating Argentina's Law of Expropriation

One savvy and pragmatic legal strategy developed early on by the ERT movement's first leaders – who have been more than capable of arguing for and articulating the moral and legal legitimacy of ERTs in the Argentine public sphere – was to turn to the mechanism of expropriation, guaranteed in the Argentine constitution (Article 17) and articulated in national and provincial legislation. After forming the cooperative and securing the temporary control of the plant under usufruct from the presiding bankruptcy judge, some early ERTs began to seek and lobby for the expropriation of the firm by the state on behalf of the cooperative as a 'common good' for 'public utility'.[62] Forming an important part of what José López, former president of Salud Junín, called in Chapter 1 their worker collective's *salida política* (political solution) during their 'resist' stage, appealing to local legislatures to expropriate the firm on behalf of workers is a clear example of the creative appropriation of Argentine law by ERT protagonists.

Today, expropriation is one accepted legal solution available to Argentine workers desiring to convert their workplaces into cooperatives. While not always achievable and riddled with legal and political hurdles that workers must overcome, the mechanics of expropriation is nevertheless fairly straightforward: Regional legislatures or the nation's Congress may draft and pass a unique expropriation bill for a specific ERT seeking to be expropriated. These bills must also be ratified by the executive branch, or may be initiated by the executive branch, as the governor of Córdoba did for the expropriation of Salud Junín. The cost of the expropriation is calculated by totalling up the fiscal value of the assets and outstanding debts of the previous business at the time of the bankruptcy, which can include owed wages and other employee benefits. Once the bill is passed, the state then compensates outstanding creditors and settles the bankruptcy, while the ERT workers are required to pay back the net costs of the

---

62   Ley No. 21.499 1977, Títulos 1, 3; See also Briner and Cusamano 2003.

expropriation (normally minus owed wages and benefits) over an accessible amortisation period of between 10 to 20 years, paid in six-month instalments and usually with an initial three-year grace period. Most often, owed wages and benefits are used as 'labour credits' and are deduced from the total fiscal value of the expropriation that the workers must pay back.[63] While simple on paper, the actual deployment of expropriation solutions, however, has not been uniform and has come with challenges.

Seeking expropriation of a business thus introduces the members of the new worker cooperative into the legislative sphere of politics. In Argentina, expropriating private property as a public good is the jurisdiction of national or provincial legislatures (including the government of the Autonomous City of Buenos Aires), and has also been historically deployed by the national or provincial executive branches of power as decrees in the case of regional or national emergencies or for the creation of public infrastructure. Nationally, expropriations fall under Ley de Expropiación Numero 21.499 (Law of Expropriation Number 21,499), which was signed into law during Juán Perón's presidency in 1948 and used at the time to begin building Argentina's national road system and for nationalising particular economic sectors. At the same time, each provincial jurisdiction and the Autonomous City of Buenos Aires also have their own version of this law.[64]

Application of Argentina's expropriation laws to ERTs began early in the phenomenon and was innovated by MNER leaders such as Eduardo Murúa and José Abelli and their lawyers at the time, in particular Diego Kravetz, Vanesa Castro Borda, and Luís Caro (who, the reader will recall, was part of MNER in the early 2000s before branching off to form MNFRT in 2003).[65] ERT umbrella organisations and lawyers, spearheaded by the public debates mobilised by MNER during ERTs' first period, ground their legal and political arguments for expropriation in Article 14 (containing language concerning the right to dignified work) and Article 17 (concerning property rights and expropriation) of the Argentine constitution. Article 14bis, ERT advocates have pointed out, constitutionally guarantees the right to work in 'dignified conditions' with various social securities such as a limited workday, just remuneration, the right to union representation, and so on. These guarantees, these advocates have further argued, even hold in economically difficult times, and especially if those difficulties were brought on by unscrupulous business owners or, at a societal level, the social and economic policies of representative governments. They have then

---

63   Ranis 2016, p. 52.
64   Magnani 2003, pp. 99–102.
65   Magnani 2003; Ruggeri 2006, personal interview.

invoked the second part of Article 17 – the expropriation of private property – to argue that ERTs are of considerable public utility to the communities in which they are located. This, they contend, justifies expropriation – and all the more so given the high unemployment and poverty rates in recent years, and the social and economic value that ERTs, as *recuperated* (and thus saved) productive entities, contribute to their localities' economic security and development. Finally, these ERT advocates add, the very act of self-managing these firms that would otherwise be closed means that the state is spared from having to take on the long-term financial costs of bankruptcy and the social costs of taking care of even more unemployed workers.

The appropriation – or, better, *recuperation* – of expropriation laws by ERT protagonists and lawyers has subsequently become an important tool on a worker cooperative's path to securing the control of a failing business, because it brings to a close further bankruptcy proceedings, legally eradicates the possibility of forced eviction and the auctioning off of the recuperated company's assets, and gives the worker cooperative complete control of the plant, including its machinery, inventory, trademarks, buildings, and client base. But seeking expropriation continues to be a bumpy political road to negotiate for ERT workers, as we will review shortly. Its long-term promise for the ERT movement has been, on the whole, less than satisfactory given that most expropriations have ultimately ended up being temporary (*expropiación temporaria*), which grants an ERT's workers a period of time in which to work out remaining legal issues, rather than definitive and permanent (*expropriación difinitiva*).

Seeking the expropriation of a business on behalf of a worker cooperative was a particularly difficult and unpaved political road during ERTs' first period, when ERT workers, lawyers, and supporters were still trying to figure out how to mobilise this legal outlet, and while elected officials and their legal advisors were baffled by not only the legality of applying laws of expropriation to a troubled firm but also by the political implications of ceding private property to workers as a '*bien común ... material*' (a material public good), as Article 1 of Argentina's expropriation legislation dictates.[66] Indeed, these difficulties still persist. Because the decision to cede a failing firm to its employees as a public good is to be considered on a case-by-case basis by elected officials (complicated further by a legal or physical person's constitutional right to possess private property), ERT workers soon found themselves immersed in the task of attempting to sway and lobby political blocs and specific politicians in regional legislatures who must present their case as a unique legislative bill. To

---

66   Magnani 2003, p. 99.

prove the case that, indeed, their firm is a public good and their worker cooperative's recuperation of it is in the public's interest, ERT workers have needed
to expend much physical and mental energy lobbying politicians and garner-
ing media attention in order to *ablandar* (soften) politicians or political blocs
within regional legislatures to their cause. This is what Palomino meant earlier
on in this chapter when he points out that the second 'terrain of conflict' for
ERT workers after occupying their firm tends to be the streets and the houses
of power.[67]

The tactic of the 'war of bodies' now takes on new spatiality, extending
workplace-specific conflicts out onto another political terrain within the community as ERT workers and supporters must attend countless parliament-
ary debates or, at times, even be physically present in, and thus symbolically 'occupy', legislative buildings during sessions in order to force politicians
(*ablandar los políticos*) to present their cases as bills of expropriation in local
legislatures. Additionally, workers must often take their cause out onto the
streets by blocking roads, conducting public rallies, or participating in sit-ins in
front of legislative or other government buildings in order to gain media attention and make their case in the public sphere. This extended political terrain
again mobilises the community, now outside of the factory or shop, in order
to persuade elected officials by swaying their voting constituents. Chilavert's
Cándido González underscored the importance of these tactics in the public
sphere in a radio interview shared with the principal author of this book in
Buenos Aires in 2005:

> Looking back at our days of struggle, three years on, one thing that we did
> right, without knowing it at the time – and that worked coincidently in
> our favour – was to move our conflict to the streets. That move gave us lots
> of results. What we tell many of our *compañeros* when we go and support
> them in another workers' conflict is that the first thing they have to do
> is to take their conflict to the streets. Let the neighbours know, let all the
> community organisations know about your struggle because those who
> will first come to support you [when you need it most] will be the people
> from the neighbourhood.[68]

Due to the intense political organisation and lobbying required to achieve
expropriation, this legal road has thus been, despite its promise, far from

---

67   Palomino 2003.
68   González and Vieta 2005.

smooth. At the political level, ERT workers seeking expropriation are beholden to the political tendencies of politicians. By 2005 numerous temporary expropriations had been sanctioned, but many less definitive ones.[69] That some legislative political blocs and government leaders still, to this day, refuse to definitively expropriate ERTs[70] is witness to how the neo-liberal experiment that seemingly collapsed in 2001–2 has continued to exert its effects, fracturing and polarising Argentine political and economic life. At times, local governments have vacillated on granting permanent expropriations to fledgling worker cooperatives because elected officials find themselves caught in a web of conflicting interests between workers' right to work and the rights of private property owners. Even those legislators who are sympathetic to the plight of ERT workers, such as left political blocs including the Kirchnerist Frente para la Victoria, find themselves torn between the push and pull of sundry lobby groups advocating for business owners or workers and politicians' perceptions of voters' interests. Moreover, both property rights and the right to work are guaranteed in the Argentine constitution, adding to the legal confusion.

Notwithstanding these challenges, struggling over permanent expropriation has been deemed to be vital to the ERT movement. So much so that in 2003 Eduardo Murúa and Diego Kravetz decided to run for legislative seats, Murúa as a left-Peronist candidate representing the province of Buenos Aires in the national Chamber of Deputies,[71] and Kravetz for a seat in the city of Buenos Aires's municipal legislature as a candidate for the Frente para la Victoria. And MNFRT president Luís Caro would also run for mayor of the Buenos Aires suburb of Avellaneda as part of a right-wing bloc of the Peronist party, while in the city of Buenos Aires elections ten other ERT protagonists would run for various left political blocs.[72] While Murúa, Caro, and the other ERT movement candidates would lose their campaigns, Kravetz ended up winning his seat in the city of Buenos Aires and was instrumental in drafting and sponsoring the first two expropriation laws for ERTs in the city of Buenos Aires in 2003 (for Chilavert and chocolate and creamery manufacturer Ghelco), and in 2004 was a key player in the passage of Law 1529/04 that had 17 ERTs head towards permanent

---

69   Ruggeri et al. 2005.

70   Such as with Mauricio Macri's veto of the expropriation of city of Buenos Aires ERTs while chief of government of the city of Buenos Aires (2007–15), and now with his veto of the expropriation of the Hotel BAUEN as president of Argentina. The *macrista* governor of the province of Buenos Aires, María Eugenia Vidal, had also vetoed the expropriation of several ERTs in that province.

71   Vales 2003.

72   Rebón 2007.

expropriation in the city of Buenos Aires.[73] By 2013, however, in a preview of what would come by 2016, then city of Buenos Aires government chief Mauricio Macri would veto the previous 17 expropriations, returning these ERTs to legal limbo.

The case of the Hotel BAUEN cooperative, the large hotel taken over by its workers in 2003 in the heart of the City of Buenos Aires, which continues to struggle over its permanent expropriation as of this writing in early 2017, serves to illustrate how ERTs' continued legal difficulties challenge their self-management projects. The lack of a solution to the Hotel BAUEN's legal situation over its entire existence as a worker cooperative marks how legal uncertainty adds additional stressors to the complexities that workers must face as they navigate both the institutional and practical processes of taking control of a firm, forming a cooperative, and learning how to transition from managed employees to self-managed workers.

The Hotel BAUEN's workers' many years of successful self-management has not been enough proof for the government of the city of Buenos Aires to take the initiative to finally expropriate the hotel on behalf of its workers in order to, as the workers say, 'make what's legitimate legal'. It was only in late 2015, 12 years after the cooperative's founding, that the Hotel BAUEN workers managed to begin to secure legal stability after a partial law of expropriation was passed by Cristina Fernández de Kirchner's Frente para la Victoria bloc in the Chamber of Deputies in November 2015 in one of the bloc's final initiatives before Fernández de Kirchner's government ceded power to Macri's Cambiemos coalition. The full law of expropriation for the Hotel BAUEN workers was finally ratified at the legislative level on 1 December 2016 when a coalition of senators led by the Frente para la Victoria bloc finally approved the law in the upper chamber.[74] However, not unexpectedly, President Macri went on to veto the law in early 2017, and a judge ruled for the eviction of the workers, which was to happen on 20 April 2017. In a show of massive national and international solidarity, the BAUEN workers, with the assistance of FACTA, the Programa Facultad Abierta, and other solidarity groups, initiated an international letter-writing campaign (which included the endorsement of Bernie Sanders and other internationally recognised names), numerous large demonstrations in front of the hotel and Congress, and a dinner gala night attended by a plethora of Argentine politicians and celebrities at the hotel in mid-April 2017. With just hours to go before the eviction would take effect, the National Court of Appeals, via the arguments

---

73   Ciudad Autónoma de Buenos Aires 2011.
74   Vales 2016.

of the hotel's lawyers, temporarily stayed the eviction order due to a technicality. While this has given breathing room to the Hotel BAUEN workers to regroup and appeal to Congress to veto Macri's initial veto and reapply the expropriation bill, there is no guarantee that this will happen and the struggle for the survival of the hotel continues.[75]

Indeed, the Hotel BAUEN is possibly the ERT case that has suffered through the longest period of legal limbo in Argentina; throughout its 14 years as an ERT, the government of the city of Buenos Aires, bankruptcy judges, and now even the president of Argentina have made consistent pronouncements against expropriation and for the eviction of its workers in favour of the very former owners that had actually defrauded the state in the first place. The Hotel BAUEN workers have, however, resiliently resisted these eviction attempts over the years by drawing on the solidarity of other ERTs and the broader social and solidarity economy, while engraining the hotel deeply into the Argentine public sphere by, for instance, housing FACTA and hosting myriad social and solidarity economy initiatives.

The Hotel BAUEN's long struggle for expropriation underscores how ongoing legal challenges negatively impact ERTs. Most notably, the Hotel BAUEN's chronic legal challenges have meant that its workers have not been able to adequately consolidate their level of service delivery to hotel guests. Rather than focus their work on fully upgrading the hotel's infrastructure and attending to the needs of guests, the BAUEN workers have had to redirect much of their energy to their legal and political struggle, which has included: dedicating inordinate amounts of time to lobbying the municipal and national legislatures for the definitive expropriation of the hotel; carrying out street protests and other forms of political mobilisation; engaging with bankruptcy courts that have yet to settle the previous owners' debt obligations; dealing with the previous owners' outstanding legal claims on the hotel; and seeking solidarity from other ERTs, sympathetic social movement groups, and self-managed workers' associations such as FACTA and CNCT.[76]

On the other hand, and as we have analysed in depth elsewhere,[77] the Hotel BAUEN workers have consistently and clearly shown how moments of conflict and having to traverse situations of difficulty together build resiliency within a workers' collective and help them coalesce into a more united and solidary group, contributing to the eventual strengthening of the worker cooperative

---

75   Página/12 2017b.

76   Bevilacqua 2009, personal interview. For more on the Hotel BAUEN, see Faulk 2008, 2016.

77   Ruggeri and Vieta 2009; Vieta 2012, 2014a.

and its ultimate involvement with other social movements and community-focused initiatives. In the case of the Hotel BAUEN, its continued existence as an ERT under workers' self-management despite its continued legal challenges has also been due to the legitimacy and broad support that its workers have received from Buenos Aires citizens; Argentine and international media outlets; and numerous social justice organisations and cooperative associations and federations. Indeed, its continued existence as an ERT while experiencing a prolonged state of legal precariousness highlights the ability of ERT workers to go much further than what was expected of them when they first came onto the scene.[78]

2.2.3   Re-appropriating Argentina's Bankruptcy Law

Another major legal contribution by protagonists of the ERT movement has been in how its legal representatives have not only creatively adopted contemporary bankruptcy law, but also re-appropriated and transformed it. While promising, the outcomes for ERTs, have been, as with expropriation, far from perfect.

According to Argentina's national bankruptcy law that was in effect until 2011, Ley Nacional de Concursos y Quiebras Numero 24.522 (National Law of Creditor's Meetings and Bankruptcy Number 24,522), a firm that could not meet its debt obligations had to first arrange a debt repayment plan or, if needed, engage in business restructuring proceedings. In Argentina this initial phase before bankruptcy is declared is called the *concurso preventivo* (preventive hearing), the phase equivalent to the US's Chapter 11. Ley 24.522 stipulated that a *concurso preventivo* had to be carried out before a firm officially declared *quiebra* (bankruptcy). Made up of insolvency hearings and creditors' meetings with the bankruptcy court in order to reorganise debt repayments, either the companies owner(s) or the collective of creditors could seek to enter the *concurso preventivo*.[79] One of the first legal areas where ERT workers' lawyers began to justify the practice of taking over the firm by workers in order to continue the 'productive activity' of the business entity was in this section of Ley 24.522 because, ERT lawyers pointed out, the first responsibility for the *concurso preventivo*, according to the legislation, was to attempt to save the firm in order to preserve the jobs therein. Indeed, these lawyers argued, only if there is no possibility for the firm to remain open is the *concurso preventivo* to seek ways of selling off the firm's assets and pay back creditors. Moreover, since the workers

---

78   Ranis 2010.

79   Magnani 2003.

were, they further noted, amongst the firm's first creditors due to their unpaid wages and benefits, the *concurso preventivo* judge had an obligation to cede control of the plant to the workers.[80]

But the *concurso preventivo* phase also posed a challenge for ERT workers. This phase includes the appointment of a court trustee, known as a *síndico* in Argentina. Usually an accountant, the *síndico*'s main job is to administer the firm during the *concurso*. As was the case with Chilavert, the appointment of a *síndico* is a weak point in Argentine bankruptcy proceedings because of the degree of control of the firm this legal representative is given during the *concurso preventivo* stage. Indeed, many of the fraudulent bankruptcy schemes in Argentina, especially prevalent during its neo-liberal convertability years in the 1990s and early 2000s, occurred with the appointment of the *síndico* during the *concurso preventivo*. In a common situation played out in countless firm closures, the trustee would engage in under the table deals with the firm's owners or creditors, as the Chilavert case made clear. One common practice often concocted between a *síndico* and a business's owners – one that, according to Gabriel Fajn, has taken place in innumerable firms in Argentina beginning with rise of neo-liberal policies with the last military dictatorship, and still occurring to this day – is related to the practice of the *vaciamiento* of the firm.[81] This often includes owners illegally selling a firm's assets during the *concurso preventivo*, giving a cut of the sales to the *síndico*, and then not showing these fraudulently sold assets in the final inventory list presented by the *síndico* to the bankruptcy court for calculating the fiscal value of the firm. This is exactly what happened at Chilavert. Another weak point with the *síndico*'s appointment is that he or she only gets compensated from a percentage of the financial value of the firm once its assets are auctioned off or from initial revenues if the firm reopens again.[82] Hence, as happened in many bankruptcies in Argentina in recent decades, a firm might declare bankruptcy prematurely when the *síndico* demands his or her fee. Because it is more likely that the *síndico* will get paid and paid more quickly with the auctioning off of the firm, the *síndico* has a vested interest in seeing the firm shut down and sold off. As Fajn explains, clearly articulating what occurred at Chilavert and countless other firms that eventually would become ERTs, and underscoring the extent of fraudulent bankruptcies in Argentina during its last neo-liberal era:

---

80   Fajn 2003; Magnani 2003.

81   Fajn 2003.

82   *Síndicos* can receive up to to 12 percent commission on the final value of the bankruptcy (Ranis 2016, p. 57; see also Fajn 2003).

In Argentina, fraudulent bankruptcies are not few, as the numerous lawyers we have consulted have told us. Indeed, there exist 'manuals' for how
to realise this type of operation that often include the active participation
of *síndicos*. On the whole, the final steps of [the *concurso preventivo*] will
often see [*síndicos*] cutting deals with fleeing owners. One of the lawyers
we interviewed figured that in the last 25 years 90 percent of Argentina's
bankruptcies were fraudulent [in this manner].[83]

But some progressive bankruptcy judges during ERTs' first period, encouraged
by the legal arguments of savvy ERT lawyers who were well aware of the fraudulent activities occurring, began to counter these fraudulent bankruptcy practices and rule in favour of ceding the plant to its remaining employees rather
than to court trustees.[84] Eventually, these supportive judges, convinced by the
arguments of ERT lawyers, began to find sufficient loopholes in Argentina's
bankruptcy law in favour of the remaining workers, or began interpreting sections of the law in ways that would allow workers who could prove the financial
viability of the firm and their capacity to manage it to be 'caretakers' of the
business and begin to operate it in usufruct while the legal status and debts
were being negotiated (see Figure 16).[85] Indeed, the proof that ERT workers
possessed the capacities to take care of a productive entity was amply available as workers showed, time and time again, that they were more than capable
of reviving a firm and keeping it afloat, especially when compared to previous
owners who were, on the other hand, too eager to abandon the firm or corruptly
sell it off or give it away in shady auctions or to bribed court trustees.

Article 189 of Ley 24.522, sanctioned originally during then-president Carlos Menem's labour and commercial law reforms of 1995, already addressed
the possibility of the 'continuity' of production of a failing business if it was
deemed favourable to creditors (not surprising, given the neo-liberal character of the Menem years). But this 'continuity' was to be at the discretion of
the *síndico* administering the firm during the *concurso preventivo*, a discretion
that was also often used for the countless aforementioned fraudulent bankruptcies.[86] In order to directly address the issue of 'continuity' and begin to

---

83   Fajn 2003, p. 102.
84   Fajn 2003; Magnani 2003.
85   There are sections of Ley 24.522 that permit the presiding judge to override the appoint-
      ment of a *síndico* or the administrative decisions of the *síndico* and instead appoint
      another party to administer the firm as caretaker during the *concurso preventivo* (Fajn
      2003; Ley No. 24.522 1995).
86   As Article 189 stipulated: '*Immediate Continuity*. The court trustee [*síndico*] can, without

regularise the possibility for employees to resume production in failing firms, a vital reform of the Ley Nacional de Concursos y Quiebras was spearheaded by ERT protagonists in early 2002. These 2002 reforms were led by, amongst others, MNER (again taking their case to the legislative sphere, as they had done when proposing the expropriation solution) and Víctor Turquet, a founding member of one of the first ERTs, the meat-packing plant Yaguané in the greater Buenos Aires municipality of La Matanza, and by 2002 the specialist on ERTs for the Instituto Nacional de Asociativismo y Economía Social (INAES, National Institute for Associationalism and the Social Economy).[87] These reforms to Ley 24.522 were subsequently passed into law by the national congress on 15 May 2002 as part of larger reforms of the Ley de Concursos y Quiebras at the time.[88]

ERT advocates' contribution to these reforms of 2002 was to further clarify how the 'continuity' of a financially troubled business could unfold by introducing changes in the procedural aspects of bankruptcy that lengthened the period of negotiation between debtors and creditors before reaching a resolution. The political arguments for changing the language of 'continuity' used by these ERT advocates was that such a reform would counteract the soaring unemployment and bankruptcy rates that were plaguing the country in the months following December 2001, during the height of the socio-economic crisis. Most directly related to the eventual creation of an ERT, the 2002 reforms explicitly made possible the 'extraordinary' recourse in granting 'productive continuity' by transferring the management of a firm in the midst of a *concurso preventivo* to a group of two-thirds or more of the remaining employees that reorganised into a worker cooperative.[89] While this in essence turned former employees into 'caretakers' of the goods and assets of the business, the worker cooperative continued to face uncertainty since the firm could still technically

---

delay, continue the exploitation of the enterprise or its establishments, except when the continuity of the firm could result in grave damages against the interests of the creditors or the conservation of the patrimony' (Ministerio de Economía y Producción 2007).

87   Magnani 2003, p. 98. INAES is Argentina's cooperative regulating body within the national Ministry of Social Development in charge of overseeing the registration of cooperatives throughout the country.

88   These 2002 reforms are to be found in Ley 25.563 (Ley No. 25.563 2002).

89   Caro 2004; Concursos y Quiebras n.d. Article 189 of Argentina's national bankruptcy law, partly overridden by Article 16 of the 2011 reforms (Ley No. 26.684 2011), now stipulates the following concerning employee ownership of a failed firm: '[T]he continuity of the enterprise [in the case of bankruptcy] will consider the formal requests of its employees in their relation of dependency that represent two thirds of active personnel, or from labour creditors, who must act in the subsequent period of continuity under the form of a worker cooperative' (Ley No. 26.684 2011, Artículo 16).

be eventually auctioned off. This issue would be addressed in the coming years, again through the efforts of ERT protagonists.

The continued work of individuals such as Turquet, ERT lawyers, political lobby groups, and umbrella organisations such as MNER, MNFRT, FACTA, and CNCT, working closely with national legislators and senators within presidents Néstor Kirchner and Cristina Fernández de Kirchner's Frente para la Victoria political bloc in the upper and lower houses of Congress, added further significant reforms to Argentina's bankruptcy law in March 2006.[90] Most poignant for ERTs, however, were the more sweeping reforms to Argentina's bankruptcy law passed as a new Ley Nacional de Concursos y Quiebras in June of 2011,[91] which we will assess in detail next. The 2011 reforms added new articles to Argentina's national bankruptcy law that sought to more clearly facilitate the conversion of failing firms into worker cooperatives by, for example, easing the transference of control of a financially troubled firm to workers *before* the firm enters the *concurso preventivo* stage, and explicitly delinking previous credit accumulated by former owners from the new worker cooperative.[92] The introduction of the new 2011 bankruptcy law, however, has paradoxically led to new challenges for workers contemplating creating a new ERT, going some way to explaining why the amount of time that must now be spent in the 'resist' stage has increased since its passing.

2.2.4   The Paradoxes of the New Bankruptcy Law in ERTs' Third and
         Fourth Periods

The impending approval of the reform of Argentina's national bankruptcy law proposed by the government of Fernández de Kirchner brought great expectations to ERT protagonists by the end of 2010.[93] As mentioned, this had been one of the first demands of the ERT movement, especially MNER. While the bulk of the bankruptcy law that was in effect until 2011, Ley 24.522, dated back to 1995, it was built on the foundations of Ley 22.917, the bankruptcy law approved in 1983 by the military dictatorship prior to leaving power.[94] Carrying over the spirit of the preceding law, and until its first reform in 2002, Ley 24.522 maintained a marked neo-liberal imprint on Argentine businesses, facilitating exiting owners while disfavouring workers. Ley 24.522 primarily enabled the quick disposal of inventory and assets to pay creditors, especially banks,

---

90   Clarín 2006.
91   Página/12 2011; CNCT 2011; Feser and Lazarini 2011.
92   CNCT 2011; Feser and Lazarini 2011.
93   Ruggeri and Vieta 2015.
94   Ranis 2016, p. 53; Ruggeri and Vieta 2015.

while ultimately neglecting to consider workers' unpaid wages or severance, for instance, and overlooked more broadly the social and economic costs of closing a business. It also facilitated successive bankruptcies (reducing the time in which the same enterprise could again declare bankruptcy to a year), and eliminated asset stripping (*vaciamiento*) as an economic crime. It was essentially a law of business liquidation that facilitated the practice of asset stripping that preceded (and still precedes) many business bankruptcies in the country and that often motivates the eventually creation of an ERT. Under the auspices of Ley 24.522, the mission of judges and trustees intervening in bankruptcies was thus the quick liquidation of inventory and assets without taking into account the potential operability of a firm or the negative effects to a local community wrought by the loss of jobs or the closing of a productive entity. Because of this, ERT protagonists early on deemed law 24.522 to be anathema to their interests.

In June 2011, a new and far-reaching reform of the Ley de Concursos y Quiebras – Ley 26.684 – was approved almost unanimously in both houses of Argentina's Congress, which was at the time under the control of the Frente para la Victoria bloc. For cases of businesses in the process of being recuperated by ex-employees, Ley 26.684 introduced more important changes to the bankruptcy process than did the 2002 and 2006 reforms. The political driver of this reform was the prioritisation of 'productive continuity' over the liquidation of assets, which is now no longer only considered as an 'extraordinary' recourse. The legislative authors of the new law, with ERTs specifically in mind, sought to make the process of ceding financially troubled businesses to employees an explicit possibility so that presiding bankruptcy judges now *must* take this option into consideration when certain requirements are met. Now, during the *concurso preventivo* phase and before bankruptcy is declared, Ley 26.684 gives explicit priority to employees to carry on the operation of the business when they are organised as a cooperative. Most broadly, Ley 26.684 now enables the involvement of workers in negotiating bankruptcy proceedings and conversions, specifies that workers should be the first to be paid back any bankruptcy-related debts owed, and essentially provisions a 'right of first refusal' for employees to buy out bankrupted companies. Specifically, Ley 26.684 stipulates that when the debts owed to workers are equivalent to the capital of the business at the time of the bankruptcy, the bankruptcy judge can adjudicate in favour of the conversion of the firm via an employees' 'purchase' of the business. This means that workers can now buy out the firm through the mechanism of 'wage compensation' claims (or labour credits), which essentially consist of the wages, overtime pay, *aguinaldos* (year-end benefits), or severance that the previous firm owed to workers. In short, debts owed to employees can now explicitly serve as capital for the new worker cooperative to purchase the business as a form of worker buyout.

While indeed a promising reform, there were, however, several objections presented by some ERT workers and their legal representatives in the months leading up to the passing of Ley 26.684 regarding the practical application of this legal mechanism. First, it was pointed out that assigning to bankruptcy judges the fundamental decision of whether or not to cede the firm to its employees (who would also be guided by the opinions of court trustees)[95] would give the courts too much arbitrary discretion. Their concern here was that there was too large a margin for ideologically-based decisions by court officials, who could potentially judge the worker cooperative to be incapable of running the firm without clarifying the actual criteria used for these negative evaluations. Moreover, ERT protagonists further suggested, the reform did not account for an independent consultative public body or ombudsperson that could give an alternative opinion on specific cases based, for instance, on the precedents established by prior experiences of ERTs or cooperatives. A second objection focused on the new law's requirement that, before a conversion can take place, a cooperative must be formed by two-thirds of the firm's employees. In some cases, it was pointed out (and subsequent experience has borne out), it might be difficult to reach this number, thus blocking the possibilities of conversion with, for instance, the departure of administrative personnel, or those workers who do not agree with the proposal to form an ERT, or those who have found jobs elsewhere. Finally, as has been the case in numerous conversion attempts since the passing of the new law, workers' claims on outstanding company debts can fall short of compensating for the financial value of the bankruptcy, which again ultimately means that the workers either cannot take over the firm or end up being responsible for part of the former owners' debts. These early objections have been confirmed in actual experience since the passing of Ley 26.684, and foreshadowed some of the new challenges faced by workers today wanting to begin an ERT project.

Before assessing the actual outcomes of Ley 26.684 for new ERTs surveyed by the Programa Facultad Abierta that emerged between 2009–13 (two-thirds of which had begun the recuperation process after the new bankruptcy law came into effect), we must first take a step back to explain the various legal processes that newer ERTs have resorted to in light of the lack of a unified national

---

95   The latter potentially gaining, as has been already mentioned, hefty commissions on the
       sell off of the firm's assets.

policy for business conversions in Argentina. In doing so we will be able to more clearly see the paradoxical results of Ley 26.684.

In the first place, there has been a notable decline in the application of the law of expropriation in the newest ERT cases since 2010. Up to 2010, 63 percent of the surveyed ERTs had been expropriated by the state on behalf of its workers. Of this group, only 19 percent had won 'definitive expropriation', while the rest were granted 'temporary expropriation'. 'Definitive expropriation' laws generally corresponded to ERTs in the city of Buenos Aires affected by Ley 1529/04 and in a few other experiences in the province of Buenos Aires and other provinces. In the majority of the city of Buenos Aires ERTs, however, 'definitive expropriation' was not ultimately applied, mainly due to then head of the city government Mauricio Macri's systematic vetoing of its use. The percentage of ERTs denied definitive expropriation in recent years has been significant, prolonging the legal uncertainty for many of them. This scenario has resulted in a legal landscape pockmarked by a wide range of often ad hoc resolutions to the legal situations of new ERTs, including: a handful of definitive and a greater number of temporary expropriations; many more ERTs with expropriation laws in process which as yet remain unresolved; ERTs granted operational continuity but without expropriation in sight; several (although still few) outright purchases of bankrupted firms by workers at auction; ERTs that have emerged as a result of workers swapping owed severance or pay for machinery and other assets; concessions, agreements, and co-ownership schemes with external administrators or the original owners of the firm; renting back the property, at times from previous owners; or other sundry scenarios.

Given these new challenges, the context of ERTs legal situation changed dramatically between 2010 and 2013. Before 2010, the main legal solution for ERTs was temporary expropriation with the promise of eventual definitive expropriation. After 2010, however, ERTs' legal situations in relation to the control and especially final ownership of the business had become more complex and diverse, as detailed in Figure 16. Scarcely 16 percent of newer ERTs were able to obtain an expropriation law in their favour, while a similar number of ERTs remained under worker occupation without any legal progress or, more worrisome for the ERT movement, had in some cases been returned to previous owners (a situation that threatened to increase with Macri's national Cambiemos coalition government). An even smaller number (10 percent) were in situations where workers had successfully been able to rely on favourable provisions under the new bankruptcy law (and these represent even fewer cases if we consider them against the total universe of ERTs). At the same time, we now find a wide variety of legal situations that fall under the category of 'other', including the list of legal scenarios provided in the preceding paragraph.

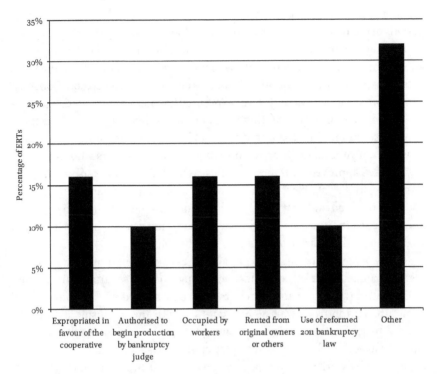

FIGURE 16   The legal situation of third-period ERTS (2010–13)
            Note: *N*=63 ERTS.
            SOURCE: RUGGERI ET AL. 2014, P. 26

This disparity allows us to assess the less-than-optimal and even paradoxical effects of the new 2011 bankruptcy law. What we can characterise as the anemic use of Ley 26.684 underscores the challenges that had been anticipated by its critics within the ERT movement. The Programa Facultad Abierta data explicitly shows that the expected hopes for the new bankruptcy law – that all, or at least the large majority, of new ERTs would be channelled through it – has not come to pass. On the contrary, as Figure 16 shows, only 10 percent had been able to use its mechanisms to move along workers' recuperation processes by the end of 2013, and the situation remained virtually the same by late 2016. Moreover, even considering that a similar percentage of ERTs that had been authorised to work by the bankruptcy judge were in a position to use this law, there still remains a substantial number of cases since the passing of Ley 26.684 where, for various reasons, the law cannot or will not be used by the presiding bankruptcy judge.

The introduction of Ley 26.684 has, thus, paradoxically had an opposite effect from that which was intended by its authors and promoters, adding new challenges today for workers intending to form an ERT, such as prolonging the periods of conflict and having to cobble together ad hoc legal solutions. Indeed, a large majority of new ERTs – 80–90 percent – face a miscellany of legal situations where the new bankruptcy law seems to actually have *blocked* the usual path of expropriation used prior to the introduction of Ley 26.684. Considering this, we see today not only fewer expropriation bills being passed, but also a growing number of ERT cases that have not even opted to try to find an expropriation solution. What the introduction of Ley 26.684 did do was to privilege its worker buyout model over expropriation, giving legislators who would otherwise have approved expropriation bills, as well as ERT workers, the impression that with Ley 26.684 the legal problems of worker-recuperated businesses could be resolved and that it was no longer necessary to go through expropriation. The reality, however, shows that, on the contrary, with the passing of Ley 26.684 the legal precariousness of ERTs has increased.

Finally, when we correlate the increased average length of time in resolving the conflicts that workers must go through before securing a firm under their control (from four to five months in ERTs' second era to an average of 11 months currently, as we saw in Figure 15) with the confusing assortment of hard to secure legal tools for resolving the various conflicts ERTs face, we can conclude the following: Bankruptcy court officials presiding over conflicts engaged in by workers who aspire to convert the firm into an ERT now have at their discretion the ability to place workers in a situation of further vulnerability and dependence due to the particular whims or apathy of judges or bankruptcy court trustees. Moreover, rather than pursuing laws of expropriation (which come with many precedents from ERTs' first and second periods), the pursuit of bankruptcy law solutions, which necessarily must be filtered through the discretion of judges, are in many cases extending the length of conflict and uncertainty for workers seeking out a conversion solution and thus prolonging the time it takes to secure, consolidate, and stabilise a new ERT.

2.3   '... Produce'

In general, if all goes well with ERTs' first two stages of occupation and resistance and the first years of temporary expropriation or some other form of legal guarantee or shared-control of the ERT – and there is, of course, no guarantees that things will go well, as we have seen throughout this chapter – then the goal of the third stage of a worker-recuperated firm is to begin self-managed production as an official worker cooperative, fully controlled by its workers under the perpetual protection of, it is hoped, a permanent law of expropriation, or with the worker buyout provisions of Ley 26.684, or with other sundry legal mechanisms. As with the overlap between the 'occupy' and 'resist' stages, there is no clear demarcation between the 'resist' and 'produce' stages. Indeed, beginning production as soon as possible after taking over the plant, as the Chilavert and Salud Junín cases showed, is often an important part of an ERT collective's resistance phase.

Because of the financial and legal tenuousness of the first years of *autogestión*, it is important for young ERTs to begin production runs as soon as possible in order to hold on to as many customers and as much market share as they can. Workers often continue to struggle for the first years after the worker cooperative has gained control of the firm, due in large part to the precarious financial situations many ERTs find themselves in from the start. As we have already seen, this is in no small part usually due to the degenerated conditions of the firm when it is taken over by its workers on account of the previous owners' mismanagement or due to sector-wide economic downturns. In some unfortunate cases, as we have also seen, some ERT worker collectives that have not managed to secure expropriations or that have not been able to buy out the firm outright have been forced to take on some or all of the outstanding debts of the previous firm. This was the case, for instance, with the publishing house Cefomar in the city of Buenos Aires and the meat-packing plant Yaguané in the Buenos Aires suburb of La Matanza.[96]

There are other pragmatic, legal, psychological, and symbolic reasons for beginning production runs as soon as possible: ERT workers feel that they must prove to themselves, the community at large, customers, judges, politicians, and Argentine society as a whole the viability of their ERT as well as the legitimacy of the notion of *autogestión* more broadly. This need is further heightened by the fact that there is also a legal and pragmatic obligation to separate the newly formed worker cooperative from the disreputable business practices and the debts of previous owners as quickly as possible. We saw some of these sentiments in the words of Salud Junín's workers, for instance, in Chapter 1. Thus, the broad goal driving most ERTs during the first months of *autogestión*, as the key informants of this book's case studies related, is not necessarily ownership of the firm's assets, but rather to be able to *secure* their jobs and hence *control* the machines and tools of their trade, and, ultimately, ensure that their means of production – encapsulating the ensemble made up of ERTs' building, land, machines, supplies, products or services, customers, and workforce – remain free from threats of closure, eviction, or repression. This is why many ERT protagonists feel that controlling the plant as soon as possible is an

---

96   Lavaca 2004.

important guarantee – something that would be secured with the creation of
a new national law of expropriation specifically geared to ERTs and other self-
managed enterprises, which is still a victory to be won by the ERT movement. As
Raul Godoy, co-founder and leader of Zanón/FaSinPat, clearly stated in 2004,
reflecting the views of many ERT leaders then and since:

> Today we have initiated a different phase [of our struggle], which seeks
> to put our struggle in the national spotlight in a much stronger way ... We
> are now seeking a concrete response from the National Chamber of Depu-
> ties and the national government, and so we are demanding not only the
> definitive expropriation of this factory by law, but also demanding for our
> *compañeros* in other recuperated enterprises the definitive expropriation
> of all of these factories taken by their workers and reopened in the ser-
> vice of their communities. This is our project ... and ... it is the fight we
> are opening up ... in a much stronger way.[97]

2.3.1   Why ERTs Become Worker Cooperatives

As the Programa Facultad Abierta team reported in 2005, during the ERT phenomenon's first period, 94 percent of ERTs would eventually self-organise
under the organisational and legal framework of a worker cooperative. By 2010,
the total number of ERTs that were worker cooperatives had risen slightly to
include just over 95.3 percent of all ERTs.[98] What is astounding in these consistently high numbers, which remained virtually intact by mid-2016, is that,
while some ERT workers have had previous experience in union organising or
community politics, most workers just starting an ERT have had *no* experience
in any form of cooperativism.[99]

---

97 Godoy, in El Militante 2004, para. 5.
98 Ruggeri et al. 2010, p. 22. Similarly, Fajn found that 93 percent of ERTs were worker
    cooperatives (Fajn 2003, p. 105). The Programa Facultad Abierta research team points
    out that those ERTs that were not yet worker cooperatives either desired to become
    worker cooperatives but had not yet done so, or had chosen other business organisa-
    tional models for pragmatic reasons. For instance, the teacher-recuperated kindergarten
    and primary school Escuela Fishbach converted into a service cooperative (rather than a
    worker cooperative) when it sought funding from city of Buenos Aires's Dirección General
    de Educación Privada (General Directorate for Private Education). The Gráficos Grupos
    y Proyectos ERT became a *sociedad de responsabilidad limitada* (SRL, or limited liability
    company) in an agreement its workers forged with its only corporate client. Finally, Clín-
    ica Medrano has proven to be to date the only ERT to have been nationalised, with its
    workers becoming municipal employees of the city of Buenos Aires's Ministerio de Salud
    (Ministry of Health) (Ruggeri et al. 2010, pp. 22–3).
99 Fajn 2003; Martí, Bertullo, Soria, Barrios, Silveira, Camalletti, et al. 2004; Rebón 2007.

Formally constituting the worker cooperative usually occurs during or just after a group of ex-employees choose to regroup and occupy the firm, taking form during an ERT's 'resist' stage and consolidating over the ensuing months and years, most usually when production starts. The challenges ERT workers face in self-managing their firms increases due to the fact that not only do they have to self-organise depleted workspaces and reinsert themselves into markets, they also have to learn the intricacies of forming and running a cooperative and self-managing a firm – something we will delve into in the next two chapters. If learning how to become cooperators compounds the challenges ERTs face early on, and if most ERT workers have not had previous experiences in cooperativism, why is it then that they overwhelmingly turn to the legal rubric of a worker cooperative?

One answer is to be found in the public debates that were, in the early years of the ERT phenomenon, preoccupying workers, social economy and social movement activists, academics working with ERTs, and the phenomenon's first political leaders. Two of these crucial early debates were held in front of the then-occupied Brukman textile factory on 13 April and 7 September 2002, still in the thick of the turn-of-millennium socio-economic crisis. In attendance at these meetings, called respectively the 'Primer' and 'Segundo Encuentro Nacional de Empresas Ocupadas' (the 'First' and 'Second National Gathering of Occupied Enterprises'), were key ERT figures at the time, such as MNER's Eduardo Murúa, the lawyer Luís Caro, Víctor Turquet from Yaguané and INAES, Zanón/FaSinPat's Raul Godoy; numerous workers from many of the earliest ERTs, such as Brukman and Chilavert from the city of Buenos Aires, Salud Junín from Córdoba, Supermercado Tigre from Rosario, and Renacer from the Tierra del Fuego; and other key figures from *piquetero* groups such as Coordinadora Aníbal Veron, the Corriente Clasista y Combativa (CCC), supportive left parties such as the Partido de los Trabajadores Socialistas (PTS, Socialist Workers' Party), activist media groups such as Indymedia, university research teams, and various other key players.[100] One of the major issues on the table at these gatherings was the legal and administrative framework that ERTs were to take: nationalisation under workers' control, as the Zanón and Brukman workers and the representatives of the PTS had been seeking, or worker cooperativism.[101] While nationalisation under workers' control was theoretically and historically plausible in Argentina,[102] most early ERT protagonists eventually scrapped the option when it became clear that the Argentine state was refusing to go along

---

100   Gaggero 2002; Godoy 2002.
101   Gaggero 2002; Fajn 2003, pp. 105–6; Ruggeri et al. 2005, p. 67.
102   Petras and Veltmeyer 2003.

with the proposal.[103] The only practical and legally sound alternative for ERTs, it was decided in these debates, was, out of 'convenience', to turn to the already viable and long-established cooperative model, especially in light of a state that could not, because of its strong commitments to capitalist enterprise, set the precedent of nationalising once-proprietary firms.[104]

At first, then, ERT workers reopen their firms as cooperatives for pragmatic reasons: in order to as quickly as possible re-establish the business as a formal productive entity legally recognised by the state, the financial system, markets, and its customer-base. As Murúa articulated in a 2006 interview:

> In the beginning I have to say that we didn't set out to study the question of *autogestión*. Rather, we began by defining what juridical form would serve us best during that historical moment and in order to ensure that the factory would be able to continue to function. We thus decided that the cooperative form of organisation would be best because it would permit workers to self-manage their enterprise, enable decisions to be made within an assembly, and ensure that revenues would be distributed equitably.[105]

At the same time, becoming a worker cooperative rather than another form of entity (such as a partnership) protects the worker-members from the seizure of their personal property should the cooperative fail, offering a form of limited liability under Argentine cooperative and business law. Additionally, the cooperative model ensures that the ERT does not have to pay taxes on revenues.[106] Argentine cooperative law, reformed somewhat in recent years, again

---

103   Fajn 2003, p. 60; Martí et al. 2004.

104   The importance of these early debates in establishing *la salida cooperativa* (the cooperative 'out' or solution) for ERT protagonists – both in formal, public debates in numerous *encuentros* and roundtables that were held at the turn of the millennium in Argentina, and in informal discussions between ERT protagonists, academics, and supportive social movements – is without question. Many worker protagonists and other participants such as Cooperativa Chilavert's Cándido González, MNER's Eduardo Murúa, the workers at the Hotel BAUEN, and UST's Mario Barrios, amongst others, have personally commented to us on the importance of these early debates in establishing the worker cooperative model as the most viable legal solution for restarting failing plants as ERTs. One of us (Andrés) was also an active participant in these early debates.

105   Murúa 2006, para. 7.

106   Cracogna 2013. Argentine cooperatives are exempted from income taxes on revenues because they are organisations that primarily benefit members, distribute surpluses between members, and are thus deemed to be non-profi and non-speculative entities in Argentine legislation. Cooperative members receiving income from their work in cooper-

in no small part by the efforts of ERT advocates such as the already mentioned Victor Turquet from within INAES, also guarantees that legally a worker-recuperated business under the control of a worker cooperative is considered a new business entity separate from the previous private firm, thus protecting the ERT cooperative from assuming most of the debts incurred by the previous owner-controlled firm.[107] And, as already mentioned in the previous section, the 2002, 2006, and 2011 reforms to Argentine bankruptcy law further facilitate the continuity of a firm under the administration of a worker cooperative formed by a group of the firm's former employees during the *concurso preventivo* phase of bankruptcy (yet again, because of the lobbying efforts of ERT protagonists).

ERT workers also take on the identity of cooperative practitioners gradually and pragmatically, associating more, as will be elaborated on in Chapter 8, with their working-class roots as *laburantes* (workers) rather than *cooperativistas*. As Matías Peralta, a UST worker-member, told this book's main author in 2009, summarising the view of a majority of the ERT workers interviewed for this text who we have spoken to over the years:

> We became *cooperativistas* out of obligation, not because we wanted to be *cooperativistas*. First we are *laburantes*, then *cooperativistas*. We formed cooperatives as an alternative for the continuity of our jobs, in order for us to keep on working. From there, from that starting point, we begin to work as a cooperative. I formed into a *cooperativista* from inside, from here, in the process of working here. I don't know if I am a complete *cooperativista* yet! I don't think this is either good nor bad, it's just the way it is.[108]

---

atives, though, must pay taxes on their personal income. Argentine cooperatives must, however, pay value added taxes (VAT) and taxes on credits and debits as with other taxable entities (Cracogna 2013).

107   Fajn 2003, p. 106. There have been cases, as with the recuperated editorial house Cefomar and as with Chilavert, where outstanding utility bills from the previous firm continue to be billed to the cooperative. This is because utility providers are not legally bound to recognise the ERT as a new entity. Additionally, as mentioned in the previous footnote, Argentine cooperatives still must pay the value added tax (VAT) when purchasing supplies and other production inputs (Cracogna 2013). One of the current struggles of ERT political lobby groups and umbrella associations such as CNCT and FACTA is to reform Argentine cooperative law to better reflect the particularities of ERTs in order to, amongst other things, ease the tax burdens of ERTs and remove the possibility of taking on *any* previous debts incurred by the old firm's administration. For more on these proposed reforms, see Chapter 7.

108   Peralta 2009, personal interview.

Julián Rebón also found this ambivalence – or, perhaps better, pragmatism – towards cooperativism in his study of ERTs, where one of the workers he interviewed commented as follows:

> We are a cooperative because it was the only legal form of being able to hold on to our jobs ... The form we took happened to be a cooperative because ... we were told that that would be how we would be able to [take advantage of] expropriation.[109]

But despite these pragmatic beginnings, most ERT workers that were interviewed for this book, as we will see in more detail in Chapter 8, have also stated that they do eventually come to realise that the worker cooperative model is indeed the most robust organisational form from which to restructure their production, collective decision-making, and remuneration processes within the more transparent work and administrative structures they eventually seek.

This brings us to a major distinguishing characteristic of ERTs when contrasted to other cooperative projects that will be elaborated on in Chapters 8 and 9: Most ERTs reorganise their self-management projects within the legal rubric of a worker cooperative – and usually after many weeks if not months of struggle – *not* because the recuperated firm's workers come to the struggle with a vision of becoming cooperators, nor because they possess pre-existing political ambitions, or were pushed into cooperativism by leftist political parties or radical unions, nor because they had connections with Argentina's more traditional cooperative sector. Rather, workers turn to cooperativism as a *legally viable* and *pragmatically defensive strategy* that emerged in the early years of the ERT phenomenon from out of the early debates engaged in by its workers and leaders. The cooperative option usually becomes known to a new struggling worker collective contemplating taking over a firm only during or after their fight to occupy and seize their workplaces.

The worker cooperative model, in sum, essentially serves to eventually give procedural shape to an ERT collective's project of *autogestión*, helping to organise their newly associated labour processes and socialised production while organisationally articulating the desires of ERT workers to collectively self-determine and control their working lives. Moreover, an ERT collective comes to the realisation that the legal framework of a worker cooperative symbolically serves to counteract and remind them of the managerial excesses they faced when they worked for a boss. There are other psychological and practical bene-

---

109   Rebón 2007, p. 184.

fits to forming a cooperative for their new socialised production model: becoming a legally recognised entity legitimates the ERT in the minds of returning or potential customers, other firms within their market sector, and in the minds of workers themselves; it facilitates access to government technical assistance programmes and subsidies; and, as we already mentioned, together with expropriation, it makes it infinitely easier for an ERT to seek legal protection from outstanding claims by the previous firm's creditors or returning owners wanting to reclaim their business. The worker cooperative model, in short, solidifies ERT workers' values of *compañerismo* and *esto es de todos*, in a process we will explore in Chapter 8.

2.3.2 Other Less Common Legal Structures

While most newly constituted worker cooperatives that take over the failing firms that had been employing its members do not seek to negotiate with previous owners or the old management, who more often than not have lost all legitimacy with the ex-employees of the former firm, some chose to do so. As Figure 16 shows, in order to begin production as soon as possible or avoid getting into drawn out court cases or political lobbying efforts, some ERT cooperatives (16 percent of cases) decide early on to sacrifice some aspect of full control of the firm by renting or leasing back the property and facilities from previous owners or new landlords. This is what transpired with the snack foods manufacturer Malvinas Argentinas located in the city of Buenos Aires and the shipyard Navales Unidos in the Buenos Aires suburb of Dock Sud.[110]

Another less common scenario is for ex-employees to seek a worker buyout solution without appeal to expropriation or lengthy court proceedings. Such was the case with the already introduced recuperated newspaper *Comercio y Justicia*, whose workers voted early on to buy out the firm completely via a lease-to-own agreement after securing first-rights to bid for the bankrupt firm. The workers then negotiated with the Cordoban bankruptcy judge to pay for half of the business via a mortgage secured with the personal assets of the founding members, and the other half via a deal with the province of Córdoba to recognise the workers' owed salaries as down payment on the mortgage.[111]

Other firms, such as the tractor manufacturer PAUNY in the town of Las Varillas, Córdoba, managed to overcome bankruptcy proceedings when its blue-collar production line workers formed a worker cooperative, Cooperativa de Trabajo Metalúrgica Las Varillas Ltda., and struck a co-ownership arrangement

---

110 Lavaca 2004, p. 125.
111 Martín 2009, personal interview. This was, at the time, the only case of this kind in Argentina that we are aware of and the first ERT to be fully bought out by its workers.

with the plant's former managers, a network of dealerships, and the municipality. In the case of PAUNY, the Las Varillas worker cooperative controls 33 percent of the enterprise, their former managers and administrators control another 33 percent of the firm, a group of dealers another 33 percent, and the municipality of Las Varillas the remaining one percent.[112] Other co-ownership schemes, for example, can involve co-management arrangements with local unions, such as with the worker-recuperated supermarket and community centre Trabajadores en Lucha/ex Supermercado Tigre in the city of Rosario, or co-ownership schemes with the firm's original owners via the issuing of shares for owed salaries, as Chilavert's workers initially proposed to their former boss.

3   Re-appropriating Relevant Laws, Deploying Cooperative Values

In sum, the political and micro-economic strategies and tactics of occupation, resistance, and self-managed production of a once troubled firm have not only become important defensive outlets for workers in Argentina over the past two decades, but also new strategic tools in labour's arsenal against capitalist exploitation and recurrent macro- and micro-economic crises. Indeed, ERT protagonists have been paving the way for the recuperation of proactive strategies and tactics of struggle and working-class self-activity. These strategies and tactics, immersed in the 'moral economy of work', suggest, as Murúa has already stated for us, 'a new form of struggle ... no longer limited to the common type of union demands for increased wages or for better work'.[113] The new forms of struggle being spearheaded by Argentina's ERTs both directly challenge the roadblocks put up by Argentina's intractable capitalist establishment and its neo-liberal model in recent decades, *and* returns a powerful form of militant working-class agency and self-activity to Argentina's working people. The return of this form of direct action-based working-class self-activity spearheaded by ERT workers is specifically reconnecting workplaces, as we will see in the remaining chapters, to the neighbourhoods and communities that surround them. It is a form of working-class self-activity that had once been widespread in Argentina in other eras, as was argued in Chapter 3, and that to some degree had been withering away under the neo-liberal production regime and its seductions of consumerism and individualism in recent decades. Moreover,

---

112   The makeup of the administrative council of the firm parallels this co-ownership scenario, with the worker cooperative, in turn, having its own council and holding its own assemblies for specific issues affecting the cooperative.

113   Murúa 2005b, personal interview.

ERT protagonists recuperate and mobilise moral arguments in order to creatively appropriate legal recognition from extant laws, gradually transforming Argentina's labour, cooperative, expropriation, and bankruptcy laws in ways that are legitimating workers' demands for the collective control and direction of economic and social life. In short, ERT protagonists are beginning to recompose aspects of an Argentine working class 'for itself'.

From out of the case studies presented in Chapter 1 and the analysis of the most common worker experiences in the stages of 'occupy, resist, produce' laid out in this chapter, we arrive at *the second radical social innovation* forged by Argentina's ERTs:

> *The ongoing lobbying of the political and legal establishments, the reappropriation and reform of extant laws, and the application of cooperative values in order to reconstitute their work and begin to consolidate their projects of* autogestión.

On the whole, the subsequent restructuring of once privately owned workplaces as self-managed firms most immediately arises from out of the convergence of: (1) workers' lived experiences of macro- and micro-economic crises; (2) the realities that these crises reproduce at the micro-political level on shop floors; (3) ERT protagonists' efforts of political mobilisation that have helped transform and re-appropriate national labour, business, and cooperative laws and policies; (4) their collective overcoming of the many challenges they must subsequently face in restarting self-managed production; and (5) the coming together and strengthening of the solidarity of the worker collective in times of crisis that undergirds their direct action tactics and strategies of *autogestión*. As will be explored in more detail in the remaining chapters, these macro-economic and micro-political convergences, experiences, crises, and challenges intimately shape the labour processes, divisions of labour, and solidarity economies being innovated by ERT protagonists.

The Challenges of *Autogestión* and ERT Workers' Responses

> Our challenges? They are very big. Anxieties accompany us along the path
> toward lifting ourselves out of the difficulties we faced ... Lifting yourself
> out of the void is hard, and you already know that in this country there
> are, or I should say, *there aren't* regulatory frameworks in place that permit
> [*empresas recuperadas*] – for various political reasons – to have access to
> the means of slowly emerging out of [our] difficulties, to walk along the
> path of production, grow, build more jobs ... So then, [we] fall out of the
> system, [we] aren't a subject of credit, [we] don't have access to working
> capital (no one gives it to you), [we] can't access credits or funds alloc-
> ated to small- and medium-sized businesses because we are a formerly
> bankrupted enterprise, and as a bankrupted enterprise now managed by
> its workers, we are not [completely] recognised in this system.
>
> EDITH OVIEDO[1]

∴

Despite the tenacity of ERT workers in recuperating their places of work and
self-managing them, the surprising longevity of the ERT movement, and their
protagonists' successes in taking their plight to Argentina's streets and houses
of political power, difficulties continue to plague individual ERTs. To some
degree, these challenges can be seen as the result of chronic micro-economic
hardships that linger from the worst days of the firm under private ownership
and as carryovers of the long days of *lucha* during the occupation and resistance stages. Other ongoing challenges are more systemic and due, for instance,
to inadequate policies, laws, or supports from the state, or from having to compete in volatile or competitive markets. While ERTs' struggles are uniquely
nuanced by their particular micro-economic circumstances, ERT protagonists

---

1 Oviedo 2005, personal interview (co-founder and president of Cooperativa de Trabajo Cefomar).

and researchers have identified commonly shared challenges.[2] Overall, and historically, these challenges tend to encompass two issues: *under-production* (mainly due to *under-capitalisation*) and *the continued precarious life conditions of workers*. These challenges are rooted in various economic, political, and legal factors that we reviewed in Part 1 and in the previous chapter. While, today, these challenges are increasingly being overcome as older ERTs consolidate as cooperatives and secure their footing as viable firms, they nevertheless persist with every new ERT. Indeed, these two overarching challenges have tended to, at one point or another, dominate the everyday concerns of most ERT workers, shaping how their projects of *autogestión* unfold within each ERT.[3]

In this chapter, I endeavour to more explicitly map out the details and analyse some of the potential causes of ERTs' major challenges, their undergirding effects on the labour process and in the lives of ERT workers, and workers' innovative responses to their challenges. These challenges were particularly heightened during ERTs' first period when government support programmes and access to credit were virtually non-existent for ERTs, and when the process of converting troubled private firms into worker cooperatives was still being worked out. Combining secondary quantitative survey data with my own qualitative findings, in the following pages I particularly show how ERTs' two overarching challenges have been exacerbated by seven factors:

(1) the depleted conditions that most of these firms emerge from, and the depreciated conditions of their technological infrastructure when starting out;

(2) the continued pressures these firms face within competitive markets;

(3) the steep learning curves for their workers as they have to learn the ins and outs of running a cooperative;

(4) the political and legal quagmires they must wade through to make a go of *autogestión*;

(5) the lack of consistent or effective national and regional government policies for assisting ERTs;

(6) the historical paucity of favourable bankruptcy, expropriation, or specific worker cooperative legislation that recognise the particularities of these firms;[4] and

(7) the state's general indifference towards these self-managed firms.

---

2   See, for instance, Fajn 2003; Fajn and Rebón 2005; Ozarow and Croucher 2014; Rebón 2007; Ruggeri and Vieta 2015; Vieta and Ruggeri 2010; and Wyczykier 2009a, 2009b.

3   Atzeni and Ghigliani 2007; Rebón 2007; Ruggeri and Vieta 2015; Vieta and Ruggeri 2009; Vieta 2010a, 2012.

4   Reviewed in depth already in Chapter 6.

The chapter also aims to explore how ERTS' principal challenges and their underlying causes have changed and shifted over the years. We will see how some of these challenges began to be overcome during ERTS' second and third periods, as worker-recuperated firms gained political, legal, and even economic legitimacy in recent years. This increased legitimacy, the reader will recall, has had much to do with the intense political work, lobbying efforts, and organisational strategies of ERT protagonists, leaders, and the movement's various representative organisations. These joint efforts have mostly taken place at the national and provincial levels in order to reform business, labour, and cooperative laws and policies so as to better favour self-managed workers, as we saw in Chapter 6. We will also see how some of these challenges had returned in recent years with the coming to power of President Mauricio Macri's Cambiemos coalition. Ultimately, ERTS' coordinated responses to their challenges point to the *empresas recuperadas*' third radical social innovation, underscoring how their workers are recuperating not only their self-activity and self-organisation on shop floors, as I will articulate further in Chapter 8, but also their capacities to organise *between* ERTS in order to begin to *collectively respond* to their production, financial, and legal issues.

1   Section 1: Production Challenges

When one considers ERT protagonists' long periods of struggle, the political and structural barriers they face in accessing funds for labour processes and technical renewal, and weak state support, it is not surprising that many ERTS have historically produced at levels much lower than their original production runs during the most economically stable days of the firm under capitalist ownership. For example, according to the self-reported testimony of ERT workers captured in Figure 17, only 25 percent of all ERTS existing as of 2004 were producing at more than 60 percent of their installed productive capacity.[5] While

---

5   'Productive capacity' here generally refers to the collective capacities of a firm's workers and the technical infrastructure available to produce the firm's products or deliver services, as well as the physical space that is used for this production. In more contemporary liberal economic terms, this could be calculated as the 'total factor productivity' of a firm, which 'divides output [which might be measured as total revenue] by a weighted sum of all inputs, taking account of each input's share in total cost' (Dow 2003, p. 180). Of course, this measure, despite the assertions of liberal economists, is not exact, particularly for a self-managed firm (Dow 2003, pp. 180–1; see also Craig 1993; Kruse and Blasi 1995; Wadhwani and Wall 1990). For example, how does an accountant or economist measure the particular effects of workers' self-management on productivity, or most accurately report on the extra costs associated with

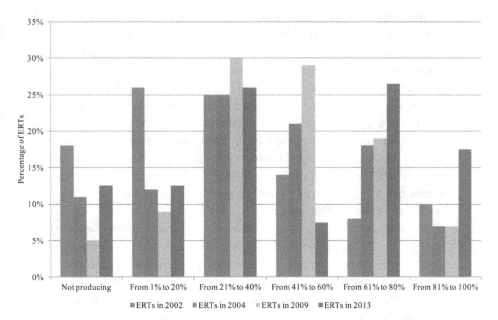

FIGURE 17   Comparing ERTs' production over installed capacity in 2002, 2004, 2009, and 2013
Note: As of Dec. 2002, *N*=59 ERTs. As of Dec. 2004, *N*=72 ERTs. As of Dec. 2009,
N=85 ERTs. As of Dec. 2013, *N*=31 ERTs.
SOURCE: RUGGERI, MARTÍNEZ, AND TRINCHERO 2005; RUGGERI, POLTI,
CLARK, ANTIVERO, DELEGDISCH, ET AL. 2010; RUGGERI, ANTIVERO, ELENA,
POLTI, ET AL. 2014

this was a jump from 2002 numbers, when only 18 percent of ERTs were producing at more than 60 percent capacity, by 2009 not much had changed from
2004 productivity estimates. While older, already consolidated ERTs have been
performing better in recent years, and 44 percent of ERTs existing as of 2013
were performing at over 60 percent capacity, this still means that the plural-
ity of ERTs were operating at 60 percent capacity or less by that year. From
another angle, however, ERTs have experienced recent improvements in production capacity between those in operation in 2004 and 2009 and those in

---

the time needed to make decisions in self-managed firms and balance this cost with other
factors of productivity? Or, how is one to measure how self-management affects the lives of
workers or the social benefits or positive externalities the practice can bring to communities? While the question of productivity that I discuss here was open to the interpretation and
judgment of workers answering the surveys, it does, however, offer general approximations of
the productive state of these firms, informing us about how they now compare to the previous firm's productivity under capitalist ownership, and doing so on the basis of the first-hand
accounts of ERTs' most well-positioned and well-informed experts: the workers themselves.

existence more recently in 2013: in 2013, 33.5 percent of ERTs were operating at between 20 to 60 percent of their installed capacity compared to 46 percent of them operating at these levels in 2004 and 59 percent of ERTs performing at these lower levels by 2009. The greatest improvement in production capacity between 2002 and 2013 can be gauged in the drop in ERTs that *were not* producing at all or producing at less than 20 percent capacity: In 2002, 44 percent of all ERTs existing at that time were either not producing or producing at less than 20 percent of installed capacity. By 2004, this number had dropped to 23 percent; and by 2009, to only 14 percent of ERTs. With the surge in new ERTs in recent years, the number of them producing at less than 20 percent has risen somewhat, to 25 percent of all existing ERTs in 2013, but was still far less then the 2002 numbers in this category.

Moreover, as we can gauge from Table 6, rough comparative trends in production levels between ERTs in different economic sectors can be deduced. For example, ERTs in certain sectors that depend on less complicated infrastructure or smaller machines operated by one or two operators (such as enterprises in the printing and publishing sector; smaller metal shops; or those ERTs dedicated to textiles, glassware, and carpentry), or that do business in service sectors with less technical requirements (such as gastronomy and education) tend to produce at higher capacity rates than those in heavier industries or in businesses that require more sophisticated technology, larger infrastructure, or more complex production processes. This is the case for larger metal-based manufacturers or ERTs in shipbuilding, pulp and paper, hydrocarbons, meatpacking, some plastic manufacturers, and recuperated hotels, which depend on much larger, more expensive, or more complex machinery or service delivery infrastructures. Because the latter, more capital-intensive sectors require higher levels of automation or adequate infrastructure using more sophisticated machinery or more complex production or service delivery cycles, ongoing operational necessities such as machine repairs and technological renewal tend to be generally hard to come by without access to regular and reliable funds for capital investments or, as I will outline below, sufficient start-up or infrastructure renewal subsidies or grants from the state. In the former, less capital-intensive sectors, the tendency is for worker-operators themselves to repair their own machines or, as I will detail in Chapter 8, to mediate structural barriers to production by engaging in just-in-time and small-batch production practices, as is the case now at Chilavert and other smaller ERTs.

Some sectors or particular ERTs, of course, do go against these rough trends due to their historical or actual conjunctural specificities. Recall the case of the PAUNY tractor manufacturer in Chapter 6, for example. That firm has managed to keep producing (and producing at high levels) comparable to the best days

TABLE 6   Level of ERT production over installed capacity by sector, as at December 2004

Sector	Level of production over installed capacity (in percents)				
	60–100%	30–60%	1–30%	Not producing	No answer
Metallurgy	33	33	28	6	0
Printing and publishing	33	17	33	0	17
Textile	17	33	33	0	17
Gastronomy	25	75	0	0	0
Glassware	0	50	50	0	0
Chemical	25	0	75	0	0
Plastics	33	33	33	0	0
Meatpacking	33	33	0	33	0
Shipbuilding	0	0	0	100	0
Foodstuffs	33	33	17	0	17
Ceramics, tiles, and brickworks	0	50	50	0	0
Tannery and leather	0	100	0	0	0
Health[a]	0	0	0	75	25
Education	50	50	0	0	0
Hotel and tourism	0	0	100	0	0
Wood products	0	50	50	0	0
Hydrocarbons and fuel	0	0	0	100	0
Pulp and paper	100	0	0	0	0

a   Note that Salud Junín (one of this book's case studies), which was offering health services in
   2004–5, was most likely within the 25 percent of ERTs in this category that did not answer.
Note: More recent data measuring and comparing ERT productivity levels *per sector* do not exist,
hence my reliance here on 2004 data.
SOURCE: RUGGERI ET AL. 2005, P. 72

of production under the previous owners due to the unique co-management
arrangement its worker cooperative managed to strike with the firm's administrators, dealerships, and the municipality of Las Varillas, as well as to the fact
that the firm did not experience a situation of *vaciamiento*.[6] Similarly, the recuperated newspaper *Comercio y Justicia*, also introduced in Chapter 6, was able

---

6   Buffa, Roitman, and Martínez 2009; Palomino, Bleynat, Garro, and Giacomuzzi 2010.

to not only increase its flagship newspaper's subscription rates substantially when compared to the previous capitalist firm, it has also expanded its production considerably by contracting out its printing facilitates to other newspapers and clients, managing moreover to upgrade its printing machines and technology and purchase new computers and a computer-to-print (CPT) system of publishing by 2009. Indeed, the *Comercio y Justicia* worker cooperative has from its early days owned its business outright without its workers needing to pursue the long road to expropriation due, in part, to the willingness and ability of its journalists and print shop worker-members to take on personal mortgages in order to buy out the firm from the bankruptcy auction.[7]

But these two cases are exceptions rather than the norm in the universe of ERTs. In the next chapter, I contrast the state of the labour processes and the compromises that ERTs such as these two exceptional cases have had to make in their cooperative business structures with the more common, conflict-riddled case studies I presented in Chapter 1. There, I will particularly make connections and comparisons to how the legal and organisational structures of an ERT and their past histories of high or low conflictivity and current market situation relate to their new labour processes as self-managed firms.[8]

1.1   *ERT Workers' Self-Reported Reasons for Under-Production*

ERTs' under-production issues, it is vital to point out, are not related to something intrinsic to the 'nature' of a worker-controlled, cooperative, or labour-managed firm (LMF). Nor are under-production issues due to ERT workers' lack of motivation or capacities to self-administer their work. These issues, rather, are related to the depleted nature of ERTs upon conversion and the paucity

---

7   Buffa et al. 2009; De Pascuale 2009, personal interview; Mario Rodríguez 2009, personal interview.

8   One more point related to how ERTs respond to production difficulties deserves mention here: The ongoing structural, financial, and operational difficulties faced by most ERTs also suggest reasons for why Argentine ERTs participate almost exclusively within national markets (Rebón 2007; Ruggeri 2009). Under such chronically volatile conditions, accessing international markets proves to be extremely difficult. Hence, few Argentine ERTs that I am aware of as of this writing were exporting to foreign markets (see also Fajn 2003; Rebón 2007; and Vieta and Ruggeri 2009). Three exceptions here, amongst a few others, are the Yaguané meatpacking plant, the ceramics manufacturer Zanón/FaSinPat, and the PAUNY tractor manufacturer, all of whom are actively involved in exporting their products. However, these three firms were, it must be pointed out, already exporting when under private management. Other, much smaller arrangements for selling to international markets have been organised in recent years by NGOs such as The Working World, which I will discuss in the last section of this chapter.

of sources of assistance in Argentina for investment in refurbishing the firm once it becomes a worker cooperative.

Studies have been showing for some years now that healthy LMFs, even considered from a more liberal economic paradigm, can be as productive and 'efficient' – if not more so – than the capital-managed firm.[9] Evidence for this has been provided by heterodox economists such as Samuel Bowles and Herbert Gintis, Gregory Dow, John Bonin, Derek C. Jones, Jan Svejnar, and Louis Putterman;[10] self-management and cooperative theorists such as John Craig, Hans Münkner, and Michael Howard;[11] and, more recently, by empirical work with Italian worker buyouts and European worker cooperatives.[12] As Dow points out via countless examples and heterodox economic arguments that primarily address work incentive and workplace control criteria in labour-managed firms, 'LMFs have no evident problem with respect to labour productivity'.[13] Howard arrives at similar conclusions from his review of the literature assessing productivity at worker-owned and -controlled firms: 'Economists have examined the relative efficiency of [LMFs], capitalist, and state-managed enterprises', he writes, 'and the evidence on that score clearly supports workplace democracy'.[14] Indeed, in what can be seen as an extension of Peter Kropotkin's historical arguments for the primacy of 'mutual aid' and cooperation over individualism, competition, and private property, cooperative theorists Robert Oakeshott and David Erdal[15] have both concluded, in separate studies of numerous worker-owned and cooperative firms and the socio-economic conditions of the communities in which these firms are located, that 'people will flourish in more egalitarian communities, such as those with widespread worker co-operatives'.[16] Amongst other social and economic

---

9   This is in contrast to the often-assumed liberal mantra that posits hierarchical divisions of labour as the most efficient way of organising production, or as the most effective way of facilitating and maximising entrepreneurial effort (for studies critical of this position, see Marglin 1974; and Noble 1984). Indeed, the take-up of workteams and other self-management practices in otherwise capitalist workplaces in recent decades, which I reviewed in Chapter 5, attests to the viability of workers controlling more and more aspects of the labour process.

10   Ben-Ner and Jones 1995; Bonin, Jones, and Putterman 1993; Bowles and Gintis 1993a, 1993b; Dow 2003; Estrin, Jones, and Svejnar 1987; Jones and Svejnar 1984.

11   Craig 1993; Münkner 1995; Howard 2000.

12   Vieta, Depedri, and Carrano 2017; Zevi, Zanotti, Soulage, and Zelaia 2011.

13   Dow 2003, p. 240.

14   Howard 2000, p. 3. For similar findings from a market socialist perspective similar to Howard's, see David Schweickart's *Against Capitalism* (1996) and *After Capitalism* (2011).

15   Erdal 2011, 2012; Oakeshott 1990, 2000.

16   Erdal 2012, p. 3. French cooperative economist Virginie Pérotin has arrived at similar con-

indicators these researchers have looked at, such as health, sick days, absentee rates, and so on, the positive nature of worker ownership and control is also reflected in robust rates of workplace productivity and worker happiness.[17]

These findings also resonated throughout my interviews, especially Oakeshott's and Erdal's correlations between worker happiness and self-reported productivity levels. One of Chilavert's founders and its bookbinding specialist, Manuel Basualdo, for example, gave me a response similar to those of other workers in other ERTs when asked to compare working at the ERT with working for a boss:

> No, no, I like working here now much better! Things are much calmer now. There's no comparison with what this place used to be like. Before you couldn't even drink a *mate*[18] during work hours. Now we're all so much more relaxed! ... But when we have to work, when we're on a deadline, we work hard, too ... Yes, it is so much better now. Even if there wasn't any work to do, the manager would insist that we grab a broom and sweep the floor; we had to always be doing something, picking up a piece of paper, whatever, ... we couldn't be seen not doing anything. You just work in a calmer way now, with a much lighter spirit. Now you definitely still know that you have to do a good job. But with a manager or owner things are

---

clusions, finding that worker cooperatives have documented 'spill-over effects ... for communities', such as creating inclusive workplaces and more fulfilling jobs where workers' 'potential and creativity can flourish', improving the overall health of workers and the community, and contributing to economic stability (Pérotin, in Atzeni and Vieta 2014, p. 56).

17   For similar recent findings, see Becchetti, Castriota, and Depedri 2010; Pérotin 2006, 2014; and Vieta et al. 2017. Jaroslav Vanek had similar claims for the potential productivity of LMFs at the level of a national economy such as Yugoslavia, wherein worker-controlled firms predominated. Such firms would, at minimum, produce as efficiently as KMFs (capital-managed firms), Vanek found, if all technological levels are equal: 'We make the observation that when all firms of an industry use the same technology and free entry is guaranteed, the labour-managed economy will be Pareto optimal. In other words, just like its ideal capitalistic counterpart, the labour-managed economy will be producing the maximum producible output from given resources, and the maximum social satisfaction for a prescribed distribution of income. These conclusions follow from the fact that the competitive labour-managed firms equalize factor marginal products to factor returns for all factors including labor, from competition in non-labour factor markets, free entry of firms and identical technologies' (Vanek 1977, p. 17). For similar arguments I make from a more explicitly Marxist perspective regarding the viability and ethical place of cooperatives and associated labour for a socialised economy, see Chapters 4, 5, and 9.

18   The bitter green tea sipped through a metal straw out of a gourd and consumed throughout South America's Southern Cone region. For more on the role of the *mate* and the change of the pace of work in ERTs, see Chapter 8.

so different. Sometimes they didn't even care if it was a job well done as long as we were seen to be producing. Now, we do very good work all the time, I would say.[19]

Rather, as with other 'abrupt transitions to workers' control [involving] a firm that is in financial distress' in other conjunctures,[20] ERTs' tendencies to under-produce are directly related to their disproportionate emergence from 'the ashes of failed capitalist firms',[21] and their lack of financing for capitalisation issues when compared to the more stable situation of capital-managed competitors or other non-ERT LMFs that have not had to go through traumatic founding experiences and that, thus, have more ready access to loans or equity-capital financing.[22] To underline the point, drawing on examples of business conversions to LMFs in the global North, Dow cites Avner Ben-Ner's data comparing conversions to LMFs in several European countries and Quarter and Brown's data for 39 worker buyouts in Canada in 1990.[23] In all of these examples, as Dow points out, difficulties in production were primarily due to the depleted nature and financial precariousness of these firms upon conversion.

In short, ERTs' under-production and other related challenges, especially during their first years of operation, have little if anything to do with their workers' lack of capacities, skills, or motivation. Indeed, ERT worker-protagonists'

---

19   M. Basualdo 2005, personal interview. There is a caveat that I need to make here given Manuel's response to my question of whether he preferred to work in the old firm with a boss or now in the cooperative. I am not suggesting here that all ERT workers are always happier working at an ERT. In fact, as I will discuss in Chapter 8, two ERT workers I interviewed said to me quite clearly that when working for a paycheque under a boss, things were 'all much easier', as one of them told me, because they had 'less responsibility'. They also said that they never wanted to self-manage a business or be their own boss in the first place (Cossarini 2009, personal interview). Moreover, in contrast to the question I asked Manuel that led to his answer above, when I would ask this question in a different way – whether they feel 'freer' or 'more liberated' now working as a self-managed worker when compared to working for a boss and for a wage – the answers were nuanced in a different way; almost to a person, they would answer that they did not feel freer in the sense of less responsibility but that they have much more responsibility now as workers of an ERT. But, they would continue, they nevertheless would not go back to working for a boss even if they got paid more. I specifically delve deeper into the tension between the concepts of 'freedom' versus 'responsibility' with self-managed work at ERTs in Chapter 8.

20   Dow 2003, p. 213.

21   Ibid.

22   For similar findings for Argentina's ERTs, see Fajn 2003; Ruggeri et al. 2010; Rebón 2007; Wyczykier 2009b.

23   Ben-Ner 1988; Quarter and Brown 1992.

actual skills, capacities, and motivations for self-managing their firms are most vividly witnessed in ERTs' high survivability rates,[24] their workers' commitments to keeping their firms afloat throughout economic downturns, and the extension of their productive endeavours to include community, cultural, and social development projects, as I will explore further in Chapter 8. Rather, under-production, under-capitalisation, and worker precariousness are most directly related to the depleted conditions inherited from the previous capitalist firm and the lack of consistent state supports or access to credit for ERTs given these conditions, placing Argentina's *empresas recuperadas* at a competitive disadvantage from the get go.[25]

Figure 18 sketches out ERTs' main self-reported causes of under-production and the main changes in these causes between ERTs' first and second periods. During ERTs' first period, production challenges tended to be mostly related to a lack of prime materials for production inputs, out-of-date or inadequate machinery, the need for funds to buy new machines or repair old ones, the lack of labour capital due to a reduced workforce roster (which I will address shortly), and difficulties in accessing new customers and markets for selling their goods or services. These problems are not surprising given that, as I showed in Chapters 1, 2 and 6, most ERTs that emerged during this period did so from situations of crisis and conflict at the point of production, many of them having gone through intense situations of *vaciamiento* and business depletion. By ERTs' second period, with a more stable national economy and with greater familiarisation and acceptance on the part of the legal and political establishments, unions, and workers to the process of converting failing capitalist firms into worker cooperatives, the main causes of under-production had changed. As Figure 18 shows, more recent reasons for ERTs' under-production are not attributed as much by workers to the bad conditions of their technological infrastructure, lack of workers, nor, most dramatically, to the lack of prime materials, but, rather, to 'difficulties in accessing markets'.[26] Indeed, in a separate but related question asked more recently by the Programa Facultad Abierta research team, over 66 percent of ERTs surveyed in 2013 claimed that their technological installations were now in 'good condition', with only 28 percent saying that some of their machines were 'obsolete'.[27]

---

24   As discussed in Chapter 2.
25   For similar findings, see also Palomino 2003; Rebón 2007; Ruggeri 2009; Ruggeri et al. 2010; Wyczykier 2009b.
26   Ruggeri et al. 2014, p. 31.
27   Ibid. Note that multiple answers were permitted for this question.

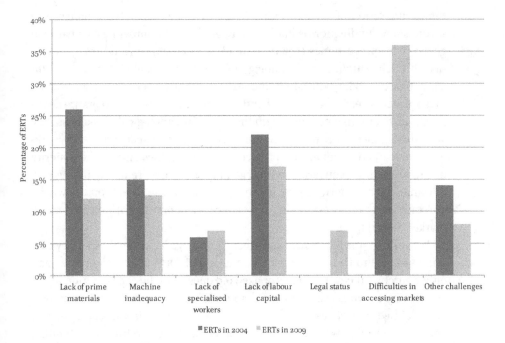

FIGURE 18   Comparing ERTs' main causes of under-production in 2004 and 2009
Note: As of Dec. 2004, *N*=72 ERTS. As of Dec. 2009, *N*=68 ERTS. Multiple answers permitted. Note that the question regarding the 'legal status' of the firm in relation to its challenges was not asked in 2004–5 survey.
SOURCE: RUGGERI ET AL. 2005, P. 74; RUGGERI ET AL. 2010, P. 68

These more recent findings need some qualifications. As I personally witnessed in the ERTs that I have visited over the years, and especially as seen in the three case studies in Chapter 1, having machines in 'good condition' or, similarly, deeming machines to be 'adequate', to link the point to Figure 18, does not mean that these firms necessarily have the latest technology, that all the technological infrastructure they have is being used, nor even that all of their technology is operational. What workers mean here is that the technology that they *can* or *do* use is in the best operational condition possible to meet the current production needs of the cooperative. This is because ERT workers in recent years have either: learned to adapt the depreciated machinery that they inherited to their new conditions of self-management (as was the case at Chilavert in Chapter 1 where they still use the two two-colour printers originally bought in the 1980s by the former owner); have accepted (reluctantly or by choice) the reduced production outputs that older machines and a reduced labour force have conditioned (again, as is the case with Chilavert); have bought *some* new machines (as with Chilavert, UST, and Salud Junín); have fixed old ones from the capitalisation of their revenues (as in all three cases); have managed to secure some funding for technological upgrading from provincial or national government programmes (again, as in all three cases) or from foreign NGOs (as with Salud Junín's ophthalmology machines from Cuba's Operación Milagro); or are working with some combination of these scenarios. It seems that, in more recent years, the causes of under-production for ERT workers are not as much related to their concerns with their firms' technological capacity as they were during ERTs' first period. In more recent years, it seems that ERT workers have learned to adapt to their technological realities and, in the majority of cases, are more concerned with regaining market share or expanding into new markets or otherwise growing their customer-base. These, on the whole, are concerns that any expanding and viable firm operating within competitive markets would have.

As the Programa Facultad Abierta team found by 2010 (from their survey covering ERTs up to December 2009), 60 percent of ERTs claimed that they had either purchased new machines or fixed old ones from the capitalisation of the cooperative's own revenues rather than from loans or state subsidies, 20 percent claimed to have done so from a combination of their own capitalisation and state subsidies, while another ten percent had done so from state funding alone.[28] This is a marked improvement in ERTs' level of self-capitalisation from the research team's 2005 survey work (covering ERTs up to December 2004), if one takes higher levels of capitalisation from revenues as one marker of the success of these firms. Moreover, further achievements in production capacity can be gauged amongst ERTs over the last six years of the first decade of the 2000s if we return to the data from Figure 18 where we see that, at the end of 2004, a combined number of 63 percent of ERTs either claimed to be experiencing 'machine inadequacy', 'lack of labour capital', or 'lack of prime materials', while by the end of 2009 only 42 percent of ERTs claimed to be experiencing these difficulties. Moreover, when we take into account from Figure 17 that 55 percent of ERTs claimed to be producing at over 40 percent of their installed technological capacity by 2009 and 51.5 percent still claimed to do so by 2013, even given the rise in new ERTs in recent years (again, all an improvement from 2004 numbers of 32 percent of ERTs claiming to be producing at over 40 percent capacity), we can safely say that, on the whole, ERTs have been testimony to the resilience and innovative capabilities of their workers to make the best of less-than-perfect business scenarios.

---

28   Rugeri 2010, p. 33. The other ten percent of firms surveyed did not provide an answer to
      this question.

Returning to the main production issue for ERTs by 2009 – that is, difficulties in accessing markets (Figure 18) – a combination of three likely factors have been at play: (1) a perceived need for market growth is the logical next step for older ERT businesses that are in growth mode; (2) the intensification of competition with most markets in expansion in Argentina between 2005 and the early 2010s;[29] and (3) ERTs' continued relatively disadvantaged conditions, given that they have been producing within competitive markets populated mainly by private enterprises that have easier access to loans and capital and that have no qualms about extracting surplus-value from employees, hiring and firing at will, and rationalising the labour process when required. As Ruggeri et al. summarise:

> [T]he numbers [we have been gathering over the years with regard to ERTs' production capacities] show the enormous difficulties [their workers have had] in capitalising firms that have had to get going, in general, with a complete lack of start-up investment necessary for beginning production runs ...[,] and under conditions of work that would not be tolerated in private enterprises ... The determinant question for these firms now is the problem of market insertion ... Most evidently, there is a relation between the capitalisation of ERTs and how they manage to cope in a market reality that has as its main rule competition and where the concepts delineating self-managed work are absolutely foreign to its logics.[30]

In sum, Figures 17 and 18 illustrate that, from the perspective of micro-economic growth and stability, ERTs have, in general, shown clear improvements in productivity and business stability since 2004. They have done so primarily because of an admixture of a more stable national economic climate of growth when compared to the crisis years spanning the turn of the millennium (i.e., during ERT's first period) and, in particular, ERT workers' own ingenuity, creativity, cooperation, and innovations, as I am arguing throughout this book. On the other hand, and again on purely micro-economic terms (and not foreseeing the socialisation, or 'de-commodification', of Argentina's national economy anytime soon), sustaining an ERT's growth by reaching new markets and producing more products or delivering services to more clients or customers, and securing the phenomenon's overall long-term viability and high survivability rates will all depend on how effectively each ERT can compete with private

---

29   Forcinito and Basualdo 2007; Kraul 2011; Kulfas 2016.
30   Ruggeri et al. 2010, p. 31.

firms in their respective markets and how they will tackle ongoing challenges in production that continue to place them within situations of competitive disadvantage.

Indeed, ensconced in market situations with mainly capitalistic firms, LMFs such as ERTs are already at a competitive disadvantage from a purely liberal economic lens since capitalist managers and business owners do not have to concern themselves with the same social issues demanded of members of worker cooperatives wherein 'labour hires capital'. The flipside to ERTs' historical production challenges, as I will analyse further in Chapter 8, is that ERT workers are compelled to continue to develop new skills and capacities that remained untapped when the firm was in private hands, showing that these workers can indeed add much potential value to the worker cooperative model in Argentina. ERT workers' practices of continuous learning and skills development, as well as their innovative ways of democratising shops and extending their initiatives out into the community (themes that will be developed in Chapter 8), also show how ERTs contribute, prefiguratively, to new forms of organising production and socio-economic exchange.

1.2   Productivist Discourses or 'Dual Realities'?

ERTs ongoing micro-economic issues have continued to bring with them, as I have been alluding to thus far, new challenges and tensions that extend beyond the merely economic. Seen from the angle of the social, goals of greater productivity or, at minimum, more stable output levels, as well as workers' desires for greater market penetration requiring direct competition with capital-managed firms, can all be seen as placing ERTs' socially focused cooperative model at risk. That is, the compulsion of some ERT workers to focus too much on keeping up with competition or with rationalising the firm can diminish or set aside the community projects many ERTs take on and dilute the values of solidarity most of them were founded upon. In the words of J.K. Gibson-Graham, another kind of 'economic imaginary'[31] – a more socialised and community-oriented one – can be compromised by business growth aspirations, market demand, and the drive to competition. Indeed, in describing in particular what they measure their ERTs' success against, some of the ERT workers I have had conversations with over the years have used what critical social theorists and economists call 'productivist assumptions'.[32] Such discourses privilege economic

---

31   Gibson-Graham 2006, pp. 6–21.
32   Weeks 2005, p. 110; See also Baudrillard 1975; Gibson-Graham 2006; Giddens 1994.

growth over other social values and practices such as solidarity and cooper-ative economics, community-focused development, and social inclusion that have also been championed by many ERTs.[33]

The contradictory values and practices of economic growth and competi-tion versus cooperation, solidarity, and social aims were constantly in tension in almost all interviews with ERT workers I conducted as well as in informal conversations I have had with ERT protagonists over the years. That is, ERT workers both recognise the need for taking care of each other and taking care of the communities that surround them while also acknowledging, almost in the same breath and at times as if apologetically added on, their cooperative's need to stay competitive, upgrade their technologies, or keep growing economically. The discourse of economic growth is also rooted in a sense of pride for these workers, showing that they can actually run a business on their own. Moreover, this discourse takes up how they in part measure success (for example, in ERT workers' comparisons of their productive output or current economic stabil-ity to the previous firm from which they emerged), and evidences some of the benchmarks ERT workers use in assessing their post-takeover performance. Recall, for example, what UST's Pablo Rolandi expressed in Chapter 1: 'Showing that you can indeed self-manage your business – and actually doing it – is a matter of survival for us'.[34] Or Salud Junín's Alejandro Torres's comment: 'If we look back, it is incredible to see how we have grown. It fills us with pride'.[35] In the same interview, a few minutes earlier, Alejandro qualified this sentiment, suggesting that the health clinic's growth is not only necessary for the cooper-ative's own survival, but also to 'prove to others' – the community, their market, the state, and even themselves – that ERTs are viable entities that matter both for social *and* economic reasons:

> As treasurer, I try and take to the workers' assembly proof that we are growing. We have to eat and live; this is one major responsibility [we have as a cooperative], but *this project also has to grow*. I am of the idea that the clinic has to show growth in order for people to say that 'Yes, *las empre-sas recuperadas* function'. If we divvy up amongst ourselves *everything* we make, then this thing will all fall apart. We have to put some of our earn-ings back into the firm, right? We have to grow so people – society, our patients, the state, our competitors – won't doubt the ERTs. So, as ERTs

---

33   For more on the social dimensions of Argentina's ERTs, see this book's Introduction and Chapters 1 and 8.

34   Rolandi 2009, personal intrerview.

35   Torres 2009, personal interview.

we have to always take two things into account: One, are your *compañeros* satisfied with what they take home as salary? And, two, is your enterprise growing?[36]

The former president of *Comercio y Justicia*, Javier De Pascuale, editorial director of the ERT at the time of my interview with him, articulated this tension between solidarity and economic growth in perhaps starker terms when I asked him how his firm measures success. Notice, in particular, how he first starts out by telling me about how strong their internal solidarity is at the cooperative and then quickly turns to discussing how the democratic decision-making structures of the cooperative slow down productivity:

> I think our major success has been at the human level here. As an [economic] organisation, however, I think we have a long road ahead of us. At the human level, we have great solidarity, and with minimal conflicts. At the organisational level we have great challenges, I think. We have to analyse the time it takes, first of all, to resolve internal issues between us. After that, we have challenges at the organisational level that have to do with bettering our products, making decisions to introduce new and improved quality standards for our newspaper's layout, for example, and improving our production processes and even standards for our internal competition so that we produce the best product possible. You see, we have issues, I would say, with our times – that is, the time it takes for us to turn around ideas into products, because we always have to consult things with the membership. Then we have challenges in the area of technical innovation, for example in creating and introducing new products, investing more than the eight percent a year that we now do from our revenues for technological upgrading.[37]

While there were similar tensions between values of solidarity and productivity in the discourses of workers at UST, Chilavert, and the other ERTs I visited throughout the years, one can understand how unavoidable these tensions are given the insertion of almost all ERTs within competitive markets *out of necessity rather than by choice*. With little effective ongoing state assistance or subsidies, a lack of comprehensive policy considerations for privileging ERTs' procurement of goods or services to the state, a need for more favourable tax

---

36   Ibid.
37   De Pascuale 2009, personal interview.

treatment, and so on, ERTs are mostly left to fend for themselves in a sea of capitalist firms that are entrenched in the interests of profit above all else and that, unlike ERT cooperatives, have no social missions to 'encumber' the pursuit of their most immediate sales objectives and revenue goals.

In a sense, then, ERTs live *dual realities*: On the one hand, out of a sheer need for survival, they must attempt to maximise production and revenues as much as they can within competitive markets. On the other hand, they must also take into account the social and solidarity objectives and values of the cooperative, which include keeping its members working and making a living and, with a good number of ERTs, redistributing portions of revenues or dedicating time and resources to community projects. This, of course, is a situation not uncommon to worker cooperatives generally, especially those existing within capitalist national economies where worker cooperatives must, at the same time, compete with capital-managed firms while being further tasked with needing to live by the dictates of the International Co-operative Alliance's seven cooperative principles.[38] Moreover, given the stubbornly depleted or less-than-optimal conditions of ERTs' technical infrastructures overall, the lack of consistent and meaningful state support, and their highly conflictive origins, the burdens piled up on an ERT cooperative are perhaps even greater than what would normally be the case with other worker cooperatives that have their start in better economic circumstances or within national conjunctures that offer more robust support structures for coops. Thus, I believe levelling the 'productivist' critique at these firms might be an unfair and 'unproductive' endeavour, given the lack of other clear choices for these workers who have had to, first and foremost, pragmatically secure their jobs and make a living.

This dual reality also necessarily means that ERT workers must always carefully consider how they will reinvest funds that are hard to come by back into the firm. As I address in more detail in Chapter 8, it also means that the role of the second, third, and seventh cooperative principles – namely, 'democratic member control', 'member economic participation', and 'concern for community' – is constantly being debated within each particular ERT. Furthermore, this dual reality means that ERT workers are faced with the need to continually reassess and even redesign the organisation of their production to most effectively meet customer orders and market demands *while also* taking into account workers' internal democratic and egalitarian obligations and the cooperative's external community commitments and social missions. Needing to juggle such multifaceted obligations, then, and given ERTs' other challenges,

---

38   Craig 1993; Cornforth 1983; Diamantopolous 2012; Melnyk 1985. See also Chapter 5.

it is not surprising that these firms are chronically under-producing or that some ERTS – such as *Comercio y Justicia*, ensconced as it is in the highly competitive newspaper publishing business[39] – choose not to engage in community projects for fear of distracting their workers from their main business goals.

The case of UST contrasts with most other ERTS in that there is not such a sharp tension with its dual reality. Without negating the strength of the social commitments of its members and the force of their political consiousness developed throughout their years of self-management, it is nevertheless important to note that UST is able to engage in its extensive community projects partly because it is mostly exempt from having to deal with competitive markets; over 90 percent of UST's revenues come from guaranteed and long-term contracts with two major state entities, CEAMSE[40] and the municipality of Avellaneda.[41] Perhaps, then, as I will further explore in Chapter 8, UST serves as a model to emulate for other ERTS and that the Argentine state should consider, not only for assisting these firms in, for example, privileging state contracts and goods and services procurement policies, but also as a non-assistentialist model for concretely carrying out locally run neighbourhood development and community revitalisation projects by that community's very members.

Three final points deserve mention in relation to ERTS' production-related difficulties and their existence in a dual reality. First, the challenges faced by ERTS that I have been reviewing so far underscore some of the reasons why the literature on cooperatives and labour-managed firms conclude that the rate of formation of LMFS tend to be far below those of capital-managed firms (KMFS), that LMFS are 'rarer' than KMFS, and that, moreover, LMFS and worker cooperatives tend to form in sectors with low capital intensity.[42] Second, the fact that almost all of Argentina's ERTS emerge out of circumstances of micro-economic crises and conflict that have a tendency to continue to resonate on these firms' shop floors well after self-management has commenced also highlights the general observation by researchers and theorists that worker cooperatives often emerge out of situations of economic distress.[43] Finally, that so many ERT prot-

39   Mario Rodríguez, 2009, personal interview.

40   CEAMSE, as I discussed at some length in Chapter 1 in the UST case study, is the public sector waste management entity that UST is contracted to service.

41   Rolandi 2009, personal interview.

42   See, for instance, Ben-Ner 1988; Craig 1993; Dow 1993, 2003; Estrin 1989; Gamson and Levin 1984; Hansmann 1996; and Quarter, Mook, and Armstrong 2009. As we suggested in Chapter 2, however, ERTS are also present in capital-intensive sectors and thus tend to buck this last trend. On this point, see also Vieta et al. 2017.

43   Briscoe and Ward 2005; Craig 1993; and Melnyk 1985.

agonists have been able to keep ERTs open, learn how to be cooperators and collectively manage these firms despite these multiple challenges, and that many of them have extended these firms out into the community in so many innovative ways, is a testament to workers' innate capacities to self-manage their own productive lives.

1.3   A Reduced Labour Force and Older Workers

Another major challenge to the competitive advantage and productivity levels of ERTs is related to their depleted workforces. On average, the workforces of most ERTs shrink by around 80 percent when compared to the situation of the most successful days of the previous firm.[44] More specifically, as the Programa Facultad Abierta team discovered, 84 percent of ERTs reported having lost workers when compared to the previous firm either because they found jobs elsewhere or due to retirement.[45] And while a fair number of ERTs were originally medium-sized or larger enterprises with several hundred workers during their heyday as capitalist firms,[46] over 75 percent of ERTs now employ less than 50 workers. In general, it is safe to say that a vastly depleted labour force further compromises ERTs' short- and medium-term productivity goals and, for some, their long-term sustainability.[47]

ERT workers also tend to be older than the average Argentine worker. While the majority of the full-time Argentine national workforce is between 20 and 40 years of age,[48] the vast majority of ERT workers, over 75 percent in fact, are over 36 years of age, and 20 percent are over 55.[49] In general, there is an older age mean with ERTs when compared to the overall Argentine workforce because most of the workers that leave before the *toma* (takeover) of a firm or that eventually decide not to be a part of an ERT project tend to be younger than those who stay. This is the case for two main reasons: First, younger people in Argentina's well-known ageist job markets generally have an easier time finding alternative work. Rather than face the challenges and uncertainties of self-managing a firm, many younger workers decide therefore to face the lesser

---

44   Fajn 2003; Fournier and Vázquez 2007; Rebón 2007; Ruggeri et al. 2005; Ruggeri et al. 2010.

45   Ruggeri et al. 2010, p. 41.

46   For example, Salud Junín, Chilavert, UST, the Pigüé (ex-Gatic) textile plant, the Forja San Martín metal shop, the aluminium products manufacturer IMPA, and the meat packing plant Yaguané were all once medium-to-large companies that lost large portions of their labour force during their years of crises and labour conflict.

47   Ruggeri et al. 2010, p. 40.

48   ILO 2011.

49   Ruggeri et al. 2010, p. 42.

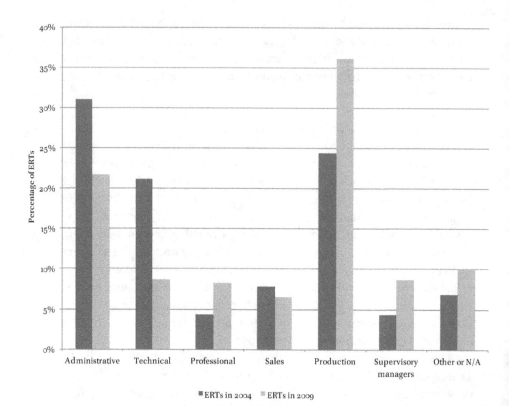

FIGURE 19   Comparing the percentage of ERT workers that leave just before, during, or just
             after the recuperation of the firm, by job classification in 2004 and 2009
             Note: N=72 ERTs for both surveys.
             SOURCE: RUGGERI ET AL. 2005, P. 70; RUGGERI ET AL. 2010, P. 42

uncertainties of the job market and look for greater job 'security' in other, usually private firms. Second, and conversely, older workers have much more to
lose with the closure of the firm, especially for those closer to retirement age,
and thus older workers will more readily risk the takeover and conversion process.

ERT labour trends also differ by profession, and differences here have also
been documented between ERTs' first and second periods. In the Programa
Facultad Abierta's survey covering ERTs up to the end of 2004,[50] as we can see
in Figure 19, the job classifications of workers who decided to leave and not stay
to self-manage their firms, or who were forced to leave for other reasons, tended

---

50   Ruggeri et al. 2005.

to be, in order of job disappearance percentages and out of the total ERT labour force sampled: administrators; highly specialised technicians, production staff, sales and marketing experts; and, lastly professionals and supervisory managers. This workforce shrinkage meant that early on in the ERT phenomenon there was a paucity of technical and administrative staff left at most ERTs by the time the remaining worker collective took over and began to self-manage their firms. Again, this is because it still was, even at the height of Argentina's economic crisis, relatively easier for administrative or technical workers with more portable skills to find jobs elsewhere as compared to blue-collar or service sector workers. Moreover, these administrative and technical workers tended to be, again, usually younger than the mostly older blue-collar workers who had no options but to stay on to take over their troubled firms. There is no doubt amongst the ERT workers I spoke to that these younger, more technically inclined, or administrative workers would have helped immensely in the reorganisation of an ERT's production processes.

By ERTs' second period, however, there was a shift in the kinds of workers who left new ERTs. By 2009, for instance, most workers who left an ERT were production line workers, followed by administrative workers, and then, at virtually the same rates, technical, professional, and supervisory managers. Why was it that more than 12 percent more production line workers had left by the 2009 survey as compared to the 2004 survey? The answer, the Programa Facultad Abierta team suggest, is simple: with a more regularised and stable economic and labour climate throughout the country during the period covered by the 2009 survey (that is, ERTs in existence between 2005–9), as compared to the still-present after-effects of the deep economic recession of the first years of the new millennium, it was easier for blue-collar, service, and production line workers and even older workers to find jobs elsewhere, and some did. In addition, many ERT workers who were nearing retirement age had actually started to retire by the 2009 survey; according to the Programa Facultad Abierta team, as of 2009, 22 percent of workers who were no longer part of an ERT were founders of the cooperative that had retired.[51]

1.4   *ERTs as Job Creators*
On the other hand, while ERTs do initially see a substantial drop in the number of workers when self-managed production begins compared to their most economically stable days as private capitalist firms, once a firm is fully under workers' control it tends, on the whole, to create new jobs – that is, it begins

---

51   Ruggeri et al. 2010, p. 42.

to take on new worker-members.[52] This is in line with the extant literature on worker cooperatives and labour-managed firms as job creators.[53]

As Marisa Fournier and Gonzalo Vazquez found, 58 percent of the 50 ERTs they surveyed created a total of 498 new jobs after their founding as an ERT, with only three of their cases seeing further losses of workers after having started self-managed production.[54] The Programa Facultad Abierta team, Gabriel Fajn, and Julian Rebón, have reported similar findings.[55] Due to the sample size and recentness of their data, the Programa Facultad Abierta researchers[56] offer the most robust overall figures concerning job growth within the ERT phenomenon: As we saw in Figure 10 in Chapter 2, between their 2004 and 2009 surveys, the number of total ERT workers grew by almost 2,900, from 8,341 workers in 2004 to 11,217 workers by 2009. By their 2013 survey, over 2,400 more ERT workers were present (totalling 13,644 ERT workers), while by early 2016, more than 2,000 additional workers made up the ERT phenomenon (totalling 15,684 workers). This growth has come both from more ERTs entering the scene between each survey and from older ERTs actually expanding their businesses and taking on new workers.

Another noteworthy and related finding of the Facultad Abierta team is that the older the ERT, the more likely it is that it will have taken on new workers. For example, in their 2010 report the team reported that 91 percent of the oldest ERTs that were founded before 2001 had incorporated new members by the time of the 2009 survey, 83 percent of those founded in 2001 had taken on new workers, 85 percent founded between the years 2002–4 had done so, and 75 percent of ERTs founded between 2005–7 had hired new workers, while 45 percent of ERTs founded after 2007 had taken on new workers.[57] The reasons for these findings are varied. We can assume, however, from the relation between the level of conflictivity during a given ERT's founding and its members' commitments to solidarity and cooperativist values (as found by Fajn and Ruggeri et al.,[58] and as suggested by my own research in the next chapter), that the link between the age of the ERT and its higher likelihood of having taken on new workers is related to two major factors: First, the more intensive levels of solid-

52   Fajn 2003; Fournier and Vázquez 2007; Rebón 2004, 2007; Ruggeri et al. 2010.

53   See, for instance, Artz and Kim 2011; Birchall and Hammond Ketilson 2009; Burdín 2014; Burdín and Dean 2009; Jossa 2014; Pérotin 2006, 2014; Rosen and Klein 1983; Sánchez Bajo and Roelants 2011; Vieta et al. 2017; and Zevi et al. 2011.

54   Fournier and Vázquez 2007, p. 42.

55   Rugeri et al. 2010; Rugeri et al. 2014; Fajn 2003; Rebón 2007.

56   Rugeri et al. 2010; Rugeri et al. 2014.

57   Ruggeri et al. 2010.

58   Fajn 2003; Ruggeri et al. 2005.

arity experienced by workers from older ERTs founded during the years of deep macro-economic crises between the end of the 1990s and early 2000s express themselves in part in a higher likelihood of taking on new workers or bringing back former workers – *compañeros* who had been laid off or fired by the former boss or workers of the former firm that had retired and who need jobs again. The other, more straightforward explanation is that older ERT firms have simply experienced more cycles of business expansion and have had more time to stabilise, thus having more opportunities to take on new workers. These two explanations for taking on new workers, as I will expand on in Chapter 8, are suggested in two of this book's case studies. Chilavert, for instance, had by 2009 expanded from eight to 14 members and UST from 34 to close to 100 members, while Salud Junín had maintained its membership level at 35 with the additional contracting of the services of more than 60 doctors.

1.5 *Issues Related to Taking on New Workers*
But taking on new workers, while usually done during the growth phase of an ERT, also brings challenges. Indeed, which new workers should be hired, when to take them on, and how to incorporate them into the firm are ongoing issues at most ERTs. For example, the issues of how much decision-making capacity the ERT cooperative should give to new workers, how much they should be remunerated, and, indeed, whether their wages should be the same as the wages of more senior members, all remain crucial points of debate within many ERT workers' assemblies. These debates are in no small part related to the uncertainty that incumbent workers have concerning a newer worker's understanding of or level of commitment to cooperative values that for many founding members of ERTs began taking shape during and just after the long months of occupation and resistance. Hence, new hires add further uncertainty concerning the future 'returns' on hiring 'investments'. As a consequence, the first cooperative principle – 'voluntary and open membership' – gets worked out immanently at each ERT as the self-management project unfolds over the years.[59]

Argentina's national legislation for cooperatives stipulates that a cooperative's full-time 'hires' must eventually be incorporated as members after a pro-

---

59   The potential uncertainties related to hiring new workers, it must be noted, are, while nuanced to each ERT's particular circumstances, not necessarily limited to Argentina's ERTs. They are generally experienced by incumbent members of most worker cooperatives, who must also think clearly about the long-term continuity and future succession plans of their firms (Craig 1993; Dow 2003). For similar issues related to worker-run and -managed firms in Italy, see Vieta et al. 2017.

bationary period.[60] Moreover, once a new worker becomes a *socio* (associate) of the cooperative, any subsequent decision to exclude him or her from membership is a long and complicated process.[61] The decision to incorporate new workers thus takes on a level of gravity and consideration not experienced by capitalist firms in Argentina. Salud Junín's Alejandro Torres made this challenge clear to me when he described a failed attempt at hiring a new worker several years before our interview. The worker ultimately did not live up to expectations as had been set out by Salud Junín's job contract. Although she became a full member of the cooperative after her probationary period, the other members ultimately voted to let her go, a decision that led to a legal confrontation between the worker and the cooperative at the province of Córdoba's labour board. This example clearly illustrates how ERTs that decide to incorporate new workers must be doubly sure that they will be able to execute and maintain a level and quality of work that will justify their salaries. Indeed, a bad hiring decision could negatively affect an ERT's already tight bottom line and the workplace's values of *compañerismo*, possibly taking it into a crisis situation once again.

In addition, the high rates at which founding members are nearing retirement age at many ERTs add more long-term worries for an ERT cooperative's incumbent members.[62] If eventually the number of new associates at an ERT were to supersede the number of founders or more senior members of the cooperative, the firm could be voted out of existence one day by being sold off or demutualised. These scenarios, of course, are not unheard of in the lifecycle of cooperatives. Indeed, the temptation of demutualisation becomes attractive if future generations of members, perhaps not as beholden to the original values of founding members, perceive the capitalist business model to be more 'efficient' or 'effective' for securing jobs and tackling competitive markets. Due to these risks, many ERT cooperatives decide to at first incorporate new hires as temporary, non-member contract workers or interns without making them members of the cooperative. Sometimes these contracts are renewed beyond the probationary period that a particular ERT would have had to respect had

---

60   Ley No. 20.337 1973. Since Argentine cooperatives must primarily serve the needs of its members (and since worker cooperatives are first and foremost organised, according to Argentine law, to provide work to its members), Argentina's cooperative law thus 'limits the work of non-members to exceptional situations of circumstantial work overload, specialized technical tasks or candidate trial periods, but always for a limited period of time' (Cracogna 2013, p. 195).
61   Cracogna 2013.
62   Calderón et al. 2009.

it planned to take on these contract workers as outright members. Of course, how not to exploit the labour of these non-member contract workers becomes another issue that ERTs must confront; ironically, these situations risk reproducing the very exploitative and alienating capitalist labour practices that led to the labour instability that ERT protagonists were contesting in the first place.

But, again, not all is black and white with these hiring practices. Take, for example, the case of Salud Junín's contractual relationship with its 60 plus doctors. As the reader will recall from Chapter 1, Salud Junín's membership is reserved for the clinic's nurses, maintenance workers, and administrative and office staff. The clinic's troubled past relationship with *los profesionales* (the professionals, that is, its doctors) has marked its current membership policy; recall that none of its contracted doctors are, as of this writing, members of the health cooperative, nor was there originally an intention to make them members when the firm was founded (although one of the clinic's founding cooperative members was a doctor who happened to be the only *profesional* to have participated in the takeover of the clinic). The clinic's past relationship with doctors is most prominently etched in the minds of the cooperative's members by its troubled relationship with the clinic's former owners who were, as I presented in Chapter 1, all health care *profesionales*. This past relationship with doctors has thus lingered in the institutional memory of the clinic and is now manifested in the fact that the doctors the clinic works with are contracted to do so and are not members of the cooperative. Furthermore, that it was the clinic's nurses, maintenance staff, and office support workers who suffered through the clinic's founding crises and subsequently went through the struggle to recuperate it, has further shaped the cooperative's membership policy. It was thus decided early on to not open the cooperative's membership base to doctors for fear that the clinic might be once again privatised by these *profesionales*. This decision, however, was not taken lightly at Salud Junín. Over the years, its members have constantly debated in whose major interest it is to be a member and what kind of members would be best for the cooperative. The answers to these two questions for the ERT's founders were clear: Those who went through the struggles of recuperating the clinic were the ones, they felt, who would secure the cooperative nature of the firm and best impart the cooperative values they had adopted to future members. Moreover, Salud Junín's founding members reasoned, doctors in the province of Córdoba already enjoy the relative job security guaranteed by their profession, while the cooperative, in turn, was the only real security its members had. As an interesting compromise, the doctors, who grant their services to the clinic under contract (and

all on a part-time basis), can attend and even participate in the cooperative's weekly Wednesday workers' assembly but as non-members without voting
rights.[63]

In most ERTs in Argentina, the balance between hiring new workers, taking on new members, and securing the future of the cooperative is maintained
by tapping into their social networks, a strategy that could be interpreted by
some critics as nepotistic (although certainly also not uncommon in capitalist
firms). This includes preferential hiring of family members, ex-workers of the
cooperative (including returning retired workers), or workers recommended to
them by the ERT's members, friends, or other ERTs. These hiring practices were
prominent in all three of my case studies because, as Salud Junín's Alejandro
Torres asserted, 'they know well the struggles we have gone through because
they also lived them out with us, and this guarantees that they are pretty much
as committed to this project as we [the founders] are'.[64] ERT researchers such
as Fajn, Rebón, Ruggeri, and Wyczykier[65] have also found that this is a common hiring practice across most ERTs for the very reasons that Alejandro told
me.

Chilavert, too, has taken on new members from personal social networks
but has also, as at Salud Junín and UST, hired workers who were previously
unknown to them. Tellingly, when I asked Chilavert's president Plácido Peñarrieta about the future of the cooperative in relation to the next generation of
workers, he prefaced his answer by talking about the risks of hiring new workers
for the future continuity of the ERT given that new workers have not experienced the same struggles that founders have, and thus might also not share
their cooperative values.[66] Indeed, in his answer, Plácido implicitly suggested a
theme that I will expand on further in the next chapter: the importance of the
memory and the stories of the cooperative's founding struggle for securing the
solidarity of their workplace and the long-term commitment of its workers to
the self-management project.

---

63   López 2007, 2009, personal interviews.
64   Torres 2009, personal interview.
65   Fajn 2003; Rebón 2007; Ruggeri 2009; Wyczykier 2009b.
66   As George Melnyk (1985) and John Craig (1993) both discuss, these are common dilemmas
      and concerns amongst most first-generation worker cooperatives contemplating taking
      on new members. Recent studies of the Mondragón cooperatives in the Basque country
      have found similar gaps between the commitments of older and younger members (Kas-
      mir 1996; MacLeod 1997).

And when the founders here retire? Will the same solidarity you all have now
endure? In other words, how do you guarantee the continuity of the cooper-
ative when the next generation of workers becomes the majority here?

Yes, of course, the risk with newer or younger members is that they won't
keep our values that we have here now in the future. We've thought lots
about this and we've even seen it a bit with our new hires. Actually,
IMPA's[67] challenges are a result of this issue. They accepted too many new
people into the cooperative. They then began to overwhelm the founders
when these newer members began to think that 'The founders are all a
bunch of useless old guys!' without taking into account the history of
[the cooperative], its values, or the effort that the 'old guys' had to go
through to recuperate it. And this is something that we see to some degree
in all of the cooperatives we are in touch with, where the coop's newer
and younger members start sweeping the old guys aside; this, as you can
imagine, causes suffering at these *empresas recuperadas* ... And knowing that this might happen to your coop is sad for us old guys who went
through all of the struggles to get here. That's why we founders remind
the younger members all the time that 'You are benefiting from this, from
our struggles, that is why you now have a job, because of our struggles!'
We old guys, the founders, we always try to lead by example. This is especially important for the three people whom we hired literally off the street
when they came knocking at our door. We didn't know them then, but we
liked their humility, what they were like as people, so we took them on.
Fortunately, all three have worked out for us ... and they really want to
know the stories of how it is that we became what we are today.[68]

In sum, in most ERTs – including Salud Junín, Chilavert, and UST – there is a
marked preoccupation with balancing the equitable treatment of *all* its workers with the ERT's new horizontalised organisational and production processes,
the needs of taking on new members, and the long-term viability of the cooperative. In this way, the issue of 'voluntary and open membership' is continually
being worked out and guided by the particular economic situation, social obligations, and the unique characteristics of the social networks of each ERT.

---

67   Recall that the IMPA metal shop was one of the first ERTs (founded as such in 1997), the
      first ERT to open up its shop to community initiatives, and the place where MNER was
      founded. It also worked closely with Chilavert during the latter ERT's 'occupy' and 'resist'
      phases. For more on IMPA, see Chapters 6 and 8.
68   Peñarrieta 2009, personal interview.

1.6   *Drops in Remuneration Rates*

While ERTs have undoubtedly been net job creators, members' salaries have remained below sector averages on the whole. Indeed, with lower production rates as compared to the previous firm and decreased revenues in general, ERT workers experience much lower remuneration rates when compared to the purchasing power of their previous wages as employees. This, of course, is one of the major sources of ERT workers' continued precarious life conditions.[69] Recall what Chilavert's Cándido González testified in Chapter 1: '[O]ne earned more before [when under owner-management] and we had fixed hours ... We started here in 2002 [as an ERT] earning $200 pesos a month, then $400 pesos, and now [in 2003] we earn $800 pesos'.[70] For Chilavert, a once lucrative arts book print shop, these were huge salary cuts for the eight founding workers. Since then, it must be pointed out, Chilavert's workers have managed to increase their pay but, with a salary fixed at $400 pesos per week as of August 2009,[71] they were still only receiving just $100 pesos above the national minimum wage of $1,500 pesos per month at that time.[72]

At the other end of the spectrum, UST's workers, with their more secure revenue stream based on their state contracts, saw their worker-members earn much more than the minimum wage in August 2009, when the average worker there made $2,277 pesos per month.[73] As I will discuss further in Chapter 8,

---

69   Fournier and Vázquez 2007; Rebón 2007. It is important to reiterate here, as we have already reviewed in Chapter 2, that traditional union bargaining structures, whereby the union negotiates salaries with management or business owners, is a non-starter for ERTs given that there is no longer any management or owners with whom to negotiate. Moreover, and while this situation has changed since ERTs' second period, some of the first ERTs were not able to tap into the sector-wide collective agreements (where pay scales are negotiated and set industry-wide) given the labour reforms of the Menem–de la Rúa years that facilitated company-specific labour contracts and bargaining (see Chapter 3). Additionally, being labour-managed firms, ERTs' salaries are directly related to revenue streams – when revenues fluctuate, salaries do as well. Thus, one of the major struggles that ERT umbrella groups such as ANTA, FACTA, and CNCT were recently engaging in was for the reform of Argentina's worker cooperative law and for the recognition of the self-managed worker as a unique juridical person so that, in part, state assistance would include salary top-ups in order to secure industry-wide or sector-wide remuneration standards for self-managed firms. As a side note, the proposal for a 'basic income' or a 'living wage' replacing the minimum wage from some ERT protagonists, radical academics, and activists in Argentina and elsewhere could begin to resolve some of the fluctuating salary issues of self-managed firms.

70   González 2003, p. 5.

71   Peñarrieta 2009, personal interview; Gráfica 2007.

72   La Nación 2009.

73   Barrios 2009, personal interview.

50 percent of UST's revenues are allocated to member salaries.[74] In some ERTs this rate is even higher. This suggests that ERTs are at core, like most labour-managed firms, 'income maximisers' that strive to maximise revenues in order to secure the highest salaries possible for members.[75] This is in contrast to the 'profit maximising' characteristics of capital-managed firms, where the main aim is profit accumulation and maximising future returns on private investments for shareholders.

UST's higher salaries, however, are an exception in the universe of Argentine ERTs. Fournier and Vázquez found in 2005 that across most ERTs, as Figure 20 shows, salaries mostly spanned between $150 to $1,500 pesos per month, and that the average salary for ERT workers by the end of 2005 was $724 pesos per month.[76] At the time, this was just above the country's *salario mínimo* (minimum wage) for the second half of that year, which was set by Néstor Kirchner's administration in July 2005 at $630 pesos per month.[77] As Fournier and Vázquez quite correctly point out, 'it is clear that the $724 [pesos] is not enough to cover all of the necessities stipulated by [Argentina's] law of labour contracts' for ERT workers, especially given that this law specifies that the minimum wage should be

> the minimum remuneration [that a single worker without family obligations should receive so that] adequate food, dignified housing, education, clothing, sanitary assistance, transport, vacation, and social security previsions are assured.[78]

'The deterioration of workers' real salaries', Fournier and Vázquez conclude, 'is a process that has been taking place for more than 30 years [in Argentina] and there is still much to recuperate in this respect'.[79] Indeed, almost all ERTs I have visited throughout the years witnessed drastic drops in remuneration rates, and one of the major challenges faced by the ERT movement is, to expand on Fournier and Vázquez's term, to 'recuperate' a dignified and living wage for all self-managed workers. The ERT movements' struggles for such a living wage has taken place both pragmatically at the level of the firm, as its worker-

---

74   Ibid.
75   Dow 2003; Vanek 1975, 1977.
76   Fournier and Vázquez 2007, p. 43. At 2005 average exchange rates to the US dollar, the Argentine peso was valued at US$0.345901.
77   La Nación 2011.
78   Fournier and Vázquez 2007, p. 44.
79   Ibid (emphasis added).

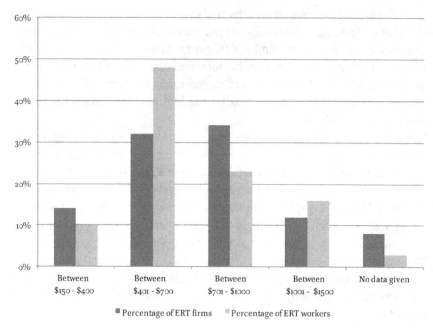

FIGURE 20   Salary levels per month (in pesos) by percentage of ERT firms and workers, as of
December 2005
Note: *N*=50 ERTs.
SOURCE: FOURNIER AND VÁZQUEZ 2007, P. 42

members find ways to increase revenues in order to maximise workers' salaries,
and politically, through workers' engagement with their unions and ERT workers' associations in order to lobby the state to raise pay scales to their sector's
standards and to ultimately combat chronic worker precariousness.

'It has been amazing that we were nothing and that now we can offer jobs
to 80 people here', *Comercio y Justicia*'s Javier De Pascuale emphasised to me in
2009.[80] But ensuring fair remuneration for all ERT workers that, at minimum,
corresponds to sector-wide pay scales continues to be one of the movement's
major challenges. As Javier continued:

> While we can say that we have managed to succeed economically in many
> ways [as a cooperative], this is relative in relation to our salaries because,
> to this day, we can't pay some of our *compañeros* what they would be able
> to get [at a private newspaper] with the same responsibilities. And this

80   De Pascuale 2009, personal interview.

also has to do with the internal decisions we need to make here because, as I already told you, nobody here can make that much more than their workmates; the pay differential here is only three times the difference in pay between a section's leaders and everybody else.[81] Regardless, this challenges us because, as you know, in our society there are those who earn lots of money and those who earn very little, and we have to compete against firms that use wages and salaries as incentives for their workers.

1.7   *Financial Challenges*

The epigraph for this chapter is from Edith Oviedo, member of the worker-recuperated editorial house Cefomar and president of the cooperative at the time that I interviewed her. It precisely captures the varied financial challenges faced by ERTs. In short, because ERT cooperatives are viewed by Argentina's financial institutions as 'risky investments' and fledgling 'entrepreneurial' initiatives by groups of 'self-employed' (or 'autonomous') workers, most ERTs find it hard to secure loans from banks (now all mostly foreign-owned after the market liberalisations of the 1990s). ERTs also find it difficult to secure money from private investors or to receive subsidies from government programmes, which are mostly geared towards investor-funded SME start-ups.[82] Thus, ERTs are constantly challenged in their pursuit of capital for upgrading, fixing, or buying new machinery; to assist with wages and benefits; or otherwise help in market expansion. Given this lack of institutional or government support, it is perhaps even more remarkable, and a testament to the potentiality for self-determination that these workers are modelling, that ERTs have survived as long as they have.

Because of the difficulties of securing funds for the capitalisation and production needs of these firms, non-traditional methods of financing have emerged, again underscoring the innovative zeal of many ERT workers as well

---

81   I discuss pay differentials and equity in more detail in Chapter 8. Overall, while a majority of ERTs practice egalitarian pay schemes for all members, some ERTs, such as *Comercio y Justicia*, do practice salary differentials based on seniority or responsibility. Having said this, for those that do practice pay differentials, most differences in salaries tend to be similar to *Comercio y Justicia*'s.

82   In many ways, as Gregory Dow argues, the lack of investor funding or equity financing is the plight of most labour-managed firms, which constantly face 'capital constraints' and 'debt' and 'equity' financing issues that contribute to making LMFs a 'rarity' when compared to capital-managed firms (Dow 2003, pp. 165–79). The reasons, according to Dow in his review of the relevant economic literature, are, again, linked to the income – rather than capital – maximising nature of LMFs and the lack of incentives for private investors to invest in such firms if they are not going to hold a controlling stake in the business.

as illustrating further promising routes leading beyond the subsumption of labour to capital and the possibility of creating more robust social and solidarity economies. Some of these new financial models include:

(1) approaching lenders as collective coalitions of loosely organised ERTs, as with the Red Gráfica and other second-tier cooperative organisations (see Chapter 3);

(2) individual ERTs organising community 'solidarity fundraising' drives (as all three of this book's case studies, Salud Junín, Chilavert, and UST, have engaged in), or at times with the assistance of ERT workers' associations;

(3) asking customers to pay for the cost of all raw materials up front when making purchase orders (a common practice with smaller, less capital-intensive ERTs such as Chilavert);

(4) recycling waste or trading the waste products of one ERT with other ERTs or cooperatives where these products become useful and cheap inputs to production (as with the Chilavert and IMPA exchange of aluminum products discussed briefly in Chapter 1);

(5) engaging in the nascent but increasingly popular practices of sharing customers and raw materials between ERTs (again, a practice being experimented with by the Red Gráfica and other second-tier cooperative organisations);[83]

(6) appropriating 'day-to-day' or 'just-in-time' production techniques;

(7) working *a façón* (a practice that sees ERTs producing under contract as a third-party contractor or as a sub-contracted part of another firm's production run); and

(8) flexible wage schemes (as, for instance, Chilavert's workers have had to exercise during downturns in their business cycle – a subject we reviewed in Chapter 1).

Of course, the last two points – working *a façón* and deploying flexible wage schemes – are double-edged swords, leading at times to further short-term difficulties and even, arguably, exploitative relations for ERT workers, thereby further challenging ERTs.

First, working *a façon* on a detailed aspect of another firm's production cycle in order to produce a component of the contracting firm's final product (as, for example, is widely practised in the global automobile industry), could be interpreted as ERT workers entering into a situation where the contracting firm is really engaging in a highly exploitative relation of production with

---

83   See, for example, the agreement between DyPRA and the Argentine news agency, TELAM, whereby 'more than 80 [mostly small and cooperative] graphic media [outlets] shall be entitled to receive the national news agency's service' (Télam 2011).

the ERT. This is similar to what Techint was proposing in the *terciarización* of the SYUSA/UST workers by outsourcing a part of Technint's production cycle within the newly formed coop of former SYUSA workers in the UST case study in Chapter 1. Such practices can be seen as a way to drastically lower the cost of production for the contracting firm, as it does not have to contribute to any of the costs of labour beyond paying the contracted firm its fee.[84] Such views highlight how self-management can and is being deployed in the service of capital in the 'post-Fordist', neo-liberal era, reminding us of how practices of workers' self-management and autonomous workteams have been co-opted into capitalist labour processes. On the other hand, such practices could be seen as a way for ERTs to tap into and return to the flexibility and autonomy still afforded to craft producers in the early days of capitalism, at which time labour was 'formally subsumed' into capital. Given ERTs' dual realities and the paucity of choices that some of these firms must face within competitive markets, producing *a façon* for some ERTs has been, especially during times of business cycle downturns, a matter of survival. I return to the implication of this aspect of some ERTs' new production regimes in light of the tensions of having to work within competitive markets in Chapter 8.

Second, the implementation of flexible wage schemes, often touted in the literature as a way that labour-managed firms ride out difficult times and save jobs, has with ERTs often led to the obvious prolonging of workers' personal hardships and to the continued precariousness of these firms. Of the three case studies, fluctuating salaries has happened most often at Chilavert, where in the past its workers' assembly has voted to make drastic cuts to or even temporarily suspend salaries until more revenues could be generated by the cooperative. As Chilavert's Plácido Peñarrieta related to me, with some disappointment:

> So, yes, we now get $400 pesos per week, but of course it still doesn't cover our necessities. And we've even made less money at times because we didn't have enough to pay for our supplies or utilities, or because we had to buy or fix a certain machine, so we took cuts to our salaries. It has reached ridiculous levels, so much so that there have been times when we have had to convince our newer members here to keep on coming to work and that things would get better! But we managed to survive those times.[85]

---

84   Rebón 2007; Ruggeri et al. 2010.
85   Peñarietta 2009, personal interview. While obviously problematic from one perspective, as Peñarrieta explicitly mentions, adding to the personal difficulties of worker-members, flexibilising wages has also been viewed as a strength of labour-managed firms in the

While such irregular financing schemes show promise, hinting at ways in which ERT workers might extricate themselves from the capitalist market system and enter into an alternative social and solidarity economy, on the whole they are still too nascent to map out a sustained and workable economic alternative for such firms in the present. ERTs' micro-economic realities continue to be shaped by the competitive markets they find themselves in. Moreover, the germinal character of these alternative financial arrangements, in addition to the two caveats just mentioned, means that ERTs cannot, at the time of this writing, determine any overarching trends that might reveal more secure sources of revenues and financing in the present or near future outside of competitive markets.

On the other hand, several of the unusual financing schemes mentioned above do prefigure possibilities that exist in Argentina for creating new, non-capitalist (or, at minimum, less capitalist) economic interchanges. These prefigurative arrangements allude to what ERT workers begin to recuperate for themselves, such as extending the boundaries of the workplace into the community and the community into the workplace; moving beyond capitalist forms of production, distribution, and capital accumulation; and, in general, transforming unifunctional factories and workplaces from enclosed spaces with the sole purpose of producing a product or delivering a service to the market into multifunctional open spaces – in the concept of *la fábrica abierta* (the open factory) taken up by ERT protagonists – serving to gather diverse collectives of actors from the surrounding communities into new socialised and solidarity-based economic activity.[86]

2   Section 2: An Ambivalent Relationship with the State

As mentioned in Chapter 6, the increasingly well-understood possibilities offered by ERTs for ameliorating some of Argentina's chronic socio-economic problems provide some reasons for why the Argentine state has, on the whole, permitted these business occupations and conversions to take place. This hav-

---

literature, especially during market downturns. As the evidence has been showing, labour-managed firms such as worker cooperatives tend to deal with labour costs during market downturns not by firing or laying off workers but, rather, by varying wages, thus experiencing fewer job losses when compared to capital-managed firms. See, for instance, Birchall and Hammond Ketilson 2009; Burdín 2014; Burdín and Dean 2009; Pérotin 2006, 2014; Rosen and Klein 1983; Sánchez Bajo and Roelants 2011; Vieta et al. 2017; Zevi et al. 2011.

86   For more on these themes, see Chapter 8.

ing been said, it must be pointed out again that the national governments of presidents Néstor Kirchner and Cristina Fernández de Kirchner, while definitely more sympathetic to the plight of self-managed workers in Argentina when compared to previous regimes, had not provided sufficient and consistent nationwide policies and financial support for worker-recuperated workplaces and for assisting the conversion of new failing firms into cooperatives.[87] By 2016, this situation risked deteriorating further with the return to explicitly neo-liberal policies of president Mauricio Macri's Cambiemos coalition, which I will return to shortly. Thus, the challenges faced by ERTs are compounded by the state's continued ambivalent relationship with the growing ERT phenomenon and with other self-managed enterprises in the country.

The Argentine state has, of course, not been completely absent from encouraging or enacting policies meant to support Argentina's social and solidarity economy. In August of 2009, as I already mentioned in earlier chapters, Fernandez de Kirchner's government, for example, introduced the programme called Plan Argentina Trabaja (Argentina Works Plan), mostly a work integration welfare programme administered by the Ministerio de Desarollo Social (Ministry of Social Development) that oversees social assistance funds funnelled through municipalities that are in turn distributed to underemployed and otherwise unemployed people that form worker cooperatives mandated to maintain local infrastructure.[88] Already by early 2010, this programme had incorporated 70,000 participants in thousands of new worker cooperatives throughout the country and was set to complement or replace the work-for-welfare initiatives for Argentina's marginalised and unemployed that began to be implemented during the crisis years at the turn of the millennium and throughout the 2000s.[89] Through this and other social assistance projects led by the Ministry of Social Development and the Ministry of Labour over the twelve years of the three Kirchner administrations (2003–15),[90] there is no

---

87   Castillo 2007; Rebón 2007; Ruggeri et al. 2014; Vieta and Ruggeri 2009; Wyczykier 2009a.

88   Piva 2015; Vuotto 2011, 2014a. For a discussion of how this and other social assistance plans linked to worker cooperatives have exponentially expanded Argentina's universe of cooperatives – and also the phenomenon of 'false cooperatives' – see Chapters 3 and 5.

89   Such programmes include, for example, Planes Jefes y Jefas de Hogar (Heads of Households Plan), Manos a la Obra (Hands to Work), and Plan Agua Más Trabajo (Water Plus Work Plan) (Guimenez 2011; INAES 2009; Piva 2015; Somoza Zanuy 2011; Vuotto 2011, 2014b). Also see Chapter 5.

90   Other social assistance-based work-for-welfare programmes have included, amongst others: Manos a la Obra (Hands to Work), Plan Agua Más Trabajo (Water Plus Work Plan), Centros Integradores Comunitarios (Integrating Community Centres), Capacitación con

doubt that the Argentine state had been much more invested in local community development work than had previous administrations.[91] According to Ana Dinerstein, these community-focused social policies constituted a 'tendency towards institutionalisation of' ERTs and other grassroots movements as one solution to unemployment, lost productivity, and social exclusion.[92] As Dinerstein elaborates, the Kirchner administrations' social assistance policies geared to the unemployed, underemployed, and workers at risk had been

> taking place within a broad policy framework, celebrated by many social movements, which (i) encourages the 'culture of work' and solidarity within a context of unemployment, informality and crisis of union representation at the workplace; (ii) takes on board the collective and solidarity principles put forward by workers and supporters; and (iii) punishes capitalist speculative behaviour on behalf of workers [as] priorities.[93]

More specifically related to ERTs, state-based programmes that mostly divvy out one-time subsidies for self-managed firms had also increased substantially since 2004 under the Kirchner administrations. In 2004, only 46 percent of ERTs in existence had received some form of state support.[94] By 2009, 85 percent of surveyed ERTs claimed to have received some sort of subsidy, technological upgrading grant, legal assessment, or other state-sponsored assistance, although this had fallen somewhat to 61 percent of all ERTs by 2013.[95] As of 2013, the main source of state subsidies and assistance for ERTs came from the national government (73 percent of all state subsidies and assistance to ERTs, up from 55 percent in 2009), followed by municipal programmes (32 percent) and provincial programmes (26 percent) of subsidies and assistance (up from 22.5 percent for both municipal and provincial assistance programmes respectively in 2009).[96] By 2009, the state organisms that delivered these programmes, in order of the number of subsidies received by ERTs at the time, included: the

Obra (Training with Work), and Obra Pública Provincial y/o Municipal (Provincial and/or Municipal Public Works) (Vuotto 2014a, 2014b).

91   Piqué 2009; Vales 2009; Vuotto 2011, 2014a. As I will also explore shortly, these social assistance programmes were increasingly at risk under Mauricio Macri's national government.

92   Dinerstein 2007, p. 545.

93   Dinerstein 2006, p. 12. See also Piva 2015.

94   Ruggeri et al. 2010, p. 71.

95   Ruggeri et al. 2014, p. 59.

96   Ruggeri et al. 2010, p. 71; Ruggeri et al. 2014, p. 59. For both surveys, multiple answers were permitted.

national Ministry of Labour (39 percent of all subsidies and assistance programmes to ERTs); the Instituto Nacional de Asociativismo y Economía Social (INAES, National Institute of Associationalism and the Social Economy), the national body that oversees cooperatives and mutual associations under the national Ministry of Social Development (18 percent); directly from the Ministry of Social Development (13 percent); the government of the city of Buenos Aires (12 percent); the government of the province of Buenos Aires (four percent); municipalities (three percent); and from 'other sources' of subsidies and assistance from state bodies including those made available by other provinces' initiatives (10 percent).[97]

During the Kirchner years, one direct source of grants and supports for ERTs came from the national Ministry of Labour's Programa Trabajo Autogestionado (Self-Managed Work Programme), formed in 2004 in order to deliver technical assistance and training and for ERTs with technological renovation issues, hygiene and workplace safety upgrading, modest salary top-ups at start-up, and to facilitate other business consulting needs. The programme was partly funded by the Inter-American Development Bank, which in August of 2005 provided US$1.5 million of seed funding to the programme.[98] Other notable state-based funding and support sources for ERTs, cooperatives, and micro-enterprises have included some infrastructure support and training from the Instituto Nacional de Tecnología Industrial (INTI, National Institute of Industrial Technology),[99] the city of Buenos Aires's Dirección General de la Economía social (Directorate of the Social Economy), and programmes out of the province of Buenos Aires's Ministerio de la Producción (Ministry of Production). Also started during the Kirchner years, the national Ministry of Social Development as well as provincial governments have organised numerous national and regional Ferias de Microemprendedores (Micro-Enterprise Fairs), where ERTs and other cooperatives and micro-enterprises highlight their products and services and vie for private sector and state contracts.[100] Finally, some ERTs, especially in the textile and printing and graphics sectors, had managed to secure state social procurement projects for products such as uniforms for state-employees and government publications. Chilavert, for instance, had been contracted to print government documents for the Presidency of Argentina and several national ministries.

---

97   Ruggeri et al. 2010, p. 72.
98   Berasatián 2009, personal interview; Ruggeri et al. 2010, p. 72; Ranis 2016, p. 57.
99   INTI is an autonomous organisation facilitating technological innovation in industry at arm's length from the national government.
100   Ministerio de Desarrollo Social 2017.

Already by the first semester of 2016, however, in the first months of Macri's Cambiemos coalition government, most of these supportive state initiatives had been placed on hold as the Macri administration introduced its economic policy of '*sinceramiento*'.[101] While the Programa Trabajo Autogestionado still existed as of this writing, the programme had been essentially frozen throughout 2016 and early 2017 with no new subsidies delivered.[102] The Macri regime's position as regards social and solidarity economy (SSE) organisations such as ERTS, taking on the explicitly neo-liberal and entrepreneurial hues of the executive branch of Argentina's government, was to focus strictly on their market viability as businesses without taking into account any of the social value these firms might have built up over the years. More to the point, the regime's position regards SSE organisations by 2016 was to 'let the market decide' their fate, thus opening up the possibility for entrepreneurial interventions into SSE firms such as ERTs. In practice, this has meant that the national government openly advocated for SSE businesses to be bought out by private investors (including returning owners) or be allowed to close if the market would not bear them. Together with the sharp rise in the costs of production for SMEs due to the increase in utility rates since 2016 (*el Tarifazo*, as reviewed earlier in the book), an inflation-based drop in consumer and business market demand in recent years, and a return to lukewarm or deleterious responses to the needs of cooperatives and other SSE organisations,[103] this meant that, during the Macri years, the ERT movement faced its most challenging period since the crisis years at the turn of the millennium.

On the whole, and notwithstanding the new challenges to ERTs brought on by *macrismo*, the level of state support for Argentina's *empresas recuperadas* had already proven to be less-than sufficient during the Kirchner era. These state-based programmes have been fragmentary and incoherent for meeting the short- and long-term production, financial, and business stabilisation needs of ERTs.[104] Specifically, they have been insufficient for assisting with the complex processes of converting firms into cooperatives, for ERTs' ongoing capitalisation needs, for addressing the ongoing social security needs of their workers, or for making available fair loans or more substantial grants that can truly assist the transition of firms from depleted and disadvantaged micro-economic conditions to fully productive self-managed (and competitive) enterprises. Moreover, there has also been a dearth of consistent skills

---

101   See Chapter 1 and 3.
102   Ruggeri 2016.
103   For more on this situation, see Ruggeri 2016.
104   See also Dinerstein 2007; Rebón 2007; and Ruggeri 2009.

upgrading or retraining programmes for ERT workers who, more often than not, have to learn new tasks such as marketing, administration, accounting, or sales, and often have to perform these new tasks as additional duties on top of their regular work. At the worker-recuperated Hotel BAUEN, for example, in the heart of the city of Buenos Aires, workers have had to literally transition from being chambermaids, bellhops, front desk workers, cooks, machinists, and bartenders to self-managed cooperators without any assistance from the state to date. As we reviewed in Chapter 6, this situation has exacerbated the challenges of administrating the hotel, maintaining its infrastructure, and delivering customer service.[105] And as Chapter 1 made clear, Chilavert's and Salud Junín's workers had also experienced many issues with new skills acquisition and have had to mostly learn new administrative and marketing tasks on their own on a trial-and-error basis or with some assistance by supportive community groups or other ERTs.[106] We need only compare this situation to Italy, Spain, and France, where, as we saw in Chapter 2, ERTs and cooperatives enjoy ample state support and grants, while their cooperative federations and other NGO agencies offer them substantial assistance in business and administrative know-how and skills upgrading.

This historically complex relationship with the Argentine state is particularly frustrating for ERT protagonists given that their existence is a testament to workers' tenaciousness and ingenuity in saving their businesses; that they provide an object lesson in how to avoid burdening the Argentine economy with more closed firms and unemployed workers; and that they contribute much added value to the economic, social, and cultural wellbeing of the neighbourhoods where they are situated. Moreover, save for a few emblematic ERTs that national or local governments have assisted with more enthusiasm (such as the PAUNY tractor factory), or that certain politicians have appeared at for photo-ops and public relations purposes (such as at the sites of our three case studies or Zanón/FaSinPat or the Brukman textile plant, after they were expropriated on behalf of their workers), it has been surprising to outside observers to learn that the extent of the state's support for ERTs has essentially been to offer them occasional small subsidies or salary supplements from the national ministries of Labour or Social Development or from other programmes sponsored by provincial governments or municipalities, or to offer occasional and often undelivered educational or technological

---

105   Dennis 2010; Resino 2008.
106   I discuss some of the informal ways that ERT workers have had to learn and adopt new business and work skills in the next chapter.

assistance from the Ministry of Social Development, INAES, or INTI. In short, as Ruggeri et al. poignantly put it:

> What is clear is that ... [state assistance plans for ERTs only offer] circumstantial and fragmentary support that would seem to be rooted in the discrepancies of each particular institutional organism, without coherency of action between them. In other words, there has been an absence of unified policies [for ERTs] ... that are dependent on the different intentions and limited [programs] that exist at each ministry or state organism. Moreover, it is the actual workers, their legal representatives, or their [umbrella] organisations that have had to pressure and look under every nook and cranny of the assistance-granting organisation for how to actually access these subsidies.[107]

Julián Rebón further articulates this fragmented policy reality in even more critical, class-based terms, placing the blame on the hierarchical and contradictory nature of the state form and its hegemonic political position, when he writes that:

> The state, as the organisational institution [of command] by the dominant classes ... [and as] ... a factor for social cohesion, represents, in hierarchical and contradictory form, society's existent social forces. Its social contradictions are manifested in the constitution of its organisms and powers, in the composition of its different parts, and in the delimitations of its attributes and actions ... [Thus,] one of the main spheres that [ERTs' struggles] have had to traverse is the institution of the state. The executive, legislative, and judicial branches of the state have expressed themselves differentially [with respect to ERTs], with all of their variegated and fractured layers. [With respect to ERT workers, the state's] practices, competencies, and the predisposition of its actions have been incongruent.[108]

Underscoring how well placed the critiques of Ruggeri et al. and Rebón are, senior government bureaucrats responsible for administering subsidies and assistance packages to ERTs at national, provincial, and municipal levels confirmed to me in interviews with them the fragmentary nature of their policies, their institutions' case-by-case treatment of ERTs, and their lack of solid or

---

107   Ruggeri et al. 2010, p. 72.
108   Rebón 2007, pp. 110–11.

correct information concerning the characteristics of the ERTs within their jurisdiction, including how many of them exist and in what sectors they are to be
found. For instance, as Susana Berasatián, a senior bureaucrat in the national
Ministry of Labour's Programa Trabajo Autogestionado, related to me in a 2009
interview:

> With regard to how we deploy our subsidies, we deal directly with each
> cooperative, not directly with any of the ERT movements [that is, their
> workers' associations and umbrella organisations], although we did meet
> with the various ERT movements originally to work out the details of
> our assistance programme. But, on the whole, our Trabajo Autogestion-
> ado programme deals with each ERT on a case-by-case basis. The workers
> come here, we deal with them directly, we go to their cooperatives, they
> show us their establishment and produce their own business plans and
> business projections that they then present to us, and so forth. This, we
> think, gives us a closer relationship of confidence with each ERT ... In
> general, we feel that it makes more sense to enter a process of negotiation
> with each ERT and tackle the specific situations of each ERT separately.[109]

Despite how the Programa Trabajo Autogestionado positions their case-by-
case policy as a better way of establishing 'a relationship of confidence' with
individual ERTs, having to 'look under every nook and cranny' for these government assistance programmes and figure out how to position their self-
management project favourably with the Ministry of Labour in order to be
'legitimate' candidates for support, as Ruggeri et al. write above, places further
burdens on these firms. Treated on a case-by-case basis, the pursuit of state
subsidies demands that workers' invest their valuable time and energy into
unproductive, non-work activities such as researching what subsidies are available and where they are to be found, lobbying bureaucrats for their time, and
filling out paperwork in order to 'prove' their assistance worthiness. As Joyce
Rothschild and Allen Whitt found in their study of several Californian cooperatives in the 1970s,[110] the constant pursuit of limited funding resources can
drastically alter a cooperative's autonomy, risking their eventual closure in the
face of having to radically alter the values and goals with which the company
was founded.[111] Such too could be the fate of ERTs pursuing limited state-based
funding.

---

109   Berasatián 2009, personal interview.
110   Rothschild and Whitt 1986.
111   For similar findings concerning cooperatives' and social enterprises' pursuit of state-based

But the critique of the state in regards to ERTs by some observers goes deeper. Some ERT researchers explicitly critical of state-based policies, such as Dinerstein[112] and Rebón,[113] have argued that the subsidy-hunt risks making *empresas recuperadas* and other social and solidarity economy cooperatives and collectives into less radical spaces and, ultimately, less likely experiments in socio-economic alternatives, because the pursuit of subsidies and grants further indebts ERTs to the state within a paternalistic relationship.[114] State subsidies and programmes that often also come with requirements to 'normalise' and 'regularise' cooperative workplaces (such as ensuring adequate hygiene procedures are being met, for example) essentially form, these critics claim, relationships of dependency between cooperatives and the state, overly committing them to situations of *asistencialismo* (assistentialism), and thus degrading a cooperative's potential autonomy. At the same time, this forces cooperatives to compete with other cooperatives in pursuit of limited and hard-to-access pots of cash from a confusing potpourri of state organisms. Furthermore, these critics also argue, the subsidy game acts as a carrot dangled in front of desperate cooperative workers' noses, whereby the pursuit of subsidies has the effect of co-opting and de-politicising them.[115]

National, provincial, and municipal government programmes for ERTs during the Kirchner years were part of the numerous policy instruments of the period centred on make-work or work-for-welfare initiatives. Officially and broadly known as policies of *contención social* (social welfare, or literally 'social containment'), these initiatives were promoted as social assistance mechanisms geared towards social inclusion and work integration.[116] Critics of these initiatives, such as Dinerstein and Rebón, argue that government programmes linked to policies of *contención social* have in practice led to the co-optation of protagonists of popular movements and social and solidarity economy initiatives such as ERTs in ways that de-politicise them while curtailing social protest and diffusing the radical potential of these initiatives more generally.[117] In sum, critics argue, government programmes of *contención social* implicitly

---

grants, funds, and supports and the isomorphic tendencies of this constant pursuit, see Akingbola 2006; Cheney, Christensen, Zorn, and Ganesh 2011; Dart 2004; Mason 2012.

112 Dinerstein 2006, 2007.

113 Rebón 2007.

114 See also D'Amico 2013; and Danani 2008.

115 Álvarez Leguizamón 2005; D'Amico 2013; Danani 2008; Dinerstein 2006, 2007; Heller 2004; Rebón 2007.

116 Gallardo 2009, personal interview; Suarez 2009, personal interview; Wert 2009, personal interview.

117 Dinerstein 2007; Rebón 2007.

contribute to regimes of soft coercion by the state towards social and labour movements such as ERTs. Dinerstein explicitly relates these critiques to the Programa Trabajo Autogestionado:

> The [Ministry of Labour's Programa Trabajo Autogestionado] reflects both a renewal in policy making and a change in the attitude of the movement of factory occupations, which have held a positive disposition towards institutional support to develop autonomy and self-management ... [The] government's approach to social movements aims at depoliticising radical action by 'assisting' the workers and making their needs a priority in a way that absorbs their ethos of *social policy from below*. The [Programa Trabajo Autogestionado] pre-empts the political meaning of the *tomas* and celebrates them as innovative survival strategies ... By 'institutionalisation' of the *tomas* we mean that the most challenging and radical aspects of workers' actions are discouraged by the state. As the *tomas* are accepted and habitualised, they are depoliticised and restricted to the purpose of the recovery of factories rather than making them an element of the 'struggle for liberation' anticipated by many workers.[118]

I am sympathetic to the de-politicisation, co-optation, and soft coercion critiques presented by these authors. I do not agree, however, that *all* forms of state support need to be coercive or sidestepped by progressive movements seeking social transformation, nor that, indeed, accepting *any* form of state support necessarily means the de-politicisation and loss of autonomy of social movements such as ERTs. No doubt, some social movement groups have been de-politicised in Argentina as a result of government assistance and co-optation. But the evidence of many ERTs' continued progressive stance towards social justice issues and their radical transformation of once-capitalist workplaces, *despite having received some form of state support*, assuages to some extent this risk and problematises the hard critique of state assistance. Allow me to explain.

There is, on the one hand, ample evidence to suggest that the social assistance programmes of the three Kirchner administrations and various provincial governments between 2003–15 that focused on assisting marginalised groups, social movements, and experiences like ERTs were indeed rooted in the state's desire for the 'institutionalisation' of these grassroots initiatives in the sense

---

118   Dinerstein 2007, p. 540.

in which Dinerstein deploys the term. Indeed, government bureaucrats from Argentina's national and provincial governments with whom I have talked over the years have used the terms *contención social* and *institucionalización* to characterise the goals of the social programmes they oversee, which include curbing social protest, securing social peace, and regularising and normalising social movement organisations. Undoubtedly, *kirchnerista* policies in pursuit of *contención social*, while executed in more indirect and diffuse ways when compared to the more heavy-handed social policies of past governments and *macrismo*, had co-optive outcomes. Policies aimed at *contención social* during the Kirchner era hearkened back to traditional Peronist methods of investing heavily in social assistance programmes or work-for-welfare schemes that in some ways couched their aims of containment and co-optation within a politics of inclusion and ongoing dialogue between a paternalistic state and social movement actors. Critical social scientists, historians, and theorists in Argentina such as Adamovsky, Danani, Dinerstein, Heller, Mercatante, Piva, Rebón, and Svampa and Pereyra,[119] amongst others, have provided considerable evidence that government policies of *contención social* were driven by soft forms of coercion, co-optation, and, ultimately, control over the activities of labour activists, social movements, and other social actors. Dinerstein, Piva, Mercatante, and others have gone as far as to suggest that policies of *contención social* directed at grassroots groups were one of the defining characteristics of the method of governance and exertion of power during the years of *kirchnerismo*. As Dinerstein further contends:

> Institutionalisation [via various social assistance programmes] does not mean that state coercion and sources of conflict between workers and the state are eradicated. The instruments of coercion remain latent in the state's monopoly on force ... Rather, institutionalisation ... implies a controlling character that facilitates the transformation of coercion into consent, by finding areas of agreement between social and labour movements and the state on which to work new and stable channels of dialogue and participation.[120]

On the other hand, however, when assessing the role of state programmes geared to ERTs, these hard critiques of state assistance must also be mitig-

---

119   Adamovsky 2007; Danani 2008; Dinerstein 2007; Heller 2004; Mercatante 2015; Piva 2015; Rebón 2007; and Svampa and Pereyra 2004.
120   Dinerstein 2007, pp. 537–8.

ated by the pragmatic realities and life situations of ERT workers and their cooperative project's dual realities. Moreover, self-described democratic states that claim to represent the needs of all of its people are ethically beholden to support social actors that also contribute to the economic and social well-being of its society, especially when these social actors also unburden the state from many of its socio-economic responsibilities. It is also clear, as I have been suggesting here and in Chapter 6, that the future continuity of the ERT phenomenon could be in jeopardy without solid legal protections and focused state interventions that directly address the wellbeing of the country's self-managed workers. Especially given that these firms must continue to operate within competitive markets from disadvantaged positions, these state-based protections and interventions could, at minimum, ensure a level playing field between all of the country's economic actors. Tellingly, ERTs' challenges have been further compounded since early 2016 with the virtual halt to these assistance programmes decreed by the Macri government.

The lack of coherent state assistance for ERTs has challenged their worker-protagonists in one additional and crucial way that further burdens the possible sustainability of these worker cooperatives: Many ERT workers also continue to experience precariousness in their personal lives due to the paucity of social security benefits available to them as cooperators.[121] When workers in Argentina take over firms and reopen them as cooperatives, they pass from being 'dependent' workers enjoying all of the social security guarantees of full-time workers working under a wage-contract as legislated by Argentine labour law to being 'independent' or 'self-employed' workers known legally in Argentina as *trabajadores autónomos* (autonomous workers). In practice, this means that ERT workers lose most of the social security benefits they enjoyed when working under a boss, including crucial employer pension contributions for ERT workers nearing retirement, personal and family health benefits, unemployment insurance, and workers' compensation insurance. In essence, Argentina lacks specific legislation that would more adequately benefit this new type of self-managed worker, lumping them all into the 'self-employed' category. Under this category, self-managed workers in Argentina fall into the contribution regime of the *monotributo* – a single payment social security, value-added tax, and income tax contribution scheme for the self-employed and the self-managed – which, as far as social security contributions go, only covers retirement contributions and some healthcare benefits.[122] In effect, this

---

121   Calderón, Mazzoli, Polti, Sarlinga, and Vázquez 2009; Ruggeri et al. 2010; Ruggeri et al. 2014; Ruggeri et al. 2016.

122   Calderón et al. 2009. To note, union-based healthcare benefits continued to be recognised

means that ERT workers lose the previous employers' contributions to social security they once received, making the situation of workers that have already absorbed large cuts in remuneration even more tenuous. In practice, on ERT shop floors, this has led at times to tensions between co-workers, as the cooperative's members must often depend on the collective resources and goodwill of their *compañeros* in order to compensate for certain healthcare needs, personal sick days, for absences due to injuries that are not covered by their *monotributo* contributions or for topping up the pensions of retired ERT workers. All of these efforts, again, end up being extra costs that the entire cooperative must bear, ultimately cutting into the membership's total share of revenues. As Calderón et al. stress in their study of the social security challenges faced by ERTs:

> These problems emerge because of the non-existence of a specific national law concerning worker cooperatives that contemplates all of the particularities that this type of [self-managed firm] faces. This legal vacuum places concrete shackles on these workers' social security needs, in effect placing ERT workers on the margins of social (in)security.[123]

In response to these social security challenges, ANTA, FACTA, and CNCT[124] are three second- and third-tier self-managed worker organisations with ERTs as members that have in recent years taken on the political task of lobbying the national government for the juridical recognition of the 'self-managed worker' as a third employment category in addition to the already legally recognised 'dependent' and 'autonomous worker' categories. Moreover, in recent years these and other cooperative and ERT umbrella organisations have been lobbying for the reform of worker cooperative law and, as we already analysed in Chapter 6, national bankruptcy laws, in order to recognise the unique needs of self-managed workers in Argentina. In particular, these organisations have been avidly advocating for these workers to, at minimum, receive the same social benefits enjoyed by the country's 'dependent workers'. Their arguments here, in the main, are grounded in the International Labour Organization's principles of social security.[125]

---

in ERT workplaces that remain with their unions, although these too are placed at risk with ERTs that have tenuous relations with their sector's union.

123   Calderón et al. 2009, p. 116.
124   For more on these and other self-managed workers' associations, see Chapter 3.
125   See Calderón et al. 2009, p. 117.

What explanations can we begin to offer regarding the lack of a coherent state policy in Argentina for ERTs? Generally, this scenario can be attributed to the fact that the Argentine state – equally in the Macri era as during the Kirchner era – remains heavily beholden to its capitalist-entrepreneurial commitments. In more Marxist terms, it is intimately related to the fact that the Argentine state has been and still is an instrument of social control for its capitalist class and for ensuring that private property rights and the privatisation of economic gain continue to be privileged over other socio-economic relations.[126] Although there is no doubt that the three Kirchner governments had stronger social democratic impulses compared to other recent national governments or the more recent Macri regime, even during the Kirchner era the Argentine state remained caught in a conundrum in relation to ERTs: actively support these workers by setting up explicit, robust, and wide-reaching policies and programmes to help convert and sustain *any* troubled firm in Argentina into worker cooperatives (perhaps more justifiable in the early 2000s when the state was severely weakened and when high rates of under- and unemployment and indigence plagued the Argentine economy), or continue to officially uphold, first and foremost, private gain and property rights and treat ERTs on a case-by-case basis, if at all? If the Argentine government were to take on the former position as official policy, there is little doubt that the country's capitalist and neo-conservative elites would view it as a dangerous precedent and respond as they historically have – by imposing countrywide lockouts, advocating for state-sanctioned evictions and even state repression, and engaging in capital flight. Indeed, these tactics were at the heart of the anti-labour climate and socio-economic crisis at the turn of the millennium. Moreover, they have continued to be practised in Argentina to this day, especially during labour disputes at multinationals or when workers, the unemployed, or the homeless attempt to take over larger businesses or potentially lucrative property. Consider, for example, the repression and state-sponsored arbitration of the worker occupation and shut down of the Terabussi-Kraft multinational in 2009 (workers there were demanding safer working conditions, more shop floor control, and the restitution of fired workers), or recent cases of police threats of eviction or other forms of repression of workers occupying and attempting to convert firms into worker cooperatives (as with the print shop Indugraf and the textile plant Textil Quilmes ERTs in 2009, or with the ERT newspaper *El Tiempo Argentino* in 2016). In sum, there is no doubt that the Argentine state has continued to believe that implementing strong and explicit pro-labour policies of work-

---

126   Vieta and Ruggeri 2009.

place conversions to worker cooperatives would compromise its standing with the capitalist-entrepreneurial class and, it is argued, risk a return to economic and political free fall.

3   Section 3: Local and Transnational Solidarity Networks of *Autogestión*

One way that ERTs have attempted to overcome the unsatisfactory support offered by the state and address some of the continued collective challenges faced by their worker-protagonists has been to look to the social and solidarity economy and begin to establish local and transnational solidarity networks. While still nascent, these local and transnational solidarity networks suggest promising solutions for addressing ERTs' challenges, defending the movement's achievements, and further expanding the ERT phenomenon.

3.1   *Local Solidarity Networks in Support of ERTs*
I have already extensively reviewed in Chapter 3 some of the solidarity-based networks and associations of ERTs that have been established since the turn of the millennium, such as MNER, MNFRT, ANTA, FACTA, and other self-managed and cooperative workers' associations; the network of recuperated metal shops organised by UOM Quilmes; and the network of cooperative print shops of the Red Gráfica. Regional networks of ERTs have also formed over the years, including those representing groups of ERTs in the provinces of Buenos Aries, Mendoza, Córdoba, and Santa Fé.

In addition, several university–ERT partnerships have been established in recent years centred on action-based research collaborations, popular education programmes, and solidarity work. These university-based initiatives have missions to accompany ERTs throughout their formation and help train or assist ERT workers and new cooperatives in reorganising their labour processes, in administrative or marketing tasks, and in pursuing subsidies and loans. The already discussed University of Buenos Aires's Programa Facultad Abierta is the most active, oldest, and best organised of these university programmes. Moreover, their close relationship with Chilavert has seen this group, in collaboration with Chilavert's workers, open up and run the ERT Documentation Centre at the ERT, as we first saw in Chapter 1. Other university-based programmes working with ERTs and other social and solidarity economy initiatives include the Universidad Nacional de Quilmes's worker-based popular education programme in partnership with UST; the Tecnicatura en Cooperativismo programme (Technical Programme in Cooperativism) out of the Universidad Nacional de La Plata; the Universidad Nacional de Córdoba's Instituto de Investigación y Formación en Administración Pública (IIFAP, Institute of Reserarch and Education in Public Administration); and Trabajo y Autogestión, a collective of university students assisting ERTs in the city of Buenos Aires.[127] More research-oriented university and cooperative sector programmes that have seen faculty, researchers, and students document and work with ERTs include the Departamento de la Cooperación (Department of Cooperation) of the Centro Cultural de la Cooperación 'Floreal Gorini' (the 'Floreal Gorini' Cultural Centre for Cooperation), which also publishes the Idelcoop journal; the Observatorio Social sobre Empresas Recuperadas y Autogestionadas (OSERA, Social Observatory on Recuperated and Self-Managed Enterprises) out of the University of Buenos Aires's Faculty of Social Science's Instituto Gino Germani; and the Maestria de Economía Social (Master's in Social Economy) programme out of the Universidad Nacional General Sarmiento.[128] Other organisations that have actively accompanied ERTs throughout the years include the associations and university connected to the Madres de la Plaza de Mayo, the film production and audio-visual collective Grupo Alavío, and Lavaca, a cooperative of radical journalists formed immediately after the December 2001 events. Notably, Lavaca also developed the first ever directory of the country's ERTs in 2004.[129] These and many other social justice and civil society organisations have collectively contributed much to documenting and supporting the experiences of Argentina's ERTs.

Together with ERTs' increasing work with traditional unions and newer self-managed workers' associations of ERTs and cooperatives, which was discussed earlier in the book, these additional partnerships, collaborations, and networks between ERTs and universities and civil society organisations show promising signs of social and solidarity economy solutions to ERTs' challenges in the absence of strong state support and growing antagonism from the capitalist system. These programmes and initiatives, however, while carried out with much energy and concrete outcomes for some beneficiary ERTs and for raising awareness of issues pertinent to the country's self-managed enterprises, have to date been too few and too geographically dispersed to address all of

---

127 Trabajo y Autogestón 2009, personal focus group interview.

128 Other university programmes that have or continue to work with ERTs and that were established during ERTs' second and third periods include: Programa Relación Capital–Trabajo, CIECS–CONICET, Universidad Nacional de Córdoba; Carrera de Relaciones del Trabajo, Universidad Nacional Arturo Jauretche; Red TISA, Universidad Nacional de Quilmes; Cátedra Libre de Fábricas Recuperadas, Universidad Nacional de La Plata; and Programa de Articulación Territorial, Universidad Nacional de San Martín.

129 Lavaca 2004.

the plethora of needs and challenges faced by the ERT movement as a whole. Relying on the volunteer work or solidarity of sympathetic students, professors, journalists, or activists with selective or informal organisation or coordination between these disparate initiatives have meant uneven outcomes for the country's ERTs. While no doubt some ERTs have benefited much from these efforts, there are many more still that have not managed to form alliances with these university- or civil society-based networks and affinity groups. Promisingly, in response to new common threats and challenges brought on by the neo-liberal policies of *macrismo* and the anticipation of new systemic crises in the near future, since early 2016 a flurry of new solidarity initiatives, collaborations, collective gatherings for political organising, and a new wave of public demonstrations have been bringing together ERTs, civil society organisations, unions, and other networks of workers and activists from the social and solidarity economy. These recent collaborations and networks of working people, civil society initiatives, and social change activists have been forging a renewal of bottom-up opposition and proposals from the grassroots and will no doubt also shape the future direction of organising and solidarity work within the ERT movement.

3.2   *Transnational Solidarity Initiatives and Networks*

Early initiatives for broad network building and organising around ERTs' common goals and challenges were already being spearheaded by first-period ERT umbrella organisations such as MNER and other ERT protagonists and advocates. These included the first and second gathering of Argentina's ERTs that took place in mid-to-late 2002, which we reviewed in Chapter 6. ERT protagonists and advocates have also begun to look beyond Argentina, seeking over the years to build transnational coalitions of solidarity with other ERTs and labour movements throughout Latin American and beyond.

The Primer Encuentro Latinoamericano de Empresas Recuperadas por los Trabajadores (First Latin American Gathering of Worker-Recuperated Enterprises) that took place in Caracas, Venezuela in October of 2005 was the first and has been, to date, the largest region-wide gathering of ERTs in Latin America, beginning to articulate the first regional vision for the ERT movement. Attended by 600 worker protagonists from 235 worker-recuperated enterprises from Argentina, Brazil, Ecuador, Peru, Paraguay, Uruguay, and Venezuela, in addition to representatives from supportive unions, government officials, and activists from Argentina, Bolivia, Brazil, Ecuador, Haiti, Mexico, Peru, Panama, Uruguay, and Venezuela, the event promised to finally 'internationalise' the ERT movement.[130] Until then, the sharing of ERT experiences between countries

---

130   Lavaca 2005a, 2005b; Martín 2005; Trigona 2006a.

had been relegated to comparative academic studies[131] or occasional contacts between the region's ERT, when workers or movement leaders were invited to international or regional events and conferences such as the World Social Forum. The Argentine delegation of 300 ERT workers – the largest of the *encuentro* – took on an inspirational role at the Primer Encuentro in Caracas, while Hugo Chávez's presence promised to guarantee to the regional ERT movement the financial backing and support of the Venezuelan state.[132] For a variety of reasons, however, the Primer Encuentro failed to live up to its promises.

Prior to the Caracas meeting, ERT leaders such as MNER's Eduardo Murúa had already been spearheading a working relationship with Chávez.[133] In August 2005, two months before the Caracas meeting, MNER discussed securing a favourable loans deal with Venezuela by piggy-backing on a greater regional economic accord that Néstor Kirchner's administration had negotiated with Venezuela to more closely integrate the two economies. This greater accord between Argentina and Venezuela was intended to be part of Chávez's alternative to the US-backed Free Trade Zone of the Americas (FTAA). Chávez had dubbed this alternative regional economic initiative the Alianza Bolivariana para los Pueblos de Nuestra América (ALBA, Bolivarian Alliance[134] for the Peoples of Our America). A proposal that was planned to have benefits for all of Argentina's ERTs and other SMEs and micro-enterprises, the greater economic agreement between the two countries had the Venezuelan government use debt bond purchases valued at over US$500 million to export four million barrels of Venezuelan oil to Argentina in exchange for Argentine industrial products such as, among other goods, agricultural machinery, elevators, hydraulics equipment, and ships.[135] From this fund, low-interest loans would be directed to the growing local and alternative economy being forged by Argentina's micro-enterprises and social and solidarity economies, including ERTs. At the time, the hope expressed to me by some of Argentina's ERT protagonists was that this infusion of cash would begin to help the country's ERTs replace old machinery, grow new markets, and ultimately kick-start undeveloped export markets that would have ERTs initially producing various products that were needed in Venezuela's increasingly nationalised economy of the time.[136]

---

131   For example, Camilletti, Guidini, Herrera, Rodríguez, Martí, et al. 2005; and Martí, Bertullo, Soria, Barrios, Silveira, Camilletti, et al. 2004.
132   Vieta and Ruggeri 2009.
133   Murúa 2005b, personal interview.
134   Before 2009, the word 'Alternative' was used instead of 'Alliance'.
135   Calloni 2005.
136   From my informal discussions with various ERT protagonists and MNER leaders.

The exact amount of the financial contribution from the Venezuelan government to the region's ERTs was confirmed by Chávez in his plenary speech at the Primer Encuentro's Caracas gathering in late October 2005, where he proposed to initially make available in 2006 a fund of soft loans worth US$5 million.[137] The purpose of the fund was specifically destined to assist the region's ERTs in their efforts to resolve production issues, expand production, forge new transregional alliances, enter new markets, and provision them with much-needed investment capital without relying on extra-regional sources of financing (that is, financing from multinational banks). At the time, Chávez viewed this fund as a critical first step for facilitating the productive efforts of ERTs across Latin America. He also viewed the fund as a crucial means of spearheading what in the region was beginning to be called a greater social and solidarity economy within the greater auspices of ALBA.[138] Ultimately, however, the funds failed to reach a single Argentine ERT, although Uruguayan and Brazilian ERTs had received some money from contracts signed with Venezuela's national government at the Caracas gathering. The ultimate failure in getting these muchneeded funds to Argentina's ERTs – again – points to the historical indifference of the Argentine state in fully supporting its homegrown ERTs.

Aside from completing 75 contracts and promissory agreements between the region's ERTs, the Caracas conference participants also managed to finalise what was known as the Compromiso de Caracas (the Caracas Accord).[139] In October 2005, this accord excited many in Argentina's ERT movement. Together with spearheading the accord, the Argentine delegation managed to secure the largest number of production contracts and memoranda of understanding of any of the national delegations in Caracas.[140] But these contracts and agreements ultimately failed to materialise, due to the lack of state support and the ongoing daily commitments that ERT workers had to continue to focus on once they returned to their cooperatives. Nevertheless, the accord still holds prefigurative proposals for what a region-wide solidarity network of ERTs could look like and thus merits recalling.

The accord detailed the vision for a multinational, worker-led, and continent-wide initiative for a solidarity network of ERTs and other worker-run enter-

---

137   AUNO 2005; Fritz 2007.
138   Of course, the proposal for a regional 'social economy' is not without its contradictions, especially when the proposal emanates from the state, as I elaborated on in Chapter 5.
139   Lavaca 2005a, 2005b.
140   Of the 75 accords that were signed at the Caracas meetings, 59 Argentine ERTs signed 39 accords. Venezuelan ERTs signed 26 accords, and the other 10 accords were signed by ERTs from the other participating countries (Lavaca 2005a; Monroy 2005).

prises that Chávez termed 'Empresas Recuperadas del Sur' or 'Empresur'.[141] Empresur was envisioned as an alternative intercontinental socio-economic network that would engage not only in traditional forms of trade between the region's self-managed firms, but would also see ERTs interact with each other outside of the neo-liberal marketplace. As the Caracas gathering's participants envisaged it, such solidarity-based interactions would also include the sharing of technical know-how, the creation of funds for 'fair loans and investments', and the provisioning of raw materials rooted in bartering, all working within a transnational network of cooperation that would offer political support for the legal hurdles faced by ERTs across the region.[142] Crucially, Empresur was to be grounded in grassroots, socialist-minded, and democratic economic initiatives led by workers' self-management.[143] Indeed, as Chávez outlined in his inaugural speech of the Caracas meeting, the region's ERT workers were to be the 'soul' of contemporary Latin America, underscoring how the experiences and values of the region's ERT protagonists symbolised the antithesis of what the FTAA represented. In fact, Empresur, which was to include a regional cooperative solidarity movement of ERTs within an alternative socio-economic framework, was subversively labelled at the Caracas meeting 'a multinational without a boss'.[144]

But, while a smaller Segundo Encuentro Latinoamericano de Empresas Recuperadas took place in late June 2009 in Venezuela,[145] in reality the Primer Encuentro in 2005 and its final accord would prove to be the apogee of these early moves to internationalise the ERT phenomenon across the region. Subsequent to the 2005 Caracas meetings, most of the contracts and initiatives that were signed, especially with the Argentine ERTs, did not come to fruition, and the accord was not subsequently carried forward. This was highly discouraging for Argentina's ERT worker-delegates who had gone to Caracas with high expectations of fulfilling numerous lucrative contracts. And while the Caracas gathering witnessed Chávez officially launch Venezuela's nationalisation and factory expropriation plans,[146] the vision for an alternative Latin American network of ERTs that would create 'a multinational without a boss' fell far short of its promise.

---

141   Fritz 2007, p. 12. See also Martín 2005; and Movimiento 13 de Abril 2005.
142   Martín 2005.
143   Fritz 2007; Vieta and Ruggeri 2009.
144   Lavaca 2005a.
145   FRETECO 2009.
146   See Chapter 2.

One reading of why the commitments of the Caracas Accord failed to materialise for Argentina's ERTs is linked to the substantial differences between ERTs
in Argentina and those in Brazil, Venezuela, and Uruguay.[147] It is, again, related
to the indifference of the Argentine state regarding the long-term fate of ERTs.
Argentina's official government delegation to the Caracas gathering, which was
made up of third-string bureaucrats with little political power, clearly showed
the government's lacklustre position towards ERTs and presaged its ultimate
unwillingness to co-finance or add anything to the US$ 50 million in total invest-
ments for the region's ERTs that Venezuela put on the table at the Caracas
gathering.[148] This had real material consequences for Argentina's ERTs at the
time: While a series of deals initiated at the Caracas gathering were consummated between the Venezuelan state and ERTs in Brazil and Uruguay, thanks to
these states' more robust support of their ERTs, diplomatic protocol prevented
Venezuela from allocating these funds to or finalising deals struck with individual Argentine ERTs without the mediation of the Argentine state.

Something similar occurred with union representation at the Caracas meeting. While, as we have already seen, Argentina's ERTs initially emerged without
the support of most unions, in Brazil, Venezuela, and Uruguay ERTs have
been intimately linked to major unions as central players in national labour
struggles. Recognising this central role, the Uruguayan ERTs at the Caracas
gathering, for example, were accompanied by representatives from the country's union central PIT–CNT. And Brazil's ERTs in Caracas were also grouped
with representatives from its union central, CUT. Argentina's unions, on the
other hand, were represented by a handful of observers.[149]

Because of the mixed outcomes of the Caracas meetings and the lack of
robust government and widespread union support for Argentina's ERTs at the
time, it was impossible for them to activate the contracts they had secured at
the Caracas meeting, while the agreements signed between the Venezuelan
government and Argentina's ERTs have long been forgotten. Moreover, while
regional conferences on self-management, such as the 2005 and 2009 Caracas
meetings, the transnational 'Workers' Economy' conferences (a growing network since 2007 and which I address next), and smaller academic gatherings
have guaranteed some continuing cross-pollination of experiences in *autogestión* across the region, the bulk of the organisational decisions, daily economic
challenges, and socio-political realities faced by the region's ERTs still remain
uniquely tied to the national economic and political conjunctures they find

147   Vieta and Ruggeri 2009.
148   Also see Lavaca 2005a.
149   Lavaca 2005a.

themselves in. Consequently, the Caracas Accord's dream for Empresur – 'a multinational without a boss' – has remained just that. In Argentina, this has meant that most ERTs have had to put the project of forging a network of solidarity across Latin America to the side as they continue to rely on their own micro-economic innovations, the ingenuity and drive of their own workers, the solidarity of the surrounding neighbourhoods and community groups, and fledgling national ERT networks.

In contrast to the Encuentro Latinoamericano de Empresas Recuperadas por los Trabajadores, another network of ERTs and other experiences in self-management that has been actively growing in recent years began in 2007 with the Encuentro Internacional de la 'Economía de los Trabajadores' (International Gathering of the 'Workers' Economy') conferences.[150] A coming together of workers from recuperated enterprises, cooperative and social and solidarity economy protagonists, radical unions, social justice advocates, and activist academics from around the world,[151] the 'Workers' Economy' network has so far organized seven international *encuentros* (gatherings): Buenos Aires in 2007 and 2009; Mexico City in 2011; Joao Pessoa, Brazil in 2013; Punto Fijo, Venezuela in 2015; Argentina again in 2017, held at two worker-recuperated firms, the city of Buenos Aires's Hotel BAUEN and Textiles Pigüé in the province of Buenos Aires; and near Sao Paulo, Brazil in 2019 at the Florestan Fernandes National School of the MST. In 2014, the 'Workers' Economy' network initiated regional chapters and bi-annual conferences representing South America; North America, Central America, and the Caribbean; and the Euromediterranean region. Originally initiated by the University of Buenos Aries's Programa Facultad Abierta and several Argentine worker-recuperated firms, the 'Workers' Economy' gatherings have hosted hundreds of participants at each *encuentro* from over 40 countries from around the world over the years. Participants have included: workers from numerous ERTs in Argentina, across Latin America, and from international ERT experiences such as Greece's Vio.Me, France's Fralib, Italy's Ri-Maflow and Officine Zero, and Chicago's New Era Windows Cooperative; social and solidarity economy initiatives; delegations from Rojava's women's cooperatives; the Zapatistas and various other Indigenous groups; and progressive union leaders from Canada, the US, South Africa, and throughout Europe and Latin America. Administered collectively and democratically by an international committee that works with local organisers for each *encuentro*, taking an inclusive approach to participation, and charging

---

150   La Economía de los/las Trabajadores/as 2017.
151   Including this author.

no fees, the 'Workers' Economy' *encuentros* have served to establish valuable linkages and networking opportunities for self-managed workers and other alternative economy protagonists from around the world.

Argentina's ERT workers and protagonists have also been building transnational linkages by speaking at international venues and conferences and exchanging experiences with other ERTs and cooperative movements in other countries. MNER's Eduardo Murúa was invited by the Canadian Association for Studies in Co-operation (CASC) in 2006 as a keynote speaker at its annual conference, and also spoke at community events and made important connections with the Canadian cooperative and labour movements. A year later, UST's and ANTA's Mario Barrios was invited by the Canadian Autoworkers (CAW) and Steelworkers (USW) to tour Southern Ontario and speak about the experiences of ERTs and alternative forms of labour organising. Other ERT workers and leaders have also toured Europe, Latin America, and North America, including two Chilavert workers' tours of Europe in 2008–9 to present a book of photographs documenting Argentina's ERT movement[152] and tours of Brazil, Italy, France, Spain, India, and Senegal by workers from Cooperativa Textil Pigüé.[153] Zanón/FaSinPat's Raul Godoy has also visited Greee's Vio.Me, where Godoy and the Vio.Me workers shared their experiences.[154] And Argentine ERT expert and director of the Programa Facultad Abierta, Andrés Ruggeri, has travelled extensively throughout the world over the past decade, presenting on the Programa's reports and books and giving talks and interviews on Argentina's ERT phenomenon in numerous media outlets. All of these transnational linkages have served to make Argentina's ERT movement and other nascent ERT experiences widely known, to exchange know-how between *autogestión* projects across the world, and to begin to build encouraging connections between Argentina's ERTs and other self-management experiences in other countries.

Yet other transnational exchanges that have extended linkages of solidarity and even provided funds to Argentina's ERTs from time to time have included initiatives financed by governments in the global North, most notably the Proyecto Redes initiative that I briefly reviewed in Chapter 3 encompassing ERT metal shops of UOM Quilmes that formed a partnership with Italy's Legacoop Bologna and Legacoop Marche in 2006,[155] as well as the presence of a number of Italy's worker buyout-generated ERTs at the ERT expo in the city of Buenos Aires in November 2007, supported by Italy's Cooperazione Finanza

---

152   Lofiego 2007; E. González 2009, personal interview.
153   Ruggeri, Bourlot, Marino, and Peláez 2017.
154   Ranis 2015.
155   NUDOS 2006a.

Impresa (CFI) (see Chapter 2), the Italian Ministry of International Commerce, and Italy's two major cooperative confederations, Legacoop and Confcooperative.[156]

Another innovative path for transnational solidarity networks for Argentina's ERTs has been the 'student tourism' or 'activist tourist' approach whereby university students or travellers from the global North take credit courses in Argentina while spending time working at ERTs or other cooperatives. Participating ERTs and cooperatives, in turn, receive a portion of the fees paid by the students and visitors. Organisations engaged in these educational solidarity exchanges have included the Argentina Automista Project, led by Graciela Monteagudo from the University of Massachusetts-Amherst in collaboration with the University of Buenos Aires and several Argentine ERTs,[157] and the similarly organised OpenMovements project.[158]

One initiative that could be foreshadowing how a specifically transnational social and solidarity economy of *autogestión* might begin to be implemented is The Working World.[159] Launched in December 2005 in Buenos Aires by American philanthropist Brendan Martin and further spearheaded by a collective of North and South American radical journalists and activists such as Avi Lewis, Esteban Magnani, and the Argentine collective La Base, The Working World has been set up as an NGO and consists of a donations-based community development programme that provides micro-lending towards the establishment of new worker cooperatives in Argentina, Nicaragua, and the US (which, as the reader will recall from Chapter 2, has recently included The Working World assisting in securing start-up funds for the New Era Windows ERT in Chicago). The Working World has also hosted an e-commerce site that allowed for customers to purchase products from the cooperatives it supports and has also been a central player in the just-mentioned OpenMovements project.

The Working World has been, since its founding, a promising example of how the strategies of online crowdfunding, product provisioning, and e-commerce could be appropriated by Argentina's ERTs. Indeed, The Working World might provide a model for ERTs to tap into the decentralised and globally available capabilities offered by internet communication technologies in order to meet their production and marketing needs. An expansion of this type of initiative could also fund other fledgling workers' self-management initiatives with much needed cash, offer invaluable support in the pursuit of larger markets,

---

156   ICE 2007.
157   Rhoads and Szelényi 2011, pp. 177–8.
158   OpenMovements 2013.
159   The Working World 2016.

and assist in building relays of affinity with the growing social and solidarity economy movement around the world. Strategically, The Working World has been purposefully tapping into a worldwide market increasingly interested in products made from firms that engage in less exploitative and more environmentally and worker-friendly labour practices, as exemplified by the popularity of the fair trade movement. Indeed, at one point MNER had been proposing branding products and services provisioned by Argentina's ERTs with a '*trabajo justo*' ('fair work') label.[160] This type of online platform could also serve as a customer-focused information portal for ERTs, provide marketing and website development services, and perhaps become a centralised web space with the capabilities of collecting donations for a 'fund that provides productive capital directly to workers through fair loans and investments', as the The Working World itself promotes on its website. While The Working World's e-commerce programme had only offered products produced by a few of Argentina's ERTs, it would not take much to considerably expand such an initiative to cover most of the country's ERTs.

Such transnational initiatives, however nascent they may still be, carry with them hopes of extending a social and solidarity economy and online community economic development model to other Argentine ERTs and similar *autogestión* movements around the world. They hold the possibility of continuing to build, as The Working World further advocated for on an earlier iteration of its website, an 'international solidarity economy, where economic justice and self-determination replace exploitation and inequality'.[161]

4   Organising Between ERTs and the Community to Collectively Overcome Challenges

In this chapter I have endeavoured to lay out the most salient challenges facing projects of *autogestión* at Argentina's ERTs and, where most relevant, have compared these challenges to those suggested by the literature on worker cooperatives and the labour-managed firm. As unusual forms of cooperatives that overwhelmingly emerged from the employee takeover of troubled private firms within a particular national conjuncture delineated by the deep socioeconomic crises of its neo-liberal model, ERTs confront several unique issues. As their members subsequently consolidate their labour processes within the

---

160   Murúa 2006, n. 12.
161   See also Ranis 2016.

organisational framework of a worker cooperative, ERT workers are further challenged by: (1) the need to return production or service delivery to levels that can ensure a decent income stream for worker-members within competitive markets; (2) the difficulty in accessing favourable loans or government grants and subsidies in order to meet their start-up or ongoing capitalisation needs; (3) the struggle to secure organisational stability; (4) securing market share; (5) hiring new workers; (6) fixing or replacing depreciated machinery; and both (7) attempting to adapt their situation to existing legislation while (8) also needing to lobby for the reform of cooperative, business, and social security laws that would improve the labour and competitive conditions of ERTs.

Considering ERTs' long-term struggles for self-management, the deteriorated technological infrastructure inherited by ERT workers, the reduced size of their workforces when compared to the previous capitalist firm, the limited access to credit, and scarce government assistance, it is not surprising that most ERTs are producing below their potential capacity as compared to their production runs under owner management. Although national and regional governments have yet to implement coherent policies and procedures for assisting ERTs, mainly due to the state's continued acquiescence to the capitalist economic model and its continued privileging of private property, the processes of starting up a worker cooperative from the ashes of a failed capitalist firm is now, together with traditional business norms of declaring bankruptcy or 'restructuring', one more option available for failing enterprises. Thus, and as I argued explicitly in Chapter 6 and implicitly in this chapter, almost twenty years after their initial surge, ERTs have managed to secure considerable legitimacy with Argentina's public and some members of the political and judiciary establishments, a legitimacy that is rooted in their positive influence on the communities that they touch and work within and in their 'moral economy of work', extending their social value far beyond their numerical size.

ERT's challenges, nevertheless, have demanded of their workers important strategic decisions in relation to which they cannot afford to err. Despite – or perhaps because of – these difficulties, ERT protagonists have had to turn to their own resourcefulness, inventiveness, and cooperation in order to strengthen their production processes and upgrade skills or acquire new abilities. As I have addressed in this chapter and will articulate further in the next, collective solutions to their ongoing challenges have included: teaching themselves new skills; adopting job rotation schemes and just-in-time production processes; collaborating with other ERTs and local universities in order to upgrade technological capacity and skill sets; seeking national and transnational solidarity linkages; building networks of solidarity between ERTs; creating new forms of social movement-based self-managed workers' associations (see Chapter 3); and innovating nascent forms of promising, non-marketised solidarity economies in conjunction with the neighbourhoods and communities that surround them. The latter initiatives include community fundraising drives; open houses; temporarily taking on interns or hiring students from local technical schools; or raising awareness and solidifying the relevance of the ERT within the local community by hosting community centres, community schools, and free health clinics on their premises, or sponsoring community economic and social development initiatives beyond the walls of their firms.

It is these collective, organisational, cooperatively driven, and community-based solutions to their myriad challenges that bring us to ERTs' *third radical social innovation*, bridging the themes of this chapter with the next:

> *The reincorporation of working-class organising strategies between ERTs and between ERTs and the community in order to collectively respond to their production, financial, and legal challenges and begin to create a new organised labour environment that extends beyond traditional union strategies and tactics.*

Ultimately, this third radical social innovation begins to illustrate how these firms are practising (again, if still nascently) the sixth and seventh cooperative principles: 'cooperation among cooperatives' and 'concern for community'.[162] In turn, this third innovation implicitly threads through the rest of the radical social innovations that embrace ERTs' new labour processes and community commitments, as well as the new shop floor learning strategies and personal transformations of its workers. These are themes I touch on in the next chapter.

---

162   ICA 2016.

Recuperating the Labour Process, Transforming Subjectivities: From *Empleados* to *Compañeros* and *Trabajadores Autogestionados*[1]

Early on in the fight to reclaim our work, we started fighting for our salaries, for getting out of our severe debt-loads that the boss had left us ... But now I know, looking back on our struggle three years on. Now I can see where the change in me started, because it begins during your struggles. First, you fight for not being left out on the street with nothing. And then, suddenly, you see that you've formed a cooperative and you start getting involved in the struggle of other ERTs. You don't realise it at the time, but within your own self there's a change that's taking place; you don't see it directly at the time. You realise it afterwards, when time has transpired ... Then, suddenly, you find yourself protesting in the local legislature, you find yourself fighting, yelling inside of the legislature to the point where you're actually stopping the official proceedings taking place, influencing change inside and outside the factory ... something that you would never imagine yourself doing.

CÁNDIDO GONZÁLEZ[2]

••

This chapter homes in on the new cooperative work cultures that ERT protagonists subsequently forge after founding the ERT, as well as the personal and collective changes workers experience when they take control of a firm, start and consolidate a cooperative, and unfold their projects of *autogestión* – that is, their transformations from managed employees to self-managed workers. The chapter explicitly returns to the case studies we first encountered in detail

---

1 Translation: "From employees to comrades and self-managed workers."
2 Co-founder and retired member of Cooperativa Artes Gráficas Chilavert, interviewed together with the author on Buenos Aires's *La Tribu* FM 88.7 on 2 August 2005 (González and Vieta 2005). The author transcribed the interview and the quote first appeared in Toronto School of Creativity and Inquiry (2007). The quote also appears in Sitrin (2012).

in Chapter 1 as well as other ERTs I have engaged with throughout the years, delving deeper into some of their inner workings as worker cooperatives. In particular, the following pages look at some of the most salient changes in ERTs' labour processes, the transformation of their workers' subjectivities, their collaborative learning processes, as well as these firms' new ways of participating with and helping develop the communities and neighbourhoods that surround them as a consequence of their members' new cooperative attitudes and values.

The chapter is divided into three sections. The first section discusses ERTs' 'dual reality' and inherent tensions with the technological realm of production. It then moves to analyse their two major labour process innovations – *marked organisational horizontality* and *pay equity*. From the evidence in the cooperative literature reviewed earlier, I argue here that the preponderance of and degree to which these two innovations are taken up across most ERTs are unique for worker cooperatives and prefigurative of another socio-economic reality. On the other hand, I also show that the predominance of competitive markets and the demands of the particular sector ERTs are ensconced in are the reasons why the labour processes of some ERTs are less horizontal and their remuneration practices less equitable as compared to others. The chapter's second section reports on some of the specific ways that ERT workers transform from managed employees to self-managed workers. To gauge for these subjective transformations, I analyse the results of a series of 'learning indicators' I embedded in my interviews. What I found was that, since engaging in their projects of *autogestión*, most ERT workers experience some degree of positive changes in their connections to and practices of community participation and solidarity building both within the ERT and outside of it, in their perceptions of their own political efficacy outside of the ERT compared to their lack of involvement in any form of politics (representative or participative) before being a part of the ERT, and in their actual collective decision-making and management skills within the cooperative. Finally, the last section of the chapter looks at how some ERTs begin to practice socialised production and exchange within economies of solidarity, in essence engaging in the sixth and seventh cooperative principles: 'cooperation between cooperatives' and 'concern for community'. Here, we will specifically explore how ERTs' sixth and seventh radical social innovations – opening up shop floors to the community and extending out the productive capacities of the ERT into its surrounding communities in non-commodified ways – serve to exponentially increase their social value and to recuperate notions of social wealth and more equitable distribution of community resources. I conclude the chapter by suggesting how ERT protagonists are challenging their 'dual reality'.

1   Section 1: Cooperatively Working and Democratising the Shop

1.1   *The Pursuit of Technological Adequacy, or Technological Fetishisation?*

In Chapter 7 of *Capital* Volume I, entitled 'The Labour-Process and the Process of Producing Surplus-Value',[3] Karl Marx offers a compelling theory of the deep subjective connections between workers and the labour process, in particular between workers and their activity of 'work itself', the 'subject of work' (that is, 'raw materials'), and 'the instrument[s] of labour'.[4] There, and elsewhere in *Capital* Volume I and the *Grundrisse*, Marx points to the profound links between the skills and capacities of 'living labour' and the tools and machinery of production.[5] Dozens of ERT workers' stories that I had the privilege of hearing first-hand over the years reminds one of these passages on the labour process, the tools of production, and work in *Capital*, a book that not all ERT protagonists have read but that many now know experientially from taking over and self-managing the firms that had once employed them. It was clear to me from talking to workers how their machines indeed are, as Marx articulated 150 years ago, extensions of their working capacities – of their 'living labour'. As ERT workers' testimonies in Chapter 1 vividly showed, many of them become motivated to take over their firms once in sight of the imminent loss of their tools and machines of work, when they begin to realise the centrality of their tools and machines for preserving their livelihoods and for manifesting their capacities to mould and create useful products from raw materials. They also come to realise that it is actually themselves, and not their employers, that possess the skills and capacities to run the machines and craft the products that their bosses once profited from. The central role played by the machines and tools of production in ERT workers' own accounts of the recuperations of their firms highlight the significance of this technology–worker nexus in their struggles for *autogestión*.

---

3   Marx 1967, pp. 177–98.
4   Marx 1967, pp. 178–9.
5   As Marx writes: 'An instrument of labour is a thing, or a complex of things, which the labourer interposes between himself and the subject of his labour, and which serves as the conductor of his activities ... *A machine which does not serve the purposes of labour, is useless* ... *Living labour must seize upon these things and rouse them from their death sleep*, change them from mere possible use-values into real and effective ones. Bathed in the fire of labour, appropriated as part and parcel of labour's organism, and, as it were, made alive for the performance of their functions in the process, they are in truth consumed ... with a purpose, as elementary constituents of new use-values, of new products, ever ready as means of subsistence for

As the stories of the ERT workers that I spoke with make clear, ERT protagonists seem to intuitively know that the connections between themselves and their tools and machines of work are crucial not only for the recuperation of their livelihoods, but also for the preservation of their dignity and self-worth as productive people contributing to the wellbeing of their society. These connections, for example, were evident in the words of Chilavert's González brothers, Cándido and Fermín, when they recounted how the machines of the print shop had to be protected at all costs during the most harrowing days of occupation in order for their jobs – and dignity – to be saved. They were also evident in the importance that Salud Junín's Alejandro Torres and José Lopéz placed on the technological renewal and infrastructural growth of the clinic since starting their project of *autogestión*. For Alejandro and José, the technological renewal they were able to oversee since taking over the firm was a testament to the viability of their clinic, as well as to the tenacity, ingenuity, and sound stewardship of their cooperatives' members.

In sum, all of these workers seemed to intuitively know when contemplating the takeover of their places of work that to face the possible loss of their machines (tools which many of them had worked with for dozens of years) was to risk losing not only the tangible expression of their skills, but also their very sense of *self-worth*. In other words, the possibility of losing their machines was also a direct threat to their very identity as workers, their *pride* as human beings, and their *dignity* as capable individuals who had managed, up until the chaos brought into their lives by the neo-liberal system of the 1990s and the subsequent micro-economic crises in their workplaces, to ably provide for themselves and their families. Pride, dignity, self-worth. These were words that almost all of the workers I spoke with used to describe their lived experiences with their jobs, their tools and machines of work, and their projects of *autogestión*. They were often deployed in the conversations I had with them to conceptualise their self-understanding as workers. These concepts had become immanently clearer in their minds during and after their collective struggles to save their jobs and restart production as a worker cooperative. As I articulated in the second section of Chapter 4, one of the ways that ERT protagonists resist losing their jobs and begin to move beyond the dominative capitalist system that had encased and limited their working lives embraces, to deploy Andrew Feenberg's concept, the 'creative appropriation'[6] of the technologies and labour processes that former bosses had used to control and exploit them.

---

individual consumption, or as means of production for some new labour-process' (Marx 1967, pp. 179, 183 emphasis added; see also Marx 1967, pp. 386–9; 1973, pp. 690–5, 702–4).

6   Feenberg 1999, pp. 125–7.

But there is a flipside to the re-appropriation of a capitalist firm's technical infrastructure by workers that often gets forgotten in the growing sociological studies of ERTs. Within the milieu of challenges ERT protagonists face in making a go of their cooperative projects, one also begins to notice when studying the ERT phenomenon in depth what Henrique Novaes has called the 'fetish of technology'.[7] By fetishising the technological and productive dimensions of *autogestión*, ERT workers risk falling into the trap of over-instrumentalising their projects and thus privileging the technical and the economic over the social possibilities of their collective endeavours. This, in essence, risks reproducing key aspects of the previous capitalist firm that their self-managed projects promise to contest and begin to transcend. As I discussed in detail in Chapter 7, this is evident, for example, in how ERT workers tend to measure their success in economic terms via their market growth since taking over the firm, their capitalisation needs, the efficiency of their production techniques, and other similar economistic criteria of production. Such instrumantalisation – or, in Herbert Marcuse's words, 'technological rationalisation'[8] – is implicitly and explicitly present in the words some ERT members' use to measure their own success, which I discussed in the context of what I called 'productivist discourses' in Chapter 7: *'crecimiento'* (growth), *'responsabilidad'* (responsibility), *'eficiencia'* (efficiency), *'compromiso'* (commitment), and so on. Such concepts guide the continued application of economic growth indicators on the part of an ERT's leaders and workers' councils in a continuation of the practices of the former firm, which practically manifest themselves in the pursuit of meeting production requirements and maximising revenues to stay afloat within a sea of competitive pressures. Central to these pursuits is the importance some ERT workers I interviewed placed on what could be termed the 'technological adequacy' of their processes of production, or finding the proper fit between their self-management projects, their technologies of production, and the market demands they confront. These technological rationalisations (or fetishisations) highlight some of the tensions that ERT progagonists must tussle with, linked to the 'dual reality' of ERTs discussed in Chapter 7. To recall, ERTs exist in a 'dual reality' in the contemporary Argentine conjuncture: On the one hand, ERT protagonists must do everything they can to maximise production and revenues within competitive market pressures. On the other hand, they must also take into account the social and solidarity objectives and values of the cooperative.

---

7   Novaes 2007.
8   Marcuse 1964.

There are two moments in which this tendency towards technological rationalisation comes to the surface upon visiting an ERT. The first moment is when one first enters an ERT as a visitor and is given the initial tour of the firm by one of its workers. During these introductory visits, the host worker almost immediately begins to talk about their production processes, usually with noticeable pride at their accomplishments and know-how, while, almost in the same breath, also mentioning the less-than-adequate conditions of their machines, often in apologetic tones. Moreover, the initial tour of the plant usually does not, at first, focus on their project of *autogestión per se*, but rather on how they *do* things in their workplace and economic sector, on the ins and outs of the different jobs at the firm, and generally how their products or services get made or are offered to customers. In other words, during these introductory tours, ERT workers will often discuss in great detail their machines, the condition they are in, how they are operated, and their firms' production processes more broadly. Workers also discuss during these introductory tours how they came to refurbish the plant or how they plan on carrying out the repairs and upgrading that still need to get done. It is only after their discussions of their production processes and how they came to refurbish their plant that they begin to tell their story of *autogestión* – that is, their processes of occupy, resist, and produce. This has been my experience at virtually all ERTs I have visited.

Secondly, one is struck by the lack of people often present in the promotional and marketing literature that one receives from ERT workers at the end of the visit. Rather than pictures of people, we tend to see in this promotional literature images of things – of buildings, assets, fixed capital, and products. Rather than focusing on the members of the cooperative, how their project saved jobs, the stories of their recuperation, the details of their social mission statements, or explaining what it means to be a cooperative and the social advantages of working with or buying from a social enterprise, an ERT's promotional literature tends to highlight the firm's technical infrastructure, their tools of the trade, their installations, their products or services, and other assets. And when an ERT's promotional literature does make mention of the story of how they became an ERT or the makeup of their membership or how many jobs they have saved or created, the tendency is to relegate these themes to the back pages of their brochures.[9] In short, the themes chosen by ERT workers for their promo-

---

9 Note that UST's promotional literature goes against this trend. Heavily marked by their social mission, as Chapter 1 and the last section of this chapter make clear, UST openly promotes its people, community projects, values, and new ways of producing and doing business that privilege the social over the economic in their brochures, on their website, and in most of their organisational materials (see Cooperativa 'Unión Solidaria de Trabajadores' 2007, 2017).

tional materials handed out to visitors, customers, providers, and the general public do not explicitly distinguish the self-management aspect of their business from the literature one would receive from capital-managed firms in their sectors.

This infrastructure-and-product-over-people approach to promoting their enterprises is perhaps not surprising given that ERTs need to position themselves within competitive market sectors, show government assistance-granting agencies and credit-granting institutions that they are first and foremost viable businesses, and, more generally, that they must compete with private capitalist firms that practice similar fetishisations of their products and technology. The market-driven scenarios that compel ERT workers to deploy such instrumentalist discourses are, ultimately, ensconced in their dual realities; it is a conundrum ultimately not of their choosing. They are, in short, pushed to this instrumentalisation due to their positioning within competitive markets. Pointing out ERTs' technological rationalisations – this fetish of technology – when positioning themselves in relation to their potential customers, suppliers, and markets serves to remind us of the complex socio-economic conjunctures within which ERTs still find themselves in the Argentina of today. ERTs, after all, exist within the dual reality of, on the one hand, being social economy businesses that engage in solidarity and socio-economic practices – that is, labour hiring capital, saving jobs, and, as I will discuss further in the last section of this chapter, contributing to community socio-economic development – and, on the other hand, having to still sell products within competitive markets. When it comes to reinvesting in their enterprises in light of the lack of state-based and other support, the reality is stark: ERTs must still, on the whole, generate capital by reinvesting portions of revenues back into their production by selling their goods or services on open markets. Here, ERTs, as with all worker cooperatives that must still operate within competitive markets, underscore Marx's critique of worker/producer cooperatives – that, pushed to sell products valued by socially-necessary labour-times, 'they naturally reproduce ... the defects of the existing system'.[10]

Caught within this dual reality of needing to meet economic ends via socialised means, ERTs exist in a constant tension. On the one hand, ERTs, as Marx[11] also pointed out with regard to the worker/producer cooperatives of his day, contest the capitalist framework in their very projects of *autogestión* by showing that managers and private owners are superfluous given the technological

---

10   Marx 1981, p. 571.

11   Marx 1981.

achievements of modern systems of production and the capacities of workers. On the other hand, given Argentina's contemporary capitalist system, ERTs need to be competitive businesses operating within market realities. With little state assistance and a solidarity and social economy still in its infancy with regard to alternative modes of non-commodified exchange, this is, at core, what ERT workers are left with. But, alternatively, it is precisely in the social and solidarity activities being forged between ERTs and the communities that surround them, within ERT networks of solidarity and in ERTs' recuperative moments touched on throughout this book (and discussed theoretically in Chapter 4) that they prefigure another socio-economic reality. In Sections 2 and 3 of this chapter and the concluding chapter of this book I will expand on the prefigurative potential of ERTs that are serving to counteract, and, promisingly, to look beyond their dual realities and the technological and economic fetishisations of their productive endeavours.

1.2 Self-Exploitation or Not? Taking Stock

The compensatory production strategies that ERTs have had to take on to contend with their technological shortfalls, under-production challenges, and their precarious situations within competitive markets (such as spending inordinate amounts of time attempting to improve their technological infrastructures by pursuing hard-to-come-by loans and government funding to upgrade them, working *a façón*, and other irregular sources of funding I mapped out in Chapter 7) have undoubtedly helped to sustain many ERTs thus far. Such strategies have also, however, added to their tenuous existence and the continued instability of their workers.

As Gabriel Fajn and Julián Rebón[12] contend, the financial precariousness undergirding irregular and unstable business practices, such as having to take on outsourced work *a façón*, coupled with the difficulty in meeting production demands and reaching new markets – mostly due to the originally depleted nature of their inherited technology and production processes – often push ERTs to focus primarily on generating as much revenue as possible from the insufficient inputs available to them. This insecurity heightens the daily pressures and precariousness of a given ERT cooperative. For instance, many ERT workers work with the constant awareness that not being able to reach either established or new markets due to a lack of productive capacity, capital investment, or raw materials necessarily means that sufficient revenues might not be generated to pay salaries. These material difficulties underscore a large part of

---

12   Fajn and Rebón 2005.

the daily concerns of many ERTs. They also illustrate the two main contradictions implicit in self-management within a greater capitalist system.

First, when staying afloat becomes the primary focus of ERT workers, they risk losing sight of the collective spirit that drove them to become a worker cooperative in the first place. As Maurizio Atzeni and Pablo Ghigliani[13] point out, situations of micro-economic desperation place undue limits on an ERT's social mission and values and have in real material ways compromised the radical potential of ERTs as sites of less hierarchical and more democratic workplaces. In other words, the most obvious challenge faced by each ERT encountering survival pressures is the risk of falling into situations of what some critical left theorists have called 'self-exploitation'[14] emerging from the despair of having to stay afloat and maximise revenues.

The second contradiction is perhaps not so obvious, but is nevertheless arguably inevitable to labour-managed firms (LMFs) when they must still produce for capitalist markets and within the commodity form. In these situations, the LMF also risks entering into relations of 'self-exploitation'. This occurs, for example, when worker cooperatives continue to produce *commodities* for competitive markets, pushing their member-workers to 'accumulate in order to meet socially necessary labour-times, which are determined on the market'.[15] As Peter Marcuse has recently written:

> Co-ops, inevitably bound by market pressures, are thus pushed to become their own capitalists and so self-exploit – better than being exploited by others, but still. It is as true in consumer co-ops as in producer co-ops; volunteers working without pay are, in economic terms, simply zero-paid workers.[16]

As Fajn and Rebón[17] further observe, the resulting pressures that come with the desperate pursuit of sufficient returns within competitive markets serve to refocus the attention of the ERT from its cooperativist possibilities, reorienting it toward the very capitalist system that it originally contested. For Fajn and Rebón, the effects of these economic pressures are reflected in the tend-

---

13   Atzeni and Ghigliani 2007.
14   As I reviewed from a critical theoretical perspective in Chapter 4 and touched on regarding the historical critique of labour-managed firms by some libertarian Marxists in Chapter 5. See, for instance, Gasper 2014; Marcuse 2015; and Ratner 2015.
15   McNally 1993, p. 181.
16   Marcuse 2015, p. 36.
17   Fajn and Rebón 2005.

ency with some ERTs to return to a business and management style in tune
with capitalist norms. What 'self-exploitation' thus means for LMFs in practice is the reinstitution of fragmented and repetitive work tasks, increased
job intensification, pressures to work overtime without adequate compensation 'for the good of the team', and situations where the control once exercised
by the shop floor supervisor is resumed in what could be called the 'collective foreman'. Subjected to these market-driven demands, ERTs risk compromising their social possibilities and values by returning to primarily capitalist
values and practices, such as: the pursuit of economic growth above all else,
labour process rationalisation, an overt focus on the quality and newness of the
machines of production over the quality of life of workers and making due with
the technologies at hand, the reproduction of capitalist management hierarchies, and ultimately – as has already happened with some ERTs – the temptation
to return the cooperative to former owners or new proprietors. Overall, market-
driven pressures risk transforming ERT workers into cooperative capitalists as
they begin to privilege, once again, the maximisation of profits. Fajn and Rebón
succinctly lay bare the results of this push in what we could call 'cooperative
accumulation': In these regressive situations, 'what was formerly abandoned
[by the cooperative] is desired once again' as workers, in essence, either give
up the vision of self-management or become 'new capitalists'[18] in their drive
to, as David McNally adds succinctly, 'meet the survival conditions established
on the market'.[19]

ERT protagonists' complex relations to their technologies of production, self-
managed labour processes, and the products of their collective labour that
unfold within their dual realities subject their projects of *autogestión* to a constant tension, brought on by having to compete in open markets while striving
to uphold social objectives. For Atzeni and Ghigliani, the tensions augmented by this dual existence can compromise an ERT's possibilities for social
production and their realisation as radicalised spaces of democratised labour
processes, embracing the full participation and actualisation of the collective
of workers.[20] On the other hand, critiques of self-management projects such
as ERTs must be tempered, as I argued in Chapters 5 and 7, in light of the
lived experiences and situated realities of their workers. The case of Argentina's ERTs, I contend, must be assessed in light of the lived realities of each ERT
collective attempting to, first and foremost, provide for the needs of its workers. Eventually, we must recall, as an ERT project unfolds over the months and

18   Fajn and Rebón 2005 p. 7.
19   McNally 1993, p. 181.
20   Atzeni and Ghigliani 2007.

years, the collective project of *autogestión* tends to become much more than just about saving jobs. One must also consider closely, as I have attempted to do throughout this book, how, over time, these workers begin to collaborate in more communally sensitive projects that commit their experiments with *autogestión* to producing more than the immediate services or products that they sell. This is certainly the case in the great majority of ERTs, contrasting these self-managed firms sharply with the capitalist firms from which they grew, and even to many traditional cooperatives in Argentina that did not emerge from out of capitalist firms in crisis. First growing out of intense situations of microeconomic crises at the point of production or point of service delivery, ERTs tend to embrace values and practices that privilege social production and social wealth creation. Indeed, most ERTs witness their workers transforming businesses into more humane workplaces that, via their commitments to horizontalism and care for one another, contest self-exploitation as much as possible while helping transform communities in the process.

It is clear from the evidence provided by Argentina's ERTs, in sum, that workers not only can but *do* begin to transform personally and collectively when they are involved in projects of *autogestión*, showing that they not only can effectively self-manage themselves, but that they also *can* and *do* imbue their collectively managed productive endeavours with social values and community commitments far beyond what capitalist enterprises offer. The subsequent discussion in the remainder of this chapter and the concluding chapter attempts to work out these *actual* and *prefigurative* alternative socio-economic dimensions innovated by ERT workers, dimensions that emerge out of and despite the challenges and barriers placed before them by a tenacious capitalist system and its subservient state.

1.3   *Two Main Tendencies Distinguishing ERTs' Renewed Labour Processes: Pay-Equity and Marked Horizontality*
The specific form of the cooperative restructuring of the shop tends to be worked out within each ERT pragmatically as it matures and lives out the intricacies of *autogestión*. While, as Ruggeri et al. point out, the transformation of firms into more egalitarian workplaces is not homogenous across all ERTs, there is a marked tendency for ERTs to become much more equitable workplaces, especially when compared to the previous capitalist firms from which they emerged.[21]

---

21   Ruggeri, Antivero, Elena, Polti, et al. 2014, p. 40.

There are two crucial ways that ERTs, at the same time, contest the market-imposed conditions just reviewed and point to how an alternative model of production begins to prefiguratively entrench itself within each ERT, even as these firms continue to live within a capitalist system: their practices of *pay equity* and their tendencies to *reorganise their labour processes horizontally*. Directly related to the second and third principles of cooperativism, respectively 'democratic member control' and 'member economic participation',[22] these two tendencies also directly address how ERT protagonists begin to recuperate the labour process, their own surpluses, and ultimately their labour-power.[23] In their longer-term possibilities for economic alternatives, these practices continue to make ERTs promising projects of *autogestión* that ultimately show paths beyond capitalist forms of surplus-value extraction and private wealth accumulation.

1.3.1   Equitable Remuneration Schemes

The practical question of how the third principle of cooperatives – 'member economic participation'[24] – is to be taken up is continuously debated within most ERTs. For instance, revenue capitalisation and salary amounts, salary adjustments due to ebbs and flows of the firm's business cycles, and patronage refunds[25] and other year-end bonuses are regularly discussed collectively, voted on democratically, and adjusted by an ERT's workers' assembly. In addition, as practised in most worker cooperatives and as entrenched in Argentine cooperative legislation,[26] all members contribute (while usually nominal in the case of ERTs) a 'membership fee' (*cuotas sociales*) to the cooperative's 'share capital', forming an important part of how 'members contribute equitably to, and democratically control, the capital of their co-operative'.[27] As in other worker coops, and also according to Argentine cooperative law, this membership fee is returned to the member with limited interest when they leave the cooperative or upon retirement. Additionally, ERT members are also entitled to patronage

---

22   ICA 2016.

23   See Chapters 4 and 9.

24   MacPherson 1996, par. 46.

25   'Patronage refunds' are usually yearly payouts to a cooperative's members based on the value of the proportional mutual exchanges (or transactions) between members and the cooperative over a given year. In the case of worker cooperatives, the mutual exchange is the labour-time given to the cooperative by each cooperative member. Essentially, patronage refunds include yearly or occasional redistributions of a cooperative's remaining income once production costs (including salaries) have been covered.

26   Cracogna 2013.

27   ICA 2016, para. 8.

refunds based on their contribution to the cooperative (which is connected to the work done by the member), divvied out usually at the end of the cooperative's fiscal year when possible. At some ERTs, these occasional refunds can replace the traditional Argentine practice of the *aguinaldo* (the 'thirteenth month's' pay at the end of the year).

Besides the widespread agreement amongst ERTs of the value and necessity of members controlling the capital of the firm – further encouraged by the horizontal organisational model and small size of most ERTs (see below) – there is no defining trend across ERTs, however, concerning how much revenue is to go back to the capital needs of the firm or how members are to 'receive limited compensation ... on capital subscribed as a condition of membership'.[28] In the case of ERTs, this means that what percentage of revenues should return to the cooperative as capital; how much should be allocated to salaries, benefits, and patronage refunds;[29] whether or not a certain percentage of revenues should go to local community needs; and how losses are to be contended with continue to be worked out pragmatically and debated within each ERT as it matures and lives out its project of *autogestión*.

More often than not, decisions concerning how ERTs' surpluses are to be allocated and losses handled are often susceptible to market cycles. Recall from Chapter 1 Chilavert's tenuous situation within the print and publishing sector and the way their salaries fluctuate based on production demands. As the Chilavert case study made clear, more financially challenging months are most often bridged with cuts to salaries and, at times, community development contributions for those firms that engage in community work. Difficulties in normalising salaries have multiple causes, but tend to be rooted in, as we saw in the previous chapter, chronically low cash reserves, a fleeting customer-base, difficult orders to fulfil due to depreciated machinery, or challenges in securing loans. UST proved to be the exception here amongst the ERTs that I visited. The fact that UST works primarily with the public sector makes their financial situation more stable. Unlike other ERTs that have to primarily sell

---

28 Ibid. See also Fontenia 2008.

29 As Cracogna (2013), Fontenia (2008), and Nieves Simonetti (2004) underscore, according to Argentina's cooperative law (Ley No. 20.337 passed in 1973 and still in force), technically there are no 'wages' or 'salaries' in Argentine worker cooperatives but rather the collective distribution of a cooperative's remaining annual surpluses to members based on their social contribution of labour to the cooperative, net allocations of revenues to production costs and legal reserves. Nevertheless, Ruggeri et al. (2014) remind us that ERT workers, given that they identify primarily as workers rather than as members of a cooperative, continue to consider this redistribution of surpluses to members as their *salarios* (salaries).

their products or services on open markets, UST's production expectations are clearly marked out, their revenue projections and expenses are understood well ahead of time, and their revenues are mostly guaranteed for the duration of their state contracts with the municipality of Avellaneda and the nationally owned CEAMSE.[30] On the whole, UST's production and revenues unfold outside of market pressures. UST takes on smaller independent contracts on open markets as extra income, such as their work with the reconstruction of a major local football stadium in the late 2000s. Mostly free from market pressures, this is also why, as I will discuss in more detail shortly, UST has been able to more fully develop its unique community development outreach projects that, I argue, could serve as a model for cooperative-based community development and social assistance delivery to local communities. Additionally, UST's relationship with the state via its public sector contracts also show a way out of the tensions and contradictions of ERTs' dual reality and, I argue, is an example of a social procurement model that deserves to continue to be struggled over in the search for more non-commodified forms of production.

The most promising and widely practised example of how ERT protagonists are recuperating their surpluses for themselves – and, again, overcoming their dual realities despite their continued market-driven challenges and tensions – is *the preponderance of pay equity schemes no matter how senior a worker is or what skills she or he possesses.*[31] Empirical research carried out by two separate teams from the University of Buenos Aires have found that between 56 percent[32] and 71 percent[33] of ERTs practice complete pay equity. While this coincides with the general tendencies of LMFs to be more equitable in remuneration practices than in capital-managed firms,[34] the degree to which pay equity is practised across the universe of ERTs is one noticeable innovation that differentiates ERTs from the practices of other, non-recuperated LMFs in Argentina and beyond its borders.

The Programa Facultad Abierta's research discovered further nuances to the preponderance of pay equity: First, the *age of the firm* is related to pay equity. It seems that older recuperated firms (especially those recuperated during the most turbulent years of Argentina's neo-liberal crisis during ERTs' first period) are more likely to practice pay equity when compared to more recently recuper-

30   CEAMSE, as will be recalled from Chapter 1, is the public sector entity mandated to manage greater Buenos Aires's waste and the vast recycled eco-park located next to UST's facilities.
31   Fajn 2003; Palomino 2003; Ruggeri, Martinez, and Trinchero 2005; Ruggeri 2009.
32   Ruggeri et al. 2005, p. 80.
33   Fajn 2003, p. 161.
34   Craig 1993, pp. 93–102; Dow 2003, p. 25.

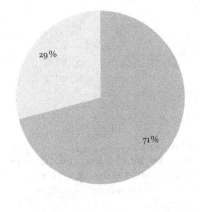

FIGURE 21
Pay equity linked to acts of occupation or
level of conflict in the early days of the ERT,
in 'occupied or highly conflictual ERTs'
Note: N=72.
SOURCE: RUGGERI ET AL. 2005, P. 82

■ Egalitarian pay schemes   ▨ Non-egalitarian pay schemes

ated firms. For example, the Programa Facultad Abierta team discovered that 70 percent of ERTs recuperated during or before 2001 practised complete pay equity while only 39 percent of those recuperated during 2003–4 did so.[35] In addition, the *size* of the firm tends to also be linked to pay equity: 64 percent of firms with 20 workers or less practice pay equity, compared to 47 percent of firms having between 20 to 50 workers and 54 percent with 50 or more workers.[36]

There are several explanations for these differing remuneration practices linked to the age and size of an ERT: It seems that the strong role of *compañerismo* (solidarity in camaraderie) that I began discussing in Chapters 6 and 7, fostered by worker solidarity that solidifies during an ERT's stages of most intense struggles, has a strong part to play in egalitarian remuneration practices. That is, the intensity of the conflicts and struggles that a worker collective goes through in the founding of an ERT are related to later practices of pay equity. And, as first-period ERTs are more likely to have experienced conflictivity in their founding days when compared to second- and third-period ERTs, older, first period ERTs are also more likely to practice pay equity. Figures 21 and 22 vividly compare how an increased likelihood of pay parity is specifically linked to an ERT cooperative's most economically and socially harrowing early days. For instance, in Figure 21 we see that 71 percent of ERTs that were involved in lengthy acts of occupation or other intense conflicts in their early days subsequently practiced pay equity, while Figure 22 shows only 37 percent

---

35   Ruggeri et al. 2005, p. 80.
36   Ruggeri et al. 2005, p. 81.

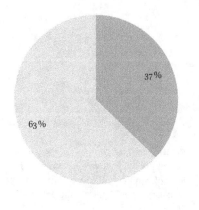

Egalitarian pay schemes   Non-egalitarian pay schemes

FIGURE 22
Pay equity linked to acts of occupation or
level of conflict in the early days of the ERT,
in 'non-occupied or not-as-conflictual ERTs'
Note: N=72.
SOURCE: RUGGERI ET AL. 2005, P. 82

of ERTs that were not occupied or had not experienced intense conflicts do so. Tellingly, workers at ERTs that incorporate equitable pay schemes told the Programa Facultad Abierta team, as they also told me, that their desire to practice pay equity was one specific way of counterbalancing the most exploitative practices they experienced under owner-management.[37]

Moreover, the Programa Facultad Abierta data suggest that the collective of workers belonging to smaller ERTs are more likely to practice pay equity when compared to larger ERTs because workers from smaller ERTs tend to spend more time interacting with each other on a daily basis than those in larger ERTs and thus have more intimate knowledge of each other's jobs and personal lives.[38] In other words, workers from smaller ERTs, underscoring Maurice Merleau-Ponty's[39] theory of intersubjective class formation and class consciousness that I reviewed earlier, more readily develop commonly-shared values and concerns via stronger bonds of solidarity and camaraderie when compared to larger firms with more complex divisions of labour or multiple and more dispersed work teams, or when compared to ERTs that engage in shift work. The values and practices of *compañerismo*, it seems, has a chance to gel more amongst the entire collective of workers at smaller ERTs, and one way that this *compañerismo* plays out is in equal salaries no matter the skill sets or member seniority.

All three of this book's case studies show nuances of how this tendency of pay equity is linked to the intensity of *compañerismo* forged during periods of

---

37   Ruggeri et al. 2005, pp. 81–2. For similar findings, see also Fajn 2003; and Rebón 2007.
38   Ruggeri et al. 2005.
39   Merleau-Ponty 1962.

struggle, and the size and age of the firm. For example, in my time at Chilavert and Salud Junín, two of the small- and medium-sized ERTs amongst the many I visited that also emerged from intense periods of struggle, I did not perceive any chronic factionalism or shop floor competition in my in situ observations and in my analysis of the narratives of the workers with whom I engaged. And almost all of these small- to medium-sized ERTs I visited practised total or near-total pay equity amongst members. The general lack of conflicts between workers at these smaller ERTs were specifically communicated to me by the workers I interviewed and talked to, both implicitly in the general lack of stories about workplace conflict in our informal conversations and explicitly when I would ask them about it in formal interviews. While I did not personally witness worker antagonisms in the larger ERTs I spent time in, their workers' stories did at times contain themes of interpersonal, shop floor, and work team conflicts. In the larger firms I visited, workers in positions of leadership tended to, for instance, spend more time discussing the lack of commitment to the ERT project of some of their *compañeros*, or had complaints about some of their *compañeros* 'slacking off' on the job or not pulling their weight, while these types of critiques were virtually absent in the smaller firms I visited. Of course, it can be argued that in the smaller firms I visited, the fact that workers knew each other well made them self-censor sensitive and intimate details of inter-worker conflictivity inside the ERT, while in larger firms, workers felt more free to discuss such matters because they did not know each other as well. Notwithstanding these possibilities, it was clear from my observations of the interactions of workers at smaller ERTs and from the many conversations I had with them that the intensity of *compañerismo* was stronger when compared to larger ERTs. I observed this in, for example, the more informal ways workers at smaller ERTs spoke to each other, and their many shared daily activities together such as communal eating practices, joking around with each other, and the degree to which they engaged in more non-work activities together as compared to the social interactions and more interpersonal formality I witnessed at larger ERTs.

On the other hand, one of the larger ERTs I have visited, the newspaper *Comercio y Justicia*, also had the least conflictual beginnings of all of the ERTs I engaged with. Not surprisingly, it also has one of the most differentiated salary schemes of all of the ERTs I have been to, basing this salary differential on a mix of experience, seniority, and position. *Comercio y Justicia* in many ways continues the same salary schemes and hierarchical structure that the previous private iteration of the newspaper had. While the ERT loosely bases its salaries on the news industry standard, especially amongst its journalists, its former president Javier De Pascuale informed me that the cooperative nevertheless tries to keep salary differentials within 3:1. Moreover, the salary differential is also based on whether or not workers have a supervisory role (see below). In addition, because *Comercio y Justicia* sees a considerable part of its revenues coming from selling advertising space in its print and online editions, the three coop members dedicated to selling advertising space in the newspaper enjoy both a base salary linked to the average salary at the newspaper plus a commission from ad sales, thereby making considerably more than other members of the ERT. When I probed Javier on these salary differentials and asked him why they do not practice complete pay parity as in other ERTs, his answer was both straightforward and telling:

> *¡Por la competencia!* [Because of the competition!] ... We have to keep good journalists here because the competition in this sector is tough ... And the sales guys? Well, they bring in a considerable amount of revenue for us which helps pay the other members' salaries, so we need to keep them motivated![40]

That remuneration practices are not as equitable at the newspaper *Comercio y Justicia* as in other ERTs illustrates the flipside of the Programa Facultad Abierta findings with regard to the relation between conflictive beginnings and subsequent pay equity: As already mentioned in Chapter 6, *Comercio y Justicia*'s beginnings were not as conflictual as most other ERTs, including this book's three case studies. This ERT happened to be the first in the country to have negotiated a worker buyout settlement with the bankruptcy courts, and so its workers did not have to enter into the usually long struggle of 'occupy, resist, produce' mapped out in Chapter 6.[41]

Somewhere in the middle of the spectrum of pay schemes – from Chilavert and Salud Junín on one end practising complete or almost complete pay equity, and *Comercio y Justicia* on the other – UST introduced in 2009 a slightly more differentiated salary level based on experience. Moreover, UST includes a unique 'community work/activism' remuneration plan for workers participating in social movement activities during working hours, and overtime pay for

---

40   De Pascuale 2009, personal interview.

41   Recall that *Comercio y Justicia*'s founders decided to take the path of negotiating with bankruptcy courts and buying out the firm instead of the more usual 'occupy and resist' path taken by most ERTs. Indeed, as my interviews at the newspaper reveal, most of its journalist members already possessed the strong critical writing skills necessary to negotiate the legal quagmire of re-negotiating bankruptcy, not to mention that the main coverage of the newspaper is commercial and legal affairs in the province of Córdoba.

doing so in the name of UST during non-work hours. While UST workers rotate in these activist and community tasks, some workers participate in social activist work more often than others and thus end up getting paid slightly more than *compañeros* who do not engage in activist work as much.

Overall, a more recent study by the Programa Facultad Abierta team found that in ERTs where salary differentials exist, 34 percent of cases had pay differences of 25 percent or less between the highest to lowest paid worker, while 33 percent of cases practised salary differentials at between 25–50 percent difference.[42] Of the ERTs that practice pay differentials in their study, reasons include hours worked (61.5 percent of cases) and seniority (23.1 percent of cases), with some ERTs paying its founders slightly more than newer members.[43] Moreover, of those ERTs that do have pay differences, 83.3 percent rely on the collective agreements of the sector for salary scales.[44] Of note, the size of pay differences in those ERTs that have such a policy is significantly smaller than at many other non-ERT worker cooperatives, including Mondragón's practices,[45] the worker cooperative 'par excellence' that, as Chilavert's Plácido Peñarrieta confirmed to me in a 2009 conversation, many ERTs compare themselves to. At the Basque country's Mondragón cooperatives, for example, the pay differential in its various cooperatives averaged out at 6:1 between the highest and lowest paid members in the early 2000s.[46] The gap in pay had, by the last years of the decade, increased even more at Mondragón, with Greg MacLeod and Darryl Reed reporting it to be 12:1 on average across Mondragón's cooperatives by the late 2000s,[47] while some studies report that in some cooperatives pay differentials in more recent years were even as high as 20:1.[48]

Finally, as Atzeni and Ghigliani, Fajn and Rebón, Rebón, Ruggeri, and Ruggeri et al. have all pointed out,[49] ERTs in more competitive market sectors also might use some form of pay differential in order to retain workers. Such is the case with *Comercio y Justicia*'s practice of paying some of its more experienced journalists and its sales people more than other members in order to, in part, retain them. Also, in larger ERTs, where practices of *compañerismo* might not

---

42   Ruggeri et al. 2014, p. 40.
43   Ruggeri et al. 2014, pp. 40–1.
44   Ruggeri et al. 2014, p. 41.
45   MacLeod and Reed 2009; Webb and Cheney 2014.
46   Christiansen 2014, p. 23.
47   MacLeod and Reed 2009, p. 134. See also Arando et al. 2010; and Maheshvaranandan 2007.
48   Christiansen 2014, p. 23.
49   Atzeni and Ghigliani 2007; Fajn and Rebón 2005; Rebón 2007; Ruggeri 2009; and Ruggeri et al. 2005.

be as strong as in smaller ERTs, it seems some remuneration is more likely to be tied to performance or participation in certain activities deemed critical to the firm. On the whole, however, it is undeniable from the evidence that ERTs certainly practice much more equitable salary schemes than capitalist firms, even when compared to other labour-managed firms in other conjunctures, pointing, perhaps, to the generally high degree of consiousness of its workers and their strong sense of solidarity developed from out of their common struggles.

These empirical findings suggest that (again as Merleau-Ponty described for us) a tight, intersubjectively existential social structure rooted in necessity, common bonds, shared experiences, and struggling to overcome situations of crises together permeates the ways ERTs organise their remuneration schemes. From out of moments of conflict and shared struggles, and also from ERT protagonists' moral economy of work, which serves to coalesce common bonds via shared experiences, new cultures of solidarity emerge.[50] Moreover, while it is true that not all ERT firms practice egalitarian salary schemes, it is nevertheless also clear that the strong tendency amongst ERTs is to practice far more egalitarian forms of remuneration then when they were under the control of bosses and owners. Thus, on the whole, struggle, cooperation, and workers' own shared sense of the communal value of their collective (and living) labour, not particular skill sets or hierarchical divisions of labour, tend to dictate the measures of compensation and reward at Argentina's ERTs.

1.3.2   Horizontalised Labour Processes

While the degree and nature of member economic participation is continually debated within and displays some variation between ERTs, one aspect of ERTs that has seen almost universal take-up across the phenomenon has been the importance that ERT protagonists give generally to the cooperative principle of 'democratic member control'.[51] Indeed, the continued discussions within each ERT concerning the form that member economic participation should take accentuates the importance that many ERT protagonists give to the principle of democratic member control. More often than not, I witnessed in ERTs I visited a strong culture of active member participation 'in setting ... policies and making decisions'.[52] These democratically mitigated and flexible organisational policies highlight the strength of the cooperative structure mentioned in the literature, underscoring what Ian MacPherson has characterised as one of

---

50   Fantasia 1988.

51   ICA 2016, para. 7.

52   MacPherson 1996, para. 33.

the 'remarkable special characteristics' of the International Co-operative Alliance's principles: their 'inherent flexibility' to adapt to the economic and political particularities of a cooperative and to the collective needs of its members.[53] And it is this aspect of Argentina's ERTs – the high number of members at an ERT who 'actively participate in setting ... policies and making decisions' – that many journalistic and academic research reports often highlight. My research found there is also, not surprisingly, a wide range of nuances in how democratic member control is carried out in practice.

On the whole, ERTs (and especially larger ones) tend to be administered more formally by a *consejo administrativo* (administrative council) or *consejo de trabajadores* (workers' council) made up of at least a president, a treasurer, a secretary, and sometimes members at large (*vocales*) elected from the membership and with renewable mandates of two or three years. Unlike in many cooperatives throughout the world, but similar to many smaller worker coops, management responsibilities do not tend to be taken up by hired managerial staff, nor are they reserved for a select group separate from the membership. Rather, managerial duties are divvied up amongst the general workers' assembly and the workers' council. The workers' council of an ERT, or worker-members who directly report to it, usually take on the role of running the business on a day-to-day basis, engaging in duties such as ordering supplies, signing cheques for accounts payable, following up on accounts receivable, preparing and distributing paycheques, keeping the books up to date, dealing with overarching production issues, customer relations, strategic marketing issues, and the like. Also, members of the administrative or workers' council, emulating in practice (if not consciously in most ERTs) the anarcho-syndicalist and council communist model of recallable delegates, can be removed from office at any time if a majority of an ERTs' members decide to do so.[54]

All ERTs also hold regular meetings of the workers' assembly, which consists of all of the cooperative's members. Usually, workers' assemblies meet either on a regular periodic basis (sometimes weekly, usually monthly), or when major issues arise, or both. (This practice, by the way, far exceeds Argentine cooperative legislations' requirements of having an annual members' meeting.) The workers' assembly is involved in debating larger issues that will affect most if not all of the ERTs' membership on an ongoing basis, such as voting for the workers' or administrative council members; deciding on when to hire new members and whom to hire; whether or not to enter new markets, engage in

---

53   MacPherson 1996, para. 32.

54   I am grateful to Chilavert's Ernesto González, who mentioned this similarity to me in an informal conversation with him in 2009.

producing new product lines, pursue grants or loans, buy new machinery, and so on; and whether or not the ERT should collaborate with certain community groups, involve itself in certain political issues, or support certain social movements or other ERTs, and so forth. In addition, the workers' assembly is also tasked with the implicit and, at times, explicit disciplining and reprimanding of members who 'free load', steal, or otherwise shirk their cooperative responsibilities. Often, social pressure is how wayward members are disciplined at assembly meetings and on shop floors,[55] while with more severe offences, such as theft or personal injury to another member, the option to remove a member from the cooperative is voted on and decided at the assembly.[56]

Communication flows between the administrative workers' council and the broader member assembly is usually informal, and acting workers' council members usually continue, at least on a part-time basis, the job tasks they perform at the firm when not in office. In larger ERTs, however, the jobs of president and treasurer in particular tend to preoccupy the incumbents on a full-time basis. The latter is the case at UST, but also at the medium-sized Salud Junín, while the former is the case at Chilavert. Smaller ERTs, such as Chilavert, tend to administer themselves primarily via regular and informal workers' assemblies as needs arise and from the collective solidarity of their members. At Chilavert, day-to-day concerns relating to production issues are more often than not worked out on an ad hoc basis on actual shop floors via the adoption of production processes that are (re)organised around flexible work teams, consensus driven, and informally led by the expert in that product line or labour process on a per-project basis. Chilavert's Walter Basualdo mapped out the cooperatives' consensus-based and flexible decision-making processes for me in my 2005 interview with him:

> How do we make decisions? Well, here we don't have a *caudillo* who says, 'OK, today you'll do this because I tell you so'. No, no. Here we take the

---

55   A good example of social pressure as disciplining mechanism at ERTs can be seen in one of the scenes in Avi Lewis and Naomi Klein's documentary *The Take* (Lewis and Klein 2004), shot during the presidential election campaign of 2003. In the scene, the only *menemista* member of a group of workers is roasted by the rest of his *compañeros* who are seen to actively support Néstor Kirchner's candidacy. Other documentaries on ERTs, especially Darío Doria and Luis Camardella's *Grissinopoli: El país de los grisines* (Doria and Camardella 2005) and Isaac Isitan's *The Women of Brukman* (Isitan and Poliquin 2007) are also full of scenes of assemblies and shop floor gatherings at ERTs in which the social pressure of the group (often couched in jesting and gentle but public reprimands) is used at times to impose discipline on wayward members.

56   The incident at Salud Junín I mentioned in Chapter 6 is an example of this.

things we have to do, we put them on the table, and we hash things out amongst ourselves. If the majority of us agree, or better said, if we all agree, then it gets done. But if anyone has a doubt as to what has to get done, or if there are any outstanding issues, then we discuss things so that we can all come to some workable agreement. All of our decisions are made in a group made up of the personalities of this cooperative. Now, if there are certain decisions that have to be made in the moment, a group of us, or all of us, will stop working. We'll get together and discuss what has to get done, what has to get worked out, what we have to set up first, and we'll decide things at that moment, as a group. Sometimes we don't have to get together as an assembly of the entire cooperative. Sometimes a situation requires that only a small group of us get together, so we stop working and clear things up right on the spot, right then and there. And that's it: we come to a decision right there. But whenever we have substantial issues to clear up we bring these to the cooperative's assembly that we hold each month. That's where we lay out and hash out everything we need to work out as a cooperative, and the decisions are made amongst all of us.[57]

In some contrast to Chilavert, larger or more complex ERTs such as UST and Salud Junín deploy more regular or formalised decision-making structures, especially concerning issues of new contracts and production runs, while a representative from the workers' council, or even a full-time production organiser, might be responsible for allocating particular tasks to certain work teams, such as with Pablo Rolandi's job at UST (see Chapter 1). In most ERTs, once a job or task is given to a particular work team, decision-making around that job or task tends to be immediately transferred to the work team. Usually the expert in the particular job leads the temporary work team, or the team decides to collectively manage the job on an ad-hoc basis based on the tasks to be done.

Some ERTs involved in sectors with traditionally hierarchical shop floors, such as the newspaper *Comercio y Justicia*, might choose to continue the old firm's labour processes and division of labour. Here, again, the degree of competitiveness of the economic sector plays a part in how hierarchical the ERT's labour process remains. *Comercio y Justicia*, for instance, is involved in perhaps the most competitive market of the many ERTs I visited. Argentina's newspaper sector is dominated by the country's largest media conglomerate, Grupo Clarín, which controls newspapers in most major urban markets. At the same time, dozens of other smaller papers, such as *Comercio y Justicia*, compete,

---

57   W. Basualdo 2005, personal interview.

often at some disadvantage, with this media giant in most major urban markets, particularly due to the fact that Grupo Clarín also dominates the street kiosk distribution system in almost all urban centres in the country. This highly centralised market, one that has seen in recent years many local papers bought up by Grupo Clarín, has had a large part to play in encouraging this ERT to continue to organise itself within a hierarchical production process, emulating the divisions of labour of traditional newspapers, as *Comercio y Justicia*'s Mario Rodríguez and Javier De Pascuale explained to me in 2009. For example, each of the newspaper's production sectors is headed by an appointed *encargado* (or chief, as in 'chief correspondent', 'editor-in-chief', 'chief of publication', and so on). Moreover, and not surprisingly, it was evident in my visits to this ERT that it tends to mostly focus on the task of producing a newspaper rather than further horizontalising their cooperative model or being more involved in the community or with other social movements. Moreover, *Comercio y Justicia* was the only ERT I visited where attendance at regular workers' assemblies is not mandatory (only attendance at the year-end assembly, as stipulated by Argentine coop law, is mandatory). Not coincidentally, perhaps, the ERT members I interviewed here also tended to have the weakest personal changes in the community-focused values and attitudes that I will touch on shortly.

The complexity of the labour process at an ERT also affects the degree to which horizontality is introduced. Salud Junín's at times highly intensive and fluctuating workflows, for instance, deeply affect how each of the clinic's core areas carry out patient care. With more intensive or emergency medical interventions, or during busy times at the clinic, the otherwise horizontal labour process can transform into a comparatively hierarchical structure in which the particular expertise of the medical personnel on hand dictates the decision-making hierarchy of the team given the particular needs of the patient. On a broad level, it was clear to me that members working at each of the clinic's sectors well understand where they fit into the general flow of patient care and who has to be contacted if further procedures are needed at the clinic, or if the patient has to be referred to another medical facility.[58] In less acute medical situations, each nurse at the clinic will rotate their decision-making responsibilities at the particular sector of the clinic they are working in, relying on the leadership of specialist doctors only when caring for patients under the direct supervision of a doctor.[59] Thus, a worker-member's expertise for a

---

58   See Chapter 1.

59   Recall from Chapter 1 that at Salud Junín doctors are not members of the cooperative but rather contract out their services to the coop for a fee.

given medical intervention guides who delegates and who follows instructions at any given sector of the clinic. When not involved in a task related to the immediate caring of patients, on the other hand, an organic and situational dynamic of job rotation takes place. In these less pressing daily routines, there is a constant flux of informal job sharing amongst the cooperative's members; for instance, nurses with downtime might relieve the patient care duties of other nurse members, for nurses on personal leave, or for colleagues who are off-shift. Indeed, it is not unheard of at Salud Junín to see nurses and other coop members engaging in janitorial duties or repairs of medical instruments, or falling into a support role during an emergency triage procedure.

1.3.3   Transforming the Pace of Work: The Merger of Work and Play

Another promising innovation in many of the ERTs I visited – loosening and arguably even humanising an ERT's labour process – is the incorporation of unstructured moments of rest and play into the working day. This was present to some degree in all of the ERTs I visited, although predictably less so in busy ERTs engaged in critical care work such as Salud Junín, or in ERTs ensconced in highly competitive markets, such as *Comercio y Justicia*. Overall, ERTs' transformations of the pace of work suggest one promising way that its worker-protagonists are reclaiming their time on shop floors and reconceptualising the labour process. Throughout my visits to Argentina's ERTs, for example, I observed countless instances of workers eating and playing together regularly, embracing practices such as daily communal lunches or social activities such as weekly football games or barbeques, and so on; varying work hours on the basis of specific deliverables, contracts, jobs, or even the personal needs of members; and taking many breaks throughout the day. ERT workers have told me on numerous occasions that these less-intense production processes worked well with their fluctuating work demands, for dealing with the non-work life needs of workers such as when they need to attend to personal matters or medical visits during working hours, and for generally helping to ease the tensions and stresses that come with the daily routines of work.

An illustrative Argentine working-class cultural practice that transforms the rhythm of the working day at ERTs deserves particular mention here to highlight the importance of the incorporation of play and rest into the new labour processes. At all of the ERTs I have visited in Argentina, the Southern Cone's[60] cultural tradition of collectively sipping *mate*, the bitter green tea served in a

---

60   The Southern Cone is the region of South America consisting of Argentina, Uruguay, Chile, Paraguay, and Southern Brazil.

shared gourd and a metal *bombilla* (straw), is alive and well. The *mate* station and its paraphernalia – the *mate* gourd, the *bombilla*, the paper bags of *mate* tea, and the water kettle – are always visibly located at prominent and easily accessed places right on ERTS' shop floors. Often, there are several *mate* stations throughout the shop. I have often seen workers making *mate*, meeting at the station, and drinking together throughout the working day. I even had the recurring pleasure of sharing with the workers this tradition right on the shop floor, partaking of the *mate* break with them, and at times even sharing the complementary *factura* (baked sweets) that is customarily eaten with *mate* in Argentina. I was told by several workers, especially at UST and Chilavert, that this particular act for them was not only a way to break up the monotony of the working day, but also a symbolic gesture that helped them reclaim their working-class cultural practices. The cultural practice of the *mate*, these workers stated, was a purposeful act that served to remind them of what they could not readily do when they worked for a boss. (Indeed, bringing two-dozen *facturas* with me to an ERT as a gift to share with all during *mate* breaks and interviews respects a centuries-old Argentine social tradition and was always pleasantly received and much appreciated.) For me, this practice, while seemingly modest, has the powerful effect of rethinking and prefiguring another pace to working life and shows yet again how ERT workers are recuperating their time and cultural practices and beginning to reconceptualise work in non-capitalist and, thus, non-commodified ways. Chilavert's Manuel Basualdo synthesised to me the importance of the *mate* break for their new work culture and labour process as follows:

> [Now, as a cooperative, we] work but we also drink *mate*. Sometimes during the middle of the workday we'll sit down and have a *mate*. It's important to have a chat and drink *mate* with each other. Before [when we had a boss] we couldn't do this.[61]

The regular *mate* break is, I argue, a small moment with much broader resonances for the reconceptualisation of work as a social act, entrenched in the production of one particular dimension of social wealth that suggests ways of uniting cultural practice with economic needs. In sum, incorporating the working-class cultural practice of the *mate* on shop floors begins to break down the capitalist obsession with dividing work time from the rest of life.

---

61   M. Basualdo 2005, personal interview.

Other mergers of work and play incorporated into the labour process in many ERTs I visited include the mid-week or Friday afternoon barbeque and informal football matches played by members of an ERT's collective, between ERTs, or with neighbours. Besides being moments when *compañerismo* is further solidified, and when, again, Argentine popular culture is recuperated and merged with work, these social spaces also act as informal places to share and figure out work issues and, in particular, engage in or plan political activist activity in support of other ERTs or when a collective's own ERT is experiencing a particularly difficult moment. Here, ERTs again show their working-class roots by incorporating organising practices that historically have been used by unions and workers' collectives in Argentina to develop and work out political strategies and tactics for mobilisation outside of the reach of bosses or the state.[62]

1.4   *Democratising the Labour Process, Reclaiming Surpluses, and Socialising Production*

In this section of the chapter, I first showed how ERTs' existence within dual realities of having to balance social values within competitive markets place their self-management projects in situations of tension, directly and indirectly affecting how *autogestión* unfolds at the firm. Secondly, I discussed how working out the intricacies of self-managed production in common contests these tensions and shapes the two main distinguishing features of ERTs' labour processes: *a widespread prevalence of pay-equity* and *flattened and horizontalised decision-making and organisational structures*. The degree to which these two features are incorporated, in turn, is linked to the solidarity forged by ERT workers collectively living through moments of micro-economic crises, the intensity of the struggles to recuperate the workplace, the age of the ERT firm, and the size of the ERT. I showed how smaller and older ERTs and ERTs with more combative histories tend to favour more horizontal organisational structures and more equitable remuneration practices. Within the Argentine conjuncture of the past two decades or so, as I will discuss further in Chapter 9, the widespread adaptation of ERTs' two major labour process characteristics distinguish them from other forms of cooperatives in Argentina, as well as from labour-managed firms in other conjunctures. These characteristics, rooted in the relation between external macro-political and internal micro-economic conflict and solidarity on shop floors, bring us to the ERT phenomenon's *fourth*

---

62   Such informal gatherings in Argentina were particularly used by workers during the dictatorship years in order to avoid state repression.

radical social innovation, an innovation that points to how ERTs overcome key aspects of capitalist exploitation, worker alienation, surplus-value extraction, and the capitalist valorisation process rooted in the capital–labour relation:

> *The redefinition of social production as ERT workers democratise the labour process, reclaim their surpluses and, ultimately, contest notions of surplus-value, surplus-labour, and worker alienation, even as they produce in part for capitalist markets.*

2   Section 2: Recuperating Cooperative Skills and Values, Informal Shop Floor Learning, and Transformed Subjectivities

In this section, we explore how ERT workers transform from employees to self-managed workers. I discuss how all of the key ERT informants in this book's three case studies self-reported that, since engaging in their projects of *autogestión,* they have experienced some degree of positive transformations in their *knowledge, skills, attitudes,* or *values* in six key areas:

(1)   in their democratic and cooperative practices at work;

(2)   in their personal behaviours towards and interactions with others at the ERT and outside of the ERT;

(3)   in their ability to influence political decisions both inside and outside of the ERT;

(4)   in their concern and interest in community affairs beyond the ERT;

(5)   in how connected they feel to the broader community; and

(6)   in their actual participation in community within and outside of the ERT.

These are some of the key social dimensions of ERT workers' critical consciousness that are developed beginning with their shared struggles. They underscore how ERT protagonists construct solidarity, politicise, and become conscious within an immanent process of a class-in-the-making first discussed in this book's Introduction and elaborated theoretically in Chapter 4. Eventually contributing to new subjectivities, ERT protagonists' transformations from *empleados* to *trabajadores autogestionados* (from employees to self-managed workers) tend to, on the whole, happen immanently and in praxis, in intentional and in unintentional ways, and on the path of doing and working out the intricacies of *autogestión* collectively. Moreover, ERT workers' cooperative aptitudes and job-related skill sets, we will shortly see, are learned primarily from experiential knowledge transferred from older or veteran ERT workers to younger or newer workers by the traditional working-class practice of the mentor–apprentice relationship. I ultimately argue that these immanent worker transformations from managed employees to self-managed workers, and their informal and social learning practices, ultimately reveal that, rather than being a fixed trait or a social category, class is an 'active *process* and an historical *relationship*'.[63]

In order to assess how these ERT workers acquire and share the skills, values, and attitudes needed to self-manage their firms and, in the process, personally and collectively transform themselves, I embedded a series of more structured questions into my otherwise semi-structured interview protocol that I deployed in order to elicit workers' own perceptions of their personal transformations and learning dynamics since working at their ERT. Specifically, these 'learning indicator' questions sought to draw out ERT workers' own reflections on changes in their *knowledge, skills, attitudes,* and *values* concerning their democratic, cooperative, and community practices over the time they have been participating in the ERT project. In support of the theory of an immanent process of class-in-the-making, what I discovered is that, for most ERT workers, their *emergent consiousness, politicisation, and transformed subjectivities emerge from out of their collective actions and struggles.* These transformations are catalysed and shaped by the conjunctures of micro-economic crises these workers must initially traverse and, subsequently, in the process of struggling and working together to make a go of their cooperatives. In other words, these subjective transformations are intimately embedded in forging a project of *autogestión* between *compañeros.*

The development and subsequent analysis of the learning indicator questions I deployed were informed, amongst others, by David Livingstone and associates' critical working-class learning research;[64] Jack Quarter and Harish Midha's investigations into informal learning processes within worker cooperatives[65] and Ian MacPhearson's theory of cooperatives as sites of 'associative intelligence';[66] and Griff Foley's, Daniel Schugurensky's, and Bud Hall and Darlene Clover's theories of social movement and social action learning.[67] This literature suggests that a collective of people engaged in associated, sustained, and socio-politically or socio-economically motivated projects – such as with

---

63   Thompson, in Wood 1982, p. 45 (emphasis in original).
64   Livingstone and Sawchuk 2003; Livingstone and Schultz 2007.
65   Quarter and Midha 2001.
66   MacPherson 2002.
67   Foley 1999; Hall and Clover 2005; Schugurensky 2000. For other related theories and approaches that informed this part of my research, see also Bandura 1977; Choudry 2015; Gouin 2009; Hall and Turay 2006; Lave and Wenger 1991; Overwien 2000; Livingstone, Smith, and Smith 2011; Larrabure, Vieta, and Schugurensky 2011; Smith and Dobson 2010; Vieta, Larrabure, and Schugurensky 2012; Wenger 1996; Wenger and Snyder 2000; and Worthen 2014.

cooperative members, social movement activists, or even colleagues in a work-place – experience rich moments of learning and personal changes. These changes happen mostly through collaborative learning processes that are inter-subjective (that is, social) in nature, often go unnoticed by members, and are mediated by concrete lived situations and experiences that arise in contested cultural, social, and political spaces. Moreover, these studies show how workers on shop floors or in union settings, participants in social movements, or cooper-ative members tend to mostly learn their political, democratic, and cooperative skills *informally*, in the act of 'doing' collaborative work *together*.[68] As we will see, the theoretical positions and research findings of this workplace, social action, and social movement learning literature overlap with the political eco-nomy of the working class and class struggle theoretical framework of this book.

In the accounts of almost all of the ERT workers I interviewed, there was a noticeable change in their *attitudes* and *values* that led them to possess a stronger sense of *bien común* (common good, or, more exactly, a 'being-in-common' or 'in community' with others), *compañerismo*, and concern for one's community as compared to their accounts of their attitudes towards others and their communities prior to being part of the ERT project. ERT workers' every-day practices of cooperation, interpersonal communication, and community involvement have, in general, also tended to improve since being a part of the ERT project, according to my interviews. In conversations extending out from the learning indicator questions I posed,[69] ERT workers tended to say that they listen better now, that they can now talk in public with more confidence, and that they can now organise meetings or are much more effective participants in meetings. These changes in interpersonal and cooperative skills, in contrast to the degree of change in the values and attitudes of *compañerismo* and *bien*

---

68   For Daniel Schugurensky, *informal learning* 'includes all learning that occurs outside the curriculum of formal and non-formal educational institutions and programs' and is exper-iential and social in nature (Schugurensky 2000, p. 1). Moreover, when learning informally the learner is often not aware that she or he is learning, but rather engages in tacit learning. Given that, as this informal and social action learning literature suggests, these experien-tial learning dimensions often go unnoticed by participants, for researchers to understand them they need to be drawn out or elicited (Hall and Clover 2005; Larrabure, Vieta, and Schugurensky 2011). I thus specifically embedded 17 personal change or 'learning indic-ator' questions in my interviews that attempted to solicit conversations tapping into key informants' changes in *knowledge*, *skills*, *attitudes*, and *values* in the six key areas I men-tioned above.

69   Following Schugurensky, eliciting these conversations were the most important reasons for embedding the learning indicators into my interviews (Lerner and Schugurensky 2007; Schugurensky 2000, 2001; Schugurensky, Mündel, and Duguid 2006).

común, were especially marked with ERT founders given that they have had more time to develop these skills at the ERT as compared to newer members. In what follows, I specifically turn to how ERT protagonists learn and adopt values, behaviours, and practices of cooperation and community participation.

2.1   Laburantes *First,* cooperativistas *Second*

Most ERT workers self-identify as *laburantes* or *obreros* (workers or labourers) and not as *cooperativistas*. As UST's Matías Peralta revealed for us in Chapter 6: 'First we are *laburantes*, then *cooperativistas*. We formed cooperatives as an alternative for the continuity of our jobs, in order for us to keep on working'.[70] Juán Vera, the expert bulldozer operator at UST, said something similar when I asked him if he felt like a worker or a cooperator:

> No, I feel that I am a *laburante*, and I will continue to be one! When we go to community meetings, we go with our overalls. And wearing our overalls all the time here is important to remind us of where we came from.[71]

These responses to my questions intimate how Argentina's ERTs are a new type of cooperative experience and working-class organisation unique to the current post-convertability Argentine conjuncture. ERT protagonists' identification first and foremost with their working-class roots underscores how ERTs emerge not out of the traditional cooperative movement but, rather, as I elaborated on in Chapter 3, from Argentina's traditional, Peronist- and *clasista*-influenced labour movement merging with the contagion of bottom-up and horizontally organised social justice movements that surged in the country in the past two decades as responses to the implosion of the neo-liberal model of the 1990s. Indeed, only three of the ERT workers I interviewed had had previous experiences with cooperativism. From how they expressed themselves to me, it was evidently easier for these three workers to conceive of themselves as cooperators when I compared their responses to the rest of their *compañeros* who had not had previous experiences with cooperativism. At the same time, however, almost all of the ERT workers I interviewed had had previous union experiences, some had been union organisers, and most of my interviewees had periodically attended union assemblies and had, at minimum, voted for their *delegados* (shop stewards) prior to being a part of the ERT.[72] So how is it, then,

---

70   Peralta 2009, personal interview.
71   Vera 2009, personal interview.
72   To recall from Chapter 3, Argentine trade unionism has had a long tradition of shop floor *asambleas* (assemblies) and a high turnout rate amongst the rank and file when electing

that ERT workers learn and adopt cooperative values? How do they, in other words, become cooperators?

Tellingly, ERT workers who have gone through previous cooperative or union organising or leadership experiences are considered point-people within the worker cooperative, holding either formal leadership positions at the ERT or informal places of standing in the minds of their *compañeros*. These point-people tend to, again informally, convey the values and practices of shop floor democracy, cooperativism, and so on to the rest of their *compañeros*, helping communicate over time to the rest of the collective how to actually go about organising workers' assemblies and how to carry out democratic decision-making. Together with the educative role played by ERTs' self-managed workers' associations[73] and some university programmes that partner with ERTs,[74] these point-people in each cooperative help teach the dispositions of mutual aid and solidarity that members need to have in order to ensure the proper functioning of the cooperative. A small subset of workers I interviewed who had either cooperative or union organising experience – namely, Chilavert's Plácido Peñarrieta and Cándido González, UST's Mario Barrios, and, to a lesser degree, Salud Junín's José López – were all instrumental in motivating their co-workers in the takeover of the failing former firm or in getting production started again as cooperatives. In addition to having to recompose a deteriorated plant, deal with continuing legal issues, learn new administrative and marketing skills, reorganise purchases and customer orders, and generally run a firm in difficulty, learning how to be cooperators adds to the challenges ERT workers face. In this light, the role of these leaders in each ERT seems to be paramount to how smoothly or not the project of *autogestión* and its inherent cooperative values unfold.

2.2 Deepening Solidarities at Work: An Emerging Sense of compañerismo *and an Ethics of* 'es de todos'

To reiterate, with all ERT protagonists I interviewed, the transformation of their previous disposition as individualist and competitive employees to that

---

shop stewards (in Argentina, *delegados*) that then vote on key national union issues and make decisions during processes of collective bargaining (Godio 2000; Munck, Falcón, and Galitelli 1987). The reader will also recall that many ERTs used to be former union shops when owner-run and most ERT workers that belonged to unions before still belong to their unions at the ERT. ERTs' current practices of holding regular workers' assemblies and electing the coop's administrative positions thus have deep roots in these traditional, union-based shop floor practices (Clark and Antivero 2009).

73   See Chapter 3.
74   See Chapter 7.

of cooperative *socios* (associates) occurs mostly *informally*, as, together with their workmates, they unfold their cooperative projects over time and struggle collectively to address the ongoing challenges that face them. Matías Peralta, one of the newest *socios* of UST when I interviewed him in 2009, put it this way for us in Chapter 6: '[Most of us] formed into ... *cooperativista*[s] from inside, from here, in the process of working here'.[75] For UST's Mario Barrios: 'We learn together as we do things ... our commitments are expressed in our everyday practices'.[76] And José López from Salud Junín underscored the collective and immanent nature of how they learned and adopted cooperative values when he stated: 'We learned the ins and outs of cooperativism *sobre la marcha, como todos acá* [on the path of doing, like all of us here]'.[77]

This immanent, informal learning *sobre la marcha* occurs most noticeably *intra-cooperatively* via both the social bonds that form organically on shop floors from having to collectively self-manage a firm and from the attitudinal and behavioural examples of the ERT's leaders and their previous experiences with political or union organising. Second, this informal learning occurs *inter-cooperatively*, via the networks that form between ERTs; from the influence of ERT workers' associations such as MNER, MNFRT, and FACTA; and between ERTs and other social movement groups that forge affinity relations with each other. Inter-cooperative exchanges especially occur during an ERT's first days, weeks, and months of high conflictivity when other ERTs and social movement organisations come to support workers occupying a firm. During these moments of high political conflict and turmoil, supporting affinity groups begin to transfer their knowledge of the political and judicial system and the values and attitudes of *compañerismo* and cooperativism to the new ERT workers. José López clearly illustrated for me the inter-cooperative and network-based informal learning and support that Salud Junín experienced:

> Meanwhile, what continued to strengthen the processes [of workplace takeovers] was the unity and solidarity of other sectors helping out: students, sympathetic unions, neighbourhood groups, human rights organisations ... That's what permitted all of these processes to sustain themselves over time ... We've had close relations with other ERTs and we have participated in national gatherings of ERTs, as well. There is a common saying among ERTs: 'If they touch one of us, they touch us all'.[78] Ever since,

---

75   Peralta 2009, personal interview.
76   Barrios 2009, personal interview.
77   López 2007, personal interview.
78   See also Faulk 2008.

if there were other ERTs that were being threatened with eviction, many of us would also go to support them. Like what happened at Zanón/FaSinPat – we travelled there to support those *compañeros* on two occasions. We also went to help the Brukman workers, and the *compañeros* from the Hotel BAUEN. And *compañeros* from Brukman and Zanón also came here to help us out. There's been a permanent exchange [and process of learning] between many of us [for some time].[79]

Subsequently, from out of this intra- and inter-cooperative informal learning and the deep-seated practices and attitudes of *compañerismo*, an ethical dimension of '*esto es de todos*' (it belongs to all of us) emerges within an ERT and between ERTs. One of the things that, in practice, more *compeñerismo* and an ethics of *es de todos* mean for ERTs is that they are now much more likely to help out their workmates as well as other ERTs in their moments of need when, in the past, they would have stuck to their job-related tasks and responsibilities and worried primarily about their own individual interests.

Most concretely on a day-to-day basis, the values of *compañerismo* and the ethic of *es de todos* have innumerable consequences for re-shaping the labour process along more humane lines than the strictly capitalist workplace promotes. Chilavert's Plácido Peñarrieta fills in the details of the collective commitment to *compañerismo* and the ethic of *es de todos* and their impact on the labour process when he emphatically told me the following:

Before, under owner-management, there was always someone marking out the rhythm of your work. You would work because you got paid. Things are now different. Now, we have other obligations based on our own responsibility to one another and our jobs ... Everything we do [and produce] now passes through our own hands ... We have different responsibilities to each other and our work nowadays ... Before we were 'workmates', but today we aren't workmates anymore. We're now more like 'associates', where the problem of one associate affects us all. And there are times when we have to look at the problems of each *compañero*

---

79   López 2009, personal interview. Salud Junín's Ana Maria Barrionuevo's comments recorded in Chapter 1 also emphasise the deep importance many ERT workers give to the community groups that came to support them, especially in the early days of occupation. Recalling her words from Chapter 1: 'Many social organisations came to help us throughout our first days ... Many, many groups from the left, neighbours from the community, and folks from other ERTs came to help us during those days ... it just takes my breath away still thinking about it!'

and try to resolve them so they won't affect the entire society that we have formed here. Before, if something happened to someone, it was the boss's responsibility ... we were all just mere acquaintances with each other, nothing more ... we didn't have direct contact with all of our workmates. But now, we're a much tighter unit, and what binds us together is the fact that we're all responsible for this cooperative as a society and we all have to contribute to moving it forward. In other words, we all have to know everyone's everyday problems for the simple reason that we have to protect our work.[80]

Comercio y Justicia's Javier De Pascuale, echoing and summing up Plácido's analysis in my interview with him four years later, articulated *compañerismo* and the complementary notion of *es de todos* as follows: '*Este proyecto es un compromiso, necesita un sentido de ética, y es una lucha por el otro* [This project is a commitment, it requires a sense of ethics, and is a struggle for each other]'.[81]

It must be pointed out, however, that ERT workers' transformations embracing increased 'obligations' and 'responsibility' to each other and that emerge from solidarity-based interpersonal relations on ERT shop floors are not a given for all workers, nor are they present to the same degree in all ERTs. As Eduardo Murúa explained in 2006:

The change in subjectivity in some workers is much more powerful than in others. The subjectivity and culture of some workers have not changed. Some workers go to work every day and just do their tasks in the recuperated enterprise; they do them very well, perhaps with more effort than before when they worked under a boss. But they finish their job for the day and then they go home like they did in their old jobs. Other workers are different. They have reconceptualised the factory differently. They begin to talk and think in a new way. They have come to understand how their former bosses were exploiting them. They have come to understand how the economic system functions in Argentina, how the capitalist system destroys each one of our workplaces.[82]

According to Murúa, and complementing the findings of the Programa Facultad Abierta team illustrated in Figures 21 and 22, it seems that those workers

---

80   Peñarrieta 2005, personal interview.
81   De Pascuale 2009, personal interview.
82   Murúa 2006, para. 5.

who ultimately experience the greatest take-up of the values and ethics of *compañerismo* and *es de todos* are those who actually experienced and struggled through conflictual situations during the founding of their ERTs and who have had to traverse further challenges in converting their workplaces into worker cooperatives:

> The strongest change in subjectivity occurs in those workers who entrenched themselves the most in the issues of the recuperation of the enterprise and that struggled to turn them into cooperatives, especially during the early days of occupation.[83]

These different degrees of transformation in the subjectivities of individual ERT workers, their varying commitments to *compañerismo*, and the degree of change in the ethics of *es de todos* linked to the degree to which they experienced conflicts collectively stood out when looking at the entire set of interviews I conducted over the years. It was obvious from my interviews that tensions – and sometimes, deep tensions – still exist between the commitment to cooperativism and *compañerismo* of some members and the continued individualism, competitiveness, or indifference of other members. Indeed, these tensions sometimes co-exist within the same worker. Some workers have said to me things such as: 'I didn't sign up for self-managing my workplace', or 'All I ever wanted was to do an honest day's work and get my regular paycheque'. Some workers, it was obvious, are more aware of these tensions within themselves than others as they reflected critically on their own contradictions between the desire to self-manage their places of work and their longing at times for 'simpler' days when they would only need to 'keep their heads down', work their shift, and go home.

My interviews showed that the degree of these tensions and how intensely *compañerismo* is taken up tend to follow the general pattern of whether or not an ERT worker was or was not involved in the periods of high conflict related to the founding of an ERT. It is also connected, with some ERT workers, to whether or not they had previously been involved in union organising or activism. Newer members of an ERT do not come into the ERT project with full knowledge of its history of struggle, and are certainly not as invested at first in this history as an ERT's founders (that is, those who were present during the occupation and resistance stages). While most new *socios* of the ERT cooperative are familiar with the ERT movement in Argentina, and some new *socios*, such

---

83   Ibid.

as Chilavert's Martín Cossarini (who ran the cultural centre there until 2007), join their ERT specifically because of their self-professed socio-political and ideological commitments to social justice issues and broader social change,[84] most new ERT members at first primarily desire to be employed. While obviously not uniformly experienced, most new ERT members do begin to develop to some degree their political commitments to the ERT movement and their sense of *compañerismo* on shop floors once they form part of the membership of an ERT, begin to struggle collectively with their workmates, and thus begin to feel like they are a central part of the cooperative project. They begin to learn the values and ethics of *compañerismo* informally and through the shared founding story of the ERT from the more senior members of the cooperative, and from the gradual process of living out *autogestión* collectively over time. Further, ERT founders who were already involved in union activity or social movement participation before their involvement with the ERT,[85] such as UST's Mario Barrios, Chilavert's Plácido Peñarrieta and Cándido González, and MNER and IMPA's Eduardo Murúa, are also important teachers for newer and younger ERT members. These more seasoned senior members of an ERT impart to newer members their understanding of the importance of practices and values of *compañerismo* and the ethic of *es de todos* by modelling these practices and values, and through informal conversations and storytelling.

On the whole, almost all workers I talked to and formally interviewed at ERTs over the years reported changes in their commitments to each other as they engage in a common project of *autogestión* together. Clearly present in the words and thoughts of most ERT workers I dialogued with were notions of *compañerismo*, 'esto es de todos', responsibility to the project and to each other, their deeper commitments to the communities that surround the ERT, and their greater sense of being an important part of creating a more socially sensitive economic reality for Argentina. Here, then, I found compelling connections between ERTs as *sites of learning* for workers' sense of solidarity and for self-managing their working lives and as spaces to begin to forge other, less capitalist productive relations, as Proudhon, Bakunin, Kropotkin, Gramsci, and contemporary *autogestión* theorists suggested for us in Chapters 4 and

---

84   Cossarini 2005, personal interview.
85   Recall that many of these more seasoned ERT protagonists had already been engaging in participative democratic practices in their union-based *asambleas* (assemblies) or *cuerpos de delegados* (shop-stewards' committees) or in other social justice struggles well before being a part of an ERT cooperative and impart these ideas and experiences to their ERT *compañeros*.

5. In short, the subjective transformations that take place with ERT workers are, as I have expressed it elsewhere, etched in collectively situated 'learning in struggle'.[86]

2.2.1   *Autogestión*: More Freedom or More Responsibility?

It was also evident in my conversations and interviews with ERT workers that there is a lingering tension between the greater freedoms for self-determination that *autogestión* suggests and the equally prominent sense of *responsibility* each worker feels for his or her *compañeros* and their project of *autogestión* more broadly. When, for example, I would ask workers what *autogestión* meant to them, almost none of them would initially say to me 'more freedom', as I had hypothesised early on in my research project. They would rather immediately respond, at times in a begrudging voice, with phrases like 'more responsibility' and 'a larger amount of commitment to my work', complementing the comments of Plácido, Eduardo, and Javier earlier on in this chapter. But when I would delve deeper and ask them if they would ever consider returning to their previous work situation, even if they received higher salaries, virtually all of the ERT workers I interviewed – with the exception of one worker – said that they would not. Chilavert's Manuel Basualdo captured this notion of responsibility vividly when he compared his work life at the cooperative now with the conditions of work intensity under his former boss:

> Things were very different before, mainly because, before, someone told you what to do, and you did it. Now nobody orders you around. Now you're more responsible, because our work depends on us and nobody else. It's just us. Before, with the owner, it was different, because you would put in your hours and leave. But now you sometimes have to work a bit harder, or a bit longer, do a little more. Before we were controlled so much. That's why they built the office with windows as walls. It was their way of controlling us, making sure we were doing something all the time.[87]

Again, Eduardo Murúa, who as the former president of MNER has been very close to the pulse of the average ERT worker in dozens of ERTs across Argentina since they first began to emerge, articulates how an implicit notion of freedom

---

86   Vieta 2014b. For the notion of 'learning in struggle' in the context of social movements for social change, see also Foley 1999.

87   M. Basualdo 2005, personal interview.

intermingles with an explicit understanding of increased responsibility that is inherent to ERT workers' projects of *autogestión* and their commitments to *compañerismo*:

> Another change that for us was very fundamental was that, given the same salary with the same work conditions, we are most certain that a worker in Argentina today would choose to work in a recuperated enterprise over an enterprise under the management of a boss. No *compañero* that has gone through the experience of working in a recuperated enterprise will want to return to a job managed by a boss. For sure if there is an offer of x amount in wages that is more than what a worker would make in a recuperated enterprise, it is possible that he would migrate to a capitalist enterprise. But under similar conditions, it is certain that that worker would not want to work under a boss. Do you understand? This has to do with the degree of internal democracy, the degree of freedom that that worker feels by working in a recuperated enterprise. That is, the change in subjectivity, I would say, happens even within the relations of production within the firm. Today the worker in a recuperated enterprise doesn't feel like an employee any more; inside of a recuperated factory the worker feels like a *compañero*. He doesn't feel like an employee utilised within an alienating job.[88]

What was similarly clear to me in talking to workers and being present at dozens of ERTs is that notions and practices of solidarity and *compañerismo*, although not uniformly conceived of and practised even within the same ERT by any means, palpably exist to some degree in all ERTs I have been in, and with all ERT workers I have talked to over the years. At the same time, each worker feels and knows from lived experience that there is a vast difference from the workplace atmosphere present at these firms when they worked for a boss and the new workplace environment under *autogestión*.

When thinking through this tension between more freedom and more responsibility in the conversations and interviews I have had with ERT workers, I am reminded of the tensions already understood by classical social anarchists between the responsibility to each other that members of a community must embrace and their pull towards the realm of freedom as autonomous individuals.[89] This is perhaps one of the central tensions in the stream of

---

88   Murúa 2006, para. 8.
89   Marshall 1992; Woodcock 2004. See also Bauman 2001.

self-determination of modern socialist thought. Recall from my discussion in Chapter 4 how classical social anarchists sought a balance between individual freedom and autonomy and the responsibility latent to participation in economic life that is implicit in the anarchist and socialist maxim 'from each according to their ability, to each according to their need'. In this sense, *autogestión* is rooted in the desire for individual freedom via self-determination and self-reliance, but also bears with it a strong sense of the shared responsibilities needed to carry out a collective project. Finding equilibrium between the realms of association and autonomy is a constant thread running throughout the works of Proudhon, for example, as I also pointed out in Chapter 4. It also resonates in the discourses of ERT workers.

2.3 *Keeping up and Upgrading Skills Informally: The Mentor-Apprentice Relationship*

Other, more top-down and sometimes more formal types of learning processes occur when NGO-based or university-led affinity initiatives approach and work with ERTs directly, or when state-based institutions and ministries assist ERTs. For example, as I reviewed in Chapter 7, several university–ERT partnerships have formed in recent years around action-based research projects and popular education programmes. But in the everyday activity of the firm, new ERT workers are, again, mostly *informally* trained on the job, both in the ins-and-outs of cooperativism and in job-specific skills, via apprenticing. Tellingly, this emulates the principal way that job training has traditionally taken place in blue-collar economic sectors in Argentina.[90] But now, in ERTs, cooperative values and ideals are layered into apprenticing scenarios on shop floors. Indeed, shadowing a more senior *socio* for a period of time on the job or on actual shop floors, I observed time and again, is the key way that ERT workers tend to informally learn new job tasks, skills, and cooperative values, often intermingled with the founding stories of the ERT. As UST's Juán Vera related to me, outlining the continuity of mentor-apprentice practices between traditional working-class life in Argentina and ERTs:

> I started as an apprentice here [twenty years ago]. I wanted to learn how to use the machines here, and the old guys taught me as jobs came up.

---

90   Of course, mentor–apprentice forms of learning, also called 'communities of practice' (Lave and Wenger 1991; Wenger 1996; Worthen 2014), are (and have been) prevalent in many work environments throughout the world. They are a fundamental way in which skills and trades are learned and passed on and, historically, long predate the capitalist era.

They would take breaks during peak hours and let me use the machines while they supervised ... And I do the same with my apprentice now. If a job comes up, I try to go but sometimes I can't [because of the other duties I have to do] so I send my apprentice, whom I'm teaching, and he replaces me also during my vacations or when I have meetings. When we have to attend political rallies to support other social movements, we take turns with who goes to the rally and who stays and works. And that's how it is here. He's already starting to replace me! Just like the old guys gave me a chance, I've also been teaching many of the young guys here and giving them a chance.[91]

On the whole, ERT *socios* tend to learn not only job skills through the mentor–apprentice model, but the model also serves to relay new values and practices of cooperativism informally to newer and younger workers. Moreover, workers learn informally from each other – again, intra-cooperatively – and on a trial-and-error basis as they work out the daily practicalities of self-management together.

2.4   The Rediscovery of Working-Class Practices, Informal Learning, and Sharing Knowledge and Skill Sets

In this section, I have shown that, on the whole, ERT workers' subjective changes tend to happen informally and immanently '*sobre la marcha*' (on the path of doing), and, as Mario Barrios termed it, as they 'learn together'. This informal and collective learning also often happens by trial and error and in the process of actually working out the details of *autogestión*, and collaboratively working through the myriad challenges each ERT faces. Moreover, ERT workers' job skills *and* cooperative aptitudes and values are transferred primarily from more senior workers and the ERTs' founders to newer workers via the traditional working-class strategy of the mentor–apprentice relationship. These mentoring relationships are important for both transferring job skills to the next generation of workers as well as for passing on the shared stories of the cooperative and the ERTs' founding, and for imparting broader interests in community wellbeing to newer workers, as well as the values of *compañerismo* and the ethical disposition of *es de todos*.

In essence, this section has shown that ERT protagonists' *politicisation and transformed subjectivities emerge from out of their collective actions* learned immanently within the conjunctures of micro-economic crises they originally

---

91   Vera 2009, personal interview.

found themselves in when working for bosses, in the actions of taking over their firms and needing to manage them collectively, and, informally, in the daily practices of *autogestión*. This personal and collective transformation – what we could also call an 'immanent becoming' within each worker and within each ERT that occurs '*sobre la marcha*', on the path and in the act of doing *autogestión* collaboratively – underscores the intimate connections between the transformations of workers and workplaces. It also underscores the connections between the micro-political and -economic conflictivity at the point of production they traverse, the challenges they collectively tackle, and the collaborative and informal learning that takes place within each ERT. With these findings, we arrive at ERTS' *fifth radical social innovation*:

> The recomposition of working-class subjectivities and multidimensional skills via informal learning processes such as shop floor apprenticing and the sharing of expertise and knowledge.

3 Section 3: Recuperating Social Production for Social Wealth

Jobs, the means of production, horizontalised labour processes, participatory decision-making structures, and informal working-class modes of learning are certainly key things that ERT protagonists recuperate. But they are not the only things recuperated. Part of the transformation of workers' subjectivities entails the recuperation of control over their capacities to cooperate – between workers at an ERT, between different ERTS, *and* in many cases with the communities that surround them. Here, the values and practices of *compañerismo* and the ethic of *es de todos* can also mean inviting the community onto the recuperated shop or extending the shop out into the community in practices of solidary economic and social development. This is an integral part of ERT protagonists' emergent class-in-the-making and demonstrates promising steps towards (if still nascent) alternative, non-capitalist economic arrangements for Argentina.

Francesco Vigliarolo suggests that Argentina's ERTS follow two directions: one with an economic focus concerned with saving jobs, reorganising the labour process, and restarting production, and another 'territorial model' that sees ERTS sharing surpluses and socialising wealth with surrounding communities.[92] These do not have to be, however, mutually exclusive. The Programa Facultad Abierta research team has found that almost two-thirds of

---

92   Vigliarolo 2016, p. 47.

ERTs are involved in community projects of some kind beyond the main business activity of the firm.[93] I conceptualise the community-based 'territorial model' of ERTs along two paths: one that brings the community into the cooperative, and another that extends the cooperative out into the community.

3.1 Creating Community-Based Solidarity Economies within the Shop

Like other social and solidarity economy organisations, ERTs tend to also have strong social missions and objectives. ERTs' new forms of *social production* and, as cooperatives, the *social wealth* they generate and redistribute amongst the coop's members can also be expansive, with some of the most promising ERTs extending their activity from just producing for the business concerns of the firm. Some ERTs actively provide for the social and economic needs of the surrounding *barrio* by opening up the shop to community initiatives. These ERTs share their space with other projects and thus essentially double as cultural and community centres, free community health clinics, spaces for popular education programmes for marginalised children and adults, alternative media projects, or community dining rooms, all run by workers, neighbours, or volunteers. As I introduced in Chapter 1, Chilavert and UST, two of the three ERTs I worked with closely, and like other emblematic ERTs such as Zanón/FaSinPat, IMPA, and the Hotel BAUEN, regularly open their workspaces to other uses besides their daily business interests.

For instance, Chilavert hosts the ERT Documentation Centre, which is run by staff and student volunteers associated with the University of Buenos Aires's Programa Facultad Abierta and used frequently by national and international researchers interested in the ERT phenomenon and its history. Indeed, I relied heavily on this centre for much of my documentary research for this book. A vibrant community centre called Chilavert Recupera (Chilavert Recuperates) also operates on its mezzanine level, hosting plays, art classes, music concerts, and community events linked to Argentina's social justice movements. During one of my weekend visits to the print shop in 2005, as I mentioned in the Chilavert case study in Chapter 1, volunteers from the community were giving a class on the dying *porteño* signage art called *filete*, while workers and visitors from the community were playing ping-pong in the cultural centre. On another occasion in July 2007, I witnessed a community play about the ERT movement, whereby Chilavert itself became a living theatre as the play was performed in the midst of stacks of papers and printing machinery.[94] Furthermore,

---

93   Ruggeri, Polti, Clark, Antivero, Delegdisch, et al. 2010, p. 79.
94   This was the play about the recuperation of the ERT Gráfica Patricios entitled *Maquinando: La historia de la lucha de la Gráfica Patricios*, collectively written by the popular

Chilavert houses a *bachillerato popular*, an adult high school equivalency and an after-school K-12 programme focused on a popular education curriculum. Organised as worker cooperatives by teachers employed in the public school system and other educators, *bachillerato populares* are present in several ERTs across the country and are heavily used by local marginalised communities. Another emblematic ERT, IMPA, the large metallurgic shop on the border of the Caballito and Almagro *barrios* of Buenos Aires, is also known as La Fábrica Ciudad Cultural (The Cultural City Factory), dedicating a large portion of its space to an art school, silk-screen shop, free health clinic, community theatre, and a *bachillerato popular*. Here I have also witnessed live theatre run by community-based artists' collectives wherein the factory itself becomes the stage. And Artes Gráficas Patricios, a medium-sized print shop located in the economically depressed southern Buenos Aires neighbourhood of Barracas (and the particular subject of the play I saw at Chilavert in 2007), houses a *bachillerato popular*, a community radio station, and a medical clinic that is run by local community volunteers. In August 2007 I attended a community fundraising concert on the blocked-off streets outside of Patricios where several thousand spectators listened to numerous bands playing on a temporary stage improvised from the print shop's flatbed truck, with local musicians donating their time and equipment to the occasion.

While changes in ERT workers' desires for spearheading community solidarity practices were less marked for most workers I interviewed when compared to their changes in values, attitudes, and commitment to cooperativism within the walls of the ERT, thinking about and proposing ways to reach out to the community in solidary ways beyond the cooperative were, nevertheless, at least somewhat important for almost all of the interviewed workers. This of course is, again, a marked difference from workers' individualistic perspectives regarding the role of their jobs and their workplace since the days they were employed by a boss. While participation in community projects was most evident in my three cases at Chilavert and UST, even amongst members of Salud Junín (who, due to its workers' lack of time[95] and the intensity and complexity of their jobs, are less involved in community work outside of the ERT), there is a tangible sense of the importance of their project for a different, less individualistic and

---

theatre troupe Grupo de Teatro Popular Olifante and directed by Argentine playwright, actor, and director Norman Briski. It has been shown in numerous ERTs across Argentina since 2007.

95   Recall from Chapter 1 that most of its nurse-members work double-shifts, both at Salud Junín and at other private clinics.

more communitarian kind of social and economic project for Argentina. As Salud Junín's Ana María Barrionuevo related to me:

> No, I was never involved in a community project of any sort before help-ing to start this cooperative ... And now I am only, unfortunately, involved in this cooperative, not in other movements. I just don't have the time. I'd like to do more work in a disadvantaged neighbourhood, for example, or some such thing. But time is limited! For us, it's about doing as much as we can for the community from here, from our cooperative.[96]

While time constraints might prohibit some workers, like Ana María, and some ERTs, like Salud Junín, from getting involved in community projects, my inter-view data suggest that after beginning to work at an ERT, workers tend to feel a stronger desire to personally take up community-oriented practices beyond their everyday work when compared to their attitudes towards community involvement when they worked for a boss. Some ERT workers get engaged in community work in their spare time if their ERT is not involved in community projects, while, for others, such desires might express themselves in the worker becoming more confident in speaking to neighbours about community issues and attending community meetings. As UST's Maxi Rodriguez, a new *socio* of the ERT and in his early twenties at the time of my conversation with him, told me:

> I never worried about community problems or problems in my neigh-bourhood before coming to work here. I just couldn't see them before, in reality. Now, from here, you start to see these problems and you start to work [to alleviate them].[97]

Save for five of the workers I interviewed that had community activist or union activist backgrounds, it is important to underscore here that most of the work-ers I interviewed did not have previous experiences with community organ-ising or activism, and that it was the specific involvement with the ERT project that fundamentally changed them into more community-minded individuals.

For ERTs such as Chilavert and UST which host cultural and community spaces within the firm and involve themselves intimately with the needs of the local community, being involved in such projects does not emerge from

---

96   Barrionuevo 2009, personal interview.
97   Maxi Rodríguez 2009, personal interview.

self-interest or the public relations exercises of 'goodwill' or 'corporate social responsibility' (CSR). Instead, workers from ERTs that host community projects tend to eventually see their workspaces as *continuations and integral parts of the neighbourhoods they are located in.* ERTs that host community spaces and participate in the social and economic development of surrounding communities also view these projects as ways of giving back to the communities that assisted them during their most harrowing days of struggle. Moreover, and thinking back to the discussions of ERTs and their community service strategies in Chapters 1, 6, and 7, the first ERT protagonists to open up cultural centres and other community projects within an ERT, encouraged by MNER during ERTs' first period, also believed that such projects within a once-capitalist business had valuable pragmatic and political ramifications. In these earlier chapters, we saw how, by ensconcing the ERT deep in the heart of the community, it becomes infinitely more difficult for the state to close the ERT while increasing the social value of the firm both within a neighbourhood and the broader surrounding communities.

The notion of *la fábrica abierta* (the open factory) has thus been taken up by many ERT protagonists in order to vividly communicate how ERTs counter the hegemonic capitalist discourses and practices of individualism and competition. *La fábrica abierta* also prefigures another mode of economic life that merges the production of culture with the production of social wealth within the otherwise strictly economic entity of a factory. Eduardo Múrua articulated this multi-pronged community strategy to me this way:

> When we took [IMPA], we set out to open up the factory to the community, and that's why we generated the cultural centre ... Here – in the middle of the city, and against the one-sided discourse in favour of globalisation and neo-liberalism that existed in the country at the time, from this recuperated enterprise – we said, 'Okay, we are going to dispute this one-sided discourse of globalisation'. That's why we generated the cultural centre that was to be a factory of ideas where people could go and discuss another discourse, create new cultural expressions, and generate at least from this location a space of resistance against the model.
>
> Having a cultural centre in a fully functioning factory is a unique development in the world. Yes, there have been experiences in other parts of the world where closed factories have been converted into cultural centres. But the central difference with our experience here is that at the same time that the factory is producing, it also has a cultural centre that is also producing, but *producing culture.* This affords us the possibility of instating the theme of the recuperated enterprises into the mainstream

media. And perhaps without meaning to – no, *definitely* without meaning to – the media contributed to the general awareness of this new method of struggle that was the recuperation of factories by workers.[98]

During my extended stays in Argentina since 2005, I quickly learned that with many ERTs their workspace walls do not demarcate enclosures that protect the work inside from the community outside. Rather, as many ERT protagonists told me, recuperated workspaces are recognised as being deeply rooted in the needs and desires of the local community and, as such, their participation in and collaboration with the communities that surround them make up vital parts of their projects of *autogestión*.

3.2   *Opening up Shops to the Community*

Argentina's ERT protagonists, then, are recuperating more than just jobs. They are also returning the practices of work and the organisation of the workplace to the neighbourhoods and communities that surround them by creating inventive ways of both symbolically and practically breaking down the walls that divide work inside a factory or shop from the rest of life outside of it. Confirmed by my own observations during my time spent in several Argentine ERTs, these community projects point to the communal values that many ERT protagonists have managed to fuse with work life, further collapsing the paradigm that encloses labour within capitalist logics and work within proprietary walls. Evocatively, such creative workplace–community fusions being fashioned by ERTs have been said to penetrate and rupture 'the capitalist secret'[99] – the proprietary nature of the capitalist paradigm enclosing the production and work that occurs within the walls of a firm from the community outside. These workplace–community fusions, it can be further argued, point to productive practices that extend beyond competitive ones. In Argentina, this has been called '*la fabrica abierta*', the open factory. With this, we arrive at ERTs' *sixth radical social innovation*:

> *The production and redistribution of social wealth that inwardly open up workplaces to the communities and neighbourhoods that surround them and, in the process, strengthen the social value of ERTS.*

---

98   Múrua 2005b, personal interview.
99   Ruggeri 2009, p. 79.

3.3   *Creating Solidarity Economies and Networks beyond the Shop*

While some ERTs open up their doors to the community, the deep transformations in community and solidary values and attitudes experienced by ERT workers have encouraged some ERTs to integrate into their very business practices social missions that see them *sharing* portions of their revenues with the community, which essentially extends their productive efforts out into the surrounding neighbourhoods spatially. Here, these ERTs both invite the community into their shops while also breaking down the barriers dividing private firms from the public sphere by extending the shop out into the community. Some of the most celebrated ERTs – such as UST, Zanón/FaSinPat, and Hotel BAUEN, for example – have expanded their business focus to include community social and economic development projects right into their *raison d'être*. The Hotel BAUEN has become a meeting place for myriad social justice initiatives and community gatherings over the years, and often subsidises accommodations for social movement actors visiting Buenos Aires. Zanón/FaSinPat has used portions of its revenues to help build a local health clinic while also provisioning tiles and other building supplies to local community initiatives. In fact, UST and Zanón/FaSinPat, in particular, are renowned for their practices of divvying up revenues between the capitalisation needs of the firm, workers' salaries, and community service. These outward focused community– ERT solidarity partnerships are especially auspicious in Argentina given the depleted and neglected reality of many working-class and popular neighbourhoods that, unfortunately, still remain far from the reach of government development programmes.

UST is an especially promising case of how to rethink the social, cultural, and economic role of a social enterprise within the immediate geographic spaces and the myriad communities that it finds itself immersed within. Like Zanón/FaSinPat and the Hotel BAUEN, UST consistently redirects a significant portion of its revenues – one quarter of revenues, in fact – to community development, such as an affordable housing project it has spearheaded for its workers and the surrounding community. This initiative has, as I specified in Chapter 1, already built 100 attractive town homes to replace precarious housing for some of its own members and other neighbours. In addition, UST built and continues to support a community centre and youth sports complex in the neighbourhood, sponsors local youth football teams and a *bachillerato popular*, initiated an alternative media workshop and radio programme, started a community bank, at one point headed a unique plastics recycling initiative for the large low-income housing project located near its plant, and has supported several other spin-off micro-enterprises. All of these projects are themselves organised as cooperatives, which has also transformed UST into a network of coops, becoming in essence a multi-stakeholder cooperative of cooperatives with UST as the organising hub of the network. What is also noticeable about UST's community projects is how they seem to interlace its locally rooted development with cultural projects and popular histories that resonate with the *barrio*. This is witnessed in its promotion of traditional Argentine music festivals, theatre productions, mural making, and in the cultural texts it produces, such as its monthly newspaper *Pluma*, all of which identify the cooperative's community work with past Argentine workers' struggles and even with the images of Eva Perón. In short, UST's community work is of deep importance to its workers, and improving the quality of life of the surrounding neighbourhoods is key to its broader social mission. As Mario Barrios, UST's president at the time of my interviews with him, explained to me, providing for the life-needs of workers *and* the surrounding neighbourhood in areas such as decent housing, sports, education, and in the vital project of eradicating illiteracy amongst workers and neighbours are key motivators for the cooperative and integral parts of their mission. Indeed, Barrios added, UST is not only in the waste management and construction business, but is also in the business of assisting in the provisioning of the life-needs of its workers and neighbouring communities.[100]

3.4   *Repurposing Surpluses for Community Development*
Symbolically tearing down the walls that, in the capitalist economic model, divide the business inside a workplace from the community outside of it, we arrive at ERTs' *seventh radical social innovation*:

> *The reclamation and redistribution of portions of workers' surpluses for outward community development, and their engagement in economies of solidarity with other cooperatives, ERTs, and community organisations.*

Summarising the discussion in this section, this is an innovation that markedly separates these new worker coops from solely for-profit, capitalist business interests, reclaiming the social wealth and surpluses produced in a socialised productive entity not only for the benefit of a cooperative's members, but also for the myriad communities it touches. In sum, ERTs' sixth and seventh radical social innovations further develop the seventh cooperative principle: 'concern for community'.

---

100   Barrios 2007, 2009, personal interviews.

4   Challenging ERTs' 'Dual Reality'

This chapter first highlighted the various tensions that ERT protagonists must work within – their 'dual reality' – especially brought on by competitive market pressures and other challenges analysed in Chapters 1, 6, and especially 7. In the case of Argentina, these challenges are compounded by the lack of coherent state policies geared towards self-managed workers. However, we also saw in earlier chapters how this had been changing with the pro-labour and pro-cooperative policies of Cristina Fernández de Kirchner's government during ERTs' second and third periods, which were also due in no small way to the consistent lobbying efforts and political work of ERT protagonists themselves; ERT workers' associations such as MNER and MNFRT; and more recent self-managed workers' organisations such ANTA, FACTA, CNCT, and others. In many ways, it is worth reiterating, ERTs' challenges parallel the historical challenges faced by worker cooperatives in other capitalist conjunctures in which having to produce for the commodity form pushes them at times either to marginal existence and ultimate failure, or to take on more capitalist practices.[101] At the same time, I showed in this chapter how ERTs begin to actively resist the push to self-exploit and become 'their own capitalist'[102] in the very ways that their workers restructure their labour processes, take on equitable pay practices, horizontalise their workplaces, democratise their decision-making structures, learn cooperative values, and tightly engrain themselves into the communities that surround them via social and solidarity economic practices. In this respect, I implicitly argued in this chapter that ERTs prefigure another, non-capitalist socio-economic model: one based on solidary economic values and practices over competitive ones.

---

101   Craig 1993; McNally 1993. See also Chapters 2, 5, and 7.
102   Marx 1981 p. 571.

PART 4

Recuperating Autogestión

∴

Recuperating *Autogestión*, Prefiguring Alternatives: Some Possible Conclusions

> Our dominant classes have always ensured that the workers should have no history, no doctrines, no heroes, nor martyrs. Each struggle must begin anew, separated from previous struggles – collective experiences get lost, lessons forgotten. History appears in this way like private property whose owners are the owners of everything. This time, it is possible for this circle to be broken.
>
> RODOLFO WALSH[1]

••

Perhaps what remains to be revisited now, at the end of our journey, are the following two overarching questions implicitly present throughout the entire book: 'Why is it that the *empresas recuperadas por sus trabajadores* emerged in Argentina when they did?' and 'What do the workers of the *empresas recupradas* actually recuperate?'. In this concluding chapter, I would like to return to these two questions so that we may continue to contemplate what Argentina's ERTs ultimately teach those of us struggling to forge a new type of non-capitalist economic reality.

1 On Workers' Recuperations of *Autogestión*

The Spanish language dictionary of the Real Academia Española[2] defines the verb *recuperar* (to recuperate) as follows:
– *tr. Volver a tomar o adquirir lo que antes se tenía* (transitive verb: To take back or acquire again what was once had).

---

1 Walsh 1969, paras. 8–9 ('Cordobazo', *Periódico CGT de los Argentinos*).
2 Real Academia Española oversees the Spanish language dictionary equivalent in status and widespread usage to the *Oxford English Dictionary* for the English language.

- *tr. Volver a poner en servicio lo que ya estaba inservible* (tr. v.: To put back into service or use that which was at one time unusable).
- *tr. Trabajar un determinado tiempo para compensar lo que no se había hecho por algún motivo* (tr. v.: To work for a determined period in order to compensate or make up for what had not been done for some reason) ...
- *prnl. Volver en sí* (pronominal verb: To return to itself, or to a former state).
- *prnl. Volver a un estado de normalidad después de haber pasado por una situación difícil.* (pn. v.: To return to a state of normalcy after having gone through a difficult situation).[3]

From the evidence presented in this book, all of these definitions can be applied to the strategies, tactics, and actions of the protagonists of Argentina's *empresas recuperadas por sus trabajadores.*[4] In taking over a failed enterprise and putting it back into production again under collective self-management, ERT workers 'put back in service or use that which was at one time unusable'. In recomposing their places of employment and securing their jobs, ERT workers 'return' their workplaces – as well as their salaried and non-salaried lives – to some 'state of normalcy' 'after having gone through a difficult situation'. But ERT workers accomplish much more during their longer processes of occupying workspaces, resisting eviction and repression, transforming a formerly capitalist workplace into a cooperative, and struggling to legitimise and consolidate their projects of *autogestión*.

In taking over the businesses that had formerly employed them and controlling the means of production therein, ERT workers most fundamentally begin to recuperate crucial aspects of their human capacities, especially their abilities to creatively produce useful things in association and without coercion from bosses. In recuperating the machines and tools of their trade, ERT workers 'take back or acquire again what was once' historically theirs. Relatedly, they also recuperate control over surpluses and the products of their labours – what they themselves had been, in Marxian terms, valorising all along. And in recuperating control of the labour process and their labouring capacities (that is, their labour-power), which they had once sold to their bosses for a wage, they also 'return to a former state' those things which all workers possess but that remain in control of others within the capitalist mode of production: their own abilities to make decisions; their capacities to imagine, conceptualise, plan, coordinate, and cooperatively shape the products of their labours; and the freedom to choose how and when to work the materials and resources mediated

---

3   Real Academia Española 2011.
4   Recall also my initial discussion of the term 'recuperation' in the Introduction. See also Sitrin and Azzellini 2012, p. 12.

by their skills and tools. In sum, in first embarking on the recuperation of their jobs and their places of work, and then producing useful things under *autogestión*, ERT protagonists go beyond merely rectifying perceived injustices in the workplace. Ultimately, and more vitally, ERT protagonists 'work for a determined period in order to compensate or make up for what has not been done for some reason' – that is, *they start to collaboratively self-determine and self-control their own places of work, their own productive lives, and the creation of social wealth*. These recuperations are embraced by what I have called ERT protagonists' 'recuperative moments' and reside at the heart of ERTs' radical social innovations in *autogestión*. At core, ERT workers, via the takeover and recuperation of workplaces once privately owned by capitalist interests and the subsequent restructuring of these workplaces under cooperative practices and values, directly redress the ways that capital alienates and exploits actual producers while prefiguring another socio-economic reality.

As I implicitly and at times explicitly considered throughout this book, the recuperative characteristics of ERTs – their 'recuperative moments' – both put into relief what workers most fundamentally struggle against in the 'real subsumption' of labour under capital – that is, 'the appropriation of unpaid labour' for the creation of surplus-value, or the process of valorisation[5] – and prefigure an alternative reality to work beyond capital. As Marx said of the worker cooperative movement of his time, Argentina's ERTs are showing, '[b]y deed, instead of by argument', that

> production ... may be carried on without the existence of a class of masters employing a class of hands; that to bear fruit, the means of labour need not be monopolised as a means of dominion over, and of extortion against, the labouring man [sic] himself; and that, like slave labour, like serf labour, hired labour is but a transitory and inferior form, destined to disappear before associated labour plying its toil with a willing hand, a ready mind, and a joyous heart.[6]

The experiences of Argentina's ERTs are rich with creative force and prefigurative possibilities for another possible world rooted in *autogestión*, what Marx termed 'associated labour'. This book has attempted to home in on the most salient ways that ERTs and their worker-protagonists embrace the recuperations of *autogestión*. I have attempted throughout to let the *actual voices* and *experiences* of these workers guide the narrative and the subsequent analysis

---

5   Engels 1978, p. 700.
6   Marx 1978a, p. 518.

as much as possible. From out of their own stories and shared memories of struggle, we have tried to better understand the many challenges that motivate ERT workers' collective actions and cooperative innovations by grounding this work in critical theoretical and historically materialist traditions that both critically assess the capitalist system that pervades production on a planetary scale, and that consider the ways workers always already strive to better their lives and move beyond the enclosures that define the present system. In critically evaluating the capitalist system of production through critical theoretical lenses and the point of view of the working class – that is, from a political economy of the working class – we can, I have argued, more clearly understand *what* ERT workers, and indeed all workers toiling under capitalist modes of production, *struggle against*. In also considering *how* and *why* workers struggle within the capitalist system of production to make their lives more secure, more meaningful, more dignified, and less alienated, we can come to know *what* workers – and ERT workers, in particular – are *struggling for*.

From out of the political economy of the working class approach embedded in the class-struggle tradition, this book has thus focused on the ERT phenomenon from the perspective of its workers' self-activity and self-determination to both perserve their work and diginity *and*, in the process, begin to move beyond status-quo practices of producing things under the capitalist mantle. What has thus inspired this book are the real accomplishments of Argentina's ERT protagonists: their tenacity in recuperating jobs and once-failing capitalist workplaces against great odds; their creative and innovative responses to the many challenges they have had to traverse in order to consolidate *autogestión*; and their forging of new forms of work, production, and social relations in the face of an often callously anti-labour national economic conjuncture and a neo-liberal order in perpetual crisis.

In a final recapitulation that should lead to many more future research codas, in the remaining pages I revisit the evidence presented in this book's empirical chapters (Chapters 1, 2, and 6–8) in order to continue the exercise of theorising how exactly the experiences of Argentina's ERTs are helping us rethink working-class agency and self-activity, cooperativism and associated labour, and the notion of *autogestión* from the perspective of workers' own lived experiences. The final paragraphs of this book explicitly return to the prefigurative potential of ERTs in light of our recent moment of global economic crisis, proposing that ERTs suggest how the radical transformation of economic life can continue to unfold in Argentina, and perhaps even in other places.

2 The Conjunctural Realities of Argentina's ERTS

In the introductory pages and then in a more detailed way throughout Part 1, I began this book by looking at why ERTs emerged in Argentina over the past two decades – that is, why in Argentina and why at this historical moment? In attempting to answer this question, I was compelled in Chapter 3 to take on a political economic and conjunctural analysis that helped to historically frame the details of ERTs' emergence and their protagonists' lived experiences of *autogestión* that are described in the book's empirical chapters.

According to Antonio Gramsci, *the conjuncture* is 'defined as the set of circumstances which determine the market in a given phase, provided that these are conceived of as being in the moment, i.e. as constituting a process of ever-changing combinations, a process which is the economic cycle'.[7] For Gramsci, the economic base's 'organic ... situation' is intimately connected to the superstructure's conjunctural moments.[8] Immanent to a given moment, *the conjunctural* can emerge out of the inevitability of capitalist economic crisis and may potentially open up the 'terrain [for] the forces of opposition to organise'.[9] 'The conjuncture', in other words, 'is a set of immediate and ephemeral characteristics of the economic situation', Gramsci further explains, and '[the] study of the conjuncture is thus more closely linked to [bottom-up] immediate politics, to "tactics" and agitation'.[10] Adopting a conjunctural approach therefore takes into consideration aspects of a particular economic situation that may incite collective actions, tactics, and struggles against a particular economic order by those most directly and negatively affected by this order's socio-political and socio-economic structures. Given the neo-liberal capitalist order out of which ERTs emerged, a conjunctural analysis helps us come to grips with how and why its workers resisted and attempted to move beyond its enclosures, alienations, and exploitations at a particular historical moment of its development within a particular national setting.

In a similar vein, Italian autonomist social theorist Maurizio Lazzarato asserts that the 'political event' – congruent in many ways with Gramsci's conjuncture – emerges out of crisis moments, coalescing individuals and collectives via creative and collaborative actions spurred on by the realisation of what is intolerable with the historical moment they live in. From within certain benchmark historical moments of crisis and conflict, moreover, 'new possib-

---

7   Gramsci 1971a, p. 177.
8   Forgacs, 2000, p. 201.
9   Ibid.
10 Gramsci 1971a, p. 177.

ilities for living' get articulated through particular events.[11] Ethico-politically charged and immanently bottom-up, the political event for Lazzarato may not only place capital's contradictions into sharp relief, it may also reveal openings for recomposing life for those oppressed by constituted power. Argentina's mass protests of 19 and 20 December 2001 represented one such event.

Other recent crisis moments of neo-liberalism that inspired or incited particular political events within conjunctures that pointed to 'new possibilities for living' include: 'The Battle for Seattle' in 1999; Québec City and Genoa 2001; the global protests against the US invasion of Iraq in March of 2003; the Arab Spring, *Indignados*, and Occupy movements of 2011–12; Turkey's Taksim Square mass mobilisations of 2013; and, in more recent years, the anti-austerity movements of Greece and France and Indigenous movements against colonial-capitalist interests the world over. These and other bottom-up movements of the oppressed, the marginalised, and the exploited have arisen conjuncturally with the ebbs and flows of the neo-liberal world order as direct responses to the ongoing crisis of global capital. They are still unfolding all over the world as I write these final lines. Importantly, these conjunctural events should not be understood as merely momentary and fleeting reactions to the inevitable glitches and cracks present in constituted power. Rather, 'the event' is the intensified and collective eruption of alternative or anti-systemic actions, images, and statements within an ongoing social struggle against established forms of capitalist and imperialist power. It is the creative climax in the long narrative of class-based conflicts instigated by the preponderance of the commodity form and the exclusionary and exploitative political economic structures that uphold the circuits and logics of production, exchange, and accumulation. In Argentina, events that emerged out of these conjunctural crisis moments throughout the 1990s and early 2000s began to rouse the collective actions of working people, the oppressed, and the dispossessed, forcing them to collectively question the dominant neo-liberal values and regimes of production that ruptured workers' and marginalised people's established ways of life. And in these people's collective responses to these conjunctural moments of crises, alternative ways of social and productive relations began to emerge, articulating other possibilities for living.

What were the specific conjunctural moments, then, that served as midwives to Argentina's ERTs? We can conclude from the evidence presented in this book that five conjunctural realities have existed in Argentina in recent decades that directly relate to the emergence of ERTs: heightened economic

---

11   Lazzarato 2003, p. 1.

precariousness, the entrenchment of deep class divisions, the rise of resistive subjectivities, the concretisation of tight community bonds, and new forms of cooperativism and workplace solidarity.

2.1 Heightened Economic Precariousness

Beginning around 1995 and coming to a head during the crisis years of 2001–3, thousands of small- and medium-sized businesses (SMEs) in Argentina began to lose market share while amassing unwieldy debt loads due to the drying up of local and export markets during the country's economic liberalisations of the 1990s. In the name of curbing hyperinflation and reducing a surging national debt that, paradoxically, continued to rise throughout the 1990s, Argentina's IMF-sanctioned liberalisations included the 'dollarisation' of the peso (officially, the Plan de Convertibilidad), the privatisation of dozens of once-nationalised or public sector firms, the erosion of decades-old labour protections, and the foreign capitalisation of large portions of Argentina's industrial and agricultural base. By the mid-1990s, it was clear that these neo-liberal policies were negatively affecting the competitive advantage of Argentine products in foreign and national markets. Specifically, the large wave of privatisation schemes, company downsizings, outsourcing, and the deregulation of labour markets and other anti-labour practices were underpinned by a mass outflow of capital to foreign economic interests, compromising the competitiveness of thousands of Argentine firms. Producing ruthless micro-economic crises at the point of production that cut across all urban economic sectors, starting around 1995 this macro-economic situation eventually caused a growing number of firms (especially SMEs) to declare bankruptcy at historically unprecedented rates, reaching its apex at the historical moment that saw the temporary collapse of the neo-liberal model in Argentina in late 2001 and early 2002.

In danger of entering the ranks of the structurally unemployed that by the first quarter of 2002 affected well over 20 percent of Argentina's active, urban-based workers, the response by some Argentine workers was to occupy and attempt to subsequently self-manage their failing or failed firms under the legal rubric of a worker cooperative. Rather than being impelled by a revolutionary cause, traditional union demands, or the leadership of mainstream political parties, in actuality these responses were, at first, highly risky and localised tactics carried out by desperate workers willing to face violent repression by the state and returning owners in order to save their jobs, continue to feed their families, and safeguard their self-dignity. Initially, then, ERT protagonists took on the challenges of self-management defensively and out of necessity, a decision that was further encouraged during the crisis years spanning the turn of the millennium by the lack of alternative employment within an ethically bankrupted political-economic system that looked the other way while countless business owners engaged in nefarious schemes to save their dying firms at the expense of the wellbeing of employees. These motivating factors for creating ERTs have persisted over the years. In sum, workers' initial actions involving the seizure of deteriorating or bankrupted companies, the occupation of them for weeks or months, and their reopening as worker cooperatives have tended to initially arise most directly and pragmatically out of commonly shared lived experiences of anger over their mistreatment and their deep worries of becoming structurally (and permanently) unemployed.[12]

2.2   The Entrenchment of Deep Class Divisions

In Argentina throughout the decade of the 1990s and into the first decade of the 2000s, conspicuous consumption by the country's upper and middle classes, due primarily to easily obtainable consumer credit, intermingled with historically high levels of poverty, indigence, and eventually unemployment. This reality was still visible even during the relative recomposition of the country's national economy during the first Kirchner presidency (a recovery in part due to more developmentalist economic policy combining with the favourable

---

12   In light of the widespread nature of micro-economic crises on shop floors during the late 1990s and early 2000s in Argentina and the country's subsequent waves of economic downturns, one question that perhaps remains unanswered is why have more ERTs not emerged? Why is it that slightly over 400 ERTs have existed to date in Argentina? While answers might initially appear to be self-evident, the question is vexed and has been under-researched by the ERT literature to date. Immediately, one might be tempted to hypothesise that workers from troubled or closing companies that do not become ERTs are not as radicalised compared to workers that eventually do decide to form ERTs. I am not convinced that this is the case overall in Argentina, especially given how well-known the ERT solution is among working people, the Argentine working class's long history of militancy, and the widespread nature of the ERT phenomenon when we consider that they are found in most urban-based economic sectors and across the Argentine territory. What is perhaps more likely is that owner-led or state-based repression tactics in countless workplaces over the years, together with the lukewarm support of the ERT solution on the part of the Argentine state, have had the intended effect of denying workers the chance to convert more firms to worker cooperatives. As a result, many of the country's workers have had no choice but to either continue to give their consent to reduced wages or worsening working conditions, disperse into the ranks of the structurally unemployed, or try to find work elsewhere for those lucky enough to do so. It is also not unreasonable to conjecture that some of Argentina's unions have taken an active interest in the plight of workers in failing firms, thus helping to prevent the closure of some of these firms, securing owed severance for fired workers, or assisting redundant workers in finding work elsewhere. In addition, of course, not all workplaces that are in trouble eventually close; many troubled firms

world commodity markets of the early-to-mid 2000s). Especially between the years 1995 and 2005 – the decade that saw the country's cycle of neo-liberal crisis most dramatically rise, peak, and ebb – deeply structurated economic and social divisions perceptibly etched everyday life in Argentina as continued social tensions between the haves and have-nots fuelled a culture of combativeness amongst the country's marginalised groups – the underemployed, the unemployed, the poor, the indigent, and those workers whose work situation was becoming increasingly precarious.

2.3   The Rise of Resistive Subjectivities

With a dearth of options left for working people on the brink of structural unemployment, between 1995 and 2005 – and especially between the years 2001 and 2003 – growing class divisions crystallised into the strident radicalisation of marginalised groups. A contagion of bottom-up popular resistance and horizontalism spread across Argentina's marginalised sectors throughout this period, witnessed in the widespread direct-action tactics of property occupations, squattings, the *piquetero*'s now-famous road blockages, spontaneous community mobilisation, and horizontal organising structures. What spilled over from these grassroots mobilisations onto all forms of popular struggle emerging from the cities' *barrios* and industrialised towns of the country at the time was a revived collective purpose against a callous and overtly exploitative system; a growing ethos of self-organisation and direct participatory democracy from below; and a massive recomposition of community-based social experiences. In turn, this contagion intermingled with a long history of working-class militancy and workers' collective memories of Argentina's 'golden years', which had in the past included a strong labour movement, a prosperous and at times combative working class, and a mostly nationalised and self-sustaining economy. By the early years of the new millennium, much cross-pollination took place between grassroots social justice groups. Thus, up until 2005 and the relative recomposition of Argentina's economy (which, it should be recalled, also included the government's co-optation of some of these grass-

---

manage to stay open either because some owners are sympathetic to the broader social consequences of closing, because some firms manage to secure adequate capital reserves to ride out hard times, or because economically challenging times have not affected all economic sectors in the same way. Moreover, it is also highly likely that many Argentine workers employed in companies that could have become ERTs over the years either succumbed to unfavourable bankruptcy court rulings, chose to take severance packages, chose to retire, or found work elsewhere in other firms or in the growing informal sector or the social and solidarity economy.

roots groups via strategies of assistentialism and clientelism), much of daily life in urban Argentina was infused with constant protests, land and road occupations, workplace takeovers, and work stoppages by myriad marginalised groups demanding better living conditions and social change.

2.4   The Concretisation of Tight Community Bonds

Over the past almost three decades in Argentina, theories and practices of *autogestión* have emerged via the intermingling of spatial/territorial dimensions and social/community imaginaries. ERTs embrace both of these aspects of *autogestión*. Geographically, for instance, ERTS are situated deep within the communities and *barrios* where they are located. As I described in the empirical chapters of this book, especially Chapters 1 and 6–8, economies of solidarity between a recuperated enterprise, the neighbourhood, and other ERTs have in some cases formed into rich community networks of mutual aid. This outcome was driven in part by the fact that most workers live in or near the neighbourhoods where the ERT is located. Moreover, neighbours and other community groups are often supportive of and at times active players in the recuperation of workplaces. Consequently, neighbourhood cultural centres and other community services have tended to emerge within many recuperated enterprises as a way for ERT workers to give back to the communities that have supported them, as a way of further valorising the ERT within the community, and also as a strategy for protecting the ERT from ongoing repression and threats of closure via the bonds of solidarity that form within these networks of mutual assistance.

2.5   New Forms of Cooperativism and Workplace Solidarity

As I analysed in Chapters 3, 5 and 6, cooperativism and union-based democratic shop floor institutions such as shop-stewards' committees and workers' councils are long-held traditions of Argentina's working class that extend as far back as the early waves of European immigration in the late nineteenth and early twentieth centuries. Many of these immigrants brought to their new country the anarchist, socialist, and cooperativist ideals of their homelands, ideals that guided the early Argentine labour movement in the first years of the twentieth century.[13] Moreover, democratic workplace institutions and practices that have often side-stepped official union hierarchies and helped infuse strong bonds of shop floor solidarity have equally imprinted themselves onto the everyday practices of Argentina's working class over the decades. Sub-

---

13   Munck, Falcón, and Galitelli 1987; Wyczykier 2009b.

sequently practised in myriad economic sectors, the country's ERTs have prag-matically adopted these democratic practices. The model of the worker cooper-ative, in particular, has served ERTs as an important organising framework for restructuring these worker-recuperated firms.

ERTS have also embraced a new form of anti-systemic cooperativism that has emerged across the world in recent years, what I have elsewhere called 'the new cooperativism'.[14] Directly addressing the worst effects of globalisation on working people, the new cooperativism encompasses socio-economic and cultural collectives and alternative work organisations that are intimately con-nected to contemporary social movements and experiments struggling against and attempting to move beyond neo-liberal capitalism. While overwhelmingly organised horizontally and democratically, experiments in the new cooperativ-ism are not necessarily preoccupied with formal cooperative organisational structures as such. They are, rather, more concerned with envisioning inclusive and solidary socio-economic practices, prefiguring the future or non-capitalist world desired by its protagonists. I explored the implications of this broad adoption of new cooperative values, structures, and practices in the horizont-ally transformed labour processes of ERTs in Chapters 6–8.

Overall, the merger of traditional working-class traditions with the practices and values of the new cooperativism – especially as re-articulated on shop floors over the past two to three decades – has played a central role in how *auto-gestión* unfolds within each ERT, as well as in the phenomenon's seven radical social innovations that I will revisit shortly.

2.6   *ERTs' Conjunctural Realities: Taking Stock*

These five conjunctural realities suggest the most direct roots of Argentina's ERTS. ERT protagonists' tactics and strategies of workplace occupations and recuperations, while distantly rooted in the social and cultural memory of past labour struggles and working-class militancy, were most directly modelled after the new social transformations and mobilisations that were taking shape around them at the time, and most directly responded to the rise of precari-ousness and insecurity impinging on workers' expectations of dignified work, stable livelihoods, and social security. At the same time, workplace occupations and recuperations were themselves inspiring other social and cultural expres-sions and movements for self-determination. Moreover, the intensification of 'communitarian social experiences' in Argentina, as Maristella Svampa and

---

14   Vieta 2010b; Lionais and Vieta 2017.

Sebastián Pereyra[15] articulated for us early on in this book, were also encouraged by the contagion of directly democratic and popular forms of resistance surging at the time across Latin America.

Peter Ranis's recent assessment of Argentina's vibrant civil society merging with – he borrows the phrase from Sidney Tarrow – the 'contentious politics' that has infused its myriad social justice movements[16] serves to summarise the five conjunctural realities that nurtured the rise of ERTs. Using metropolitan Buenos Aires as his example, Ranis suggests that:

> Within the ... context of the capital city, greater Buenos Aires, and the province of Buenos Aires, where over one third of the entire Argentine population resides, ... we observe a rich mélange of associational life with high union density, multiparty proliferation and high levels of participatory cultural outlets, while not many kilometres away one sees clear strongholds of elitism, verticality, religiosity, political clientelism and party patronage. The worker cooperative movements have been active within these cross-cultural geographies, and through their various capabilities have mounted a certain challenge to the Argentine political, economic and legal systems. Though they have come away with some victories and some defeats, they have managed to combine certain features that allow one to perceive them as proponents of 'contentious politics', as social movements.[17]

Immersed, then, in this vibrant cross-current of contentious politics and social movements operating within an effervescent civil society, for some workers in Argentina participation in direct actions to recuperate their workplaces and forge their projects of *autogestión* have become viable solutions for securing their livelihoods and dignity. Going down the long and challenging road of starting an ERT in Argentina becomes particularly compelling for workers when they face the stark possibility of permanent unemployment; an unresponsive or antagonistic neo-liberal state committed to the interests of capital; and often unresponsive union bureaucracies perceived to be dedicated more to their own self-preservation than representing the interests of working people.

---

15   Svampa and Pereyra 2004.
16   Ranis 2016, pp. 88 ff.
17   Ranis 2016, p. 88.

2.6.1   The Cooperation of Workers within the Labour Process

ERT workers' direct actions of workplace occupation and resistance and their eventual take up of *autogestión* also have deep roots in how workers' solidarity and cooperation develops organically within the capitalist labour process. A brief return to Marx's analysis of cooperation within the labour process can help us see this more clearly.

The unleashing of value creation with workers' cooperation in the capitalist labour process is, for Marx, the prime motivator for capital's mustering of the 'socially productive power of labour', which is 'a free gift to capital'.[18] But there is a contradiction in this 'free gift': through the ideological lenses of capitalism, '[c]ooperation, which is a productive power of social labour, *appears* as a productive power of capital, not of labour'.[19] Since, despite this appearance, this socially productive power resides in the embodied and social capacities of labourers, the harnessing of workers' cooperative capacities within the labour process also compels the capitalist to mobilise 'the work of control' specifically because of '*the antagonism of interests* between capitalist and labourer'.[20] However, Marx reasserts, capital is really only the mediator here, rather than the cause of 'the productive power'; it is the organiser of the cooperative forces and valorising capacities of labour within the capitalist labour process.[21] Since this productive power in cooperation is not embodied in the capitalist but rather in the worker, the capitalist must organise the labour process by exerting forms of explicit or implicit control over the worker in order to contain and channel the 'unavoidable antagonism between the exploiter and the living and labouring raw material he exploits'.[22]

Hence, cooperation within the capitalist labour process is – like labour and technologies of production within capitalism – twofold: On the one hand, cooperation in the capitalist labour process requires workers' consensus under

---

18   Marx 1976b, p. 451.

19   Marx 1988, p. 260 (emphasis added).

20   Marx 1967, p. 332 (emphasis added).

21   As Marx clarifies, while 'cooperation [within capitalist processes of production] only begins with the labour process', and that 'by then [cooperation and the labour process] have ceased to belong to [workers]' (Marx 1976b, p. 451), 'the connexion existing between their various labours *appears* to them, *ideally*, in the shape of a preconceived plan of the capitalist, and practically in the shape of the authority of the same capitalist' (Marx 1967, p. 331, emphasis added). As we know from our critical theoretical analysis in Chapter 4, these *appearances*, in practice, incorporate the actual valorising capacities of workers into capital via workers' consensus, managerial control, and the wage-labour contract which secures workers' incorporation into capital '[a]s cooperators, as members of a working organism' (Marx 1976b, p. 451). See also Lebowitz 2003, p. 87.

22   Marx 1967, p. 331.

the suasion of the wage-labour contract 'negotiated' between two ostensibly 'equal' and 'free' agents (that is, employers and employees). When this consensus is not attainable or is breached, workers' cooperation is enforced via strategies of outright managerial control in order to rein in the disparate capacities of workers who have negotiated their labour contracts individually. On the other hand, when labourers are brought together 'under one roof',[23] the capitalist not only assembles the 'socially productive power of labour' but also unintentionally unleashes interdependence between workers. In this respect, cooperation on capitalist shop floors brings workers together and forms 'the collective worker'. This is the positive side of capital, the side that 'socializes the worker'[24] and begins to create solidarity between them based on common interests, shared experiences, and common struggles.[25]

Why, then, asks Michael Lebowitz, 'are the producers [that is, workers] themselves not able to capture the fruits of cooperation in production?'[26] Because the capitalist's 'planned cooperation',[27] mixed with detailed divisions of labour and managerial control, focuses cooperation squarely on the extraction 'of the greatest possible amount of surplus-value'.[28] The '[d]riving motive and determining purpose of capitalist production', Marx asserts, is not the full-sided development of the worker, after all, but 'the self-valorization of capital'.[29] For workers to achieve true self-development and self-determination, therefore, they must, according to Lebowitz, 'reduce their degree of separation' that results when each individual labourer sells their labour-power to the capitalist.[30] This can be done by *recuperating* from the control of capitalists a power capital does not really possess and that belongs, in essence, to workers in the first place: *the power of cooperation*. And workers can begin to recuperate the power of cooperation for themselves by struggling to control the means of production and, ultimately, take hold of their work time and 'disposable time' – time in order to self-develop and self-actualise – for themselves.[31] This crucial recuperation effectively begins to replace 'capital as the mediator for wage-labour, separating the worker from her labour-power as property' and as 'the mediator between

---

23   Marx 1967, p. 473.
24   Lebowitz 2003, p. 87.
25   Marx 1967, p. 763. See also Atzeni 2010; and Lebowitz 2003.
26   Lebowitz 2003, p. 87.
27   Ibid.
28   Marx 1967, p. 331.
29   Marx 1976b, p. 449.
30   Lebowitz 2003, p. 87.
31   As Marx writes: 'If the labourer consumes his disposable time for himself, he robs the capitalist' (Marx 1967, p. 233).

wage-labourers in each moment of the circuits of capital'.[32] When workers collectively control and self-organise the means of production and their labour in a worker cooperative, they recuperate the 'productive power of social labour' for themselves, break the mediating role of capital, do away with wage-labour as property, and take back control of their working *and* non-working lives.[33]

2.6.2 Recuperating the Power of Cooperative Labour within Moments of Crisis

For class-struggle Marxists, the possibility for workers' re-appropriations (that is, recuperations) of the means of production – and, ultimately, of their time – begins with materialising, or bringing to the surface, the historical reshaping of the power of cooperative labour by capital.[34] For workers, this realisation can happen within moments of crises that interrupt the smooth flow of capitalist circuits of production and exchange. During periods when the capitalist system experiences intensive and far-reaching ruptures, as happened during the Argentine December of 2001, these moments of crises can bring for labouring people critical awareness of the exploitative and alienating character of capitalist work. Often fostered by the inherent nature of the capitalist system itself to centralise and over-accumulate, acute moments of crises may put into sharp relief for workers their place in the class struggle and the antagonisms and contradictions between 'collective capital, i.e., the class of capitalists' and 'collective labour, i.e., the working class'.[35] Moments of social and economic crises have, in other words, the potential to monkey wrench the circuits of capitalist production and exchange by bringing the exploitative tendencies of capital to the surface, problematising capital's obscuring and securing of surplus-value extraction, making painfully evident to working people the vastly divergent interests between themselves and the capitalist class, and leading workers to see the need to channel their cooperative power into resistance and revolt.[36]

---

32   Lebowitz 2003, p. 88.

33   As Marx asserts: 'It is ... clear that in any given economic formation of society, where not the exchange-value but the use-value of the product predominates, surplus-labour will be limited by a greater set of wants which will be greater or less, and that here no boundless thirst for surplus-labour arises from the nature of the production itself' (Marx 1967, p. 235).

34   See, for instance, Feenberg 2002; Lebowitz 2003; Marcuse 1964; and Vieta 2016a.

35   Marx 1967, p. 235.

36   'Along with the constantly diminishing number of the magnates of capital', writes Marx in the final pages of *Capital* Volume I, 'who usurp and monopolise all advantages of this process of transformation [of labour, land, and 'other means of production' via the centralisation of capitals and the intensification of the capitalist mode of production], grows the mass of misery, oppression, slavery, degradation, exploitation; but with this too *grows*

But we must also remember that the potential for crises within capitalism is perpetually present – if dormant during periods of class compromise and labour peace – in the labour process itself. The same social relations of capitalist work that compel workers to combine into unions and to agitate and bargain for shop floor improvements and better wages also open up the potential for conflict to extend to other areas of working life beyond the shop and the wage-labour contract.[37] The always already contradictory and exploitative nature of the labour process under capitalism is at the heart of this conflict; the capitalist labour process is already charged with the possibility for conflict to explode beyond the point of production. 'For our understanding of workers' mobilization', Maurizio Atzeni argues, 'the contradictory and conflicting nature of the capitalist labour process, as an organization of production driven by valorization, is crucial'.[38] And this contradictory and conflictual nature of the labour process under capitalism can come to the surface when situations of exploitation at the point of production are ratcheted up to extremes, or when the wage-labour contract is explicitly or callously breached by employers, or when workers' quality of life diminishes beyond acceptable levels whereby workers can no longer consent to capitalist processes of production, or when the obscuring and securing of surplus-value extraction is clearly revealed and made painfully obvious to workers.

In the Argentina of the mid-1990s and early 2000s, as Chapters 1, 3, and 6 made clear, these otherwise latent conflicts and contradictions in the capitalist labour process, gradually revealed to workers with owners' increasing violations of the labour contract, would finally intensify to the point of rupturing. In this milieu, more and more sacrifices were asked of workers by desperate (and, too often, greedily cunning) owners and managers as they attempted to cheapen labour costs by initiating rationalisation drives, intensifying work, asking employees to take salary cuts 'for the good of the team', holding back wages (or not paying them at all), locking out workers, and eventually firing them. And as the consent of increasingly restless workers slipped away from capitalist overseers during Argentina's neo-liberal crisis years, employers would resort

---

the revolt of the working class, a class always increasing in numbers, and disciplined, united, organised by the very mechanism of the process of capitalist production itself ... Centralisation of the means of production and socialisation of labour at last reach a point where they become incompatible with their capitalist integument. Thus integument is burst asunder. The knell of capitalist private property sounds. The expropriators are expropriated' (Marx 1967, p. 763, emphasis added).

37   Atzeni 2010, p. 22.
38   Ibid.

to openly coercive methods of control.[39] These explicit employer actions – accompanied more broadly by a collapsing neo-liberal order – brought into sharp relief for workers the real exploitation that is always present (but usually obscured under the rubric of consensus)[40] in the capital–labour relation.

In turn-of-the-millennium Argentina, the intersubjectively shared struggles of some workers' collectives would merge with the solidarity already fostered on troubled shop floors – solidarities that would increasingly crystallise during times of rising micro-economic crises at the point of production, within the broader situation of intensifying political economic crisis. As more and more workers in Argentina were experiencing obviously exploitative labour processes, as an increasing number of firms began to fail, and as workers across the country began to learn of how other workplaces were being taken over and self-managed by their workers, a contagion of workplace recuperations began to emerge by the late 1990s and early 2000s in workplaces that were experiencing some of the most egregious forms of exploitation. From the perspective of workers, such times of micro- or macro-economic crises can reveal the real nature of capitalist production – the exploitation of workers – and the real interests of capital – accumulation and profit-seeking at the expense of workers' wellbeing.

From out of these revelations there can emerge, as with Argentina's ERTs, spontaneous and bottom-up workers' resistances and revolts that may eventually unfold into workers' organised self-activity that fundamentally challenges the capital–labour relation itself. These initially spontaneous or organic working-class resistances and revolts begin to tear through 'previously accepted practices of management control' that now are, to workers, an 'unbearable invasion into [their] lives'.[41] In times of labour peace, it is easier to attribute '[e]very improvement in society' to capital, effectively keeping out of sight its exploitative nature.[42] However, in times of acute macro- or micro-economic crises spawned either by failing markets, contentious anti-labour policies, or broader crises in the capitalist system, the class compromise is put into question and can make workers acutely aware that their dependence 'on particular capitals' is actually vulnerable to the whims of market fluctuations and the

---

39   'So long as trade is good, the capitalist is too much absorbed in money-grubbing to take notice of [the] gratuitous gift of labour [that is, valorisation, surplus-value]. A violent interruption of the labour-process by a crisis makes him sensitively aware of it' (Marx 1967, pp. 206–7).

40   Burawoy 1985.

41   Atzeni 2010, pp. 22–3.

42   Atzeni 2010, p. 23.

capitalist compulsion for profit above all else.[43] 'At different times and places, but continuously', writes Atzeni, workers' struggles 'against the system that is exploiting them' surface, especially during hard economic times. As Atzeni clearly puts it:

> When the impelling need of capitalists for profitability breaks even the illusion of an equal exchange relation, exploitation is revealed. Changes in the workers' everyday working conditions (longer hours, harder work or greater danger), despotic managerial control (less freedom of movement, tighter definition of tasks or separation of workers), reduction of wages and redundancies are some of the forms in which this exploitation is represented.[44]

Certainly, then, not all workers' struggles are about the specific factors that occupy the thoughts and actions of trade unions under normal conditions of class peace, such as pushing up wage rates, improving the conditions at work while preserving capitalist ownership and management structures, and sundry collective bargaining issues. In times when the accustomed forms of work – those that are central to workers' consent and the class compromise – are violated or put at risk by employers or crises in the broader capitalist system, workers can and at times do organise in more extreme ways that see them go far beyond laying down tools or engaging in walkouts, strike threats, or actual strikes. In situations where the accustomed forms of working life are put at risk, a moral economy of work kicks in.[45] As Atzeni goes on to say: 'Workers' struggles are not just about money but also about their conditions as human beings'.[46] At particular conjunctures, workers' struggles can transform into 'a question of freedom against control and authority, the creativity of each individual as against the dehumanization produced by machines and the existence of fully developed human beings as against alienation'.[47]

Such have been the conjunctural roots and characteristics of Argentina's ERTS.

---

43   Atzeni 2010, p. 24.
44   Atzeni 2010, p. 25.
45   For my discussions of ERT protagonists' 'moral economy of work', see this book's Introduction and Chapters 4 and 6.
46   Ibid.
47   Ibid.

3   *Autogestión* and Argentina's ERTs

As I genealogically defined it in Chapter 5, the current struggle in Argentina for *autogestión* is the struggle to *self-organise and self-direct working life cooperatively* as responses to the perpetual crises of (neo-liberal) capital and as alternatives to capitalist work organisation. To *autogestionar* is the verb that delineates how more and more groups throughout Argentina are democratically and ethically reconstituting productive life. *Autogestión*, so crucial for how ERT protagonists conceive of their cooperative work projects, has equally been the key concept framing this book. The concept has assisted us in better understanding ERT protagonists' strategies and tactics of 'occupy, resist, produce'; the cooperativised workplaces they eventually form; the radical social innovations that directly address and begin to move beyond their challenges; and the recuperative moments they unleash.

Under the auspices of *autogestión*, the ERT phenomenon in numerous ways problematises the very notion of wage-labour and the privileging of property rights over not only the right to work, but also the right for workers to self-control their capacities to labour and the products of their labours. In Marxian terms, what Argentina's ERT protagonists fundamentally challenge is the capitalist practice of extracting value from the surplus-labour of workers' expended labour-power. What ERTs' very existence suggests is that to live lives beyond alienation and exploitation necessarily means that working people must struggle to collectively control and own the means of production and the products of their labours by self-directing their productive lives in common. One of the major breakthroughs of the practice of *autogestión* in Argentina, then, is that it begins to open up the social divisions of labour enclosed within capitalist logics of production to other values and practices that lie outside of the profit motive and the compulsion to accumulate. *Autogestión* centres economic life in working people's needs, desires, and collective self-determination. In this respect, Argentina's ERTs share many of the values and practices of the worldwide social and solidarity economy, including the cooperative movement's democratic organisational principles, participatory economics' theories of equitable work-sharing, Kropotkin's ethics of mutual aid, and the everyday bottom-up practices of countless people's collectives that have emerged within the alter-globalisation and anti-capitalist social justice movements in recent years.

Moreover, *autogestión* has made those practising it in Argentina increasingly aware that, on the one hand, any stark separation between 'working life' and 'the rest of life' is a fantasy – human sociability, needs, and desires elide artificial divisions between 'work' and 'the rest of life'. On the other hand, there is also an increasing awareness that the neo-liberal drive to merge capitalist production with the reproduction of life itself is a move by this contemporary form of capital to more totally capture for its projects of accumulation and incessant pursuits of profit the moments that Marx called 'the interval between the buying and the selling'[48] – the spaces of life that had for capital been about 'unproductive consumption'[49] and 'unproductive labour'.[50] The crisis of the neo-liberal model in Argentina has made many workers who were standing on the precipice of permanent structural unemployment realise the emptiness of neo-liberalism's absolutist promises of abundance and wellbeing 'for all' within free markets, unencumbered competition, and perpetual growth. In actuality, they now realise, these 'promises' are not about increasing working people's wellbeing, but rather ideologically driven moves by contemporary capital – especially during hard economic times – to further secure workers' dependence on the system, defend the power base of an elite minority, maximise productivity while minimising labour costs, and assure the socialisation of risk and the privatisation of wealth.

The worker cooperative model is the most effective form of organising ERT protagonists' projects of *autogestión* because it specifically addresses other values and practices, such as caring for one another, horizontality, self-reliance, and equity – values and practices that gradually and immanently grow in the imaginary of ERT workers during the process of fighting for the control of their workplaces, securing their jobs, and ensuring dignified and humane working conditions. The worker cooperative model also symbolically and practically counters the abusive and exploitative relations ERT workers suffered under former bosses. Additionally, the worker cooperative model serves to place a workable organisational framework around ERT protagonists' desires to self-manage their work by, for instance, encouraging each worker member to have an equal say in the running of the recuperated shop. This is most readily visible in the regular workers' assemblies and elected workers' councils that administer ERTs. As well, and due in part to the political lobbying and direct action pressure tactics of ERT protagonists and their self-managed workers' organisations such as MNER, MNFRT, ANTA, and FACTA, the worker cooperative organisational framework has become one of the only recognised legal models in Argentina for former employees to begin to self-manage bankrupted enterprises. Furthermore, the potential for workers' liberation from alienation and exploitation implicit in the worker cooperative form emerges out of the different productive world that it reveals to workers due to its focus on self-reliant

---

48   Marx 1967, p. 155.
49   Marx 1967, p. 573.
50   Marx 1976b, pp. 1038–44.

labour processes grounded in the notions and practices of 'labour hir[ing] capital' (rather than the other way around), 'work' as the common contribution of each member, and 'control linked to work'.[51] In sum, for ERT workers the worker cooperative model most effectively articulates and organises their projects of *autogestión*.

Rather than predetermined blueprints for alternative economic spaces, the notion of 'the labour commons' that Greg de Peuter and Nick Dyer-Witheford introduced to us in Chapter 4 expresses how experiments in *autogestión* can be thought of as emergent, radical, and bottom-up labour and social movements that can arise from workers' organised responses to deep macro-economic crises reverberating onto shop floors. The labour commons is also suggestive of how experiments in *autogestión* can proliferate within 'new economic imaginaries' that incite the creation of more radical and horizontal workplaces in a process akin to what J.K. Gibson-Graham call the 'generative commons'.[52] An open-ended, generative vision of the labour commons recalls the open-ended, under-determined processual 'becoming' of *autogestión* I historicised and theorised in Chapter 5. Here, *autogestión* as labour commons is not a new 'hegemonic imaginary', as Stevphen Shukaitis warns, but rather a generative process of 'developing such spaces with the intent of *creating resources and possibilities to expand and deepen other struggles* as well'.[53] Similarly, Ethan Miller has called for the continual building of a 'wider economic movement' that embraces 'an alternative [solidarity-based] ecosystem ... [that] ... generate[s] interventions at every point in the economic cycle'.[54]

I believe that the possibility for the proliferation of such new economic movements and ecosystems of *autogestión* as labour commons is what is being prefigured by Argentina's ERTs. In assessing throughout this book how ERT protagonists are forging projects for the collective provisioning of their own needs *and* for the production and distribution of social wealth (that is, for broader socio-economic needs), their practices of *autogestión* are, in the spirit of de Peuter and Dyer-Witheford's, Shukaitis', and Miller's rejoinders, beginning to re-imagine a world where bottom-up and community-based practices of cooperative self-provisioning can flourish. In other words and simply put, ERTs map – *prefiguratively* – another socio-economic reality.

---

51 Oakeshott 1990, p. 27; Smith, Chivers, and Goodfellow 1988, p. 25.
52 Gibson-Graham, in de Peuter and Dyer Witheford, 2010, p. 46. See also Lionais and Vieta 2017; and Vieta, 2010b.
53 Shukaitis 2010, p. 72 (emphasis added).
54 Miller, in Miller and Albert 2009, p. 13.

Prefigurative practices of *autogestión*, the reader will recall, chart aspects of a post-capitalist world 'by experimenting with alternatives that develop the seeds of the future in the present society',[55] creating, to paraphrase the constitution of the IWW, the new society out of the shell of the old one.[56] Workers' organisations and self-activity rooted in *autogestión*, as I laid out in Chapters 4 and 5, have prefigurative force for delineating a different socio-economic reality for the future in the present. ERTS, as worker cooperatives – like other historical workers' combinations – are organisations pregnant with possibilities for working-class recomposition, mapping out another life beyond capital.

ERTS, as I have been arguing throughout this book, are imbued with such prefigurations. José Luís Coraggio and María Sol Arroyo's ethnographic analysis of the transformations they witnessed in five ERTS in the Buenos Aires metropolitan area parallels and helps summarise my own findings regarding ERTS' prefigurative force.[57] In struggling to shape new worker cooperatives from out of the ashes of former capitalist firms, ERT workers, Coraggio and Arroyo argue, move from thinking of themselves as mere employees to something more akin to associated producers who place themselves at the centre of a new, infinitely more democratic work life. As I have also discussed often throughout this book, these transformations come about gradually, intersubjectively, and from within the struggle to self-manage their places of work. These transformations unfold as ERT workers involve themselves in working out their challenges collectively by, as Coraggio and Arroyo conceptualise, 'multi-skilling' and 'multitasking'.[58] We can connect their concept of 'multi-skilling' to the new labour processes forged by Argentina's ERTS that we paid attention to in Chapter 8, including: flexible production processes moving beyond alienating capitalist specialisation, adaptable work patterns based on the job at hand, workers taking more breaks throughout the day and eating and socialising together, collective learning practices such as workers teaching each other new skills or mentor–apprentice relationships, and so on. In turn, we can relate 'multitasking' to ERT workers' practices of job sharing and rotation, the use of ad hoc work groups, opening up shop floors to the community, collaborative production processes shared between ERTS or with other cooperatives, and so forth. For Coraggio and Arroyo, as with my findings, these transformations are centred around workers' very responses to the challenges of *autogestión*, which include changes in 'working patterns' that create new, more participative processes of

---

55   Larrabure, Vieta, and Schugurensky 2011, p. 183.
56   IWW 2017, p. 3.
57   Coraggio and Arroyo 2009.
58   Coraggio and Arroyo 2009, p. 146.

production, more directly democratic decision-making processes, and merged 'time-space distances of factory, neighbourhood, home, and work' that, as I have underscored with ERTs' fourth to seventh radical social innovations (see below), 'replace the heteronomy of the capitalist production line and its distance from the life-world'.[59]

ERTs ground their new social and economic practices in *a new moral economy of work* that re-calibrates for its worker-protagonists what should be considered fair, just, and legitimate for their collective efforts and cooperative labour. This new moral economy of work infuses ERTs' radical social innovations and recuperative moments, which we will return to shortly. In sum, the practices of *autogestión* being forged by ERT protagonists prefiguratively sketch out different possibilities for economic and productive life, including:

(1)   the ethics and practices of mutual aid, *compañerismo*, and '*es de todos*' etched right onto shop floors;

(2)   a spirit of collaborative and informal learning amongst workers, both out of need (that is, responding to market demands) and eventually out of their own desires to learn new cooperative skills;

(3)   a greater desire to 'confront social injustice'[60] stemming from ERT workers' own experiences of having suffered injustices;

(4)   a view of self-managed work as 'more dignified', especially because of the 'joint effort' now needed to sustain a cooperative firm;[61] and,

(5)   a changed 'social subjectivity no longer harnessed to capitalist work (pay in exchange for labour) but to a principle of worker solidarity'[62] (cooperative work).

4   Revisiting ERTs' 'Dual Reality'

But, as we have also seen throughout the book, ERTs, as with most worker cooperatives today, still must operate within a capitalist market system and this brings tensions and challenges to ERTs' projects of *autogestión*. ERTs must thus continue to deal with the contradictions inherent to all labour-managed organisations still operating within a capitalist order, as Marx previously pointed out for us in his two-fold view of worker cooperatives. The major factor burdening worker cooperatives such as ERTs that must still operate within capitalist

---

59   Ibid.
60   Coraggio and Arroyo 2009, p. 143.
61   Ibid.
62   Coraggio and Arroyo 2009, p. 147.

markets is rooted in the continued preponderance of the commodity form. As David McNally reminds us, also drawing from Marx's nuanced critique of worker cooperatives:

> [W]hen workers' cooperatives are forced to accumulate in order to meet socially necessary labour-times, which are determined on the market ... workers [are forced] to utilize a quality and quantity of the means of production [to] ensure the market viability of the firm. This is why even workers' cooperatives producing commodities for the market will tend inevitably to 'become their own capitalist' – they will be driven by market competition to accumulate a growing surplus from their own labour in order to invest in new means of production which give them a fighting chance to meet the survival conditions established on the market.[63]

In short, worker cooperatives' drive to 'meet the survival conditions established on the market', as McNally puts it, can transform them into less radical spaces, as I discussed in Chapter 8. The tensions between *autogestión* and the challenges brought on by having to produce commodities for obstinately competitive markets – what I called ERTs' 'dual reality' – get played out in each ERT on a daily basis, creating tensions within and shaping their cooperative labour processes. Indeed, ERTs' many challenges are fundamentally rooted in this dual reality and begin with the exigent conditions out of which most ERTs emerge.

That many worker cooperatives and most workplace takeovers and conversions (such as ERTs) emerge historically as 'children of distress' – that is, as defensive solutions to socio-economic crises[64] – means that, from the get-go, these firms find themselves in situations of economic tenuousness, particularly where capitalist markets remain intact. This economic precariousness pressures workers to 'fix' their firms as quickly as possible so that they can adequately perform and compete with other, usually capitalist firms that have not had to experience such difficulties. As these difficulties persist in the search for consistent inputs for production and for upgrading the labour process within competitive markets, labour-managed firms may continue to struggle to simply stay afloat, which can compromise, stunt, or derail their cooperative reorganisation, values, and social objectives. Striving to overcome these challenges and pressures, labour-managed firms such as ERTs face heightened temptations to reconvert back at some point into firms motivated by profit

---

63   McNally 1993, p. 181.
64   Craig 1993; Bayat 1991; Briscoe and Ward 2005.

maximisation and accumulation, which can overshadow the solidarity and collective values and practices that inspired their creation in the first place.

With Argentina's ERTs, as Gabriel Fajn and Julián Rebón[65] pointed out for us in Chapter 8 (and echoing McNally's assessment), when workers become overwhelmed by the daunting demands of self-management within competitive markets, compensatory tendencies set in. With some Argentine ERTs, these have included: returning to the hierarchical organisation of the original firm, rationalising the labour process, privileging once again technical and marketing skills above other skill sets, increasing work intensity, and reintroducing a new form of authoritarianism rooted in the workers' administrative council that becomes a kind of 'collective foreman'.[66] With some ERTs, these tendencies have led to practices of 'self-exploitation' that have risked returning the cooperative back to an ideology of capitalist technological rationality above other values. As with a handful of ERTs to date, these tendencies have meant returning the firm to former owners, selling it to new owners, or entering into a mixed-model capital–cooperative ownership scheme. In short, beginning to privilege, once again, the maximisation of profits over other social objectives risks reconverting the ERT into the primarily capitalist labour process that its workers had originally contested.

It is important to note here, as I argued in Chapters 4 and 5, that the issue of course is not with the validity of workers' control of the means of production. Indeed, the return of the means of production to workers organised in association is a crucial step in any socialist vision that aspires towards the fundamental transformation of society beyond capitalist divisions of labour and circuits of production and exchange. More pragmatically, as the literature showed us in Chapters 5–7, worker cooperatives and other forms of labour-managed firms have proven to be viable, efficacious, and even 'efficient' ways of organising the production of socially useful goods and services. But, as with Argentina today, the real issue still stymieing a more complete social transformation of society, even with the promising successes of the ERT phenomenon and other social and solidarity economy experiments, rests with *the continued presence of the political economic structures that enable the commodity form and competitive capitalist markets*. As McNally explains it: 'the key issue' blocking a true socialist transformation lies in the stubborn continuation of a system that still supports the commodity form and the buying and selling of labour-power under the abstractions of socially necessary labour-times.[67] The continuation

---

65   Fajn and Rebón 2005.
66   For a related analysis by Marx, see Marx 1981, pp. 511, 571; and also Marx 1978a, 1978b.
67   McNally 1993, p. 181.

of this economic system guarantees that even worker cooperatives will always live in a tension that may include 'the compulsion to competitive accumulation which entails the domination of living labour by dead labour – something which can occur even within a worker-managed firm producing for exchange'.[68]

It is true that Argentina has been nowhere close to transforming into a directly democratic, socialist, or workers' society where the actual producers decide what, how, and when to produce socially useful products at a societal level (rather than the market 'deciding'), and where there does not exist a market for wage-labour. This is especially so with the wave of neo-liberal policies reintroduced with vigour by the government of Mauricio Macri after coming to power in December 2015. Nevertheless, the ERT phenomenon *is* showing ways – prefiguratively – that a cooperatively inspired and worker-centred social transformation could take place, one workplace at a time. And perhaps the ERT phenomenon shows how this transformation can gradually emerge in a manner that does not rely on a party led by 'the vanguard', or await the 'total revolution', but that is instead guided by smaller pockets of change eventually fanning out contagiously as more and more workspaces become autonomously run workers' collectives, engrained tightly within their neighbourhoods and communities. This transformation can begin to emerge, in other words, in the gradual proliferation of workplaces where control is linked to work, where work is not based on hired wage-labour, and where workers and communities are 'associated' in the productive enterprise as members and co-owners of the labour process and the means of production therein.

The possibilities for this social transformation are solidly grounded in ERTs' prefigurative force. It is a force that I believe in many ways echoes the proposals of modern socialism's stream of self-determination and the radical theories of *autogestión* reviewed in some detail in Part 2 of this book. ERTs' prefigurative force particularly reverberates with the key things that are at stake in their projects of *autogestión*: the reclamation of social labour for the production of social wealth; the recovery of workers' control of what, how, and when to produce; and, ultimately, the recuperation of working people's autonomy over their *time* – time for work to satisfy needs *and* time to dedicate to life's other pursuits, aspirations, and passions.[69] Indeed, in many ways ERTs bring to the surface and even begin to make possible the other side of Marx's critique of cap-

---

68   Ibid.

69   '[F]ree time, *disposable time*', was for Marx 'wealth itself'. In disposable time Marx saw the possibility for human self-development, 'partly for the enjoyment of the product, partly for free activity which – unlike labour – is not dominated by the pressure of an extraneous purpose which must be fulfilled' (Marx 1969, p. 860).

italist production – the side that underscores the normative and liberational hopes that drove much of his writing and that is echoed in the other side of ERTS' dual reality:

> Labour-time, even if exchange-value is eliminated, always remains the creative substance of wealth and the measure of the cost of its production. But free time, disposable time, is wealth itself, partly for the enjoyment of the product, partly for free activity which – unlike labour – is not dominated by the pressure of an extraneous purpose which must be fulfilled, and the fulfilment of which is regarded as a natural necessity or a social duty ... It is self-evident that *if labour-time is reduced* to a normal length and, furthermore, [if] *labour is no longer performed for someone else*, but for myself, and, at the same time, [if] the social contradictions between master and men [sic] ... [are] abolished, *it acquires a quite different, a free character, it becomes real social labour,* and finally *the basis of disposable time* – the labour of a man who has also disposable time, must be of a much higher quality than [labour is in capitalist modes of production, where it resembles a] ... beast of burden.[70]

In sum, it is not easy for workers to attempt to rebuild and reconfigure a broken company within a capitalist system, especially given the financial and production challenges that still plague many ERTs, the stubborn market competition they must still face, and a state that remains, on the whole, indifferent and even antagonistic to their plight. But, despite their challenges, ERTs begin to forge a different world, or, at minimum, point to the possible socio-economic dimensions that such a world could embrace. With ERTs, this possible world is prefigured in their radical social innovations and recuperative moments that emerge organically and immanently as they carry out their projects of *autogestión*.

5   Revisiting ERTS' Radical Social Innovations and Recuperative Moments

Throughout this book, we learned that ERT protagonists co-create seven *radical social innovations* that delineate their projects of *autogestión*. These radical social innovations, as I introduced early on in this study, include both new

---

70   Marx 1969, p. 860.

processes of socialised and cooperativised production and new *outcomes* of social wealth generation. Moreover, they directly address ERTs' myriad challenges while beginning to prefiguratively move beyond capital–labour relations. ERTs' radical social innovations, I believe, should provide much inspiration for workers facing growing job losses, business closures, and the perpetual socio-economic challenges and crises of the global neo-liberal order. To recall, ERTs' seven radical social innovations include:

(1) The mobilisation of direct action strategies and the re-forging of workplace solidarity in order for workers to keep their jobs and safeguard their places of work via the occupation of the firms that had been employing them and their subsequent pursuit of self-managed production.

(2) The ongoing lobbying of the political and legal establishments, the re-appropriation and reform of extant laws, and the application of cooperative values in order to reconstitute ERTs' work and begin to consolidate their projects of *autogestión*.

(3) The re-incorporation of working-class organising strategies between ERTs and between ERTs and the community in order to collectively respond to their production, financial, and legal challenges and begin to create a new organised labour environment that extends beyond traditional union strategies and tactics.

(4) The redefinition of social production as ERT workers democratise the labour process, reclaim their surpluses and, ultimately, contest notions of surplus-value, surplus-labour, and worker alienation, even as they produce in part for capitalist markets.

(5) The recomposition of working-class subjectivities and multidimensional skills via informal learning processes such as shop floor apprenticing and the sharing of expertise and knowledge.

(6) The production and redistribution of social wealth that inwardly open up workplaces to the communities and neighbourhoods that surround them and, in the process, strengthen the social value of ERTs.

(7) The reclamation and redistribution of portions of workers' surpluses for outward community development, and their engagement in economies of solidarity with other cooperatives, ERTs, and community organisations.

As I first presented in the Introduction, these seven radical social innovations can be condensed into the following four overarching social innovations: (1) *responding collectively and creatively* to socio-economic crises, intensive market competition, and financial and production challenges; (2) *embracing practices of direct democracy* that, at the level of the firm, re-contour a work organisation's governance and decision-making; (3) *re-rationalising labour processes and divisions of labour* in such a way that ERTs reconstruct workplaces horizontally, humanise work, and return surpluses to workers and local communities; and (4) *nurturing tight bonds of solidarity* that open up workplaces to the community, extend them out territorially into the community, and can be co-created between workers, different ERTs, surrounding communities, and other groups struggling for socio-economic justice in Argentina. Taken together, ERTs' radical social innovations revitalise social and economic life by reclaiming productive entities for workers and the community and rediscovering, producing, and redistributing social wealth.

Rearticulating ERTs' seven radical social innovations into these four overarching dimensions of social innovation helps us, in turn, grasp ERT protagonists' six key *recuperative moments*. As I elaborated on in detail in Chapter 4 and implicitly throughout the book, these moments of recuperation are spread across the usually long road of occupying failing workplaces, resisting repression from the state or returning owners, struggling for legal recognition, and beginning production under the auspices of *autogestión*. They are, in other words, moments that deeply mark the paths of occupy, resist, produce – the processes through which workers begin to liberate their living labour from the constraints of the capital–labour relation and take back for themselves vital characteristics of their productive and creative capacities. These six recuperative moments are:

(1)   the recuperation of the creative skills inherent to workers' *labour-power*;
(2)   the recuperation of workers' *surpluses*;
(3)   the recuperation of workers' expansive powers of production in *voluntary cooperation* (that is, 'associated labour'), forged by workplace solidarity in the labour process;
(4)   the recuperation of *the labour process* in general;
(5)   the recuperation of *the division of labour*; and
(6)   the recuperation of *social production* for producing *social wealth*.

Perhaps the reader has been questioning my claims for these six recuperative moments, arguing that ERT workers cannot take back these things since they did not possess them before being a part of an ERT. The reader might further add that it is actually the 'entrepreneurial' capitalist that invests in, organises, mobilises, and even innovates these things. So, this sceptical reader might ask, how is it that workers are *recuperating* them? Let me address this question by recapping Marx's twofold analysis of labour in capitalism and, specifically, the unique nature of the commodity labour-power.

Certainly, in partial agreement with this sceptical reader, when workers sign on to become employees – that is, when they sell their labour-power by agreeing to take a wage from the owners of the means of production in compensation for the deployment of their labouring capacities over the working day – they sell (or, perhaps more accurately, 'lease' or 'hire out') their productive and creative capacities. In doing so, workers can be seen to 'choose' to relinquish full autonomy and control over their productivity and creativity. When workers become employees they also forsake their rights to directly control, benefit from, or use the products they have created (unless buying them back on open markets as commodities). Finally, workers, as employees, forsake full claims to the surpluses they have helped to create.

To be clear, then, I agree that in the capitalist system of production the direct producers *renounce control over* their labour-power, surpluses, cooperation in the labour process, the labour process itself, the division of labour, and the ultimate wealth they create. However, this renunciation is not total. To renounce control over these things is, rather, a legal issue. Since workers' labour-power is embodied in them, and since they are not slaves, workers 'own' their labour-power and are thus 'free' to sell this commodity and can thus decide to enter a contractual agreement with the purchaser of this commodity and cede to this purchaser control over its deployment, how much of it will be deployed, under what conditions, and the outcomes of its deployment. More precisely, then, in the standard capitalist employment agreement that underwrites wage-labour, workers give up the *legal right* to self-determine what, when, where, and how to produce throughout the working day for the duration of the contract. It is a 'right' that, as Marx points out, underscores the 'double sense' of 'free' as regards 'free labourer[s]' in the capitalist system: Workers are at once free to 'dispose' of their labour-power as their 'own commodity' *and* free from possessing any other consequential commodities to sell save for their labour-power.[71] What are the consequences of this 'right' for 'free' labourers in the capitalist mode of production? Compelled to work for a wage in order to provide for their necessities, when the direct producers are at work for the capitalist they become *separated* from (that is, lose control over) key aspects of their very humanity, including: their human associations, the raw materials transformed in their acts of working, the products of their labour, and their creativity for self-development (that is, their 'species being').[72] Indeed, the young Marx's theory of alienation rests precisely on these four crucial separations, and these separations are at the heart of social relations in the capital–labour nexus.

But these separations are never totally consummated; the capital–labour relation is, after all, a social relation situated in class struggle. Separation (or ali-

---

71　Marx 1967, pp. 168–9.

72　Or 'humanity's capacity to transform itself through intentional social activity', including 'the cooperative organization of labour' (Dyer-Witheford 2006, p. 17).

enation, estrangement) from these things within the capitalist framework does not mean that waged-workers completely lose or absolutely give up their productive and creative *capacities* and *potential*. Indeed, the commodity labour-power that is purchased by the capitalist at the price of the wage is constituted precisely by our very creative capacities and the potential to put these capacities to work. In this exchange, workers do not completely surrender their entire bodies and lives to capital. Even under the real subsumption of labour to capital, the potential and actual capacities of our bodies and minds to be productive and to create socially useful things – that is, to create social wealth – remain aspects of our humanness that we continue to corporeally possess and still, to some degree, wilfully direct, despite what the capitalist ideology of private property and contract law might stipulate. Moreover, to reiterate what I argued in Chapter 4, the six things recuperated by ERT workers – labour-power, surpluses, cooperation, the labour process, the division of labour, and the capacity to create social wealth collectively – are certainly *not* capitalist inventions; they are, rather, first and foremost embodied in living labour and emerge out of the capacities of human beings as creative beings.

Thus, *when workers recuperate a capitalist firm where they had been employed and eventually self-manage it cooperatively*, two things happen simultaneously: Workers put into sharp relief what is at stake in their struggles against capital, and they *take back* – for themselves and for their collective control – *their* labour-power, *their* surpluses, *their* capacities to cooperate, *their* labour processes, *their* divisions of labour, and, ultimately, the wealth *they* have created in common. These are all critical aspects of workers' very humanity as social beings that they had once legally surrendered to capital when they signed the wage-labour contract. In these recuperative moments, ERT workers also implicitly renounce the basic assumptions of the wage-labour contract and begin to move beyond capital–labour social relations. In other words, ERT workers most fundamentally contest the following rules and ideologies of capitalism: that others should dictate when, where, what, and how workers are to produce; that part of the working day of the direct producers should go to enriching the non-producers; that private ownership of the means of production is the most effective way of provisioning for life's needs and wants; and that competition is part of human nature and guarantees efficient production and the wellbeing of all. In sum, ERTs' six recuperative moments at once embrace the most obvious things that their workers recover – jobs, tools, machines, workplaces – while also suggesting that they recuperate much more in the process: *In their direct actions and in their subsequent projects of* autogestión, *ERT worker-protagonists most vitally unleash the recuperation of key aspects of what it means to be fuller, more complete human beings creating socially useful things and social wealth in association.*

6   Revisiting the Definition of Argentina's *Empresas Recuperadas por sus Trabajadores*

As we saw in Chapters 2, 4, and 5, workers' occupations and takeovers of firms are not new and have recurred throughout the historical development of capitalism. With a few exceptions, however, as we also saw in Chapters 2 and 5, earlier experiences with workplace occupations in other historical conjunctures did not become ERTs as we know them today.[73] Historically, instances of workplace occupations by workers have tended to be centred on union tactics occurring over short periods of time in the pursuit of bargaining demands; occasional and dispersed responses by workers to mass redundancies, restructurings, or firm closures; or carried out in support of other political ends and led by vanguardist parties or nationalist policies in particular periods of revolutionary fervour or turbulent socio-political circumstances. Instead, what we know today as *empresas recuperadas por sus trabajadores* more resemble the historical establishment of worker cooperatives or collectives in other historical conjunctures during periods of downward economic cycles or deeper socio-political crises of the extant capitalist system. Next to other contemporary Latin American experiences with ERTs that we reviewed in Chapter 2, similar surges in conversions to worker cooperatives as solutions to the growing rate of unemployment and economic crisis occurred with the Industrial Common Ownership Movement (ICOM) in the United Kingdom during its deep economic recessions in the late 1970s and early 1980s,[74] or with the conversions of troubled workplaces to cooperatives in Italy, Spain, and France in the 1970s and 1980s.[75]

But something undoubtedly different has also transpired with the surge of ERTs in Argentina and elsewhere today as compared to the growth in worker cooperatives and workplace occupations in other historical conjunctures. Today's ERT phenomenon is, in a nutshell, a working-class experience responding to a particular historical moment and socio-economic situation characterised by a hegemonic neo-liberal political and economic order in perpetual crisis in semi-industrialised or industrialised national or regional contexts with tradi-

---

73   Two historical exceptions here akin to today's ERTs might include the experiences of the Paris Commune of 1871 and the anarchist communes and collectives of revolutionary Spain in 1936. For short periods in both cases, the takeovers of factories, shops, and public services by the working class transitioned firms into communal and democratically organised enterprises. However, the deep connections of these two earlier experiences to specific revolutionary aims and broader socio-political transformations, together with their brief existence, differentiate them from today's ERTs.

74   Melnyk 1985; Oakeshott, 1990; Vieta, Quarter, Spear, and Moskovskaya 2016.

75   Vieta, Depedri, and Carrano 2017; Zevi, Zanotti, Soulage, and Zelaia 2011.

tions of cooperativism or bottom-up labour militancy. In turn, Argentina's ERT phenomenon is distinguished from ERT experiences in other national contexts in the following ways: it includes the largest number of worker cooperatives in the world emerging from the conversion of capitalist firms in crisis; it is widespread, including firms in multiple economic sectors and throughout the entire national territory; it is not strongly affiliated with traditional or established political parties; it tends not to be closely aligned with traditional union bureaucracies; it has an ambivalent relationship with the state, at once lobbying it for better support and using extant laws pragmatically while forging new federations of self-managed workplaces and affinities with broader social and solidarity economy initiatives that are also antagonistic to the state-capitalist order; and it is populated by surprisingly long-lasting experiments in workers' control that, in almost all cases, transform troubled capitalist firms into viable solidarity-based cooperatives with strong links to the communities where they are located.

Most promisingly, Argentina's ERTs have been inspiring new 'economic imaginaries'[76] in their radical and socially innovative practices of *autogestión*, which include: almost across-the-board transformations of shop floors via horizontal and egalitarian labour processes; workers' direct and unmediated control of their creative and productive capacities, thus de-commodifying their labour-power; and the socialisation of wealth via widespread inclusion of affinity projects with other social movements and surrounding communities. The new cooperativism taken up by ERTs – a cooperativism that both responds directly to macro- and micro-economic crises and that dramatically converts a capitalist firm into a community focused, labour-managed one – is the direct outcome of what their worker-protagonists recuperate and transform. Thus, while we can, on the one hand, definitively say that ERTs are inextricably linked to the long history of workers' struggles for control of their working lives, on the other hand we can also point to aspects of today's ERTs that suggest new forms of working-class self-activity that directly respond to the distresses experienced by working people in the 'regime of production'[77] under the neo-liberal system of capitalism.

Now, then, at the end of our journey and from the evidence provided by the lived experiences of ERT protagonists articulated in their own words throughout this book, we can more precisely define Argentina's ERTs as follows:

---

76 Gibson-Graham 2006, pp. xix–xxxvii.

77 Recall from Chapter 3 that production regimes are regimes of regulation that affect the point of production, including how economic, social, and political dimensions resonate in the labour process (see also Burawoy 1985).

(1)   ERTs are formerly investor- or privately-owned capitalist businesses taken over and reopened by embattled former employees after either risky occupations or confrontations with former owners or with the juridical-political establishment. These actions are motivated by, at first, workers' fears and desperation at having to face the closure of their workplaces and falling into the ranks of the structurally unemployed.

(2)   ERTs overwhelmingly become worker cooperatives redesigned by workers along the lines of extremely flat, or horizontal, production processes, and almost all to some degree take up governance structures guided by one worker, one vote direct democracy via workers' councils and workers' assemblies.

(3)   Unlike most traditional cooperative practices, ERT worker cooperatives are distinguished by a predominance of near across-the-board egalitarian remuneration schemes despite variations in worker seniority or skill sets.

(4)   ERTs endeavour, as much as they can and where possible, to not replicate the management hierarchy and exploitative practices of the former firm they have emerged from.

(5)   Many ERTs open up their workspaces to the community or engage in outwardly focused community economic development, intimately embracing the seventh principle of cooperativism – 'concern for community'.

And finally,

(6)   these five characteristics at once emerge out of and directly address ERTs' legal, production, financial, and other challenges, interplaying intimately with their protagonists' conceptualisations and practices of *autogestión*.

Of course, other worker cooperatives in other conjunctures have encompassed one or more of these features. But overall, and in the context of the waxing and waning neo-liberal conjuncture from which Argentina's ERTs emerge, the pervasiveness of these characteristics in almost all of the country's ERTs also mark them as unique experiences in the history of working-class struggles against capital. I believe this book has provided ample evidence for maintaining this assertion, beginning with the three stories of recuperating workplaces highlighted in Chapter 1 and the subsequent empirical evidence detailed in Chapters 2 and 6–8. In these chapters, I sought to underscore how *autogestión* is being lived and practised in Argentina's ERTs. Most astounding, I believe, has been ERTs' longevity as self-managed productive entities and as a movement, as well as their protagonists' innovative zeal in forging new forms of work and social relations in spite of the many challenges they face along the path to a collectively self-determined life.

7   Closing Thoughts, Continued Openings

Guided by the concept of *autogestión* and organised as worker cooperatives, Argentina's ERTs exemplify innovative ways in which working people can reconceptualise work so as to directly address and cut paths through the instability and inequalities wrought by the global neo-liberal system. They offer viable community-based alternatives to business and economic restructuring, firm closures, under- and unemployment, and assistentialist welfare schemes. At core, ERTs articulate ways of moving beyond the capital–labour relation, illustrating for working people how to overturn the power vested in employers to determine the working conditions and life circumstances of employees. The ERT phenomenon is also modelling for Argentina's historically precarious political economy alternative forms of socio-economic relations within a broader social and solidarity economy. ERTs model these new socio-economic relations via the solidary economic networks they forge with surrounding communities and in their socialised forms of production, including sharing customer orders, prime materials, technological know-how, and even machinery and labour processes between workplaces that practice infinitely more horizontalised and egalitarian labour processes when contrasted with capitalist firms. Most importantly, these alternative socio-economic relations are pointing to worker-led paths beyond recurrent macro-economic crises. Rooted deeply in the neighbourhoods and communities where they are located, ERTs rely more on the principle of subsidiarity – intimately engaging in production practices that privilege the local – rather than in the globalised and financialised capitalist system that is inherently unresponsive and even detrimental to local needs.

Indeed, the case of Argentina's ERTs should be of particular interest to all working people affected by and suffering from the ill effects of the global neo-liberal economic order and its state-led austerity measures promulgated by undemocratic international financial institutions. Neo-liberalism's ill effects, well known by now, include: environmental degradation leading to devastated communities, depleted resources, and climate change; the intractable presence of stark inequality created by the brazen hoarding of wealth; stubbornly high rates of underemployment, unemployment, and poverty; and lingering precarious life conditions for millions around the world. Not just the plight of the global South, these circumstances, of course, are planetary and have also been intensifying in the global North. In the so-called 'developed' or 'advanced' capitalist economies, the ills of neo-liberalism for working people over the past 40 years have come in no small way from their growing entanglements with financialised global capital.[78] Some of the ways that these entanglements in

---

78   Albo, Gindin, and Panitch 2010.

the global North are most existentially felt in everyday life include: the decline of real wages and dwindling employment prospects (as jobs are increasingly outsourced or automated out of existence), an over-reliance on consumerism fuelled by the easy availability of personal credit (as panacea to both the loss of purchasing power and to rising psychological angst and social isolation), the erosion of old-age security via the financialisation of workers' pension plans and the privatisation of health care, skyrocketing housing costs, and foreclosures on excessively mortgaged homes.

Argentina's ERTs teach us that the remedies for these socio-economic ills can be found in delinking working people's lives from the prerogatives of global capital and wage-labour and reconnecting them back to each other and their local communities through the creation of new cooperatives and the expansion of social and solidarity economies. Rather than competing for limited jobs, or remaining in unfulfilling ones, working people can come together via their collective energies and pooled resources and create their own jobs in new worker cooperatives, or propose buying out or converting troubled or shuttered firms into cooperatives or social enterprises. Argentina's ERTs and ERT experiences throughout the global South and North are increasingly showing that such worker- and community-led solutions are possible and viable.

Indeed, workers taking over and self-managing workplaces in trouble are not just experiences of the global South, as we saw in Chapter 2. Recall, for instance, the case of workplace sit-ins during the Great Depression in the United States; the worker takeover and self-management of the LIP factory in France and the factory sit-ins and subsequent ICOM movement in the UK in the early 1970s; or the US's and Canada's conversions of steel mills, paper mills, and workplaces in other sectors since at least the 1940s. Or take the more recent conversion of Republic Windows and Doors by its workers to the New Era Windows Cooperative in Chicago, or the new wave of conversions of failing firms in Italy, Spain, France, Greece, and South Korea in recent years. It is worth reiterating that in the global North, worker buyouts of firms have been legally possible in Canada, the US, and in numerous European countries for decades; a fact that, given recent experiences with austerity and socio-economic crises, surprisingly remains virtually unknown to most workers and the population at-large and inadequately addressed by policymakers, business pundits, economists, and intellectual and political leaders. Inspired by Argentine ERTs' re-appropriation and use of national expropriation laws, US labour sociologist and political scientist Peter Ranis has even gathered compelling case study evidence mapping out the legal precedents in the US for municipalities and states to deploy 'eminent domain' laws for converting shuttered or troubled firms to worker cooperatives.[79] Though the possibilities of labour-managed firms emerging in the global North *en masse* as workers' responses to recent crises or industry restructuring and outsourcing has to be looked at in light of each conjunctural particularity, worker- and community-led conversions of firms into worker coops in developed industrial economies such as Canada, the United States, and throughout Europe are not as far-fetched as neo-liberal ideologues or sceptics might have one believe.[80]

I believe the most crucial thing that the protagonists of Argentina's *empresas recuperadas* teach us – and I have attempted to show this in some detail in this book – is that working people *can* forge an alternative reality for their working and non-working lives; *can* overcome situations of socio-economic crises, industrial restructuring, and exploitation on their own terms; and *can*, in the process of securing their livelihoods by self-managing their places of work, begin to recuperate key aspects of their very humanity and dignity. The alternatives ERT workers begin to recuperate are actually assets and capacities that already exist and remain alive within each of us and in every community, latently present in our very human capacities to creatively produce useful things *cooperatively*. And this, as I have implicitly argued, is even the case as workers continue to toil away as wage-labourers. By experimenting with *autogestión* and putting into play the possibilities it opens up for both confronting micro- and macro-economic crises and reinventing productive life on the basis of more cooperative and directly democratic principles and practices, ERTs are pointing to viable paths for workers to take back self-determination of and control over their own skills, labour-power, surpluses, labour processes, and ultimately their own *time* (which is, after all, true wealth, as Marx reminds us).

ERT workers' everyday practices of *autogestión* and their promising radical social innovations are, while emergent and always in tension with the capitalist system that surrounds them, living testimonies of a commitment to another, less exploitative and less alienating mode of productive life. Most inspirational to me are the many personal testimonies I have had the privilege of hearing in hundreds of conversations I have had with ERT workers since 2005. Significantly, ERT protagonists I have spoken with have told me time and time again that they would not go back to the exploitative working conditions they previously experienced when working for bosses, even despite the long struggles needed to achieve *autogestión* in Argentina. This is the case, most insisted, even

---

79 Ranis 2007, 2014, 2016.
80 In this regard, see the arguments provided by DuRand 2016; Ranis 2016; Schweickart 1996, 2011, 2012; Vieta et al. 2017; Malleson 2014; and Wolff 2012.

if their salaries or wages were to increase with an employer and, most surprising to me early on in my research, despite the many challenges to material security that the pursuit of *autogestión* continues to entail in Argentina.

We can better understand what ERTs prefigure if we think about what exactly it is that their worker-progatonists recuperate. This is, ultimately, what I have attempted to do in this book. In thinking through ERT protagonists' recuperative moments and radical social innovations, we begin to see the *other world* that is emerging with their projects of *autogestión* – slowly perhaps, in suggestive hues and outlines maybe, not without contradictions certainly, yet nevertheless emerging. This other world that ERTs suggest is not-yet-here entirely, but palpable nonetheless. It is a world rich with other potential arrangements for meeting our social, economic, and cultural needs and desires.

Appendix: Formal Interviews Conducted, Meetings Attended, and Cooperatives Visited

Key informants	Organization and role	Interview dates
Mario Alberto Barrios	Former President, Coop. Unión Solidaria de Trabajadores (ERT); President, Asociación Nacional de Trabajadores Autogestionados; Executive Committee member, Central de Trabajadores de la Argentina	April 2007 August 2009 August 2017
Diego Ledezma	President, Coop. Unión Solidaria de Trabajadores (ERT)	August 2009 August 2017
Oscar Barrios	Member, Coop. Unión Solidaria de Trabajadores (ERT)	July 2007 August 2009
Pablo Rolandi	Employee (by choice), Coop. Unión Solidaria de Trabajadores (ERT)	August 2009 August 2017
Maximiliano 'Maxi' Rodríguez	Member, Coop. Unión Solidaria de Trabajadores (ERT)	July 2009
Juán Vera	Member, Coop. Unión Solidaria de Trabajadores (ERT)	August 2009
Matías Perralta	Member, Coop. Unión Solidaria de Trabajadores (ERT)	August 2009
Carlos Mamud	Member, Coop. Unión Solidaria de Trabajadores (ERT)	August 2009
Claudia Álvarez	Professor, Teoría y Práctica de la Economía Social, Universidad Nacional de Quilmes; Director of the university extension program Trabajo Autogestionado between Universidad Nacional de Quilmes and UST	December 2009
Fermín González	Member, Coop. Chilavert (ERT)	July 2005a August 2005b August 2009
Cándido González	Member, Coop. Chilavert (ERT)	July 2005a August 2005b August 2005c July 2007
Plácido Peñarrieta	President, Coop. Chilavert (ERT); President Coop. Red Gráfica	July 2005 September 2009 August 2017
Jorge Luján Gutierrez	Member, Coop. Chilavert (ERT)	August 2005
Hector Francisco Gamboa	Member, Coop. Chilavert (ERT)	August 2005
Walter Basualdo	Member, Coop. Chilavert (ERT)	August 2005
Manuel Basualdo	Member, Coop. Chilavert (ERT)	August 2005
Daniel Suárez	Member, Coop. Chilavert (ERT)	August 2005
Martín Cossarini	Member, Coop. Chilavert (ERT)	August 2005
Raúl Herrera	Member, Coop. Chilavert (ERT)	September 2009
Belén Ludovico	Intern, Coop. Chilavert (ERT)	August 2005

(cont.)

Key informants	Organization and role	Interview dates
Ernesto González	Member, Coop. Chilavert (ERT)	August 2009 August 2017
José López	Former President, Coop. Salud Junín (ERT)	July 2007 July 2009
Alejandro Torres	Treasurer, Coop. Salud Junín (ERT)	August 2009
Ana María Barri-onuevo	Member, Coop. Salud Junín (ERT)	August 2009
Edith Allende	Member, Coop. Salud Junín (ERT)	August 2009
Esteban Torletti	President, Coop. Salud Junín (ERT)	August 2017
Javier De Pascuale	Former President, Coop. Comercio y Justícia (ERT)	July 2009
Eduardo Martín	Member, Comercio y Justícia (ERT)	July 2009
Mario Rodriquez	Member, Comercio y Justícia (ERT)	July 2009
Daniel 'Dante' Aguirre	Member, Comercio y Justícia (ERT)	July 2009
Carolina Klepp	Member, Comercio y Justícia (ERT)	July 2009
Aracely Maldonado	Member, Comercio y Justícia (ERT)	July 2009
Gustavo Ojeda	President, Grafíco Patricios (ERT)	August 2005
Edith Oviedo	President, Cefomar (ERT)	August 2005
Jorge Bevilaqua	Federación Argentina de Cooperativas de Trabajadores Autogestionados (FACTA)	September 2009
Eduardo Murúa	Member, IMPA (ERT); former President, Movimiento Nacional de Empresas Recuperadas (MNER)	July 2005a July 2005b June 2006 February 2007 July 2009
Julio Tomada	President, Asamblea Barrial "Pompeya"	July 2005
Eduardo Amorín	Trabajo y Autogestión (ERT support organization)	August 2009
Soledad Guerriere	Trabajo y Autogestión (ERT support organization)	August 2009
Andrés Ruggeri	Director, Programa Facultad Abierta Universidad de Buenos Aires and Centro de Documentación de Empresas Recuperadas	August 2005 March 2006
Natalia Polti	Coordinator, Programa Facultad Abierta, Universidad de Buenos Aires and Centro de Documentación de Empresas Recuperadas	September 2009
Santiago Luzain	Researcher and policy analyst, Centro Cultural de la Cooperación 'Floreal Gorini'	July 2009
Verónica Montes	Co-director, Tecnicatura en Cooperativas program, Universidad de La Plata	September 2009
Alicia Ressel	Co-director, Tecnicatura en Cooperativas program, Universidad de La Plata	September 2009
Julián Almadoraggione	Cooperative developer and student, Tecnicatura en Cooperativas, Universidad de La Plata	September 2009
Martín Guerrero	Cooperative developer and student, Tecnicatura en Cooperativas, Universidad de La Plata	September 2009
José Luís Coraggio	Director, Maestría en Economía Social, Universidad Nacional General San Martin	August 2009

(cont.)

Key informants	Organization and role	Interview dates
Francoise Blanc	Community activist and student, Maestría en Economía Social, Universidad Nacional General San Martin	August 2009
Carlos La Serna	Director, Instituto de Investigación y Formación en Administración Pública, Universidad Nacional de Córdoba	July 2009
Sandra Gallardo	Researcher and funding lead for support programs for cooperatives and self-managed workplaces, Ministerio de Producción, Province of Buenos Aires	August 2009
Cristián Wertmuller	Director of support programs for cooperatives and self-managed workplaces, Ministerio de Producción, Province of Buenos Aires	August 2009
Jorge Suarez	Government lawyer, Autonomous City of Buenos Aires	July 2005
José Roselli	National Senator of Argentina	August 2005
Susana Berasatián	Programa Trabajo Autogestionado, Ministerio de Trabajo, Argentina	July 2005
Hector Palomino	Director, Estudios en Relaciones del Trabajo, Ministerio de Trabajo, Argentina; Professor, Cátedra de Relaciones del Trabajo, Facultad de Ciencias Sociales, Universidad de Buenos Aires	July 2009 August 2009
Pablo Pozzi	Professor, Cátedra de Historia Oral, Facultad de Filosofía y Letras, Universidad de Buenos Aires	August 2005
Mario Hernandez	Bachillerato Popular Darío Santillán	August 2017

Focus group		Date conducted
	Autogestión y Trabajo (various members)	August 2009

Meetings attended and recorded		Date attended
	Programa Facultad Abierta, Facultad de Filosofía y Letras, Univesidad de Buenos Aires	Numerous meetings attended between 2005 and 2017
	Movimiento Nacional de Empresas Recuperadas (MNER) assemblies	July 2005 August 2005 February 2007 August 2009
	IMPA assembly	August 2009
	Hotel BAUEN/FACTA meeting	July 2009
	ANTA assemblies	July 2009 August 2009
	Joint ANTA-MNER assembly	August 2009
	CNCT assembly	August 2009

(cont.)

Other ERTs and cooperatives visited	Date visited
Cooperativa Patricios (ERT)	July 2005
	August 2005
	February 2007
	August 2009
Cooperativa 'La Juanita' (educational and community development cooperative founded by former *piqueteros*)	July 2005
Cooperativa La Nueva Esperanza/Global (ERT)	August 2009
Cooperativa Vallese (ERT)	July 2009
Cooperativa Hotel BAUEN (ERT)	July 2009
	August 2009
Cooperativa 'La Cacerola'	August 2009
	December 2016
	August 2017
Cooperativa IMPA (ERT)	August 2009
Complejo de Vivienda Monteagudo, Movimiento de Liberación Territorial (MTL)	August 2009
Cooperativa Alé Alé (ERT)	August 2017
Cooperativa Téxtiles Pigüé (ERT)	August 2017
Bachillerato Popular Darío Santillán	August 2017

Glossary of Spanish and Other Foreign Terms and Phrases

Ablandar   To soften. The tactic of politically 'softening' politicians, lawyers, and judges by lobbying or mobilising near or occupying the offices of politicians and judges or the country's legislative houses or courts, in order to sway decisions or legislation in favour of the group doing the lobbying or mobilising. This is an old practice in Argentine labour and social movement history.

Aguinaldo   The extra month's pay – or 'the thirteenth month' – given to employees in many Argentine firms in the formal economy around Christmas.

Argentinazo, el   Moniker for the massive social uprisings and economic and political upheavals throughout Argentina that took place on 19 and 20 December 2001.

Asambleas barriales   Neighbourhood assemblies

Asistencialismo   Assistentialism. The critical term used in Argentina to encompass an array of state-driven policies of social welfare delivery linked to containing social unrest and building a political coalition for the party in power by addressing the demands of popular sectors via co-optive strategies.

Autogestión   Self-management

Avenida (Av.)   Avenue

Bachillerato popular   Literally 'popular high school'. A popular education-based, cooperatively run high school equivalency and K-12 education program that has emerged in conjunction with the ERT movement and that is run out of several ERTs across Argentina.

Barrio   Neighbourhood

Bien común   Common good, as in 'for the good of the community', also related to the commons and being in community with others.

Bombilla   The metal straw used to sip *mate* throughout the Southern Cone region of South America.

Calle   Street

Cartoneros   Colloquial name for the cardboard recyclers in Argentina's urban centres that emerged as a consequence of the massive unemployment caused by the crisis of the neo-liberal model in the 1990s and into the early years of the 2000s.

Caudillo   Used as a synonym for dictator, strongman, or authoritarian political or military leader, especially during Argentina's colonial and revolutionary years. Colloquial name given to personalist, populist, sometimes ruthless, and always male leaders.

Clasismo   An anti-capitalist, anti-imperialist, and pro-nationalist stream of Argentina's labour movement that emerged in the late 1960s and early 1970s, strongly identified with a subversive or radicalised tendency in various working-class organisations.

Clubes de trueque   Barter clubs

Cogestión   Co-management

Compañerismo   Literally 'camaraderie', from *compañero* (comrade). The solidarity developed between a group of people engaging in a common project.

Compañero   Comrade

Comisiones internas   Shop floor workers' commissions or factory committees.

Compromiso   Commitment

Concurso Preventivo de Acreedores   Preventive hearing of creditors. Argentina's debt restructuring proceedings of troubled firms similar to the US's Chapter 11. This is the phase carried out under law in Argentina before a firm officially declares *quiebra* (bankruptcy) or to prevent bankruptcy.

Consejo administrativo   Administrative council

Consejo de trabajadores   Workers' council

Contención social   Literally, 'social containment'. Referring to social welfare and related programmes and policies.

Convertibilidad   Convertability. The policy of fixing the Argentine peso to the US dollar that was introduced by Argentina's economics minister Domingo Cavallo during the first term of Carlos Menem's presidency. Officially known as the Plan de Convertibilidad (Convertability Plan see below), it was passed into law in the first trimester of 1991 as the Ley de Convertibilidad (Convertability Law). The 'epoca' or 'periodo de la convertibilidad' (era or period of convertability) also denominates the years influenced by this neo-liberal policy during the 1990s and early 2000s.

Coordinadores interfabriles   Coordinating bodies of factory and workers' commissions by district, especially during the labour unrests in Argentina in the mid-1970s.

Coopératives de solidarité   Solidarity cooperatives. Multistakeholder cooperatives in Québec.

Cordobazo, el   Monicker for the social uprisings and political upheavals that took place in the city of Córdoba in late May and into the first days of June of 1969.

Crecimiento   Growth

Criollo   A Latin American of direct Spanish ancestry or lineage, ranking below the *peninsulares* (Spaniards born in Spain but living in Latin America) in the Spanish colonial caste system. The term is still used in colloquial conversations and in literary texts in Argentina to describe the autochthonous character of something or someone.

Cuerpos de delegados   Shop-stewards' committees or plenaries

Delegados (de fábrica)   (Factory) shop stewards

Economía social y solidaria   Social and solidarity economy

Empresa   Enterprise, business, firm, company

Empresas autogeridas   Self-managed enterprises

Empresas recuperadas por trabalhadores (no Brasil)   Worker-recuperated enterprises (in Brazil)

Empresas recuperadas por sus trabajadores   Worker-recuperated enterprises. Also *empresas recuperadas por los trabajadores* (enterprises recuperated by the workers). The acronym used in this book, ERT, is most commonly used in Argentina.

Empresas de trabajadores   Workers' enterprises. The term for factories nationalised under workers' control in Salvador Allende's Chile.

Encargado   Manager, or the person responsible for a particular sector of the firm.

Encuentro   Literally, an encounter. Formal or informal gatherings of people with the same interests in events such as conferences, plenaries, workshops, and debates.

El otro   The other. In the case of ERTs, as in looking out for each other.

Es de todos / esto es de todos   It belongs to all of us / this belongs to all of us

Estafado   Shafted, ripped off

Expropiación   Expropriation

Façón, producción a   A production practice that sees a firm producing under contract as a third-party contractor or as a sub-contracted part of another firm's production run.

Factura   The general term used by Argentines to name their wide selec-tion of baked sweets, usually eaten with *mate* and in the afternoons and on Sunday mornings.

Filete   A highly stylised art form from Buenos Aires, visible in many public spaces in the capital city of Argentina and, to a lesser extent, in the city of Rosario and in other urban centres of Argentina, filete signage decorates buses and taxis and is also promin-ently visible in the city's cafes and bars.

Guerra de cuerpos   War of bodies

Horizontalidad   Horizontality. A concept that has historical roots in the practices of European anarch-ist and autonomist collectives and that embraces the organisational practices of numerous contempor-ary Latin American groups engaging in solidarity economics, bottom-up community development, and social justice issues. It specifically refers to the forms of structuring organisations along flatter, less vertical administrative and par-ticipative lines, usually involving direct democracy and consensus decision-making and grounded in values of mutual aid and self-help.

Kirchnerismo   Kirchnerism. The polit-ical economic era, policies, and socio-economic practices during the 12 years of the national govern-ments of Néstor Kirchner (2003–7) and Cristina Férnandez de Kirchner (2007–15).

Laburante   In the Argentine slang called *lunfardo*, a worker or labourer.

La lucha por el otro   The struggle for the other

La fábrica abierta   The open factory

La fábrica cultural   The cultural factory

Ley   Law

Lucha   Struggle

Macrismo   Macrism. The political economic era, policies, and socio-economic practices of the national government of Mauricio Macri (2015–19).

Menemismo   Menemism. The political economic era, policies, and socio-economic practices of the national government of Carlos Menem (1989–99).

Mate   The bitter green tea sipped through a metal straw out of a gourd and consumed throughout South America's Southern Cone region.

Monotributo   Literally, 'single contribution'. A single payment social security, value-added tax, and income tax contribution scheme for the self-employed, the self-managed, and worker cooperative members.

Muerte en vida   Death in life

Mutuellisme   Mutualism

Obras Sociales   Argentina's entities insuring and delivering health services and run either by unions or business associations to cover the health needs of members.

Obrero   Labourer, worker

Ocupar, resistir, producir   Occupy, resist, produce. The slogan used by many ERT protagonists to articulate the three-staged process of converting a troubled privately owned firm into an ERT.

Ocupaciones   Occupations

Pago único   Sole contribution. A legal mechanism in Spain whereby redundant workers can use their unemployment insurance for buying out their employers' firms or for creating new worker cooperatives or SALS.

Patrón, el   The boss

Patronal, el   Bosses, management, administrators

Penisulares   First generation Spanish immigrants that made up the elite classes of colonial Latin America.

Peronismo   Peronism. The political-economic eras and varied policies and socio-economic practices influenenced by the ideologies and political vision of Juán Domingo Perón, Eva Perón, and other leaders and thinkers of the Partido Justicialista (Justicialist Party).

Personería gremial   An Argentine labour policy giving one union per sector the legal right to negotiate sector-wide collective agreements and to represent all workers in that sector or in a particular workplace.

Piqueteros, los   Literally, 'picketers'. The colloquial name for the diverse movement of unemployed workers also known as the Movimiento de Trabajadores Desocupados (MTD, Movement of Unemployed Workers) that emerged circa 1995–6.

Plan de Convertibilidad   The fixed-rate exchange policy introduced by

President Carlos Menem's economics minister Domingo Cavallo in the first trimester of 1991 pegging the peso to the US dollar.

Porteño Literally, 'one from the port' or 'of the port'. The Argentine-Spanish demonym for a native of the city of Buenos Aires, also applied as an adjective for anything from the 'port city' of Buenos Aires.

Proceso de Reorganización Nacional National Process of Reorganisation. The euphemistic name the military dictatorships of 1976–83 gave to their project to 'reorganise' Argentina under more conservative social values and more liberal markets.

'¡Qué se vayan todos, que no quede ni uno sólo!' 'Everyone [in the political and economic establishment] must leave now, let not even one stay!' Part of the slogan chanted by those taking part in the massive social protests leading up to, during, and in the weeks and months following the events of 19 and 20 December 2001.

Quiebra Bankruptcy

Recuperaciones Recuperations, as in the recuperation or recovery of failing firms by its workers.

Responsabilidad Responsibility

Salida Literally, 'exit'. In Argentina the term *salida* is also used to mean an 'out' or a solution to a problem.

Sindicato Labour union

Sindicalismo Unionism, syndicalism

Sobre la marcha Literally, 'on the march', also 'on the path'. Referring to change that occurs in a group or an individual in the act of doing something.

Socio Associate or member, as in a member of a cooperative.

Tarifazo, el The colloquial term given to the sharp rise in business and consumer utility rates for gas, water, and electricity during the first months of the national administration of Mauricio Macri in 2016.

Terciarización Literally, 'tertiarisation'. The Spanish term for outsourcing or being outsourced, especially the outsourcing of services.

Terrateniente Landlord, usually used to label large landholders that employ peons in the rural sector.

Tomas Takes, as in worker takeovers of businesses.

Trabajador Worker

Trabajadores autónomos Literally, 'autonomous workers'. The legal term for the self-employed in Argentina.

Trabajo Work

Trabajo 'en negro' Literally, 'work in the black'. The colloquial term given to jobs undertaken by workers who do not work under a formal labour contract, a phenomenon that in Argentina has included around 50 percent of its workforce over the past two decades.

Unidades/empresas de producción socialista/social Socialist/social production enterprises (in Bolivarian Venezuela)

Vaciamiento Literally 'emptying'. Refers to what is known in English as 'asset stripping'. Used in Argentina to describe acts by business owners of selling off or relocating a business's assets while in the process of declaring bankruptcy.

Verticalismo   Verticalism. The general moniker given to Argentina's Peronist-influenced bureaucratic form of unionism, especially consolidated by the CGT leadership in the years of Peron's exile (1955–73).

Viborazo, el   Monicker for the social uprisings, political upheavals, and factory occupations in the city of Córdoba in March 1971.

Villas de emergencia   Literally, 'towns of emergency'. Another, more inclusive and less derogatory term for *villas miserias*.

Villas miserias   Shantytowns; literally, 'towns of misery'. Considered a more derogatory alternative to 'villas de emergencia'.

Bibliography

Adamovsky, Ezequiel 2007, *Más alla de la vieja izquierda: Seis ensayos para un nuevo anticapitalismo*, Buenos Aires: Promoteo Libros.

Adorno, Theodor W. and Max Horkheimer 2002 [1947], *Dialectic of Enlightenment: Philosophical Fragments*, Stanford, CA: Stanford University Press.

Agencia Venezolana de Notícias (AVN) 2016, 'Trabajadores de empresas recuperadas trazan líneas de acción para aumentar niveles de producción', 1 February, available at: http://www.avn.info.ve/contenido/trabajadores-empresas-recuperadas-trazan-l%C3%ADneas-acci%C3%B3n-para-aumentar-niveles-producci%C3%B3n

Aguilar, Lucho 2015, 'A treinta años del desalojo de la Ford ocupada por sus obreros', *La Izquierda*, 16 July, available at: https://www.laizquierdadiario.com/A-treinta-anos-del-desalojo-de-la-Ford-ocupada-por-sus-obreros

A-Infos Anarchist News Service 1999, 'Russian Workers Beat Off Armed Attack on Occupied Factory', *Workers Solidarity Movement*, 11 October, available at: http://www.wsm.ie/c/russian-workers-beat-armed-attack-occupied-factory

Aiziczón, F. 2009, *Zanón: Una experiencia de lucha obrera*, Buenos Aires: Herramienta.

Akingbola, Kunle 2006, 'Strategic choices and change in non-profit organizations', *Strategic Change*, 15, 6: 265–81.

Albert, Michael 2005, 'Argentine Self-Management', *Autonomedia*, 24 November, available at: http://dev.autonomedia.org/node/4885

Albo, Greg, Sam Gindin, and Leo Panitch 2010, *In and Out of Crisis: The Global Financial Meltdown and Left Alternatives*, Winnipeg: Fernwood.

Alfieri, Manuel 2014, 'El modelo de las fabricas recuperadas crece en Europa', *Infonews*, 13 December, available at: http://www.infonews.com/nota/176839/el-modelo-de-las-fabricas-recuperadas-crece

Allman, Paula 2001, *Critical Education Against Global Capitalism: Karl Marx and Revolutionary Education*, London: Bergin & Garvey.

Allman, Paula, 2007, *On Marx: An Introduction to the Revolutionary Intellect of Karl Marx*, Rotterdam: Sense.

Almeyra, Guillermo 2004, *La protesta social en la Argentina, 1990–2004: Fábricas recuperadas, piquetes, cacerolazos, asambleas populares*, Buenos Aires: Continente Pax.

Altman, Morris 2014, 'Are Cooperatives a Viable Business Form? Lessons from Behavioural Economics', in *Co-operatives in a Post-Trowth Era: Creating Co-operative Economics*, edited by Sonja Novkovic and Tom Webb, London: Zed Books.

Álvarez Leguizamón, S. (ed.) 2005, *Trabajo y producción de la pobreza en Latinoamérica y el Caribe: Estrucutras, discursos y actores*, Buenos Aires: Consejo Latinoamericano de Ciencias Sociales (CLACSO).

Ámbito.com 2016a, 'Patota desalojó por la fuerza a trabajadores de Tiempo Argentino', 4 July, available at: http://www.ambito.com/845695-patota-desalojo-por-la-fuerza-a -trabajadores-de-tiempo-argentino

Ámbito.com 2016b, 'Fuerte crítica a medidas del gobierno: Hay 1.400.000 de nuevos pobres en Argentina, según un informe de la UCA', 11 August, available at: http://www .ambito.com/850778-hay-1400000-de-nuevos-pobres-en-argentina-segun-un-infor me-de-la-uca

Amin, Ash (ed.) 2009, *The Social Economy: International Perspectives on Economic Solidarity*, London: Zed Books.

Anarchist FAQ Collective 2009, 'An Anarchist FAQ', *The Anarchist Library*, available at: http://theanarchistlibrary.org/library/the-anarchist-faq-editorial-collective-an-an archist-faq

ANTA 2007, 'Asociación Nacional de Trabajadores Autogestionados', Archivos de la Central de Trabajadores de la Argentina, available at: http://archivo.cta.org.ar/IMG/ pdf/Anuario_FINAL.pdf

Antunes, Ricardo 2013, *The Meanings of Work: Essay on the Affirmation and Negation of Work*, Leiden: Brill.

Aracoop 2016, 'Què és aracoop', organisational website, available at: http://aracoop .coop/aracoop/que-es-aracoop/

Arango Jaramillo, Mario 2005, *Manual de cooperativismo y economía solidaria*, Bogotá: Universidad Cooperativa de Colombia.

Arendt, Hannah 1998, *The Human Condition*, Chicago: University of Chicago Press.

Aroskind, Ricardo C. 2001, *Más cerca o más lejos del desarollo: Transformaciones económicas en los '90*, Buenos Aires: Libros del Rogas-Serie Extramuros.

Arroyo, D. 2006, 'Estado y economía social en la Argentina actual', *Cuadernos Argentina Reciente: A 5 años del 19 y 20 de diciembre*, 3, December: 148–53.

Artz, Georgeanne M. and Younjun Kim 2011, 'Business Ownership by Workers: Are Worker Cooperatives a Viable Option?', Working Papers No. 11020, Department of Economics, Iowa State University.

Arvon, Henri 1980, *La autogestión*, Buenos Aires: Fondo de Cultura Económica/Edición Nuevo País.

Ase, Iván 2006, 'La descentralización de servicios de salud en Córdoba (Argentina): Entre la confianza democrática y el desencanto neoliberal', *Salud Colectiva*, 2, 2; 199– 218.

Ashforth, Blake E. and Barrie W. Gibbs 1990, 'The Double-Edge of Organizational Legitimation', *Organization Science*, 1, 2: 177–94.

Askew, Kate and Marcelo Vieta 2012a, 'Artes Gráficas Chilavert', in *Building a Better World: 100 Stories of Co-operation*, edited by Kate Askew, Brussels: International Cooperative Alliance.

Askew, Kate and Marcelo Vieta 2012b, 'Argentinean Workers Take Destiny Into Their

Own Hands: Unión Solidaria de Trabajadores', in *Building a Better World: 100 Stories of Co-operation*, edited by Kate Askew, Brussels: International Co-operative Alliance.

Askew, Kate and Marcelo Vieta 2012c, 'From Nothing to the Fastest Growing Medical Clinic in the Province: Cooperativa de Trabajo Salud Junín', in *Building a Better World: 100 Stories of Co-operation*, edited by Kate Askew, Brussels: International Co-operative Alliance.

Atzeni, Maurizio 2010, *Workplace Conflict: Mobilization and Solidarity in Argentina*, Houndmills, Basingstoke, UK: Palgrave Macmillan.

Atzeni, Maurizio and Pablo Ghigliani 2007, 'Labour Process and Decision-Making in Factories Under Workers' Self-Management: Empirical Evidence from Argentina', *Work, Employment and Society*, 21, 4: 653–71.

Atzeni, Maurizio and Pablo Ghigliani 2008, 'Nature and Limits of Trade Unions' Mobilisations in Contemporary Argentina', Amsterdam: LabourAgain Publications, International Institute of Social History, available at: http://www.iisg.nl/labouragain/documents/atzeni-ghigliani.pdf

Atzeni, Maurizio and Marcelo Vieta 2014, 'Self-Management in Theory and in the Practice of Worker-Recuperated Enterprises in Argentina', in *The Routledge Companion to Alternative Organization*, edited by Parker, Martin, George Cheney, Valérie Fournier, and Chris Land, London: Routledge.

AUNO 2005, 'Se realizó el Primer Encuentro Latinoamericano de Empresas Recuperadas', *Agencia Universitaria de Noticias*, 18 November, available at: https://www.auno.org.ar/article/se-realizo-el-primer-encuentro-latinoamericano-de-/

Azzellini, Dario and Oliver Ressler 2014, 'Occupy, Resist, Produce – RiMaflow', *Workerscontrol.net*, 26 December, available at: http://www.workerscontrol.net/authors/occupy-resist-produce-rimaflow

Azzellini, Dario and Oliver Ressler 2015, 'Occupy, Resist, Produce – Officine Zero', *Workerscontrol.net*, 30 December, available at: http://www.workerscontrol.net/experiences/officine-zero

Azzellini, Dario 2011, 'De las cooperativas a las empresas de propiedad social directa en el proceso venezolano', in *Cooperativas y Socialismo: Una Mirada desde Cuba*, edited by Camila Piñeiro Harnecker, Havana: Editorial Caminos.

Azzellini, Dario 2017, *Communes and Workers' Control in Venezuela: Building 21st Century Socialism from Below*, Leiden: Brill.

Babilón Poma, L. 2005, *Autogestión empresarial peruana: Reflotamiento, recuperación, sector social económico*, Lima: Escuela Sindical CGTP.

Baer, Werner, Diego Margot, and Gabriel Montes-Rojas 2011, 'Argentina's Default and the Lack of Dire Consequences', *Economía Aplicada*, 15, 1, available at: http://www.scielo.br/scielo.php?script=sci_arttext&pid=S1413-80502011000100007

Bagnasco, Arnaldo 1977, *Tre italie: La problematica territoriale dello sviluppo italiano*. Bologna: Il Mulino.

Baillie, Caroline and Eric Feinblatt 2010, 'Recycling Technologies and Cooperativism: Waste-For-Life', *Affinities: A Journal of Radical Theory, Culture, and Action*, 4, 1: 205–24.

Bakunin, Mikhail 1953, *The Political Philosophy of Bakunin: Scientific Anarchism*, edited by G.P. Maximoff, London: Collier-Macmillan.

Bakunin, Mikhail 1990 [1873], *Statism and Anarchy*, Cambridge: Cambridge University Press.

Bakunin, Mikhail 1974, *Selected Writings*, edited by Arthur Lehning, New York: Grove Press.

Bakunin, Mikhail 2005 [1871], 'The Organization of the International', in *Anarchism: A Documentary History of Libertarian Ideas, Volume One: From Anarchy to Anarchism (300 CE to 1939)*, edited by Robert Graham, Montreal: Black Rose Books.

Balladares, Carina 2009, 'Dilemas de la autogestión en una empresa recuperada de la provincia de Buenos Aires', paper presented at the Séptimo Congreso Nacional de Estudios de Trabajo, Asocación Argentina de Especialistas en Estudios de Trabajo (ASET), La Plata, Buenos Aires, Argentina.

Bandura, Albert 1977, *Social Learning Theory*, New York: General Learning Press.

Basañes, Carlos C. 1999, 'Nuevas estrategias de las cooperativas agropecuarias: Algunos ejes pare el debate.', in *Nueva vision del cooperativisim argentina: Homenaje al 80° aniversario del primer congreso argentino de la cooperación*, edited by F.R. Arella. Buenos Aires: Colegio de Graduados en Cooperativismo y Mutualismo de la República Argentina.

Battisacco, Aldo 2016, 'El neoliberalism siempre produjo destrucción de producción y empleo (entrevista con José Abelli)', *Conclusón*, 24 May, available at: http://www.conclusion.com.ar/2016/05/jose-abelli-cuando-escuche-hablar-de-competitividad-mercado-o-capitales-me-llamaron-para-recuperar-empresas/

Battistini, Osvaldo 2005, 'Trabajadores, identidad y clase', *El Correo de Económicas*, 1, 1: 70–92.

Baudrillard, Jean 1975, *The Mirror of Production*, St. Louis: Telos Press.

Bauman, Zygmunt 2001, *Community: Seeking Safety in an Insecure World*. New York: Polity.

Bayat, Asef 1991, *Work, Politics, and Power: An International Perspective on Workers' Control and Self-Management*, New York: Monthly Review Press.

Becattini, Giacomo, and Gabi Dei Ottati 2006, 'The Performance of Italian Industrial Districts and Large Enterprise Areas in the 1990s', *European Planning Studies*, 14, 8: 1139–62.

Becchetti, Leonardo, Stefano Castriota, and Sara Depedri 2010, 'Working in the Profit Versus Non-For-Profit Sector: What Difference Does it Make? An Inquiry of Preferences of Voluntary and Involuntary Movers', Working Papers No. 005–10, European Research Institute on Cooperative and Social Enterprises (EURICSE), Trento, Italy.

Bell, Peter and Harry Cleaver 2002, 'Marx's Theory of Crisis as a Theory of Class Struggle', *The Commoner*, 5, Autumn, available at: http://pdfs.semanticscholar.org/dc1d/ccf569feof7d5c801dd7be74fec70ab389ff.pdf

Belmartino, Susana 2000, 'The Context and Process of Health Care Reform in Argentina', in *Reshaping Health Care in Latin America: A Comparative Analysis of Health Care Reform in Argentina, Brazil, and Mexico*, edited by Sonia Fleury, Susana Belmartino, and Enis Baris, Ottawa: International Development Research Centre.

Belmartino, Susana 2005, 'Crisis y reformulación de las políticas sociales', in *Nueva historia argentina: Dictadura y democracia (1976–2001) (Vol. 10)*, edited by Juán Suriano, Buenos Aires: Editorial Sudamericana.

Ben-Ner, Avner 1984, 'On the Stability of the Cooperative Type of Organization', *Journal of Comparative Economics*, 8, 3: 247–60.

Ben-Ner, Avner 1988, 'Comparative Empirical Observations on Worker-Owned and Capitalist Firms', *International Journal of Industrial Organization*, 6, 1: 7–31.

Ben-Ner, Avner and Derek C. Jones 1995, 'Employee Participation, Ownership, and Productivity: A Theoretical Framework', *Industrial Relations: A Journal of Economy and Society* 34, 4: 532–54.

Bentivogli, Chiara and Eliana Viviano 2012, 'Changes in the Italian Economy: The Cooperatives', Bank of Italy Occasional Papers No. 112, available at: https://ssrn.com/abstract=2023189

Berardi, Franco 2003, 'What is the Meaning of Autonomy Today? Subjectivation, Social Composition, Refusal of Work', *Multitudes*, available at: http://www.multitudes.net/what-is-the-meaning-of-autonomy/

Berkman, Alexander 1972 [1929], *The ABC of Anarchism [Now and After: The ABC of Communist Anarchism]*, New York: Dover Publications.

Berlin, Isaiah 1969 [1958], *Two Concepts of Liberty*, Oxford: Oxford University Press.

Bernard, Elaine 2011, 'Recipe for Anarchy: British Columbia's Telephone Workers' Occupation of 1981', in *Ours to Master and to Own: Workers' Control from the Commune to the Present*, edited by Immanuel Ness and Dario Azzellini, Chicago: Haymarket Books.

Bernstein, Paul 2012 [1976], *Workplace Democratization: Its Internal Dynamics*, Kent, OH: Kent State University Press.

Bielsa, Rafael, Miguel Bonasso, Stella Calloni, Cristina Feijóo, Lucio Salas Oroño, José Pablo Feinmann, Alicia Le Fur, Luis Mattini, et al. 2002, *¿Qué son las asambleas populares?*, Buenos Aires: Peña Lillo/Ediciones Continente.

Birchall, Johnston 1994, *Co-op: The People's Business*, Manchester: Manchester University Press.

Birchall, Johnston 1997, *The International Co-operative Movement*, Manchester: Manchester University Press.

Birchall, Johnston 2003, *Rediscovering the Cooperative Advantage: Poverty Reduction through Self-Help*, Geneva: International Labour Organization.

Birchall, Johnston 2004, *Cooperatives and the Millennium Development Goals*, Geneva: International Labour Organization.

Birchall, Johnston and Lou Hammond Ketilson 2009, *Resilience of the Cooperative Business Model in Times of Crisis*, Geneva: International Labour Organization.

Bocangel, Danilo 2001, 'Small-Scale Mining in Bolivia: National study', Report No. 71, Mining, Minerals and Sustainable Development of the International Institute for Environment and Development, available at: http://pubs.iied.org/pdfs/G00713.pdf

Boggs, Carl 1977, 'Marxism, Prefigurative Communism, and the Problem of Workers' Control', *Radical America* 11, 6: 99–122.

Boltanski, Luc, and Eve Chiapello 2007, *The New Spirit of Capitalism*, London: Verso.

Bonefeld, Werner 1994, 'Human Practice and Perversion: Beyond Autonomy and Structure', *Common Sense*, 15: 43–52.

Bonefeld, Werner, Richard Gunn, John Holloway, and Kosmas Psychopedis (eds.) 1995, *Open Marxism, Volume 3: Emancipating Marx*, London: Pluto.

Bonin, John P., Derek C. Jones, and Louis Putterman 1993, 'Theoretical and Empircial Studies of Producer Cooperatives: Will Ever the Twain Meet?', *Journal of Economic Literature*, 31, 3: 1290–1320.

Bookchin, Murray 1971, *Post-Scarcity Anarchism*, Berkley, CA: Ramparts.

Bookchin, Murray 1990, *Remaking Society*, Montreal: Black Rose Books.

Boorstin, Julia 2016, 'Sun Valley Conference: Argentine President Macri Explains Economic Turnaround', CNBC, 7 July, available at: http://www.cnbc.com/2016/07/07/sun-valley-conference-argentine-president-macri-explains-economic-turnaround.html

Borda-Rodriguez, Alexander and Sara Vicari 2016, 'Resilience', in *The Co-operative Firm: Kewords*, edited by Andrea Bernardi and Salvatore Monni, Rome: RomaTrE-Press.

Boron, Atilio and Mabel Thwaites Rey 2004, 'La expropiación en la Argentina: Genesis, desarollo, y los impactos estructurales', in *Las privatizaciones y la desnacionalización de América Latin*, edited by James Petras and Henry Veltmeyer, Buenos Aires: Promoteo Libros.

Borzaga, Carlo and Ermanno Tortia 2007, 'Social Economy Organisations in the Theory of the Firm', in *The Social Economy: Building Inclusive Communities*, edited by Antonella Noya and Emma Clarence, Paris: OECD Publishing.

Borzaga, Carlo, Sara Depedri, and Ermanno C. Tortia 2009, 'The Role of Cooperative and Social Enterprises: A Multifaceted Approach for an Economic Pluralism', Working Papers No. 000–09, Trento, Italy: European Research Institute on Cooperative and Social Enterprises (EURICSE), Trento, available at: https://papers.ssrn.com/sol3/papers.cfm?abstract_id=1622143

Borzaga, Carlo, Sara Depedri, and Ermanno Tortia 2010, 'The Growth of Organizational Variety in Market Economies: The Case of Social Enterprises', Working Papers No. 003–10, Trento, Italy: European Research Institute on Cooperative and Social Enterprises (EURICSE), available at: https://papers.ssrn.com/sol3/papers.cfm?abstract_id=1622155

Bowles, Samuel and Herbert Gintis 1993a, *Markets and Democracy: Participation, Accountability and Efficiency*, Cambridge: Cambridge University Press.

Bowles, Samuel and Herbert Gintis 1993b, 'A Political and Economic Case for the Democratic Enterprise', *Economics and Philosophy*, 9, 1: 75–100.

Bowman, Betsy, and Bob Stone 2006, 'Venezuela's Cooperative Revolution: An Economic Experiment is the Hidden Story Behind Chávez's "Bolivarian Revolution"', *Dollars & Sense*, 266: 16–23.

Bratton, John, Jean Helms Mills, Timothy Pyrch, and Peter Sawchuk 2004, *Workplace Learning: A Critical Introduction*, Aurora, ON: Garamond Press.

Braverman, Harry 1974, *Labor and Monopoly Capital: The Degradation of Work in the Twentieth Century*, New York: Monthly Review Press.

Bray, John F. 1839, *Labour's Wrongs and Labour's Remedy; or, The Age of Might and the Age of Right*, Leeds: David Green.

Brenner, Neil and Stuart Elden 2009, 'Introduction: State, Space, World: Lefebvre and the Survival of Capitalism', in *State, Space, World: Selected Essays / Henri Lefebvre*, edited by Neil Brenner and Stuart Elden, Minneapolis: University of Minnesota Press.

Briner, Maria Agustina, and Adriana Cusmano 2003, 'Las empresas recuperadas en la Ciudad de Buenos Aires: Una aproximación a partir del estudio de siete experiencias', in *Empresas recuperadas: Ciudad de Buenos Aires*. Buenos Aires: Secretaria de Desarollo Económica del Gobierno de la Ciudad Autónoma de Buenos Aires.

Brinton, Maurice 1970, *The Bolsheviks and Workers' Control, 1917–1921: The State and Counter-Revolution*, Montreal: Black Rose Books.

Briscoe, Robert and Michael Ward (ed.) 2005, *Helping Ourselves: Success Stories in Cooperative Business and Social Enterprises*, Dublin: Oak Tree.

Brouard, François and Sophie Larivet 2011, 'Social Enterprises: Definitions and Boundaries', paper presented at the annual conference of the Association for Nonprofit and Social Economy Research, Fredricton, New Brunswick, Canada, 1–3 June.

Broué, Pierre and Emile Témime 1962, *La revolución y la guerra de España*, México: Fondo de Cultura Económica.

Brouwer, Steve 2011, *Revolutionary Doctors: How Venezuela and Cuba Are Changing the World's Conception of Health Care*, New York: New York University Press.

Bryman, Alan 1988, 'The debate about quantitative and qualitative research.', in *Quantity and quality in social research*, edited by Alan Bryman. London: Unwin.

Buber, Martin 1996 [1949], *Paths in Utopia*, Syracuse: Syracuse University Press.

Buendía Garcia, Luis 2005, *Destrucción económica y recuperación de empresas en Argentina en la última década*, unpublished Pre-Doctoral thesis, Madrid: Universidad Complutense de Madrid

Buffa, Adolfo, Susana Roitman, and Carlos Martínez 2009, 'Empresas recuperadas en Córdoba: Memoria y balance', in *Las empresas recuperadas: Autogestión obrera en Argentina y América Latina* edited by Andrés Ruggeri, Buenos Aires: Facultad de Filosofía y Letras, Universidad de Buenos Aires.

Burawoy, Michael 1979, *Manufacturing Consent: Changes in the Labour Process Under Capitalism*, Chicago: University of Chicago Press.

Burawoy, Michael 1984, 'Organizing Consent on the Shop Floor: The Game of Making Out', in *Critical Studies in Organization and Bureaucracy*, edited by Frank Fischer and Carmen Sirianni, Philadelphia: Temple University Press.

Burawoy, Michael 1985, *The Politics of Production: Factory Regimes Under Capitalism and Socialism*, London: Verso.

Burawoy, Michael 1998, 'The Extended Case Method', *Sociological Theory*, 16, 1: 4–33.

Burawoy, Michael 2000, 'Introduction: Reaching for the Global', in *Global Ethnography: Forces, Connections, and Imaginations in a Postmodern World*, edited by Michal Buawoy, Joseph A. Blum, Sheba George, Zsuzsa Gille, Millie Thayer, et al., Berkley and Los Angeles: University of California Press.

Burdín, Gabriel 2014, 'Are Worker-Managed Firms More Likely to Fail than Conventional Enterprises? Evidence from Uruguay', *Industrial and Labor Relations Review* (*ILR Review*) 67, 1: 202–38.

Burdin, Gabriel and Andrés Dean 2009, 'New Evidence on Wages and Employment in Worker Cooperatives Compared with Capitalist Firms', *Journal of Comparative Economics* 37, 4: 517–33.

Burijovich, Jacinta and Laura C. Pautassi 2005, 'Calidad del empleo y calidad de la atención en la salud en Córdoba, Argentina: Aportes para políticas laborales más equitativas', Santiago: Comisión Económica para América Latina y el Caribe (CEPAL), United Nations.

Burkett, Paul 2005, 'Marx's Vision of Sustainable Human Development', *Monthly Review*, 57, 5: 34–62.

Cabrera, Hugo and Gabriel Rojas n.d. 'Prologo', *Curso básico sobre cooperativas de trabajo*, Red Gráfica Cooperativa, in archives of Centro de Documentación de Empresas Recuperadas, Programa Facultad Abierta, Facultad de Filosofía y Letras, Universidad de Buenos Aires.

Calderón, Soledad, Penélope Mazzoli, Natalia Polti, Mariela Sarlinga, and Verónica Vázquez 2009, 'Las empresas recuperadas y la seguridad social: Trabas a la hora de enfrentar problemas relacionados con los riesgos del trabajo y la (im)previsión social', in *Las empresas recuperadas: Autogestión obrera en Argentina y América Latina*, edited by Andrés Ruggeri, Buenos Aires: Facultad de Filosofía y Letras, Universidad de Buenos Aires.

Callejas, Bruno Rojas 2014, 'Las "empresas sociales": ¿Una alternativa real para los trabajadores o una forma de eludir las obligaciones de los empresarios?', La Paz: Centro de Estudios para el Desarollo Laboral y Agrario, available at: http://www.cedla.org/obess/43249

Calloni, Stella 2005, 'Compró Venezuela 500 millones de dólares en bonos de deuda argentina', La Jornada, 13 August, available at: http://www.jornada.unam.mx/2005/08/12/index.php?section=economia&article=025n1eco

Camilletti, Alfredo, Javier Guidini, Andrea Herrera, Mónica Rodríguez, Juan Pablo Martí, et al. 2005, 'Cooperativas de trabajo en el Cono Sur: Matrices de surgimiento y modelos de gestión', Revista UniRcoop 3, 1: 32–56.

Campos, Miguel 2007, 'Miguel Campos of FRETECO speaks on workers' control in Venezuela', Socialist Appeal, 4 January, available at: http://socialistappeal.org/news-analysis/46-general-solidarity/298-miguel-campos-of-freteco-speaks-about-workers-control.html

Careforce 2016, organisational website, available at: http://www.careforce.ca/

Carey, David 2017, Oral History in Latin America: Unlocking the Spoken Archive, London: Routledge.

Caro, Luís 2004, 'Cada fábrica es una revolución: Entravista a Luís Caro', in Sin patrón: Fábricas y empresas recuperadas por sus trabajadores: Una historia, una guía, edited by Lavaca, Buenos Aires: Lavaca.

Carpintero, Enrique and Mario Hernández (eds.) 2002, Produciendo realidad: Las empresas comunitarias: Grissinopoli, Río Turbio, Zanón, Brukman y General Mosconi, Buenos Aires: Topia Editorial/La Maza.

Carrell, Severin 2007, 'Strike Rochdale from the Record Books: The Co-op Began in Scotland', The Guardian, 7 August, available at: https://www.theguardian.com/business/2007/aug/07/retail.uknews

Carretero Miramar, José Luís 2010, 'Las empresas recuperadas: Hacia una comprensión de la autogestión obrera real', Nómadas, 25, January–June, available at: http://www.redalyc.org/articulo.oa?id=18112179024

Castells, Manuel 2000, 'Toward a Sociology of the Network Society', Contemporary Sociology, 29, 5: 693–9.

Castiglioni, Luisina 2006, 'Autogestión: Crisis dentro de la principal organización de compañías tomadas por los trabajadores: Varias empresas recuperadas argentinas crean una coordinadora más participativa', Diagonal, 12 October, available at: https://www.diagonalperiodico.net/movimientos/varias-empresas-recuperadas-argentinas-crean-coordinadora-mas-participativa.html

Castillo, Christian 2007, 'Acumulación de experiencias y desafíos de la clase trabajadora argentina', in Los '90: Fin de ciclo: El retorno a la contradicción, edited by José Enrique, Buenos Aires: Final Abierto.

Castro Soto, Gutavo 2008, 'Las fábricas recuperadas en Argentina, ¿experiencia antisistémica?', *LaHaine.org*, 14 July, available at: http://www.lahaine.org/mundo.php/las _fabricas_recuperadas_en_argentina_ie

Cattani, Antonio David (ed.) 2004, *La otra economía*, Buenos Aires: Altamira.

Ceceña, Ana Esther 2005, *La guerra por el agua y por la vida: Cochabamba, una experiencia de construcción comunitaria frente al neoliberalismo*, Buenos Aires: Ediciones Madres de la Plaza de Mayo.

CECOP–CICOPA Europe 2012a, 'CECOP Position on EC's Green Paper: Restructuring and Anticipation of Change: What Lessons from Recent Experience?', Brussels: The European Confederation of Cooperatives and Worker-Owned Enterprises Active in Industries and Services, available at: http://www.cecop.coop/IMG/pdf/cecop _position_green_paper_restructuring_en.pdf

CECOP–CICOPA Europe 2012b, 'The Resilience of the Cooperative Model: How Worker Cooperatives, Social Cooperatives and Other Worker-Owned Enterprises Respond to the Crisis and its Consequences', Brussels: The European Confederation of Cooperatives and Worker-Owned Enterprises Active in Industries and Services, available at: http://www.cecop.coop/IMG/pdf/report_cecop_2012_en_web.pdf

CECOP–CICOPA Europe 2013, 'Business Transfers to Employees Under the Form of a Cooperative in Europe: Opportunities and Challenges', Brussels: The European Confederation of Cooperatives and Worker-Owned Enterprises Active in Industries and Services, available at: http://www.cecop.coop/IMG/pdf/bussiness_transfers_to _employees_under_the_form_of_a_cooperative_in_europe_cecop-4.pdf

Chávez, Miriam 2016, 'Tres empresas que pasaron a trabajadores sobreviven en la incertidumbre', *La Rázon*, 9 May, available at: http://www.la-razon.com/economia/ empresas-pasaron-trabajadores-sobreviven-incertidumbre_0_2484351545.html

Chedid Henriques, Flávio 2014, *Autogestão em empresas recuperadas por trabalhadores: Brasil e Argentina*, Florianópolis: Insular Livros.

Chedid Henriques, Flávio, Vanessa Moreira Sígolo, Sandra Rufino, Fernanda Santos Araújo, Vicente Nepomuceno, et al. 2013, 'Empresas recuperadas por trabalhadores no Brasil: Resultados de um levantamento nacional', *Mercado de Trabalho*, 55, August, available at: http://repositorio.ipea.gov.br/bitstream/11058/3830/1/bmt55_ econo2_empresas.pdf

Cheney, George, Lars Thøger Christensen, Theodore E. Zorn, Jr., and Shiv Ganesh 2011, *Organizational Communication in an Age of Globalization: Issues, Reflections, Practices*, Long Grove, IL: Waveland.

Choudry, Aziz 2015, *Learning Activism: The Intellectual Life of Contemporary Social Movements*, Toronto: University of Toronto Press.

Christiansen, Anders Asa 2014, *Evaluating Workplace Democracy in Mondragon*, unpublished honor's thesis, University of Vermont, Burlington, Vermont.

Chun, Lin 2006, *The Transformation of Chinese Socialism*. Durham: Duke University Press.

Ciccarelli, Roberto 2015, 'Non bruciate il sogno delle Officine Zero', *Focus*, Camere del Lavoro Autonomo e Precario (CLAP), 25 November, available at: http://www.clap -info.net/2015/11/non-bruciate-il-sogno-delle-officine-zero/

Ciudad Autónoma de Buenos Aires 2011, 'Catálogo de empresas recuperadas', Departamento de Comunicación Social, Gobierno de la Ciudad Autónoma de Buenos Aires.

Chase, William J. 1987, *Workers, Society, and the Soviet State: Labor and Life in Moscow, 1918–1929*, Urbana and Chicago: University of Illinois Press.

Claeys, Gregory 1991, 'Introduction', in *A New View of Society and Other Writings* (*Robert Owen*), edited by Gregory Claeys, London: Penguin.

Clarín 2005, 'La pobreza bajó, pero se mantiene a niveles muy altos', 22 September, available at: http://www.clarin.com/ediciones-anteriores/pobreza-mantiene-niveles-al tos_o_SJbWCKwkRFl.html

Clarin 2006, 'Nueva ley de quiebras', 23 March, available at: http://www.clarin.com/ ediciones-anteriores/nueva-ley-quiebras_o_rkSeicHkAYx.html

Clarín 2009, 'Para el INDEC, la pobreza está en el nivel más bajo de la era K', 4 August, available at: https://www.clarin.com/ediciones-anteriores/indec-pobreza-nivel_o_r kwbP6LCaYg.html

Clark, Gabriel and Javier Antivero 2009, 'La intervención sindical en las empresas recuperadas en la Argentina: Hacia la reconstrucción selectiva de un model de justicia social', in *Las empresas recuperadas: Autogestión obrera en Argentina y América Latina*, edited by Andrés Ruggeri, Buenos Aires: Facultad de Filosofía y Letras, Universidad de Buenos Aires.

Clark, Martin 1977, *Antonio Gramsci and the Revolution that Failed*, New Haven, CT: Yale University Press.

Clay, John 2013, 'Can Union Co-ops Help Save Democracy?', *Truthout*, 4 July, available at: http://www.truth-out.org/news/item/17381-can-union-co-ops-help-save-democra cy

Cleaver, Harry n.d., '[Notes on] Capital, Vol. 1, Chapter 15, Machinery and Modern Industry', in *Study Guide to Capital*, available at: https://la.utexas.edu/users/hcleav er/357k/357ksg15.htm

Cleaver, Harry 1992a, 'The Inversion of Class Perspective in Marxian Theory: From Valorization to Self-Valorization', in *Open Marxism, Volume II: Theory and Practice*, edited by Werner Bonefeld, Richard Gunn, and Kosmas Psychopedis, London: Pluto.

Cleaver Harry 1992b, 'Kropotkin, Self-Valorization and the Crisis of Marxism', paper presented at the Pyotr Alexeevich Kropotkin conference, Russian Academy of Science, 8–14 December, Moscow, St. Petersburg, and Dmitrov, Russia.

Cleaver, Harry 2000, *Reading Capital Politically*, Oakland: AK Press/AntiThesis.

CNCT 2011, 'CNCT. Se aprobó la Ley de Concursos y Quebras: Con la ley a nuestro favor', Gacetilla de Prensa de la Confederación Nacional de Cooperativas de Trabajo, in *mutualcoop.org.ar*, available at: http://www.mutualcoop.org.ar/noticias.php?id=204

CNCT 2016, 'Argentina. Movilización de cooperativistas en defense del trabajo, por más obras y menos Tarifazos', Gacetilla de Prensa de la Confederación Nacional de Cooperativas de Trabajo, in *Resumen*, 20 July, available at: http://www.resumenlati noamericano.org/2016/07/20/argentina-movilizacion-de-cooperativistas-en-defen sa-del-trabajo-por-mas-obras-y-menos-tarifazos/

CNT–AIT n.d., 'Proudhon & l'autogestion anarchiste', *L'autogestion: D'hier à demain?*, available at: http://datao.eklablog.com/ae-editions/perso/bibliotheque%20-% 20pdf/autogestion%20d-hier%20a%20demain.pdf

Coady, Moses 1939, *Masters of Their Own Destiny: The Story of the Antigonish Movement of Adult Education Through Economic Cooperation*, New York: Harper & Row.

Cohen, Patricia 2015, 'Oxfam Study Finds Richest 1% Is Likely to Control Half of Global Wealth by 2016', *New York Times*, 19 January, available at: https://www.nytimes.com/2015/01/19/business/richest-1-percent-likely-to-control-half-of-global-wealth-by-2016-study-finds.html

Cole, George Douglas Howard 1920, *Guild Socialism Restated*, London: Leonard Parsons.

Colectivo Situaciones 2002, 'Asambleas, cacerolas, y piquetes (sobre las nuevas formas de protagonismo social): Boradores de investigación #3', available at: http://www .nodo50.org/colectivosituaciones/borradores_03.html

Colectivo Situaciones 2004, 'Causes and Happenstance (Dilemmas of Argentina's New Social Protagonism): Research Manuscript #4', *The Commoner*, 8, Autumn/Winter, available at: http://www.ainfos.ca/03/dec/ainfos00368.html

Colletti, Lucio 1972, *From Rousseau to Lenin: Studies in Ideology and Society*, London: New Left Books.

Cooley, Mike 1980, *Architect or Bee? The Human/Technology Relationship*, Slough, UK: Langley Technical Services.

Cooperativa 'Unión Solidaria de Trabajadores' 2007, promotional pamphlet on the history of Unión Solidaria de Trabajadores, in archives of Centro de Documentación de Empreasas Recuperadas, Programa Facultad Abierta, Facultad de Filosofía y Letras, Universidad de Buenos Aires.

Cooperativa 'Unión Solidaria de Trabajadores' 2017, organisational website, available at: http://cooperativaust.com.ar/

Co-operatives UK 2017, 'The Co-operative Economy [2017]', available at: http://uk.coop/open-data/organisations

Coraggio, José Luis 1999, 'De la economía de los sectores populares a la economía del trabajo', paper presented at the Seminario 'Economía dos Setores Populares: Entre a Realidade e a Utopia', Universidad Católica de Salvador, Salvador, Bahia, Brazil, 8–9 November, available at: http://municipios.unq.edu.ar/modules/mislibros/archi vos/De_la_econo.pdf

Coraggio, José Luis 2003, 'La economía social como vía para otro desarrollo social', *Urbared: Red de Pólíticas Sociales*, available at: http://biblioteca.municipios.unq.edu.ar/modules/mislibros/archivos/laeconomia.pdf

Coraggio, José Luis 2004, 'Una alternativa socioeconómica necesaria: La economía social', in *Política social y economía social. Debates fundamentales*, edited by Caudia Danani, Buenos Aires: Universidad Nacional de General Sarmiento and Editorial Altamira.

Coraggio, José Luis and María Sol Arroyo 2009, 'A Path to the Social Economy in Argentina: Worker Takeovers of Bankrupt Companies', in *The Social Economy: International Perspectives on Economic Solidarity*, edited by Ash Amin, London: Zed Books.

Corcoran, Hazel and David Wilson 2010, 'The Worker Co-operative Movements in Italy, Mondragon and France: Context, Success Factors and Lessons', Canadian Social Economy Research Partnerships and Canadian Worker Co-operative Federation, 31 May, available at: http://community-wealth.org/sites/clone.community-wealth.org/files/downloads/paper-corcoran-wilson.pdf

Cornforth, Chris 1983, 'Some Factors Affecting the Success or Failure of Worker Co-operatives: A Review of the Empricial Research in the United Kingdom', *Economic and Industrial Democracy*, 4: 163–90.

Coté, Daniel 2007, 'Best Practices in Co-operative Development in Québec', in *Effective Practices in Starting Co-ops: The Voice of Canadian Co-op Developers*, edited by Joy Emmanuel and Lyn Cayo: Victoria, BC: New Rochdale Press.

Cox, Laurence and Alf Gunvald Nilsen 2014, *We Make Our Own History: Marxism and Social Movements in the Twilight of Neoliberalism*, London: Pluto.

Cracogna, Dante 2013, 'Argentina', in *International Handbook of Cooperative Law*, edited by Dante Cracogna, Antonio Fici, and Hagen Henrÿ, Heidelberg: Springer.

Craddock, Trent and Sarah Kennedy 2006, 'Worker Cooperative Trends in North America and Europe', *GEO Newsletter*, available at: http://www.geo.coop/archives/InternationalTrendsinWorkerCoops.htm

Craig, John G. 1993, *The Nature of Co-operation*, Montreal: Black Rose Books.

Craig, John G. and Saxena, Suren K. 1986, 'The Cooperative Principles and the Community', in *Community and Cooperatives in Participatory Development*, edited by Yair Levi and Howard Litwin, Aldershot, Hants, UK: Gower.

Critchley, Simon 2007, *Infinitely Demanding: Ethics of Commitment, Politics of Resistance*, London: Verso.

Cúneo, Martín 2014, 'Fábricas recuperadas en España, ¿por qué no?', *Diagonal*, 14 August, available at: https://www.diagonalperiodico.net/global/23617-fabricas-recuperadas-espana-por-no.html

Cuninghame, Robert Patrick 2016, 'Self-Management, Cooperatives and Workers' Control in Mexico: Scope and Limits', paper presented at the 'Moral Economies,

Economic Morality' conference, University of California, Berkeley, USA, 24–26 June.

Curl, John 2009, *For All the People: Uncovering the Hidden History of Cooperation, Cooperative Movements, and Communalism in America*, Oakland, CA: PM Press.

Curl, John 2010, 'The Cooperative Movement in Century 21', *Affinities: A Journal of Radical Theory, Culture and Action*, 4, 1: 12–29.

Dahl, Robert Alan 1985, *A Preface to Economic Democracy*, Berkeley and Los Angeles: University of California Press.

Dahrendorf, Ralf 1959, *Class and Class Conflict in Industrial Society*, Stanford, CA: Stanford University Press.

D'Amico, Victoria 2013, 'La política social en debate. Desigualdades, intervención estatal e inclusión social en la Argentina democrática', Revistras de la Facultad de Humanidades y Ciencias Sociales de la Educación (FaHCE, Universidad Nacional de La Plata), 9, available at: http://www.cuestionessociologia.fahce.unlp.edu.ar/article/view/CSn09a27/4586

Damill, Mario 2005, 'La economía y la pólitica económica: Del viejo al nuevo endeudamiento.', in *Nueva historia argentina: Dictadura y democracia (1976–2001)*, edited by Sariano J., Buenos Aires: Editorial Sudamericana.

Danani, Claudia C. 2008, 'América Latina luego del mito del progreso neo-liberal: Las ciencias sociales y el problema de la desigualdad', *Ciências Sociais Unisinos*, 44, 1:39–48.

Dandolo, Francesco 2009, *L'industria in Italia tra crisi e cooperazione: La partecipazione dei lavoratori all agestione d'impresa dall'autunno caldo alla legge Marcora (1969–1985)*. Torino: Bruno Mondadori.

Dangl, Ben 2009, 'Common ground: Learning from Latin American social movements', *ZNet*, 26 July, available at: http://venezuelanalysis.com/analysis/4661

Darlington, Ralph 2013, *Radical Unionism: The Rise and Fall of Revolutionary Syndicalism*, Chicago: Haymarket Books.

Dart, Raymond 2004, 'The Legitimacy of Social Enterprise', *Nonprofit Management & Leadership*, 14, 4: 411–24.

Dávolos, Patricia and Laura Perelman 2004, 'Acción colectiva y representaciones sociales: Los trabajadores de empresas recuperadas', Amsterdam: LabourAgain Publications, International Institute of Social History, available at: http://www.workerscontrol.net/system/files/docs/davolos_perelman.pdf

Day, Richard J.F. 2004, 'From Hegemony to Affinity: The Political Logic of the Newest Social Movements', *Cultural Studies*, 18, 5: 716–48.

Day, Richard J.F. 2005, *Gramsci is Dead: Anarchist Currents in the Newest Social Movements*, London: Pluto.

De Angelis, Massimo 1995, 'Beyond the Technological and Social Paradigms: A Political Reading of Abstract Labour as the Substance of Value', *Capital & Class*, 57, Autumn: 107–34.

De Angelis, Massimo 2007, *The Beginning of History: Value Struggles and Global Capital*, London: Pluto.

De Angelis, Massimo and David Harvie 2014, 'The Commons', in *The Routledge Companion to Alternative Organization*, edited by Martin Parker George Cheney, Valérie Fournier, and Chris Land, London: Routledge.

Defourny, Jacques and Marthe Nyssens 2010, 'Conceptions of Social Enterprise and Social Entrepreneurship in Europe and the United States: Convergences and Divergences', *Journal of Social Entrepreneurship*, 1, 1: 32–53.

de Peuter, Greig 2010, *The Contested Convergence of Immaterial Labour*, unpublished doctoral dissertation, School of Communication, Simon Fraser University, Vancouver and Burnaby, BC, Canada.

de Peuter, Greig and Nick Dyer-Witheford 2010, 'Commons and Cooperatives', *Affinities: A Journal of Radical Theory, Culture and Action*, 4, 1: 30–56.

Del Campo, Hugo 2005, *Sindicalismo y peronismo: Los comienzos de un vínculo perdurable*, Buenos Aires: Siglo Veintiuno Editores.

Del Mar Araus, María 2004, 'Autogestión: Una nueva cultura,' *solidaridad.net*, available at: https://antigua.solidaridad.net/noticia/320/autogesti-o-n-una-nueva-cultura

del Pont, Tomás Marcó 2016, 'Un grupo de violentos irrumpió en el edificio de Tiempo Argentino y destrozó la redacción', *La Nación*, 4 July, available at: http://www.lana cion.com.ar/1915190-irrumpieron-en-el-edificio-de-tiempo-argentino-y-echaron-a-los-trabajadores

Della Paolera, Gerardo, and Alan M. Taylor (eds.) 2003, *A New Economic History of Argentina. Volume 1.*, Cambridge, UK: Cambridge University Press.

Dellatorre, Raúl 2013, 'Otro modelo es posible, y autogestionado', Página/12, 27 October, available at: https://www.pagina12.com.ar/diario/economia/2-232223-2013-10-27 .html

De Martino, George 2003, 'Realizing Class Justice', *Rethinking Marxism*, 15, 1: 1–31.

Dennis, Elissa 2010, 'Hope and exhaustion at the Hotel BAUEN: Seven years in, workers trudge on and forge ahead at Argentina's recuperated businesses', *Dollars & Sense*, 290, September/October: 24–8.

Dévadhar, Y.C. 1971, 'Alfred Marshall on Cooperation', *Annals of Public and Cooperative Economics*, 42, 2: 285–301.

Devita, Marina 2016, 'Un giro total en relaciones con otros países con la idea de "desideologizar la política exterior"', *La Capital*, 11 June, available at: http://www .lacapitalmdp.com/un-giro-total-en-relaciones-con-otros-paises-con-la-idea-de-desideologizar-la-politica-exterior/

Diamantopolous, Mitch 2012, 'Breaking Out of Co-operation's 'Iron Cage': From Movement Degeneration to Building a Developmental Movement', *Annals of Public and Co-operative Economics*, 83, 2: 197–212.

Diario Popular 2014, 'Más de 3 millones de personas trabajan en negro', 16 June, available at: https://www.diariopopular.com.ar/general/mas-3-millones-personas-trabajan-negro-n194824

Díaz-Bonilla, Carolina, Eugenio Díaz-Bonilla, Valeria Piñeiro, and Sherman Robinson 2004, 'El plan de convertibilidad, apertura de la economía y empleo en Argentina: Una simulación macro de pobreza y desigualdad', in *Quien se beneficia del libre comercio? Promoción de exportaciones en America Latina y el Caribe en los 90*, edited by Enrique Ganuza, Samuiel Morley, Sherman Robinson, and Rob Vos, Bogotá: Alfaomega Colombiana.

Dickstein, Carl 1991, 'The Promise and Problems of Worker Cooperatives', *Journal of Planning Literature*, 6, 1: 16–33.

Dillon, Alfredo 2016, 'Argentina, con el desempleo joven más alto de la región', Clarín, 3 August, available at: http://www.clarin.com/sociedad/Argentina-desempleo-joven-alto-region_0_1625237666.html

Dinerstein, Ana Cecilia 2002, 'The Battle of Buenos Aires: Crisis, Insurrection and the Reinvention of Politics in Argentina', *Historical Materialism*, 10, 4: 5–38.

Dinerstein, Ana Cecilia 2007, 'Workers' Factory Takeovers and New State Policies: Towards the "Institutionalisation" of Non-Governmental Public Action in Argentina', *Policy and Politics*, 35, 3: 529–50.

Dinerstein, Ana Cecilia 2015, *The Politics of Autonomy in Latin America: The Art of Organizing Hope*, Houndmills, Basingstoke, UK: Palgrave Macmillan.

Doob, Christopher B. 2015, *Social Inequality and Social Stratification in US Society*, London: Routledge.

Doria, Darío and Luis Camardella 2004, *Grissinopoli: El país de los grisines* [film], Argentina: A4 Films and Insituto Nacional de Cine y Artes Audiovisuales (INCAA).

Dow, Gregory 1993, 'Democracy Versus Appropriability: Can Labor-Managed Firms Flourish in a Capitalist World?', in *Markets and Democracy: Participation, Accountability, and Efficiency*, edited by Samuel Bowles, Herbert Gintis, and Bo Gustafsson Cambridge, UK: Cambridge University Press.

Dow, Gregory 2003, *Governing the Firm: Workers' Control in Theory and Practice*, Cambridge, UK: Cambridge University Press.

Dowd, Douglas F. 2012, 'Robert Owen: British Social Reformer', in *Encyclopedia Britannica*, available at: https://www.britannica.com/biography/Robert-Owen#ref221950

Drèze, Jacques 1976, 'Some Theory of Labour Management and Participation', *Econometrica*, 44, 6: 1125–39.

Drèze, Jacques 1993, 'Self-Management and Economic Theory: Efficiency, Funding, and Employment.', in *Market Socialism: The Current Debate*, edited Pranab K. Bardhan and John E. Roemer, Oxford: Oxford University Press.

Duguid, Fiona, Mümtaz Derya Tarhan, and Marcelo Vieta 2015, *New Co-operative Development in Canada: Findings from Research Emerging from the Co-operative Development Initiative (2009–2013)*, final report submitted to the Co-operative Difference in Canada project and Measuring the Co-opertive Difference Research Network, available at: http://www.cooperativedifference.coop/co-operatives-in-canada/new -co-operative-development-in-canada/

DuRand, Cliff, (ed.) 2016, *Moving Beyond Capitalism*, London: Routledge.

Dyer-Witheford, Nick 1999, *Cyber-Marx: Cycles and Circuits of Struggle in High-Technology Capitalism*, Chicago: University of Illinois Press.

Dyer-Witheford, Nick 2006, 'Species-Being and the New Commonism: Notes on an Interrupted Cycle of Struggles,' *The Commoner*, 11, Spring: 15–32.

Dyer-Witheford, Nick 2015, *Cyber-Proletariat: Labour in the Digital Vortex*, London: Pluto.

DyPRA 2011, 'Diaros y Períodicos Regionales Argentinos', organisational website, available at: http://www.dypra.com.ar/

Earle, John 1986, *The Italian Cooperative Movement: A Portrait of the Lega Nazionale delle Cooperative e Mutue*, New York: HarperCollins.

Economía de los/las Trabajadores/as 2017, 'VI Encuentro Internacional de la Economía de los/las Trabajadores/as / VI International Gathering of the Workers' Economy', Buenos Aires and Pigüé, Argentina, 30 August–2 September, organisational website, available at: https://laeconomiadelostrabajadores.wordpress.com/

Eckstein, Susan 2006, 'Urban Resistance to Neoliberal Democracy in Latin America', *Colombia Internacional*, 63: 12–39.

El Destape 2016, 'Grave informe sobre la violencia estatal en los primeros seis meses del macrismo', 21 September, available at: http://www.eldestapeweb.com/grave-informe -la-violencia-estatal-los-primeros-seis-meses-del-macrismo-n21030

El Economista 2018. 'El pago único o la capitalización del desempleo'. *elEconomista.ca*, 28 May, available at: https://infoautonomos.eleconomista.es/ayudas-subvenciones -autonomos/el-pago-unico-o-la-capitalizacion-del-desempleo/

El Militante 2004, 'Mantenemos la pelea por la estatización de la fábrica bajo control obrero', 25 November, 25 November, available at: http://argentina.elmilitante.org/ fbricas-ocupadas-othermenu-98/1024-fbricas-ocupadas/707-qmantenemos-la-pe lea-por-la-estatizacin-de-la-fbrica-bajo-control-obreroq.html

El Universal 2012, 'Venezuelan Government Wedded to Direct Social Property', 4 February, available at: http://www.eluniversal.com/economia/120204/venezuelan-govern ment-wedded-to-direct-social-property

Eley, Tom 2009, 'Autoworkers End Factory Occupation in Windsor, Ontario', *World Socialist Website*, 20 March, available at: https://www.wsws.org/en/articles/2009/ 03/wind-m20.html

Elgue, Mario César (ed.) 2007, *La economía social: Por un empresariado nacional y democrático*, Buenos Aires: Capital Intelectual.

Elgue, Mario César (ed.) 2015, *La economía social del siglo XXI: Ideas y experiencias argentinas y latinoamericanas*, Buenos Aires: Ediciones Corregidor.

Elgue, Mario César and Daniel Cieza 2007, 'La economía social y el peronismo his-
    tórico', paper presented at the II Foro Federal de Investigadores y Docentes en
    Economía Social, Centro Cultural General San Martín, Buenos Aires, 2–3 August,
    available at: http://siare.clad.org/fulltext/2058800.pdf

Ellerman, David 1985, 'ESOPS & CO-OPS: Worker Capitalism & Worker Democracy',
    Labor Research Review, 1, 6: 55–69.

Elliott, Anthony 2002, 'Subjectivity, Culture, Autonomy: Castoriadis and Social Theory',
    in Jennifer Lehmann (ed.), Critical Theory: Diverse Objects, Diverse Subjects. Bingley,
    UK: Emerald Group Publishing.

Engels, Friedrich 1968 [1845], The Condition of the Working Class in England, Stanford,
    CA: Stanford University Press.

Engels, Friedrich 1978 [1880], 'Socialism: Utopian and Scientific', in The Marx-Engels
    Reader, edited by Robert C. Tucker, New York: W.W. Norton.

EnRedAndo 2006, 'Rosario fue sede del acto fundacional de la Federación Argentina
    de Cooperativas de Trabajadores Autogestionados (Facta)', Boletín de EnRedAndo,
    12 December, available at: http://www.boletin.enredando.org.ar/noticias_desarrollo
    .shtml?x=32018

EnRedAndo 2007, 'Quién dijo que todo está perdido', Boletín de EnRedAndo, 26 July,
    available at: http://boletin.enredando.org.ar/noticias_desarrollo.shtml?x=34396

Erdal, David 2011, Beyond the Corporation: Humanity Working, New York: Random
    House.

Erdal, David 2012, 'Employee Ownership is Good for Your Health: People Thrive in a
    Social Environment Characterized by Employee Ownership', Journal of Cooperative
    Thought and Practice, 1, 1: 3–6.

Escobedo, Martín, and María Victoria Deux Marzi 2007, Autogestión obrera en la Argen-
    tina: Historia y presente, Rosario: Universidad Nacional de Rosario Editora.

Estrin, Saul 1989, 'Workers' Co-operatives: Their Merits and Their Limitations', in Mar-
    ket Socialism, edited by Julian Le Grand and Saul Estrin, Oxford: Clarendon
    Press.

Estrin, Saul, Derek C. Jones, and Jan Svejnar 1987, 'The Productivity Effects of Worker
    Participation: Producer Cooperatives in Western Economies', Journal of Comparat-
    ive Economics, 11: 40–61.

Etchemendy, Sebastian, and Ruth Berins Collier 2007, 'Down but not out: The Recovery
    of a Downsized Labor Movement in Argentina (2002–2006)', IRLE Working Paper
    Series No. 141–07, Berkeley, CA: Institute for Research on Labor and Employment,
    University of California at Berkeley.

Evans, Peter and Chris Tilly 2016, 'The Future of Work: Escaping the Current Dystopian
    Trajectory and Building Better Alternatives', in The SAGE Handbook of the Sociology
    of Work and Employment, edited by Stephen Edgell, Heidi Gottfried, and Edward
    Granter, Thousand Oaks, CA: Sage.

FACTA 2016a, 'Senadores provincials privilegian a empresario y peligran 100 puestos de trabajo cooperativos', Prensa de la Federación Argentina de Cooperativas de Trabajadores Autogestionados, 15 July, available at: http://www.facta.org.ar/news/senadores-provinciales-privilegian-a-empresario-y-quitan-la-explotacion-del-frigo rifico-recuperar-a-la-cooperativa/ [accessed on 30 July 2016]

FACTA 2016b, '25 mil cooperativistas participaron de la Marcha Federal "En defense del trabajo"', Prensa de la Federación Argentina de Cooperativas de Trabajadores Auto-gestionados, 20 July, available at: http://www.facta.org.ar/news/25-mil-cooperativis tas-participaron-de-la-marcha-federal-en-defensa-del-trabajo/ [accessed on 30 July 2016]

FACTA 2016c, 'Yasky participará del lanziamiento de la Secretaría de Economía Social de CTA', Prensa de la Federación Argentina de Cooperativas de Trabajadores Auto-gestionados, 20 July, available at: http://www.facta.org.ar/news/yasky-participara -del-lanzamiento-de-la-secretaria-de-economia-social-de-cta/ [accessed on 30 July 2016]

FACTA 2016d, 'Plaini se comprometió a acompañar los procesos de recuperación de empresas', Prensa de la Federación Argentina de Cooperativas de Trabajadores Autogestionados, 6 September, available at: http://www.facta.org.ar/news/plaini-se -comprometio-a-acompanar-los-procesos-de-recuperacion-de-empresas/ [accessed on 19 September 2016]

FACTA 2017, 'Quienes somos', Federación Argentina de Cooperativas de Trabajadores Autogestionados, organisational website, available at: http://www.facta.org.ar/quie nes-somos/ [accessed on 1 February 2017]

Fairbairn, Brett 1994, *The Meaning of Rochdale: The Rochdale Pioneers and the Co-operative Principles*, Ocassional Paper Series, Saskatoon: Centre for the Study of Cooperatives, University of Saskatchewan.

Fajn, Gabriel 2003, *Fábricas y empresas recuperadas: Protesta social, auotgestión, y rup-turas en la subjectividad*, Buenos Aires: Centro Cultural de la Cooperación/ Instituto Movilizador de Fondos Cooperativos.

Fajn, Gabriel and Julián Rebón 2005, 'El taller ¿sin cronometro? Apuntes acerca de las empresas recuperadas', *Herramienta*, 28, available at: http://www.herramienta.com .ar/revista-herramienta-n-28/el-taller-sin-cronometro-apuntes-acerca-de-las-em presas-recuperadas

Fakhfakh, Fathi, Virginie Pérotin, and Mónica Gago 2012, 'Productivity, Capital, and Labor in Labor-Managed and Conventional Firms: An Investigation on French Data', *Industrial and Labor Relations Review (ILR Review)*, 65, 4: 847–79.

Fals Borda, Orlando 1971, *Cooperatives and Rural Development in Latin America: An Analytical Report*, Geneva: United Nations Research Institute for Social Develop-ment.

Fals Borda, Orlando 2001, 'Participatory (Action) Research and Social Theory: Origins and Challenges', in *Handbook of Action Research: Participative Inquiry and Practice*, edited by Peter Reason and Hilary Bradbury, Thousand Oaks, CA: Sage.

Fantasia, Rick 1988, *Cultures of Solidarity: Consciousness, Action, and Contemporary American Workers*, Berkeley and Los Angeles: University of California Press.

Farmer, Paul 1979, 'Enjoying Language: An Adventure with Words', *The English Journal*, 68, 5: 58–61.

Faulk, Karen Ann 2008, 'If They Touch One of Us, They Touch All of Us: Cooperativism as a Counterlogic to Neoliberal Capitalism', *Anthropological Quarterly*, 81, 3: 579–614.

Faulk, Karen Ann 2016, '"Recuperar el trabajo": Utopia and the Work of Recovery in an Argentine Cooperativist Movement', *The Journal of Latin American and Caribbean Anthropology*, 21, 2: 294–316.

Fay, C.R. 1947 [1920], *Life and Labour in the Nineteenth Century*, Cambridge, UK: Cambridge University Press.

FECOOTRA 2017, 'Federación de Cooperativas de Trabajo de la República Argentina', organisational website, available at: http://www.fecootra.org.ar/

Feenberg, Andrew 1995, *Alternative Modernity: The Technical Turn in Philosophy and Social Theory*, Berkeley and Los Angeles: University of California Press

Feenberg, Andrew 1999, *Questioning Technology*, New York: Routledge.

Feenberg, Andrew 2002, *Transforming Technology: A Critical Theory Revisited*, Oxford: Oxford University Press.

Feenberg, Andrew 2004, *Heidegger and Marcuse: The Catastrophe and Redemption of History*, London: Routledge.

Feinmann, Juan Pablo 2010, *Peronismo: Filosofía política de una persistencia argentina. Tomo 1: De 1943 a primer regreso de Perón (1972)*, Buenos Aires: Planeta.

Felder, Ruth and Viviana Patroni 2011, 'Austerity and its Aftermath: Neoliberalism and Labour in Argentina', *Socialist Studies*, 7, 1/2, Spring/Fall: 259–81.

Fentress, James and Chris Wickham 1992, *Social Memory*, Oxford: Blackwell.

Fernández Álvarez, Ana María 2006, *Política y subjetividades recuperadas: Asambleas barriales y fábricas recuperadas*, Buenos Aires: Tinta y Limón.

Fernández Álvarez, María Inés 2004, 'Proceso de trabajo y fábricas recuperadas: Algunas reflexiones a partir de un caso de la cuidad de Buenos Aires', Amsterdam: LabourAgain Publications, International Institute of Social History, available at: http://www.iisg.nl/labouragain/documents/fernandez-alvarez.pdf

Ferreyra, P. 2002, 'Decisión unanime de la legislatura de la ciudad: Expropian dos firmas y se las dan a sus empleados', *Clarín*, 13 September, in archives of Centro de Documentación de Empreasas Recuperadas, Programa Facultad Abierta, Facultad de Filosofía y Letras, Universidad de Buenos.

Feser, María Eleonora and Valeria Mutuberría Lazarini 2011, 'Reforma de la Ley de Concursos y Quiebras: Desafíos para las futuras empresas recuperadas por sus trabajadores', *Revista Idelcoop*, 38, 205: 284–94.

Fidler, Richard 2013, 'Bolivian Government Authorizes Workers to Take Over Closed or Abandoned Firms', *The Bullet*, Socialist Project E-Bulletin No. 888, 18 October: available at: https://www.socialistproject.ca/bullet/888.php

Fine, Ben and Alfredo Saad-Filho 2004, *Marx's Capital*, London: Pluto.

Fitzpatrick, Sheila 2008, *The Russian Revolution*, Oxford: Oxford University Press.

Foley, Griff 1999, *Learning in Social Action: A Contribution to Understanding Informal Education*, London: Zed Books.

Fontan, Jean-Marc and Eric Shragge 2000, 'Tendencies, Tensions and Visions in the Social Economy', in *Social Economy: International Debates and Perspectives*, edited by Jean-Marc Fontan and Eric Shragge, Montreal: Black Rose Books.

Forcinito, Karina, and Victoria Basualdo (eds.) 2007, *Transformaciones recientes en la economía argentina: Tendencias y perspectivas*, Buenos Aires and Los Polvorines, Buenos Aires: Prometeo Libros and Universidad Nacional de General Sarmiento.

Forgacs, David (ed.) 2000, *The Antonio Gramsci Reader: Selected Writings, 1916–1935*, New York: New York University Press.

Fontenia, Eduardo 2008, *Cooperativas de trabajo y empresas recupadas*, Buenos Aires: InterCoop Editorial Cooperativa.

Fourier, Charles 1971, *Design for Utopia: Selected Writings of Charles Fourier*, New York: Schocken Books.

Fournier, Marisa and Gonzalo Vázquez 2007, *Experiencias y aprendizajes en la construcción de otra economía: Estudio sobre emprendimientos socioeconómicos asociativos*, Los Polvorines, Buenos Aires: Instituto del Conurbano, Universidad Nacional de General Sarmiento.

Fraga, Rosendo 2006, 'Cambios políticos post-crisis 2001–2002', *Cuadernos Argentina Reciente: A 5 años del 19 y 20 de diciembre*, 3, December, 138–41.

Franks, Benjamin 2006, *Rebel Alliances. The Means and Ends of Contemporary British Anarchisms*, Oakland, CA: AK Press.

Franks, Benjamin 2010, 'Vanguards and Paternalism', in *New Perspectives on Anarchism*, edited by Nathan J. Nun and Shane Wahl, New York: Lexington Books.

Freire, Paulo 1970, *Pedagogy of the Oppressed*, New York: Continuum.

FRETECO 2009, 'Balance del IIo Encuentro Latinoamericano de Empresas Recuperadas por sus Trabajadores', *Lucha de Clases: Corriente Marxista Internacional*, 7 July, available at: http://www.luchadeclases.org.bo/internacional/americas/199-balance-del-ii-encuentro-latinoamericano-de-empresas-recuperadas-por-sus-trabajadores.html

Friedman, Andrew L. 1977, *Industry and Labour: Class Struggle at Work and Monopoly Capitalism*, London: Macmillan.

Fritz, Thomas 2007, *ALBA contra ALCA: La Alternativa Bolivariana par alas Américas: Una nueva vía para la integración regional en latinoamérica*, Berlin: Centro de Investigación y Documentación Chile Latinoamérica (FDCL), available at: http://www

.alternative-regionalisms.org/wp-content/uploads/2009/07/fritz-albacontraalca1
.pdf

Fromm, Erich 1968, *The Revolution of Hope: Toward a Humanized Technology*, New York: Harper & Row.

Fundación Fundemos 2016, 'Historia', organisational website, available at: http://www .fundemos.org.ar/

Furubotn, Eirik G. and Svetozar Pejovich 1970, 'Property Rights and the Behaviour of the Firm in a Socialist State: The Example of Yugoslavia', *Zeitschrift für Nationalökonomie / Journal of Economics*, 30, 3/4: 431–54.

Furubotn, Eirik G. and Svetozar Pejovich 1974, *The Economics of Property Rights*, Cambridge, MA: Ballinger.

Gaggero, Alejandro 2002, 'Algunos por la autonomía, otros con la estatización', *Página/ 12*, 8 September, available at: https://www.pagina12.com.ar/diario/elpais/1-9886-2002-09-08.html

Gaiger, Luiz Inácio 2003, 'A economia solidária diante do modo de produção capitalista', *Caderno CRH*, 16, 39: 181–211.

Gaiger, Luiz Inácio and Eliene Dos Anjos 2013, 'Solidarity Economy in Brazil: The Relevance of Cooperatives for the Historic Emancipation of Workers', in *Cooperatives and Socialism: A View from Cuba*, edited by Camila Piñeiro Harnecker, Houndmills, Basingstoke, UK: Palgrave Macmillan.

Galiani, Sebastian, Paul J. Gertler, Ernesto Schargrodsky, and Federico Sturzenegger 2003, 'The costs and benefits of privatization in Argentina: A microeconomic analysis', Research Network Working Paper #R-454. Washington, DC: Inter-American Development Bank, Latin American Research Network/Banco Interamericano de Desarrollo Red de Centros de Investigación.

Gallego, Juan Luis 2014, 'Guía para tumbar el capitalismo (1/2)', *Numeros Rojos*, 30 July, available at: http://blogs.publico.es/numeros-rojos/2014/07/30/guia-para-tumbar-el-capitalismo-12/

Gambina, Julio 2005, 'Los aportes de la economía social para el desarrollo: El caso de las empresas recuperadas en la Argentina.', *El Correo de Económicas*, 1, 1: 13–22.

Gambina, Julio and Daniel Campione 2002, *Los años de Menem: Cirugía mayor*, Buenos Aires: Centro Cultural de la Cooperación.

Gamson, Zelda F. and Henry M. Levin 1984, 'Obstacles to the Survival of Democratic Workplaces', in *Worker Cooperatives in America*, edited by Jackall R. and Levin H.M., Berkeley and Los Angeles: University of California Press.

García Allegrone, Verónica, Florencia Partenio, and María Inés Fernández Álvarez 2004, 'Los procesos de recuperación de fábricas: Una mirada retrospectiva', in *El trabajo frente al espejo: Continuidades y rupturas en los procesos de contrucción identitatria de los trabajadores*, edited by Osvaldo Battistini, Buenos Aires: Promoteo.

Garnett, Ronald G. 1972, *Co-operation and the Owenite Socialist Communities in Britain, 1825–45*, Manchester: Manchester University Press.

Gasper, Phil 2014, 'Are Workers' Cooperatives the Alternative to Capitalism?', *International Socialist Review*, 93, available at: http://isreview.org/issue/93/are-workers-cooperatives-alternative-capitalism

Geras, Norman 2000, 'Minimum Utopia: Ten Theses', *Socialist Register 2000*, 36: 41–52.

Germani, Gino and Sibila S. de Yujnovsky 1973, 'El surgimiento del peronismo: El rol de los obreros y de los migrantes internos.' *Desarrollo Económico*, 13, 51: 435–88.

Ghibaudi, Javier 2004, 'Una aproximación comparativa a las empresas recuperadas argentinas y las autogeridas en Brasil', Amsterdam: LabourAgain Publications, International Institute of Social History, available at: http://base.socioeco.org/docs/ghibaudi.pdf

Gibson-Graham, J.K. 2006, *A Postcapitalist Politics*, Minneapolis: University of Minnesota Press.

Giddens, Anthony 1979, *Central Problems in Social Theory: Action, Structure and Contradiction in Social Analysis*, Berkley and Los Angeles: University of California Press.

Giddens, Anthony 1994, *Beyond Left and Right: The Future of RadicalPpolitics*, Stanford, CA: Stanford University Press.

Gide, Charles 1905, *Économie sociale. Les institutions du progrès social au début du XXe siècle*. Paris, Larose.

Gil de San Vicente, Iñaki 2013, *Cooperativismo obrero, consejismo y autogestión socialista: Algunas lecciones para Euskal Herria*, Bilbao: Boltxe Liburuak.

Gillespie, Cillian and Stephen Boyd 2009, 'Waterford Crystal: Nationalisation was the Key', *Socialism Today*, 129, June: available at: http://www.socialismtoday.org/129/waterford.html

Gindin, Sam, 2016, 'Chasing Utopia: Worker Ownership and Cooperatives Will Not Succeed by Competing on Capitalism's Terms,' *Jacobin*, March 10, available at: https://www.jacobinmag.com/2016/03/workers-control-coops-wright-wolff-alperovitz/

Giovannini, Michela and Marcelo Vieta 2017, 'Cooperatives in Latin America', in *The Oxford Handbook of Mutual, Co-Operative, and Co-Owned Business*, edited by Jonathan Michie, Joseph R. Blasi, and Carlo Borzaga, Oxford: Oxford University Press.

Glenn, John 2009, 'Welfare Spending in an Era of Globalization: The North – South Divide', *International Relations*, 23, 1: 27–50.

Godio, Julio 2000, *Historia del movimiento obrero argentino: 1870–2000*, Buenos Aires: Corregidor.

Godoy, Raul 2002, 'Segundo encuentro nacional de fabricas ocupadas y empresas en lucha', *Argentina IndyMedia*, 5 August, available at: http://argentina.indymedia.org/news/2002/08/41768_comment.php

González, Cándido 2003, 'Entrevista con Cándido González', in archives of Centro de Documentación de Empreasas Recuperadas, Programa Facultad Abierta, Facultad de Filosofía y Letras, Universidad de Buenos Aires.

González, Cándido and Marcelo Vieta 2005, Interview with Cándido González and

Marcelo Vieta on the show *La Cuadrilla*, La Tribu FM 88.7, 2 August, Buenos Aires, Argentina, available at: http://www.vieta.ca/thoughts/2005/08/fm-la-tribu-887-buenos-aires.html [accessed on 20 February 2018]

Gordon, Uri 2008, *Anarchy Alive! Anti-Authoritarian Politics from Practice to Theory*, London: Pluto.

Gorz, André 1973, 'Workers' Control Is More Than Just That', in *Workers' Control: A Reader on Labor and Social Change*, edited by Gerry Hunnius, G. David Garson, and John Case, New York: Vintage.

Gorz, André 1982, *Farewell to the Working Class: An Essay on Post-Industrial Socialism*, London: Pluto.

Gouin, Rachel 2009, 'An Antiracist Feminist Analysis for the Study of Learning and Social Struggle', *Adult Education Quarterly*, 59, 2: 158–75.

Gracia, Amalia and Sandra Cavaliere 2007, 'Repertorios en fábrica: La experiencia de recuperación fabril en Argentina, 2000–2006', *Estudios Sociológicos*, 25, 73: 155– 86.

Graeber David 2004, *Fragments of an Anarchist Anthropology*, Chicago: Prickly Paradigm Press.

Graeber, David 2009, *Direct Action: An Ethnography*, Oakland, CA: AK Press.

Grahame, Peter R. 1998, 'Ethnography, Institutions, and the Problematic of the Everyday World', *Human Studies*, 21, 4: 347–60.

Gramsci, Antonio 1919, 'Workers and Peasants', *L'Ordine Nuovo*, 2 August, available at: https://www.marxists.org/archive/gramsci/1919/08/workers-peasants.htm

Gramsci, Antonio 1971a, *Selections from the Prison Notebooks*, edited by Quintin Hoare and Geoffrey Nowell Smith, New York: International Publishers.

Gramsci, Antonio 1971b, 'Americanism and Fordism', in *Selections from the Prison Notebooks*, edited by Quintin Hoare and Geoffrey Nowell Smith, New York: International Publishers.

Gramsci, Antonio 2000 [1919], 'Workers' Democracy', in *The Antonio Gramsci Reader: Selected Writings, 1916–1935*, edited by David Forgacs, New York: New York University Press.

Gray, John 1825, *A Lecture on Human Happiness* [short title]. London: Sherwood Jones.

Gray, John 1831, *The Social System: A Treatise on the Principle of Exchange*, Edinburgh: William Tait.

Grevatt, Martha 2009, 'Irish Workers Occupy Waterford Glass Factory', *Workers World*, 22 February, available at: http://www.workers.org/2009/world/waterford_0226/

Grint, Keith 2005, *The Sociology of Work*. Cambridge, UK: Polity.

Grupo de Boedo Films 2002, *Brukman: La trilogia + Cuatro estaciones* [film], Argentina: Grupo de Boedo Films, Kino Nuestra Lucha.

Guerra, Pablo 2013, *Autogestión empresarial en Uruguay: Análisis de caso del FONDES*, Montevideo: Facultad de Derecho, Universidad de la República.

Guimenez, Sandra 2011, 'Una salida colectiva', *Página/12*, 12 June, available at: https://www.pagina12.com.ar/diario/economia/2-169984-2011-06-13.html

Gurney, Peter 1988, 'George Jacob Holyoake: Socialism, Association and Cooperation in Nineteenth-Century England', in *New Views of Cooperation (History Workshop)*, edited by Stephen Yeo, London: Routledge.

Gutiérrez, José Antonio 2005, 'Workers Without Bosses: Workers' Self-Management in Argentina', *anarkismo.net*, 31 May, available at: http://www.anarkismo.net/newswire .php?story_id=627%203%20Jul.%202005

Halbwachs, Maurice 1980, *The Collective Memory*, New York: Harper Colophone Books.

Hall, Budd L. and Darlene E. Clover 2005, 'Social Movement Learning', in *The Encyclopedia of Adult Education*, edited by Leona M. English, Houndmills, Basingstoke, UK: Palgrave Macmillan.

Hall, Budd L. and Thomas Turray 2006, 'A Review of the State of the Field of Adult Learning: Social Movement Learning', The State of the Field Review, Canadian Council on Learning, available at: http://en.copian.ca/library/research/sotfr/socialmv/ socialmv.pdf

Hansmann, Henry 1988, 'Ownership of the Firm', *Law, Economics, and Organization*, 4, 2: 267–304.

Hansmann, Henry 1996, *The Ownership of Enterprise*. Cambridge, MA: Belknap.

Hardt, Michael and Antonio Negri 2004, *Multitude: War and Democracy in the Age of Empire*, New York: Penguin.

Harvey, David 2005, *A Brief History of Neoliberalism*, Oxford: Oxford University Press.

Harvie, David 2005, 'All Labour Produces Value for Capital: And We All Struggle Against Value', *The Commoner*, 10: 132–71.

Heilbroner, Robert L. & William S. Milberg 2008, *The Making of Economic Society*, Upper Saddle River, NJ: Prentice Hall.

Heller, Pablo 2004, *Fábricas Recuperadas: Argentina 2000–2004*, Buenos Aires: Ediciones Rumbos.

Henley, Jon, Ashifa Kassam, Constanze Letsch, and Uki Goñi 2015, 'May Day: Workers of the World Unite and Take Over – Their Factories', *The Guardian*, 1 May, available at: https://www.theguardian.com/world/2015/may/01/may-day-workers-of-the -world-unite-and-take-over-their-factories

Hernandez, Mario 2013, *El movimiento de autogestión obrera en Argentina: Empresas recuperadas y movimientos de trabajadores desocupados*, Buenos Aires: Topia.

Hill, Christopher 1986, 'The Poor and the People', in *The Collected Essays of Christopher Hill, Volume 3: People and Ideas in 17th Century England*, Amherst, MA: University of Massachuettes Press.

Hirtz, Natalia Vanesa, and Marta Susana Giacone 2013, 'The Recovered Companies Workers' Struggle in Argentina: Between Autonomy and New Forms of Control.', *Latin American Perspectives*, 40, 4: 88–100.

Hobsbawm, Eric 1964, *Labouring Men: Studies in the History of Labour*, London: Weiden-feld & Nicolson.

Hobsbawm, Eric 2011, *How to Change the World: Reflections on Marx and Marxism*, New Haven and London: Yale University Press.

Hodgskin, Thomas 1825, *Labour Defended Against the Claims of Capital, or the Unproductiveness of Capital Proved with Reference to the Present Combinations Amongst Journeymen*, London: B. Steil.

Hoe, Susanna 1978, *The Man Who Gave His Company Away: A Biography of Ernest Bader, Founder of the Scott Bader Commonwealth*. Portsmouth, NH: Heinemann.

Holloway, John 2002, *Change the World Without Taking Power: The Meaning of Revolution today*, London: Pluto.

Holloway, John 2011, 'Zapatismo', personal website, available at: http://www.johnhollo way.com.mx/2011/07/30/zapatismo/

Holyoake, George Jacob 1875, *The History of Co-operation*, London: T. Fisher Unwin.

Hopkins, Kathryn, Dan Milmo, and Henry MacDonald 2009, 'Sit-ins at Three Factories after Vehicle Parts Company Goes Into Administration', *The Guardian*, 2 April, available at: https://www.theguardian.com/business/2009/apr/02/car-industry-unions-visteon-ford

Horkheimer, Max 1947, *Eclipse of Reason*, Oxford: Oxford University Press.

Horkheimer, Max 2002 [1937], 'Traditional and Critical Theory', in *Critical Theory: Selected Essays*, New York: Continuum.

Horvat, Branko 1982, *The Political Economy of Socialism: A Marxist Social Theory*, Armonk, NY: M.E. Sharpe.

Hough, Peter, David Wilson, and Hazel Corcoran 2010, 'The Worker Co-op Sector in Canada: Success Factors, and Planning for Growth', Canadian Social Economy Research Partnerships and Canadian Worker Co-operative Federation, 31 May, available at: http://canadianworker.coop/wp-content/uploads/2011/03/CWCF_Canadi an_SSHRC_Paper_16-6-2010_fnl.pdf

Howard, Michael W. 2000, *Self-Management and the Crisis of Socialism: The Rose in the Fist of the Present*. New York: Rowman & Littlefield.

Howarth, Melanie 2007, *Worker Co-operatives and the Phenomenon of Empresas Recuperadas in Argentina: An Analysis of Their Potential for Replication*, Geneva: International Labour Organization.

Huang, Daniel 2014, 'Don't Cry for Them: The World's Biggest Sovereign Defaults Since 2000', *The Wall Street Journal*, 2 July, available at: http://blogs.wsj.com/moneybeat/ 2014/07/02/dont-cry-for-them-the-worlds-biggest-sovereign-defaults-since-2000/

Hudis, Peter 2012, *Marx's Concept of the Alternative to Capitalism*, Leiden: Brill.

Hudson, Juan Pablo 2010, 'Formulaciones teóricos-conceptuales de la autogestión.', *Revista Méxicana de Sociologia*, 74, 4: 571–97.

Huertas, Olga, Ricardo Dávila Ladron de Guevara, and Dario Castillo 2011, 'Transform-

aciones en las subjetividades de los trabajadores: Casos de empresas recuperadas',
Universitas Psychologica, 10, 2: 581–94.

Hunnius, Gerry, G. David Garson, and John Case 1973, *Workers' Control: A Reader on Labor and Social Change*, New York: Vintage.

Hunt, E.K. 1986, 'The Putative Defects of Socialist Economic Planning: Reply to Rattansi', *Science & Society*, 50, 1: 102–7.

Hutchinson, Frances and Brian Burkitt 2005, *The Political Economy of Social Credit and Guild Socialism*, Charlbury, UK: John Carpenter Publishing.

Huws, Ursula 2014, *Labor in the Global Digital Economy: The Cyberteriat Comes of Age*, New York: Monthly Review Press.

Iacoponi, Ricardo Díaz and Néstor Sánchez Sotelo 2012, *Industria Argentina: La Fábrica Es Para los que Trabajan* [film], Argentina: Insituto Nacional de Cine y Artes Audiovisuales (INCAA).

ICA 2013, 'Argentina's Cooperative Sector Continues to Grow', *Recent News*, International Co-operative Alliance, 12 March, available at: http://ica.coop/en/media/news/argentinas-co-operative-sector-continues-grow

ICA 2014, 'French National Assembly Passes New Social Economy Law 2014', *Recent News*, International Co-operative Alliance, 20 August, available at: https://ica.coop/en/media/news/french-national-assembly-passes-new-social-economy-law

ICA 2016, 'Co-operative Identity, Values & Principles', International Co-operative Alliance organisational website, available at: http://ica.coop/en/whats-co-op/co-operative-identity-values-principles

ICA Group 2016, 'The ICA Group About Us', organisational website, available at: http://icagroup.org/about/

ICE 2007, 'Italia en la Exposición de Empresas y Fábricas Recuperadas por los Trabajadores: Catálogo de los participantes italianos', Istituto Nazionale per il Commercio Estero, 23–25 November, in archives of Centro de Documentación de Empreasas Recuperadas, Programa Facultad Abierta, Facultad de Filosofía y Letras, Universidad de Buenos Aires.

INAES 2007, 'Que es una cooperativa: Definición, valores, principios, tipos', Instituto Nacional de Asociativismo y Economía Social, Ministerio Nacional de Desarollo Social, Gobierno Nacional de la República Argentina, available at: http://www.alimentosargentinos.gob.ar/contenido/valorAr/redypa/Cooperativas_INAES.pdf

INAES 2008, 'Cantidad de cooperativas por actividad', Instituto Nacional de Asociativismo y Economía Social, Ministerio Nacional de Desarollo Social, Gobierno Nacional de la República Argentina, available at: http://www.inaes.gov.ar/es/Enlaces/estadisticas_c2.asp [accessed on 20 December 2008]

INAES 2009, 'Las cooperativas y las mutuales en la República Argentina', Instituto Nacional de Asociativismo y Economía Social, Ministerio Nacional de Desarollo

Social, Gobierno Nacional de la República Argentina. Available at: http://www.inaes
.gov.ar/es/Entidades/cooperativas [accessed on 11 November 2009]

INDEC 2011, 'Encuesta permanente de hogares (EPH): Línea de pobreza y canasta
básica: Serie histórica', Instituto Nacional de Estadísticas y Censos de la República
Argentina, available at: http://www.indec.gob.ar/informesdeprensa_anteriores.asp
?id_tema_1=4&id_tema_2=27&id_tema_3=64

INDEC 2016, 'Mercado de trabajo: Principales indicadores (Segundo trimestre de 2016)',
Instituto Nacional de Estadísticas y Censos de la República Argentina, 23 August,
available at: http://www.indec.gov.ar/uploads/informesdeprensa/EPH_cont_2trim
16.pdf

Indymedia UK 2007, 'Major Victory for Worker Recovered Factory "Jugoremedija" in
Serbia', 31 January, available at: https://www.indymedia.org.uk/en/2007/01/360564
.html

Infield, Henrik F. 1947, Co-operative Communities at Work, London: Keegan.

Infield, Henrik F. 1956, The Sociological Study of Co-operation: An Outline, Loughbor-
ough: Co-operative College.

Instituto de Investigaciones Gino Germani 2012, 'Encuesta: Formas Económicas Altern-
ativas', Buenos Aires: Facultad de Ciencias Sociales, Universidad de Buenos Aires,
available at: http://webiigg.sociales.uba.ar/empresasrecuperadas/PDF/PDF_07/
FORMAS_ECO.pdf

Intercentar n.d., 'Fact Sheet: French Employee Buy-Out Mutual Fund "FCPE de reprise"',
Kelso Professorship of Comparative Law, East European Business Law and European
Legal Policy, Europa Universität Viadrina, available at: http://intercentar.de/filead
min/files/Conference/7d_Fact%20Sheet%20French%20FCPE%20de%20Reprise
%20EN.pdf

Isitan, Isaac and Carole Poliquin 2007, The Women of Brukman [film], Canada: Canadian Heritage, Radio Canada, Les Productions ISCA.

Iturraspe, Francisco 1986, Participación, cogestión y autogestión en América Latina:
América Latina, Argentina, Bolivia, Caribe, y Centro América, Caracas: Nueva Sociedad.

IWW 2017, 'Preamble, Constitution, and General Bylaws of the Industrial Workers of
the World', organisational website, available at: https://iww.org/PDF/Constitutions/
CurrentIWWConstitution.pdf

Jainchill, Andrew, and Samuel Moyn 2004, 'French Democracy Between Totalitarian-
ism and Solidarity: Pierre Rosanvallon and Revisionist Historiography', The Journal
of Modern History, 76, 1: 107–54.

James, Daniel 1978, 'Power and Politics in the Peronist Trade Unions', Journal of Inter-
american Studies and World Affairs, 20, 1: 3–36.

James, Daniel 1988, From Resistance to Integration: Peronism and the Argentine Working
Class, 1946–1976, Cambridge, UK: Cambridge University Press.

James, Steve 2011, 'Vita Cortex Factory Occupied in Cork, Ireland', *World Socialist Web Site*, 29 December, available at: https://www.wsws.org/en/articles/2011/12/occu-d28.html

Jay, Martin 1973, *The Dialectical Imagination: A History of the Frankfurt School and the Institute of Social Research, 1923–1950*, Boston: Little, Brown and Company.

Jelin, Elizabeth 2003, *State Repression and the Labors of Memory*, Minneapolis: University of Minnesota Press.

Jensen, Anthony 2011, 'Saving Companies Worth Saving: Spain Pioneers a Sustainable Model of Democratic Corporate Governance', *Economic and Industrial Democracy*, 32, 4: 697–720.

Jensen, Anthony 2012, *Insolvency, Employee Rights, and Employee Buy-Outs: A Strategy for Restructuring*, unpublished doctoral dissertation, University of Sydney, Sydney, Australia.

Jensen, Michael C. and William H. Meckling 1976, 'Theory of the Firm: Managerial Behavior, Agency Costs and Ownership Structure', *Journal of Financial Economics*, 3, 4: 305–60.

Jensen, Michael C. and William H. Meckling 1979, 'Rights and Production Functions: An Application to Labour-Managed Firms and Codetermination', *Journal of Business*, 52: 469–506.

Jones, Derek C. and Jan Svejnar 1984, 'Participation, Profit Sharing, Worker Ownership and Efficiency in Italian Producer Cooperatives', *Economica*, 52, 208: 449–65.

Jones, Jack and D. Seabrook 1969, 'Industrial Democracy', in *Trade Union Register*, edited by Ken Coates, Tony Topham, and M.B. Barrett, London: Merlin Press.

Jossa, Bruno 2005, 'Marx, Marxism and the Cooperative Movement', *Cambridge Journal of Economics*, 29, 1: 3–18.

Jossa, Bruno 2014, *Producer Cooperatives as a New Mode of Production*. London: Routledge.

Jossa, Bruno 2015, 'A Few Reflections on the Reasons Why Cooperative Firms Have Failed to Gain a Firm Foothold', *Open Journal of Business and Management*, 3: 265–80.

Jossa, Bruno 2016, 'Production Modes, Marx's Method and the Feasible Revolution', *European Scientific Journal*, 12, 31: 20–49.

Jossa, Bruno 2017, *Labour Managed Firms and Post-Capitalism*, London: Routledge.

Jukic, Elvira M. 2015, 'Much-Loved Bosnian Company Rises from the Ashes', *BalkanInsight*, 12 June, available at: http://www.balkaninsight.com/en/article/once-leading-bosnia-detergent-company-rises-from-ashes

Juncal, Luis 2005, 'Desarollo del cooperativismo y la economía social en la Argentina.', *El Correo de Económicas*, 1, 1: 104–13.

Juravich, Tom 1988, *Chaos on the Shop Floor: A Worker's View of Quality, Productivity, and Management*, Philadelphia: Temple University Press.

Karyotis, Theodoros 2014a, 'Workers of Self-Managed Factories Meet in Marseille for the "Workers' Economy" International Meeting', *Workerscontrol.net*, 14 February, available at: http://www.workerscontrol.net/authors/workers-self-managed-facto ries-meet-marseille-%E2%80%9Cworkers-economy%E2%80%9D-international-meeting

Karyotis, Theodoros 2014b, 'Vio.Me: Workers' Control in the Greek Crisis', *ROAR Magazine*, 1 May, available at: https://roarmag.org/essays/viome-workers-control-greek -crisis/

Kasmir, Sharryn 1996, *The Myth of Mondragon: Cooperatives, Politics and Working-Class Life in a Basque Town*, Albany, NY: University of New York Press.

Kasparian, Denise 2012, 'Presentación de la Unión Productiva de Empresas Autogestionadas (UPEA)', *Revista OSERA*, 4: available at: http://webiigg.sociales.uba.ar/em presasrecuperadas/PDF/PDF_04/upea4.pdf

Katz, Claudio 2007, 'Gobiernos y regimenes en América Latina', in *Los '90: Fin de ciclo: El retorno a la contradicción*, edited by José Enrique, Buenos Aires: Final Abierto.

Kennard, Matt and Ana Caistor-Arendar 2016, 'Occupy Buenos Aires: The Workers' Movement that Transformed a City, and Inspired the World', *The Guardian*, 10 March, available at: https://www.theguardian.com/cities/2016/mar/10/occupy-buenos-ai res-argentina-workers-cooperative-movement

Kelso, Louis and Mortimer Adler 1958, *The Capitalist Manifesto*, New York: Random House.

Kim, Hwalshin and Seungkwon Jang, 2015, *A Worker-Owned Firm's Organizatonal Change from the Perspective of Organizational Learning: The Case of Woojin Traffic*, paper presented at the 'Co-operatives and the World of Work Research Conference', International Labour Organization and the International Co-operative Alliance Committee on Co-operative Research, Antalya, Turkey, 10–11 November.

Klein, Naomi 2003, 'Snapshot of a Nation: How Argentina's New President Deals with the Occupied Factories will be Hugely Significant', 28 April, available at: https://www .theguardian.com/world/2003/apr/28/usa.globalisation

Kosacoff, Bernardo 2007, *Hacia un nuevo modelo industrial: Ideas y vueltas del desarrollo argentine*, Buenos Aires: Capital Intelectual.

Koselleck, Reinhart 2004, *Futures Past: On the Semantics of Historical Time*, New York: Columbia University Press.

Kotkin, Stephen 1991, *Steeltown, USSR: Soviet Society in the Gorbachev Era*, Berkeley and Los Angeles: University of California Press.

Kozloff, Nikolas 2008, *Revolution! South America and The Rise of the New Left*, Houndmills, Basingstoke, UK: Palgrave Macmillan.

Kraul, Chris 2011, 'Are Good Times in Argentina for Real or an Illusion?', *Los Angeles Times*, 2 August, available at: http://www.latimes.com/business/la-xpm-2011-aug-02 -la-fi-argentina-economy-20110802-story.html

Kropotkin, Peter 1989 [1902], *Mutual Aid: A Factor of Evolution*, Montreal: Black Rose Books.

Kropotkin, Peter 1995 [1892], *The Conquest of Bread and Other Writings*, edited by Marshall S. Shatz, Cambridge, UK: Cambridge University Press.

Kruse, Douglas L., Richard B. Freeman, and Joseph R. Blasi, (eds.) 2010, *Shared Capitalism at Work: Employee Ownership, Profit and Gain Sharing, and Broad-Based Stock Options*, Chicago: University of Chicago Press.

Kruse, Douglas and Joseph Blasi 1995, 'Employee Ownership, Employee Attitudes, and Firm Performance', NBER Working Papers No. 5277, National Bureau of Economic Research, available at: http://www.nber.org/papers/w5277.pdf

Kulfas, Matías 2016, *Los tres kirchnerismos: Una historia de la economía argentina, 2003–2015*, Buenos Aires: Siglo Veintiuno Editores.

La Coperacha 2016, 'Cooperativa Trabajadores de Pascual, refrenda su compromiso social', 4 July, available at: http://lacoperacha.org.mx/Cooperativa-Pascual-refrenda -compromiso-social.php

La Economía de los/las Trabajadores/as 2017, 'La Economía de Los/Las Trabajadores/as: VI Encuentro Internacional (Buenos Aires–Pigüé, 30 de agosto al 2 de septiembre)', organisational website, available at: https://laeconomiadelostrabajadores.word press.com/

La Nación 2009, 'Acordaron un salario mímimo de 1.500 pesos a partir de 2010', 29 July, available at: http://www.lanacion.com.ar/1156136-acordaron-un-salario-minimo-de -1500-pesos-a-partir-de-2010

La Nación 2011, 'La carrera del salario mínimo y la inflación', 21 July, available at: www .lanacion.com.ar/1391262-la-carrera-del-salario-minimo-y-la-inflacion

La Nación 2015, 'En 2014 empeoró el número de trabajadores "en negro"', 13 March, available at: http://www.lanacion.com.ar/1775995-en-2014-empeoro-el-numero-de- trabajadores-en-negro

La Repubblica 2014, 'La storia di Ri-Maflow, da ex fabbrica iper tecnologica a modello anti liberista', 19 Nobember, available at: http://www.repubblica.it/solidarieta/ cooperazione/2014/11/19/news/la_storia_di_rimaflow-100918928/

La Serna, Carlos 2004, *La economía solidaria en Argentina: Entre las necesidades y las aspiraciones*, Córdoba, Argentina: Programa Modernidad y Políticas Sociales, Instítuto de Investigación y Formación en Administración Pública (IIFAP), Universidad Nacional de Córdoba.

Laidler, Harry 1938, *A History of Socialist Thought*, New York: Thomas Y. Crowell Company.

Larrabure, Manuel, Marcelo Vieta, and Daniel Schugurensky 2011, 'The 'New Cooperativism' in Latin America: Worker-Recuperated Enterprises and Socialist Production Units', *Studies in the Education of Adults*, 43, 2: 181–96.

Lavaca 2004, *Sin patrón: Fábricas y empresas recuperadas por sus trabajadores: Una historia, una guía*. Buenos Aires: Cooperativa de Trabajo Lavaca.

Lavaca 2005a, 'Lavaca en Venezuela: Una multinacional sin patrón', 1 November, available at: http://www.lavaca.org/seccion/actualidad/1/1195.shtml

Lavaca 2005b, 'Documento Final: Compromiso de Caracas', 1 November, available at: http://www.lavaca.org/seccion/actualidad/1/1196.shtml

Lave, Jean and Etienne Wenger 1991, *Situated Learning: Legitimate Peripheral Participation*, Cambridge, UK: Cambridge University Press.

Laville, Jean-Louis, Benoît Lévesque, and Marguerite Mendell 2007, 'The Social Economy: Diverse Approaches and Practices in Europe and Canada', in *The Social Economy: Building Inclusive Economies*, edited by Antonella Noya and Emma Clarence, Paris: OECD Publishing.

Lazzarato, Maurizio 2003, 'Struggle, Event, Media', *RepublicArt/European Institute for Progressive Cultural Politics*, available at: http://eipcp.net/transversal/1003/lazzarato/en.html

Lebowitz, Michael 2003, *Beyond Capital: Marx's Political Economy of the Working Class*, Houndmills, Basingstoke, UK: Palgrave Macmillan.

Lebowitz, Michael 2005, 'Constructing Co-Management in Venezuela: Contradictions Along the Path', *Monthly Review Online*, 24 October, available at: http://mrzine.monthlyreview.org/lebowitz241005.html

Lebowitz, Michael 2008, 'The Spectre of Socialism for the Twenty-First Century', *Links: International Journal of Socialist Renewal*, available at: http://links.org.au/node/503

Lebowitz, Michael 2009, *Following Marx: Method, Critique and Crisis*, Leiden: Brill.

Lebowitz, Michael 2011, 'The Unifying Element in All Struggles Against Capital Is the Right of Everyone to Full Human Development', *Monthly Review*, 63, 6: 46–51.

Lefevbre, Henri 2009, *State, Space, World: Selected Essays*, edited by Neil Brenner and Stuart Elden, Minneapolis: University of Minnesota Press.

Lenin, Vladimir Ilyich 1965 [1923], 'On Cooperation', in *V.I. Lenin: Collected Works, Volume 33, August 1921–March 1923*, Moscow: Progress Publishers.

Lerner, Josh and Daniel Schugurensky 2007, 'Who Learns What in Participatory Democracy? Participatory Budgeting in Rosario, Argentina', in *Democratic Practices and Learning Opportunities*, edited by Ruud van der Veen, Danny Wildemeersch, Janet Youngblood, and Victoria Marsic, Rotterdam: Sense.

Leverink, Joris 2015, 'Kazova Workers Claim Historic Victory in Turkey', *ROAR Magazine*, 1 May, available at: https://roarmag.org/essays/free-kazova-cooperative-turkey/

Levin, Andrea and Verbeke, Griselda 1997, 'El cooperativismo argentino en cifras: Tendencias en su evolución: 1927–1997', Buenos Aires: Documentos del Centro de Estudios de Sociología del Trabajo, Facltad de Ciencias Económicas, Universidad de Buenos Aires.

Levitsky, Steven 2003, *Transforming Labor-Based Parties in Latin America: Argentine Peronism in Comparative Perspective*, Cambridge, UK: Cambridge University Press.

Levy Yeyati, Eduardo and Diego Valenzuela 2013, *La resurrección: Historia de la poscrisis argentina*, Buenos Aires: Eudeba.

Labour Party 2017, 'For the Many, Not the Few: The Labour Party Manifesto 2017,' Labour Party of the United Kingdom, available at: http://www.labour.org.uk/index .php/manifesto2017

Lewis, Avi and Naomi Klein 2004, *The Take: Occupy, Resist, Produce* [film], Canada: National Film Board of Canada, Canadian Broadcasting Corporation, Odeon Films.

Lewis, Daniel K. 2001, *The History of Argentina*, London: Greenwood Press.

Lewkowicz, Javier 2016, 'Recuperadas contra las cuerdas', *Pagina/12*, 30 May, available at: https://www.pagina12.com.ar/diario/economia/2-300542-2016-05-30.html

Ley No. 21.499 1977, 'Expropiaciones', Ministerio de Hacienda y Finanzas Públicas, Gobierno Nacional de la República Argentina, available at: http://www.mecon.gov.ar/concursos/biblio/LEY%2021499-77%20EXPROPIACIONES.pdf

Ley No. 20.337 1973, 'Ley de cooperativas', InfoLEG Información Legislativa, Ministerio de Justicia y Derechos Humanos, Gobierno Nacional de la República Argentina, available at: http://servicios.infoleg.gob.ar/infolegInternet/anexos/15000-19999/18462/texact.htm

Ley No. 24.522 1995, 'Ley de concursos y quiebras', InfoLEG Información Legislativa, Ministerio de Justicia y Derechos Humanos, Gobierno Nacional de la República Argentina, available at: http://servicios.infoleg.gob.ar/infolegInternet/anexos/25000-29999/25379/texact.htm

Ley No. 25.563 2002, 'Concursos y quiebras', InfoLEG Información Legislativa, Ministerio de Justicia y Derechos Humanos, Gobierno Nacional de la República Argentina, available at: http://servicios.infoleg.gob.ar/infolegInternet/anexos/70000-74999/72339/texact.htm

Ley No. 26.684 2011, 'Modificación de la Ley No. 24.522', Senado y Cámara de Diputados de la Nación Argentina, available at: https://www.santafe.gob.ar/index.php/web/content/download/215664/1119390/file/Ley%2026.684.pdf

Lichtheim, George 1970, *A Short History of Socialism*, London: Weidenfeld & Nicolson.

Liendo, Mónica, and Adriana Martínez 2001, 'Asociatividad: Una alternativa para el desarollo y crecimiento de las PyMEs', paper presented at the Sextas Jornadas 'Investigaciones en la Facultad de Ciencias Económicas y Estadísticas,' Universidad Nacional de Rosario, Rosario, Argentina.

Linebaugh, Peter and Marcus Rediker 2000, *The Many-Headed Hydra: Sailors, Slaves, Commoners, and the Hidden History of the Revolutionary Atlantic*, Boston: Beacon.

Lionais, Doug and Marcelo Vieta 2017, 'The New Cooperativism and the Commons: Lessons from Nova Scotia's Antigonish Movement and Argentina's Worker Recuperated Enterprises', paper presented at the annual conference of the Canadian Association for Studies in Co-operation, Ryerson University, Toronto, Canada, 31 May–2 June.

Livingstone, David and Peter Sawchuk 2003, *Hidden Knowledge: Organized Labour in the Information Age*, Toronto: University of Toronto Press.

Livingstone, David and Antonie Scholtz 2007, 'Contradictions of Labour Processes and Workers' Use of Skills in Advanced Capitalist Economies', in *Work in Tumultuous Times: Critical Perspectives*, edited by Vivian Shalla and Wallace Clement, Montreal and Kingston: McGill-Queen's University Press.

Livingstone, David, Dorothy E. Smith, and Warren Smith 2011, *Manufacturing Meltdown: Reshaping Steel and Work*, Winnipeg: Fernwood.

Llorens, María and Luana Ferroni 2017, 'De las comisiones internas y las ocupaciones de lugares de trabajo a las empresas recuperadas: Autogestión y democracia obrera en la historia argentina', in *Autogestión y luchas obreras: Del 2001 al nuevo neoliberalismo*, edited by Andrés Ruggeri, Natalia Polti, and Javier Antivero, Buenos Aires: Callao Cooperativa Cultural.

Lofiego, Andrés 2007, *No pasar: Una mirada desde el trabajo autogestionado*, Buenos Aires: Cooperativa Chilavert Artes Gráficas.

López, Fernando M. 2016, 'Para los que piden trabajo, el macrismo sólo tiene represión', *Contexto*, 25 August, available at: http://www.diariocontexto.com.ar/2016/08/25/para-los-que-piden-trabajo-el-macrismo-solo-tiene-represion/

Lo Vuolo, Rubén Mario, and Alberto C. Barbeito 1998, *La nueva oscuridad de la política social: Del estado populista al neoconservador*, Buenos Aires: Miño y Dávila.

Lozano, Claudio 2005, 'Los problemas del empleo, la distribución del ingreso, y el crecimiento en la Argentina actual', *El Correo de Económicas*, 1, 1: 50–69.

Lundgaard Andersen, Linda, Malin Gawell, and Roger Spear (eds.) 2016, *Social Entrepreneurship and Social Enterprises: Nordic Perspectives*, London: Routledge.

Luxemburg, Rosa 2006 [1900], *Reform or Revolution and Other Writings*, Mineola, NY: Dover Publications.

MacLeod, Greg 1997, *From Mondragon to America: Experiments in Community Economic Devfelopment*, Sydney, NS: Cape Breton University Press.

MacLeod, Greg and Daryl Reed 2009, 'Mondragon's Response to The Challenges of Globalization: A Multi-Localization Strategy', in *Co-operatives in a Global Economy: The Challenges of Co-operation Across Borders*, edited by Darryl Reed and J.J. McMurtry, Newcastle-Upon-Tyne, UK: Cambridge Scholars Publishing.

MacPherson, Ian 1996, 'Co-operative Principles, ICA Review 1995', Brussels: International Co-operative Alliance, available at: http://www.uwcc.wisc.edu/icic/orgs/ica/pubs/review/ICA-Review-Vol--88-No--4--19951/Co-operative-Principles--ICA-Review-19951.html

MacPherson, Ian 2002, 'Encouraging Associative Intelligence: Co-operatives, Shared Learning and Responsible Citizenship', *Journal of Co-operative Studies*, 35, 2: 89–98.

Magnani, Esteban 2003, *El cambio silencioso: Empresas y fábricas recuperadas por los trabajadores en la Argentina*, Buenos Aires: Promoteo Libros.

Magnani, Esteban 2009, *The Silent Change: Recovered Businesses in Argentina*, Buenos Aires: Teseo.

Maheshvarananda, Dada 2007, 'Visit to Mondragón', *Prout*, 13 January, available at: http://proutaftercapitalism.blogspot.it/2007/01/visit-to-mondragn.html

Malleson, Tom 2014, *After Occupy: Economic Democracy for the 21st Century*, Oxford: Oxford University Press.

Mandel, David 2001, 'Why is There No Revolt? The Russian Working Class and Labour Movement', *Socialist Register*, 31: 171–95.

Mandel, Ernest 1973, 'The Debate on Workers' Control', in *Workers' Control: A Reader on Labor and Social Change*, edited by Gerry Hunnius, G. David Garson, and John Case, New York: Vintage.

Manjoo, Farhad 2002, 'United's ESOP Fable: Did Employee Stock Ownership Drive the Airline Into Bankruptcy?', *Salon*, 12 December, available at: http://www.salon.com/2002/12/12/esop/

Marcuse, Herbert 1964, *One-Dimensional man: Studies in the Ideology of Advanced Industrial Society*, Boston: Beacon.

Marcuse, Herbert 1966, *Eros and Civilization: A Philosophical Inquiry into Freud*, Boston: Beacon.

Marcuse, Herbert 1968, *Negations: Essays in Critical Theory*, Boston: Beacon.

Marcuse, Herbert 1969, *An Essay on Liberation*, Boston: Beacon.

Marcuse, Peter 2015, 'Cooperatives on the Path to Socialism?', *Monthly Review*, 66, 9: 31–38.

Marglin, Stephen A. 1974, 'What Do Bosses Do? The Origins and Functions of Hierarchy in Capitalist Production', *Review of Radical Political Economics*, 6, 2: 60–112.

Marshall, Peter 1992, *Demanding the Impossible: A History of Anarchism*, London: HarperCollins.

Martí, Juan Pablo 2006, *Impactos de la integración regional del MERCOSUR sobre el movimiento cooperativo*, Buenos Aires: Cooperativas e Integración Regional Mercosur.

Martí, Juan Pablo, Jorge Bertullo, Cecilia Soria, Diego Barrios, Milton Silveira, Alfredo Camilletti et al. 2004, 'Empresas recuperadas mediante cooperativas de trabajo: Viabilidad de una alternativa', *Revista UniRcoop*, 2, 1: 80–105.

Martí, Juan Pablo, Florencia Thul, and Valentina Cancela 2013, 'Las empresas recuperadas como cooperativas de trabajo en Uruguay: Entre la crisis y la oportunidad', *CIRIEC-España*, 82: 5.

Martín, Jorge 2005, 'Primer Encuentro Latinoamericano de Empresas Recupardas por los Trabajadores', *elmilitante.org*, 30 November, available at: http://www.elmilitante.org/amrica-latina-principal-137/venezuela-principal-146/2770-primer-encuentro-latinoamericano-de-empresas-recuperadas-por-los-trabajadores.html

Marx, Karl 1967 [1867], *Capital: A Critique of Political Economy, Volume I: A Critical Analysis of Capitalist Production*, New York: International Publishers.

Marx, Karl, 1969 [1863], *Theories of Surplus Value*, Moscow: Progress Publishers.

Marx, Karl 1973 [1857–61], *Grundrisse: Foundations of the Critique of Political Economy (Rough Draft)*, London: Penguin.

Marx, Karl 1976a [1845], 'Theses on Feuerbach' [original version], in *Marx & Engels Collected Works, Volume 5 (Marx and Engels: 1845–47)*, London: Lawrence & Wishart.

Marx, Karl 1976b [1867], *Capital: A Critique of Political Economy, Volume I*, London: Penguin.

Marx, Karl 1978a [1864], 'Inaugural Address of the Working Men's International Association', in *The Marx-Engels Reader*, edited by Robert C. Tucker, New York: W.W. Norton.

Marx, Karl 1978b [1875], 'The Critique of the Gotha Program', in *The Marx-Engels Reader*, edited by Robert C. Tucker, New York: W.W. Norton.

Marx, Karl 1978c [1871], 'The Civil War in France', in *The Marx-Engels Reader*, edited by Robert C. Tucker, New York: W.W. Norton.

Marx, Karl 1981 [1894], *Capital: A Critique of Political Economy, Volume III*, London: Penguin.

Marx, Karl 1985 [1866–67], 'Instructions for the Delegates of the Provisional General Council. The Different Questions, 5. Co-operative Labour', in *Marx & Engels Collected Works, Volume 20 (Marx and Engels: 1864–68)*, London: Lawrence & Wishart.

Marx, Karl 1988 [1863], 'a) Cooperation', in *Marx & Engels Collected Works, Volume 30 (Karl Marx: 1861–63 [Marx's Economic Manuscripts of 1861–63])*, London: Lawrence & Wishart.

Marx, Karl 2007 [1844], *Economic and Philosophic Manuscripts of 1844*, Mineola, NY: Dover Publications.

Marx, Karl and Friedrich Engels 1970 [1846], *The German Ideology*, London: Lawrence & Wishart.

Marx, Karl and Friedrich Engels 1998 [1848], *The Communist Manifesto: A Modern Edition*, London: Verso.

Mason, Ronald M. 1982, *Participatory and Workplace Democracy: A Theoretical Development in Critique of Liberalism*, Carbondale, IL: Southern Illinois University Press.

Mason, Rowena 2016, 'Labour Backs Employees' Right to Own Shares in Their Workplace', The Guardian, 20 January, available at: https://www.theguardian.com/politics/2016/jan/20/labour-backs-employees-right-own-shares-workplace

Mason, Paul 2016, *Postcapitalism: A Guide to Our Future*, New York: Ferrar, Straus and Giroux.

Mathews, Race 1999, *Jobs of Our Own: Building a Stakeholder Society: Alternatives to the Market and the State*, Sydney: Pluto.

Matsushita, Hiroshi 1983, *Movimiento obrero argentino, 1930–1945: Sus proyecciones en los orígenes del peronismo*, Buenos Aires: Ediciones Siglo Veinte.

Mattick, Paul 1969, 'Workers' Control', in *The New Left: A Collection of Essays*, edited by Priscilla Long, Boston: Porter Sargent.

McBride, Jo and Ian Greenwood (eds.) 2009, *Community Unionism: A Comparative Analysis of Concepts and Contexts*, Houndmills, Basingstoke, UK: Palgrave Macmillan.

McCain, R.A. 1999, 'The Mystery of Worker Buyouts of Bankrupt Firms: An Explanation in Terms of Learning by Doing and Specific Human Capital', *Economic Analysis*, 2, 3: 165–77.

McInerney, Paul-Brian 2012, 'Social Enterprise in Mixed-Form Fields: Challenges and Prospects', in *Social Enterprises: An Organizational Perspective*, edited by Benjamin Gidron and Yeheskel Hasenfeld, Houndmills, Basingstoke, UK: Palgrave Macmillan.

McLellan, David 1973, *Karl Marx: His Life and Thought*, New York: Harper Colophon Books.

McMurtry, J.J. (ed.) 2010, *Living Economics: Canadian Perspectives on the Social Economy, Co-operatives, and Community Economic Development*, Toronto: Emond Montgomery.

McNally, David 1993, *Against the Market: Political Economy, Market Socialism and the Marxist Critique*, London: Verso.

McNally, David 1997, *Socialism From Below*, Toronto: New Socialists Canada, available at: http://www.marxsite.com/socialism_from_below_by_david_mc.htm

Meiksins, Peter 1987, 'New Classes and Old Theories: The Impasse of Contemporary Class Analysis', in *Recapturing Marxism: An Appraisal of Recent Trends in Sociological Theory*, edited by Rhonda Levine and Jerry Lembcke, New York: Praeger.

Melman, Seymour 1975, 'Industrial Efficiency Under Managerial Versus Co-operartive Decision-Making: A Comparative Study of Manufacturing Enterprises in Israel', *In Self-governing Socialism, Volume 2*, edited by Branko Horvat, Mihailo Markovic, and Rudi Supek, Armonk, NY: M.E. Sharpe.

Melnyk, George 1985, *The Search for Community: From Utopia to a Co-operative Society*, Montreal: Black Rose Books.

Mendizábal, Antxon and Anjel Errasti 2008, 'Premisas teóricas de la autogestión', paper presented at the 'EcoCri 2008: XI Jornadas de Economía Crítica' conference, Bilbao, Basque Country, 27–29 March.

Mercatante, Esteban 2015, *Le economía argentina en su laberinto: Lo que dejan doce años de kirchnerismo*, Buenos Aires: Ediciones IPS.

Merleau-Ponty, Maurice 1962, *Phenomenology of Perception*, London: Routledge & Kegan Paul.

Mészáros, Istvan 1995, *Beyond Capital: Toward a Theory of Transition*, London: The Merlin Press.

Mill, John Stuart 1909 [1848], 'On the Probable Futurity of the Labouring Classes', in *Principles of Political Economy with Some of Their Applications to Social Philosophy*, Book IV, Chapter VII. London: Longmans, Green and Company, available at: http://www.econlib.org/library/Mill/mlP62.html

Miller, Ethan and Michael Albert 2009, *Post-Capitalist Alternatives: New Perspectives on Economic Democracy*, London, ON: Socialist Renewal Publishing Project.

Miller, Ethan 2004, 'Solidarity Economics: Strategies for Building New Economies from the Bottom-Up and the Inside-Out', Community Economies Collective, available at: http://www.communityeconomies.org/site/assets/media/Ethan_Miller/Miller_Soli darity%20Economics%20(2005).pdf

Ministerio de Coordinacion y Desarrollo Social 2010, 'Informe de rendición de cuentas, 2007–2010', Gobierno de la República del Ecuador, available at: http://www.desarrol losocial.gob.ec/wp-content/uploads/downloads/2012/07/14_rendicion_de_cuentas _2007-2010.pdf

Ministerio de Desarrollo Social 2017, 'Ferias y mercados', Presidencia de la Nación, Gobierno Nacional de la República Argentina, http://www.desarrollosocial.gob.ar/ feriasymercados

Ministerio de Economía y Producción 2007, 'Artículo 21. Información Legislativa (2007)', Gobierno Nacional de la República Argentina.

Ministerio de Trabajo 2007, 'Cuadro 1.1.13: Tasas de actividad, empleo, desempleo abier- to, subempleo horario y sobreempleo (1980–2003)', Ministerio de Trabajo, Empleo, y Seguridad Social, Gobierno Nacional de la República Argentina.

Ministerio de Trabajo 2008a, 'Universo de empresas recuperadas por sus trabajadores', Programa de Trabajo Autogestionado, Ministerio de Trabajo, Empleo, y Seguridad Social, Gobierno Nacional de la República Argentina.

Ministerio de Trabajo 2008b. 'Dinámica del empleo y rotación de empresas', Ministerio de Trabajo, Empleo, y Seguridad Social, Gobierno Nacional de la República Argen- tina.

Mintz, Frank 2006, *Autogestión y anarcosindicalismo en la España revolucionaria*, Mad- rid: Traficantes de Sueños.

Miranda Lorenzo, Humberto 2011, 'Cooperativismo y autogestión en las visiones de Marx, Engels y Lenin', in *Cooperativas y socialismo: Una mirada desde Cuba*, edited by Camila Piñeiro Harnecker, La Habana: Editores Caminos.

Mittelman, Mario 2005, *Los sindicatos, las cooperativas y el socialismo hoy en nuestro país*, Buenos Aires: Departamento del Cooperativismo, Centro Cultural de la Coope- ración.

Monteagudo, Graciela 2008, 'The Clean Walls of a Recovered Factory: New Subjectivit- ies in Argentina's Recovered Factories', *Urban Anthropology*, 37, 2: 175–210.

Montes, Verónica L. and Alicia B. Ressel 2003, 'Presencia del cooperativismo en Argen- tina', *Revista UniRcoop*, 1, 2: 9–26.

Moody, Kim 1997, *Workers in a Lean World: Unions in the International Economy*, Lon- don: Verso.

Monroy, Maria Elena 2005, 'Suscriben 75 acuerdos en Encuentro de Empresas Recuper- adas', *Agencia Bolivariana de Noticias*, 29 October, available at: https://www.aporrea .org/actualidad/n67971.html

Morone, Piergiuseppe and Giuseppina Testa 2008, 'Firms Growth, Size, and Innovation: An Investigation into the Italian Manufacturing Sector', *Economics of Innovation and New Technology*, 17, 4: 311–29.

Movimiento 13 de Abril 2005, 'Instalado 1er encuentro latinoamericano de empresas recuperadas,' 27 October, available at: http://www.sencamer.gob.ve/sencamer/action/get-news?id=33204

Munck, Ronaldo 2002, *Globalisation and Labour: The New Great Transformation*, London: Zed Books.

Munck, Ronaldo, Ricardo Falcón, and Bernardo Galitelli 1987, *Argentina: From Anarchism to Peronism: Workers, Unions, and Politics, 1855–1985*, London: Zed Books.

Münkner, Hans-H. 1995, *Chances of Cooperatives in the Future: Contribution to the International Co-operative Alliance Centennial, 1895–1995*, Marburg: Institute for Cooperation in Developing Countries, Philipps-Universitä.

Muñoz, Alberto D. 2005, 'Cooperativas de agua en la Argentina', in *Por un modelo público de agua: Triunfos, luchas y sueños*, edited by Brid Brennan, Olivier Hoedeman, Phillip Terhorst, Satoko Kishimoto, and Belén Belanyá, Buenos Aires: El Viejo Topo.

Murmis, Miguel and Juan Carlos Portantiero 1971, *Estudios sobre los orígenes del peronismo*, Buenos Aires: Siglo Veintiuno Editores.

Murúa, Eduardo 2006, 'On the Crisis of Capitalism, Argentina's Worker-Recuprated Enterprises, and the Possibilities for Another World: An Interview with Eduardo Murúa', interviewed by Jennifer Moore, translated by Marcelo Vieta, *Workerscontrol.net*, 3 June, available at: http://www.workerscontrol.net/authors/crisis-capitalism-argentina%E2%80%99s-worker-recuperated-enterprises-and-possibilities-an other-world

Narvaez, Alfonso A. 1991, 'Louis O. Kelso, Who Advocated Worker-Capitalism, Is Dead at 77', *New York Times*, 21 February, available at: http://www.nytimes.com/1991/02/21/obituaries/louis-o-kelso-who-advocated-worker-capitalism-is-dead-at-77.html

NCEO 2014, 'ESOP (Employee Stock Ownership Plan) Facts', National Centre for Employee Ownership, organisational website, available at: http://www.esop.org/

Négation 1975, *LIP and the Self-Managed Counter-Revolution*, Detroit: Black and Red.

Negri, Antonio 1988, *Revolution Retrieved: Selected Writings on Marx, Keynes, Capitalist Crisis and New Social Subjects, 1967–83*, London: Red Notes.

Negri, Antonio 1991, *Marx Beyond Marx: Lessons on the Grundrisse*, New York: Autonomedia.

Negri, Antonio 2005 [1989], *The Politics of Subversion: A Manifesto for the Twenty-First Century*, Cambridge, UK: Polity Press.

Negri, Antonio 2003, 'The Ballad of Buenos Aires', *Generation Online*, available at: http://www.generation-online.org/t/sitcol.htm

Ness, Immanuel (ed.) 2009, *The International Encyclopedia of Revolution and Protest: 1500 to the Present*, Hoboken, NJ: Wiley-Blackwell.

Ness, Immanuel 2011, 'Workers' Direct Action and Factory Control in the United States', in *Ours to Master and to Own: Workers' Control from the Commune to the Present*, edited by Immanuel Ness and Dario Azzellini, Chicago: Haymarket Books.

Ness, Immanuel, and Dario Azzellini (eds.) 2011, *Ours to Master and to Own: Workers' Control from the Commune to the Present*, Chicago: Haymarket.

Nieves Simonetti, Ester 2004. *Las cooperativas de trabajo*, available at: http://www.monografias.com/trabajos16/cooperativa-de-trabajo/cooperativa-de-trabajo.shtml

Noble, David F. 1984, *Forces of Production: A Social History of Industrial Automation*, Oxford: Oxford University Press.

Noble, David 1993, *Progress Without People: In Defense of Luddism*, Chicago: Charles H. Kerr Publishing.

Novaes, Henrique T. 2007, *O fetiche da tecnologia: A experiência das fábricas recuperadas*, São Paolo: Expressão Popular.

Novkovic, Sonja and Tom Webb 2014, *Co-operatives in a Post-Trowth Era: Creating Co-operative Economics*, London: Zed Books.

NUDOS 2006a, 'Cuando más compartimos, más tenemos', Redes de Empresas, Redes de Personas (Proyecto Redes), organisational magazine, 1, 1: 3.

NUDOS 2006b, 'Como organizarse', Redes de Empresas, Redes de Personas (Proyecto Redes), organisational magazine, 1, 6: 4–5.

Nueva Mayoria 2016, 'La conflictividad laboral (1980–2015)', *NuevaMayoria.com*, 5 February, available at: http://nuevamayoria.com/images/stories/celaforum/lab1602conflictos.pdf

Oakeshott, Robert 1990, *The Case for Workers' Co-ops*, Houndmills, Basingstoke, UK: Palgrave Macmillan.

Oakeshott, Robert 2000, *Jobs and Fairness: The Logic and Experience of Employee Ownership*, Norwich, UK: Michael Russell.

OEOC 2016, Ohio Employee Ownership Centre, organisational website, available at: http://www.oeockent.org/

Olivera, Lucía Verónica 2007, 'Lideres de América Latina: El daño institucional en Argentina durante los primeros años de gobierno menemista (1989–1992)', *Revista de Ciencia Política*, 2, December: available at: http://www.revcienciapolitica.com.ar/num2art7.php

Ollman, Bertell (ed.) 1998, *Market Socialism: The Debate Amongst Socialists*, London: Routledge.

Olmedo, Clara and Martin J. Murray 2002, 'The Formalization of Informal/Precarious Labor in Contemporary Argentina.', *International Sociology*, 17, 3: 421–43.

OpenMovements 2013, organisational website, available at: https://www.facebook.com/OpenMovements/

Operación Milagro 2016, organisational website, available at: http://www.operacion milagro.org.ar/nueva/

OSERA 2010, 'Cooperativa Unión Solidaria de Trabajadores (UST): Fragmentos de una entrevista a Mario Barrios, presidente de la cooperative, Observatorio Social Empresa Recuperadas y Autogestionadas', Buenos Aires: Facultad de Ciencias Sociales, Universidad de Buenos Aires, available at: http://webiigg.sociales.uba.ar/empresas recuperadas/PDF/PDF_03/UST.pdf

Ottawa Citizen 1985, 'Bolivian Workers Seize Plants, Hold 180 Executives Hostage', 19 January.

Overwien, Bernd 2000, 'Informal Learning and the Role of Social Movements', *International Review of Education*, 46, 6: 621–40.

Owen, R. 1991a, *A New View of Society and Other Writings*, edited by Gregory Claeys, New York: Penguin.

Owen, Robert 1991b [1817], 'Observations on the Effects of the Manufacturing System', in *A New View of Society and Other Writings*, edited by Gregory Claeys, New York: Penguin.

Owen, Robert 1991c [1921], 'Report to the County of Lanark', in *A New View of Society and Other Writings*, edited by Gregory Claeys, New York: Penguin.

Ozarow, Daniel and Richard Croucher 2014, 'Workers' Self-Management, Recovered Companies and the Sociology of Work', *Sociology*, 48, 5: 989–1006.

Página/12 2011, 'CFK promulgó la reforma de la Ley de Quiebras', 29 June, available at: https://www.pagina12.com.ar/diario/ultimas/20-171094-2011-06-29.html

Página/12 2010, 'El trabajo en negro un poco más oscuro', 18 September, available at: https://www.pagina12.com.ar/diario/economia/2-153375-2010-09-18.html

Página/12 2016a, 'Primera protesta contra el tarifazo', 14 July, available at: https://www .pagina12.com.ar/diario/ultimas/20-304238-2016-07-14.html

Página/12 2016b, 'La CGT confirmó que vuelve a la calle', 18 November, available at: https://www.pagina12.com.ar/diario/ultimas/20-312836-2016-10-27.html

Página/12 2016c, 'Queremos respuestas ya', 19 November, available at: https://www.pagi na12.com.ar/edicion-impresa/19-11-2016

Página/12 2017a, 'Para mirar la película y no sólo la foto', 14 March, available at: https:// www.pagina12.com.ar/25564-para-mirar-la-pelicula-y-no-solo-la-foto

Página/12 2017b, 'Se suspendió el desalojo del Bauen', 18 April, available at: https://www .pagina12.com.ar/32555-se-suspendio-el-desalojo-del-bauen

Palmer, Tim 2015, 'Craft Beer: Worker Cooperative Industry Research Series', Democracy at Work Institute, US Federation of Worker Cooperatives, available at: http://institute .coop/resources/industry-research-series-craft-beer

Palomino, Hector 2003, 'The Workers' Movement in Occupied Enterprises: A Survey', *Canadian Journal of Latin American and Caribbean Studies*, 28, 55: 71–96.

Palomino, Hector 2005a, 'Los cambios en el mundo del trabajo y los dilemas sindicales', in *Nueva historia argentina: Dictadura y democracia (1976–2001)*, edited by Juan Suriano, Buenos Aires: Editorial Sudamericana.

Palomino, Hector 2005b, 'Los sindicatos y los movimientos sociales emergentes del colapso neoliberal en Argentina', in *Sindicatos y nuevos movimientos sociales en América Latina*, edited by Enrique de la Garza Toledo, Buenos Aires: CLACSO.

Palomino, Héctor, Ivanna Bleynat, Silvia Garro, and Carla Giacomuzzi 2010, 'The Universe of Worker-Recovered Companies in Argentina (2002–2008): Continuity and Changes Inside the Movement', *Affinities: A Journal of Radical Theory, Culture, and Action*, 4, 1: 252–87.

Pannekoek, Anton 2003 [1950], *Workers' Councils*, Oakland, CA: AK Press.

Panzieri, Raniero 1980, 'The Capitalist Use of Machinery: Marx Versus the Objectivists', in *Outlines of a Critique of Technology*, edited by Phil Slater, London: Ink Links.

Parker, Martin, George Cheney, Valérie Fournier, and Chris Land (eds.) 2014, *The Routledge Companion to Alternative Organization*, London: Routledge.

Parsons Lee 1999, 'Molson Brewery Workers Occupy Ontario Plant', World Socialist Web Site, 1 December, available at: https://www.wsws.org/en/articles/1999/12/mols-d01.html

Pastore, Rodolfo 2010, 'Un panorama del resurgimiento de la economía social y solidaria en la Argentina', *Revista de Ciencias Sociales*, 2, 18: 47–74.

Pateman, Carole 1970, *Participation and Democratic Theory*, Cambridge, UK: Cambridge University Press.

Paton, Rob 1989, *Reluctant Entrepreneurs: The Extent, Achievements, and Significance of Worker Takeovers in Europe*, Milton Keynes, UK: Open University Press.

Patroni, Viviana 2002, 'Structural Reforms and the Labour Movement in Argentina', *Labour, Capital, and Society*, 35, 2: 252–80.

Patroni, Viviana 2004, 'Disciplining Labour, Producing Poverty: Neo-liberal Structural Reforms and Political Conflict in Argentina', *Research in Political Economy*, 21: 91–119.

Paulucci, Maria Alejandra 2013, 'As empresas recuperadas pelos trabalhadores na Argentina e no Brasil', *Em Tese*, 10, 1: 136–64.

Pearce, John 2009, 'Social Economy: Engaging as a Third System?', in *The Social Economy: International Perspectives on Economic Solidarity*, edited by Ash Amin, London: Zed Books.

Peixoto de Albuquerque, Paulo 2004, 'Autogestión', in *La otra economía* edited by Antonio David Cattani, Buenos Aires: Editorial Altamira.

Peredo, Ana Maria, and James J. Chrisman 2006, 'Toward a Theory of Community-Based Enterprise', *Academy of Management Review*, 31, 2: 309–28.

Pérotin, Virginie 2006, 'Entry, Exit, and the Business Cycle: Are Cooperatives Different?', *Journal of Comparative Economics*, 34, 2: 295–316.

Pérotin, Virginie 2014, 'Worker Cooperatives: Good, Sustainable Jobs in the Community', *Journal of Entrepreneurial and Organizational Diversity*, 2, 2: 34–47.

Pérotin, Virginie, and Andrew Robinson (eds.) 2004, *Employee Participation, Firm Performance and Survival*, Bingley, UK: Emerald Group Publishing.

Petit, Mercedes 2009, 'Frigorífico Lisandro de la Torre: Huelga y repression', *El Socialista*, available at: http://www.izquierdasocialista.org.ar/viejos_es/cgi-bin/elsocialista.cgi .php?es=124&nota=15

Petras, James and Henry Veltmeyer 2002, 'Autogestión de trabajadores en una perspectiva histórica', in *Produciendo realidad: Las empresas comunitarias: Grissinopoli, Río Turbio, Zanón, Brukman y General Mosconi*, edited by Enrique Carpintero and Mario Hernández, Buenos Aires: Topía Editorial/La Maza.

Petras, James and Henry Veltmeyer (eds.) 2004, *Las privatizaciones y la desnacionalización de América Latina*, Buenos Aires: Promoteo Libros.

Phebus, Nicolas 2004, 'Canada, ALCAN: Worker's control in Jonquière', Collectif La Nuit and *A-Infos*, available at: http://www.ainfos.ca/04/feb/ainfos00074.html

Phillips, Paul 2003, *Inside Capitalism: An Introduction to Political Economy*, Winnipeg: Fernwood.

Phills, James A., Kriss Deiglmeier, and Dale T. Miller 2008, 'Rediscovering Social Innovation', *Stanford Social Innovation Review*, Fall: 34–43, available at: www.ssireview.org/ images/articles/2008FA_feature_phills_deiglmeier_miller.pdf

Picchetti, Valentina 2002, 'Fábricas tomadas, fábricas de esperanzas: La experiencia de Zanón y de Brukman', in *Produciendo realidad: Las empresas comunitarias: Grissinopoli, Río Turbio, Zanón, Brukman y General Mosconi*, edited by Enrique Carpintero and Miguel Hernández, Buenos Aires, Argentina: Topia Editorial/La Maza.

Piketty, Thomas 2014, *Capital in the Twenty-First Century*, Cambridge, MA: Harvard University Press.

Piñeiro Harnecker, Camila 2007, 'Workplace Democracy and Collective Consciousness: An Empirical Study of Venezuelan Cooperatives', *Monthly Review*, 59, 6: 27–40.

Piñeiro Harnecker, C. (ed.) 2011, *Cooperativas y socialismo: Una Mirada desde Cuba*, Havana: Editorial Caminos.

Piñeiro Harnecker, Camila (ed.) 2013, *Cooperatives and Socialism: A View from Cuba*, Houndmills, Basingstoke, UK: Palgrave Macmillan.

Piñeiro Harnecker, Camila 2016, 'Cuba's Cooperatives: Their Contribution to Cuba's New Socialism', *Moving Beyond Capitalism*, London: Routledge.

Piore, Michael J. and Charles F. Sabel 1984, *The Second Industrial Divide: Possibilities for Prosperity*, New York: Basic Books.

Piqué, Martin 2009, 'Un plan para crear 100 mil puestos de trabajo', *Pagina/12*, 14 August, available at: www.pagina12.com.ar/diario/elpais/1-129967-2009-08-14.html

Piva, Adrián 2015, *Economía y política en la Argentina kirchnerista*, Buenos Aires: Batalla de Ideas.

Plys, Kristin 2016, 'Worker Self-Management in the Third World, 1952–1979', *International Journal of Comparative Sociology*, 57, 1–2: 3–29.

Polanyi, Karl 2001 [1944], *The Great Transformation: The Political and Economic Origins of Our Time*, Boston: Beacon.

Portal de Economía Solidaria 2014, 'Crece la experiencia de fábricas recuperadas por sus trabajadores en Europa,' 27 December, available at: http://www.economiasolidaria .org/noticias/crece_la_experiencia_de_fabricas_recuperadas_por_sus_trabajadores _en_europa

Portes, Alejandro 1985, 'Latin American Class Structures: Their Composition and Change During the Last Decades', *Latin American Research Review*, 20, 3: 7–39.

Portes, Alejandro and Kelly Hoffman 2003, 'Latin American Class Structures: Their Composition and Change During the Neo-liberal Era', *Latin American Research Review*, 38, 1: 41–82.

Potter, Beatrice 1904, *The Co-Operative Movement in Great Britain*, London: Swan Sonnenschein & Company.

Pozzi, Pablo 1988, *La oposición obrera a la dictadura (1976–1982)*, Buenos Aires: Editorial Contrapunto.

Pozzi, Pablo 1998, 'Popular Upheaval and Capitalist Transformation in Argentina', *Latin American Perspectives*, 27, 114: 63–8.

Pablo Pozzi, 2012, 'Oral History in Latin America', *Oral History Forum*, 32: 1–7.

Pozzi, Pablo and Fabio Nigra 2015a, 'Argentina a Decade after the Collapse: The Causes of the Crisis and Structural Changes', *Latin American Perspectives*, 42, 1: 3–10.

Pozzi, Pablo and Fabio Nigra 2015b, 'Argentina a Decade after the Collapse: Old and New Social Movements', *Latin American Perspectives*, 42, 2: 3–11.

Price, Richard (ed.) 1996, *Maroon Societies: Rebel Slave Communities in the Americas*, Baltimore: Johns Hopkins University Press.

Price, Wayne 2012, 'Marx's Economics for Anarchists: An Anarchist's Introduction to Marx's Critique of Political Economy', *The Anarchist Library*, available at: https:// theanarchistlibrary.org/library/wayne-price-marx-s-economics-for-anarchists

Programa Facultad Abierta 2002, 'Informe del relevamiento entre empresas recuperadas por los trabajadores', Buenos Aires: Programa Facultad Abierta, Facultad de Filosofía y Letras, Universidad de Buenos Aires, available at: http://www.recuperadasdoc .com.ar/Informes%20relevamientos/Informe%20Primer%20relevamiento% 202003.pdf

Programa Facultad Abierta 2016, ERT dataset made available to author, Programa Facultad Abierta, Facultad de Filosofía y Letras, Universidad de Buenos Aires

Programa Facultad Abierta 2017, 'VI Encuentro Internacional "La economía de los/as Trabajadores/as"', available at: http://www.recuperadasdoc.com.ar/

Project Equity 2015, 'Case Studies: Business Conversions to Worker Cooperatives: Insights and Readiness Facotors for Owners and Employees', April, available at: http:// www.uwcc.wisc.edu/pdf/Case%20Studies_Business%20Conversions%20to%20 Worker%20Cooperatives_ProjectEquity.pdf

Proudhon, Pierre-Joseph 1970 [1840], *What is Property? An Inquiry into the Principle of Right and of Government*, New York: Dover Publications.

Proudhon, Pierre-Joseph 1972 [1847], *System of Economic Contradictions: or, The Philosophy of Misery*, New York: Arno Press. https://www.marxists.org/reference/subject/economics/proudhon/philosophy/index.htm

Proudhon, Pierre-Joseph 1979 [1863], *The Principle of Federation*, Toronto: University of Toronto Press.

Proudhon, Pierre-Joseph 1989 [1851], *General Idea of the Revolution in the Nineteenth Century*, London: Pluto.

Proudhon, Pierre-Joseph 2011, *Property is Theft! A Pierre-Joseph Proudhon Anthology*, edited by Iain McKay, Oakland, CA: AK Press.

Proudhon, Pierre-Joseph 2014, 'Political Capacity of the Working Classes', available at: http://libertarian-labyrinth.blogspot.ca/2014/02/from-proudhons-political-capacity-of.html

Pusey, Andre 2010, 'Social Centres and the New Cooperativism of the Common.', *Affinities: A Journal of Radical Theory, Culture and Action*, 4, 1: 176–98.

Pushkar, Jha 2012, 'Is Employee Ownership the Answer to Our Economic Woes?', *The Guardian*, 25 September, available at: http://www.theguardian.com/sustainable-business/blog/employee-ownership-answer-economic-woes

Quarter, Jack 1992, *Canada's Social Economy: Co-opeartives, Non-profits, and Other Community Enterprises*, Toronto: James Lorimer & Company.

Quarter, Jack 1995, *Crossing the Line: Unionized Employee Ownership and Investment Funds*, Toronto: James Lorimer & Company.

Quarter, Jack 2000, *Beyond the Bottom Line: Socially Innovative Business Owners*, London: Quorum Books.

Quarter, Jack and Harish Midha 2001, 'Informal Learning Processes in a Worker Cooperative', NALL Working Paper No. 37, New Approaches to Lifelong Learning (NALL), Centre for the Studies of Education and Work, Ontario Institute for Studies in Education of the University of Toronto.

Quarter, Jack and Judith Brown 1992, 'Worker Buyouts in Canada: A Social Network Analysis', *Economic and Industrial Democracy*, 13: 95–117.

Quarter, Jack, Laurie Mook, and Ann Armstrong 2009, *Understanding the Social Economy: A Canadian Perspective*, Toronto: University of Toronto Press.

Quispe, Aline 2013, 'Norma autoriza a trabajadores a administrar empresas quebradas', *La Razón*, 8 October, available at: http://www.la-razon.com/economia/Norma-trabajadores-administrar-empresas-quebradas_0_1921007928.html

Radio Nacional 2016, 'Entrevista con Hugo Cabrera, Federico Tonarreli, y Andrés Ruggeri sobre las emrpesas recuperadas argentinas', *Gente de a pie*, 25 June, available at: http://radiocut.fm/audiocut/gente-de-a-pie-25062016-situacion-de-empresas-recuperadas/

Ragan, Christopher T.S. and Richard G. Lipsey 2004, *Macroeconomics*, Toronto: Pearson Canada.

Rama, Carlos M. 1962, *Revolución social en el siglo veinte*, Montevideo: Nuestro Tiempo.

Rancière, Jacques 1989, *The Nights of Labor: The Workers' Dream in Nineteenth-Century France*, Philadelphia: Temple University Press.

Ranis, Peter 2006, 'Factories Without Bosses: Argentina's Experience with Worker-Run Enterprises', *Labour: Studies in Working Class History of the Americas*, 3, 1: 11–24.

Ranis, Peter 2007, 'Eminent Domain: Unused Tool for American Labor?' *Working USA: The Journal of Labor and Society*, 10, 2: 198–208.

Ranis, Peter 2010, 'Argentine Worker Cooperatives In Civil Society: A Challenge To Capital–Labor Relations', *WorkingUSA*, 13, 1: 77–105.

Ranis, Peter 2014, 'Promoting Cooperatives by the Use of Eminent Domain: Argentina and the United States', *Socialism and Democracy*, 28, 1: 51–69.

Ranis, Peter 2016, *Cooperatives Confront Capitalism: Challenging the Neoliberal Economy*, London: Zed Books.

Ratner, Carl 2015, 'Neoliberal Co-optation of Leading Co-op Organizations, and a Socialist Counterpolitics of Co-operation', *Monthly Review*, 66, 9: 18–30.

Raus, D.M. 2006, 'Gobernabilidad y democracía: La cuestión social y los desafíos políticos en la Argentina post-crisis 2001', *Cuadernos Argentina Reciente: A 5 años del 19 y 20 de diciembre*, 3, December: 142–7.

Rebón, Julián 2004, *Desobedeciendo al desempleo: La experiencia de las empresas recuperadas*, Buenos Aires: Ediciones Picaso/La Rosa Blindada.

Rebón, Julián 2007, *La empresa de la autonomía: Trabajadores recuperando la producción*, Buenos Aires: Colectivo Ediciones-Picaso.

Recalde, Hector 2012, *Una historia jamas contada: El relato empresario ante conquistas y nuevos derechos de los trabajadores en Argentina (1869–2012)*, Buenos Aires: Corregidor.

Real Academia Española 2017, 'Recuperar', *Diccionario de la lengua española (edición del tricentanario)*, Madrid: Asociación de Academias de la Lengua Española, available at: http://dle.rae.es/?id=VXJKMGZ

Red Gráfica Cooperativa 2008, promotional brochure, in archives of Centro de Documentación de Empreasas Recuperadas, Programa Facultad Abierta, Facultad de Filosofía y Letras, Universidad de Buenos Aires.

Red Gráfica Cooperativa 2011, '¿Quienes somos?', organisational website, available at: http://rutacoop.com.ar/cooperativas/red-gra-iexcl-fica-cooperativa.html/1292

Resino, Fabio 2008, 'Los limites de la autonomía: El hotel BAUEN', in *El trabajo por venir: Autogestión y emancipación social*, edited by Norma Giarraca and Gabriela Massuh, Buenos Aires: Editorial Antropofagía.

Restakis, John 2010, *Humanizing the Economy: Co-operatives in the Age of Capital*, Gabriola Island, BC: New Society Publishers.

Reuters 2016, 'Argentina 2016 Inflation seen at 40 Percent to 42 Percent: Finance Minister', available at: http://www.reuters.com/article/us-argentina-investment-idUSK CN0ZA2TY

Rhoads, Robert A. and Katalin Szelényi 2011, *Global Citizenship and the University: Advancing Social Life and Relations in an Interdependent World*, Stanford, CA: Stanford University Press.

Ricoeur, Paul 2004, *Memory, history, forgetting*, Chicago: University of Chicago Press.

Rieiro, Anabel 2017, 'Uruguay en el cono sur: Metamorfosis y continuidades del campo autogestionario', paper presented at the 'VI Encuentro Internacional de la Economía de los/las Trabajadores/as / VI International Gathering of the Workers' Economy', Buenos Aires and Pigüé, Argentina, 30 August–2 September.

Rigby, Elizabeth 2013, 'Chancellor's 'Shares for Rights' Plan Flops', *Financial Times*, 28 June, https://www.ft.com/content/6ec7934e-e005-11e2-bf9d-00144feab7de

Rigby, Elizabeth, Andrew Bounds, and Arash Massoudi 2015, 'Business Attacks Labour Plan for Employee Buyouts', *Financial Times*, 7 February, available at: https://www.ft.com/content/8b5442e4-aeof-11e4-8188-00144feab7de

Rinehart, James, Christopher Huxley, and David Robertson 1997, *Just Another Car Factory? Lean Production and its Discontents*, Ithacy, NY: Cornell University Press.

Rock, David 1987, *Argentina, 1516–1987: From Spanish Colonization to Alfonsín*, Berkeley and Los Angeles: University of California Press.

Rocker, Rudolf 1978 [1933], *Nationalism and Culture*, Montreal: Black Rose Books

Rocker, Rudolf 1989 [1938], *Anarcho-syndicalism*, London: Pluto.

Rofman, Adriana 2005, 'Argentina: Pobreza urbana en el nuevo siglo: La politica del estado y respuesta alternatives en el marco de la economía social', *El Correo de Económicas*, 1, 1: 4–12.

Romero, Luis Alberto 2003, *La crisis argentina: Una mirada al siglo XX*, Buenos Aires: Siglo Veintiuno Editores.

Ronchi, Veronica 2012, *La cooperazione integrale: Storia di 'El Hogar Obrero' avanguardia dell'economia sociale argentina (1905–2005)*, Rome: Edizioni di Storia e Letteratura.

Rosanvallon, Pierre 1979, *La autogestión*, Madrid: Editorial Fundamentos.

Rosen, Corey and Katherine Klein 1983, 'Job-Creating Performance of Employee-Owned Firms', *Monthly Labor Review*, 106, 8: 15–19.

Rothschild-Whitt, Joyce 1979, 'The Collectivist Organization: An Alternative to Rational-Bureaucratic Models', *American Sociological Review*, 44, 4: 509–27.

Rothschild, Joyce, and J. Allen Whitt 1986, *The Cooperative Workplace: Potentials and Dilemmas of Organizational Democracy and Participation*, Cambridge, UK: Cambridge University Press.

Rougier, Marcelo and Martín Schorr 2012, *La industria en los cuatro peronismos: Estrategias, políticas y resultados*, Buenos Aires: Capital Intelectual.

Rudi, Daniel M. 1974, *Los derechos constitucionales del trabajador*, Buenos Aires: EUDEBA.

Ruggeri, Andrés 2006, 'The Worker-Recovered Enterprises in Argentina: The Political
    and Socio-Economic Challenges of Self-Management', paper presented at 'Another
    World is Necessary' Center for Global Justice Annual Workshop, San Miguel de
    Allende, Mexico.

Ruggeri, Andrés (ed.) 2009, *Las empresas recuperadas: Autogestión obrera en Argen-
    tina y América Latina*, Buenos Aires: Facultad de Filosofía y Letras, Universidad de
    Buenos Aires.

Ruggeri, Andrés (ed.) 2016, *Las empresas recuperadaos por los trabajadores en los comi-
    enzos del gobierno de Mauricio Macri: Estado de situación a mayo de 2016*, Buenos
    Aires: Programa Facultad Abierta, Facultad de Filosofía y Letras, Universidad de
    Buenos Aires, available at: http://www.recuperadasdoc.com.ar/informe-mayo-2016
    .pdf

Ruggeri, Andrés, Carlos Martínez, and Hugo Trinchero 2005, *Las empresas recuperadas
    en la Argentina*, Buenos Aires: Programa Facultad Abierta, Facultad de Filosofía y
    Letras, Universidad de Buenos Aires, Programa de Transferencia Científico-Técnica
    con Empresas Recuperadas por sus Trabajadores (UBACyT de Urgencia Social F-
    701).

Ruggeri, Andrés, Natalia Polti, Gabriel Clark, Javier Antivero, Dan Delegdisch, et al.
    2010, *Informe del tercer relevamiento de empresas recuperadas por sus trabajadores:
    Las empresas recuperadas en la Argentina, 2010*, Buenos Aires: Programa Facultad
    Abierta, Facultad de Filosofía y Letras, Universidad de Buenos Aires, available at:
    http://www.recuperadasdoc.com.ar/Informes%20relevamientos/informe_Tercer_
    Relevamiento_2010.pdf

Ruggeri, Andrés, Javier Antivero, Paloma Elena, Natalia Polti, et al. 2014, *Informe del
    IV relevamiento de empresas recuperadas en la Argentina, 2014: Las empresas recu-
    peradas en el período 2010–2013*, Buenos Aires: Programa Facultad Abierta, Fac-
    ultad de Filosofía y Letras, Universidad de Buenos Aires, available at: http://www
    .recuperadasdoc.com.ar/Informe_IV_relevamiento_2014.pdf

Ruggeri, Andrés and Marcelo Vieta 2015, 'Argentina's Worker-Recuperated Enterprises,
    2010–2013: A Synthesis of Recent Empirical Findings', *Journal of Entrepreneurial and
    Organizational Diversity*, 4, 1: 75–103.

Ruggeri, Andrés, Luciana Bourlot, Fernando Marino, and Pablo Peláez 2017, *Cooperativa
    Textiles Pigüe: Historia de la recuperación de una fábrica de Gatic*, Buenos Aires: Peña
    Lillo/Ediciones Continente.

Rouco, Miguel Angel 2016, 'Primer semestre y economía: Apogeo y decepción', *La Cap-
    ital*, 11 June, available at: http://www.lacapitalmdp.com/primer-semestre-y-econo
    mia-apogeo-y-decepcion/

Saad-Filho, Alfredo 2005, 'The Political Economy of Neoliberalism in Latin America',
    in *Neoliberalism: A Critical Reader*, edited by Alfredo Saad-Filho and Deborah John-
    ston, London: Pluto.

Saad-Filho, Alfredo, Francesca Iannini, and Elizabeth Jean Molinari 2007, 'Neoliberalism, Democracy and Economic Policy in Latin America', in *Political Economy of Latin America: Recent Economic Performance*, edited by Philip Aristis P. and Malcolm C. Sawyer, Houndmills, Basingstoke, UK: Palgrave Macmillan.

Sale, Kirkpatrick 1996, *Rebels Against the Future: The Luddites and Their War On the Industrial Revolution: Lessons for the Computer Age*, New York: Basic Books.

Salı, Ocak 2015, 'Occupy, Resist and Produce: "Özgür Kazova" Textile Cooperative', *Tekhne*, 27 January, available at: http://tekhnede.blogspot.ca/2015/01/occupy-resist-and-produce-ozgur-kazova.html

Sánchez Bajo, Claudia and Bruno Roelants 2011, *Capital and the Debt Trap: Learning From Cooperatives in the Global Crisis*, Houndmills, Basingstoke, UK: Palgrave Macmillan.

Sandoval, Marisol 2016, 'What Would Rosa Do? Co-operatives and Radical Politics', *Soundings: A Journal of Politics and Culture*, 63, Summer: 98–111.

Sardá de Faria, Maurício and Henrique T. Novaes 2011, 'Brazilian Recovered Factories: The Constraints of Workers' Control', in *Ours to Master and to Own: Workers' Control from the Commune to the Present*, edited by Immanuel Ness and Dario Azzellini, Chicago: Haymarket Books.

Sarria Icaza, Ana Mercedes, and Lia Tiriba 2004, 'Economía popular', in *La otra economía* edited by Antonio David Cattani, Buenos Aires: Editorial Altamira.

Sartelli, Eduardo 2005, *La plaza es nuestra: El Argentinazo a la luz de la lucha de la clase obrera en la Argentina del siglo XX*, Buenos Aires: Ediciones Razón y Revolución.

Sauser, William I. 2009, 'Sustaining Employee Owned Companies: Seven Recommendations', *Journal of Business Ethics*, 84, 2: 151–64.

Schneider, Alejandro 2005, *Los compañeros: Trabajadores, izquierda y peronismo, 1955–1973*, Buenos Aires: Imago Mundi.

Schugurensky, Daniel 2000 'The Forms of Informal Learning: Towards a Conceptualization of the Field', NALL Working Paper No. 19, New Approaches to Lifelong Learning (NALL), Centre for the Studies of Education and Work, Ontario Institute for Studies in Education of the University of Toronto.

Schugurensky, Daniel 2001, 'Grass Roots Democracy: The Participatory Budget of Porto Alegre', *Canadian Dimension*, 35, 1: 30–2.

Schugurensky, Daniel, Karsten Mündel, and Fiona Duguid 2006, 'Learning From Each Other: Housing Cooperative Members' Acquisition of Skills, Knowledge, Attitudes and Values', *Cooperative Housing Journal*, Fall: 2–15.

Schuster, Federico L. 2008, 'Argentina: The Left, Parties and Movements: Strategies and Prospects' in *The New Latin American Left: Utopia Reborn*, edited by Patrick S. Barrett, Daniel Chavez, and Cesar A. Rodriguez Garavito, London: Pluto.

Schvarzer, Jorge 1998, *Implantación de un modelo económico: La experiencia argentina entre 1975 y el 2000*, Buenos Aires: A–Z Editora.

Schweickart, David 1996, *Against Capitalism*, Boulder: Westview.

Schweickart, David 2011, *After Capitalism*, Lanham, MD: Rowman & Littlefield.

Schweickart, David 2012, 'An Economic Democracy Reform Agenda', *Perspectives on Global Development and Technology*, 11, 1: 244–57.

Scott, Hal S. 2010, 'Obama's Troubling Acceptance of Sovereign Default', *Forbes*, 30 November, available at: https://www.forbes.com/2010/11/30/sovereign-default-econo my-debt-opinions-contributors-hal-s-scott.html

Seibel, Hans Dieter and Ukandi Godwin Damachi 1982, *Self-Management in Yugoslavia and the Developing World*, London: Macmillan.

Seidman, Gay W. 1994, *Manufacturing Militance: Workers' Movements in Brazil and South Africa, 1970–1985*, Berkeley and Los Angeles: University of California Press.

Sen, Arup Kumar 2011, 'Workers' Control in India's Communist-Ruled State: Labor Struggles and Trade Unions in West Bengal', in *Ours to Master and to Own: Workers' Control from the Commune to the Present*, edited by Immanuel Ness and Dario Azzellini, Chicago: Haymarket Books.

Serdar, Ayse 2015, 'Reconsidering Social Movement Unionism in Postcrisis Argentina', *Latin American Perspectives*, 201, 42, 2: 74–89

Shaffer, Jack 1999, *Historical Dictionary of the Cooperative Movement*, Lanham, MD: Scarecrow.

Shukaitis, Stevphen 2010, 'Sisyphus and the Labour of Imagination: Autonomy, Cultural Production, and the Antinomies of Worker Self-Management', *Affinities: A Journal of Radical Theory, Culture, and Action*, 4, 1: 57–82.

Sidicaro, Ricardo 2010, *Los tres peronismos: Estado y poder económico*, Buenos Aires: Siglo Veintiuno Editores.

Singer, Paul 2004, 'Economía solidaria', in *La otra economía*, edited by Antonio David Cattani, Buenos Aires: Editorial Altamira.

Singer, Paul and André Ricardo de Souza (eds.) 2000, *A economia solidária no Brasil: A autogestão como resposta ao desemprego*, São Paulo: Contexto.

Singh, Val and Point, Sébastien 2009, 'Diversity Statements for Leveraging Organizational Legitimacy', *Management International/International Management/Gestión Internacional*, 13, 2: 23–34.

Sitrin, Marina (ed.) 2005, *Horizontalidad: Voces de Poder Popular en Argentina*, Buenos Aires: Chilavert Art Gráficas.

Sitrin, Marina (ed.) 2006, *Horizontalism: Voices of Popular Power in Argentina*, Oakland, CA: AK Press.

Sitrin, Marina 2012, *Everyday Revolutions: Horizontalism and Autonomy in Argentina*, London: Zed Books.

Sitrin, Marina, and Dario Azzellini 2012, *Occupying Language: The Secret Rendezvous with History and the Present*, New York: Zuccotti Park Press.

Sitrin, Marina, and Dario Azzellini 2014, *They Can't Represent Us! Reinventing Democracy from Greece to Occupy*, London: Verso Books.

Slatman, Melisa, Florencia Rodriquez, and Natalia Lascano 2009, 'Las coordinadoras interfabriles de Capital y Gran Buenos Aires (1975–1976): Un estado del arte', *Revista THEMAI*, First Semester, available at: http://revista-theomai.unq.edu.ar/numero19/ArtSlatman.pdf

Smith, Adam 1976 [1776], *An Inquiry into the Nature and Causes of the Wealth of Nations*, Oxford: Oxford University Press.

Smith, Dorothy E. 2005, *Institutional Ethnography: A Sociology for People*, Lanham, MD: Rowman & Littlefield.

Smith, Dorothy E. and Stephan Dobson 2010, 'Storing and Transmitting Skills: The Expropriation of Working-Class Control', in *Manufacturing Meltdown: Reshaping Steel Work*, edited by David W. Livingstone, Dorothy E. Smith, and Warren Smith, Winnipeg: Fernwood.

Smith, Paddy, and David Chivers, and Giles Goodfellow 1988, *Cooperatives that Work: New Constitutions, Conversions, and Tax*, Nottinghamm UK: Spokesman.

Smith, Stephen C. and Jonathan Rothbaum 2014, 'Co-operatives in a Global Economy: Key Issues, Recent Trends and Potential for Development', in *Co-operatives in a Post-Trowth Era: Creating Co-operative Economics*, edited by Sonja Novkovic and Tom Webb, London: Zed.

Smith, William C. 1991, *Authoritarianism and the Crisis of the Argentine Political Economy*, Stanford, CA: Stanford University Press.

Snow, David A. and Sarah A. Soule 2010, *A Primer on Social Movements*, New York: W.W. Norton.

So, Alvin Y. 1991, 'Class Atruggle Analysis: A Critique of Class Structure Analysis', *Sociological Perspectives*, 34, 1: 39–59.

So, Alvin Y. and Muhammad Hikam 1989, '"Class" in the Writings of Wallerstein and Thompson: Toward a Class Struggle Analysis', *Sociological Perspectives*, 32, 4: 453–67.

Somoza Zanuy, Ariadna 2011, 'Integrador social', *Pagina/12*, 13 June, available at: https://www.pagina12.com.ar/diario/economia/2-169984-2011-06-13.html

Soulage, François 2011, 'France: An Endeavour in Enterprise Transformation', in *Beyond the Crisis: Cooperatives, Work, and Finance: Generating Wealth for the Long Term*, edited by Alberto Zevi, Antonio Zanotti, François Soulage, & Adrian Zelaia, Brussels: CECOP Publications.

Spronk, Susan and Jeffry Webber (eds.) 2014, *Crisis and Contradiction: Marxist Perspectives on Latin America in the Global Political Economy*, Ledien: Brill.

Stiglitz, Joseph E. 2012, *The Price of Inequality: How Today's Divided Society Endangers Our Future*, New York: W.W. Norton & Company.

Street, John 1983, 'Socialist Arguments for Industrial Democracy', *Economic and Industrial Democracy*, 4: 519–39.

Subsecretaría de Comercio Internacional 2009, 'Informe sectorial: Sector de industria gráfica, libros, revistas y otras publicaciones', Ministerio de Economía y Producción, Gobierno Nacional de la República Argentina, available at: http://docplayer.es/3938067-Informe-sectorial-sector-de-industria-grafica-libros-revistas-y-otras-publicaciones.html

Suchman, Mark C. 1995, 'Managing Legitimacy: Strategic and Institutional Approaches', *Academy of Management Review*, 20, 3: 571–610.

Suriano, Juan (ed.) 2005a, *Nueva historia argentina: Dictadura y democracia (1976–2001)*, Buenos Aires: Editorial Sudamericana.

Suriano, Juan 2005b, 'Introducción: Una Argentina diferente', in *Nueva historia argentina: Dictadura y democracia (1976–2001)* edited by Juan Suriano, Buenos Aires: Editorial Sudamericana.

Svampa, Maristella and Sebastián Pereyra 2004, *Entre la ruta y el barrio: La experiencia de las organizaciones piqueteras*, Buenos Aires: Editorial Biblos.

Télam 2011, 'Télam Signs Agreement with a Cooperative of Regional Newspapers', 25 February, available at: http://english.telam.com.ar/index.php?option=com_content&view=article&id=11281:telam-signs-agreement-with-a-cooperative-of-regional-newspapers&catid=34:society

Télam 2016, 'El Indec informó que la desocupación es del 9,3%', 23 August, available at: http://www.telam.com.ar/notas/201608/160192-desocupacion-indec.html

The Working World 2016, organisational website, available at: http://www.theworkingworld.org/us/

Theorell, Töres 2003, 'Democracy at Work and its Relationship to Health', in *Emotional and Physiological Processes and Positive Intervention Strategies (Research in Occupational Stress and Well-Being, Volume 3)*, edited by Pamela L. Perrewe and Daniel C. Ganster, Bingley, UK: Emerald Group Publishing.

Thoburn, Nicholas 2003, *Deleuze, Marx and Politics*, London: Routledge.

Thompson, Edward Palmer 1963, *The Making of the English Working Class*, New York: Vintage.

Thompson, Edward Palmer 1993 [1971], 'The Moral Economy of the English Crowd in the Eighteenth Century', in *Customs in Common: Studies in Traditional Popular Culture*, New York: The New Press.

Thompson, Edward Palmer 2001, *The Essential E.P. Thompson*, New York: The New Press.

Thompson, William 1824, *An Inquiry into the Principles of the Distribution of Wealth Most Conducive to Human Happiness; Applied to the Newly Proposed System of Voluntary Equality of Wealth*, London: Longman, Hurst, Rees, Orme, Brown & Green.

Thompson, William 1827, *Labor Rewarded: The Claims of Labor and Capital Conciliated, or, How to Secure to Labor the Whole Products of its Exertions*, London: Hunt & Clarke.

Tiempo Argentino 2016, 'Campaña contra el desalojo de Tiempo', 2 July, available at: http://www.tiempoar.com.ar/articulo/view/57674/campana-contra-el-desalojo-de-tiempo

Tierney, Brian 1999, *The Middle Ages*, New York: McGraw-Hill.

Toronto School of Creativity and Inquiry 2007, 'Recovering and Recreating Spaces of Production: A Virtual Roundtable with Protagonists of Argentina's Worker-Recovered Enterprises Movement', *Affinities: A Journal of Radical Theory, Culture, and Action*, 1, 1: 33–48.

Torre, Juan Carlos 2012, *Ensayos sobre movimiento obrero y peronismo*, Buenos Aires: Siglo Veintiuno Editores.

Triglia, Carlo and Luigi Burroni 2009, Italy: Rise, Decline and Restructuring of a Regionalized Capitalism, *Economy and Society*, 38, 4: 630–53.

Trigona, Marie 2006a, 'Recuperated Enterprises in Argentina: Reversing the Logic of Capitalism', *Upside Down World*, 27 March, available at: http://upsidedownworld .org/archives/argentina/recuperated-enterprises-in-argentina-reversing-the-logic-of-capitalism/

Trigona, Marie 2006b, 'Workers Without Bosses at a Turning Point', *Upside Down World*, 13 November, http://upsidedownworld.org/archives/argentina/workers-without-bosses-at-a-turning-point-2/

Trigona, Marie 2006c, 'Zanon: Worker Managed Production, Community and Dignity', *Toward Freedom*, 13 July, available at: http://towardfreedom.com/archives/labor/za non-worker-managed-production-community-and-dignity/

Trigona, Marie 2006d, 'Workers in Control: Venezuela's Occupied Factories', *venezuela nalysis.com*, 9 November, available at: http://venezuelanalysis.com/analysis/ 2055

Trigona, Marie 2010, 'Strategic Lessons from Latin America: Workplace Resistance and Self-Management', *Synthesis/Regeneration*, 51, Winter, available at: http://www .greens.org/s-r/51/51-11.html

Tronti, Mario 1973, 'Social Capital', *Telos*, 17, Fall: 98–121.

Tronti, Mario 2007 [1980], 'The Strategy of Refusal', in *Autonomia: Post-Political Politics*, edited by Sylvére Lotringer and Christian Marazzi, Los Angeles: Semiotext(e).

Truthout 2013, 'Can Unions and Cooperatives Join Forces? An Interview With United Steelworkers President Leo Gerard', 24 May, available at: http://www.truth-out.org/ news/item/16418-can-unions-and-cooperatives-join-forces-an-interview-with-unit ed-steelworkers-president-leo-gerard

Tuckman, Alan 2012, 'Factory Occupation, Workers' Cooperatives and Alternative Production: Lessons from Britain in the 1970s', in *Alternative Work Organizations*, edited by Maurizio Atzeni, Houndmills, Basingstoke, UK: Palgrave Macmillan.

Urien, Paula 2016, 'Para la UCA, crece la cantidad de "nuevos pobres"', *La Nación*, 12 August, available at: http://www.lanacion.com.ar/1927350-para-la-uca-crece-la-cantidad-de-nuevos-pobres

USFWC 2016, United States Federation of Worker Cooperatives, organisational website, available at: https://usworker.coop/home/

Vales, Laura 2003, 'Desde una quiebra a una esperanza', *Pagina/12*, 19 September, available at: http://www.pagina12.com.ar/diario/elpais/1-26093-2003-09-29.html

Vales, Laura 2005, 'Un sindicato propio para los "recuperados"', *Pagina/12*, 18 December, available at: https://www.pagina12.com.ar/diario/elpais/1-60656-2005-12-18.html

Vales, Laura 2009, 'Para que tengan autonomía', *Pagina/12*, 30 August, available at: https://www.pagina12.com.ar/diario/elpais/subnotas/1-42172-2009-08-30.html

Vales, Laura 2016, 'El combo viene con despidos y represión', *Pagina/12*, 4 July, available at: https://www.pagina12.com.ar/diario/elpais/1-303342-2016-07-04.html

Van de Sande, Mathijs 2015, 'Fight with Tools: Prefiguration and Radical Politicas in the Twenty-First Century', *Rethinking Marxism*, 27, 2: 177–94.

Vanek, Jaroslav 1975, *Self-Management: Economic Liberation of Man: Selected Readings*, Harmondsworth, UK: Penguin.

Vanek, Jaroslav 1977, *The Labor-Managed Economy: Essays*, Ithaca, NY: Cornell University Press.

Velde, François R. and Marcelo Veracierto 2000, 'Dollarization in Argentina', *Economic Perspectives*, Federal Reserve Bank of Chicago, 24, 1: 24–37

Venezuelanalysis.com 2005, 'Chavez Says Venezuela Will Expropriate Closed Enterprises', 18 July, available at: http://www.venezuelanalysis.com/news.php?newsno=1692

Vieta, Marcelo 2006, 'Argentina's Worker-Recovered Enterprises Movement: Reconstituting Working Lives', *New Socialist: Ideas for Radical Change*, 57: 21–3.

Vieta, Marcelo 2009a, 'Las empresas recuperadas por sus trabajadores como cooperativas de trabajo', in *Las empresas recuperadas: Autogestión obrera en Argentina y América Latina*, edited by Andrés Ruggeri, Buenos Aires: Facultad de Filosofía y Letras, Universidad de Buenos Aires.

Vieta, Marcelo 2009b, 'Desafíos e innovaciones sociales en las empresas recuperadas por sus trabajadores,' in *Las empresas recuperadas: Autogestión obrera en Argentina y América Latina*, edited by Andrés Ruggeri, Buenos Aires: Facultad de Filosofía y Letras, Universidad de Buenos Aires.

Vieta, Marcelo 2010a, 'The Social Innovations of *Autogestión* in Argentina's Worker-Recuperated Enterprises: Cooperatively Organizing Productive Life in Hard Times', *Labor Studies Journal*, 35, 3: 295–321.

Vieta, Marcelo 2010b, 'Editorial: The New Cooperativism', *Affinities: A Journal of Radical Theory, Culture, and Action*, 4, 1: 1–11.

Vieta, Marcelo 2012, 'From Managed Employees to Self-Managed Workers: The Transformations of Labour at Argentina's Worker-Recuperated Enterprises', in *Alternative Work Organizations*, edited by Maurizio Atzeni, Houndmills, Basingstoke, UK: Palgrave Macmillan.

Vieta, Marcelo 2013, 'Recuperating a Workplace, Creating a Community Space: The Story of Cooperativa Chilavert Artes Gráficas', *Scapegoat: Architecture, Landscape, Political Economy*, 4: 161–78.

Vieta, Marcelo 2014a, 'The Stream of Self-Determination and *Autogestión*: Prefiguring Alternative Economic Realities', *Ephemera*, 14, 4: 781–809.

Vieta, Marcelo 2014b, 'Learning in Struggle: Argentina's New Worker Cooperatives as Transformative Learning Organizations', *Relations Industrielles/Industrial Relations*, 69, 1: 186–218.

Vieta, Marcelo 2015, 'The Italian Road to Creating Worker Cooperatives from Worker Buyouts: Italy's Worker-Recuperated Enterprises and the Legge Marcora Framework', Working Papers No. 078–15, Trento, Italy: European Research Institute on Cooperative and Social Enterprises (EURICSE), available at: http://www.euricse.eu/wp-content/uploads/2015/08/WP-78_15_Vieta.pdf

Vieta, Marcelo 2016a, 'Marcuse's "Transcendent Project" at 50: Post-Technological Rationality for Our Times', *Radical Philosophy Review*, 19, 1: 143–72.

Vieta, Marcelo 2016b, 'Autogestión: Prefiguring a "New Cooperativism" and "the Labour Commons"', in *Moving Beyond Capitalism*, edited by Cliff DuRand, London: Routledge.

Vieta, Marcelo 2017, 'Inklings of the Great Refusal: Echoes of Marcuse's Post-Technological Rationality Today', in *The Great Refusal: Herbert Marcuse and Contemporary Social Movements*, edited by Andrew Lamas, Todd Wolfson and Peter N. Funke, Philadelphia: Temple University Press.

Vieta, Marcelo 2018a, 'New Co-operativism in Latin America: Implications for Cuba', in *Co-operativism and Local Development in Cuba: An Agenda for Democratic Social Change*, edited by Henry Veltmeyer and Sonja Novkovic, London: Routledge.

Vieta, Marcelo 2018b, 'Recuperating and (Re)Learning *Autogestión* in Argentina's *Empresas Recuperadas* Worker Cooperatives', *Journal of Cultural Economy*, published online first, available at: https://doi.org/10.1080/17530350.2018.1544164

Vieta, Marcelo and Andrés Ruggeri 2009, 'Worker-Recovered Enterprises as Workers' Co-operatives: The Conjunctures, Challenges, and Innovations of Self-Management in Argentina and Latin America', in *Co-operatives in a Global Economy: The Challenges of Co-operation Across Borders*, edited by Darryl Reed and J.J. McMurtry, Newcastle Upon-Tyne: Cambridge Scholars Publishing.

Vieta, Marcelo, Manuel Larrabure, and Daniel Schugurensky 2012, 'Social Businesses in Twenty-First Century Latin America: The Cases of Argentina and Venezuela', in *Businesses With a Difference: Balancing the Social and the Economic*, edited by Jack Quarter, Laurie Mook, and Sherida Ryan, Toronto: University of Toronto Press.

Vieta, Marcelo, Jack Quarter, Roger Spear, and Aleksandra Moskovskaya 2016, 'Participation in Worker Cooperatives', in *The Palgrave Handbook of Volunteering, Civic Participation, and Nonprofit Associations*, edited by David Horton Smith, Robert A. Stebbins, and Jurgen Grotz, Houndmills, Basingstoke, UK: Palgrave Macmillan.

Vieta, Marcelo, Sara Depedri, and Antonella Carrano 2017, *The Italian Road to Recuperating Enterprises and the Legged Marcora Framework: Italy's Worker Buyouts in Times of Crisis*, Research Report No. 015–17, Trento, Italy: Trento, Italy: European Research Institute on Cooperative and Social Enterprises (EURICSE), available at: http://www .euricse.eu/publications/italys-worker-buyouts-in-times-of-crisis/

Vigliarolo, Francesco 2016, 'Recovered Factories', in *The Co-operative Firm: Kewords*, edited by Andrea Bernardi and Salvatore Monni, Rome: RomaTrE-Press.

Virno, Paolo 2004, *A Grammar of the Multitude: For an Analysis of Contemporary Forms of Life*, Los Angeles: Semiotext(e).

Vitabar, Lourdes 2005, 'Empresas recuperadas: Ayer un sueño imposible, hoy una realidad fértil', *LaRed21*, 18 December, available at: http://www.lr21.com.uy/comunidad/ 197737-empresas-recuperadas-ayer-un-sueno-imposible-hoy-una-realidad-fertil

Vlaisavljevic, Milos 2016, 'Los herederos de la autogestión', *Autogestión para Otra Economía*, December, 1, 1: 42.

Volkov, Vladimir 2000, 'Struggle of Russian workers for control of Vyborg Cellulose Combine', World Socialist Web Site, 16 February, available at: https://www.wsws.org/ en/articles/2000/02/russ-f16.html

Vosko, Leah F. 2006, *Precarious Employment: Understanding Labour Market Insecurity in Canada*, Montreal and Kingston: McGill-Queen's University Press.

Vuotto, Mirta 2011, *El cooperativismo de trabajo en la Argentina: Contribuciones para el diálogo social*, Buenos Aires: Oficina Regional para América Latina y el Caribe, Programa Regional para la Promoción del Diálogo y la Cohesión Social en América Latina, Oficina International del Trabajo/International Labour Organization.

Vuotto, Mirta 2012, 'Organizational Dynamics of Worker Cooperatives in Argentina', *Service Business*, 6, 1: 85–97.

Vuotto, Mirta 2014a, 'La economía social y las cooperativas en la Argentina', *Voces en el Fenix*, 38, October: 46–53.

Vuotto, Mirta 2014b, 'El desarrollo reciente del cooperativismo de trabajo en la argentina y el rol de las políticas públicas dirigidas al sector', in *Ciudadanía, desarrollo territorial y paz desde el accionar de cooperative*, edited by Juan Fernando Álvarez, Bogotá: Universidad Católica de Colombia.

Wadhwani, Sushil, and Martin Wall 1990, 'The Effects of Profit-Sharing on Employment, Wages, Stock Returns, and Productivity: Evidence from UK Micro-Data', *The Economic Journal*, 100, 399: 1–17.

Wainfeld, Mario 2016, *Kirchner: El tipo que supo*, Buenos Aires: Siglo Veintiuno Editores.

Walsh, Rodolfo 1969, 'Cordobazo', *Periódico de la CGT de los Argentinos*, available at: http://www.cgtargentinos.org/documentos6.htm

Walsh, Sebastian 2011, 'A History of Debt Defaults: Argentina 2001', *Financial News*, 29 July, available at: https://www.fnlondon.com/articles/history-of-debt-defaults-argentina-2001-20110725

Walzer, Michael 1983, *Spheres of Justice: A Defense of Pluralism and Equality*, New York: Basic Books.

Ward, Benjamin 1958, 'The Firm in Illyria: Market Syndicalism', *American Economic Review*, 48, 4: 566–89.

Waterman, Peter 1999, 'The New Social Unionism: A New Union Model for a New World Order', in *Labour Worldwide in the Era of Globalization: Alternative Union Models in the New World Order*, edited by Ronaldo Munck and Peter Waterman, Houndmills, Basingstoke, UK: Macmillan Press.

Waterman, Peter 2001, *Globalization, Social Movements, and the New Internationalisms*, New York: Continuum.

Webb, Tom, and George Cheney 2014, 'Worker-Owned-and-Governed Co-Operatives and the Wider Co-Operative Movement: Challenges and Opportunities Within and Beyond the Global Economic Crisis', in *The Routledge Companion to Alternative Organization*, edited by Parker, Martin, George Cheney, Valérie Fournier, and Chris Land, London: Routledge.

Webb, Tom, and Sonja Novkovic (eds.) 2014, *Co-operatives in a Post-Growth Era: Creating Co-operative Economics*, London: Zed Books.

Webster, Edward 1988, 'The rise of Social Movement Unionism: The Two Faces of the Black Trade Union Movement in South Africa', in *State, Resistance and Change in South Africa*, edited by Philip Frankel, Noam Pines, and Mark Swilling, London: Croom Helm.

Weeks, Kathi 2005, 'The Refusal of Work as Demand and Desire', in *Resistance in Practice: The Philosophy of Antonio Negri*, edited by Timothy S. Murphy and Abdul-Karim Mustapha, London: Pluto.

Weeks, Kathi 2011, *The Problem with Work: Feminism, Marxism, Antiwork Politics, and Postwork Imaginaries*, Durham: Duke University Press.

Weitzman, Martin L. and Chenggang Xu, 1994, 'Chinese Township-Village Enterprises as Vaguely Defined Cooperatives', *Journal of Comparative Economics* 18, 2: 121–45.

Wenger, Etienne 1996, *Communities of Practice: Learning, Meaning, and Identity*, Cambridge, UK: Cambridge University Press.

Wenger, Etienne and William M. Snyder 2000, 'Communities of Practice: The Organizational Frontier', *Harvard Business Review*, 78, 1: 139–46.

Werner, Ruth and Facundo Aguirre 2007, *Insurgencia obrera en la Argentina, 1969–1976: Clasismo, coordinadoras interfabriles y estrategias de la izquierda*, Buenos Aires: Ediciones IPS.

Whitford, Josh 2001, 'The Decline of a Model? Challenge and Response in the Italian Industrial Districts', *Economy and Society*, 30, 1: 38–65.

Wilkinson, Richard and Kate Pickett 2010, *The Spirit Level: Why Greater Equality Makes Society Stronger*, New York: Bloomsbury.

Willis, Paul E. 1977, *Learning to Labor: How Working-Class Kids get Working-Class Jobs*, New York: Columbia University Press.

Witherell, Rob, Chris Cooper, and Michael Peck 2012, 'Sustainable Jobs, Sustainable Communities: The Union Co-op Model', United Steelworkers of America, Mondragón, and Ohio Employee Ownership Center, available at: http://www.usw.org/union/allies/The-Union-Co-op-Model-March-26-2012.pdf

Wolff, Richard D. 2012, *Democracy at Work: A Cure for Capitalism*, Chicago: Haymarket Books.

Won, Jong Ho and Seungkwon Jang 2015, 'Becoming a Cooperative with Self-Organizing Process: The Case of Happy-Bridge Cooperative', paper presented at the 'Co-operatives and the World of Work Research Conference', International Labour Organization and the International Co-operative Alliance Committee on Co-operative Research, Antalya, Turkey, 10–11 November.

Wood, Ellen Meiksins 1982, 'The Politics of Theory and the Concept of Class: E.P. Thompson and his Critics', *Studies in Political Economy*, 9, 1: 45–75.

Wood, Ellen Meiksins 1983, 'Marxism Without Class Struggle?', *Socialist Register*, 20: 239–71.

Wood, Ellen Meiksins 1986, *The Retreat from Class: A New 'True' Socialism*, London: Verso.

Wood, Ellen Meiksins 1988, 'Capitalism and Human Emancipation', *New Left Review*, 167, Jan/Feb: 3–20.

Wood, Ellen Meiksins 1995, *Democracy Against Capitalism: Renewing Historical Materialism*, Cambridge, UK: Cambridge University Press.

Wood, Ellen Meiksins 2002, *The Origin of Capitalism: A Longer View*, London: Verso.

Woodcock, George 2004, *Anarchism: A History of Libertarian Ideas and Movements*, Peterborough, ON: Broadview.

Workerscontrol.net 2012, 'Solidarity Petition: Support Jugoremedija Workers' Struggle in Serbia', 24 January, available at: http://www.workerscontrol.net/geographical/solidarity-petition-support-jugoremedija-workers-struggle-serbia

Working World, The 2016, organizational website, http://theworkingworld.org/

World Bank 2003, 'The Health Sector in Argentina: Current Situation and Options for Improvement', Report No. 26144-AR, Washingon, DC: Human Development Department, World Bank.

World Bank 2016a, 'Unemployment, Total (% of Total Labor Force) (Modeled ILO Estimate): Argentina', available at: http://data.worldbank.org/indicator/SL.UEM.TOTL.ZS?locations=AR

World Bank 2016b, 'GDP Growth (Annual %): Argentina', available at: http://data.world bank.org/indicator/NY.GDP.MKTP.KD.ZG?locations=AR

Worthen, Helena 2014, *What Did You Learng at Work Today? The Forbidden Lessons of Labor Education*, New York: Hardball Press.

Wright, Erik Olin 2010, *Envisioning Real Utopias*, London: Verso.

Wright, Steve 2002, *Storming Heaven: Class Composition and Struggle in Italian Autonomist Marxism*, London: Pluto.

Wyczykier, Gabriela 2009a, 'Sobre procesos de autogestión y recolectivzación laboral en la Argentina actual', *Polis: Revista Académica de la Universidad Bolivariana* 8, 24: 197–220.

Wyczykier, Gabriela 2009b, *De la dependencia a la autogestión laboral: Sobre la reconstrucción de expériencias colectivas de trabajo en la Argentina contemporánea*, Buenos Aires: Universidad Nacional de General Sarmiento and Promoteo Libros.

Wylde, Christopher 2011, 'State, Society and Markets in Argentina: The Political Economy of Neodesarrollismo Under Néstor Kirchner, 2003–2007', *Bulletin of Latin American Research*, 30, 4: 436–52.

Zamagni, Stefano 2014, 'Choices, Incentives and Co-operative Organization', in *Cooperatives in a Post-Growth Era: Creating Co-operative Economics*, edited by Tom Webb and Sonja Novkovic, London: Zed Books.

Zamagni, Stefano, and Vera Zamagni 2010, *Cooperative Enterprise: Facing the Challenge of Globalization*, Chettenham, UK: Edward Elgar Publishing.

Zanotti, Antonio 2011, 'Italy: The Strength of an Inter-Sectoral Network', in *Beyond the Crisis: Cooperatives, Work, and Finance: Generating Wealth for the Long Term*, edited by Alberto Zevi, Antonio Zanotti, François Soulage, and Adrian Zelaia, Brussels: CECOP Publications.

Zibechi, Raúl 2010, 'Una década de fábricas recuperadas: Reinventar la vida desde el trabajo', *Tlaxcala*, 18 December, available at: http://www.tlaxcala-int.org/article.asp?reference=3009

Zibechi, Raúl 2012, *Territories in Resistance: A Cartography of Latin American Social Movements*, Oakland, CA: AK Press.

Zevi, Alberto, Antonio Zanotti, François Soulage, and Adrian Zelaia 2011, *Beyond the Crisis: Cooperatives, Work, and Finance: Generating Wealth for the Long Term*, edited by Alberto Zevi, Antonio Zanotti, François Soulage, & Adrian Zelaia, Brussels: CECOP Publications.

Index

For a list of all abbreviations and acronyms, see pp. xxxi–xxxv.

CPSIA information can be obtained
at www.ICGtesting.com
Printed in the USA
JSHW030827291120
9842JS00003B/6